Walter Dean Myers

McFarland Literary Companions
by Mary Ellen Snodgrass

1. *August Wilson* (2004)

2. *Barbara Kingsolver* (2004)

3. *Amy Tan* (2004)

4. *Walter Dean Myers* (2006)

Walter Dean Myers

A Literary Companion

Mary Ellen Snodgrass

McFarland Literary Companions, 4

McFarland & Company, Inc., Publishers
Jefferson, North Carolina, and London

LIBRARY OF CONGRESS CATALOGUING-IN-PUBLICATION DATA

Snodgrass, Mary Ellen.
Walter Dean Myers : a literary companion / Mary Ellen Snodgrass.
p. cm. — (McFarland literary companions ; 4)
Includes bibliographical references and index.

ISBN 0-7864-2456-7 (softcover : 50# alkaline paper) 

1. Myers, Walter Dean, 1937– —Criticism and interpretation.
2. Young adult literature, American — History and criticism.
3. Children's literature, American — History and criticism.
4. African Americans in literature. I. Title. II. Series.
PS3563.Y48Z87 2006 813'.54 — dc22 2006001514

British Library cataloguing data are available

On the cover: Walter Dean Myers; background image ©2006 PhotoAlto

Manufactured in the United States of America

McFarland & Company, Inc., Publishers
Box 611, Jefferson, North Carolina 28640
www.mcfarlandpub.com

Acknowledgments

I owe many thanks to Walter Dean Myers, who has answered my queries promptly in person and by telephone and email. I am particularly appreciative of Wanda Rozzelle, reference librarian at the Catawba County Library in Newton, North Carolina, for locating obscure book reviews, articles, and copies of Myers's lesser known works. In addition, I acknowledge the advice and research assistance of the following people and institutions:

Judy Foster, reference librarian
Catawba County Library
Newton, North Carolina

Avis Gachet, Book Buyer
Wonderland Books
5008 Hickory Boulevard
Hickory, North Carolina 28601

Susan Keller, reference librarian
Western Piedmont Community College
Morganton, North Carolina

Hannah Owen
Deputy Director
Patrick Beaver Library
Hickory, North Carolina

Mark Schumacher, reference librarian
Jackson Library, UNC-G
Greensboro, North Carolina

Contents

Even in our wealthy country, there are always children
that need to be rescued from some obscure hell.
1994 Margaret A. Edwards Award Acceptance Speech

Let us hear the questions in their hearts
and let us hear them with our hearts.
Let us celebrate the children.
Glorious Angels (1995)

Everyone wants to have value as a human being,
and you have to find that value.
"Turning Memories into Memoir" (2000)

It is not only the wicked that travel with pain.
Sometimes it is the innocent as well.
The Dream Bearer (2003)

Strong grows the rising heart
Stronger still the deepening mind.
Here in Harlem: Poems in Many Voices (2004)

Preface

For those who have limited knowledge or understanding of Walter Dean Myers's literary contributions, *Walter Dean Myers: A Literary Companion* is the ideal introduction. It provides the reader, student, researcher, teacher, historian, reviewer, and librarian with personal data and analyses of characters, dates, events, motifs, and themes from the canon of America's beloved exponent of honest teen literature.

The text opens with an annotated chronology of Myers's life and works followed by a two-stage family tree. The 101 A-to-Z entries combine insights from a variety of titles and themes along with generous citations from primary and secondary sources. Each entry concludes with selected bibliography on such subjects as segregation, Malcolm X, urbanism, rootlessness, writing, metafiction, drugs and alcohol, slavery, and the Vietnam War. A map of Harlem particularizes the author's settings; charts elucidate the genealogies of Tarik, Tippy, Godoy, Lewis, Loper, Owens, and the Collins, Little and Perry families. Generous cross references point to divergent strands of thought and guide the reader into peripheral territory, e.g., from irony to athletics, fable to humor, music to folk artist Jacob Lawrence, and storytelling to diaspora, the global movement that spread black people and their vibrant culture over agrarian and urban settings.

Back matter is designed to aid the student, teacher, and researcher. It orients the beginner with a time line of historical events in Myers's writings and those of his characters, beginning with the importation of slaves to North America in 1619. A coding system connects each event to one or more of the author's titles. A second appendix provides forty topics for group or individual projects, composition, oral analysis, background material, and theme development.

The back matter concludes with an exhaustive listing of primary sources and general bibliography, many of which derive from journal articles, books on young adult literature, and reviews of Myers's works in the newspapers of major cities. These secondary sources are particularly useful for study of adolescent psychology and the themes of powerlessness, education, coming of age, achievement, juvenile crime, and parenthood.

A comprehensive index directs users of the literary companion to major and minor characters, historical figures, movements, titles, culture, places, and issues, e.g., Tippy, "Mr. Moses" Littlejohn, Marcus Garvey, Jackie Robinson, Robert Gould Shaw, King Gezo, Black Is Beautiful, civil rights, spirituals, Schomburg Center for Research in Black Culture, Sierra Leone, *Roots*, "Lift Every Voice and Sing," bullying, and volunteerism.

Introduction

In an era when adults have despaired of ways to rescue youth from a surfeit of temptations, Walter Dean Myers has made an innovative path through a tangle of urban ills. His realistic fiction, biography, history, storybooks, memoir, and verse examine the growing-up years with humor and hope. Neither didactic nor Pollyanna, his canon dramatizes the issues of his day with an eye toward retrieving children and teens from self-destruction. As a template, he poses characters on the streets that he walked in childhood — the avenues, parks, subways, schools, playing fields, museums, and libraries that broadened his world from the Dean family flat to all of Harlem. His joy in black people — their food, wisdom, wit, and music — permeates his picture books and invigorates poems that look beyond poverty and racial bias to the solid character of old friends, neighbors, and kin.

Critics anticipate new installments in Myers's lengthy canon and welcome his fresh take on humankind through photojournal, saga, war story, and animal fable. Parents, librarians, textbook editors, and educators trust his writings for their touches of grace to unforgiving urban landscapes. Amid the hardships of parents at work, siblings in jail, and neighborhoods riddled by petty crime and drug dealing, his fictional characters come of age with dignity and self-confidence. They carry to the outer world the sportsmanship and courtesies that formed their earliest lessons. Crucial to their maturation are the frequent matchups of naive or wayward child with wise elder, an intergenerational training system that dates to ancient Greece, China, and the Americas. The pairing of young heads with seasoned mentors halts some characters on the route to perdition and channels others toward the longings and ambitions that frame their adult character.

Myers's works outdistance fad fiction in popularity, longevity, and literary merit. Children who grew up loving *Fast Sam, Cool Clyde, and Stuff* direct their sons and daughters toward the author's late masterworks, *Fallen Angels*, *Monster: A Novel*, *Shooter*, and "Wolf Song." Teachers who remember a satisfying read of *The Dragon Takes a Wife* or *It Ain't All for Nothin'* in their past recommend to young readers Myers's *Now Is Your Time!* and biographies of Sarah Forbes Bonetta, Muhammad Ali, Malcolm X, Colonel Fred. V. Cherry, and Dr. Martin Luther King, Jr. Arrangers of

Black History Month celebrations rely on Myers at his best — the saga *The Glory Field*, the history *U.S.S. Constellation*, *Bad Boy: A Memoir*, the teen novel *The Young Landlords*, and a verse portrait gallery, *Here in Harlem*. Whatever title suits the occasion, Myers approaches the human need for pride and self-fulfillment with the same unhurried pacing, the same reverence for human variables. The rhythms and dialogue of his rap and repartee reward readers with elements of their own lives. His unforeseen epiphanies implant nuggets of wisdom as investments for the future.

Chronology of Myers's Life and Works

Walter Dean Myers, a pre-eminent author of teen fiction and verse, refines the image of black characters that are frequently trivialized or vilified in juvenile literature, advertising, television, and film. His canon surveys the complex realm of the teen years as colliding settings in home, school, and the street, areas in which he has experienced difficulties as well as success. His biography is complicated by faulty information about the Green side of the family, his several stepmothers and numerous step-siblings, and his three brothers' violent deaths.

Before 1865 Author Walter Dean Myers accounts for his family's role in American history. He traces his lineage to a great-grandmother, Dolly Dennis, and her son, slaves who were the property of the Dandridges of Leetown in King William County, Virginia. The white family owned a plantation called the Bower, which the author visited and photographed to illustrate *Now Is Your Time! The African-American Struggle for Freedom* (1991). Captain William Dandridge served on the Virginia Council. Myers added that "Some of my family ... live in Harpers Ferry, the site of the John Brown raid of 1859. A great-great-great uncle (Lucas Dennis) claimed to have seen John Brown on his way to trial in Charlestown" (Gallo, 10).

August 12, 1937 Born on a Thursday in the industrial town of Martinsburg, West Virginia, near the end of the Great Depression, Walter Milton Myers was seventh of the eight children of George Ambrose and Mary Dolly Green Myers, whose middle name he gave to the slave matriarch Dolly in *The Glory Field* (1994), a fictionalized saga. His family lived ten miles from the Dandridge plantation on which his relatives had been enslaved. The Myers attended the Free Will Baptist Church, which opened the first freedman's school for educating ex-slaves. In 2004, the author ennobled his father by assigning his name to the verse monologue of an English teacher in the anthology *Here in Harlem: Poems in Many Voices* (2004).

1940 Mary Myers died at the birth of Imogene, leaving her youngest son longing for photographic evidence of a mother-son relationship. Still needy of proof, in the introduction to *Angel to Angel: A Mother's Gift of Love* (1998), issued 58 years later, he accounts for his collection of antique family photos: "I look at these pictures, pictures of children leaning against their mothers, standing in the shadows of their strengths, of their love, and I am made whole" (Myers, 1998, n.p.). Teri Lesesne, a reviewer for *Teacher Librarian* remarked, "Here is a book which celebrates that which connects us all: mother's love" (Lesesne, 1999, 43).

Imogene joined Walter's large circle of siblings, including Gertrude, Viola, Ethel, Geraldine, Douglas, and George, Jr. The latter brother the author honored as dedicatee of *It Ain't All for Nothin'* (1978) and pictured on the back cover of *Here in Harlem: Poems in Many Voices.* Because of racial discrimination and low-paying jobs for blacks, the widower could not care for and support his brood. He sent Walter's two half-sisters, Gerry and Viola, to their Indian-German mother, Florence Brown Dean, whom he immortalized in *Bad Boy: A Memoir* (2001). Her husband, Herbert Julius Dean, who learned to read in the navy during World War I, worked numerous jobs as a stevedore, maintenance man, mover for gangster Dutch Schultz, and shipping clerk for the U.S. Radium Corporation. It was Herbert who elected to add Walter to the family to provide the Deans with a son. The author later credited his foster father with providing the self-discipline that a writer needs.

In retrospect of accepting a new home and family, Walter remarked, "My formal education began in the Harlem apartment of my foster parents" (Myers, May 2001, 58). He traveled by Greyhound bus to an apartment on 126th Street in central Harlem as an informal adoptee, a subject he later addressed in the teen novel *Won't Know Till I Get There* (1982). The family lived one block from poet Langston Hughes and walked to Sunday school at the Abyssinian Baptist Church, where Hughes gave readings and sold his published works from a shopping bag or an old valise. Myers later extolled the poet in *Here in Harlem: Poems in Many Voices* as "Negro/Quintessential" for his concern for the underclass and for "what it meant/To Poet Black" (Myers, 2004, 39). Another narrative, "Ernest Scott, 26," describes a lover of black poetry as "the chorus, the doo-wop from dim halls" (*ibid.*, 58).

While Myers's sisters attended school, he had the full attention of a mother, whom he described as a patient listener. In 2005, he recalled, "My mother always suspected I was an angel, no matter what happened" ("Youth," 2005). After she began work at a button factory, he entered day care with a neighbor who read aloud to him. He recalled how she returned home with swollen ankles, a working-class anomaly unaddressed in the novels of white authors Jack London, Thomas Mann, and Mark Twain. Sixty years later, Myers honored her job in the short story "Fighter" (2000), in which a mother takes time off from work to discuss with a junior high school counselor her son's choice of boxing as a career goal.

1941 Myers's memories of New York include rats on piers along the Hudson River, dark-skinned children living in red brick tenements, and the babble of Jewish, Irish, and black kids in East Harlem. In a story collection *145th Street: Short Stories* (2000), he mentions La Marqueta, an outdoor marketplace near the train station "filled with fresh food just brought in to the city and fresh fish laid out neatly on beds of cracked ice" (Myers, 2000, 117). At Christmas, he visited Macy's to see Santa Claus. With friends and siblings, he played Chinese handball, ring-a-levio, stickball, relay races, and two-sewer stoopball on the streets and at Morningside Park. He fielded baseball for a sandlot on a Morningside Drive team and attended games at Ebbets Field in Brooklyn. The plays he attended at Teacher's College prefaced a consuming interest in black cultural achievements. One of his memories involves his brother's tossing a candy wrapper on the garden of Langston Hughes, who chased the boy for a block.

The Dean family enjoyed spirited conversation and informal storytelling — ghost stories and scary monster tales with sound effects from Myers's father, whom the author credits with teaching his first writing lessons. Myers heard pious Old Testament lore of Job, the tower of Babel, and the children of Israel from his paternal grandfather, William "Pap" Dean, a retired wagoneer who lived with the family after blindness limited his ability to care for himself. The author reprised the pairing of a nine-year-old boy with an elderly storyteller, Grandpa Jeremiah, in "Jeremiah's Song," collected in *The Giver and Related Readings* (1987). Myers's mother told German folk stories and described the background of Bessie Smith, a blues star. From his mother, who was semi-literate, five-year-old Walter learned to read the newspaper, classic comics, and *True Romance* magazines. His sister Geraldine gave him a collection of bible stories, from which he derived drama and "the absolute sense of good and evil" (Myers, 2003, xi). In an article for *School Library Journal*, he admitted that, among his peers, "Reading was synonymous with weakness. As a result, I became a secret reader and book lover" (Myers, June 2001, 44).

Myers remarked that "Heroes that looked anything like me were hard to come by" (Myers, *The Greatest*, ix). The Dean family welcomed soap operas on the radio and the big band music of Cab Calloway, Duke Ellington, and Glenn Miller. Family life centered on the Church of the Master, a Presbyterian sanctuary on Manhattan Avenue, where Myers made lanyards and wallets in Bible school, the place where he got his first kiss. He attended Monday night bible study and heard Josephine Baker sing to the congregation. After learning modern dance, Myers played the role of Adam in a choreographic performance of the choral epic "The Creation," one of the dialect sermons in James Weldon Johnson's *God's Trombones* (1927). The church eventually became home base for Arthur Mitchell's Dance Theater of Harlem.

As athletics began to take precedence in his life, Myers sparred with boxer Sugar Ray Robinson, who cruised in a lavender Cadillac through Harlem, and saw Joe Louis shaking his fist at children playing along 125th Street, Harlem's main thoroughfare. The author perfected a flat jump shot in the church's basement gym. He recalled the thrill of physical competition: "There was a time when there was no gulf between my mind and my body. On the basketball court I wanted to bring my strong body against other strong bodies, to feel the strength of an opponent challenging my own strength, to answer the dare of his speed with my own fleet movements" (Myers, "Private," March 16, 2005). The rush from pitting strength against strength lasted until he approached age thirty.

1942 Already a reader at age five, Myers entered Mrs. Dworkin's first grade class at P.S. 125 Ralph J. Bunche School on LaSalle Street. Throughout his public school education, all of Myers's teachers were white except Mr. Manley, the French teacher in junior high. Myers made friends with classmates Binky, Clyde, and Light Billy, the models for urban youths in his Harlem stories.

1943 During World War II, the Dean family resettled in a fourth-floor apartment on Morningside Avenue across the street from Morningside Park, where Myers became "a playground rat" (Naughton, 1989, 8). After Herbert Dean was drafted into the navy, Florence found a job in a clothing factory. In Mrs. Bower's class in the second grade, Myers enjoyed an oral reading of Laura Ingalls Wilder's *Little House in the Big Woods* (1932). He suffered bullying from mockers who mimicked his speech defect. The surname of his tormentor, Manuel Bonilla, recurred in a Hispanic family in *The Mouse Rap* (1990).

1945 In third grade, Myers suffered slaps from Mrs. Zeiss and low grades in all but physical education. Over forty years later in the essay "Gifts" for *Horn Book* magazine, the author observed, "Those of us who grew up in emotional distress bring [to the world] the capacity to deal in anguish as a social commodity" (Myers, 1986, 436). Fortunately, he was able to turn that anguish into narratives intended to relieve the emotional hurts of young readers.

Summer, 1945 Myers received math tutoring from his uncle Frank Law. For throwing orange peelings on the sidewalk, the author had to whitewash walls under the direction of the minister, the Reverend James H. Robinson.

1946 Myers began writing in his spare time because composition allowed him to succeed in a way that conversation denied him. In Mrs. Parker's fourth grade, he stumbled over works containing *r*, *u*, and *w* and with the *ch* and *sh* combinations. His frustration generated anger at kids who called him Mushmouth. The emotional turmoil turned him into a classroom behavioral problem from hyperactivity and an inability to concentrate. For fighting and throwing a book at a teacher, he spent time in the principal's office and received whippings at home. School authorities considered expelling him permanently.

Fall, 1947 The Deans parents enrolled Myers at Public School 43 for fifth grade, where he read a comic book instead of completing his math assignment. Mrs. Conway, his teacher, was responsible for the title of his memoir. Calling him a "bad boy," she ended his immersion in a comic book by tearing it up and substituting works from her own shelves (Myers, *Bad Boy*, 45). He first enjoyed *East o' the Sun, West o' the Moon* (1941), an illustrated collection of Norwegian folklore that Peter Christen Asbjornsen and Moe Jorgen collected in the 1800s. Myers also liked male-centered fiction —*Huckleberry Finn, Little Men, The Three Musketeers,* and *Robin Hood*— and the sports novels of John Roberts Tunis, a prolific writer of juvenile fiction.

Mrs. Conway circumvented Myers's problems with reading aloud by permitting him to read his original verse, which he composed from words he could pronounced. One of his poems, "My Mother," appeared in the school literary magazine. He enjoyed story time and free browsing at the George Bruce Branch of the public library at 518 West 125th Street. Myers's goal was to fill up his library card with 128 stamps, one per box. To conceal his literary leanings from pals, he carried books home in a paper bag. In 1991, he reflected on the happiness of free reading: "Libraries have become sanctuaries.... I think kids go there now because they know they are places of sanity and safety" (Decandido and Mahony, 1991, 15).

Reading helped to cure Myers's speech problems, in part by giving him confidence with written language. While flourishing at the study of literature, he wrote poems and short stories. He delivered parcels for a jewelry distributor and planned on majoring in law. He omitted writing as a career choice because of a lack of nonwhite models: "[Ralph] Ellison and [James] Baldwin were just coming along, and we weren't taught about Zora Neale Hurston or the Harlem Renaissance" (Brown, 46).

1948 At a hopeful turn in his schooling, Myers advanced in academics and entered sixth grade at Public School 125. His strict, idealistic teacher, ex–Marine Irwin Lasher, convinced Myers "that I was bright and that being smart meant something" (Myers, "Turning," 20). Lasher arranged for Myers to receive speech therapy one day per week and developed his leadership capabilities as a tutor for slow readers and flag carrier in the honor guard. As an adult, Myers encountered Lasher and realized that his teacher had no idea how greatly he had influenced the author's life and career. As a token of appreciation, Myers dedicated *Handbook for Boys: A Novel* (2002) to Lasher with the comment that his teacher "made a permanent difference in my life" (Myers, 2002, n.p.).

The budding author flourished and learned to accept the consequences of his actions. Mistreatment of colored teens worried him and alienated him from Eric Leonhardt, his best friend, whose blond, blue-eyed looks opened doors that remained closed to Myers. Eric went to engineering school and became a baker. In 1983, the author named a character Dr. Erich Leonhardt, the archeologist in *Tales of a Dead King.*

1949 Myers remarked that his "life as an adolescent was filled with troubles and inner turmoil," a threat to vulnerability that he captures in the poem "Wolf Song" (2005) (Myers, "1994," 131). He confided to Adam Graham, an interviewer for the *Detroit News* that the period as "an extremely difficult journey as I tried to figure out who I was in a world that often seemed hostile" (Graham, 2002). The murder of the author's uncle, Leroy "Lee" Dean, cast a year-long shadow on the family because the loss led to Herbert Dean's depression. While coping with emotional unrest, Myers flourished intellectually. He entered a special program for bright students at Junior High School 43 and completed the seventh and eighth grades in one year. Of his writings from this period, he mused, "I never kept a journal. I wish I had" (Myers, "YA," 2001).

1950 After his biological father moved to Harlem, Myers reunited with his siblings. Influenced by critiques in the *New York Times Book Review*, he concluded that the book business was a valid career. He began reading the verse of Welsh poet Dylan Thomas, whom he heard reading his works at the White Horse Tavern on Hudson Street in Greenwich Village. Myers wrote sonnets and won his first writing competition with an essay for *Life* magazine. For explaining why he would like to see Ernest Hemingway's *The Old Man and the Sea* filmed in Cinemascope, he received a year's subscription to the magazine. Myers retains a soft spot for his ninth-grade teacher, Mrs. Finley. In an interview for this book, he remarked, "She sensed what we were capable of achieving, and knew that we hadn't developed the character to follow through" (Myers "Private," February 25, 2005). In the article "How I Came to Love English Literature" for *English Journal*, he recalled her dedication to literature: "Not only did she love poetry but she actually expected us to appreciate her attempts at metric immersion" (Myers, 1985, 93). Under her direction, Myers memorized two sections of Samuel Taylor Coleridge's symbolic poem *The Rime of the Ancient Mariner* (1798), a text he refers to in *The Dream Bearer* (2003). At Christmas, Mrs. Finley, whom he honored as a character in the novel, supplied Myers with eight Shakespearean plays and inspired his love of British poets.

As the author's perceptions of literature laid the groundwork for his career, he played pennywhistle in a performance of *The Stolen Prince*, a Japanese noh play. He also read a part in a stage version of *The Rime of the Ancient Mariner*, one of his favorite poems. He discovered that he could buy used books for a dime, but feared that the church deacon, Mr. Abbott, would doom him to hell for reading romance novels. Surreptitiously, Myers read under his desk passages where "swords clashed, bosoms heaved and fell like sunrises, and scintillating repartee splashed along the bitter irony" (*ibid.*).

1951 Following his friend Edward Norton, Myers studied accelerated math and science coursework at historic Stuyvesant High School, a boy's school at 345 Chambers Street. It was founded in 1904 and named for Peter Stuyvesant, a governor of New York Colony. The author used the school as the alma mater of rookie infantryman Richard "Richie" Perry, anti-hero of *Fallen Angels* (1988), and of Steve Harmon, a 16 year old charged with felony robbery and murder in *Monster* (1999). Attending a noon-to-5:30 schedule meant Myers had a 45-minute subway ride each morning and evening. He enjoyed writing short fiction in Mr. Brant's class. Norton also thrived, became an attorney, and married Eleanor Holmes Norton, the Democratic congresswoman from Washington, D.C.

1952 In English class, teacher Bonnie Liebow was the first adult to assure Myers that he had the talent to earn a living as a professional writer. She provided individualized instruction in literature and composition for her students. For Myers, she outlined difficult readings by European authors— Albert Camus's *The Stranger*, Émile Zola's *Nana*, Thomas Mann's *Buddenbrooks*, Anatole France's *Penguin Island*, and Honoré de Balzac's *Pere Goriot*. In the article "And Then I Read..." for *Voices-from-the-Middle*, Myers asserted, "Reading has given me a fair education" (Myers, May 2001, 58). To Allen O. Pierleoni, an interviewer for the *Sacramento Bee*, he acknowledged a pitfall of intense reading: "I was an excellent reader when I was coming up, but I never saw black people reading the books I read" (Pierleoni, 2005). In *Fallen Angels*, his powerful examination of the Vietnam War, he patterns protagonist Richie Perry after himself, setting him in Harlem at Stuyvesant High School under an English teacher named Mrs. Liebow. She explains to Richie the qualities that turn ordinary mortals into heroes and urges him not to give in.

Myers blossomed in his mid-teens from an immersion in bible analysis and the observation of moral right and wrong. He won an essay competition and earned a set of encyclopedias for winning a poetry contest. Because earnings from delivering messages for the post office were inadequate for him to purchase a portable typewriter, his father bought him a used Royal office model. In 1981, the author dedicated *Hoops* to his father for the gesture of paternal faith in his son's choice of writing as a career. He remarked in a panel discussion, "I write a lot about difficult father-son relationships.... It's an issue made fresh by being, somehow, alive in me" (Myers, "YA," 2001).

The Dean family could not afford to send Myers to college to study law on Herbert Dean's janitor's salary. Myers also lacked funds for the application fees for scholarships. He often skipped class on gym day because he couldn't afford shorts. Through a fictional alter ego in "Sunrise over Manaus" (1997), Myers admits, "I was about two inches and a phone call away from being kicked out of high school" (Myers, 1997, 73). Lured by "the mystique of the semi-hoodlum," he dropped out of school at age 15 to hang out with his cronies (Gray, 2002, 35). He later revealed his motivation, "I devalued myself as a person" ("His Goal," 2000). Over months of absence from class, he forged answers to the letters the school sent his parents. He dated a Brazilian exotic dancer and befriended Frank Hall, a young psychotic who suffered from violent outbursts and who walked the streets talking to himself. Myers retreated to the park and, in solitude, imitated the style of European novelists and poets. When a guidance counselor called, Myers's mother learned of the deception and took him back to school the next day.

1954 At age 16, Myers concluded, "I had worked after school in menial jobs in the garment center, pushed hand trucks through New York's busy midtown streets, carried packages for tips and, more important, had seen what being black and lacking a college degree would get you in 1954" (Myers, "School Days," 1). He joined a rough crowd, but later surmised, "I've never been able to approach behavior which my American and Christian upbringing considered immoral without feeling that I would be immoral to act out such behavior" (Myers, "Escalating," 701). For self-protection, he armed himself with a stiletto, which he used to rescue a younger boy and himself from three attackers. He fled an undercover cop who tried to nab the boys in a subway and left school a second time to avoid arrest. On his way out, a guidance counselor asked if Myers liked being black, a thought-provoking question that resurfaced in his fiction. He later reflected, "It was as if she knew something that I needed to know. My inner turmoil was such that I don't remember her name. What a pity" (Myers, "YA," 2001). In retrospect, the author recounted in the introductory letter to *Handbook for Boys: A Novel* (2002) that he needed "a group of worldly and knowledgeable men to counsel me" (Myers, 2002, n.p.).

June, 1954 Myers was so detached from high school life that he returned to class after the semester had ended. His friends had graduated; the building was locked for the summer. He walked away in tears. He later confirmed the value of self-education: "I had been, even at 16, better read than most Americans" (Myers, "School Days," 1).

August 12, 1954 Myers needed to leave Harlem to avoid arrest. He conceded, "I was in deep trouble and had a possibility of getting my little butt in jail" (Naughton, "Stories," C1). In a grimmer testimonial, he reported in a speech to adolescent boys in Paterson, New Jersey, "I was very lucky I didn't get killed" ("Writer," 2005). Influenced by Rupert Brooke's World War I poem "The Soldier," Myers joined the army at age 17 with "a romantic idea of what war would be like" ("Novel," 1988, 7). Sweetening his departure was the fact that his pre-admission test scores were high. In *Fallen Angels*, where he dramatized the motif of Richie Perry departing from Mabel, his mother, to enter the army, Myers pictures her crying and reminding Richie, "You don't have to go" (Myers, 1988, 74).

August 19, 1954 Leaving behind a weeping mother, Myers entered basic training at Fort Dix, New Jersey, a setting he mentions in the background of the fictional soldier Reuben Curry in *The Dream Bearer* (2003), who was also 17 when he entered the military. After studying radio repair as well as multiple ways to kill, the author starred on a military basketball team. After losing a tournament, he reaped the colonel's annoyance. Myers and other team members spent time at an Arctic missile base on Baffin Island. From his point of view—"icebound on a cargo ship"—the foggy terrain reminded him of *The Rime of the Ancient Mariner* (Myers, "How I Came," 94). He marveled at scenery that included habitats of polar bears and seals.

1957 After military service, Myers returned home in uniform, a guise that impressed his youngest brother, Thomas Wayne "Sonny" Myers. The author settled with his parents in Morristown, New Jersey, loaded trucks, and worked in an electronic cable factory. Contributing to family strife was his father's disapproval of fiction as a suitable career. In an article for *Instructor* magazine, the author recalled that his father "remembered me writing stories when I was a child, and was more than a little concerned that I was still writing stories as an adult" (Lewis, 1996, 73).

Myers moved to the Cort Hotel in Manhattan at 48th Street, which he describes in "Sunrise over Manaus" as smelling "like somebody had sprayed stuff around to cover up the way the place stunk. It didn't work" (Myers, 1997, 80). He found a job as mail clerk for the Peerless Brokerage while receiving rejection slips for his writing, which he published under the pseudonyms "W. Milton Dean, Tommy Enright, others I'd make up on the spot" (Myers "Private Interview," May 22, 2005). He read serious works by Honoré de Balzac, Lord Byron, Albert Camus, T. S. Eliot, André Gide, James Joyce, Friedrich Nietzsche, Eugene O'Neill, George Orwell, and Jean-Paul Sartre as well as the seamy Southern novels of Erskine Caldwell. Restless and dissatisfied because of a lack of social skills and confidence, Myers returned to Harlem, but found it changed by drug running and crime. While he continued writing, he lived off unemployment checks. Even unremunerative publication pleased him: "As long as I saw my name in print, I felt better about myself" (Graham, 2002).

1959 Myers married Joyce Smith while clerking for the post office, an occupation he reprises as the former job of Richard Perry in *Won't Know Till I Get There* (1982), the post–Vietnam War job of Sidney Rock in *Darnell Rock Reporting* (1994), and the father's employment in "The Treasure of Lemon Brown" (2001). In the author's off hours, he played percussion in a band and hung out with heavy drug users. Ironically, as his marriage foundered from his inattention to home life, he fantasized about a contented postal worker and his wife and three children in a picture book, *The Dragon Takes a Wife* (1972). While working as a messenger, he compiled ad copy for cemeteries and began publishing verse and adult adventure stories in *Black Creation, Black Digest, Black Scholar, Black World, Essence, The Liberator,* and *Negro Digest.* Writing under his own name and under pseudonyms, he earned a small return for his efforts. He later regretted that he did not learn more about the business end of the publishing world.

1960 During the Summer Olympics in Rome, Italy, Myers got his first look at an evolving athletic hero, gold-medalist Cassius Clay, a young boxer from Louisville, Kentucky. The author later extolled the boxer's heroism on a number of fronts in *The Greatest: Muhammad Ali* (2001).

1961 Joyce Myers gave birth to the couple's first child, Karen Elaine, to whom Myers dedicated the serious verse he submitted to a literary journal. After reading an ad in the *New York Post,* he enrolled in a community workshop to study composition. Under the counsel of Lajos Egri, the Hungarian-Jewish author of *The Art of Creative Writing* (1965), Myers began making impressive progress. According to fellow student Thomas C. Dent, author of *Southern Journey: A Return to the Civil Rights Movement* (1997), the class dissection of original works was harrowing: "The rule was that, after you read your work, you could not argue or try to explain what you had written. Everyone else had their say first — you had to sit there and take it. Then, and only then, could you comment" (Kalamu, 1993, 336). The discipline aided Myers in shaping his unique style and focus. For relaxation, he played basketball with the Jolly Brown Giants.

1963 Joyce had a second child, Michael Dean, who later developed a military career with the Air Force as a chaplain. Myers used his son's name in *Mojo and the Russians* (1977). In *A Time to Love: Stories from the Old Testament* (2003), Michael Dean examines his upbringing in storytelling and reading. He learned biblical stories in his early years and followed those oral stories in his teens to a greater analysis for his "journey through the scriptures" (Myers, 2003, viii). Through a tripartite study method — a family bible, dictionary, and a children's version of the bible — he came to love familiar characters and to envision himself living in their milieu. The oneness with scriptural times and places impelled him toward service to the faith.

1966 While Myers supervised the placement of employees for the New York State Department of Labor, he hung out with artists in East Village and played bongos at night clubs. Still active at basketball, he played at the Cage, a court on Sixth Avenue. In a private interview, he confided, "Somewhere along the flow of years I grew almost imperceptibly less strong, a half step slower. An athlete who would have been smothered by my abilities now proved an elusive step faster" (Myers, "Private," March 16, 2005). The match-up caused Myers to reflect on the inevitability of age: "Instead of matching him step for step, anticipating his moves, I found myself trying to slow him down, reaching for him, sometimes grabbing nothing but the flapping, sweat-encrusted jersey as he moved past. Years before, when I had come into my own as an athlete, when I had first exulted in my own basketball triumphs I had 'come of age' physically. In my early thirties I saw that period had come full circle. Someone else had 'come of age'" (*ibid.*).

Myers moved his family to Queens and bought his first house. On the G.I. Bill, he enrolled in languages at City College of the City University of New York and passed French, but failed English. While working with a therapist to eradicate his speech defect, he submitted adventure lore and sports stories on bullfighting and kick boxing to *Argosy, Blue Book, Cavalier, Delta Review, Espionage*, and *Male* and celebrity pieces to *National Enquirer* and *Star* at $15–20 per article.

1968 The era produced monochromatic young adult reading material that lacked essential data about "what it is to be a boy, of competition with other males" (Myers, "Pulling," 44). Three years after Dr. Nancy Larrick jolted literary critics with the article "The All-White World of Children's Books" (1965), the Council on Interracial Books for Children, including poet Langston Hughes and child advocate Dr. Benjamin Spock, served as go-betweens for aspiring nonwhite authors seeking to publish their manuscripts. Myers saw the brief advertisement for the council's writing contest for unpublished third world writers and surmised that "there wouldn't be much competition" ("Center," 12). He won $500, the first place prize for *Where Does the Day Go?*, a story for elementary school readers. His understanding of relationships between black parents and their children hints at the humanity and compassion that became his trademarks.

Myers breached the standard expectations for nonwhite children by having black and Hispanic youngsters develop their intellectual curiosity by asking an adult about the cosmic forces that control sunrise and sunset. Critics Zena Sutherland, Dianne L. Monson, and May Hill Arbuthnot commented in *Children and Books* (1972) on Myers's choice of a stable parent as role model for impressionable youngsters. Of his influence on readers, he remarked in a panel discussion, "The only advice I ever give is that young people believe in themselves and their ability to do well, to seek advice from people they admire, and to think of their lives in a longer time frame than most teenagers do" (Myers, "YA," 2001).

Myers's embrace of pacifism resulted from his loss of his 20-year-old brother Sonny to the Vietnam War. Sonny arrived shortly before the Tet offensive on January 31, 1968. He died on May 7, 1968, only two days after his arrival to combat in Vietnam in a firefight that erupted during a patrol. Myers carried guilt for setting an example of an older brother in uniform and wrote an essay on the death for *Essence*. Myers and son Chris went to the Vietnam Wall to make a rubbing of Sonny's name, one of the 58,200 victims inscribed on the monument in 1982. The author grieved for 20 years before writing Sonny's story in *Fallen Angels*. The narrative poses a loving mentorship of an older brother for a younger sibling in the affection of rookie infantryman Richie Perry for Kenny, a child who, from age four, has looked up to Richie as surrogate father and role model.

1969 Parents Magazine published Myers's *Where Does the Day Go?* as a picture book illustrated by Leo Carty. The story portrays a black father answering questions about nightfall for his son Steven and some Asian, black, and Hispanic companions. The characterization introduced one of Myers's interests, the relationship between black men and their sons. During this period of growth and professional development, his wife divorced him and took the two children, Karen and Michael Dean.

June, 1969 Myers issued in *Negro Digest* a bitter dilemma story about racism in white-controlled prisons, "How Long Is Forever?" The wry rejoinder to the title question is "Two to fo'teen years for a nigger" (Myers, 1969, 53). The theme of injustice goads inmate Moses over the edge into retaliation against Jenkins, a jeering, sexually brutalizing guard. The biblical allusion to Moses, the prince-turned-murderer who leads the Hebrews out of bondage in Egypt, implies an epic day of reckoning against haughty overlords. Intensified by contemporary views on prison problems, the motif of black families scarred by the incarceration of adults and children recurred in Myers's later works, particularly the novel *Somewhere in the Darkness* (1992).

1970 Lured by an advertisement in the *Amsterdam News*, Myers took a writing workshop at Columbia University under black author and writer-in-residence John Oliver Killens, a friend to black artists and the organizer of the Harlem Writers Guild. At Killens's direction, Myers left his work as an interviewer and employment supervisor for the State of New York and went to work at 57th Street and Fifth Avenue for the acquisitions editor of Bobbs-Merrill. Under a company program encouraging black authors like poet Nikki Giovanni, he advanced to senior trade book editor. In this same period, he visited his daughter Karen's elementary school in Brooklyn to peruse the adequacy of library books that met the needs of nonwhite children.

1971 To the anthology *What We Must See: Young Black Storytellers* (Dodd), edited by Orde Coombs, Myers contributed "The Fare to Crown Point." The story of a break-in pictures a young criminal discovering a baby left in its crib while the mother earns enough money to return home to Indiana. Myers and his agent negotiated with Bobbs-Merrill for a nonfiction work. About this time, he altered his middle name to Dean to honor his adoptive parents, a ritual naming that recurs in *Won't Know Till I Get There* (1982). For Parents Magazine, he completed *The Dancers*, a picture book illustrated by Anne Rockwell. The narrative portrays a white youth integrating the otherwise all-black cast of characters. The story of male interest in ballet pleased Florence Dean as well as the critics, who cited the story for its appeal to artistic boys. The book won a Child Study Association of America's Children's Books of the Year citation.

March, 1971 For *Black World*, Myers characterized solitude in "The Going On," a story of a widower's grief for his wife and his acceptance of living alone.

April, 1971 In *Black Creation*, Myers published "Juby," a short story about a troubled white woman who meets a man claiming to be a magician. By setting the plot in the Caribbean, the author makes plausible the woman's interest in voodoo and island culture, two subjects he returns to in *Mojo and the Russians* (1977) and *Mr. Monkey and the Gotcha Bird* (1984).

Fall, 1971 Myers's personal life took a setback after Florence Dean died of heart disease. In a book review he wrote for the *Washington Post*, he describes a similar break in the mother-son bond as "a deeply felt tragedy" (Myers, "Surviving," 7). In *Black Creation*, the author published "The Dark Side of the Moon," a tale of perversity and madness. An intense psychological study of a rapist and strangler named Augie, the narrative reveals escapes from reality in a budding criminal. His skill at rationalizing four deaths anticipates a similar mental maelstrom in *Monster: A Novel* (1999) and *Shooter* (2004), two of the author's most critically acclaimed works.

1972 At age 35, Myers edged closer to the needs of young black readers by composing a modern fairy tale, *The Dragon Takes a Wife* (Bobbs-Merrill), illustrated by Ann Grifalconi. The transformation of a conventional fairy into a hip, jive-talking troubleshooter named Mabel Mae Jones introduced an updated view of kindness and sweetness. Through trial and error, Mabel Mae satisfies her own need for change by giving Harry the dragon something to fight for. By concluding with an image of a stable family, Myers edges away from magic solutions to an Americanized happy ending based on the nuclear family and the work ethic.

The violation of stereotypical European fairy lore generated an uproar. In Myers's article "The Black Experience in Children's Books; One Step Forward, Two Steps Back" (1979) for *Interracial Books for Children Bulletin*, he stated that "some of the most virulent hate mail imaginable" accused him of stereotyping blacks and of corrupting white European folklore with dialect (Myers, 1979, 14). He remarked that "'obscene' was one of their milder labels" (*ibid.*). The banning of his books from school and public library shelves became the first in a series of book censorships that dogs his works into the present. Nonetheless, he anticipated the blossoming of humanistic literature for children like that written by Sharon Bell Marthis, Ray Sheppard, Virginia Driving Hawk Sneve, Margaret Musgrove, and Mildred Taylor. Moreover, he expected markets to flourish with the widening of racial and cultural appeal of young adult literature.

November, 1972 For *Essence*, Myers wrote "Bubba," a complex study of racial bias and loss in a white soldier's return of a black comrade's body to a grieving mother.

1973 Myers published his first young adult novel, first nonfiction, and short pieces in men's magazines, *McCall's, Sunday News Magazine*, and *Alfred Hitchcock Mystery Magazine*. His success with white audiences led him to doubt his aim and purpose. He struck a nerve in white readers after issuing an article on interracial adoption. He contributed the story "Gums" to *We Be Word Sorcerers: Twenty-five Stories by Black Americans* (Bantam), edited by Sonia Sanchez and containing the works of top black authors—Toni Cade Bambara, Imamu Amiri Baraka, Gwendolyn Brooks, Ed Bullins, Dudley Randall, and Alice Walker. Myers's frightening tale pictures a young man and his grandfather confronting the personified figure of Death.

1974 Myers married Constance Brendel Myers, a former clerk at the labor office who later researched her husband's six-book history series. Their son Christopher became the author's illustrator and a sounding board for his development of young characters and authentic dialogue. Myers traveled to England, France, and Italy with his older son Michael. For Putnam, Myers wrote *Fly, Jimmy, Fly!*, an urban story illustrated by Moneta Barnett. The fantasy novel empowers the main character to float aloft and look down on the city.

1975 Myers, Connie, and Christopher visited Greece, where a student demonstration resulted in police action and tear gas. Myers got his first fiction contract for *Fast Sam, Cool Clyde, and Stuff* for Viking Press, winner of a Woodward Park School Annual Book Award and an American Library Association (ALA) Notable Book citation. The ironic initiatory novella began as a short story about 12-year-old Francis, a character whom critics compared to Mark Twain's Tom Sawyer. At the suggestion of Linda Zuckerman, an editor at Viking Press, Myers turned the episode into his first young adult novel, a comedy that describes how Fast Sam and his friends create a club that directs bewildered children to "the 116th Street good people," the ones who could be counted on to protect and shelter kids from urban trouble.

Myers's venture into teen reality fiction earned the support of critics, parents, librarians, teachers, church leaders, and young readers. For his creation of an endearing teen anti-hero, critic Jim Naughton, a reviewer for the *Los Angeles Times*, dubbed the author an "accidental pioneer" and an "institution in the low-profile world of children's fiction" (Naughton, "Literary Crusader," 8). The author's method seems simple — he succeeds by "humanizing the kid. Giving the kids the same kinds of problems that everybody else has" (*ibid.*). In the estimation of critic Barbara Bader, Myers rejuvenated the teen literary market "then dominated by Robert Cormier's psychological thrillers, with their morally bankrupt characters, and Paul Zindel's dramas of self-absorbed alienation" and by Alice Childress and Sharon Bell Mathis's dreary stories of drug addicts (Bader, 147). Myers followed with *The World of Work: A Guide to Choosing a Career* for Bobbs-Merrill, a nonfiction handbook to seeking and acquiring employment in jobs that promise satisfaction and opportunities for advancement. He dedicated the text to his mentor, John Killens.

January, 1976 Myers published in *Black Scholar* an encomium, "Gordon Parks: John Henry with a Camera," the only black photographer working for *Life* and *Vogue*. Myers's essay marvels at Parks's "documentaries of American life during the depression and, later, in Harlem and South America" (Myers, 1976, 27). Through Gerald McQuillen, protagonist of *The Nicholas Factor* (1983), Myers states the value of such candid shots: "It was almost like looking into the windows of their lives" (Myers, 1983, 27).

Later that year, 1976 For Franklin Watts, Myers wrote *Social Welfare: A First Book*, a history of government programs intended to aid the poor and needy. His tutorial expresses stern condemnations of mistreatment, notably, his charge that "The poor have always been exploited" (Myers, 1976, 4). Among the photos substantiating his text is a snapshot of black children laboring on a Southern farm in 1939.

While the author and his family traveled to Peru, he worked at his own career development. As they camped among the Quechua in a rainforest on the Amazon River, he acquired data for a piece on bullfighting and material for *The Nicholas Factor*, a spy thriller that focuses on natives of Iquitos on the Colombia-Peru border. At a rhapsodic moment in the narrative, a character describes the beauty of Lima at "the end of their cloudy season, and there's no fresher air anywhere in the world" (Myers, 1983, 48). The resulting novel, which Myers calls "my weakest published book," suffered from his departure from experience into fancy (Myers, "And Then," 61).

Summer, 1977 After Bobbs-Merrill disbanded Myers's department, he, Connie, and two-year-old Christopher journeyed to Bangkok, Hong Kong, and Thailand, settings that influenced the author's writing of *Fallen Angels* and *The Hidden Shrine* (1985). During the vacation, Myers pondered what direction to take to support his family. He decided on freelance writing after resolving a serious consideration: "Are publishers buying works from black authors?.... In short, are we in vogue?" (Myers, "Gordon Parks," 28). Without hesitation, the author chose to shoulder a challenge—the "obligation to all the kids who are voiceless" (Naughton, "Literary Crusader," 8). To amuse his son during the long plane ride from Taiwan to Anchorage and on to New York, Myers made up a story that he later adapted into *Mr. Monkey and the Gotcha Bird* (1984), a fool tale that Leslie Morril illustrated in bold colors and sleek geometrics.

Myers returned to Jersey City and taught creative writing and black history. He mastered a number of genres—biography, coming-of-age, fantasy, science fiction, and mystery novels, including the four-book Arrow Series, and stories for *Black Creation, Black World, Boy's Life, Ebony, Jr., Espionage, Essence, Parents,* and *Scholastic.* His narratives featured the tradition of the griot. One novel, *Mojo and the Russians* (Viking), he dedicated to "the Martinsburg Gang," a humorous name for siblings Ethel, George, Geraldine, Imogene, and Viola. Critic Denise M. Wilms, a reviewer for *Booklist,* grasped a skill in *Mojo and the Russians* that became Myers's *raison d'etre*—his unsentimental characterizations and an "accurate feeling for the thoughts and folkways of children" that result in spontaneity and vigor (Heins, 1978, 167). Myers followed with *Victory for Jamie* (Scholastic), illustrated by Norm Walker, and *Brainstorm* (Franklin Watts), featuring photographs by Chuck Freedman. The latter, a sci-fi story for disadvantaged readers, sets teens in the role of earth's saviors after they fly a space ship to another planet to locate a threat to human life.

1978 The Myers family bought a home at 2543 Kennedy Boulevard in Jersey City, New Jersey, a site that Jim Naughton, a reporter for the *Los Angeles Times* summarized as "a modest row house on the main drag in this gritty town at the mouth of the Holland Tunnel" (Naughton, "Literary Crusader," 8). Nonetheless, the Harlem lingo and rhythms held steady with Myers's first realistic novel, *It Ain't All for Nothin'* (Viking), which earned an ALA Notable Book Citation and an ALA Best Book for Young Adults award. Of children's awareness of crime, Myers later exonerated them for staying true to their peer group by keeping mum about what they've seen and heard: "Even when kids know there's something wrong going on, they have these divided loyalties" (Myers, "Pulling," 44).

November, 1978 For *Black Scholar,* Myers wrote a tragic short story, "The Vision of Felipe," about the dangers to homeless orphans in Lima, Peru, during the brutal military dictatorship of Juan Velasco Alvarado. The author describes the tenderhearted Felipe as bereft of guidance after his grandmother's death. Like the urban survivors in Myers's young adult novels, ten-year-old Felipe leaves Iquitos and undergoes a long barge journey to Lima, 600 miles to the southwest, as the most likely place in which to thrive. The story builds pathos out of Felipe's Dickensian generosity toward others even less fortunate than he. Although Felipe begs from tourists to support himself, he contributes a few coins to a destitute mother whose infant appears close to death. The author's pity for hapless children re-emerges in later works, including the enslaved title figure in *The Legend of Tarik* (1981).

1979 *The Young Landlords* (Viking), describes teen entrepreneurs—Bubba, Dean, Gloria Wiggens, Jeannie, Omar, and Paul Williams—who buy the Stratford Arms, a dilapidated building at 356 West 122nd Street in Harlem. The story puts Paul and his 15-year-old cohorts in the position of tenement owners dealing with eccentrics, including Petey Darden, the janitor-bootlegger, and Askai Ben Kenobi, a Star Wars fan who challenges the owners with karate chops that splinter a banister. The story alters in tone after Paul and his father drive to West Virginia to the funeral of Paul's uncle Jerry and discuss along the way his father's estrangement from Jerry, whose wasted life began with petty thievery. Critic P. L. Gauch, reviewing for the *New York Times Book Review*, correctly assessed the loose connection between episodes. He also admired the engaging dialogue, a realistic element that is Myers's strength.

For its lessons in pragmatism, *The Young Landlords* won a second ALA Best Book for Young Adults award, a second ALA Notable Book Citation, and a film option from Topol Productions. Dedicated to Dr. Augusta Baker, renowned Baltimore-born author, librarian, and storyteller, the novel honors her 17-year influence on young readers at the 135th Street Branch Library in Harlem and acknowledges her prominence as the first black administrator of the New York Public Library and as a consultant to *Sesame Street*. She challenged educators and publishers to right a serious wrong against the black children "reading about the heroes and history of every country without being told the truth about the contributions of their own African and slave ancestors to the progress of this country" (Baker, 79).

In a busy year, the Myers family traveled to Morocco. He gave the film version of *The Young Landlords* a so-so rating for its attempt to turn his novel into a musical. For *Interracial Books for Children Bulletin*, the author completed a pivotal article, "The Black Experience in Children's Books: One Step Forward, Two Steps Back," which challenged publishers to address civil rights gains and ongoing social issues in books for nonwhite children. In his opinion, publishing houses "did not deliver images upon which black children could build and expand their own worlds" (Myers, 1979, 14). He remarked on the promise of the late 1960s, which withered with the phase-out of Great Society funds to schools and public libraries. He urged teachers and librarians to demand books that "reflect the experiences of all Americans," regardless of the racial and cultural makeup of individual institutions (*ibid.*). The forceful essay established a pattern in Myers's public appearances and writings, which stress the needs of nonwhite children for a literature of their own.

1980 Myers issued two children's works for Viking. The first, *The Golden Serpent*, is a mystery-fable or apologue set in India at the beginning of the 20th century. The text illustrates callous royal and upper-class disregard of human suffering. Myers followed with a seriocomic detective duo, *The Black Pearl and the Ghost; or, One Mystery After Another*, illustrated by Robert Quackenbush. The narrative offers grade-school readers a touch of parody in its description of ghost busting. *The Young Landlords* won a Coretta Scott King Award, a major acknowledgement of Myers's contribution to positive experiences for black youth. Children's Television International filmed *Mojo and the Russians* as a part of the Storybound Series, which also features fiction by Natalie Babbitt, Judy Blume, Katherine Paterson, and Armstrong Sperry.

1981 Myers earned critical acclaim for *Hoops: A Novel* (Delacorte), a suspenseful teen sports novel that won his third ALA Best Book for Young Adults citation and entered the finals for the Edgar Allan Poe Award. The text opens on a father's recognition of his son's dreams. The father predicts, "You gonna lay your days out in front of yourself like an imaginary road" (Myers, 1981, 1). The novel denounces the prostitution of poor black athletes to college and professional team sports. By portraying the consequences of shaving points for cash, the author establishes the need for integrity as well as athletic skill. Myers dedicated the book to educator and author Hoyt William Fuller, a native of Atlanta, Georgia, who edited *Negro Digest* and mentored activists and writers of the Black Arts Movement. The film version of the novel features Lou Gossett, Jr. Myers channeled his observations on Islam and Morocco into the setting and characters of *The Legend of Tarik* (Viking), the first of his fantasy and adventure lore. The author dedicated the combination fantasy-historical fiction text to financier and teacher Dr. Edward W. Robinson, Jr., a noted historian.

1982 Myers visited Aswan, Egypt, a setting he used for an exotic thriller, *Tales of a Dead King* (1983). A quest fable, *The Legend of Tarik,* earned a Notable Children's Trade Book in Social Studies citation and Myers's fourth ALA Best Book for Young Adults award. The author completed a fourth novel, *Won't Know Till I Get There* (Viking), which he dedicated to his children, Karen, Michael, and Chris. The plot covers thorny terrain—a juvenile delinquent named Earl Goins comes to live at Stephen Perry's house as a foster child. The seriocomic book won the Parents Choice Award for its realistic examination of foster parenting and its portrayal of intergeneration relationships between teens and old people. In a critique for *School Library Journal*, reviewer Hazel Rochman lauded "the move from slapstick to pathos, the sudden stabs of psychological insight" (Rochman, "Review," 72).

1983 Challenges to *Fast Sam* from Ohio school administrators, Myers's head-on encounter with book banning, had little effect on him. He published *The Nicholas Factor* (Viking), a mystery-thriller based on his visit to Peru. The plot describes the Crusade Society, an elite cadre of teenagers who battle Kohler, a German villain. After completing *Tales of a Dead King* (Morrow), an adventure book featuring details he learned on a trip to Egypt, he won a New Jersey Institute of Technology Authors Award. The novel was the subject of a Hallmark made-for-TV film, *Legend of the Lost Tomb* (1997), which starred Stacy Keach.

To reassure his father that he was a professional writer, Myers studied criminal justice and photography as adjuncts to fiction. To complete a 600-page project, he interviewed prosecutors, defense attorneys, killers, robbers, prostitutes, dope dealers, and juvenile felon wannabes in youth houses. At Greenhaven prison in Rahway, New Jersey, he profited from "hearing the heavy steel doors slam behind me, looking into the faces of the young inmates" (Myers, "And Then I Read," 61). In an interview with critic Hazel Rochman for *Booklist*, he noted that the inmates distanced themselves from issues of right and wrong: "These guys were like jailhouse lawyers, so to speak, and they knew the law backward and forward, but there was no moral discussion" (Rochman, "Interview," 1101).

Taking a more positive approach to human existence, Myers developed a passion for antique snapshots, an interest he displayed previously in his admiration for Gordon Parks's photo collection *Moments Without Proper Names* (1975). Myers's collection grew into a professional library. For *Brown Angels: An Album of Pictures and Verse* (1993), a survey of moods and postures revealing the personalities of silent figures, he wrote eleven poems to accompany sepia-toned pictures. He followed with a fully developed photo-essay, *One More River to Cross: An African American Photograph Album* (1995), which critic Anthony Edwards compared to the work of Harlem Renaissance photographer James Van Der Zee. Blending black-and-white images of ordinary people with portraits of Marian Anderson, Mary McLeod Bethune, Frederick Douglass, W. E. B. Dubois, Billie Holiday, Paul Robeson, Jackie Robinson, Madame C. J. Walker, Booker T. Washington, and Ida B. Wells, Myers establishes the success of the Great Migration in founding a black haven in Harlem. His verbal and visual success at black history elicited from critic Jackie Gropman a spontaneous burst of praise: "All incredibly expressive" (Gropman, 1996, 186). Of the need for snapshot collections as family history, Myers stressed, "It's especially sad when people die without living relatives to keep the family heirloom photographs intact" (Connors, 17). He elevates legacies to treasure in the life of a homeless man, the title character of "The Treasure of Lemon Brown" (1983), a popular story originally published in *Boys' Life*.

1984 Myers completed a B.A. in communications from Empire State College for adult learners. He studied biblical history and culture in an extension course from Hebrew University of Jerusalem that later influenced his writing of *A Time to Love: Stories from the Old Testament* (2003). He devoted more time to his younger son by coaching Little League baseball at Lincoln Park. That same year he published three more works. The first, the picture book *Mr. Monkey and the Gotcha Bird* (Delacorte), a beast fable illustrated by Leslie Morrill, is dedicated to Christopher. The second and third were sequels to *Hoops* and *It Ain't All for Nothin'— The Outside Shot* (Delacorte), winner of a Parents' Choice Award, and *Motown and Didi: A Love Story* (Viking Kestrel), which earned Myers a second Coretta Scott King Award. The latter novel is Myers's initial abandonment of first-person narration. The story honors survivalism in Motown, a foster child who respects black solidarity and personal responsibility in an environment filled with wrongdoing and temptation.

1985 Myers believes that "writing can be learned by anyone truly interested in language and literature" (Foreman, 223). In addition to writing, he taught composition and grammar bimonthly at P.S. 40, the Ezra S. Nolan junior high school on Chambers Avenue, to students called "The Creative Spirit of P.S. 40." He explained his methods of having student writers interview their elders about their education. He also likes to describe writing as a means of solving problems. He coached a star pupil, Lorraine Kenny, in polishing her original story, "The Vacation," for *Shoe Tree*, a children's magazine published in Santa Fe, New Mexico.

Myers recapped his own education in "How I Came to Love English Literature" for *English Journal* and completed for Viking Kestrel the first two works in the four-part Arrow Series: *The Hidden Shrine* and *Adventure in Granada*, illustrated by John Speirs. The latter received a Child Study Association of America award. Reflecting the style and tone of Hardy Boy mysteries, the novellas feature the exploits of fatherless brothers, Chris and Ken Arrow, at exotic sites studied by Dr. Carla Arrow, their anthropologist mother.

1986 After the death of Herbert Dean from cancer in a veterans' hospital, Myers learned family history that proved that his foster father was illiterate. The scrawl with which Dean filled out forms proved that he was poorly educated. The author bore hard feelings that Dean did not comment on his books. Myers concluded, "I realized that he had never commented on any of my books because he couldn't read them" (Gallo, 11).

Myers stood first among black authors for youth, but he expressed disillusion with the teen literary market in an essay, "I Actually Thought We Would Revolutionize the Industry," for the *New York Times Book Review*. He predicted that, if black people don't buy books written for them, "We will simply have to wait for the next round of race riots, or the next interracial conflict, and the subsequent markets thus created" (Myers, "I Actually," 50).

For Teachers & Writers Collaborative, Myers wrote a popular school text, *Sweet Illusions*, an interactive story about teen pregnancy and abortion. The imaginative text presents complex issues from the perspective of multiple characters. Each chapter provides space for composing reader response to issues like absent fathers, government funding for daycare, and the responsibility of young mothers to find workable solutions to their problems. In July, he published a pro-child essay, "Gifts," in *Horn Book*. Reflecting on 17 years as a writer for youth, he declared with hesitation that "it is those now in sneakers and jump-suits who will most affect the world's survival" (Myers, "Gifts," 437). He warned of "shadows of indifference" and foresaw that the upbringing of that generation would determine whether the world would ever achieve peace (*ibid.*).

1987 In grief over the death of his father, Myers began studying his family origins. He published a fantasy-quest novel, *Shadow of the Red Moon* (HarperCollins), a didactic sci-fi adventure that contrasts urbanism with wilderness. The narrative describes how an Okalian, 15-year-old Jon, seeks a new land after a meteorite fouls Crystal City with dust. The narrative builds tension from the paranoia and government lies that cloud issues of survival. Myers moves sure-footedly toward a pacifist conclusion: fear and faulty assumptions nurture enmity.

Myers completed the Arrow Series with *Duel in the Desert* and *Ambush in the Amazon*. He based the second novel on family's travel along the Amazon River among the Quechua of Peru. The mystery-adventure novella features the synergy of three teens who unmask two villains posing as monsters. Myers followed with "Jeremiah's Song," a short story collected in *The Giver and Related Readings* (1987), and a teen novel *Crystal* (Viking Kestrel), a cautionary tale about an identity crisis in Crystal Brown, a professional model. In the latter, Myers presents his protagonist with an approach-avoidance situation—a life of celebrity and self-absorption that precipitates demands for sexual repayment to the men who foster her career in movies and sleazy photography. Myers expresses his confidence in teens by tracing Crystal's mental and emotional retreat from a seamy life.

1988 Myers honed his talents with a fellowship to the McDowell Colony, the nation's oldest arts enclave located near Mount Monadnock Region, New Hampshire. He lived in a wooded setting while working on *The Glory Field*, a generational saga covering five layers of family history. For a city boy, the sight of raccoons and the sounds of small creatures scampering across the roof were unnerving.

Myers's masterwork, *Fallen Angels* (Scholastic), won of a third Coretta Scott King Award, a fifth ALA Best Book for Young Adults award, and a second Parents Choice Award. For background data, the author searched historic firefights from the National Archives, consulted the Vietnam Veterans Outreach Center, and interviewed war heroes and the survivors of soldiers killed in combat. He also traveled cross-country by Amtrak and visited the hometowns of his fictional cast for an impression of their lives in peacetime. For terrain and southeast Asian culture, he relied on his observations while visiting Thailand. The poignant platoon leader, Lieutenant Carroll, Myers developed from the example of a local parish priest. Carroll's prayer was Myers's own composition. The text appealed to white readers more than blacks in part because of the level of reading difficulty.

Myers wrote *Me, Mop, and the Moondance Kid* (Delacorte), a warm, funny novella illustrated by Rodney Pate with realistic pen-and-ink drawings. The author based the story on his observations of son Christopher's Little League team and focused on issues of surrogate parenting. T. J. and Moondance's effort to get Olivia "Mop" Parrish adopted enhances a multicultural camaraderie between the two black boys and the white girl. Critic Barbara Bader remarked in a review for *Horn Book*, "A few pictures and a passing reference are all the ID needed to tell us that the kids are a mixed lot" (Bader, 2003, 150). The novel won an ALA Notable Book Citation. Demco Media issued a video version along with a film of *Fallen Angels*, a powerful young adult classic that compares in combat intensity to Stephen Crane's combat story *The Red Badge of Courage* (1895), Mariano Azuela's *The Underdogs* (1914), and Gary Paulsen's *A Soldier's Heart* (1998).

Scorpions (Harper & Row) returns to a more unsettling urbanism than in *It Ain't All for Nothin'* (1978). According to Jim Naughton, an author-reviewer for the *Los Angeles Times*, the author sets the story in "a world in which there are no good choices" (Naughton, "Literary Crusader," 8). Against the violence, crack cocaine, and prison sentences of the 1980s, 12-year-old protagonist Jamal Hicks alternates between admiration for armed gangs and terror of their guns. Myers earned critical acclaim for rhetorical control and moral tone and for compassion toward wayward pre-teens. He dedicated the novel to three of his daughter Karen's children, Brandon, Brian, and Beverly.

November, 1988 At the National Council of Teachers of English in St. Louis, Missouri, Myers addressed the Adolescent Literature Assembly with the speech "The Young Adult Novel: Writing for Aliens."

1989 Myers kept current with the teen world by teaching creative writing. He was somewhat disconcerted when "instead of writing a story about a teddy bear or their favorite Christmas, they are writing about a friend who is OD'ing on crack" (*ibid.*). His teen urban novel *Scorpions* earned a Newbery Honor Book Award, an ALA Notable Book Citation, Judy Lopez Children's Books Award, Honorable Mention Children's Books from the Library of Congress, a Books for the Teen Age from the New York Public Library, and an ALA Best Books for Young Adults award. In addition, the story inspired letters from isolated, confused young readers who wanted the author's advice. For his choice of realistic situations and dialogue, he faced criticism from conservative parents and educators. The ALA listed *Hoops* among its censored or banned books after a Colorado district challenged the work.

1990 The author completed a high-spirited comedy, *The Mouse Rap* (HarperCollins), which won a Parent's Choice Award and an International Reading Association (IRA) Children's Choice selection. He based the story on two extremes—on the popularity of rap music and on legends about Tiger Moran's mob money allegedly stashed in an abandoned building. The plot pictures a situation that Myers knew from experience—a father re-emerging in the life of Frederick "The Mouse" Douglas, a 14-year-old Harlem rapper. Myers earned the regard of critic Diane Roback, a reviewer for *Publishers Weekly*, who praised him for "depth, credibility and a keen sense of humor" (Roback, 1990, 64). The author dedicated the work to New York City librarian Harriet B. Brown, the 1980 chair of the Coretta Scott King Task Force, for Brown's contributions to children's literature. He later commented on her importance to his career: "Encouragement from librarians and from people who know [my] work honors me more than awards" (Chance, *et al.*, 1994, 248).

Demco debuted a video of *Scorpions*. A second work, *Fallen Angels*, appeared on the ALA banned books list after Ohio school authorities objected to its use of language common to city streets and army barracks. In a 1994 interview with the staff of the *Journal on Reading*, he commented on age-appropriate writing style: "The only thing that makes this particular novel for older readers is my decision to use profanity" (*ibid.*, 247). Subsequent publicity about book proscription increased sales.

February, 1990 Myers's unpublished play *And There Stood a Man*, a tribute to actor Paul Robeson, opened at Rutgers University and featured five players from the dramatics department.

1991 Myers covered issues of race and human rights in *Now Is Your Time! The African-American Struggle for Freedom* (HarperCollins), his first contribution to black history. His epilogue reminds black readers, "We are not alone, but are a people" (Myers, 1991, 272). He dedicated the text to nine preservers of black history. Dr. Charles L. Blockson, an archivist from Norristown, Pennsylvania, specializing in data on the Underground Railroad, donated his world-class collection of Afro-Americana to Temple University in 1982. Dr. Theodore Brunson earned the Fred Shuttlesworth Lifetime Achievement Award for founding the Afro American Historical Society Museum. Author Howard Dodson began directing the Schomburg Center for Research in Black Culture in 1984. Another Pennsylvanian, Debra Newman Ham, was the first black female archivist at the National Archives in Washington, D.C. William W. Layton, also in the nation's capital, is an author and private collector of historical data. Chronicler and filmmaker William Miles focuses on the history of Harlem. Historian Clement Price teaches African American studies at Rutgers. Researchers Dorothy Provine and Paul E. Sluby of the Afro-American Historical and Genealogical Society compile data on blacks living in the Washington, D.C., area.

Myers collected documents and illustrations on the Myers family for a text that features slavery, the Dred Scott trial, and the 54th Massachusetts Regiment of Black Soldiers during the Civil War. Contributing to his ordering of details were his sisters, Ethel, Geraldine, Imogene, and Viola. The narrative honors orators Frederick Douglass and Malcolm X, freedom fighter Coretta Scott King, businessman James Forten, inventor Lewis Latimer, rebels Nat Turner and John Brown, journalist Ida B. Wells, and sculptor Meta Vaux Warrick Fuller. The history snagged his fourth Coretta Scott King Award, an ALA Best Books for Young Adults and Notable Books for Children, and a National Council of Teachers of English Orbis Pictus Award for Outstanding Nonfiction.

January, 1991 Myers delivered "Travelers and Translators," the main address at The Ohio State University Children's Literature Conference in Columbus.

February 27, 1991 When the Persian Gulf War ended, Michael Dean Myers returned home from serving in the Air Force. That same year Christopher Myers entered Brown University.

April, 1991 Myers received a community honor — the title of Everyday Hero from the *Jersey Journal* "News in Education" project for his work with Little League players and his tutoring of students at P.S. 40.

December, 1991 In "Telling Our Children the Stories of Their Lives," an essay for *American Visions*, Myers confronted publishers of fiction and textbooks for omitting black faces and experiences. His rhetorical question forced the issue of discounting lives: "Is it not logical for the child to assume that if the books denote who is and is not significant, and that if people of color are not represented, then they don't count?" (Myers, "Telling," 30). To relieve the dearth of worthy texts about black people, he listed quality reading, including *At the Crossroads* (1991), a fiction book by Rachel Isadora on South African children and their families under Apartheid. He concluded with advice to parents, teachers, and librarians: "It is essential that we search for those images that nurture black children" (*ibid.*, 32).

1992 In a busy year, Myers toured England, spending six weeks in London, and began for Bantam the 18 Pine Street books, the first mass-market series to star black characters. According to Dianne Johnson-Feelings in an article collected in *African-American Voices in Young Adult Literature: Tradition, Transition, Transformation* (1994), the creation of a series "indicates ... that Myers is among the upper class in the world of children's and young adult publishing — publishers know that his name alone will sell any book" (Smith, 1994, 153). Johnson-Feelings lauds Myers for his "big step in reversing for countless young adult readers of all ethnic groups the stereotype that African American experience is monolithic" (*ibid.*, 157).

Myers also published *Mop, Moondance, and the Nagasaki Knights* (Delacorte), a sequel to *Me, Mop, and the Moondance Kid* that intersperses with humor the troubling issues of poverty and homelessness. Set during an international baseball tournament, the story poses language and cultural hurdles to the understanding of players in Japan, Mexico, and France. Realism dominates *A Place Called Heartbreak: A Story of Vietnam* (Raintree Steck-Vaughn), illustrated by Frederick Porter, and *Somewhere in the Darkness* (Scholastic), a Newbery Honor Book, a Booklist Editers Choice selection, an ALA Best Books for Young Adults, an ALA Notable Books for Children, and a Boston Globe–Horn Book Honor Book. *A Place Called Heartbreak* describes the seven-year, four-month imprisonment in North Vietnam of Colonel Fred V. Cherry, the first black POW of the Vietnam War. The latter novel Myers claims to have incubated in the dark regions of his mind. The action of *Somewhere in the Darkness* portrays the odyssey of Cephus "Crab" Little, an ex-con, who leaves prison and abducts his son Jimmy from Mama Jean's care. Father and son seek wholeness during a cross-country odyssey from New York to Chicago and Arkansas and back to New York.

Reality struck close to home with the banning of Myers's works. With the issuance of a gentle children's biography, *Young Martin's Promise* (Raintree), illustrated by Barbara Higgins Bond, Myers encountered censorship, this time close to home at a Queens library. Another work, the story "Who Needs an Aries Ape?" (1992), was banned because two characters arrange the animals in a pet shop by their zoological signs.

Myers joined four associates in establishing the Center for Multicultural Children's Literature (CMCL), an outreach to publishers and writers. The cooperative brought together 50 artists and writers under the sponsorship of HarperCollins. Through the mentoring of promising talent, the consortium hoped to end the dominance of white children and white neighborhoods in young adult literature to the exclusion of other races and cultures.

August, 1992 Myers mined Western history in 1882 for *The Righteous Revenge of Artemis Bonner* (HarperCollins), the recounting of events following the murder of Uncle Ugly Ned in Tombstone, Arizona. Set in frontier towns from the Southwest to Anchorage, Alaska, the plot follows 15-year-old Artemis Bonner, a sign painter from New York City, in a parody of treasure hunting and a vengeance quest. In 1996, Demco released a video of *The Righteous Revenge of Artemis Bonner.*

1993 Myers won a Coretta Scott King Honor Book Award, this time for *Somewhere in the Darkness.* He published substantial additions to his canon: *Malcolm X: By Any Means Necessary* (Scholastic), a young adult biography that reveals "an everyday kind of guy" ("Review," 1992, B1). The author justifies the leader's lifestyle as "just surviving in this subculture after being rejected by the mainstream American culture" (*ibid.*). Myers diminishes the elements of threat and violence in Malcolm's speeches: "In scaring America, in bringing it face to face with the realities of our society in the sixties, he left it a better place" (*ibid.*).

Myers oversaw for Bantam the writing and publication of four-book 18 Pine Street Series—*The Test, Fashion by Tasha, Intensive Care*, and *Dangerous Games*—which won a Jeremiah Ludington Award. From his collection of photographs, he compiled two anthologies for HarperCollins, *Remember Us Well: An Album of Pictures and Verse* and *Brown Angels: An Album of Pictures and Verse*, a photography collection that *Parenting* named one of the year's ten best books. *Brown Angels* was the source of verse and 150 photographs exhibition at the Neward Public Library from December 1993 to January 1994. In 2001, poet Sharon Creech wrote *Love That Dog*, in which she admires "Love That Boy" from *Brown Angels* as "the best best BEST/ poem/ever" (Creech, 42).

In addition, Myers contributed the Gothic story "Things That Go Gleep in the Night" to an anthology, *Don't Give Up the Ghost: The Delacorte Book of Original Ghost Stories*, and crafted the poem "Migration" for *The Great Migration: An American Story* (HarperCollins), a colorful display of paintings that folk artist Jacob Lawrence completed in 1940 and 1941. Covering the black diaspora from 1916 to 1919, the text discloses the misgivings and hopes of black Southerners deserting their agricultural foundations for urban industrial centers in the North. *Publishers Weekly* lauded Myers's ode as a "poetic anthem" ("Review," 1993, 61). Critic Mary M. Burns, reviewing for *Horn Book*, asserted that the book salutes "a significant aspect of United States history and one which needs emphasizing" (Burns, 1994, 88).

1994 Myers, winner of the first annual Virginia Hamilton Award, earned an ALA Notable Children's Book, an IRA Teachers Choice, and a sixth Coretta Scott King award for *Malcolm X*, and a New York Public Library Books for the Teen Age citation for *Brown Angels*. He explored empathy and observation in children in *Darnell Rock Reporting* (Delacorte), which he based on the idea of a Lincoln, Nebraska, librarian who formed a reading club. The author dedicated the novel to Charles Culler Middle School in Lincoln. Veteran *Booklist* reviewer Janice Del Negro labeled the novel "a masterpiece of understatement" (Del Negro, 1994, 2044). The narrative develops a teen epiphany about human worth. The job of school reporter inspires 13-year-old Darnell to evaluate the life of Sweeby Jones, a homeless man, and to propose establishment of a garden in place of a parking lot.

In the style of Alex Haley's *Roots* (1965) and *Queen: The Story of an American Family* (1993), Myers composed *The Glory Field* (Scholastic), which covers the enslavement of 11-year-old Muhammad Bilal from Sierra Leone in 1713 through six generations of the Lewis family. The title derives from a plot of land that Elijah Lewis owned on Curry Island, South Carolina, in 1900. During the Great Depression, the story shifts to Chicago, where entrepreneur Luvenia Lewis establishes Mahogany Beauty Products. Her kinsman Tommy Lewis, the first family member to go to college, takes part in the 1964 civil rights demonstrations. In 1994, family members gather for a Lewis family reunion at Glory Field to celebrate pride in their West African forebear. The publisher celebrated the novel with a reception involving students from the New York City Laboratory School for Collaborative Studies.

February 7, 1994 Following authors S. E. Hinton, Richard Peck, Robert Cormier, Lois Duncan, and M. E. Kerr, Myers reached a career height with a prestigious honorarium, the Margaret A. Edwards Award for lifetime achievement in writing for youth. The committee singled out *Fallen Angels, Hoops, Motown and Didi*, and *Scorpions* as expressions of compassion for the urban teen. At the presentation at the

American Library Association Annual Conference in Miami, the committee chair, Judy Nelson, remarked on the universality of Myers's themes: "While his is a voice that speaks to African American youth, his appeal is not limited to any particular ethnic group" (Sutton, "Threads," 24). In an interview for the *Journal of Reading*, authors Rosemary Chance, Teri Lesesne, and Lois Buckman extolled Myers for versatility and for "[promoting] an understanding and appreciation of all people to the realization of the American dream" (Chance, 1994, 246). Myers divulged that he had reached a point in his art when narrative could "become more interesting and more personalized than in the past," in part because he was less timid about exploring his own dark thoughts (*ibid.*, 248). His acceptance speech appeared in the winter edition of *Journal of Youth Services in Libraries.*

Myers expressed an intuitive understanding of self-examination, which he called "a core element of the writer" (Myers, "1994," 129). His speech accused adults of alienation from troubled youth and of failure to identify the pervasive hate and bias that reach critical mass in the young. To avoid didacticism, he added that public demand influenced his choices of topic: "There's a fine line there that you have to navigate. Very often people want more from books than a story.... They want books to represent them well" (Sutton, 26).

April 23, 1994 In Denver, Myers was keynote speaker at the annual Young Adult Literature Conference for librarians, teachers, and parents. He led a panel discussion among junior high students about adolescent issues and literature. He told them, "My family was poor, but in those days it was OK to be poor. Now advertisers spend millions of dollars to tell young people that the value is how rich you are, how sexy you are, how bad you are" ("Myers," 1994, 17).

May, 1994 When 20-year-old Christopher Myers returned home from college, his father observed the contrast between Chris and his peers: "When he came back, many of the kids who went to high school with him had fallen by the wayside" (Feder-feitel, 2004, 14). The contrast sharpened the author's perceptions about the social ills that ruined young lives.

May 22, 1994 The author delivered a graduation address at Jersey City State College calling for a lifetime of education, a philosophy that has guided his own career. He exhorted: "Lifetime learning is vital to our communities and nation. Those who surrender and fail to become lifetime learners become superfluous" (Myers, "Jersey City").

November 19, 1994 At a breakfast assembly in Orlando, Florida, Myers received the ALAN Award for his contributions to the field of young adult literature, an honorarium extended by the Assembly on Literature for Adolescents of National Council of Teachers of English.

1995 Myers tackled a full slate of original and reissued works in one year — a new version of *The Dragon Takes a Wife* (Scholastic) reillustrated in gouache, watercolor, and crayon by Fiona French, and Scholastic's reissue of *Shadow of the Red Moon*, the first book he co-produced with his son, artist Christopher Myers. The author also completed *The Story of the Three Kingdoms* (HarperCollins), a fable dynamically illustrated by Ashley Bryan's Crayola® colors and stylized geometrics. A model of traditional storytelling, the narrative portrays the division of earth among elephant, shark, and hawk, lords of the land, sea, and sky. The emergence of humankind requires a unique empowerment unlike any of earth's animals.

Myers also compiled *One More River to Cross: An African American Photograph Album* (Harcourt Brace), which won the Golden Kite Award from the Society of Children's Book Writers and Illustrators. The picture book honors black achievements in family life, business, agriculture, education, and the military by picturing achievers like black Civil War infantrymen, the Buffalo Soldiers, athlete Jackie Robinson, orator Frederick Douglass, and singer Billie Holiday. Myers explained that photos prove to children that "a black person can be any old thing. Kids say they want to play in the NBA or rap because we haven't given them permission to consider anything else" (Brown, 1999, 45).

The fourth work, *Glorious Angels: A Celebration of Children* (HarperCollins), a multicultural sequel to the photographic collages of *Brown Angels* and *Remember Us Well*, combats the stereotypes that readers have of poetry and poets. To illustrate what critic R. D. Lane calls "the majesty of black childhood," Myers collected pictures from private homes, museums, auction houses, flea markets, dumpsters, and antique houses" (Lane, 1998, 132). In the introduction, the author declares that children's "early steps are sometimes hesitant, sometimes reckless, but they represent all that humankind can be" (Myers, *Glorious*, n.p.). Myers also contributed a contemporary urban poem, "To a Child of War," to *On the Wings of Peace: Writers and Illustrators Speak Out for Peace, In Memory of Hiroshima and Nagasaki* (Clarion), edited by Sheila Hamanaka, a collection honoring victims of two atomic bombs dropped in 1945.

1996 In the year that Myers contributed a story, "Briefcase," to editor Harry Mazer's *Twelve Shots: Outstanding Short Stories About Guns*, Myers branched out to varied venues: *Turning Points: When Everything Changes* (Troll Communications), *Smiffy Blue, Ace Crime Detective: The Case of the Missing Ruby and Other Stories* (Scholastic), illustrated by David J. A. Sims, *Harlem Blues* (Rageot), and *How Mr. Monkey Saw the Whole World* (Doubleday), a West African trickster tale illustrated in Crayola®-bright tones by minimalist artist Synthia Saint James. Myers's *Darnell Rock Reporting* was released on video.

For *Toussaint L'Ouverture: The Fight for Haiti's Freedom* (Simon & Schuster), Myers crafted a text that is both reflective and immediate. The biography features the 41 rhythmic, complex narrative artworks that Jacob Lawrence completed in earthy tones in the 1930s. In a review for *School Library Journal*, critic Melissa Hudak described the combination of text with art as "absolutely compelling" (Hudak, 1996, 116). The pictures remain on public view at the Amistad Research Center in New Orleans.

November 1, 1996 The award-winning *Slam!* (Scholastic) features 17-year-old Greg "Slam" Harris in an on-court challenge against Benny "Ice" Reese, a homey-gone-wrong who deals drugs to users in Harlem's Garvey Park. The author dedicated the novel to Jean Grace Killens, the widow of John Oliver Killens and a noted combatant against Apartheid in South Africa and racism anywhere. She opened her home as a refuge to black writers and artists and decorated her walls with photos and memorabilia of the best in black talent.

In the October 10, 1998, issue of *Education Week*, John G. Ramsay explains the value of a book like *Slam!* In a classroom vignette, he pictures Chad Kramer, the teacher, demonstrating a way to help dead-end kids connect with literature. After Jesse, a sullen non-achiever, reads Myers's novel, Kramer explains to Jesse, "That's why we read these books. So that you have some time to think about you. A book can be a safe place to go to" (Ramsay, 1998, 44). The comment rings true of biographies of troubled teens like author Gary Paulsen, who frequently remarks in school presentations the debt he owes to a librarian who rescued him in boyhood from despair by suggesting the right books.

1997 Myers made significant contributions to anthologies: the short story "Reverend Abbott and Those Bloodshot Eyes," to the collection *When I Was Your Age: Original Stories About Growing Up*, "Sunrise over Manaus" in *From One Experience to Another*, and "Stranger" to *No Easy Answers: Short Stories About Teenagers Making Tough Choices*. He published a richly allusive picture-ode, *Harlem: A Poem* (Scholastic), a sophisticated work that critics Barbara Hiron and Blake Rodman summarized for *Teacher Magazine* as "a pulsating mix of promise and pain, yellows and blues" (Hiron & Rodman, 1997, 65). The verse describes Myers's hometown as a "crucible of American culture" (Myers, 1997, flap copy). His son Christopher energized the oversized pages with paper cuts, portraits, and ink and gouache in vibrant yellow-gold, rust-red, olive, blues, and ebony-brown, a visual feast that critic Michael Cart praised as "wonderfully complementary" (Cart, 1997, 1021). The work received a Caldecott Honor Book citation for its artistry and subtlety. The string of honors to Myers continued with a Boston Globe–Horn Book Award and a Coretta Scott King Honor Book for *Harlem*, and a fifth Coretta Scott King award for *Slam!* A ten-minute Spoken Arts video of *Harlem* features the voices of Ruby Dee and Ossie Davis, a black acting couple who established their stage and film careers in Harlem.

1998 After researching details of an 1839 mutiny, three years of incarceration for murder and piracy, and the first major U.S. court battle involving slaves, Myers wrote *Amistad: A Long Road to Freedom* (Dutton). His data come from court records, news accounts, letters, and photos and accompanied the Stephen Spielberg film, *Amistad* (1997). Myers also released *Scorpions* in audio form for Recorded Books and published *Angel to Angel: A Mother's Gift of Love* (HarperCollins), a photojournal that opens on a poem he wrote for his mother at age ten. The creamy pages, silvered at the edges like a keepsake album, enhance the book's value to scrapbook makers and to readers. He dedicated the work to his big sister, Viola Law, a model of motherhood.

May, 1998 The Myers family visited Holland and Germany, where the author addressed readers and students.

1999 After thirty years of writing young adult literature, Myers published three nonfiction works for Scholastic—*My Name Is America: The Journal of Scott Pendleton Collins, a WWII Soldier, Normandy, France, 1944*; *My Name Is America: The Journal* *of Joshua Loper, a Black Cowboy on the Chisholm Trail, 1871*; and *At Her Majesty's Request: An African Princess in Victorian England.* Myers researched Scott Collins's story from basic training at Fort Dix to D-Day and the capture of St. Lô, France. He dedicated the biography to Nancy Larrick, "whose concerns helped bring me in to the field of children's literature" (Myers, "Scott," 138). Joshua Loper's cowboy story derives from data about black cowhands and from Loper's own journal. He describes the task of 11 drovers in herding 2,200 head of cattle from southern Texas to Abilene, Kansas. The book was so true to history that curators included it in material for a traveling museum program on the Chisholm Trail, which appeared in Boston, Fort Worth, Houston, Las Vegas, Memphis, Minneapolis, Quebec, and Sausalito.

In the introduction to *At Her Majesty's Request*, Myers admits that he's "always found old book stores exciting" (Myers, "At Her," ix). He developed the biography from 50 letters and clippings a London used-book dealer sold him concerning an eight-year-old Dahomian girl. A sea captain, Frederick E. Forbes, named the child Sarah Forbes Bonetta and transported her from West Africa to the British Isles in 1850. After escaping death in a cemetery ritual, Sarah came under the protection of Queen Victoria and visited Buckingham Palace, where she rode in the royal pony cart. Whoopi Goldberg optioned the story for film.

Myers earned critical acclaim for a venture into YA metafiction, *Monster: A Novel*, a taut novel noir dedicated to the author's friend and brother-in-law John Brendel. The author wrote it during a peak of public outrage at the rise in juvenile murder, theft, sexual assault, arson, and possession of drugs and weapons. The narrative of a youth's involvement in violence won favor with the movie industry, which has considered it for filming. Chris Myers illustrated the text with stylized marginalia and photos of real people and with his father's fingerprints. The story focuses on 16-year-old Steve Harmon, whose confused perspective compares to characters in J. D. Salinger's *The Catcher in the Rye* (1951), S. H. Hinton's *The Outsiders* (1967), and Robert Cormier's *The Chocolate War* (1974). In Myers's narration, police charge Steve as the lookout for a robbery that concluded in the armed robbery and shooting death of a Harlem pharmacy owner. Reviewer John A. Staunton notes that the novel "confronts the white middle class fear of black youth as public menace" (Staunton, 2002, 792).

Myers took the suggestion of HarperCollins editor Phoebe Yeh to incorporate journal entries into the screenplay that Steve writes about his quandary. For details, Myers perused the 600 pages of interviews that he conducted with street people and some 25 inmates in New York and New Jersey prisons. He took part in a seminar on criminal justice organized by the New York City prosecutor's office and attended the trial of a 17 year old charged with armed robbery and attempted murder. In his collection of data, it occurred to Myers that "kids could go from being in high school now and not much later be faced with a life sentence" (Rochman, "Interview," 1101).

The action of *Monster* pictures the crime as a film and describes Steve's emotions as entries in a journal. The problem of self-image derives from Myers's interviews with imprisoned male repeat offenders who committed crimes escalating in severity. He recognized a pattern in men who "were clearly separating their concept of self from their deeds" (Myers, "Escalating," 701). Similarly, by looking at himself like a character in a script, Steve distances himself from wrongdoing with "the luxury of the distance, the film script, the wide-angle shots, what the filmmaker wants you to see" (Rochman, "Interview," 1101). Even though he is not punished, he experiences an impermeable blot on his character. The author explained, "His legal guilt was not the issue. His moral stance was" (Myers, "Escalating," 701).

July, 1999 The experimental narrative of *Monster!*, written from a teenager's perspective, won a National Book Award nomination, Coretta Scott King Honor Book, *Booklist* Editor's Choice selection, and Boston Globe–Horn Book Honor Book Award. Critics interpreted the reception of Myers's novel as the beginning of a postmodern trend toward variety of form, including metafiction, free verse, and unreliable narrators. He won the first Michael L. Printz Award for Excellence in Young Adult Literature, which officers of ALA presented at the Annual Conference in Chicago in July during the YALSA awards luncheon.

August, 1999 Myers contributed "The Beast Is in the Labyrinth" to *Places I Never Meant to Be: Original Stories by Censored Writers*. The collection juxtaposes his work among narratives by the best writers in the young adult field — Judy Blume, Norma Fox Mazer, Katherine Paterson, and Paul Zindel. Proceeds from the book's sale fight suppression of free reading through the National Coalition against Censorship. Three months later, the Cedar Rapids PTA Reconsideration Committee voted to retain Myers's *Scorpions* over the objections of some parents.

2000 Myers completed *Malcolm X: A Fire Burning Brightly* (HarperCollins), a picture book dedicated to Jerry Weiss and illustrated in acrylics, spray paint, and pastels by Leonard Jenkins. Recorded Books released the audiocassette version of *Slam!* featuring the narration of Thomas Penny. Myers received the 2000 Audio Earphones Award for the full-cast audio version of *Monster!* from Listening Library, featuring Jeron Alston as Steve Harmon. The author also won a Boston Globe–Horn Book Awards for Excellence in Children's Literature for ten short pieces in *145th Street: Short Stories* (Delacorte), which appeared in e-book form in May 2005. The anthology describes Harlem life in ten narratives that survey street life for its character strengths. "A Christmas Story" remarks on the residence of fighter Jack Johnson and the pulpit where novelist James Baldwin's father, David Baldwin, delivered sermons. The dedication honors educator Beryle Banfield, author of *Africa in the Curriculum* (1968), *Black Focus on Multicultural Education* (1979), and *The African Diaspora Curriculum* (1991). She cofounded a drug rehabilitation center for youth, directed the Center for Urban Education, chaired the Council on Interracial Books for Children, and promoted the balancing of classic selections with multicultural authors and themes.

Myers published a picture book, *The Blues of Flats Brown* (Holiday House), a questing dog story illustrated in jewel-toned pastels by Nina Laden. The narrative features a singer and guitarist, Flats, and his flight with companion Caleb from A. J. Grubbs, a cruel owner who wants his animals to compete in the dog-fighting ring. Myers stresses redemption in the Flats's confrontation with Grubbs in New York City. By strumming and singing a soul tune, "The Gritty Grubbs Blues," the singer convinces A. J. to change his ways. An audiocassette version from Live Oak Media features the warm tones of reader Charles Turner and Mark "Dog" Deffenbaugh's slide guitar.

June 15, 2000 At the launching of Harlem U.S.A., a 285,000-square foot entertainment complex on 125th Street, Myers's *Harlem* was a featured book at a student read-a-thon encouraging literacy. Scholastic encouraged readers in grades K–8 by donating 450 copies of the book.

Late September, 2000 While retaining the spotlight for quality writing in a variety of genres, during Banned Book Week, Myers also claimed seventh place among the top ten most censored authors. In contention was *Fallen Angels*, which complainants banned for offensive language and violence and for unsuitability for young readers. The notoriety placed Myers alongside top authors— Maya Angelou, Margaret Atwood, Judy Blume, Robert Cormier, David Guterson, Stephen King, Lois Lowry, J. K. Rowling, John Steinbeck, and Alice Walker. Myers participated with Judy Blume and Robert Lipsyte in the film *Tell It Like It Is!*, a 15-minute video from the National Coalition against Censorship on the banning of children's books.

2001 Myers issued a black sports biography, *The Greatest: Muhammad Ali* (Scholastic), which he dedicated to Dr. Rudine Sims Bishop, the author of *Shadow and Substance: Afro-American Experience in Contemporary Children's Fiction* (1982), the author biography *Presenting Walter Dean Myers* (1990), and *A Centennial Salute to Arna Bontemps, Langston Hughes, and Lorenz Graham* (2002). The glimpse of the boxer's life covers Ali's childhood in Louisville, Kentucky, as well as his Olympic gold medal, major fights against Sonny Liston, Joe Frazier, and George Foreman, participation in war protests, and the abandonment of a slave name, Cassius Clay, for his Muslim name. Bill Ott, reviewing for *Booklist*, stresses that Myers's subtext enlightens readers about "the troubled business of boxing and the great physical risks the sport entails" (Ott, 2001, 952).

The author turned to his own life for *Bad Boy: A Memoir* (HarperCollins), which he dedicated to his children, Karen, Michael, and Christopher. The text also appeared in a Harper Children's Audio version narrated by Joe Morton. Myers completed short fiction, "Season's End," for James Howe's anthology *The Color of Absence: Twelve Stories About Loss* (Simon & Schuster), a collection featuring stories by Avi, Chris Lynch, Norma Fox Mazer, and Michael Rosen. To Glencoe's expanded edition of Paul Zindel's *The Pigman* (1968), Myers added "The Treasure of Lemon Brown" (1983), a touching account of fatherhood that the author set in a decaying section of Harlem.

April, 2001 *The Journal of Biddy Owens: The Negro Leagues* (Scholastic) was Myers's second contribution to the "My Name Is America" series, which showcases the talents of young adult authors Joseph Bruchac, Kathryn Lasky, Jim Murphy, and Laurence Yep. Myers's story reprises the life of an equipment manager for the Black Barons, a Negro League baseball team. The biography of Biddy Owens provides another glimpse of the black nuclear family in the closeness of Biddy with his parents, younger sister Rachel, and Aunt Jack.

May, 2001 Myers published "And Then I Read...." in *Voices-from-the-Middle: Stepping into the Real World*, a summary of his life as a writer from childhood until his establishment of a professional freelance career.

June, 2001 For *School Library Journal*, Myers interviewed author Robert Lipsyte, a fellow winner of the Margaret A. Edwards Award.

September 8, 2001 Myers joined 50 top-ranked participants in the first National Book Festival, set at the Library of Congress and sponsored by First Lady Laura Bush. He remarked in a panel discussion for *Authors on the Web*, "I've been accused of writing adult books and calling them 'Young Adult' books. Where does one stop and the other begin?" (Myers, et al., "YA," 2001). He corroborated his remarks with a comparison: "Mark Twain never thought of himself as writing for Young Adults, nor did Shakespeare set out, in *Romeo and Juliet*, to test the YA market" (*ibid.*).

2002 Myers published *The Gifts We Bring* (HarperCollins) and pursued humor and adventure in *Three Swords for Granada* (Holiday House), a swashbuckling animal fantasy illustrated by John Speirs with pen-and-ink and wash drawings. Set in Málaga, Spain, in 1420, the narrative resets the face-off between Catholics and Moors as three cat swordfighters—Askia, Lacy, and Poco—protect kittens in dog-infested terrain patrolled by the Fidorean Guard. Elaine E. Knight, a reviewer for *School Library Journal*, summarized the whimsical book's strengths as "snappy dialogue, flashing swords, and daring action" (Knight, 2002, 230).

For Amistad, the author crafted redemptive fiction in *Handbook for Boys: A Novel*, illustrated with minimalist pen-and-ink drawings by Matthew Bandsuch. The didactic story describes reclamation of boys before they turn from mischief into hard crime. A Harlem barbershop on 145th Street is the setting of a productive meeting between wise old males—Cap and Mister M—and 16-year-old Jimmy and 17-year-old Kevin. Duke Wilson's informal mentoring to the juvenile court remands offers the type of advice that Myers wished that he had received in his youth. The audiocassette version, narrated by Peter Francis James, creates a realistic contrast between youthful vernacular and the mellow tones of maturity.

For HarperCollins, Myers returned to military stories with a disturbing picture book, *Patrol: An American Soldier in Vietnam*. The text is illustrated in mixed-media and photo collage by Ann Grifalconi, who creates a claustrophic jungle milieu in green marbling and saturated forest tones. Critic Joanna Rudge Long describes the effect as "visual correlatives to discontinuous perceptions, the kind of blanks experienced during extreme stress" (Long, 2002, 450). The text reaches its peak as the soldier sees his enemy eye to eye, a shattering perception of humanity in a person the protagonist is expected to kill. In the estimation of Lynda Jones, a reviewer for *Black Issues Book Review*, the overall effect is "a haunting tale that captures the weary soul of one black American soldier" (Jones, 2003, 61). The stream-of-consciousness story won a Jane Addams Children's Book Award for stark contrasts between the land and people of Vietnam and the fire power of the American military. Through letter writing, the main character expresses the torment of killing people classed as enemies of the United States.

May 15, 2002 Children from 12 Detroit public schools chose Walter Dean Myers as the featured speaker for the city's 14th Author Day 2002. Chairwoman Ruth Birsdorf described Myers as "wow": "He is a librarian's dream come true. He writes for all ages and all interests and finds something that everybody can identify with. He is a brilliant author" (Graham, 2002).

July 17, 2002 Joining all-star Hall-of-Famer Nate "Tiny" Archibald, Myers gave a public reading in the Bronx at the New York Public Library's Mott Haven Branch. A part of the Summer Reading Season, the event was an outreach of the National Basketball Association Read to Achieve program to encourage a life-long love of reading.

August 2–4, 2002 Myers appeared at the Langston Hughes Children's Literature Festival, sponsored by the Children's Defense Fund, Scholastic Books, and HarperCollins. Held at the former Alex Haley Farm, the arts festival featured works by black authors writing about the black experience to promote the Leave No Child Behind program. As a part of the festival, HarperCollins, with matching funds from Myers, established the Walter Dean Myers Publishing Institute to inspire undergraduate students located by the Black Community Crusade for Children. His purpose was the demystification of writing: "I don't think it's something that very, very special people do. It can be learned. It can be taught" (Myers, "Walter," 15).

December, 2002 For an anthology, *Big City Cool: Short Stories About Urban Youth* (Persea), edited by educator Morton Jerome "Jerry" Weiss and his wife, Helen S. Weiss, Myers wrote "Block Party—145th Street Style." The story appeared alongside 13 multicultural works by such acclaimed authors as Judith Ortiz Cofer, Joseph Geha, John H. Ritter, Amy Tan, and Laurence Yep.

2003 Myers wrote *The Dream Bearer* (Amistad), an urban folktale, to describe the value of a gentle graybeard and the personal reformation that comes through forgiveness. In an audiocassette version from Recorded Books, reader Peter Francis James, who also narrated *Handbook for Boys: A Novel* and *Monster!* in 2002, modulates his voice to contrast youthful enthusiasm with an elderly sage's authority. In a review for *Kliatt*, critic Sally Tibbetts admires James's handling of Myers's fiction for "[achieving] an edgy feeling of frustration while simultaneously creating a sympathetic character" (Tibbetts, 2004, 48).

The basis of *The Beast* (Scholastic), an elegiac novel that Myers excerpted in *Scholastic Scope*, is the clash of a tender first love gone limp because of drug dependency. The author abandoned his spunky sassiness from earlier teen novels to develop a soulful dialogue rife with poetic lines and mythic images. Allusions to hagiography, the Black Death, Herod's slaughter of the innocents, and the Greek myth of the Minotaur in the labyrinth of ancient Crete enhance the hopelessness that promotes Gabriela "Gabi" Godoy's heroin addiction. Her personal burdens include a blind grandfather, a brother drawn to gangs, and a mother overwhelmed by cancer. While 17-year-old protagonist Anthony "Spoon" Witherspoon attempts to rescue his Dominican girlfriend, the plot develops his personal entrapment among snobbish, privileged preppies at Wallingford Academy in Connecticut. Critics responded to

Myers's introspective text with bemusement, perhaps trying to reframe their image of the author from creator of intricate urban plots to witness to the heartfelt suffering of teen lovers.

Myers teamed with son Chris to complete *A Time To Love: Stories from the Old Testament* (Scholastic), a Caldecott Honor Book that the author dedicated to his sisters Ethel, Imogene, and Viola. The author thanked Dr. Charles E. Carter, a Carnegie Scholar and teacher at Seton Hall University, for his advice on theological issues, which Myers gave immediacy and humanity. Introducing the text are the words of Chaplain Michael Myers, the author's older son, who graduated from the Interdenominational Theological Center in Atlanta. Patricia D. Lothrop, an appreciative book critic for *School Library Journal*, compliments the three Myers for "supplementary essays [that] add a worthwhile personal dimension to this contemporary effort at midrash" (Lothrop, 2003, 158).

The contemporary collection, which reviewer Graceanne A. Decandido calls "provocative," examines biblical characters from unusual perspectives, such as a boy who dies during the plagues of Egypt, the Philistine Delilah's seduction and betrayal of Hebrew strongman Samson, and a glimpse of Lot's unnamed wife from the point of view of Zillah, their confused and disillusioned daughter (Decandido, 2003, 1656). Enhancing the personal accounts are images in photo-collage, pencil sketches, and silhouettes. In the estimation of Jana Riess, a reviewer for *Publishers Weekly*, the artistic storybook proves "There are numberless ways to behold sacred stories" (Riess, 2003, 64).

For *Blues Journey* (Holiday House), the author established the uniqueness of black music in its evolution from slave call-and-response to the unique African American blues idiom. The text reveals what Roger Sutton, reviewer for *Horn Book*, calls "America's answer to haiku" (Sutton, "Review," 363). The volume, illustrated by Chris Myers with enigmatic figures in blue ink, white paint, and brown wrapping paper, won a *Bulletin of the Center for Children's Books* Blue Ribbon Nonfiction Award, Lee Bennett Hopkins Poetry citation, ALA Notable Children's Book award, and honoraria from *Horn Book* and *Kirkus*. In the opinion of Wendy Lukehart, a reviewer for *School Library Journal*, the book's "song will slide through readers' ears and settle into their souls" (Lukehart, 2003, 188).

January 28, 2003 Myers's poem *Harlem* was the kernel of a play, *Harlem: The Story*, adapted by Bill Grimmette and presented by director Susan Kelleher at the Pikes Peak Center in Colorado Springs. Christopher Myers supplied the backdrop and Kysia Bostic composed the music for the performance, which was part of the Kennedy Center Imagination Celebration's Family Theater. The next week, the play moved on to Kingsbury Hall in Salt Lake City along with a four-piece jazz ensemble, vocalist, and the focal character, Stoop Storyteller, played by Jefferson A. Russell. The staff of the Kennedy Center next planned a staging of *The Blues Journey*.

April 28, 2003 In an article for the *New York Times*, Robert Lipsyte, author of *The Contender* (1967), characterized fiction as a force powerful enough to change young lives. He named Myers among the writers for youth who "brought to the genre a grittier and even a more literary sensibility than existed in mainstream fiction" (Lipsyte, 2003, E1).

2004 For Amistad Press, Myers wrote *I've Seen the Promised Land: The Life of Dr. Martin Luther King, Jr.*, illustrated with kaleidoscopic collage of acrylic, pastel, and spray paint by Leonard Jenkins, a teacher at New York's Pratt Institute. The narrative moves from the arrest of Rosa Parks in 1955 through the Memphis strike of sanitation workers in 1968, King's last demonstration before his assassination. The interplay between text and art creates subtextual commentary on the human cost of bold leadership during the crusade for civil rights. In Myers's words, the delivery of the "I Have a Dream" speech "was a glorious day for America" (Myers, *I've Seen*, n.p.). An unnamed reviewer for *Publishers Weekly* applauded the author for a stirring biography that "soars to the heart of King's mission" ("Review: *I've*," 2004, 54).

For a second novel, *Shooter*, Myers visited Columbine High School in Littleton, Colorado, to explore the setting of a school shooting on April 20, 1999. To recreate the madness and turmoil in crazed student terrorists, he resorted to verbal collage, an art that has appealed to him from the beginning of his career. He dedicated the work to Bill Morris, a close friend, book lover, and head of library promotions at HarperCollins. In the multi-sided account of a sociopathic assassin, the author sets up a scary scenario drawn from real teen angst. He told an interviewer for the Santa Rosa, California, *Press Democrat*: "First they disconnect from their families, then they become isolated. It starts at home" ("Author," 2004). Of his protagonists, he commented in an interview for *Scholastic Choices* that "Bullying happens because bullying works" ("Bully," 5). In a summation of the tormentors' motives, critic Susan Perren of the Toronto *Globe & Mail* remarked, "A terrible emptiness lives at the heart of their darkness" (Perren, 2004, D11).

In an article for the *Newark Star-Ledger*, Myers declared a disturbing truth: "For too many teenagers, especially in urban areas, learning to cope with the threat of violence is as important as learning English or math" (Myers, "Intimidating," 21). He described the source of intimidation as the perpetrator's need for respect and noted that the success of extorting money or terrorizing weaker kids can damage lives and self-image. He advocated tough school policies that empower the underdog to fight back against bigger, stronger kids. Compared to Todd Strasser's *Give a Boy a Gun* (2000) and Robert Cormier's *The Rag and Bone Shop* (2001), Myers's novel succeeded in audio Harper CD form and on audiocassette from Recorded Books, read by Chad Coleman, Bernie McInerney, and Michelle Santopietro.

Myers ventured further into history with two nonfiction works. For Scholastic, he compiled *Antarctica: Journeys to the South Pole*, which compiles first-person citations and biographical elements of the voyages of Captain James Cook, Roald Amundsen, Douglas Mawson, Robert Falcon Scott, Ernest Shackleton, and Richard E. Byrd. The text, dedicated to Michael and Spring Myers, includes archival photography, primary documents, and tutorials on scurvy, seals, navigation by latitude and longitude, and geographical and magnetic poles. Holiday House issued *U.S.S. Constellation: Pride of the American Navy*, a study of America's last sail-rigged naval vessel that Myers dedicated to fellow young adult biographer Linda Trice. A national legend, the *Constellation* takes shape in first-person citations, sketches, photos, documents, and a glossary of naval terms.

In a more lyrical history, Myers completed *Here in Harlem: Poems in Many Voices*, which *Publishers Weekly* praised for its "pastiche of the community's fixtures" ("Review: *Here*," 2004, 61). The text coalesces into a broad view of the author's hometown from 54 perspectives, from domestic worker to beautician, hustler to guitarist. Written in the style of Edgar Lee Masters's *Spoon River Anthology* (1916), the textured poems demonstrate Myers's skill at a variety of lyric modes. In "Bill Cash, 30," a multilayered plaint by a boxer, Myers shapes pathos from an image of the self-sacrificing god Prometheus. The author employs a controlling metaphor of forgetfulness, which derives from the name of Bill's wife, Letha, a variation on Lethe, the underworld river of oblivion. Myers's reverence for black settings extends from the Harlem River to the Kalahari, Mount Kenya, Niger River, and Timbuktu. He displays a gift for distilling dramatic moments, such as the confrontation between street vendor Willie Schockley and his fed-up, out-of-sorts woman. Illustrating the text are black-and-white photos of the Reverend Al Sharpton, Winnie Mandela standing behind a poster of her husband Nelson, singer Dorothy Dandridge, composer Duke Ellington, unidentified portraits and candid street scenes, and a posed picture of the author and his brother, George "Mickey" Myers, Jr., in Easter finery before the Church of the Master.

February, 2004 In an interview with Don Gallo for *Writing* magazine, Myers disclosed that he bought a cache of photos of black aviators who fought in Ethiopia and Italy during World War II. He placed them in a file as material for a future work.

Early December, 2004 Wendy Waszkiewicz, a parent in Rochester, New York, challenged the school board to ban Myers's *Monster: A Novel* out of "[concern] her son and some of his friends might not be mature enough to handle the material" (Bauza, 2004). Her challenge lost in a 4–3 vote. The Rochester public school board president defended Myers's crime fiction for its inclusion of accountability and moral responsibility.

February 11, 2005 The American Library Association listed *Fallen Angels* at the top of the list of banned books. Complainants objected to violence, offensive language, and racism.

February 17, 2005 Myers was the featured speaker at the 37th McConnell Children's Literature Conference, a banquet held at the Radisson Plaza Hotel in Lexington, Kentucky. His topic was "Beyond Rap: Language in the Inner City."

April 2005 Myers received the Lee Bennett Hopkins Poetry Award.

May, 2005 Myers and his family visited Prague, a source of information on an eastern basketball player, the protagonist of the author's next book project. The plot pits the black protagonist against a young Czech athlete. Both teens come from urban settings with economic problems and rampant alcoholism among young residents. The author published in the May-June issue of *Horn Book* the poem "Wolf Song," an ode to hope based on an Old Testament prophecy from Isaiah 11:6. The text emphasizes Myers's familiar faith in efforts to uplift the younger generation: "We can do more/Than what is buried within us" (Myers, "Wolf," 304).

August 2005 Myers returned to familiar issues in *Autobiography of My Dead Brothers*, a YA novel on the value of friendship in a milieu beset by crime and despair.

• *Further Reading*

"Author: Teen Problems Start at Home" (Santa Rosa, California) *Press Democrat* (22 June 2004).

Bader, Barbara. "Multiculturalism Takes Root," *Horn Book* 79, no. 2 (March/April 2003): 143–152.

Baker, Augusta. "The Changing Image of the Black in Children's Literature," *Horn Book* 51 (February 1975): 79–88.

Banfield, Beryle. "Commitment to Change: The Council on Interracial Books for Children and the World of Children's Books," *African American Review* 32 (spring 1998): 17–22.

Bauza, Margarite. "Mom's Dispute May Revise Reading Policies," *Detroit News* (21 December 2004).

Beavin, Kristi. "Review: *Monster!*," *Booklist* 98 (January 2001): 123.

Brown, Jennifer M. "Walter Dean Myers Unites Two Passions," *Publishers Weekly* 246, no. 2 (22 March 1999): 45–46.

"Bully Business," *Scholastic Choices* 20, no. 3 (November-December 2004): 5.

Burns, Mary M. "Review: *The Great Migration: An American Story*," *Horn Book* 70, no. 1 (January 1994): 88–89.

Burshtein, Karen. *Walter Dean Myers*. New York: Rosen, 2003.

Cart, Michael. "Review: *Harlem: A Poem*," *Booklist* 98, no. 12 (15 February 1997): 1021.

"Center Offers Mentoring Program for Aspiring Writers," *Reading Today* 13, no. 5 (April/May 1996): 12.

Chance, Rosemary, Teri Lesesne, and Lois Buckman. "And the Winner Is...: A Teleconference with Walter Dean Myers," *Journal of Reading* 38, no. 3 (November 1994): 246–249.

Connors, Cathy. "Walter Dean Myers Captures Childhood in Its Beautiful Innocence of an Era," *New York Amsterdam News* (16 April 1994): 17.

Creech, Sharon. *Love That Dog*. New York: Joanna Cotler Books, 2001.

Decandido, Graceanne A. "Review: *A Time to Love: Stories from the Old Testament*," *Booklist* 99, no. 18 (15 May 2003): 1656.

_____, and Alan P. Mahony. "Westchester Librarians Study Multiculturalism," *School Library Journal* 37, no. 11 (November 1991): 14–15.

Del Negro, Janice. "Review: *Darnell Rock Reporting*," *Booklist* 90, no. 22 (August 1994): 2044.

Edwards, Anthony. "Review: *One More River to Cross: An African American Photograph Album*," *MultiCultural Review* 5 (September 1996): 73.

Feder-feitel, Lisa. "Writing About What's Real," *Scholastic Scope* 52, no. 12 (9 February 2004): 14.

Foreman, Carol. "Review," *School Library Journal* 50, no. 9 (September 2004): 223.

Gallo, Donald R. "A Man of Many Ideas: Walter Dean Myers," *Writing* 26, no. 5 (February/March 2004): 10–11.

Gauch, P. L. "Review: *The Young Landlords*," *New York Times Book Review* (6 January 1980): 20.

Graham, Adam. "Author's Just a Kid at Heart," *Detroit News* (6 May 2002).

Gray, Jerry. "'He Knows I Have Come to Kill Him': A Young Soldier Meets the Enemy in Vietnam, and Discovers an Unsettling Truth," *New York Times Book Review* 107, no. 40 (19 May 2002): 35.

Gropman, Jackie. "Review: *One More River to Cross: An African-American Photograph Album*," *Booklist* 42, no. 8 (August 1996): 186.

Heins, Ethel L. "Review: *Mojo and the Russians*," *Horn Book* 54, no. 2 (April 1978): 166–167.

Heins, Paul. "Review: *The Golden Serpent*," *Horn Book* 56 (December 1980): 686.

Hiron, Barbara, and Blake Rodman. "Noteworthy," *Teacher Magazine* 9, no. 1 (August/September 1997): 65.

"His Goal Is to Make Young Blacks See Themselves in Books," *Philadelphia Daily News* (4 February 2000).

Hudak, Melissa. "Review: *Toussaint L'Ouverture: The Fight for Haiti's Freedom*," *School Library Journal* 42, no. 11 (November 1996): 116.

Jones, Lynda. "Review: *Patrol: An American Soldier in Vietnam*," *Black Issues Book Review* 4, no. 5 (September-October 2002): 61.

Kalamu ya Salaam. "Enriching the Paper Trail: An Interview with Tom Dent," *African American Review* 27, no. 2 (summer 1993): 327–344.

Knight, Elaine E. "Review: *Three Swords for Granada*," *School Library Journal* 48 no. 9 (September 2002): 230.

Lane, R. D. "'Keepin' It Real': Walter Dean Myers and the Promise of African-American Children's Literature," *African American Review* 32, no. 1 (22 March 1998): 125–138.

Lesesne, Teri. "Review: *Angel to Angel: A Mother's Gift of Love*," *Teacher Librarian* 26, no. 3 (January-February 1999): 42–43.

Lewis, Valerie. "Walter Dean Myers," *Instructor* 105, no. 8 (May/June 1996): 72–73.

Lipsyte, Robert. "Novels with the Power to Change Young Lives," *New York Times* (28 April 2003): E1.

Long, Joanna Rudge. "Review: *Patrol: An American Soldier in Vietnam*," *Horn Book* 78, no. 4 (July-August 2002): 449–450.

Lothrop, Patricia D. "Review: *A Time to Love: Stories from the Old Testament*," *School Library Journal* 49, no. 5 (May 2003): 158.

Lukehart, Wendy. "Review: *Blues Journey*," *School Library Journal* 49, no. 4 (April 2003): 188.

McElmeel, Sharron L., and Carol Simpson. "Profile: Walter Dean Myers," *Book Report* 20, no. 2 (September/October 2001): 42–44.

Mehren, Elizabeth. "Fountain of Stories for Youth: Walter Dean Myers," *Los Angeles Times* (15 October 1997): E1.

Myers, Walter Dean. "And Then I Read...," *Voices-from-the-Middle* 8, no. 4 (May 2001): 58–62.

_____. *Angel to Angel: A Mother's Gift of Love*. New York: HarperCollins, 1998.

_____. *At Her Majesty's Request: An African Princess in Victorian England*. New York: Scholastic, 1999.

_____. *Bad Boy: A Memoir*. New York: HarperCollins, 2001.

_____. "The Black Experience in Children's Books: One Step Forward, Two Steps Back," *Interracial Books for Children Bulletin* 10, no. 6 (1979): 14–15.

_____. "Escalating Offenses," *Horn Book* 77, no. 6 (November-December 2001): 701–702.

_____. *Fallen Angels*. New York: Scholastic, 1988.

_____. *Fast Sam, Cool Clyde, and Stuff*. New York: Viking, 1975.

_____. "Gifts," *Horn Book* 62, no. 4 (July-August 1986): 436–437.

_____. *Glorious Angels: A Celebration of Children*. New York: Bantam, 1995.

_____. "Gordon Parks: John Henry with a Camera," *Black Scholar* 7, no. 5 (1976): 27–30.

_____. *The Greatest: Muhammad Ali*. New York: Scholastic, 2001.

_____. *Handbook for Boys: A Novel*. New York: Amistad, 2002.

_____. *Harlem: A Poem*. New York: Scholastic, 1997.

_____. *Here in Harlem: Poems in Many Voices*. New York: Holiday House, 2004.

_____. *Hoops*. New York: Delacorte, 1981.

_____. "How I Came to Love English Literature," *English Journal* 74, no. 7 (November 1985): 93–94.

_____. "How Long Is Forever?," *Negro Digest* (June 1969): 52–57.

_____. "I Actually Thought We Would Revolutionize the Industry," *New York Times Book Review* (9 November 1986): 50.

_____. "The Intimidating Foe of Bullying," *Newark Star-Ledger* (23 April 2004): 21.

_____. *I've Seen the Promised Land: The Life of Dr. Martin Luther King, Jr.* New York: Amistad, 2004.

_____. "Jersey City Class Hears Call for 'Lifetime Learning,'" *Newark Star-Ledger* (23 May 1994).
_____. *My Name Is America: The Journal of Scott Pendleton Collins, a WWII Soldier, Normandy, France, 1944*. New York: Scholastic, 1999.
_____. *The Nicholas Factor*. New York: Viking, 1983.
_____. "1994 Margaret A. Edwards Award Acceptance Speech," *Journal of Youth Services in Libraries*, 8, no. 2 (winter 1995): 129–133.
_____. *Now Is Your Time! The African-American Struggle for Freedom*. New York: HarperCollins, 1991.
_____. *145th Street: Short Stories*. New York: Delacorte, 2000.
_____. "Private Interview" (email), February 25, 2005.
_____. "Private Interview" (email), March 16, 2005.
_____. "Private Interview" (email), May 22, 2005.
_____. "Pulling No Punches," *School Library Journal* 47, no. 6 (June 2001): 44.
_____. "School Days; Least Likely to Succeed," *Washington Post* (4 August 1991): 1.
_____. *Social Welfare: A First Book*. New York: Franklin Watts, 1976.
_____. "Sunrise over Manaus," *From One Experience to Another*. New York: Forge, 1997.
_____. "Surviving Mean Streets," *Washington Post* (12 May 1991): 7.
_____. "Telling Our Children the Stories of Their Lives," *American Visions* 6, no. 6 (December 1991): 30–32.
_____. *A Time to Love: Stories from the Old Testament*. New York: Scholastic, 2003.
_____. "Turning Memories into Memoir," *Scholastic Scope* 51, no. 1 (6 September 2002): 20.
_____. "Walter Dean Myers," *Read* 54, no. 13 (25 February 2005): 14–15.
_____. "Wolf Song," *Horn Book* 81, no. 3 (May-June 2005): 304.
_____, et al. "YA Grows Up," http://www.authorsontheweb.com/features/0108-ya/0108-ya.asp, 2001.
"Myers, Teen Panel Headline Denver YA Conference," *School Library Journal* 40, no. 6 (June 1994): 17.
Naughton, Jim. "Literary Crusader Writes Stories About Real Kids," *Los Angeles Times* (29 December 1989): 8.
_____. "Stories from the Inner City; Walter Dean Myers, Writing About Reality for Black Children," *Washington Post* (9 December 1989): C1.
"Novel Depicts Black Soldier in Vietnam," [Portland, Ore.] *Skanner* 13, no. 38 (22 June 1988): 7.
Ott, Bill. "Review: *The Greatest: The Life and Career of Muhammad Ali*," *Booklist* 97, no. 1 (1 January 2001): 952.
Perren, Susan. "Children's Books: *Shooter*," *Globe & Mail* (31 July 2004), D11.
Pierleoni, Allen O. "Wrongs and the Writer," *Sacramento Bee* (29 March 2005).
Price, Michael H. "A New Look at That Old Chisholm Trail," *Fort Worth Business Press* 17, no. 51 (17 December 2004): 28.
Ramsay, John G. "When Jesse Reads *Slam!*," *Education Week* 18, no. 7 (14 October 1998): 44.
"Review: *The Great Migration: An American Story*," *Publishers Weekly* 240, no. 39 (27 September 1993): 61.
"Review: *Here in Harlem: Poems in Many Voices*," *Publishers Weekly* 251, no. 46 (15 November 2004): 61.
"Review: *How Mr. Monkey Saw the Whole World*," *Publishers Weekly* 243, no. 8 (19 February 1996): 215.
"Review: "*I've Seen the Promised Land: The Life of Dr. Martin Luther King, Jr.*," *Publishers Weekly* 251, no. 2 (12 January 2004): 53–54.
"Review: *Malcolm X: By Any Means Necessary*" (Indianapolis), *Recorder* (28 November 1992): B1.

Riess, Jana. "Review: *A Time to Love: Stories from the Old Testament*," *Publishers Weekly* 250, no. 13 (31 March 2003): 64.

Roback, Diane. "Review: *The Mouse Rap*," *Publishers Weekly* 237, no. 13 (30 March 1990): 64.

Robinson, Edward W., *et al. The Journey of the Songhai People*. Philadelphia: Pan African federation, 1987.

Rochman, Hazel. "Interview: Walter Dean Myers," *Booklist* 96, no. 12 (15 February 2000): 1101.

_____. "Review: *Won't Know Till I Get There*," *School Library Journal* 28, no. 9 (May 1982): 72–73.

Schmidt, Nancy J. "Children's Literature about Africa," *Lion and the Unicorn* 21, no. 2 (April 1997): 284–287.

Smith, Karen Patricia, ed. *African-American Voices in Young Adult Literature: Tradition, Transition, Transformation*. Lanham, Md.: Scarecrow, 1994.

Staunton, John A. "Review: *Monster: A Novel*," *Journal of Adolescent & Adult Literacy* 45, no. 8 (May 2002): 791–793.

Sutton, Roger. "Review: *Blues Journey*," *Horn Book* 79, no. 3 (May-June 2003): 363–364.

_____. "Threads in Our Cultural Fabric," *School Library Journal* 40, no. 6 (June 1994): 24–28.

Tibbets, Sally. "Review: *The Dream Bearer*," *Kliatt* 38, no. 2 (March 2004): 48.

Twichell, Ethel R. "Review: *The Legend of Tarik*," *Horn Book* 57 (August 1981): 434.

West, Mark I. "Harlem Connections: Teaching Walter Dean Myers's *Scorpions* in Conjunction with Paul Laurence Dunbar's *The Sport of the Gods*," *Alan Review* 26, no. 2 (winter 1999).

Williams, Karen. "Review: *Harlem: A Poem*," *Christian Science Monitor* (29 May 1997): 1.

"Writer Tells Kids: Future Is in Books, Not on the Streets," *Bergen (N.J.) Record* (9 March 2005).

"Youth Author Has Reasons to Write" *Syracuse Post-Standard* (21 April 2005).

Myers's Genealogy

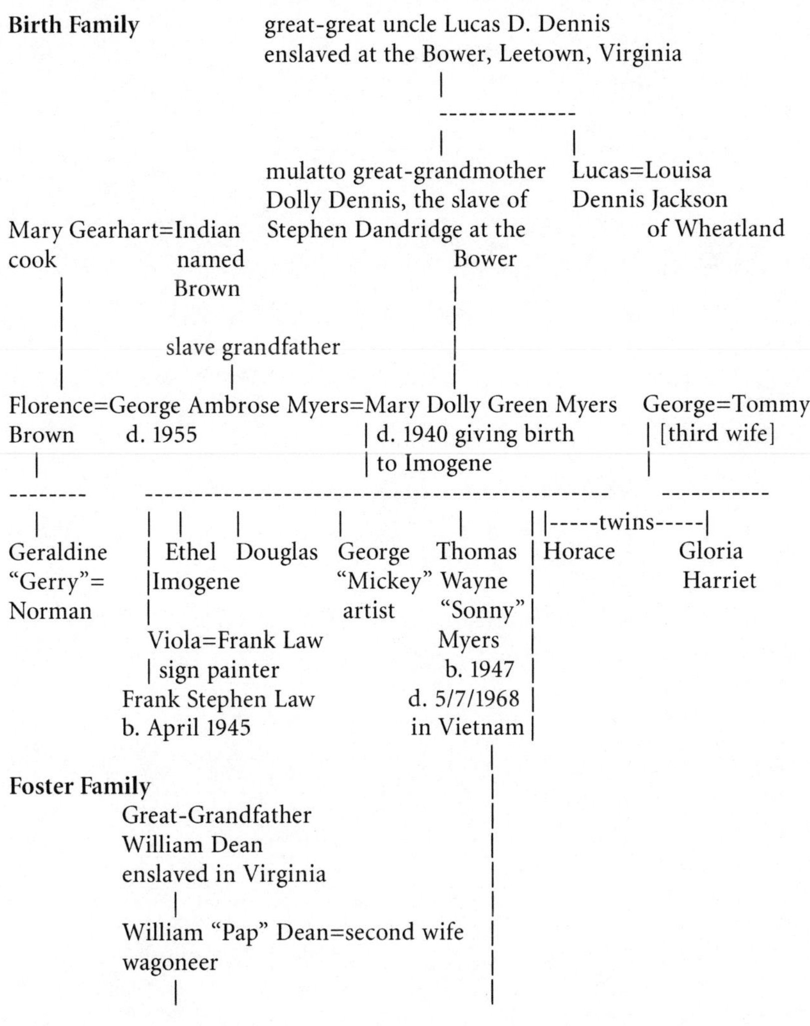

Birth Family
great-great uncle Lucas D. Dennis
enslaved at the Bower, Leetown, Virginia
mulatto great-grandmother
Dolly Dennis, the slave of
Stephen Dandridge at the
Bower
Lucas=Louisa
Dennis Jackson
of Wheatland
Mary Gearhart=Indian
cook named
Brown
slave grandfather
Florence=George Ambrose Myers=Mary Dolly Green Myers
Brown d. 1955
d. 1940 giving birth
to Imogene
George=Tommy
[third wife]
Geraldine
"Gerry"=
Norman
Ethel
Imogene
Douglas
George
"Mickey"
artist
Thomas
Wayne
"Sonny"
Myers
b. 1947
d. 5/7/1968
in Vietnam
twins
Horace
Gloria
Harriet
Viola=Frank Law
sign painter
Frank Stephen Law
b. April 1945
Foster Family
Great-Grandfather
William Dean
enslaved in Virginia
William "Pap" Dean=second wife
wagoneer

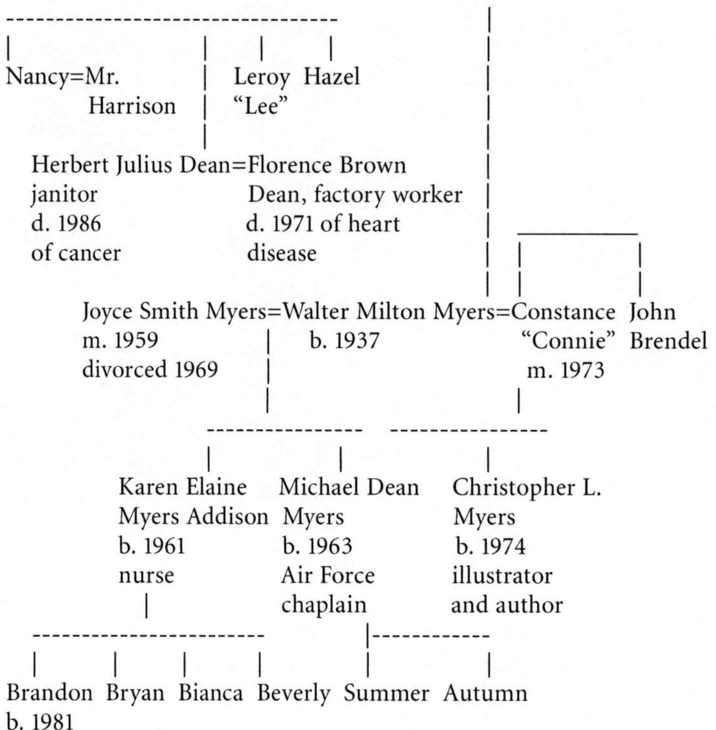
Nancy=Mr. Harrison
Leroy "Lee"
Hazel
Herbert Julius Dean=Florence Brown Dean, factory worker
janitor
d. 1986
of cancer
d. 1971 of heart
disease
Joyce Smith Myers=Walter Milton Myers=Constance "Connie"
m. 1959
divorced 1969
b. 1937
m. 1973
John
Brendel
Karen Elaine
Myers Addison
b. 1961
nurse
Michael Dean
Myers
b. 1963
Air Force
chaplain
Christopher L.
Myers
b. 1974
illustrator
and author
Brandon
b. 1981
Bryan
Bianca
Beverly
Summer
Autumn

Walter Dean Myers: A Literary Companion

achievement

Walter Dean Myers writes to give young readers hope for the future. He explained, "I want to write books where a child says, 'I'm going to feel good about myself'" (Brown, 46). His lengthy canon includes a number of texts devoted to the theme of accomplishment, notably, the short story "The Treasure of Lemon Brown" (1983), the biographical play *And There Stood a Man* (1990) about actor Paul Robeson, and the history texts *Now Is Your Time! The African-American Struggle for Freedom* (1991), *Amistad: A Long Road to Freedom* (1998), *Antarctica: Journeys to the South Pole* (2004), and *U.S.S. Constellation: Pride of the American Navy* (2004). The author's works also examine the cost of low achievement, especially in delinquent boys, particularly Jimmy Lynch and Kevin, court remands in *Handbook for Boys: A Novel* (2002). In both *Monster: A Novel* (1999) and *Shooter* (2004), Myers presents troubling scenarios in which outsiders choose the outlaw's style of excellence. In the latter novel, 16-year-old Leonard "Len" Gray rises above his high school classmates long enough to plot a murder-suicide that kills both Gray and his arch enemy, Brad Williams, a strutting jock. The subtext suggests that redirection of talented killers might have resulted in more positive, less lethal accomplishments.

Myers introduced an antidote to low self-esteem in an early picture book, *The Dragon Takes a Wife* (1972), a modernized fable in which a fairy named Mabel Mae Jones delivers straight talk to Harry, a fire-breathing dragon whose record for losses weighs heavy on his outlook. In the lingo of the day, Mabel Mae summarizes the problem: "You got that losing stuff in your system and you can't move right" (Myers, 1972, n.p.). The child-pleasing narrative generates a double happily-ever-after by ridding Harry of his hang-ups and relieving Mabel Mae of a half-hearted career as a magician. Contributing to the theme of attainment are Ann Grifalconi's pictures of Mabel Mae as costume changes alter the fairy from wand-waver to gardener, cool chick, and cheerleader to wife and mother of three small dragons. The motif lauds pragmatic solutions to problems by awarding Harry and Mabel Mae a contented nuclear family.

Myers examines the issue of classroom achievement in his seriocomic teen novel *Fast Sam, Cool Clyde, and Stuff* (1975). On report card day, Clyde Jones's mother engages him in give and take over the issue of academic coursework. Clyde, a fatherless boy, has the option to take an easier math course, but chooses to stay in the harder class, even though he received an F during the first term. Mrs. Jones builds confidence in Clyde with a "good-doing speech" that compares him to his father, who "never would give up on anything he really wanted" (Myers, 1975, 86, 84). In *It Ain't All for Nothin'* (1978), the author indicates that good performance in school is an introit to more accomplishments. Roland Sylvester, the mentor and eventual foster father of 12-year-old Tippy, examines the boy's trophies for relay racing and suggests that pride in sports acumen can lead to pride in other things, particularly academic excellence. Roland creates a visual image of the virtual trophy and urges Tippy to "try as if there is one" (Myers, 1978, 153).

In biography, fiction, verse, and snapshot, Myers fills his published pages with role models—the Harlem Hellfighters, poets Countee Cullen and Langston Hughes, singers Dorothy Dandridge and Billie Holiday, musicians Scott Joplin and Duke Ellington, preachers Al Sharpton and Dr. Martin Luther King, Jr., critic W. E. B. Dubois, and freedom fighters Malcolm X, Rosa Parks, and Winnie Mandela. Prominent in the author's thoughts are sports heroes like Jack Johnson, Joe Louis, Muhammad Ali, and members of the Negro Baseball League, the inspiration to generations of young athletes. In the teen novel *It Ain't All for Nothin'* Grandma Carrie Brown's interest in baseball peaks with the retirement of Jackie Robinson, the black player who first integrated a white team. In an essay for *Black Scholar*, "Gordon Parks: John Henry with a Camera" (1976), Myers summarized the importance of these achievers: "Young artists often forget, in their zeal to rush through the portals of success, just who it was that opened the door" (Myers, 1976, 27).

In fictional teen assessments of the people who deserve respect, some gain prominence for beauty and grace, for example, the 16-year-old title character in *Crystal* (1987), or for size and strength, like Mack, protector to a gang leader in *Scorpions* (1988), or for being pathfinders, like the first black U.S. senator, Hiram Revels, mentioned in *Fallen Angels* (1988). Others, like Lonnie Jackson, the teen basketball player in *Hoops: A Novel* (1981), and Eddie "Mack" McCormick in "Kitty and Mack: A Love Story" in *145th Street: Short Stories* (2000), earn esteem for skill at sports. In Mack's case, predictions of his acceptance in major league baseball set him apart from other teens. The narrator explains that people idolize Mack for his stardom on the diamond. For those strivers who fall short of their goals, Myers offers encouragement. In *Harlem: A Poem* (1997), he grants would-be achievers "their own slam-dunk dreams" as the legacy due all children (Myers, 1997, n.p.).

Achievement and dreams pair naturally in Myers's writing. In *Hoops*, the possibilities of college or professional careers loom on the fantasy horizon of Paul, who hopes to be scouted and awarded a scholarship to a white school. The author grants that wish for Lonnie in a sequel, *The Outside Shot* (1984), which advances the community basketball star to a college athlete on scholarship at Montclare State College in Indiana. To balance Lonnie's life, Myers emphasizes the heart-warming success at Lonnie's off-campus job at University Hospital, where he provides sports therapy for nine-year-old Eddie Brignole, an autistic child. By earning more personal satisfaction from helping Eddie and for friendships with roommates and with Sherry Jewett, Lonnie looks for achievement less from lay-ups at court and cheers of fans and more from goals suited to adults.

In contrast to the scholarship seekers and glory hounds of the basketball court, Myers pictures the children of segregation as citizens short-changed by racial inequity. A colorful character, 51-year-old Sweeby Jones, a homeless Vietnam vet in *Darnell Rock Reporting* (1994), grew up in Live Oak, Florida, a racist Southern community. He entered school in 1949, fifteen years before *Brown v. the Board of Education* in May 1954 opened schools to all races. Sweeby recalls being "expected to sit in the back of the room like a big dummy" (Myers, 1994, 88). Although he graduated with a diploma, the certificate was valueless to a young man who accomplished nothing practical or useful. Myers indicates that Sweeby's generation received no opportunity to develop their natural gifts.

The author turned to history for the achievements of Colonel Fred V. Cherry, a model of the overachiever who refused to let obstacles stand in the way. In *A Place Called Heartbreak: A Story of Vietnam* (1992), Myers reflects on the Virginian in his youth: "He thought about flying and dreamt about flying, imagining how the pilots felt" (Myers, 1992, 7). Setting the example were his parents, who worked multiple jobs. Myers comments, "There weren't any crybabies in the Cherry household" (*ibid.*, 9). The F-105 bomber pilot and Korean War veteran endured over seven years' captivity among the Vietcong. Much of his resilience was the early home training in viewing failure as just another form of opportunity.

An asset of Myers's fiction derives from frequent references to Harlem as the incubator of great people, such as star vocalists the Shirelles and boxer "Sugar" Ray Robinson. On the back cover of *Harlem: A Poem* (1997), the author's son, artist Christopher Myers, captures his father's celebration of achievement in a competitive moment of a girls' basketball game. In the foreground, the netted hoop symbolizes black strivings for greatness. In *The Beast* (2003), the author mentions poet Langston Hughes as the translator of poems by Chilean author Gabriela Mistral. When the protagonist, 16-year-old Anthony "Spoon" Witherspoon, returns home from Wallingford Academy in Connecticut for Christmas break, his mother speaks admiringly of Arctic explorer Matthew Alexander Henson, who once lived in the Paul Laurence Dunbar Apartments, the first large garden complex in Manhattan built in 1926 at Seventh Avenue and West 149th Street. These fleeting images impress the minds of readers with the ammunition to shoot down self-doubt.

When Myers turned to biblical lore for *A Time to Love: Stories from the Old Testament* (2003), he described figures who rose above others in wealth and prosperity. Of Samson, a giant of an Israelite, the king's soldiers state, "Nothing defeats him. In his hands, anything becomes a terrible weapon, a sword, a stick, even the jawbone of a donkey" (Myers, 2003, 4). The author turns pride in success against Samson, whom the Philistine temptress Delilah betrays and humbles. Even before their love flares, he admits, "Love makes us all weak" (*ibid.*, 8). A similar twist on greatness generates jealousy in the story of Joseph and Reuben. The brothers, sons of Jacob, try to limit Joseph's rise to fame and to repay him for his conceit. Asher rationalizes that Joseph's achievements are undeserved because they are "based on what he would take from us" (*ibid.*, 32). He accuses Joseph of "[putting] the bitter where the sweet should be," the author's lyric commentary on accomplishment gone awry (*ibid.*, 33). In both instances, the success stories bear a price in human suffering — the enslavement of both Samson and Joseph.

In a virtuoso verse collection, *Here in Harlem: Poems in Many Voices* (2004), Myers-the-poet showcases individual speakers exulting in unique personal triumphs. Alto saxophonist Willie Arnold blows the hot notes of bebop that rock the house. By turns rhapsodic and swinging, his music invades the mind and enlivens the feet. Mechanic William Dandridge takes comfort from the artistry of jazz saxophonist Charlie "Bird" Parker. In another mood, Myers poses the paradox of the forgotten hero in a Shakespearean sonnet, "Frank Griffin, 82." The poem honors the 369th Infantry Regiment known as the "Harlem Hellfighters," the first black U.S. combat unit to be shipped overseas during World War I. A companion poem, "Lemuel Burr, 81," draws strength from the valor of three black veterans of the Red-Ball Express, General George S. Patton's famed supply line. The Army Transportation Corps formed a trucking unit on August 21, 1944, to ferry goods, food, and fuel from St. Lô, France, to Liège, Belgium. Belying achievement is the return home to Batesville, Tennessee, where racism engulfs the trio once more, assuring even a blind man that "he was home again" (Myers, 2004, 79). The choice of Batesville as a setting freights the atmosphere with race baiting, a Southern specialty that rewards the war heroes exclusion from a bus ride home. Like Samson and Joseph, the trio must accept the fact that achievement is fleeting.

See also **adaptation, Muhammad Ali, athletics, dreams, fable, Leonard Gray, Steve Harmon, historical milieu, Malcolm X, *Now Is Your Time!***

• *Further Reading*

Brown, Jennifer M. "Walter Dean Myers Unites Two Passions," *Publishers Weekly* 246, no. 2 (22 March 1999): 45–46.
Myers, Walter Dean. *Darnell Rock Reporting*. New York: Delacorte, 1994.
_____. *The Dragon Takes a Wife*. Indianapolis: Bobbs-Merrill, 1972.
_____. *Fast Sam, Cool Clyde, and Stuff*. New York: Viking, 1975.
_____. "Gordon Parks: John Henry with a Camera," *Black Scholar* 7, no. 5 (1976): 27–30.
_____. *Harlem: A Poem*. New York: Scholastic, 1997.
_____. *Here in Harlem: Poems in Many Voices*. New York: Holiday House, 2004.
_____. *It Ain't All for Nothin'*. New York: Viking, 1978.
_____. *145th Street: Short Stories*. New York: Delacorte, 2000.
_____. *A Place Called Heartbreak: A Story of Vietnam*. Austin, Tex.: Raintree, 1992.
_____. *A Time to Love: Stories from the Old Testament*. New York: Scholastic, 2003.
Smith, Karen Patricia, ed. *African-American Voices in Young Adult Literature: Tradition, Transition, Transformation*. Lanham, Md.: Scarecrow, 1994.

adaptation

Myers's fiction frequently contrasts survival in nature with the challenges of unfamiliar customs, a situation that arises in the personal reflections of *My Name Is America: The Journal of Joshua Loper, a Black Cowboy on the Chisholm Trail, 1871* (1999) and in the naval and slave history texts *Amistad: A Long Road to Freedom* (1998) and *U.S.S. Constellation: Pride of the American Navy* (2004). Early in his career, Myers published "Gums" in *We Be Word Sorcerers: Twenty-five Stories by Black Americans* (1973), a detailed study of adjustment in a child. The tragic story of loss and orphanhood pictures nine-year-old Stevie anticipating the loss of his 69-year-old guardian, grandfather Gums, who senses that his life is ending. The likelihood that Stevie can survive alone without his grandfather's retirement and Social Security checks is dim. The falling action pictures Gums hiding from the specter of death as the boy cowers and weeps at the terrors of life.

The theme of survival invigorates "The Vision of Felipe" (1978), a short story published in *Black Scholar* that pictures another boy threatened by loss of a support system. Myers describes the destitution of ten-year-old Felipe, an orphan from Iquitos, Peru, who undergoes a 600-mile barge journey southwest to Lima. Necessary to life is his acculturation to city ways, which he learns from 12-year-old Daniel, a city-bred urchin. The action indicates that neither child, for all their street-wise begging and scavenging, can survive the hostile milieu — the brutal dictatorship of Juan Velasco Alvarado, which extended from 1968 to 1980. In place of hope, Myers provides Felipe with a vision of a dignified coffin and wake. The boy reduces his ambitions from a shoeshine business to a white shirt, a decent garment for his corpse. The decrease in expectations reflects the harsh lifestyle of Peru, a land that the author had studied in person.

For the novel *It Ain't All for Nothin'* (1978), Myers places 12-year-old Tippy in a series of temporary homes. The apartment he has shared with Grandma Carrie Brown shelters him from the time his mother hemorrhages to death at his birth. Grandma's advancing age and her fall in a stairway end a warm, nurturing arrangement. After a social worker places Tippy with Lonnie, his birth father, the boy, like Charles Dickens's Oliver Twist, adapts as best he can to living among criminals. Torn internally by his grandmother's religious beliefs and by Lonnie's erratic cruelties, Tippy escapes reality through movies, television, sleep, and alcohol. When pressures overwhelm him, he flees from the duality of good boy/bad boy by taking the subway downtown and holing up in an abandoned building. Myers indicates that adaptation for one so young requires more autonomy than Tippy possesses. His only escape from a precarious existence among armed thieves results in flight to Roland Sylvester, a bus driver and mentor who helps Tippy turn in Lonnie and his pals to the police. Without sugar-coating the ending, Myers pictures Tippy still reaching out to his birth father through letters to the prison. The novel suggests that blood ties require some response, even after home life is irrevocably broken down.

In the paired sports novels *Hoops: A Novel* (1981) and *The Outside Shot* (1984), high school basketball star Lonnie Jackson develops into a college student expanding his horizons. On scholarship to Montclare State College in Indiana, he becomes the lone Harlemite in a midwestern community, where street jive and hard-charging court play are inappropriate. The wrenching shift in attitudes and behaviors at first unsettles him, forcing him to depend on friendships with Sherry Jewett and Colin Young for moral support. Myers introduces Lonnie to the experiences that demand more intellectual responses than he is accustomed to. While dating Sherry, he learns to examine film as a mental stimulus rather than as light entertainment. In November, he visits the Young farm in Cisne, Illinois, a rural setting that demands manual labor while offering wide expanses of land and a peaceful night's sleep. More serious is Lonnie's accustoming himself to offers of easy money from gamblers, a temptation that ruins the college career of teammate Bill Larson. Myers indicates through Lonnie's emotional and ethical growth that college is a blessing to an urban teen who needs to examine an array of possibilities for achievement before he reaches manhood.

Outside cityscapes, Myers builds memorable human efforts to adapt to the most negative of human experiences, such as the post–World War II wanderings of the grieving father in "The Treasure of Lemon Brown" (1983) and the decline of a blood brother in *Autobiography of My Dead Brother* (2005). In *The Nicholas Factor* (1983), a spy thriller, Gerald McQuillen is recovering from the death of his father when John Martens, an investigator for the National Security Agency, enlists the college freshman to spy on possible neo–Nazi activities in the campus Crusade Society. The sudden shift to undercover agent requires immediate orientation to group philosophy and readiness for the society's first project, the protection of Quechuan Indians from parasitic illness indigenous to the Amazon jungles of Peru. The narrative extols Gerald for easygoing friend-making and a gradual collection of facts. In time, he realizes that elitist society members manipulate unsuspecting natives and threaten their lives. Patricia A. Morgans, in a review for *Best Sellers*, recognizes in Gerald "a young man of integrity with inner resources upon which he can rely" (Morgans, 1983, 155). Myers reprised elements of the story in *Ambush in the Amazon* (1986), in which brothers Ken and Chris Arrow investigate a *monstruo* (monster) in the Peruvian village of Los Cauchos. To acclimate themselves to the rainforest, the boys maneuver a boat and swim among crocodiles and piranha. Their habituation to dangerous territory enables them to outfox the villains who want to steal Quechuan land.

Other examples of threat force naive youths into similar life-altering situations, such as the sexual come-ons of talent packagers to young models in *Crystal* (1987) and the harsh prison environment that 16-year-old Steve Harmon endures in *Monster: A Novel* (1999). Steve remarks in his journal, "To get used to this I will have to give up what I think is real and take up something else" (Myers, 1999, 4). The taxing chore of adaptation is worse for Myers's fictional soldiers. As a member of a fighting force in the Vietnam War, Richard "Richie" Perry, a rookie infantryman in *Fallen Angels* (1988), learns the importance of day-to-day survival. He recognizes the value of keeping dry feet, cleaning and loading an M-16, obeying orders, and staying alert to night sounds during sector patrol. From a buddy, Harry "Peewee" Gates, Perry observes local wisdom: Gates assumes that salves used by the Vietnamese might be of value to soldiers contracting rashes native to the jungles of Southeast Asia. In *Somewhere in the Darkness* (1992), Cephus "Crab" Little explains to his 15-year-old son Jimmy the hardening of men to prison. To cope in a womanless world, inmates post pictures of women and pretend that someone awaits the men's release from prison. One prisoner is so desperate for a fantasy woman that he steals Cephus's pictures of his wife Dolly. The cruelty of the theft causes Cephus to remark on a tenuous situation: "Jail ain't no place to be" (Myers, 1992, 38).

In his ode "Migration," which concludes the picture book *The Great Migration: An American Story* (1993), co-authored by folk artist Jacob Lawrence, Myers speaks of ambition as an impetus to learning a new environment. The multiple images of people abandoning barren Southern fields and cotton bolls chewed to the pit by weevils prefigures a reach for success in industrialized urban centers in the North. Along with lunch baskets and rope-tied suitcases are the memories of "back cracking, heartbreaking days" that precede "humbled dreams" (Myers, 1993, n.p.). The achievement of vibrant black communities in Chicago, Cleveland, Detroit, and Harlem fulfill those ambitions in the second generation as black children flourish in Northern schools and adapt to the demands of city life.

In one of Myers's most colorful picture books, *The Story of the Three Kingdoms* (1995), he develops the concept of adaptation as the salvation of the earth's first people. When humans appear on the land, they face potential destruction from the elephant's size and weight, the shark's teeth, and the hawk's talons. To survive, the people turn to communal storytelling around the fire, a universal pose of sharing and unity. Through collected wisdom, the group pools energy to raise the elephant from a pit and develops weaving to produce a net strong enough to entrap the shark. In their final strategem, they ensnare the hawk after he settles in a baobab tree. The concept of community action produces a stylized version of the skills that prehistoric clans evolved to secure their place among bigger, stronger beings. Myers concludes with a suitable reward, human pride in accomplishment.

In his picture-ode *Harlem: A Poem* (1997), Myers carries humankind's flexibility to a higher plane. He describes the kinetic relief in a rider of the subway from lower Manhattan to 110th Street, where the outskirts of Harlem abut Central Park North. Riders on the A train advance from "unreal to real" as their arrival in home territory "[relaxes] the soul" (Myers, 1997, n.p.). The senses respond to the fragrance of fresh-rinsed collard greens, the sight of brick buildings, and the sound of women singing along with a radio broadcast of "Lady Day," a familiar nickname for jazz great Billie Holiday (*ibid.*). The cornucopia of welcoming stimuli attest to the black New Yorker's adaptation to America's black capital.

Myers dramatizes adaptation in returns of Harlemites who have broadened their horizons through travel or boarding school or who return from war or prison. As the barber Duke Wilson explains in *Handbook for Boys: A Novel* (2002), "Humans are the most adaptable animals on the planet" (Myers, 2002, 162). The truism supports his advice to a court remand, 16-year-old Jimmy Lynch, about a person who gets into trouble, goes to prison, and experiences life in a cell. Duke adds, "[The prisoner] should be struggling to raise himself out of it, and instead of that he simply adapts to it" (*ibid.*). Duke summarizes acquiescence to crime and punishment as "the path of least resistance" (*ibid.*, 163). In *The Beast* (2003), while 16-year-old protagonist Anthony "Spoon" Witherspoon walks down Nicholas Avenue during Christmas break from Wallingford Academy in Connecticut, he has difficulty reacquainting himself with a natural strut. He wonders, "Could I have forgotten it so soon?" (Myers, 2003, 31). His self-consciousness suggests that five months at prep school has shifted his perspective away from home territory.

More troubling is the perverse adaptive skills of 16-year-old Leonard "Len" Gray and his 17-year-old sycophant, Cameron Porter, in *Shooter* (2004). In a plot chillingly similar to the student terrorism on April 20, 1999, at Columbine High School, Littleton, Colorado, Myers describes the regression of Len and Cameron from normal school friendship toward the lethal posturing of outlaws. After Len introduces Cameron to guns through target practice with the right-wing Patriots club, the two boys cultivate a sullen isolationist mentality and plot revenge against Brad Williams, the bullying jock who ridicules and baits them. The worsening of Len's persecution complex concludes with a school shooting that kills Brad and forces Len to shoot himself. Myers illustrates through the interrogation of two survivors—Cameron and Carla, Len's girlfriend—that adaptation can steer disaffected teens toward criminal behavior in an environment that offers no solace for the outsider.

See also **achievement, Steve Harmon, military**

• *Further Reading*

Morgans, Patricia A. "Review: *The Nicholas Factor*," *Best Sellers* 43, no. 4 (July 1983): 155.

Myers, Walter Dean. *The Beast.* New York: Scholastic, 2003.

_____. *The Great Migration: An American Story.* New York: HarperCollins, 1993.

_____. *Handbook for Boys: A Novel.* New York: Amistad, 2002.

_____. *Harlem: A Poem.* New York: Scholastic, 1997.

_____. *Monster: A Novel.* New York: HarperCollins, 1999.

_____. *Somewhere in the Darkness.* New York: Scholastic, 1992.

_____. *The Story of the Three Kingdoms.* New York: HarperCollins, 1995.

Smith, Karen Patricia, ed. *African-American Voices in Young Adult Literature: Tradition, Transition, Transformation.* Lanham, Md.: Scarecrow, 1994.

Amistad

A precedent-setting event in American history, the slave rebellion aboard the slaver *Amistad* on July 2, 1839, thrust into headlines the plight of kidnap victims illegally sold into bondage at public auction. The event appears in two of Myers's works, *Now Is Your Time! The African-American Struggle for Freedom* (1991) and *Amistad: A Long Road to Freedom* (1998). According to the latter, in January 1839, slavers warehoused some 300 blacks kidnapped from Sierra Leone and the Congo by the minions of Birmaja, a Vai prince and son of King Shaka. For a month, Pedro Blanco, a notorious Spanish trader from Málaga, hold the captives under whip and musket at Lomboko near the Gallinas River before transferring them from the barracoons by canoe to the hold of the *Teçora*. The crew and its human cargo sail west toward the Caribbean. On the Middle Passage, over one-third of the Africans die, primarily of disease and dehydration. The rest survive on limited meals of rice and one cup of water each day. Myers implies black pride at the resilience of those who complete the voyage.

In violation of the Anglo-Spanish Treaty of 1817, the slavers slip into port by night to avoid British offshore patrols. For two weeks, captors sequester valuable black flesh under the cover of jungle. In a Havana barracoon built to hold 1,500, the 53 African *bozales* (illegal imports) known as the *Amistad* captives pass into the custody of Spanish planters Pedro Montes and Jose Ruiz. Montes purchases four children and Ruiz buys 49 adults. En route from Havana to Puerto Príncipe, Cuba, aboard the schooner *Amistad*, Joseph Cinqué, a high-born Mandingo tribesman in his mid–20s, learns from Celestino, the ship's mulatto cook, that the crew intends to dismember, cook, and eat the Africans. Terrified by the tall tale, Cinqué uses a nail to release the imprisoned blacks and, with the aid of Grabeau, arms the captives with machetes. At this point, Myers indicates that there is no turning back for men determined to liberate themselves.

The return to freedom requires more than a simple reversal of course. On July 1, Cinqué and Grabeau lead a mutiny in which two West African captives die. Murder of the captain, Ramon Ferrer, and Celestino precedes the sparing of Ruiz and Montes, who bargain for their lives with the aid of the bilingual cabin boy Antonio. The two Spaniards agree to pilot the craft back to West Africa. Montes tricks the slaves by sailing up the Atlantic coast of North America. During the lengthy voyage, eight more Africans die of disease. Survivors have to drop anchor 30 times to acquire food and fresh water wherever they can find it.

On August 2, the U.S.S. *Washington*, a Coast Guard surveying brig, seizes the *Amistad* off Culloden Point at Montauk, New York. After the *Amistad* berths at New London, Connecticut, on August 26, authorities arrest the insurrectionists for murder and piracy. Federal agents jail the Africans in New Haven and try them in Hartford under Judge Andrew T. Judson. Abolitionists seize on the controversial episode as a model of convoluted logic. Lewis Tappan and other anti-slave sympathizers clash with President Martin Van Buren, who sides with slavers demanding extradition of the Africans to Cuba. Leading the defense is 74-year-old John Quincy Adams, a former U.S. president who is serving in Congress. At issue is a question of whether the men come under the jurisdiction of their owners or whether they can exercise rights of personhood as kidnap victims. Lawyer Roger S. Baldwin demands of U.S. Supreme Court justices, "Suppose they had been impressed American seamen ... who had regained their liberty in a similar manner, would they in that case have been deemed guilty of piracy and murder?" (Myers, 1991, 86). On March 9, 1841, the appeal to the nation's highest court ends in acquittal for the 35 surviving slaves. With funds from mission societies and private donors, 32 of the former slaves leave in November aboard the *Gentleman* and reach Freetown harbor in mid–January 1842.

In Walter Dean Myers's picture book, *Amistad: A Long Road to Freedom*, he alters and enhances some of the data from encyclopedia entries and accounts of the episode from the Farmington Historical Society and the Methodist Archives of Drew University. He calls the head mutineer Sengbe Pieh, a more African name than the Spanish "Cinqué," and describes him as a rice farmer and father of three in the village of Mani in Mendeland. Myers wrings irony from two translations—the ship *La Amistad* (friendship) and the Cuban slave pen *El Misericordia* (mercy). The narrative stresses that four of the Africans incarcerated in New Haven are children, three girls— Kague, Margru, and Teme — and the boy Kali, all between the ages of six and nine. According to a September 1839 news item in the *New Haven Herald*, the jailing incurs curiosity seekers, who pay an entrance fee to the jailer, Colonel Stanton Pendleton, to stare at the Africans. Translators aid the questioning of the mutineers.

Myers takes a humanistic tone in reference to the Africans' sojourn in New England. He states that Sengbe, a dignified peacemaker, objects to being treated like an animal and that the African begs, "Give us free! ... Give us free!" (Myers, 1998, 64). Kali learns enough English from missionary teachers to write to John Quincy Adams that "Mendi people have got souls" (*ibid.*, 70). At the end of the Supreme Court deliberation, the narrative cites the prisoners' rights "to resist oppression, and to apply force against ruinous injustice" (*ibid.*, 72). After regaining freedom, the prisoners accept housing in Farmington, Connecticut, a respected abolitionist stronghold and a station of the Underground Railroad. Myers stresses the names of kindhearted people who sew clothing for the prisoners, build a barracks, and offer church membership and acreage for the men to plant. Some of the detainees appear at fund raisers to solicit money for a return voyage to Africa.

The book's resolution refutes the notion that the Africans return home unharmed. One casualty, a farmer named Foone, drowns in an estuary on August 7, perhaps deliberately out of despair of ever seeing home again. The loss spurs action on the financing of a return voyage, which begins on November 25. Seven weeks later, the survivors reach Freetown. Sengbe finds his people gone and his village empty. Teme, who becomes a Christian, stays at the Mendi Mission, as does Kali. Margru studies at Oberlin College and teaches school in Africa; her friend Kague dies of malaria. Sengbe, in his mid–60s, returns to the mission, where he dies. Myers concludes with a poignant summation: "Their lives were what they could make of them, as are the lives of all free people" (*ibid.*, 94).

• *Further Reading*

Jones, Howard. *Mutiny on the Amistad*. Oxford: Oxford University Press, 1987.

Myers, Walter Dean. *Amistad: A Long Road to Freedom*. New York: Dutton, 1998.

_____. *Now Is Your Time! The African-American Struggle for Freedom*. New York: HarperCollins, 1991.

Osagie, Iyunolu Folayan. *The Amistad Revolt: Memory, Slavery, and the Politics of Identity in the United States and Sierra Leone*. Athens: University of Georgia Press, 2000.

Owens, William A. *Black Mutiny: The Revolt on the Schooner Amistad*. New York: Plume, 1997.

Spielberg, Steven, Maya Angelou, and Debbie Allen. *Amistad: "Give Us Free."* New York: Newmarket, 1998.

anti-hero

Myers fills his narratives with protagonists who lack the expected heroic qualities of an admirable citizen or leader, particularly skill, grace, honesty, courage, and/or truth. The description fits a number of the author's characters, especially Steve Harmon in *Monster: A Novel* (1999) and Carla, Cameron Porter, and Leonard "Len" Gray, three alienated teens in *Shooter* (2004). A grouping of realistic anti-heroes in *Fast Sam, Cool Clyde, and Stuff* (1975) develops the author's belief that friendship can compensate for immaturity and wrongheadedness. Writing for the *Los Angeles Times*, author-reviewer Jim Naughton noted that "the children he wrote about were seldom particularly athletic or particularly smart," a testimony to the author's preference for the anti-hero (Naughton, 1989, 8). Although the premise is idealistic, the camaraderie and support of Sam, Clyde, Stuff, and their female comrades help Clyde through grief for his father, Gloria through sorrow that her parents separate, and Stuff over regret that the group fails to save Carnation Charley from drug addiction. By populating the fictional setting with real children in their early teens, the author illustrates that heroism arises less from valor than from spur-of-the-moment actions, particularly the retrieval of Charley from a drug den.

For "The Vision of Felipe" (1978), a short story published in *Black Scholar*, the author falls back on survivalism to dramatize the terrors of homeless orphans on the streets of Lima, Peru, during the 12-year dictatorship of Juan Velasco Alvarado. Pitting boyish guile against the predations of military patrols, the narrative approves the street wisdom of finding food at all cost, even if nutrition for the day requires swiping a mango from a market fruit stand. From 12-year-old Daniel, the ten-year-old title figure learns the deceptions and self-protective measures that keep both boys fed and clothed. To Felipe's tender-heartedness, Daniel urges him to accept vengeance as a natural emotional response to the adult soldiers who steal proceeds from tourist handouts to the boys.

That same year, Myers wrote an anti-heroic young adult novel, *It Ain't All for Nothin'* (1978). The story ends 12-year-old Tippy's reliance on a beloved, righteous grandmother, Carrie Brown, and tosses him into the custody of Lonnie, his estranged father. Living on the edge of respectability, the boy comes in daily contact with career criminals, alcohol and marijuana consumption, gambling, illicit sex, and erratic pummelings. To cope, Tippy retreats into television, movies, and sleep, but gradually gives into alcohol, the escape of choice among Lonnie and his pals. Forced into two robberies, Tippy battles the pangs of conscience while accompanying his father to dangerous encounters. Duality eventually gives place to a mature decision — to turn in his father and his gang to police and to live with Roland Sylvester, a stable mentor. Myers retains the anti-heroism in the resolution, in which Tippy maintains a correspondence with his father in prison and tries to evolve for himself a persona that is neither anti-parent nor condoning of adult criminality.

The author insists on reducing the glory of war heroes. In *Fallen Angels* (1988), young Richard "Richie" Perry joins the army and fights in the Vietnam War by default. Lacking the money for college tuition, he chooses to support his mother and younger brother Kenny with allotment checks. As a young rookie infantryman, he adjusts to the terrors and privations of a jungle war zone, in which he is alternately bored, tense, and horrified by the suddenness of destruction. He realigns his concept of heroism and courage as the action reveals the fragile assurances of survival, particularly the field treatments of medics and evacuation by helicopter to military hospitals. By accepting fear as a normal response to night patrols and sappers, he acknowledges in himself the effects of constant instability.

The narrative stresses the anti-hero's unease in hostile terrain. During the holiday season from Thanksgiving to Christmas, instead of enjoying the traditional home festivities, he fulfills his obligation to the military. Service entails physical and emotional responses to stress, cold, fear, uncertainty, thirst, fatigue, and shrapnel wounds. Deployment places Perry and his unit in unfamiliar geographic and social situations and forces them into chancy leaps from choppers. Jungle humidity and hip-deep stagnant water in rice paddies threaten Perry's feet with disease and his M-16 with muck and other contaminants. After encircling his bivouac with sandbags, he huddles from bright moonlight alongside Scotty the gunner and strains at calls and movements of advancing VC. For self-protection, Perry sensitizes himself to the throb of hovering Hueys and incoming fire, the blaze of rifle muzzles, the fall of napalm, and the needs of body and spirit. Strengthening his resolve to survive is daily proof that protracted violence can snuff out a human life and shred a living body into unrecognizable pieces.

In a less terrifying setting, Myers creates hope for the title character in *The Blues of Flats Brown* (2000), a picture book that accounts for the roots of soul music. Flats, a "blues playing dog," fears that his owner, A. J. Grubbs, will destroy him by arranging fights with vicious scrapper dogs (Myers, 2000, n.p.). After a near capture, Flats and his pal Caleb take to the roads. Sensibly, Flats rationalizes, "I can't stand no fighting" (*ibid.*). Intuitively, he finds his way to a blues club in New York City and builds a career with poignant ballads about loss, sorrow, and the situations that cause rootlessness. Myers illustrates that homelessness and retreat from aggression become the mainstays of the blues phenomenon. In the critique of Brian E. Wilson for *School Library Journal*, the author "offers meaningful messages about friendship and music without being too didactic or preachy" (Wilson, 2002, 8).

See also **Leonard Gray, Steve Harmon, Richie Perry**

• *Further Reading*

Myers, Walter Dean. *The Blues of Flats Brown*. New York: Holiday House, 2000.

Naughton, Jim. "Literary Crusader Writes Stories About Real Kids," *Los Angeles Times* (29 December 1989): 8.

Smith, Karen Patricia, ed. *African-American Voices in Young Adult Literature: Tradition, Transition, Transformation*. Lanham, Md.: Scarecrow, 1994.

Veeder, Mary. "Review: *Fallen Angels*," *Chicago Tribune Books* (13 November 1988): 6.

Wilson, Brian E. "Review: *The Blues of Flats Brown*," *School Library Journal* 48, no. 11 (November 2002): 8.

athletics

Myers is generous in his admiration of physical vigor and concentration in youth, from the relay races in *It Ain't All for Nothin'* (1978) and a phalanx of skateboarders in the park at Christmas in *The Beast* (2003) to the pick-up basketball games that precede community team participation in city-wide tournaments in the award-winning novel *Hoops: A Novel* (1981). In his first teen fiction, *Fast Sam, Cool Clyde, and Stuff* (1975), Myers describes Gloria as a worthy basketball player whose name suggests an earned reputation for competence. Later references to female athletes do little more than drop a comment about women's competitive drive without developing the complex emotions and physical attainments that precede success. In *The Mouse Rap* (1990), the author turns enthusiastically to male athleticism. He describes star basketball player Ahmed Wilson as the subject of a feature for *U.S.A. Today*. To his credit, Wilson returns from "the whole Ghetto-to-Glory trip" to talk with youngsters playing at Morningside Park (Myers, 1990, 32). Even though Myers credits young sports enthusiasts with commitment to challenge, he is persistent in suppressing the Cinderella aspect of college and professional athletics, which apparently does nothing for female contenders and rarely turns a local male player into a pro, much less a multi-millionaire.

Myers describes the tensions and frustrations of competitive basketball in *Hoops*. The story sets Lonnie Jackson, a 17-year-old star senior on a Harlem team, at a thrilling moment in his game when he has the attention of scouts. The casual remarks of a seasoned player, Sweet Man Johnson, interject the voice of reason. At one time, his main concern was playing for the National Basketball Association. The serendipity of his career is an education and a "chance to realize my own potential" (Myers, 1981, 140). Johnson parlays his opportunity into a contribution to the community. At stake for Lonnie is the Tournament of Champions, which gamblers want the coach and Lonnie to lose. A last-minute save boosts Lonnie to victory and a potential college scholarship, but costs Coach Calvin F. "Spider" Jones his life for defying brutal racketeers. The author's familiarity with the locker room and gym milieu becomes an asset to realism. In the opinion of critic Stephanie Zvirin, a reviewer for *Booklist*, the "dialogue rings with authenticity, on-court action is colorful and well integrated into the story" (Zvirin, 1981, 98).

Myers followed with two sequels, *The Outside Shot* (1984) and *Motown and Didi: A Love Story* (1984). In the first, Lonnie earns a scholarship to play for Montclare State College in Indiana. He risks his education and honor by contemplating the proceeds of illegal gambling, a temptation that Myers observed firsthand in a friend's fight to retain his reputation during a disastrous point-shaving scandal. Myers downplays the value of competitive athletics by depicting character-building events in Lonnie's life, particularly his success at turning hoop shoots into therapy for an autistic child, nine-year-old Eddie Brignole. The understated conclusion portrays Lonnie at an upswing in his maturity in which the rewards for helping Eddie and for making lasting friendships on campus outweigh temporal thrills from cheering fans. Contributing to Lonnie's adult values is the example of Ray York, an aging would-be basketball player who shoots himself out of frustration and self-blame for failing at athletics. The second sequel, the award-winning *Motown and Didi*, discloses the duality in Myers, who had to choose between playing ball at a white college or remaining with the black community in which he felt at home.

The use of athletics as a revelation of character adds to suspense in *The Nicholas Factor* (1983), a spy thriller set on a college campus in Santa Barbara, California. Before accepting an assignment from John Martens of the National Security Agency to infiltrate the campus Crusade Society, Gerald McQuillen plays tennis with a Costa Rican contact, Alfredo Santana. The early morning game becomes an unacknowledged man-to-man challenge. Gerald takes pleasure in outpacing Alfredo and smirks,

"It felt good to cream him" (Myers, 1983, 16). The afterglow increases with Alfredo's self-saving remarks about being rusty from lack of practice. The tension mounts with the author's implication that winning at tennis may overcharge Gerald with a sense of control. In the second matchup with Alfredo, Gerald admits to a gesture of conceit: "I would turn instantly away from the net when I knew I had a winner, and it ticked him off" (*ibid.*, 25). Gerald's advantage derives from Alfredo's elitism — the "need to feel that he was better than everybody else," a clue to the neo–Nazism of the Crusaders (*ibid.*, 26).

Myers reveals another down side to competence in the opening lines of *Slam!* (1996), in which the main character, 17-year-old Greg "Slam" Harris, sees court times as "the only time I'm being for real" (Myers, 1996, 1). Speaking through Assistant Coach "Goldy" Goldstein, the author reminds Slam that he needs to improve his grades if he expects an offer from a college scout. After working out some of his problems with ego and temper, Slam relaxes and enjoys the safety and comfort of the gym in what *Publishers Weekly* critic Sybil S. Steinberg terms "heart-thumping hoop action" (Steinberg, 1996, 76). Eventually, Slam must admit that sports challenges do not compare with more serious issues like schoolwork, his grandmother Ellie's battle with cancer, and his unrest around Ice, an old friend who deals dope. By recognizing the ephemeral nature of his sports self, Slam ventures closer to manhood.

Descriptions of athletes present Myers's diction and phrasing at their best. In the short story "Fighter" in *145th Street: Short Stories* (2000), he describes Billy in action against a "comer," a boxer groomed for advancement: "[Billy] faked Vegas out of position and banked his hands to the wiry body" (Myers, 2000, 33). The fight jargon enhances verisimilitude as the bout progresses. Myers chooses "backed off," "circled," "mix it up," "feinted once," and "fists flashing" as proof of the heated competition. Contrasting boxing terms are evidences of exhaustion and pain in "contort," "barely conscious," "slurred," and "slumped." The ambiguity of the conclusion characterizes the compromise expected of a professional athlete as Billy tries to hold together a life of headaches and regrets from prize fighting and the homey atmosphere of a loving wife who asks no questions.

Myers sprinkles his texts with frequent reminders that black athletes are role models to the black community. In the story "The Baddest Dog in Harlem" (2000), Harlemites of 145th Street casually discuss Joe Louis, Muhammad Ali, and Roberto Duran as though the comparison of prizefighters is a weighty issue. Another of Myers's contributions to black history is *My Name Is America: The Journal of Biddy Owens: The Negro Leagues* (2001), a reflection on black baseball teams in 1948, the last year of the Negro League functioned. His title character displays a savvy knowledge of scores and triumphs for such heroes as Willy Mays, Jackie Robinson, Satchel Paige, Buck Leonard, and Josh Gibson, black role models who retain their immediacy long after the ebb of their careers.

In a short story, "Season's End" in *The Color of Absence: Twelve Stories about Loss* (2001), Myers muses through the mind of an adult, 36-year-old James "Jimmy" Sims, on the worth of athletic competition. The protagonist, a dispirited 15-year veteran, admits on the chanciness of winning: "You guess right and you're a hero" (Myers, 2001, 170). Of the magic moment when player and serendipity come together,

Sims exults at "a fusion of mind and body that edged on greatness," a connection he is unable to achieve in the last game of his career (*ibid.*, 172). In a postscript, Myers remarks on his own experience of slowing down, realizing that his speed and agility at basketball had peaked and that a younger player was coming of age on the court.

The subject of pride in achievement recurs in "John Reese, 70," an entry in *Here in Harlem: Poems in Many Voices* (2004). In old age, Reese, now a janitor, relives the time when he and his teammates were "roaring eagles, the barons of our/Turf" (Myers, *Here*, 19). He identifies with Jackie Robinson, a victor on a par with Homer's Ajax. The next generation, epitomized by "Lawrence Hamm, 19," experiences basketball with joyous kinesis. Hamm describes his lithe court moves as "so sweet they make shadows stumble" (*ibid.*, 63). The uplift that buoys his spirit takes on a sanctity akin to a zen epiphany. He erupts in cries of "I am! I am!" (*ibid.*).

The negative side of athletics dominates the psychiatric evaluations in *Shooter* (2004), a teen novel loosely based on the teen terrorism plot at Columbine High School, Littleton, Colorado, on April 20, 1999. Cameron Porter, a 17-year-old outsider, depicts jocks as cliquish boors who bully anyone not belonging to the group. Because he fails to make the basketball team, he encounters the anger of his father, who "couldn't get over it, like I had done something to him personally" (Myers, *Shooter*, 82). The father, Norman Porter, connects sports with business success and considers Cameron's ineptness proof that he's a quitter. After Norman gets Cameron a spot on the team, the boy and his friend, 16-year-old Leonard "Len" Gray incur the hatred of jocks who bully and taunt. Because Cameron lacks the competitive spirit of an athlete, he follows Len on a downward spiral of gun worship and spite. Their anger at a school that devalues them results in Len's early-morning shooting spree, which targets Brad Williams, the school's star athlete. Myers's psychological evaluation of teen outlaws generates disturbing evidence that sports accolades, taken to the extreme, further unhealthy attitudes in misfits who function outside the stereotype of the heroic jock.

See also **achievement**

• *Further Reading*

Myers, Walter Dean. *Here in Harlem: Poems in Many Voices.* New York: Holiday House, 2004.

_____. *Hoops.* New York: Delacorte, 1981.

_____. *The Mouse Rap.* New York: HarperCollins, 1990.

_____. *The Nicholas Factor.* New York: Viking, 1983.

_____. *145th Street: Short Stories.* New York: Delacorte, 2000.

_____. "Season's End," *The Color of Absence: Twelve Stories About Loss.* New York: Simon & Schuster, 2001.

_____. *Shooter.* New York: Amistad, 2004.

_____. *Slam!* New York: Scholastic, 1996.

Steinberg, Sybil S. "Review: *Slam!*," *Publishers Weekly* 243, no. 48 (25 November 1996): 76.

Zvirin, Stephanie. "Review: *Hoops: A Novel*," *Booklist* 78, no. 2 (15 September 1981): 98.

Bad Boy: A Memoir

Myers aroused critical interest with his autobiography, *Bad Boy: A Memoir* (2001). In 20 chapters, he progresses from his ancestry to a bibliography of 45 of his works along with the awards they won. Constructed from Works Progress Administration data, photos, census records, and family oral history, the narrative reveals normal childhood memories of discarded comic books for savoring and trading and of Myers's appointment as cookie monitor. The complex relationship of the Dean and Myers families discloses some important realignments. The author reunited with his biological brother George "Mickey" Myers, Jr., after the Myers family moved around the corner from the Deans' Harlem apartment. Myers testifies to a strong sibling relationship on the back cover of *Here in Harlem: Poems in Many Voices* (2004), which pictures the brothers in Easter suits and hats in front of the Presbyterian church.

The author provides meticulous support for his choice of title. At Easter, 1947, an inflamed appendix requires surgery at Sydenham Hospital. After eight days, Myers returns home to rest, heal, and read Honeybunch and Bobbsey Twins books. Against orders, he rides his bike and runs upstairs, causing the incision to rip open. After a second hospital stay, he returns to his bed and finishes the fourth grade at home. At this point in *Bad Boy*, he recognizes color bias in black people, who favor light skin tones over dark. The discovery illustrates that the bad boy is both intelligent and perceptive.

Critically contrasted to James McBride's *The Color of Water* (1997), Myers's life story shocked his adult daughter, who was surprised that he had lived through a period of confusion, truancy, and soul searching. Sporting what critic Allison Follos calls "a too-cool armor within a tough Harlem neighborhood," the narrator explores his interests in basketball, reading, and inner-city life and accounts for his misbehavior as a means of fitting in with peers (Follos, 2004, 66). For commentary on racial issues, he dramatizes his friendship with James Baldwin. Myers drew a broader readership after excerpting an incident — hitching a ride on a cab bumper and being dragged for a block — as "Growing Pains," reprinted in a September 2002 issue of *Scholastic Scope*. Significant to the episode is his memory of urban racism: "We didn't get many yellow cabs coming to the street, because downtown cabs didn't stop for black people" (Myers, 2002, 18). He concludes with one of his worst behaviors, blaming his mother for beating him, a lie to cover up his fall from the cab bumper.

See also **chronology**

• *Further Reading*

Follos, Alison. "Review: *Bad Boy: A Memoir*," *School Library Journal* 50, no. 11 (November 2004): 66.
Myers, Walter Dean. *Bad Boy: A Memoir*. New York: HarperCollins, 2001.
_____. "Growing Pains," *Scholastic Scope* 51, no. 1 (6 September 2002): 18–19.

belonging

Myers refers frequently to the human need for the oneness of group identity, an essential in the history text *Amistad: A Long Road to Freedom* (1998), the crime story

Monster: A Novel (1999), and the sports memoir *My Name Is America: The Journal of Biddy Owens: The Negro Leagues* (2001). At the beginning of *The Nicholas Factor* (1983), John Martens piques Gerald McQuillen's interest in an altruistic campus organization called the Crusader Society. To negate Gerald's idea that Crusaders are snobs, Martens describes branches in Europe, South America, and eventually the Middle East and characterizes members as "pretty upstanding young people like you" (Myers, 1983, 8). Similarly idealistic, the concept of joining a spirited team invigorates *U.S.S. Constellation: Pride of the American Navy* (2004), an account of black and white sailors sharing the jobs of ridding the world of the slave trade and of fighting the Civil War.

The author acknowledges the importance to youth of acceptance by a group or community, such as the clutch of five black youths splashing in the stream from a hydrant in *Harlem: A Poem* (1997). Varying in shades from golden-brown to coffee and ebony, the quintet exult in acceptance in America's black capital. In *Fast Sam, Cool Clyde, and Stuff* (1975), the outsider Francis Williams, nicknamed "Stuff," longs to join the children of 116th Street. At stake is a sense of belonging among taller kids who value the ability to sink balls on the basketball court and with a group that tries to rescue Binky's ear, gnawed off in a rumble over a girl. For six teens at South Oakdale Junior High in *Darnell Rock Reporting* (1994), group identity as the Corner Crew threatens to spotlight members for the wrong reasons. To rescue them from additional notoriety as shirkers of school work, Miss Seldes, the school librarian intervenes with the principal and offers the Crew a meeting place in the library. To accentuate the positive aspects of belonging, she distributes T-shirts marked "SOCC for South Oakdale Corner Crew" (Myers, 1994, 19).

Myers moves beyond childish concerns in "Monkeyman," an entry in *145th Street: Short Stories* (2000), which depicts the narrator's longing to escape Harlem. Because he considers Africa his motherland, his Uncle Duke Wilson, the owner of the neighborhood barbershop, charges him with having "a bad attitude toward Harlem" (Myers, 2000, 73). The youth justifies his ambivalence toward the neighborhood as a desire "to be more than what I saw on the block" (*ibid.*, 74). The concept of affiliation emerges as friends rally to protect Monkeyman from gang retaliation. Myers's theme is a simplified version of the Golden Rule: "It's hip to help a brother in trouble" (*ibid.*, 76).

Camaraderie poses a variety of choices to Lonnie Jackson, one of Myers's more fully developed characters. As the protagonist in *Hoops: A Novel* (1981) and *The Outside Shot* (1984), Lonnie develops from a Harlem homeboy into a college student, but not without undergoing tests of friendship and loyalty. He manages demands of the urban scene like a native by accepting gamblers, street toughs, and addicts as the down side of city life. During the Tournament of Champions, he weathers competitive games at gyms in other parts of New York City and suits up in white shirt and tie for a business meeting on Madison Avenue. In the sequel, he works harder at belonging at Montclare State College, an Indiana campus populated with midwestern students whose experiences and values challenge his Harlem ways. By accepting Colin Young as a friend and by visiting his farm on a November weekend, Lonnie discovers new types of belonging — as teammate, roommate, and fellow student rather than as a blood brother of a fellow black.

Variant types of belonging involve fictional characters at different comfort levels. In *Fallen Angels* (1988), anti-hero Richard "Richie" Perry and his hoochmate, Harry "Peewee" Gates, form a military-style camaraderie based on humor, toughness, and commonalities of urban boyhood, Perry in Harlem and Peewee in Chicago. Out of the loop is nurse Judy Duncan, a seatmate on the flight to Southeast Asia. Unlike black males who bond with dialect and shared experiences, she remains an outsider because of her gender. In another example of group bonding, Myers collaborated with folk artist Jacob Lawrence on the picture book *The Great Migration: An American Story* (1993), which describes the wrenching up of agrarian roots as Southern wanderers head north to urban industrialized centers. To increase a sense of belonging, blacks turn to fundamentalist faith at storefront churches and build new lives that replace dirt-floored cabins with apartments and fire escapes.

The author takes opposing views of milieu in *Monster* and *The Dream Bearer* (2003). In the former, protagonist Steve Harmon's urge to hang with street toughs places him on the scene of felony robbery and murder of a pharmacy owner rather than with the affectionate parents who visit him at the Manhattan Detention Center. In the latter novel, Myers recreates David Curry's oneness with Moses Littlejohn, a homeless Harlemite who generates security and personal identity. A foil to Reuben Curry, David's fractious father, Moses directs the boy to a place in his own psyche to find peace and belonging. Unlike Steve, who negates self-respect, David engages his dreams as a source of strength during difficult times.

Myers uses alienation as a cause of mental torment in *Shooter* (2004), a teen novel loosely based on teen terrorism at Columbine High School, Littleton, Colorado, on April 20, 1999. Len Gray, a sociopathic outsider, forms *Ordo Sagittae* (Order of the Arrow) comprised of Cameron Porter, Carla Evans, and two other students, Paul and Walter Klubenspies, who belong to no clique. A parallel to the adult males in the Patriots, a right-wing adult shooting club, Len's group exists "slightly out of the mainstream" (Myers, 2004, 93). When FBI agent Victoria Lash questions Cameron, she accuses him of being a mindless follower. He gives no thought to consequences, such as random shots into a dumpster and group shooting by white racists at a photo of Dr. Martin Luther King, Jr. When Franklin Bonner completes a psychological evaluation of Carla, she explains why she values acceptance in Len's retinue: "I was part of something — a little group — and maybe that's better than liking somebody" (*ibid.*, 150). On the day preceding a murder-suicide, Len's diary scrutinizes his role as leader of the disaffected: "Can I trust them to go all the way? Can I take them?" (*ibid.*, 240). The failure of the group to stick to the plan saves Cameron and Carla from a bloody rage that costs Len his life. The outcome echoes the moral of Aesop's fable about the yapping pup: it's better to be known for something bad than not to be known at all.

See also **black identity, dialect, diaspora, displacement, gangs**

• *Further Reading*

Myers, Walter Dean. *Darnell Rock Reporting*. New York: Delacorte, 1994.
_____. *The Great Migration: An American Story*. New York: HarperCollins, 1993.

_____. *The Nicholas Factor*. New York: Viking, 1983.
_____. *145th Street: Short Stories*. New York: Delacorte, 2000.
_____. *Shooter*. New York: Amistad, 2004.
_____. "Walter Dean Myers," *Read* 54, no. 13 (25 February 2005): 14–15.
Smith, Karen Patricia, ed. *African-American Voices in Young Adult Literature: Tradition, Transition, Transformation*. Lanham, Md.: Scarecrow, 1994.

betrayal

Myers dramatizes human relations based on trust and jeopardized by betrayal, such as the bad advice Carol Brown gives her daughter about fame as a supermodel in *Crystal* (1987), comic disloyalty in *The Righteous Revenge of Artemis Bonner* (1992), and the intervention of a biased school board member in *Darnell Rock Reporting* (1994). The author ramps up the endangerment of young people in lethal situations, as described in the failure of Cameron Porter and Carla Evans from joining Leonard "Len" Gray in a school massacre in *Shooter* (2004) and in social menace to youth in the ode "Wolf Song" (2005). The theme of treachery enhances the dilemmas of storybook fables *Mr. Monkey and the Gotcha Bird* (1984) and *How Mr. Monkey Saw the Whole World* (1996) and of the shearing of Samson and the sale of Joseph into slavery in scriptural retellings in *A Time to Love: Stories from the Old Testament* (2003).

One example from Myers's teen fiction, *It Ain't All for Nothin'* (1978), portrays a wretched duality in 12-year-old Tippy, who tries to adapt to living with his criminal father Lonnie. The experiment in living with an unpredictable alcoholic results in child abuse and Lonnie's encouragement of delinquency in Tippy. By forcing the child to accompany him on dangerous robberies, Lonnie presses Tippy to the edge of endurance. For good reason, Tippy turns his father in to police. The choice represents a dual betrayal/rescue. By stymying the careers of career criminals, the boy salves an aching conscience that insists on right thinking and acceptable behavior. By precipitating a second prison sentence for Lonnie, Tippy stops his father's rapid slide into one rationalized robbery after another, each more dangerous than the last.

Like the teen fiction of Robert Cormier and Kaye Gibbons, Myers's young adult novels present betrayal from a number of perspectives. In *Hoops: A Novel* (1981), 17-year-old Lonnie Jackson hesitates to accept a wino, Calvin F. "Spider" Jones, as coach and confidante. When Cal wavers from sobriety and misses practices and games in the Tournament of Champions, Lonnie considers ending his friendship with Cal, but chooses instead to track him down and help him through a rough time. Myers presses the issue of betrayal to the final pages of the resolution by depicting Cal as the tight-lipped coach demanding trust. Because Lonnie accedes to Cal's dictates, both characters profit—Lonnie from a triumph on the basketball court and Cal from tricking racketeer Tyrone Giddins into expecting a big win from gambling on a loss. Myers rejects a happily-ever-after ending with Cal's death from a knifing in the locker room. In grief, Lonnie surveys the tenuous moral ground of trust and recognizes Cal's fortitude in risking retaliation for betraying villains.

Flagrant violations of trust precipitate anger and fear in Myers's characters. While rookie infantryman Richard "Richie" Perry copes with the Vietnam War in *Fallen Angels* (1988), bad memories of home focus on a night three years earlier when his father deserted his mother, Mabel Perry. The abandonment causes her and her young son Kenny to weep. Perry recalls, "I put my head under the cover" (Myers, 1988, 95). In an incident in *Somewhere in the Darkness* (1992), Cephus "Crab" Little flees from police officers tipped off by Rydell DePuis, Crab's former accomplice in the plotting of a robbery. The fragile link between two men who deny carrying out an armored car robbery that ends in murder results in brief cell time for the perpetrator, Richie "Frank" Dutton, and a nine-year sentence for Crab, who was at home recovering from tooth extraction at the time of the shooting. Myers's depiction of the fallout from treachery suggests that life assigns punishments arbitrarily with no semblance of fairness.

Problems of trust within a troubled family complicate *The Dream Bearer* (2003), an urban folk tale heavily laced with realism. The Currys struggle daily with Reuben's paranoia and his refusal to take daily medication, which he believes undermines his manhood. Evelyn Curry solaces her husband for his misgivings and eases the crises that create turbulence in Reuben's emotions. The couple's two sons, 12-year-old David and 17-year-old Tyrone, support Evelyn with as much understanding as they are capable of. Her momentary lapses into tears cause David to reveal Tyrone's involvement with drugs and unsavory characters. Myers indicates that betrayal falls outside the boundaries of disloyalty because David fears that Tyrone will become a victim, either of the police or of the group to whom he owes $400. Thus, David is loyal to a higher moral order. Evelyn's assurance that parents need to know about child endangerment fails to placate David, who vacillates between shielding Tyrone and informing on him. As is common to Myers's young adult fiction, the question of immaturity exonerates David for facing choices far beyond his wisdom to understand.

See also ***Crystal***, **vengeance**

• *Further Reading*

Barker, Carol Y. "Review: The Dream Bearer," *School Library Journal* 50, no. 1 (January 2004): 67.

Myers, Walter Dean. *The Dream Bearer*. New York: Amistad, 2003.

_____. *Fallen Angels*. New York: Scholastic, 1988.

_____. *Somewhere in the Darkness*. New York: Scholastic, 1992.

black identity

Myers is a master at identifying the qualities that comprise black identity. Key to his success is his loyalty to Harlem, his hometown, and to the people he revered from childhood. In an interview with Allen O. Pierleoni for the *Sacramento Bee*, Myers asked why other writers don't return to their roots: "What happened to the idea of celebrating a neighborhood and the ordinary people in it? Nobody gives them a voice, but I do" (Pierleoni, 2005).

The author's books survey strands of self in young protagonists who are still forming value systems, an element of his short story "The Treasure of Lemon Brown" (1983) and the history texts *My Name Is America: The Journal of Biddy Owens: The*

Negro Leagues (2001) and *U.S.S. Constellation: Pride of the American Navy* (2004). In repeated fictional scenarios, the author layers glimpses of home, family, conversation, food, amusement, love, and school that he refers to in a review for the *Washington Post* as "cultural substance" (Myers, 1991, 7). These themes establish an African American continuity, as with the blood oath sworn by black infantrymen Harry "Peewee" Gates and Richard "Richie" Perry in *Fallen Angels* (1988) as a sign of belonging to a black brotherhood. In another fearful resettlement of blacks in unknown environs, *The Great Migration: An American Story* (1993) pictures the centrality of scripture-based faith and memories of family members buried in the agrarian South as wanderers make a new life in the urban industrialized North. Assuring their belonging are the black villages that spring up in Chicago, Cleveland, Detroit, New York, Philadelphia, and Pittsburgh. Bursting with community belonging in the picture-ode *Harlem: A Poem* (1997) are children at play, "waiting to sing their own sweet songs" in America's black capital (Myers, 1997, n.p.).

Shoring up splintered home lives in Myers's works are the wise black matrons, like Mabel Perry, Richie's mother. Imitating them are younger females like Gabriela "Gabi" Godoy in *The Beast* (2003), who learn from their elders how to dispense love, acceptance, and a patina of religiosity that assures wayward young men of someone to call on when times turn bad. Contributing to his protagonists' self-esteem are monuments to black history — Marcus Garvey Park, Malcolm X Avenue, a school bearing Ralph Bunche's name, the songs of Billie Holiday and Duke Ellington, a framed picture of Dr. Martin Luther King, Jr., snipped from a magazine, and a photo of King next to a picture of Jesus. In *The Young Landlords* (1979), idealistic youth learn from an accountant about Jack Johnson, the first black heavyweight boxing champion and forerunner of hero Muhammad Ali. Introduction to black heroes heartens the young entrepreneurs with models of risk-taking and success.

Introspection figures in numerous characterizations in Myers's fiction, beginning in June 1969 with the contemplative character of Moses, a wronged prison inmate in "How Long Is Forever?," a dilemma story issued in *Negro Digest*. In *It Ain't All for Nothin'* (1978), Myers describes 12-year-old Tippy's struggle with duality. By being untrue to his inner self, he loses touch with reality and integrity. Forced into crime by Lonnie, his dissolute father, Tippy enjoys the high of scot-free thievery, but recognizes the danger of more night prowls. In choosing to save Bubba, Lonnie's accomplice, from a deadly wound, Tippy opts for honesty that results in the arrest of Lonnie and his cohorts. In 1987, Myers echoed Tippy's identity crisis in the misgivings of the title character in *Crystal*, the story of a 16-year-old model who suppresses her values under a facade of chic outfits and sexual allure. The inner voice that warns Crystal Brown of the perils of celebrity refuses to be ignored, particularly after Rowena, an 18-year-old colleague, chooses suicide over a career that values her only as a face and body. More troubled is Steve Harmon, a 16-year-old accused of felony murder and robbery in *Monster: A Novel* (1999). Although his mind tries to reflect goodness and worth, he fears the condemnation in other people, particularly his father and his attorney, Kathy O'Brien. Steve writes in his journal, "I wanted to open my shirt and tell her to look into my heart to see who I really was" (Myers, 1999, 92). Through self-study, these characters recognize the still small voice of self that refuses to lie.

One of Myers's most lauded picture books is *Brown Angels: An Album of Pictures and Verse* (1993), a tender arrangement of neighborhood images in child fashions long out of style. In preface to the commonplaces of a small child with his pet dog and goat cart, friends climbing a fence, and toddlers and school groups dressed up for the photographer, the author reminds us that "the child in each of us is our most precious part" (Myers, *Brown*, n.p.). His wording carefully deletes an us-vs.-them mindset by reminding readers that all people share memories of a time when personal judgments and bias were still in the future. His second motivation is a reclamation of black children from media stereotyping. His text projects youngsters loved and valued by families who scrubbed them clean and dressed them in their best caps, bonnets, and hair bows. With a touch of the father and the idealist, Myers anticipates a time when the "long stride walker" becomes a "good man" (*ibid.*, n.p.). In a parting stanza, he asks that readers "honor the memory" of black forebears (*ibid.*, n.p.). His enigmatic closure anticipates acceptance of all children for their promise.

The source of black identity in *The Glory Field* (1994) dates to 1763 and the shackling and transportation of Muhammad Bilal, an African from Sierra Leone and patriarch of the Lewis family. From plantation days, the blessing of children over his grave unites a family that prides itself in strength and solidarity. In the saga's third stave, 75-year-old Grandpa Moses Lewis blesses the burial ground in 1900. His call-and-response prayer elicits amens of commitment from younger family members who lack the fervor of those who survived enslavement at Live Oaks Plantation on fictional Curry Island, South Carolina. Grandma Saran ensures future respect to the deceased by ordering 14-year-old Elijah Lewis to tend the site every week. Contributing to family traditions is membership in a church built from the boards of dismantled slave cabins, a reminder of the Lewis family's emergence from bondage. More poignant is the leg iron that Grandpa Moses saves as evidence of Muhammad's courage and survival.

Myers introduces black identity in *Slam!* (1996) as atmosphere for a story about a teenager who is unsure of his future. Because the protagonist, 17-year-old Greg "Slam" Harris, attends Latimer Arts Magnet School, a mostly white school, he wears his race with pride. While attending a basketball game between Carver and Trinity High, he stands for the playing of the national anthem and sings the Negro anthem, "Lift Every Voice," which poet James Weldon Johnson and his brother, musician John Rosamond Johnson, wrote in 1899. Slam is pleased to see that whites from Trinity High stand respectfully along with blacks from Carver High. The gesture elevates the opposing team for its sensitivity to nonwhite people. Contrasting Trinity students is Mr. Parrish, Slam's English teachers, who mocks Slam's black English as an African trait from the "We-Be tribe" (Myers, 1996, 213). By naming his authority figure "Parrish," Myers suggests a parochial racism that is unlikely to undermine Slam's self-esteem.

In one of Myers's undervalued works, *Here in Harlem: Poems in Many Voices* (2004), an anthology of verses and candid black-and-white photos, black identity reaches its height in praise of the community known as America's black capital. In 54 first-person poems, he connects black pride to political heroes— Malcolm X, Marcus Garvey, Dr. Martin Luther King, Jr., Winnie Mandela — as well as to sports figures, educators, and jazz greats like ballplayer Jackie Robinson, educator Booker T. Washington, and singer Dorothy Dandridge. An introspective monologue by teenager Malcolm James ponders how a youth chooses a role model. The scrap of a union card belonging to his dead father earns regard as Malcolm's fount of pride, a tattered rectangle that attests to his father's career as a sailor. By picturing tangible proof of black identity as fragile, the author reminds readers to treasure ephemeral tokens of personal history.

See also **gangs, Harlem**

• *Further Reading*

Lane, R. D. "'Keepin' It Real': Walter Dean Myers and the Promise of African-American Children's Literature," *African American Review* 32, no. 1 (22 March 1998): 125–138.
Myers, Walter Dean. *Brown Angels: An Album of Pictures and Verse.* New York: HarperCollins, 1993.
_____. *The Great Migration: An American Story.* New York: HarperCollins, 1993.
_____. *Harlem: A Poem.* New York: Scholastic, 1997.
_____. *Here in Harlem: Poems in Many Voices.* New York: Holiday House, 2004.
_____. *Monster: A Novel.* New York: HarperCollins, 1999.
_____. *Slam!* New York: Scholastic, 1996.
_____. "Surviving Mean Streets," *Washington Post* (12 May 1991): 7.
Pierleoni, Allen O. "Wrongs and the Writer," *Sacramento Bee* (29 March 2005).

Bonetta, Sarah Forbes (ca. 1843–1880)

A Yoruban princess of the Egbado tribe, Sarah Forbes "Sally" Bonetta lived an extraordinary life that intrigued Walter Dean Myers to write an illustrated biography, *At Her Majesty's Request: An African Princess in Victorian England* (1999). Orphaned at age five during the Okeadon War of 1848, Bonetta survived a massacre in which only those worthy of ritual murder were spared sale as slaves. In the carnage, Bonetta witnessed the Dahomian attackers dragging her parents from their compound and decapitating them with swords. Kept safe from slave catchers, for two years she remained in Abomey at the royal court of King Gezo, who surrounded himself with a body guard of amazons. He adorned his palisades with 148 skulls, including some of those slain at Okeadon. Her biography is so submerged in the era's dehumanization of captives and slaves that Myers found no clue to her birth name. In a review for *Horn Book*, critic Marilyn Bousquin noted, "The very absence of her voice bears undeniable witness to her story" (Bousquin, 1999, 82).

In 1849, Captain Frederick Edwyn Forbes of the British Royal Navy, the author of *Five Years in China* (1848), volunteered for two diplomatic missions to the king of Dahomey. He described his African sojourns in the two-volume work *Dahomey and the Dahomans: Being the Journal of Two Missions to the King of Dahomey and Residence at His Capital in the Years 1849 and 1850* (1851). Among the gifts that Gezo presented Forbes on July 5 were fabric, footstools, rum, cowries, and an "African child" (Forbes, 1851, 206). Forbes realized that, to reject the human gift would have "signed her death-warrant" (*ibid.*, 207). He recognized that the seven-year-old's facial markings destined her to be burned to death as a royal offering to Gezo's noble ancestors in a ritual called See-qua-ah-hee (watering of the graves), which honored the king's mother, grandmother, and great-grandmother.

Forbes rescued Bonetta for presentation to Queen Victoria and, at a baptismal ceremony, named the child for himself and for his ship, the brigantine *Bonetta*. Her first name is biblical, after the Hebrew Sarah (princess), wife of the patriarch Abraham. In late July 1850, Forbes delivered the child to the port of Gravesend. The next year, he issued his illustrated commentary on his journeys and on British efforts to stop the slave trade. With typical Victorian piety, he considered Bonetta's salvation God-given and projected that "her duty leads her to rescue those who have not had the advantages of education from the mysterious ways of their ancestors" (*ibid.*, 207–208).

After she entered the protection of Queen Victoria at Windsor Castle, Bonetta lived under what *Publishers Weekly* critics Diane Roback and Jennifer M. Brown called "the prescribed rules for women in her day" (Roback & Brown, 1999, 216). By age eight, she was fluent in English and gifted with an ear for music. She resided with Frederick and Mary Forbes and enjoyed royal privileges. According to Forbes, Bonetta modeled the intelligence of black people, an excellence of thought and performance that refuted racist beliefs that black Africans are naturally mentally impaired. A signal honor of her importance to British society was a bust cast by Benedetto Pistrucci, the Roman sculptor who became chief engraver of the London mint.

Myers surmises that Bonetta suffered isolation and identity crises as a black protégé of a white queen. An analysis in *Publishers Weekly* points out the dual implications of the title, which suggests that Queen Victoria could request without impunity a number of possibilities for Bonetta's future. In 1851, Bonetta traveled to Freetown, Sierra Leone, to study at a mission school. According to an article from the *Brighton Gazette* dated August 1862, she learned sewing, English, and French and studied music before her return to England in June 1855. She lived with the Shoen family in Gillingham and later with Sophie Welsh in Brighton. Against Bonetta's wishes, she entered an arranged marriage with a 32-year-old African missionary, James Pinson Labulo Davies. On August 14, 1862, she was the bride at England's first royal African wedding, held in Brighton at St. Nicholas Church, the area's oldest structure, which dates to Norman times. The regal ceremony involved matched carriages and 16 bridesmaids.

Bonetta returned to Africa as Sarah Bonetta-Davies. While her husband conducted his business in Freetown, she taught at the Female Institution and later in Lagos, Nigeria. The couple's daughter was born in 1863; in honor of the queen, Bonetta named her daughter Victoria Davies. In early childhood, Sarah's daughter met Queen Victoria, who claimed the girl as a godchild. Sarah gave birth to two more children. After her chronic tuberculosis worsened, she went to Funchal, Madeira, to recuperate. She died in August 1880 at age 37 and was buried on the island. The queen comforted Victoria Davies upon Bonetta's death. Sarah Bonetta's life might have remained hidden in the archives of history if Myers had not located the packet of letters and written a biography based on solid research.

See also **historical milieu**

• *Further Reading*

Bousquin, Marilyn. "Review: *At Her Majesty's Request: An African Princess in Victorian England*," *Horn Book* 75, no. 1 (January 1999): 82.
Forbes, Frederick E. *Dahomey and the Dahomans: Being the Journal of Two Missions to the King of Dahomey and Residence at His Capital in the Years 1849 and 1850.* London: Longman, Brown, Green, and Longmans, 1851.
Myers, Walter Dean. *At Her Majesty's Request: An African Princess in Victorian England.* New York: Scholastic, 1999.
"Review: *At Her Majesty's Request: An African Princess in Victorian England*," *Publishers Weekly* 246, no. 6 (8 February 1999): 215.
Roback, Diane, and Jennifer M. Brown. "Forecasts: Children's Books," *Publishers Weekly* 246, no. 6 (8 February 1999): 215–216.

Collins genealogy

For a veteran of the military landing at Normandy, Myers composed *My Name Is America: The Journal of Scott Pendleton Collins, a WWII Soldier, Normandy, France, 1944* (1999), which details the family whom Scott leaves behind when he departs for the European theater during World War II:

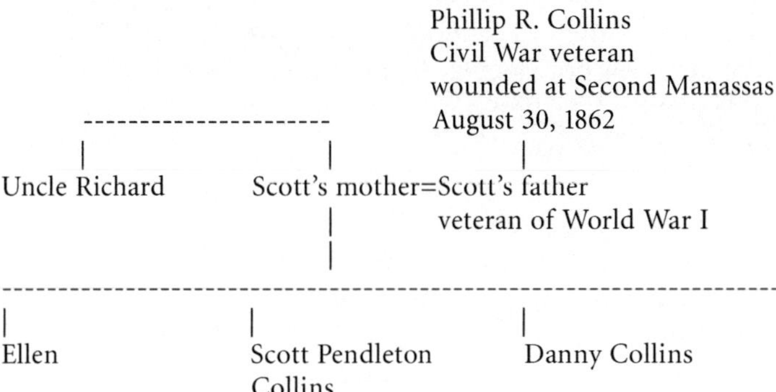

• *Further Reading*

Myers, Walter Dean. *My Name Is America: The Journal of Scott Pendleton Collins, a WWII Soldier, Normandy, France, 1944.* New York: Scholastic, 1999.

coming of age

Myers earns the respect of a wide span of people for his commitment to children and youth, whether he writes of the acceptance of man-sized responsibilities in *My Name Is America: The Journal of Joshua Loper, a Black Cowboy on the Chisholm Trail, 1871* (1999), the tension in the son of an insane father in *The Dream Bearer* (2003), the scramble of the powder monkey during the Civil War in *U.S.S. Constellation: Pride of the American Navy* (2004), or threats to the young in the ode "Wolf Song" (2005). Early in his career, the author pictured outsized challenges to youngsters, such as the specter of homelessness for nine-year-old Stevie in "Gums," anthologized in *We Be Word Sorcerers: Twenty-five Stories by Black Americans* (1973), and for the title character in "The Vision of Felipe" (1978), published in *Black Scholar*. Some 20 years later, the author stated his credo at the annual American Library Association convention in Miami in the 1994 Margaret A. Edwards Award Acceptance Speech. He promised that, through literature, he would bring youth to the foreground by presenting their unique problems. His intent to "[peel] away the labels they have been burdened with, that diminish their humanity" aimed at promoting connection with the world (Myers, 1995, 131). In addition to didactic purpose, Myers chose to entertain readers and to stimulate intellectual curiosity, two goals that enliven his seriocomic novel *Fast Sam, Cool Clyde, and Stuff* (1975) and the adventure-mystery Arrow series.

The quandaries and missteps of youth provide Myers with thought-provoking material for androcentric teen fiction. The motif fits most of his works, including the exemplum "The Treasure of Lemon Brown" (1983) and *The Legend of Tarik* (1981), an allegorical quest novel in which two wise mentors, Nongo and Docao, ready Tarik for knighthood and for the stalking of a mass murderer, El Muerte (death). In a realistic vein, Myers examines the rites of passage in the life of Lonnie Jackson, a Harlem-born basketball star in *Hoops: A Novel* (1981) and its sequel, *The Outside Shot* (1984). Lonnie's wise rejection of gambling on point spreads parallels mature behaviors at home. On leaving for Montclare State College in Indiana, he promises Sister Boone that he will stay true to his religious upbringing. At a low point, he calls his mother and admits that campus demands make him homesick. He also edges nearer a lasting male-female relationship. Unlike his shaky commitment to Mary-Ann in *Hoops*, his love for Sherry Jewett in *The Outside Shot* resembles an adult expression of affection based on more than physical attraction and sex.

The author turns his masterful historical fiction *Fallen Angels* (1988) into a coming-of-age character novel by describing the horrors and waste of the Vietnam War. Combat destroys the innocence in protagonist Richard "Richie" Perry, who grows into manhood from terrifying patrols in enemy territory. At times, his confusion about self and ambition clouds his thinking. Contributing to the mental fog are images of dead Viet Cong and the unexpected deaths of Jenkins from a land mine and of Lieutenant Carroll during a firefight at a village cemetery. Perry experiences an epiphany about fear of violating standard behavior. To him, "standing alone" as a war protester and refugee to Canada seems more terrifying than risking death in combat in Vietnam (Myers, 1988, 147).

Examining growing up from another perspective, Myers discloses faulty parenting in *Somewhere in the Darkness* (1992), an initiatory story of Jimmy Little and his father, Cephus "Crab" Little, an escaped convict. In childhood, Jimmy follows his mother's demand that he go hunting with his father, a stereotypical model of male bonding. After an afternoon's tracking through the woods, Jimmy observes the man halt for a session of drinking. Because the boy rejects liquor, his father asserts, "You in the company of men now, you got to act like a man acts" (Myers, 1992, 101). After Crab's imprisonment for robbery and murder, Jimmy deduces that manly behavior can exaggerate macho swagger into crime. Crab's misspent life, which ends in the infirmary from kidney failure, aids Jimmy in formulating a sensible gender ideal that balances masculine aggression with the nurturing he learns from Mama Jean, his legal guardian. Myers stresses the irony that Jimmy develops more fully into adulthood than his father did.

Less clear is the author's depiction of the maturing of 16-year-old Steve Harmon, the protagonist of *Monster: A Novel* (1999). In the Manhattan Detention Center awaiting trail for felony robbery and murder, he suffers a grievous confinement among hardened thugs who assault and rape other inmates with impunity. Steve mops corridors by day and weeps by night while pondering how he allowed his search for manhood to lead him into company with James King, a career criminal. Myers slices through stereotypes about dissolute black families by picturing the Harmon home as stable and encouraging. Steve lives with a religious mother and college-educated father and prospers at Stuyvesant High School under the mentoring of George Sawicki, coordinator of a three-year cinematography workshop. In view of these opportunities and encouragement, Steve must examine his conscience to determine how he became involved with the fatal shooting of a drugstore owner by simply standing watch on the sidewalk. At a crucial moment on the threshold of adulthood, the boy recognizes that decision making is complicated.

Myers returned to the subject of youth at the threshold of adulthood in *The Greatest: Muhammad Ali* (2001), a sports biography that follows Cassius Clay from the theft of his bicycle in Louisville, Kentucky, at age 12 through boxing lessons that precede the world heavyweight championship. By stressing the boy's thin limbs and awkward movements, Myers prefaces the development of an Olympic gold medalist from unpromising beginnings. The narrative reflects on "the downward spiral of young black boys" (Myers, 2001, 6). Myers lauds trainers Joe Martin at the Columbia Gym and Fred Stoner at the Grace Community Center in Louisville, for avoiding the indifference common to adults, who fail youth "by turning away, by denying that [moral decline] is happening" (*ibid.*, 7). As a result of male leadership, Clay leaves the cultural ghetto and changes both his life and the sport of boxing.

In the novel *The Beast* (2003), Myers describes the social insecurity of 16-year-old Anthony "Spoon" Witherspoon, a Harlemite who misreads the friendship of Chanelle Burnitz, an upper-class student at Wallingford Academy in Connecticut. He arrives at her apartment for a party, but faces the cold disdain of a snooty white doorman. Among mostly white guests, Spoon asserts his individuality by making a date to play basketball with classmate James Brand and by dancing with several girls. Spoon's attitude toward female peers erupts in a single cynical comment about two girls crying: "I imagined one of them had just lost a lover or an earring" (Myers, 2003, 53). His sarcasm implies that women give in to frivolous emotions. Of his own unraveling relationship with Gabriela "Gabi" Godoy, his Dominican girlfriend, he is equally sarcastic about throwing himself into a volcano, leaving behind a suicide note in haiku form. His fantasies denote how far he has to progress before becoming a man.

Tandem views of brothers approaching adulthood dramatize family dynamics in *The Dream Bearer* (2003). The tenuous hold of Evelyn Curry on her volatile paranoid husband Reuben, her street-wise 17-year-old son Tyrone, and 12-year-old David weakens under the constant disruptions of home unity. Critic Carol Y. Barker, a reviewer for *School Library Journal,* views the title figure, Moses Littlejohn, as a catalyst who encourages the ferment of David's thoughts and hopes as he enters his teens. The resulting contemporary urban folk tale provides plenty of pithy scenes and dialogues for young readers to ponder and discuss. Among them is the question of choosing a model of adult male behavior when the father figure is seriously flawed.

See also **achievement, *Crystal, Fast Sam, Cool Clyde, and Stuff, Hoops*, immaturity, juvenile crime, *Monster: A Novel*, opportunity, Richie Perry**

• *Further Reading*

Barker, Carol Y. "Review: The Dream Bearer," *School Library Journal* 50, no. 1 (January 2004): 67.
Lane, R. D. "'Keepin' It Real': Walter Dean Myers and the Promise of African-American Children's Literature," *African American Review* 32, no. 1 (22 March 1998): 125–138.
Myers, Walter Dean. *The Beast.* New York: Scholastic, 2003.
_____. *Fallen Angels.* New York: Scholastic, 1988.
_____. *The Greatest: Muhammad Ali.* New York: Scholastic, 2001.
_____. "1994 Margaret A. Edwards Award Acceptance Speech," *Journal of Youth Services in Libraries*, 8, no. 2 (winter 1995): 129–133.
_____. *Somewhere in the Darkness.* New York: Scholastic, 1992.

community

Myers honors the Greek concept of *koinonia* or community, a human gathering that generates synergy, like the fictional ousting of thugs from a tenement in "The Treasure of Lemon Brown" (1983), the apprehension of villains posing as monsters in the adventure novella *Ambush in the Amazon* (1986), the counseling and personal regard for a 16-year-old model in *Crystal* (1987), and the solution to homelessness and hunger in *Darnell Rock Reporting* (1994). In the author's view, affiliation to a group welcomes individuality at the same time that it demands allegiance to group ethics, the basis for the creation fable *The Story of the Three Kingdoms* (1995) and the tender ode "Wolf Song" (2005). In a sci-fi allegory, *Shadow of the Red Moon* (1987), the author characterizes the erasure of national enmity through the formation of a new society. He praises the courage of the young in breaching prejudices: "One day, four sick and weary souls had come together and called themselves a people" (Myers, 1987, 183). An unidentified reviewer for *American Visions* summarizes, "the Okalian youth discover that the real danger is not what everyone thinks, and that everything they have ever been told is a lie" ("Review," 1998, 35). The novel's concluding line suggests that faith in unity suffices as a new order replaced outworn traditions.

The concept of team effort inspired the author's history texts, particularly *Now Is Your Time! The African-American Struggle for Freedom* (1991), *I've Seen the Promised Land: The Life of Dr. Martin Luther King, Jr.* (2004), and *U.S.S. Constellation: Pride of the American Navy* (2004), which describes the shipboard camaraderie and interdependence of black and white sailors during the Civil War. Out of love for his growing-up years in Harlem, Myers began filling his urban fiction with evidence of community cohesion. Decades before Senator Hillary Clinton's notion of "it takes a village to raise a child," Myers depicted the surrogate parenting of old ladies sitting on their apartment steps, men gathered at the barbershop, and the street wisdom of older children, as exemplified by Daniel, a hardened Peruvian urchin in "The Vision of Felipe' (1978). The value to the author's life of neighborhood discipline, acceptance, and encouragement preceded another form of fellowship, which he summarized in the 1994 Margaret A. Edwards Award Acceptance Speech as the "vital community of writers and book people" (Myers, "1994," 133).

At a Highlights for Children conference in Chautauqua, New York, Myers made fast friends with children's author Pam Conrad, a foster parent of a black child. Their experience won Myers's interest and concern. He depicted a fostering situation in *It Ain't All for Nothin'* (1978), a story of community efforts to rescue 12-year-old Tippy from homelessness. As his grandmother, Carrie Brown, sinks under the double whammy of arthritis and injuries from a fall, neighboring women offer advice, coffee and bags of groceries, bedside care, and intervention with Social Services. After Tippy passes to the custody of Lonnie, his ex-con father, bouts of child abuse, hunger, endangerment, and neglect send the boy to the streets. Because he falls ill from consumption of alcohol, Ronald Sylvester and his wife Edna volunteer to counsel and mentor the boy. The further decline of Lonnie into robbery and shooting destroys the family, leaving Tippy with little choice but to turn his father and his gang over to police and to accept the Sylvesters as foster parents. Myers presents the makeshift arrangement as the community's response to unloved, misdirected children in a milieu beset by delinquency and wasted lives.

On a more optimistic note, the author's upbeat novel, *The Young Landlords* (1979), describes the six-member teen Action Group that takes charge of a decrepit tenement in Harlem at 356 West 122nd Street. The passage of ownership from Joseph Harley to 15-year-old Paul Williams begins with a survey of legal papers at the social services office, where Paul's father works. From there, Paul takes the papers to the Legal Aid Society, where a second lawyer, Charlie Turner, represents Paul free of charge and draws up lease agreements. Later in the narrative, Paul remarks that his neighbors tend to respect each other's privacy, but during the street clean-up campaign, residents get involved in a group effort. Myers illustrates that the backing of teens by parents, neighbors, government agencies, and volunteers contributes to a youth project that brightens the neighborhood and revives a cooperative spirit.

Myers returns to issues of foster parenting in *Won't Know Till I Get There* (1982), a seriocomic novel depicting Steve Perry's first infraction against the law. For spray-painting a train with the name of an imaginary gang, the Royal Visigoths, he earns no sympathy from a black judge. Instead of remanding Steve and his accomplices to a juvenile hall, she sends the foursome to the Micheaux House for Senior Citizens, a community retirement center, to aid elderly people from Steve's neighborhood. Enterprise infects the teens. One resident of the center, Mabel Jackson, asserts her feeling of belonging: "The old neighborhood, that's what I'm all about" (Myers, 1982, 174). Susan Williamson, a reviewer for *Voice of Youth Advocates*, applauds Myers's integration of "a successful, two-parent, black middle class family, and of senior citizens as full functioning human beings" (Williamson, 1982, 34).

A macabre sense of community permeates the spy thriller *The Nicholas Factor* (1983), which Myers sets on a college campus in Santa Barbara, California. The focus is the Crusade Society, an allegedly altruistic network that organizes letter-writing campaigns, fund raising and support for charities, and monitoring of national and international situations. The tension between protagonist Gerald McQuillen's suspicions about the basic philosophy of the Crusades and his need for involvement fuels a psychologically convoluted plot. At the outset, he admits that, since his father's death, membership "was a hook, a lifeline" (Myers, 1983, 24). The society's intrusive philosophy colors a three-week expedition to Lima, Peru, where participants provide Indians with unwanted shoes to prevent parasitic infections through the soles of the feet. Gerald collects evidence that crusaders are oblivious to the menace of their neo-Nazi organizers. Myers uses the plot to warn readers that surface altruism may cloak lethal intent.

A subsequent teen novel expresses more of Myers's concern for right thinking in unfamiliar circumstances. As scholarship-winner Lonnie Jackson prepares to depart for Montclare State College in *The Outside Shot* (1984), the author looks back through his protagonist's eyes at the black community in the early 1980s. The makeup of street scenes is realistic. Alongside a nodding addict and Sister Boone cooling her neck in front of a brownstone apartment building range examples of normal activities—while men play dominoes at a bodega, a dog rests under the table. Lonnie's mother escorts him away from home to the airport and a new phase of his life far from New York City. He muses that "everything had its place," a commentary on the rightness of the milieu in which he grew up (Myers, 1984, 2). On campus, he investigates an unfamiliar sense of community based on friendships with classmates and roomies and on loyalty to the basketball team. As he matures, he is able to commit to nine-year-old Eddie Brignole, an outpatient at University Hospital, and to Alethea York, the widow of Ray York, Lonnie's acquaintance from pick-up games with mill workers. By developing new friend-making skills, Lonnie expands his sense of community to more than his childhood home.

Critics applaud Myers's use of community action as salvation for teen criminals, drug addicts, and derelicts. In *Handbook for Boys: A Novel* (2002), a juvenile court judge sends court remands Jimmy Lynch, Kevin, and Ernesto to Wilson's barbership for daily chores and on-the-job lessons in responsibility. An unsigned review in *Publishers Weekly* characterizes the unusual book as "a penetrating profile of a community through the brief appearances of characters who file through Duke Wilson's barbershop" ("Review: *Handbook*," 2002, 70). By selecting local individuals as objects of admiration or pity or disgust, Duke illustrates to the trio of boys that Harlem provides lessons of all types. He expresses generosity and concern for unfortunates by helping Billy to move to new quarters and by cutting the hair of Irene Davis, a babbling street derelict hooked on drugs. By ridding Duke of scorn or superiority, Myers illustrates the value of charitable citizens to Harlem.

The author reminds readers that change in communities is unavoidable. In an unsettling reunion between 17-year-old Anthony "Spoon" Witherspoon and Harlem in *The Beast* (2003), corruption has settled into the neighborhood that he knew from birth. Feeling out of place after only five months at Wallingford Academy in Connecticut, he worries about his Dominican girlfriend, Gabriela "Gabi" Godoy, who escape squalor through heroin use. On the street, a rapid-fire seizure and arrest of friend Leon for theft leaves Spoon shaken. After Leon's return to tell his side of the event, he claims to know nothing about stolen baseball cards. To redeem Harlem from harsh police tactics, an unnamed man urges Leon to file a repart "to say that the New York Police Department cannot just slam people around and terrorize people without a response" (Myers, 2003, 81). The man claims that a formal complaint will prove to the authorities that Harlem's unity holds firm against unsubstantiated raids on citizens.

Myers ennobles his Harlem upbringing in reflections on the vivid community as a page in the history of a global African diaspora. He collaborated with folk artist Jacob Lawrence for the picture book *The Great Migration: An American Story* (1993), which expresses the yearning for justice and common goals in the agrarian blacks who vacated fields in the Carolinas, Alabama, and Georgia to form urban enclaves in the industrialized North. In the closing pages of Myers's *tour de force* anthology *Here in Harlem: Poems in Many Voices* (2004), he pulls together strands of personal testimony to Harlem's longevity. The final prose commentary of Clara Brown, the poet's bright seer, pictures the neighborhood's lengthy history of "its big-time people and its struggling folk" (Myers, 2004, 81). Like the Greek Pythia, the clairvoyant priestess of Delphi, Clara enlightens the reader to a paradox—the texture of good and bad fortune and of the human rises and falls that distinguishes Harlem.

See also **belonging**

• *Further Reading*

Gauch, Patricia L. "Review: *The Young Landlords*," *New York Times Book Review* (6 January 1980): 20.

Myers, Walter Dean. *The Beast.* New York: Scholastic, 2003.

_____. *Here in Harlem: Poems in Many Voices.* New York: Holiday House, 2004.

_____. *The Nicholas Factor.* New York: Viking, 1983.

_____. "1994 Margaret A. Edwards Award Acceptance Speech," *Journal of Youth Services in Libraries*, 8, no. 2 (winter 1995): 129–133.

_____. *The Outside Shot.* New York: Delacorte, 1984.

_____. *Shadow of the Red Moon.* New York: Harper Collins, 1987.

_____. *The Story of the Three Kingdoms.* New York: HarperCollins, 1995.

_____. *Won't Know Till I Get There.* New York: Viking, 1982.

"Review: *Handbook for Boys: A Novel*," *Publishers Weekly*, 249 no. 16 (22 April 2002): 70–71.

"Review: *Shadow of the Red Moon*," *American Visions* 13, no. 6 (December 1998): 35.

Williamson, Susan. "Review: *Won't Know Till I Get There*," *Voice of Youth Advocates* 5, no. 5 (December 1982): 34.

Crystal

Dedicated to storyteller Spencer Shaw, a professor emeritus from the library science school of the University of Washington, *Crystal* evolved from requests of high school girls that Myers write about a fashion model. For material, he interviewed young women who posed for book covers. The novel portrays the dilemmas of an impressionable young girl facing mature challenges and decisions. The narrative opens on 16-year-old Crystal Brown in a Brooklyn church choir singing "Jesus

Called My Name," a token of the Christianity at work in a ghetto community (Myers, 1987, 3). The title character juggles the input of a concerned father and star-struck mother as well as high school friends, agent, and photographers. Most fearful is the suicide of a colleague, Rowena, who chooses death over perpetual handling and positioning of her body before studio lights as though she has no more worth than her good looks and sexy form. In the view of Gerry Larson, a critic for *School Library Journal*, Crystal "makes a stand for personal integrity in a competitive world ... [and] shatters many illusions of stardom" (Larson, 1987, 111).

Myers aims his young adult fiction at impressionable preteen and teen females who can identify with Crystal as she progresses from child model to adult. After nine months of work, she still feels awkward about displaying her size-five body nude to a photographer, yet, she enjoys the fuss over makeup and clothes and an opportunity for night-clubbing with a handsome movie star. Inner warnings and mother-daughter unease deflate the highs of working in the modeling profession and of being admired by neighbors and fellow students. The threat of an over-developed ego arises after George ages her with professional makeup. Crystal admires her reflected image draped in ermine and asserts, "You *are* divine" (*ibid.*, 59). Bringing her back to earth is the growl of her father, Daniel Brown, when a limo brings her home in the wee hours. His complaint expresses parental concern that Crystal is moving too far too fast. He charges, "You think it's all too easy" (*ibid.*, 70). The comment is a standard in Myers's teen fiction in which hardened parents foresee difficulties ahead for naive youth.

Myers indicates that networking is valuable to women in the beauty business because it provides feedback from models who have experienced similar emotional confusion. Crystal's friendship with Rowena, an 18-year-old white model, reaps valuable insights into the perils of professional modeling. Rowena's summation of celebrity offers Crystal a warning about false identity—being "so into being something that somebody wants you to be" (*ibid.*, 75). The meat market aspect of modeling takes on new meaning after fashion photographer Marc Everby of *La Femme* magazine slides his hands over Crystal's stomach and buttocks. A succeeding scene pictures the rescue of a puffy orange kitten from a cage holding a snake, a suggestion of Crystal's endangerment in the hands of amoral talent handlers and packagers. Critic Pam Spencer in a review for *School Library Journal* remarks on the workings of Crystal's conscience: "Deep down she's bothered by the backstage maneuvering needed to achieve ... stardom" (Spencer, 1992, 164).

See also **sex**

• *Further Reading*

Betancourt, Jeanne. "Review: *Crystal*," *New York Times Book Review* (13 September 1987): 48.
Larson, Gerry. "Review: *Crystal*," *School Library Journal* 33, 10 (June/July 1987): 111.
Myers, Walter Dean. *Crystal*. New York: Viking Kestrel, 1987.
Spencer, Pam. "Winners in Their Own Right," *School Library Journal* 38, no. 3 (March 1992): 163–167.

death

Myers began surveying the human response to death early in his writings. He turns shock and grief into life-changing experiences, for example, the suicide of Rowena, the 18-year-old model in *Crystal* (1987), the assassination of a father by racists in *Malcolm X: By Any Means Necessary* (1993), and the murderous rampage of Leonard "Len" Gray, a paranoid teen gunman who kills a football player in *Shooter* (2004). In works overlaying youth activities with felonies, drugs, and war, Myers enhances the dangers of abetting or complicity in crime or of fighting in the military with killings and near-death experiences. He accounts for his interest in mortality, which puzzled him in his youth: "I felt that as a young man I had not understood the whole idea of dying" (Chance, *et al.*, 1994, 247). After joining the army, he learned more about killing in violent confrontations. To his dismay, his younger brother Sonny emulated him and enlisted in the military at the height of the Vietnam War. Sonny's death within two days of deployment heaped guilt on Myers for setting the wrong example.

In his earliest fiction, Myers returned frequently to motifs of darkness and evanescence. He heightens violent incidents in two stories, "How Long Is Forever?" (1969), and "The Dark Side of the Moon" (1971), by picturing troubled minds losing control and allowing dark inner drives to lash out. In the first story, the inmate Moses has reason to retaliate against Jenkins, a sadistic prison guard. In the second story, Augie, a psychopathic serial killer, strikes four times against people who do him no harm. The fourth victim, old Mrs. Fletcher, walks her dog on Herkimer Street and encounters sudden death with no warning of criminal intent. Myers indicates through Augie that innocence and harmlessness offer no protection against criminals who kill for obscure reasons. The motif recurs in one of the author's most popular stories, "The Treasure of Lemon Brown" (1983), which pictures a homeless man cowering in a boarded-up tenement from the random violence of roving thugs.

The author reprises the name Moses for "The Going On" (1971), a psychological study published in *Black World* that opens on a man's venture to church after the death of his 51-year-old wife Mildred Smith. The narrative describes an unfamiliar rush of detachment, which Moses has not experienced since age 17 when he arrived by bus from Shreveport, Louisiana. In his musings, he fears that death overtook Mildred when she was "all alone in her seeing, scared real bad and thinking on his name" (Myers, 1971, 65). Myers suggests that, by identifying with his wife's final thoughts, Moses expresses his own terrors of death. To protect himself from a sudden demise, the widower avoids touching the radio with wet hands and spackles cracks in the plaster to shut out encroaching evil. Myers speaks through Moses's pathetic self-protection a psychological truth about dying: Moses is unsure whether he pities Mildred or himself.

Myers reprises the fear of death in the short story "Gums" in *We Be Word Sorcerers: Twenty-five Stories by Black Americans* (1973), in which the 69-year-old protagonist protects himself from advancing age. Befuddled by senile dementia, Gums grows paranoid of knocks at the door, which he bolts and anchors with a chair under the knob, leaving his grandson Stevie in the hallway to plead for admittance. Gums prefers caution over haste since the macabre scenario of his sister Lillian's death. In ballad style, Gums recalls trios of raps at the door, but no human on the other side—only a breeze. To enhance the terror of unforeseen collapse, he describes Lillian's state as "stone dead," a comparison of the mortal state to a lifeless grave marker (Myers, 1973, 183). The contrast between living flesh and a cadaver recurs in Gums's memory of Old Man Jenkins's ignoble death, which leaves the body "cold dead, clutching on to a sty pole" (*ibid.*, 184). The story advances no hope for humanity after life has run its course.

The author tends to juxtapose the decline of old age with the promise of youth. In a child's view of recovering from loss in *Fast Sam, Cool Clyde, and Stuff* (1975), Myers poses dance and soul food as antidotes to sorrow. At first, neighborhood children fear that competing in a dance contest may insult Clyde Jones, who is recovering from the recent death of his father. Mrs. Jones cites the New Orleans attitude toward rejoicing after leaving a burial. She recalls, "They'd play up a storm on the way home, brass bands, mostly, and then they'd have a party" (Myers, 1975, 42). By rounding out a period of mourning with chicken and gumbo, family and friends reassure themselves that "life was going to keep on going on" (*ibid.*).

The author glimpses the blurred boundary between life and death in a short story, "The Vision of Felipe," which he published in *Black Scholar* in 1978. A tale of the title figure, a ten-year-old orphan living homeless in Lima, Peru, outlines the daily scramble for discarded fruit and the joy of an overripe mango, which satisfies Felipe's hunger. For shelter, he sleeps on the street facing the Plaza de Toros, a bull ring built in 1766 that symbolizes the pitiless death of innocent animals. At a pivotal moment in Felipe's struggle, he experiences a vision of himself dressed for burial and lying in a coffin on All Saint's Day, a Catholic holiday that follows Halloween and honors dead ancestors. His response to imminent death is a request that his friend Daniel buy him a shirt for a burial garment. The vision comes true during the brutal 12-year military dictatorship of Juan Velasco Alvarado, when street fighters precipitate a gun battle. Felipe's end from a bullet to the chest creates empathy for street children, the innocent victims of vengeance and power-mongering.

Myers brings random violence home to Harlem in *Hoops: A Novel* (1981), a story of camaraderie and trust. The protagonist, 17-year-old Lonnie Jackson, witnesses the assault and stabbing of a beloved mentor, Coach Calvin F. "Spider" Jones, for refusing to shave points or to condone a deliberate loss of the Tournament of Champions. The graphic images of Lonnie kneeling by Cal and trying to stem a lethal hemorrhage carries through to the funeral and graveside rites, a sobering prospect for a basketball star who resists the temptation to aid gamblers. The perils of athletics move in a different direction in the sequel, *The Outside Shot* (1984), in which mill worker Ray York, a would-be professional athlete, clings to fantasies of sports glory. After competing for a position with the Fronteras, an Italian team, Ray abandons his adult life with wife Alethea and three-year-old son Jeffrey by shooting himself. The unforeseen suicide jolts Lonnie and his roommate Colin Young into reconfiguring their ambitions away from athletics to more feasible goals.

In the short story "Jeremiah's Song," collected in *The Giver and Related Readings* (1987), Myers uses death as a link between generations. The funereal story describes a tradition of keeping declining old people within the family's watchfulness and care. After a debilitating stroke, the title character stays in bed, but his gift as a family storykeeper resurges, allowing him to contribute entertainment and enlightenment. From a thin body covered in loose skin, Jeremiah's voice resonates with the details of Old Carrie, the trickster who deceives the Devil. The comic allegory reprises tales of struggles against the powers of darkness found in folklore the world over. The restorative effect of oral tradition earns the approval of Dr. Crawford, who declares, "If it makes [Jeremiah] feel good it's as good as any medicine I can give him" (Myers, 1987, 191).

In Myers's survey of combat fatalities, death in *Fallen Angels* (1988) seems both jarring and routine. During the Vietnam War, anti-hero Richard "Richie" Perry experiences the first loss of a buddy in a leisurely walk up a path back to camp. After Jenkins sustains a shrapnel puncture to the chest from an exploding land mine, officers zip his remains into a body bag. Perry reflects that losing his grandmother unsettled him less than the sudden shredding of a fellow infantryman. The visceral terror "grabbed something inside my chest and twisted it hard" (Myers, 1988, 43). The supply clerk's casual reach for one of a stack of body bags indicates that the military must expect and prepare for heavy losses. Confusing the issue for Perry is his internal congratulations that Jenkins died and Perry is still alive. Father Santora recognizes a defense mechanism in the refusal to pray: "Figure you don't want to make your peace if you're not ready to die" (*ibid.*, 223).

After viewing the corpse of a Viet Cong the men shot on patrol, Perry contrasts the deaths of Jenkins and the enemy and concludes that the latter is "a thing, a trophy" rather than a human casualty of war (*ibid.*, 85). In a subsequent impersonal scene, he watches the shooting of an enemy: "His body jerked around like a rag puppet being dragged by a dog" (*ibid.*, 182). Shortly afterward, Perry turns away from the sound of a zipper as medics seal his friend Brew into a body bag. These wrenching visualizations of death illustrate the life-changing experiences that young soldiers see daily in wartime. Perry experiences insight into his humanity: "I needed the people in the World to be okay, and to be the same as when I left them" (*ibid.*, 187). A paradox in the conventions of war literature, the thought is both comforting and terrifying.

In 1991, Myers examined death from the eyes of the 16-year-old protagonist of *My Name Is America: The Journal of Joshua Loper, a Black Cowboy on the Chisholm Trail, 1871*, one of the author's contributions to black history. Joshua regrets having to wound two rustlers, but a subsequent shooting causes him more serious anguish. His horse, Pretty, weakens and bleeds from the nostrils. Taking a rifle to a grove of trees, he strokes the horse and tries to sing "Lorena," a popular love plaint from the Civil War era. Overcome with emotion, Joshua says a prayer and shoots Pretty to end his misery. The brutality of euthanizing a horse alters Joshua's thinking about livestock. He declares, "I will not be in this business for very long.... I do not want to be around no more cattle and no more horses" (Myers, *Joshua*, 103). The effort to shield the self from inevitable losses illustrates Joshua's immaturity.

War deaths earned prominence in Myers's history and historical fiction, particularly the dangerous work of black and white sailors during the Civil War in *U.S.S. Constellation: Pride of the American Navy* (2004). He admitted that he originally joined the military with a romanticized notion of combat. Later, when he was older and wiser, he observed that "The currency of war is fear and death, not ideals" ("Novel," 1988, 7). A sober understanding of carnage influenced the composition of *My Name Is America: The Journal of Scott Pendleton Collins, a WWII Soldier, Normandy, France, 1944* (1999). The historical fiction depicts the protagonist weeping and vomiting after the landing on Omaha Beach, where German machine gunners left bodies bobbing in the waves. The chaplain's prayers remind Scott of "spaces in our minds where friends used to be" (Myers, *Scott*, 31).

Myers dramatizes his saga *The Glory Field* (1994) with agony and terror as 11-year-old patriarch Muhammad Bilal experiences the Middle Passage, a voyage indelibly stamped on black history for its savagery. Bilal recalls the attack by Mande-speaking brigands, whose predations caused screams in the night, possibly from his parents, Odebe and Saran. In the hold of a slave ship, death comes swiftly to men packed tight. Bilal survives by quelling panic and by raising his knees to avoid the canker that leg shackles rubbed into raw flesh. The narrative describes the seesawing of composure and terror in the foul-smelling unknown where death "nestled in the darkness next to them," claiming victims who languish into silence (Myers 1994, 7).

A bit of comic relief in Myers's realistic canon is the black humor of the trickster tale "Big Joe's Funeral" (2000), a mockery of somber ritual in *145th Street: Short Stories*. The story pictures the grandstander Big Joe planning and acting out his own departure on the Fourth of July, complete with jazz band and fake burial at Jackie Robinson Memorial Park. His girlfriend's testy daughter Peaches carries a sign assuring onlookers that Joe is hoodwinking them. At the burial spot, she and her friends LaToya and Squeezie add to the mirth with a boombox playing "I'll Be Glad When You're Dead, You Rascal You" (1932), a song popularized by Louis Armstrong. When Joe pops out of his coffin, onlookers and winos vacate the park in a hurry. Big Joe leads the partiers in a life-affirming dance to reggae music. When Cassie's husband beats her that night, Myers observes, "It's almost as if the block is reminding itself that life is hard, and you have to take it seriously" (Myers, 2000, 12).

The theme of human frailty recurs in Myers's later works. In "Angela's Eyes" (2000), a second story in the collection, after Poli dies in his taxi, Angela Luz Colón recalls his reflection on death one morning at breakfast. He had spoken a philosophy similar to that of the title character in William Shakespeare's *Julius Caesar* (ca. 1599), who states that "Cowards die many times before their deaths.... Death, a necessary end/Will come when it will come" (II, ii, 33, 37–38). In Poli's view, "The bad part is when the death grows in us. When we know it's coming" (*ibid.*, 49). He speaks soberly of people's tendency to mourn themselves before they die. To reaffirm life, he polishes off his speech with a joke, that he wants to die during the World Series under a comet that falls on Yankee Stadium. The witticism comes naturally to Myers, who accepts life with all its ramifications.

The pain of losing someone dear resonates through more recent writing, especially Myers's depiction of youths who depend on adults to save them from rootlessness and neglect. In *The Beast* (2003), Gabriela "Gabi" Godoy retreats from the possibility of death by describing flu symptoms in her mother, "Mami" Lucila. After frequent visits to the hospital, Gabi accepts Mami's death in a heroin haze, which softens the hurt of standing at the bedside when her mother died. To 17-year-old Anthony "Spoon" Witherspoon, Gabi's boyfriend, she confides emotional fracturing: "Spoon, I'm broken. I'm broken!" (Myers, 2003, 106).

Myers approached a panorama of human emotions in the 53 poems of *Here in Harlem: Poems in Many Voices* (2004). In "William Dandridge, 67," a parade of funeral cars makes the "long Cadillac/Ride to loss" as his best friends, one by one, reach their graves. A more pathetic case, "Homer Grimes, 83," a blind veteran, begs on the street and ponders the emotion that lies beyond bitterness. Sensing cold enveloping his legs, he envisions the coming dark, a metaphor for his moribund state. Juxtaposed by poems of struggle and celebration, Grimes's experience provides closure to a poetry collection that surveys community experiences.

See also ***The Glory Field*****, powerlessness,** ***Monster: A Novel*****, realism,** ***Shooter*****, violence**

- *Further Reading*

Chance, Rosemary, Teri Lesesne, and Lois Buckman. "And the Winner Is ...: A Teleconference with Walter Dean Myers," *Journal of Reading* 38, no. 3 (November 1994): 246–249.
Myers, Walter Dean. *The Beast.* New York: Scholastic, 2003.
_____. *Fallen Angels.* New York: Scholastic, 1988.
_____. *Fast Sam, Cool Clyde, and Stuff.* New York: Viking, 1975.
_____. *The Glory Field.* New York: Scholastic, 1994.
_____. "The Going On," *Black World* (March 1971): 61–67.
_____. "Gums" in *We Be Word Sorcerers: Twenty-five Stories by Black Americans.* New York: Bantam, 1973.
_____. *Here in Harlem: Poems in Many Voices.* New York: Holiday House, 2004.
_____, "Jeremiah's Song" in *The Giver and Related Readings.* Boston: McDougal Littell, 1987.
_____. *My Name Is America: The Journal of Joshua Loper, a Black Cowboy on the Chisholm Trail, 1871.* New York: Scholastic, 1999.
_____. *My Name Is America: The Journal of Scott Pendleton Collins, a WWII Soldier, Normandy, France, 1944.* New York: Scholastic, 1999.
_____. *145th Street: Short Stories.* New York: Delacorte, 2000.
"Novel Depicts Black Soldier in Vietnam," [Portland, Ore.] *Skanner* 13, no. 38 (22 June 1988): 7.

dialect

Myers learned to appreciate dialect literature in boyhood by absorbing conversations and by reading black authors at the public library. At home, storytelling by his parents and his grandfather, William "Pap" Dean, filled the author's mind with rhetorical devices that packed words and phrases with punch. At church, Myers performed the part of Adam in James Weldon Johnson's epic sermon "The Creation" (1927), a dialect tableau. When Myers began writing his own stories, he was already subconsciously supplied with the cadencing and diction of the wordsmith. Examples of unusual wording appeared in his early work, especially in the short story "Gums" anthologized in *We Be Word Sorcerers: Twenty-five Stories by Black Americans* (1973). The title character, a 69-year-old grandfather, explains to his nine-year-old grandson Stevie a personal experience with death. In his youth, Gums felt the approach of death as a breeze and "didn't pay any stead to it" (Myers, 1973, 184). In contrast, Old Man Jenkins panics at the approach of death. Gums flees from the scene, describing his run as "picking them up and laying them down" (*ibid.*).

Myers created verisimilitude in his first novel, *Fast Sam, Cool Clyde, and Stuff* (1975), by echoing the vernacular and repartee of Harlem teens. Mastery of snappy rejoinders becomes a source of self-identity and belonging for pre-teens seeking respect from their peers, particularly Fast Sam, an adroit braggart and self-promoter. For humor, Myers reprises signifying, a matrix of insults, destructive innuendo, and verbal posturing intended to harass the listener with hidden messages while elevating the speaker for lingual dexterity. Subtextual messages extend from criticism of personal appearance and behavior of the victim to the "dozens," a similar set of verbal putdowns of the victim's friends and family, especially the reputation of the mother. In a subsequent teen novel, *Mojo and the Russians* (1977), Myers develops respect for Kwami, an able imagist, hyperbolist, and rapper who patterns and rhymes with the ease of Fast Sam.

More suited to adults is the Captain's scolding of Gloria with cadenced rhetoric in *The Young Landlords* (1979). Using parallelism, he informs her and her peers that the younger generation knows nothing, owns nothing, and aspires to nothing. In another scene, a protester proclaims "**RE-VO-LU-TION**" as a means of rectifying injustice to black apartment dwellers (Myers, 1979, 88). His rhetoric tends toward call and response, a group phenomenon comprised of bold statements—"This raggedy building is where our people got to live"—encouraged by supportive gestures and verbal agreement from his listeners (*ibid.*, 89). The use of dialect exhibits bonding among people who defeat squalor through group action.

Myers's verbal wizardry suits the variety of texts in his canon. Much of his award-winning novel *Hoops: A Novel* (1981) portrays the slick, patterned Harlem slang and black dialect that gains instant credibility for characters. At a tense moment between 17-year-old Lonnie Jackson and his friend Paul, Lonnie accuses his "ace boon" of engaging in a "semiwhiteything," a reference to the attempt of a black to imitate whites (Myers, 1981, 91). In a social novel, *Won't Know Till I Get There* (1982), banter, repartee, and creative insults serve a story about the inclusion of a 13-year-old delinquent, Earl Goins, in the Perry family. In 1984, Myers appealed to children with *Mr. Monkey and the Gotcha Bird*, an animal fable that reflects a Caribbean setting and West Indian dialect that the author describes as "a playful, musical language" (Myers, 1984, n.p.). Told by a smiling female griot, the tale introduces a happy simian: "Monkey he live in place you don't know about. Monkey like he live there" (*ibid.*). A gentle moral warns of self-satisfaction in the Gotcha Bird: "He thinking how he big stuff" (*ibid.*). To a winged predator four times his size, Mr. Monkey taunts, "I plenty danger!" (*ibid.*). The non-threatening text deflates Mr. Monkey's ego while the Gotcha Bird "hold string he put on Monkey tail," a metaphor for the power of the verbal expert over the *poseur* (*ibid.*).

The variety of language traits in Myers's writings attest to his versatility at fitting narrative to drama, short and long fiction, history, biography, poetry, song, and picture books. For *Brown Angels: An Album of Pictures and Verse* (1993), he supplies snapshots with light-voiced verse ranging from prayers and folk rhyme to rhythm chants suited to jumping rope. In trochaic slang, he calls to a young barefoot girl, "Zudie O, Zudie O/Where you been?" and rebuffs too serious elders with a sibilant "tizzy-busy" (Myers, 1993, n.p.). Among the criminal element in *Monster: A Novel* (1999), the author stresses tough-sounding street argot — wannabe, stoolies, dis, faggot, copping some z's— along with the euphemisms of hardened inmates— went down, locked down, light him up, dropped a dime, and lay low. In "Big Joe's Funeral" in *145th Street: Short Stories* (2000), Myers repeats the familiar insult "Maybe he ain't ugly, maybe he's just inside out"; for "A Story in Three Parts," he relies on underworld slang like "showed green," "the heavies," "crack pipe," and "freebasing," terms common to drug running (Myers, 2000, 2, 124, 127, 132). In "The Streak," another part of the collection, he leaps directly into street slang to enliven Jamie Farrell's views on bad luck. For *My Name Is America: The Journal of Biddy Owens* (2001), Myers cites the common phrase "showing your color" and depicts the exasperated mother of Rachel Owens retorting "You ain't old enough to smell your pee," an earthy phrase intended for home use between adult and child (Myers, 2001, 58, 12). Idiom is also essential to *Handbook for Boys: A Novel* (2002), a paralleling of youthful brashness with the wisdom of Duke Wilson and his friends, the men who hang around a barbershop. In a description of ill-gotten gains from drugs, Duke reminds Jimmy Lynch that youngsters are likely to admire dealers who flash a "black machine all shiny at the curb, a fist full of Benjamins and two fly hootchie mamas on either arm" (Myers, 2002, 47). The choice of slang demeans underworld symbols of achievement.

The steady rhythm of soldier slang, prattle, jocularity, banter and verbal sparring, and quiet contemplation develops the tender, immature sensibilities of inexperienced draftees like infantryman Richard "Richie" Perry, the protagonist of *Fallen Angels* (1988). Officers and buddies maintain a verbal flow that typifies the attitudes and interests of energetic rookies who have traveled little and encountered few surroundings as daunting as wartime Vietnam. Perry's buddy, Harry "Peewee" Gates, joshes a Vietnamese cleaning woman by calling her "Mama Cong" and by taunting a barracks mate as "a ugly-ass Cong, too" (Myers, 1988, 11). In contrast to ready quips, Perry struggles to write realistic and reassuring letters to his mother and little brother Kenny in Harlem to bring home to them his daily existence in a war zone.

Dialect establishes the distance between Myers's peripatetic characters and their childhood homes. With a lethal edge, Myers establishes the endangerment of 14-year-old Greg Ridley in "The Treasure of Lemon Brown" (1983). After Greg ventures into a boarded-up Harlem tenement, he encounters a threat from a voice that promises, "I got a razor here sharp enough to cut a week into nine days!" (Meyers, 1983, 84). The title character, a homeless blues musician, mellows with the mention of his boy, Jesse Brown, a casualty of World War II. Lemon murmurs nostalgically, "What else a man got 'cepting what he can pass on to his son?" (*ibid.*). Similarly, the rootlessness of the title character in *The Blues of Flats Brown* (2000) requires deft turns of idiom to picture cultural displacement and homesickness after Flats takes the Midnight Special from Memphis, Tennessee, to New York City. According to critic Diane Roback's review for *Publishers Weekly*, the author's "shaggy fantasy has the slow-and-easy pacing of a lazy Southern afternoon. His colorful phrases and dialect ... evoke the Mississippi and Tennessee settings" that anchor the story to the agrarian South (Roback, 2000, 311).

For *The Beast* (2003), Myers removes neighborhood slang and sounds from the speech of 17-year-old homeboy Anthony "Spoon" Witherspoon. While he associates with wealthy whites and privileged blacks at Wallingford Academy in Connecticut, he avoids the in-crowd vernacular of Harlem. As he nears Pennsylvania Station on Christmas break, he develops a case of nerves before taking the A train to West 122nd Street. The reason crystallizes in his mind: his classmates "had taken their lives, their successes, with them, and I had left mine behind" (Myers, 2003, 21). In *Here in Harlem: Poems in Many Voices* (2004), Myers reprises life in Harlem through fifty personal testimonials that rely on local lingo for verisimilitude. One, by Didi Taylor, pictures a change in her life if she were rich, living on Sugar Hill, and lifting a "hincty" nose in snobbery. These elements of the cultural milieu establish belonging and self-awareness among appreciative listeners.

See also **belonging**

• *Further Reading*

Hurlburt, Tom S. "Review: *Slam!*," *School Library Journal* 42, 11 (November 1996): 123.

Myers, Walter Dean. *The Beast.* New York: Scholastic, 2003.

____. *Brown Angels: An Album of Pictures and Verse.* New York: HarperCollins, 1993.

____. "Gums" in *We Be Word Sorcerers: Twenty-five Stories by Black Americans.* New York: Bantam, 1973.

____. *Handbook for Boys: A Novel.* New York: Amistad, 2002.

____. *Hoops.* New York: Delacorte, 1981.

____. *Mr. Monkey and the Gotcha Bird.* New York: Delacorte, 1984.

____. *My Name Is America: The Journal of Biddy Owens.* New York: Scholastic, 2001.

____. *145th Street: Short Stories.* New York: Delacorte, 2000.

____. "The Treasure of Lemon Brown," *Boys' Life* 73 (March 1983): 34–40.

____. *The Young Landlords.* New York: Viking, 1979.

Roback, Diane, "Review: *The Blues of Flats Brown*," *Publishers Weekly* 247, no. 4 (24 January 2000): 311.

Rochman, Hazel. "Review: *Won't Know Till I Get There*," *School Library Journal* 28, no. 9 (May 1982): 72–73.

diaspora

The displacement of black slaves from West Africa and of Southern blacks from the agrarian South recurs frequently in Myers's contemplations of black history, particularly the exemplum "The Treasure of Lemon Brown" (1983), *Now Is Your Time! The African-American Struggle for Freedom* (1991), and *U.S.S. Constellation: Pride of the American Navy* (2004), which glimpses the return of 705 slaves from the hold of the *Cora* to Liberia. Myers addresses the motifs of displacement and scattering directly in the picture book *The Great Migration: An American Story* (1993). Opening during the First World War, the narrative honors those wanderers seeking dignified work and a living wage in Northern industrial cities—Chicago, Cleveland, Detroit, New York, Philadelphia, and Pittsburgh. Jacob Lawrence's narrative folk art chronicles epic endurance in individuals and families who braved violence and racism to carve out black communities far from the agrarian South. Figures face the same direction as though sharing the determination to reach their collective objectives. Like the birds in formation above them, migrants travel light to accommodate the steady progress of one foot in front of the other. Lawrence concluded, "Out of the struggle comes a kind of power, and even beauty" (Myers, 1993, n.p.). In his ode "Migration," Myers concurs with the artist's upbeat epic of a "forever moment": "There is the hope/Of a people with yet one more river to cross" (*ibid.*).

Myers returned to the theme of restless ambition in subsequent works, including the African American saga of the Lewis clan in *The Glory Field* (1994) and his tutorial on music in *Blues Journey* (2003). In his picture history, *Harlem: A Poem.* (1997), the opening verse follows black pilgrims from Waycross and East St. Louis, from Holly Springs and Memphis, and from Trinidad and Goreé Island, a Senegalese center of the West African slave trade. Myers's appreciation for cultural exchange resonates in the calls and shouts of West Africans in a Harlem setting, a "new sound, raucous and sassy" that praises the freedom of 125th Street (Myers, 1997, n.p.). The uniqueness of Harlem's spirit is the reward for centuries of struggle and enterprise.

Myers resets the peripatetic experience in a tender dog story, the picture book *The Blues of Flats Brown* (2000). The author pictures the title figure singing and strumming soul music in New York City—"the sounds of the waterfront in Mound Bayou and the music from the little church down the street from the junkyard ... sounds of a freight train and the hot sounds of the Curley-Que" (Myers, 2000, n.p.). Within the humor of a guitar-playing dog from Mississippi, Myers inserts the roots of black soul, the homesickness of newcomers for the Southern plantation background they shunned on their way north to opportunity. Flats turns his experiences into "The New York City Blues," which bewails the "far from down home" longings (*ibid.*). His success enables him to return south with his guitar in one paw and "some fried chicken in a cardboard suitcase in the other" (*ibid.*). The contrast between the exodus and its reversal is a new self-confidence, the offshoot of black identity developed among his own kind.

Myers's offhand references to the black diaspora include other glimpses of individuals in transit. In *The Beast* (2003), 17-year-old Anthony "Spoon" Witherspoon enjoys riding trains because they are more traveler-friendly than planes. The humble duffel bags and suitcases taped shut remind him of the people who journeyed north to find more fulfilling lives and less racial injustice in large industrial centers like Chicago and New York. Myers embroiders on the motif of the expectant pilgrim in "Dennis Chapman, 40," a dramatic poem in *Here in Harlem: Poems in Many Voices* (2004). Dennis vacillates between the certainty of acreage in Alabama and dreams of "the electric kaleidoscope of boundless freedom" he anticipates in Harlem (Myers, 2004, 23). Unlike the simple travelers bearing ragged valises, Dennis pictures himself airborne, flying toward a black community that lures him from home like a beckoning flirt. The second stage of pilgrimage describes the journey of his woman, who opts for the more mundane Greyhound bus. In contrast to flight, ground travel provides her with a step-by-step replay of the diaspora from Harlem to the racist South.

See also **community, displacement, *The Glory Field*, Lewis genealogy, Moses Littlejohn, rootlessness, slavery**

• *Further Reading*

Myers, Walter Dean. *The Beast.* New York: Scholastic, 2003.
_____. *The Blues of Flats Brown.* New York: Holiday House, 2000.
_____. *The Great Migration: An American Story.* New York: HarperCollins, 1993.
_____. *Harlem: A Poem.* New York: Scholastic, 1997.
_____. *Here in Harlem: Poems in Many Voices.* New York: Holiday House, 2004.
Smith, Karen Patricia, ed. *African-American Voices in Young Adult Literature: Tradition, Transition, Transformation.* Lanham, Md.: Scarecrow, 1994.

displacement

Myers sympathizes with people who lack the assurance of welcome and belonging, particularly in a bigoted environment like the South in "The Treasure of Lemon Brown" (1983), away from family like John, a Pennsylvania college student who misses his mother and sister in "The Beast Is in the Labyrinth" (1999), or in a predominantly white world that ignores non-athletic blacks, the situation of 17-year-old Cameron Porter in *Shooter* (2004). In an overview of career possibilities for 16-year-old Crystal Brown in the teen novel *Crystal* (1987), the author depicts her talent handlers cataloguing her under "black model" as though she has no value as an individual and no choice in her assignments. His strongest comments on the subject of dislocation result in stern descriptions of the slave trade in *Now Is Your Time! The African-American Struggle for Freedom* (1991) and *U.S.S. Constellation: Pride of the American Navy* (2004), which cites an eyewitness account of the rescue of slaves at sea for repatriation in Liberia.

The theme of displacement took shape early in Myers's fiction in the dilemma story "How Long Is Forever?" published in the June 1969 issue of *Negro Digest.* Moses, the protagonist, makes the fateful choice between tolerating prison brutality and currying favor with the parole board to gain him a return to society. The elements of dignity, manhood, and survival push him to fight back against Jenkins, a sadistic guard who deserves the retaliation that Moses inflicts. Unlike Myers's popular teen fiction, the story of Moses portrays a gritty existentialism in the lives of prisoners. Moses chooses displacement from home over displacement from humanity, a decision that promises an extension of his sentence and a threat to his sanity.

A series of separation issues impacts the characters in *Fast Sam, Cool Clyde, and Stuff* (1975), a seriocomic novel about the function of neighborhood volunteers. Myers introduces the theme of displacement in the arrival of a newcomer, Francis Williams, whom the gang names Stuff and receives as a friend. More worrisome issues illustrate family difficulties after Clyde Jones's father dies, Mrs. Jones goes to work to support the family, and Gloria Chisholm's father slaps his wife and stalks out of the apartment. In retrospect, Gloria explains her father's public emotional outburst as the result of a lost job after his company relocates from Harlem to the South. Myers describes from a child's point of view the fallout from displacement in Mr. Chisholm's drinking, weeping, cursing, and marital quarreling. The family suffers from his self-destruction, which causes Gloria to hate her father. Myers commends the value of peer sympathy in the formation of the 116th Street Good People, a support group that gives Stuff "one of my best nights ever" (Myers, 1975, 80).

In *The Outside Shot* (1984), Myers describes the dilemmas of campus experience in a college freshman, Harlemite Lonnie Jackson, the protagonist of *Hoops: A Novel* (1981). In Indiana at Montclare State College, Lonnie unconsciously alters his language and manners to accommodate the expectations of Midwesterners. On a visit to the Young farm in Cisne, Illinois, he attends an all-white church and adapts to open spaces and quiet nights. He begins escorting Sherry Jewett to intellectual films that he learns to discuss afterward for their subtextual meanings. In the theater, he behaves differently from the way he viewed movies in Harlem. In unknown territory, he hesitates to put his arm around her shoulders because "This was her turf" (Myers, 1984, 82). He experiences anger and hurt from her response to his sexual overtures, which seem out of place to other theater-goers who watch Sherry depart in a huff. He concludes, "What none of them wanted was a street guy from Harlem" (*ibid.*, 88). Contributing to his feelings of displacement are the suicide of failed athlete Ray York and the racist remarks of Hauser, who denigrates Mexicans and Koreans. In a funk, Lonnie contemplates escaping to Harlem. Myers stresses the protagonist's emotional growth in Lonnie's admission that "I had a slim chance of making it after all" (*ibid.*, 136).

In *The Beast* (2003), the issue of a poor black teenager studying among the wealthy and privileged at Wallingford Academy in Connecticut sets up barriers to social acceptance similar to those Lonnie faces. Unlike Myers' more vigorous characters, 17-year-old Anthony "Spoon" Witherspoon is a contemplative youth who analyzes his reactions and emotions with an adult intensity. In trying to establish friendships with other black students, he hopes to get a ride home at semester break. Ironically, he discovers in Chanelle Burnitz a more permanent sense of displacement brought on by divorce. Of her return to New York, she muses on switching holidays between parents: "I'm the one who's being split up and I'm the one who has to jump back and forth and understand who's sleeping with who" (Myers, 2003, 11). The novel dramatizes the hurt of displacement within the family, a more severe dislocation than Spoon's homesickness for Harlem.

Myers deepens motifs of alienation during the holiday home visit, a time often fraught with abortive expectations and personal disillusion. The narrative contrasts Spoon's alienation at the prep school with the sufferings of his Dominican girlfriend Gabriela "Gabi" Godoy and of Gabi's blind grandfather. Unlike Spoon, who can travel by train from school to Harlem to reconnect with home, the blind grandfather lives in memories of island scenes that he treasured when he had sight. After the death of his daughter Lucila, he intends to flee social isolation by repatriating to the Dominican Republic. Gabi, whom heroin displaces from the real world, suffers a more terrifying disjuncture from self, from humanity. The author's dramatic novel provides teen readers with realistic views of adaptation to trying situations.

See also **diaspora, historical milieu, slavery**

• *Further Reading*

Mehren, Elizabeth. "Fountain of Stories for Youth: Walter Dean Myers," *Los Angeles Times* (15 October 1997): E1.

Micklos, J., Jr., "Author Walter Dean Myers Stresses Realism in His Writing," *Reading Today* 8, no.4 (February-March 1991): 38.
Myers, Walter Dean. *The Beast.* New York: Scholastic, 2003.
____. *Fast Sam, Cool Clyde, and Stuff.* New York: Viking, 1975.
____. *The Outside Shot.* New York: Delacorte, 1984.
Smith, Karen Patricia, ed. *African-American Voices in Young Adult Literature: Tradition, Transition, Transformation.* Lanham, Md.: Scarecrow, 1994.

dreams

Myers's use of dreams in fiction strips off layers of consciousness to disclose inner turmoil and individual yearnings. The author's coverage of dreams ranges over a variety of human concerns—the inmate Moses's hopes for parole in "How Long Is Forever?" (1969), the ambitions of parents for African American children in the picture book *The Great Migration: An American Story* (1993), and the gossamer images of tomorrow that 17-year-old Anthony "Spoon" Witherspoon envisions while he studies at Wallingford Academy in Connecticut in *The Beast* (2003). The author explains in a letter to the reader in *Handbook for Boys: A Novel* (2002) the value of ambition to lives he examined: "People who did well were, almost without exception, actively involved in pursuing their dreams" (Myers, 2002, n.p.). Extending the author's theme is a comment from barber Duke Wilson, the novel's mentor, who urges court remand Jimmy Lynch to "Figure out what you mean by success" (*ibid.*, 66). Wilson implies that Jimmy must outline the work necessary to succeed and commit to the labor required.

Myers bases realism on the intersection between the dream world and actuality. For 17-year-old Lonnie Jackson in *Hoops: A Novel* (1981), dreams play out his illusions about success as a basketball star. When surreal elements take over, Lonnie finds his dream self double dunking the winning shot, but receiving no accolades from the "la-di-da niggers" in the stands (Myers, 1981, 96). His cries of "Look at me!" prove futile (*ibid.*). In the case of 12-year-old Jamal Hicks in *Scorpions* (1988), dreams are more palatable than the downward spiral of his life at home and school. For infantryman Richard "Richie" Perry, the anti-hero of *Fallen Angels* (1988), shared fantasy trips around the world draw him closer to little brother Kenny. Reprising those mental escapes aids Perry in enduring the constant strain of patrols during the Vietnam War, which bears little resemblance to the foreign travels the brothers once fantasized. Perry clings to more attainable goals—thoughts of some relief time and possible rest and recuperation in Saigon.

In *The Outside Shot* (1984), the sequel to *Hoops*, Myers inserts a different kind of fantasy. Farm girl Ruth Young imagines leaving Illinois and taking karate lessons while living in a big city, where she would carry a derringer to protect her from felons. Off-campus student Lonnie Jackson observes the visions of glory in mill hands, older men who play against scholarship athletes at Montclare State College. Even though the outsiders lose every year, the games against future star basketball players feed the laborers' egos and "help them get their dreams off" (Myers, 1984, 35). One of the players, Ray York, clings to memories recorded in a yellowed newspaper clipping about a college game in his past. With pathetic self-importance, he spreads his dreams before Lonnie—playing in Europe or coaching and working at the mill "until I make a decision" (*ibid.*, 38). The stereotypical loser reminds Lonnie of Harlemites who hang around the streets waiting for success to find them. To Lonnie, they melt into the street scene like lampposts and fire hydrants as their dreams lose traction and slip into the past. Ray, too, fades from the scene by committing suicide.

Myers moves more vigorously through black dreamscapes in *The Glory Field* (1994), a fictional saga that pictures shackled slaves during the Middle Passage, when the rocking ship squelched dreams in a darkened hold. In the second stave of Lewis family history, Saran explains to Lizzy that all slaves are subject to a "freedom dream," which can seize the spirit by night or day (Myers, 1994, 31). Comparing themselves to birds, the dreamers picture themselves as autonomous adults rearing a family and working as they choose. The fantasy of freedom to pick flowers engulfs Lizzy as she flees Live Oaks Plantation. The reality lacks the beauties of dreams: "It was a hungry free and a tired free, but it was free" (*ibid.*, 58). After she shelters with black Union soldiers, her night visions alternate between losing a race with the master's hounds and walking at her will dressed in a white woman's gown, a contrast to the shift she put on earlier to cover whip marks on her back. The pull of the past suggests that ex-slaves are never completely rid of bondage.

Myers perpetuates the motif of black dreams into the Great Depression. Luvenia Lewis, the protagonist of the fourth stave of *The Glory Field*, experiences two unsettling night visions of working for the Deets family and losing control of their Pekingese dog Precious, which dies under an oncoming Chicago trolley. A third dream turns inward as Luvenia dances with other black women at Miss Etta Pinckney's rent party. Luvenia's body takes on the stout frame and quivering flesh of her elders as she tries to flee the tenement. The dream mirrors her efforts to find steady work while she puts herself through college to realize the ambitions of the "New Negro" (*ibid.*, 199). Contrary to her goals are the nostalgic yearnings of her father Elijah, who siphons his earnings in Chicago to the family homeplace on Curry Island, South Carolina.

Myers's most Gothic text, *The Dream Bearer* (2003), applies a common ploy of folk wisdom lore—the naive boy learning from a graybeard. "Mr. Moses" Littlejohn, a self-proclaimed dream bearer, exhibits the mystic look of the title character in *The Rime of the Ancient Mariner* (1798). An association with a man who looks beyond Harlem's problems helps 12-year-old David Curry cope with Reuben, David's mentally ill father, and with Tyrone, a 17-year-old brother drawn to drugs and gangsterism. A subplot depicts Sessi, a Kenyan friend, as a sounding board with a Kikuyu perspective on urban ills. In response to threats against her model palm leaf house on the roof, she retorts, "That's what Americans do.... You tear things down," an outsider's reflection on the short life-span of creative efforts in the United States (Myers, 2003, 2).

The Dream Bearer sets up an unusual contrast—the thwarted ambitions of urban youngsters like David and the harsh realities of early African American history, a burden that wears heavily on Moses. The old man's Jungian dreams reflect strands of black struggle, from the capture of slaves and picking cotton under the crack of the overseer's whip to a lynching amid a circle of armed whites who enjoy murdering Cammie while helpless blacks watch. Moses interweaves horrific realism with the personification of death, who stands "grinning in their midst" (*ibid.*, 117). Without understanding Karl Jung's psychological concept of recovered racial memory, David concludes that Moses's fearful dreams are somehow visceral "from someplace deep inside of him" (*ibid.*, 121).

For another form of contrast, Myers juxtaposes dreams and disappointments in the 53 dramatic monologues in *Here in Harlem: Poems in Many Voices* (2004). Against the despair of the unemployed and the frustrations of the homeless and handicapped, he poses 12-year-old Lois Smith, a middle-school student who expects to see her name in books. After she becomes "as famous as old Booker T.," she anticipates that other children will claim her as their ideal (Myers, 2004, 38). Lois embodies Myers at his best, the embrace of the coming generation as the brightest and best of black history.

See also **achievement, education, gangs, opportunity**

- *Further Reading*

Cox, Ruth. "Preteen and Young Teen Protagonists," *Teacher Librarian* 31, no. 2 (Dec 2003): 16.

Myers, Walter Dean. *The Dream Bearer.* New York: Amistad, 2003.

_____. *The Glory Field.* New York: Scholastic, 1994.

_____. *Handbook for Boys: A Novel.* New York: Amistad, 2002.

_____. *Here in Harlem: Poems in Many Voices.* New York: Holiday House, 2004.

_____. *Hoops.* New York: Delacorte, 1981.

_____. *The Outside Shot.* New York: Delacorte, 1984.

drugs and alcohol

Myers permeates his urban scenarios with frequent slang references to drinking beer and "the hard stuff," chugging 'Bird straight from the bottle, rolling "blunts," blowing dope or herb, swallowing and injecting drugs and prescription antidepressants, and stealing, buying, and selling the narcotics that lead to addiction, the focus of "The Fare to Crown Point" (1971) (Myers, 1988, 146; 2002, 171). In *Fallen Angels* (1988), Captain Stewart retreats from the Vietnam War by watching Phil Silvers on TV and sipping booze. The crime that spreads from illicit possession and sale of drugs envelops Frank Greene, who buys a stolen watch from an addict in *Handbook for Boys: A Novel* (2002). A more problematic scene in *Fast Sam, Cool Clyde, and Stuff* (1975) pictures idealistic teens trying to rescue Carnation Charley from an overdose. The intervention of Sam's father contrasts the childish efforts of Sam and his friends, who apply ice to Charley's swollen face. The adult walks Charley about, then badgers him with sensible comments: "You mess with dope you're going to die. You never see no *old* dope fiend, do you?" (Myers, 1975, 166). The lecture proves prophetic; Charley dies at a robbery. Myers maintains an even tone by separating his young characters from the crime scene, but still stirring thoughts of mortality. Stuff concludes, "The calendar didn't say that I was any older but I seemed older to me" (*ibid.*, 188).

The wisdom of elders returns in Myers's *It Ain't All for Nothin'* (1978), a social novel about 12-year-old Tippy, who loses Grandma Carrie Brown as his guardian. After passing to the custody of his dissolute father Lonnie, an ex-con, drunkard, and robber, the boy retreats into sleep, TV and movies, and alcohol as antidotes to hopelessness. The text interposes Roland Sylvester, a paternal rescuer who finds Tippy passed out in the park. The older man's advice comes from experience: "People don't do things to hurt themselves unless they got problems" (Myers, 1978, 111). In Roland's estimation, alcohol leads to self-destruction rather than escape.

To create menace in *The Nicholas Factor* (1983), a spy thriller set on a college campus in Santa Barbara, California, Myers describes the teen attitude toward indulgence in alcohol as proof of maturity. As protagonist Gerald McQuillen gets to know 16-year-old Jennifer Wells, a wealthy rice heiress, she establishes her superiority at social experience and claims to labor under "the curse of the privileged class" (Myers, 1983, 54). After her father voices his opinion that children are society's "last pretense of innocence," she becomes "a prime example of what an *un*restricted child could be like" (*ibid.*, 49). Her venture from martinis to whiskey sours at twelve resulted in secret bingeing by age fourteen. A disclosure that her father died of alcoholism enhances the menace of her risky behavior, which tends to increase during tense situations.

Another incident of substance abuse occurs early in the war novel *Fallen Angels* (1988), in which a black soldier faces court martial or transfer for getting stoned on guard duty. A later scene pictures a chopper pilot reeking of booze, a common fault in career soldiers. Anti-hero Richard "Richie" Perry, a rookie infantryman, relates to alcoholic indulgence, the burden of his family after his father deserted them and his mother, Mabel Perry, began drinking. His own experience is comic — a sip from Lieutenant Carroll's captured bottle of Jack Daniels goes down like fire, then comes up easier. The scene suggests that Perry has little background in drinking straight liquor.

In *Hoops: A Novel* (1981), a friendship sours after 17-year-old Lonnie Jackson notices changes in the behavior of his old friend Paul and assumes that Paul uses angel dust. The suspenseful narrative gains immediacy in the falling action after Tyrone roughs up Mary-Ann and tries to kill her with an overdose. The choice of a narcotic as a murder weapon attests to the ubiquitous use of drugs and the conclusions that others may draw about Mary-Ann as a user rather than a victim. The vision of a junkie nodding on the street recurs in the novel's sequel, *The Outside Shot* (1984). Lonnie recalls in childhood trying to carry groceries and prescriptions home to his mother and having to battle his way through addicts. As he departs for Montclare State College in Indiana, he observes a Harlem junkie "[trying] to pull his manhood together" on a public street (Myers, 1984, 2). In full view of passersby, the ominous failure at upright posture implies that young people grow up viewing curbside lessons in self-destruction.

The author analyzes the influence of addictive substances in a number of teen settings, for example, the casual offer of drinks to 16-year-old model Crystal Brown in *Crystal* (1987), a novel that disparages the pseudo-sophistication of the fashion world. Myers makes an intense foray into the criminal underbelly of Harlem with

Motown and Didi: A Love Story (1984), a story of Didi's attempt to save her brother Tony from addiction. The pre-teen characters in *Scorpions* (1988) navigate a city milieu pocked with drowsing potheads and the actions of young drop runners, whom their elders exploit because the authorities never subpoena minors to testify against the dealers. Within the gang, Mack displays the glazed eyes and altered attention of a user. The fact limits his value to 12-year-old Jamal Hicks, who needs backup if he is to succeed as the new Scorpion leader. Their off-kilter pairing dramatizes the uselessness of people who sink their energies and money into drugs.

The hazy links between addicts and criminality recur in *The Glory Field* (1994), the saga of the Lewis family from slave days to the late 20th century. Shep Lewis, a down-and-out resident of a Harlem men's shelter, avoids the family reunion and wastes travel funds on "the pipe," his reference to crack cocaine (Myers 1994, 343). His claim of being robbed gives way to the truth as he accepts the strength of his cousin Malcolm, who guides Shep on a journey south to Curry Island, South Carolina. Shep's weakness and vomiting are obvious signs of addiction to Dr. Jennie Lewis, a physician who supports Shep through the miserable stages of withdrawal. Without grasping at rosy predictions of her kinsman's recovery, Myers's epilogue indicates that family unity enfolds the wayward cousin and offers a share in "a good harvest" (*ibid.*, 375).

As the toll on black victims rose in the late 1990s, the author turned to bestial, monstrous images of addiction. The short story "Stranger," collected in *No Easy Answers: Short Stories about Teenagers Making Tough Choices* (1997), takes a Jekyll-and-Hyde approach to 18-year-old Cassie Holliday's lapse into drugs by revealing a stranger in the mirror. The psychological dissociation leaves her huddled in bed unable to face the estrangement that cleaves her own personality. In *The Beast* (2003), which reprises the imagery of "The Beast Is in the Labyrinth" (1999), Myers refers to the Minotaur, the man-beast that lurked in a Cretan labyrinth in Greek mythology until Theseus stalked it through the maze and slew it with his sword. The murky environs elucidate the underworld "head joint," a drug parlor on 121st Street in which Gabriela "Gabi" Godoy, the Dominican girlfriend of 17-year-old Anthony "Spoon" Witherspoon, struggles with heroin addiction among nodding, moribund fellow addicts (Myers, *Beast*, 125). Her emotional dependence begins with her mother's illness with cancer and the arrival of a blind Dominican grandfather. Emotional and monetary hardships force the family to the edge of survival, where Gabi chooses a life-altering escape from reality.

Myers establishes that the seamy underside of drug use remains hidden from the sober world. At first, Spoon fears that the estrangement from Gabi might indicate a rival for her affection, but he discerns the real reason, that she is "skin surfing" (*ibid.*, 56). Given to reading and composing verse, she speaks of drug use with metaphor: "If you see the Beast, you run away.... I didn't run fast enough" (*ibid.*, 69). When she fails to elude the beast, Spoon locates her at an abandoned building and pulls her outdoors into crisp late December air. Of the foul den she departs, Monica, a crack user, comments, "Ain't nothing pretty about it" (*ibid.*, 125). With admirable compassion, Myers identifies Monica as a knowing, soft-hearted addict who commiserates with Gabi and wishes her well. The poignant element of Spoon's rescue plot emerges from Gabi, who admits that she no longer loves herself. At the bottom of skid row, she seems ready to banish self-jeopardy and fight her way back toward survival.

Myers continued scrutinizing the deadfall of addiction in *The Dream Bearer* (2003). The erratic family life of the Currys derives from the ravings of Reuben, the paranoid father, and the drug dealings of Tyrone "Circle T" Curry, David's 17-year-old brother. Adding immediacy to the story is a police raid on the Curry apartment at 1:30 A.M., when Tyrone quickly flushes an unidentified object down the toilet. Lacking evidence and an arrest warrant, one cop threatens Tyrone with death if the police find him dealing on the streets. The outburst leaves Evelyn Curry weeping for her son and Reuben muttering about insults to his manhood. In the mother's opinion, street influences can "suck your brains out," a metaphor for the predatory enticements available to youth (Myers, *Dream*, 178). David, at age 12, despairs: "It was as if sadness had just come in and was living with our family" (*ibid.*, 26). The narrative indicates that warnings about drugs at school and home fall short of preparing a pre-teen for grave decision making about his immediate family. David seizes a predictable human escape mechanism by refusing to think about his responsibility to the family and to Tyrone. The avoidance of pain suggests Myers's sympathy for a child forced too soon into adult situations.

In *Here in Harlem: Poems in Many Voices* (2004), Myers's spectacular collection of first-person verse, the layout pairs two perspectives on the destruction wrought by self-indulgence. The first speaker, retiree Christopher Lomax, gazes down the boulevard at his daughter Junice, who leans "benumbed" and bobbing against a lamp post (Myers, 2004, 12). The father regrets spawning a "sap-poisoned flower," whom he forgives for her lapse from grace (*ibid.*). On the facing page, Junice sees his expression and becomes "his lost child again," a suggestion that the father's disappointment has often marred their relationship (*ibid.*, 13). Myers carefully chooses "frantic" and "reckless" as descriptives for her destructive behaviors. As thought he can alert a fictional character to peril, the author surrounds her with signposts to sanity.

See also **self-destruction**

• *Further Reading*

Myers, Walter Dean. *The Beast.* New York: Scholastic, 2003.

_____. *The Dream Bearer.* New York: Amistad, 2003.

_____. *Fallen Angels.* New York: Scholastic, 1988.

_____. *Fast Sam, Cool Clyde, and Stuff.* New York: Viking, 1975.

_____. *The Glory Field.* New York: Scholastic, 1994.

_____. *Handbook for Boys: A Novel.* New York: Amistad, 2002.

_____. *Here in Harlem: Poems in Many Voices.* New York: Holiday House, 2004.

_____. *It Ain't All for Nothin.'* New York: Viking, 1978.

_____. *The Nicholas Factor.* New York: Viking, 1983.

_____. *The Outside Shot.* New York: Delacorte, 1984.

_____. "Stranger," *No Easy Answers: Short Stories about Teenagers Making Tough Choices.* New York: Delacorte, 1997.

Rotella, Mark. "Review: *The Beast*," *Publishers Weekly* 250, no. 48 (1 December 2003): 57–58.

Smith, Karen Patricia, ed. *African-American Voices in Young Adult Literature: Tradition, Transition, Transformation.* Lanham, Md.: Scarecrow, 1994.

education

Myers writes from experience of the need of youth for educational opportunities. He defends schools, museums, and libraries as havens for poor kids who might otherwise turn to addictive substances, crime, or gangs. In the seriocomic novel *Won't Know Till I Get There* (1982), the narrative pictures a librarian scolding protagonist Steve Perry for owing $15.00 in fines on books that he keeps out for six months. Her reasoning provides a life lesson in responsibility: "You have to pay for the books because of your negligence" (Myers, 1982, 160). In a depiction of Gerald McQuillen, a young Californian grieving for his deceased father in *The Nicholas Factor* (1983), life issues require a similar clarification found in logic and right thinking. Gerald admits, "I was drifting as far as college was concerned. I didn't know what I wanted to study or do or where I wanted to go with my life" (Myers, 1983, 6). The structure and discipline of classes offer a framework on which he erects a foundation for the future, a coming-of-age task that the author describes in his own life in *Bad Boy: A Memoir* (2001).

In Myers's adventure story *Ambush in the Amazon* (1986), he extends urban views on education to a plot deriving from his travels in the Peruvian outback. He pictures the Quechuan translator, 14-year-old Tarija, as a victim of peasant prejudice in Los Cauchos. As she tries to help Chris and Ken Arrow solve the mystery of a *monstruo* (monster) stalking the Amazon jungle, she rejects calling in police (Myers, 1986, 10). The intrusion of outsiders tends to make local Quechua "think that is what going to school does" (*ibid.*, 36). Instead of conferring with authorities, Tarija applies her training to ensnaring the unidentified threat. As Ken explains tribal thinking, to convince a village that a monster stalks them, "The easiest way would be to convince the smartest person, and then everybody else would believe it, too" (*ibid.*, 35). In token of Tarija's courage and cool logic, the chief of Los Cauchos asks for her advice on apprehending a greedy double-dealer. Myers indicates that such a tribute from a male elder to a young female is rare.

The theme of educational opportunity is a focus of a variety of Myers's works. In *Crystal* (1987), he pictures 16-year-old model Crystal Brown staying out late for photo shoots and professional networking while her grades slide in history and geometry. The picture book *The Great Migration: An American Story* (1993) commends parents for shouldering displacement and hardship in the urban industrialized North for the sake of better education for their children. In *Handbook for Boys: A Novel* (2002), the author reminds the youth of the 20th century of past privations with a public sign in a barbershop. It cites a Virginia law dated 1849: "If a white person assemble with negroes for the purpose of instructing them to read or write.... He shall be confined in jail not exceeding six months and fined not exceeding one hundred dollars" (Myers, 2002, 77). Mentor Duke Wilson explains the purpose of keeping slaves illiterate — to conceal the possibilities of living beyond the plantations and to control geographic and economic information about running away. In *U.S.S. Constellation: Pride of the American Navy* (2004), Myers details the hands-on education of young sailors during the nation's first century. These forms of education honor varied learning styles as legitimate means to prepare for the future.

The author frequently writes from the point of view of the poorly educated adult, for example, Sweeby Jones, the homeless Vietnam vet in *Darnell Rock Reporting* (1994). In graphic terms, Sweeby emphasizes, "I ain't got a good job because I ain't got nothing between these ears that anybody is going to pay any good money for" (Myers, *Darnell*, 88). In the opinion of critic Ellen Fader, a reviewer for *Horn Book*, Sweeby "lives the legacy of some teachers' low educational expectations of African Americans" (Fader, 1995, 194). In *Fallen Angels* (1988), Myers depicts the lapsed dream of anti-hero Richard "Richie" Perry to graduate from Stuyvesant High School, go to college, and become a pharmacist. The typical obstacle to kids like Perry, whose father abandoned the family, is lack of funds for tuition. A more insidious obstacle is the high school counselor who laughs at Perry for wanting to be a philosopher. The stigma of racism and low expectations for ghetto teens rankles on the author, who stresses the value of unfettered dreams in the young. Instead of reveries of success, he experiences self-instruction in survival. On patrol, he cautions, "Don't think. Stop thinking. Stop. Look ahead of me. Don't think, don't daydream. Look" (Myers 1988, 194). He later admits, "We had all learned something about dying, and about trying to keep each other alive. It was good" (*ibid.*, 234).

In contrast to Perry's limited choices, the author depicts the good fortune of 17-year-old Anthony "Spoon" Witherspoon, protagonist of *The Beast* (2003). On scholarship, Spoon is privileged to leave Harlem and finish high school at Wallingford Academy in Connecticut. By the time Spoon returns to Harlem for Christmas vacation after five months in New England, he discovers that Scott and others have dropped out of Frederick Douglass High School. Scott describes his personal malaise as a gradual mental decline: "My life is getting raggedy.... It just slid from correct to raggedy" (Myers, 2003, 78–79). The two teens, Perry and Spoon, develop insight into self and ambition from widely variant experiences—the soldier fights to stay alive on jungle patrols in Vietnam; the college freshman wavers after one term at the academy over the lapse of his friends into self-defeat. Myers stresses that some of the best lessons in success come from scrutiny of failure.

The author's plots capture the clash between street life and school, the source of criminal allure to 16-year-old Steve Harmon in *Monster: A Novel* (1999). For teenaged students, the draw of sports, gossip about crime, swaggering punks, drugs and alcohol, and love matches interferes with their concentration on learning. In *Scorpions* (1988), the author introduces a troubling lack of adult support. A cynical principal, Mr. Davidson, uses Jamal Hicks as an example of a boy going nowhere. Mr. Davidson takes an adversarial role in his taunt, "Sooner or later you're going to do something that's going to let me put you out of the school" (Myers, 1988, 59). The remark is spiteful and unprofessional for a man employed to encourage and uplift youth. Myers denounces the principal as a coward who is unwilling to investigate Jamal's use of a gun in a fight because the school might incur a lawsuit. Davidson annoys a parent with a lame excuse and school policy "not to make hasty accusations" and further denigrates Jamal as a contaminant of other students (*ibid.*, 138). The principal further undermines his authority after he suggests that Mrs. Roberts, the school nurse, gain permission from Mrs. Hicks to sedate Jamal each school morning.

Children share with adults like Davidson a faulty vision of education. In *Somewhere in the Darkness* (1992), protagonist Jimmy Little quickly deduces that classmates retained in the detention office during achievement tests are administrators' hedge against low scores. By removing problem learners from class, school authorities hope to elevate their overall standing in the school system and to curry favor with politicians. The deception illustrates the fatal blow to the humanities after testing programs and scores became more important that the students themselves.

Learning takes another blow in Myers's saga *The Glory Field* (1994). Sixteen-year-old Tommy Lewis recognizes the prejudice of his grandmother, Mary Hardin Lewis, against educated people. In a discussion of an unnamed white woman who has expert knowledge of sweet grass baskets, Mary declares that book learning of crafts is far different from the body's experience of winnowing rice with a woven tray. She accepts Tommy's excitement about a possible scholarship to Johnson City State College, but she maintains that classroom education is worthless "if you didn't learn not to be a fool" (Myers, *Glory*, 261). Her stance on literacy places her on a fine line — between the author's contempt for blacks willing to accept the status quo and his admiration for elderly wisewomen, who appear frequently in his writings as models of prudence. In a later scene, the issue of education returns during the 1994 Lewis family reunion, where Tommy's wife, Dr. Jennie Epps Lewis, treats a parturient woman and helps Shep Lewis cope with addiction to crack. By downplaying Tommy's position on the family tree as the first college-educated Lewis, Myers honors Jennie, a female whose drive to attend Meharry Medical School results in professional skills that directly impact the Lewis family.

Myers occasionally dabbles in educational method by disclosing some of the best and worst teaching strategies. In *Slam!* (1996), he suggests a way of helping at-risk students through classroom innovation. Seventeen-year-old Greg "Slam" Harris loses interest in writing a theme on Shakespeare's *Romeo and Juliet* and avoids the hard work of learning algebra. By composing a visual introduction to his neighborhood with a video camera, he earns the regard of family, students, and faculty. At the same time, he introduces white viewers to the uniqueness of ghetto life. Like Shakespeare, who learned on the job while acting on late-16th-century London stages, Slam discovers that training in his own neighborhood provides him satisfying insights into human behavior.

Myers's young adult biography *Malcolm X: A Fire Burning Brightly* (2004) returns to Harlem to examine the alternatives for blacks who lack an education. During the title figure's term for robbery at Charlestown State Prison, from age 21 to 27, he educates himself through reading and correspondence with Nation of Islam leader Elijah Muhammad. Delighted by the value of literature to his life, Malcolm exclaims, "My alma mater was books, a good library" (Myers, 2004, n.p.). By opening his mind to new ideas, he develops into an inspirational speaker and religious leader who models an exemplary family life to other black Muslims who share Malcolm's urban background.

The author's ability to turn a number of milieus into educational material increases the value of his writings to classrooms and libraries as well as to his fans. An unsigned critique in *Kirkus Reviews* remarks on the one-on-one reclamation of

Jimmy Lynch, a juvenile court remand in *Handbook for Boys: A Novel* (2002). The reviewer comments on the value of community to the theme of life lessons from elders to youths: "Everyone who comes into Duke's barbershop relates a story of victimhood or success-fodder for discussion and a moral" ("Review," 2002, 575). By novel's end, Jimmy has enough input on right thinking that he is ready to make responsible choices about his behavior and ambitions. In the author's philosophy, such insight into life situations bears more fruit than college degrees.

See also **fable, mentoring, opportunity**

• *Further Reading*

Fader, Ellen. "Review: *Darnell Rock Reporting*," *Horn Book* 71, no. 2 (March 1995): 194, 200.
Fazioli, Carol. "Review: *Bad Boy*," *School Library Journal* 49, no. 11 (November 2003): 84.
Myers, Walter Dean. *Ambush in the Amazon*. New York: Viking Kestrel, 1986.
_____. *The Beast*. New York: Scholastic, 2003.
_____. *Darnell Rock Reporting*. New York: Delacorte, 1994.
_____. *Fallen Angels*. New York: Scholastic, 1988.
_____. *The Glory Field*. New York: Scholastic, 1994.
_____. *Handbook for Boys: A Novel*. New York: Amistad, 2002.
_____. *Malcolm X: A Fire Burning Brightly*. New York: HarperCollins, 2004.
_____. *The Nicholas Factor*. New York: Viking, 1983.
_____. *Scorpions*. New York: Harper & Row, 1988.
_____. *Somewhere in the Darkness*. New York: Scholastic, 1992.
_____. *Won't Know Till I Get There*. New York: Viking, 1982.
"Review: *Handbook for Boys*," *Kirkus Reviews* 70, no. 8 (15 April 2002): 575.

fable

Myers has achieved fame for storybooks and narratives that he fills with the wisdom of the natural world and of human interaction, for example, the fool tale of the Georgia tenant farmer saved from death in the seriocomic novel *Darnell Rock Reporting* (1994) and the animal rescue motif of *Three Swords for Granada* (2002). The author pits sensible solutions against protracted failure in *The Dragon Takes a Wife* (1972), a modernized fable that overturns the usual expectations for achievement. In "The Black Experience in Children's Books: One Step Forward, Two Steps Back" (1979), an essay for *Interracial Books for Children Bulletin*, he insists that nonwhite children deserve their own cultural and racial models, such as the hip black fairy in *The Dragon Takes a Wife*. The next year, he orchestrated his liberal ideals in *The Golden Serpent* (1980), an Eastern fable about a wise man's assessment of a self-indulgent ruler and his kingdom's underprivileged people. The author pursued more subtle narrative in *The Legend of Tarik* (1981), a complex quest story in which nested fables educate Tarik, the evolving champion, about the relationship between vengeance and self-control.

For Myers's next venture, *Mr. Monkey and the Gotcha Bird* (1984), the author chose literary conventions developed by West African and Caribbean griots. The narrative incorporates rhythmic Caribbean dialect and West African trickster lore.

The story of bestial victimization of the large against the small leads up to Mr. Monkey's escape from the rapacious bird. Myers balanced the moral of the animal fool tale with textured water color vignettes by Leslie Morrill that picture guile in action. Critic Helen E. Williams, in a review for *School Library Journal*, described the synergy of the picture book as "a perfect coordination of text and illustrations" (Williams, 1985, 66).

The picture book pays tribute to storytelling as a basis of early childhood education. The opening scene displays a female griot in a bright, self-assertive Caribbean costume — pink underskirt, yellow and blue overlayering, island patterned blouse in orange and blue, green shawl, and red head wrap. The genial smile, relaxed posture and hands, and bare feet invite the reader to an affable West African beast fable composed "Long time ago, before you born" (Myers, 1984, n.p.). The story of connivance and double dealing concludes with the same female teller gesturing farewell and returning to work with a flash of bright skirts, basket of lemons, and bare feet, an emblem of earthy informality.

The second trickster tale, *How Mr. Monkey Saw the Whole World* (1996), first appeared in *Cricket* magazine in February 1993. A reviewer for *Publishers Weekly* labeled it a "pithy and piquant fable," a description of the fine-edged cunning that saves small animals from large predators. ("Review: *How*," 1996, 215). The text describes how Mr. Monkey outfoxes the bullying Mr. Buzzard during a famine. Myers creates intimacy with an I-you personal touch, a ploy that fabulist Rudyard Kipling developed in *Just So Stories for Little Children* (1902) to involve his own daughters, Josephine and Elsie. Myers's narrative concludes with a calypso feast, a come-one, come-all communion that invites the whole animal realm to a full table. The story earned the regarded of critic Elizabeth Bush, reviewer for the *Bulletin of the Center for Children's Books*, who described the book as a pleasurable example of "folklorically monkeying around" (Bush, 1996, 348).

Between the stories of Mr. Monkey, Myers published *The Story of the Three Kingdoms* (1995), a somber creation legend that begins at an indistinct point when "the stars had not found their places in the night sky" (Myers, 1995, n.p.). The narrative follows the progress of earth's creatures from tyranny by a giant elephant, shark, and hawk, who divide earth, sea, and sky much as the mythic Greek gods separated cosmic powers. The appearance of humankind, correctly depicted in Ashley Bryan's stylized drawings as Africans, begins a one-sided power struggle that places "the People" fourth after the muscular beasts (*ibid.*). The fable commends human ingenuity in rescuing the elephant from a pit, trapping the shark in a net, and lassoing the hawk in a baobab tree. Linking the main episodes is a pervasive faith in stories, treasures from the past that, through repetitions, engender new ideas. Myers crowns humankind with "the gift of story and the wisdom it brings" (*ibid.*).

For the reclamation of two juvenile delinquents, 16-year-old Jimmy Lynch and 17-year-old Kevin, the protagonists of *Handbook for Boys: A Novel* (2002), Myers breaks into the Harlem milieu with an animal fable, "The Blind Monkey Strut" (Myers, 2002, 33). Structured like a fool tale, the story builds on the premise of a monkey trusting a tiger, an obvious lapse in judgment. The second monkey who finds the victim strung up in a tree states the moral: "You knew tigers eat monkeys.

... You didn't need to know anything else!" (*ibid.*, 36). The exemplum illustrates to Jimmy that Frank Greene is not entirely innocent of his legal quandary in buying a secondhand watch from an addict supporting his habit by selling stolen goods. A later animal fable, the story of the monkey's arrival in heaven, moves straight to unwise behaviors by picturing the newly dead soul as eager to return to earth to commit more sins. The monkey rationalizes his foolish choices as a renewed effort "to have a good time" (*ibid.*, 161). Myers employs the monkey stories as scaled-down models of unwise human behaviors.

See also ***The Golden Serpent***

• *Further Reading*

Bush, Elizabeth. "Review: *How Mr. Monkey Saw the Whole World*," *Bulletin of the Center for Children's Books* 49 (June 1996): 348.
Fader, Ellen. "Review: *How Mr. Monkey Saw the Whole World*," *Horn Book* 72, no. 4 (March 1995): 452.
Myers, Walter Dean. *Handbook for Boys: A Novel*. New York: Amistad, 2002.
_____. *How Mr. Monkey Saw the Whole World*. New York: Doubleday, 1996.
_____. *Mr. Monkey and the Gotcha Bird*. New York: Delacorte, 1984.
_____. *The Story of the Three Kingdoms*. New York: HarperCollins, 1995.
Phelan, Carolyn. "Review: *The Story of the Three Kingdoms*," *Booklist* 91, no. 19–20 (1 June 1995): 1788.
"Review: *Handbook for Boys: A Novel*," *Publishers Weekly*, 249 no. 16 (22 April 2002): 70–71.
"Review: *How Mr. Monkey Saw the Whole World*," *Publishers Weekly* 243, no. 8 (19 February 1996): 215.
"Review: *The Story of the Three Kingdoms*," *Publishers Weekly* 242, no. 19 (8 May 1995): 296.
Williams, Helen E. "Review: *Mr. Monkey and the Gotcha Bird*," *School Library Journal* 31, no. 5 (January 1985): 66.

Fallen Angels

Walter Dean Myers's masterwork, *Fallen Angels* (1988), derives from an idea that he incubated for twenty years and from detailed interviewing of veterans and research at the National Archives. Dedicated to his brother Sonny, who died at age 21 on May 7, 1968, on patrol in the Vietnam War, the novel delves into the dark confines of combat and the lasting effects on young soldiers of imminent death in a Southeast Asian war. The plot opens on September 15, 1967, a year and ten months after the conflict pitted U.S. military might against the spread of Communism into the Indochinese peninsula. In 22 months, the U.S. casualty rate already stood above 16,000. The action coincides with an historic strategic offensive to hold a hilltop position and to secure an airstrip at Khe Sanh, a hellish siege that lasted from October 1967 to April 1968. Simultaneously, Dr. Martin Luther King, Jr., addressed noncombatants at Riverside Church in Harlem in protest of national involvement that cost a disproportionate number of black casualties.

The author illustrates a no-win situation in a callow anti-hero who must shoulder man-sized burdens. The protagonist, Richard "Richie" Perry, elects to join the military rather than go to college. His home situation accounts for the high percentage of black volunteerism during the conflict: his single-parent family needs financial support, which army allotment checks immediately satisfy. The money keeps younger brother Kenny in school clothes. Meanwhile, Perry completes basic training in Massachusetts and receives assignment to the front after only seven months of military experience. On his flight to Vietnam via a refueling stop in Anchorage, Alaska, he relaxes in the company of nurse Judy Duncan of Irving, Texas, and Harry "Peewee" Gates, a high-spirited greenie from Chicago whom Myers based on a soldier he served with in the army. From the beginning of their deployment to combat, the author interjects moments of humor, one of the few sources of humanity that relieve pre-battle forebodings.

Myers stresses the screw-ups that annoy and dismay soldiers caught up in the vast and complicated war machinery operated by the faceless Pentagon bureaucracy. Perry expects to be rejected from active duty because of a bad knee injured in a fall on the basketball court during basic training. Nonetheless, on September 15, he flies to Osaka, Japan, and arrives with Gates at Alpha Company of the 22nd Replacement Company. Disbursal to Tan Son Nhut airbase in Hue City requires hours of standing in formation on the tarmac until authorities ready the men for dispersal to individual assignments. Boredom harries untried, energetic men like Perry, who grumble about guard duty and chow, pull pranks, write letters, drink beer while watching a Julie Andrews movie and playing ping-pong in the day room, listen to the news on the radio, and play checkers and chess. These activities restore normalcy to men new to a foreign land where death is a daily possibility.

In a review for the *Washington Post*, Myers described male feistiness in the ranks as a "yearning for adventure" (Myers, 1991, 7). Verbal sparring, fistfights, and war news from Dak To and Pleiku increase tensions. For reading material, the men turn to *Stars and Stripes, Playboy, Reader's Digest*, and *Ebony* magazine and watch *Gunsmoke*, a sanitized television account of savagery in the Old West. Lobel, who goes on patrol with Perry, copes with fear by pretending that he is playing a Lee Marvin role in a war movie. Perry thinks about his enjoyment of *Shane* (1945), Jack Schaefer's post–World War II classic novel of man-to-man confrontation Western style. Lobel encourages fantasy by advising Perry not to get "hooked on reality" (*ibid.*, 76). Nonetheless, Perry realizes, "We were in the middle of it, and it was deeply within us" (*ibid.*, 167). The author characterizes the rookies as youths who respond in typical teen fashion. To counter dangers in the field, Gates and Perry pledge brotherhood, a male bonding ritual that concludes with a spit oath. The act enhances the poignance of immature, idealistic young men readying themselves for killing and being killed.

Nervous anticipation of injury and death hovers over Myers's text. Officers lecture on the dangers in Vietnam — Viet Cong insurgents, malaria, crabs and venereal disease, the black market, and narcotics— and repeat warnings about staying alert and keeping weapons clean. Before the men depart to Chu Lai in a C-47 troop transport, the familiar scuttlebutt predicting a permanent truce at the Paris peace table buoys, then deflates morale. At times, Perry retreats from misconceptions of a quick end to hostilities into memories of home, where the Shirelles perform at the Apollo

Theater and Perry and his little brother Kenny dream of jetting around the world. Perry's reveries illustrate how daydreams relieve the misery of the moment, yet they endanger lives of men distracted from the business of hunting the enemy in a jungle where death "hung around our shoulders and filled the spaces between us" (*ibid.*, 129).

The narrative testifies to the value of mentoring the young. After Perry's first chopper ride and his receipt of the standard M-16 rifle, he reaches into the past for handholds of wisdom to bolster self-confidence. A stand-out among the role models who guided him in boyhood is a teacher, Mrs. Liebow, who urged him to do more than just observe life. The advice proves prophetic as Perry gets his first taste of treachery, a booby trap in a rice paddy that erupts in shards that pierce Jenkins's chest, killing him instantly. The death-laden scenario rends Perry's innocence, exposing him to the numbing of emotions and the routine act of zipping into body bags the whole or dismembered remains of buddies. Myers inserts a touching, healing consolation in the paradoxical prayer of a 23-year-old platoon leader, Lieutenant Carroll, who prays for "angel warriors," the youths who comprise the majority of the U.S. fighting force (*ibid.*, 44). The immediate shift in Perry's thinking causes him to question himself and to try to phrase his new mode of identity to his mother.

Myers characterizes Perry as a well-rounded recruit. He profits from team athletics while playing tournament basketball with the Monarchs, who taught him the importance of group action. The narrative builds up the human side of a war zone by placing Perry in a village for a public service called Chiu Hoi (open arms). To lure locals away from the Viet Cong, Americans distribute malaria pills, band-aids, aspirin, chocolate bars, and C rations, a packaged meal that soldiers carry into situations where standard food service is impossible. As fighting increases at Dak To and Pleiku, Perry nears his first face-to-face confrontation with a dead VC, an Asian the size of his little brother Kenny. During sector patrol, Myers spikes the danger by revealing one of the ironies of war, the firing on First Company, whom Perry's company misidentifies as the enemy. The result is sobering — many wounded and 15 more body bags. The emotional price of so much destruction results in nightmares and the searching of scripture for solace.

The dark atmosphere of battle conceals details much as it clouds the thinking of survivors. Perry suffers the guilt of omission after the loss of Lieutenant Carroll, who dies from a hit under the arm. Perry surmises that more gunfire might have saved Carroll, a gentle, brave veteran. The victim remains alive and inspirational in the men in his prayer, "Let us fear death, but let it not live within us. Protect us, O Lord, and be merciful unto us" (*ibid.*, 44, 128). Contributing to the surreality of normal life within carnage is an armed escort for a civilian pacification team to show Donald Duck cartoons to children in a Vietnamese hamlet. In the background, parachutes eject from a jet before it crashes.

Before Christmas, Myers escalates danger from a rocket attack and sappers from a Viet Cong suicide squad. Perry muses, "Wasn't there ever going to be a time when I wasn't scared?" (*ibid.*, p. 174). Chopper flight, strafing, and fire fights impact the senses with the feel, smell, sound, and sight of death as he makes his first kills. His tears gush from a welter of emotions— relief, anxiety, fatigue, frustration, and shock.

Worsening negative emotions are the physical discomforts of bivouacking among mosquitoes, rats and leeches, claustrophobia, rainy jungle, malodorous rice paddies, spider holes, and punji sticks. Perry reports that, on patrol, "Sleeping didn't come hard; it didn't come at all" (*ibid.*, 185). After four months in country, he sustains shrapnel wounds in his cranium, wrist, side, groin, and left leg. He snorts to himself, "I hadn't see a lot of action, but enough. Lord knows it was enough" (*ibid.*, 217). The hollow honor of a purple heart does little to revive his enthusiasm in mid-January as he returns to the fray in Tam Ky. Myers enlarges on the uplift of a familiar face after Perry reunites with Gates. In contrast to the joy of camaraderie, Perry's inability to join Chaplain Santora in prayer echoes the author's pervasive motif of the failure of religious ritual to sustain the spirit.

The pace of treachery and killing picks up at the novel's climax. The use of women and children as bearers of booby traps results in the dismemberment of a woman. Perry observes, "I saw part of her body move in one direction, and her legs in another" (*ibid.*, 321). Myers depicts another of the horrors of the Vietnam conflict, the rolling clouds of napalm, a gasoline gel that adheres to and incinerates victims. The stripping and burning of corpses, the shooting of a friend to end his suffering, and the collection of dog tags increase the numbing of the emotions. Perry responds with an out-of-body perception: "Suddenly I wasn't there" (*ibid.*, 159). Jerky scenes of patrolling, hiding in a tunnel, removal of a cumbrous flak jacket, and rescue at a pickup zone conclude in heroism after Perry rescues Monaco. After months of paperwork, on March 8, the army corrects its error and ships Perry home. Myers returns to irony with a reflection on the original trio, Perry and friends Gates and Duncan. The unlikely casualty of the three is nurse Duncan. Of the slaughter, critic Maria B. Salvadore in a review for *School Library Journal* concludes that Myers's effort is "compelling, graphic, necessarily gruesome and wholly plausible" (Salvadore, 1988, 118).

The clash of values holds steady throughout the narrative. Perry witnesses body counts and inflated numbers fed to the news media and observes the barbarity of VC chopping off enemy ears and fingers as trophies. Details cloud his view of the enemy with images of peasants tending rice paddies and gunners strafing the innocent on the ground below hovering Hueys. Reverence to Saint Jude, the patron of police officers and lost causes, and to Buddha contrasts interrogation of POWS and the search for infiltrators. The background news of the *Pueblo* incident — the capture of a Navy intelligence-gathering ship and its 83 crewmen on January 23, 1968, by a North Korean shore patrol — assaults morale. Mounting doubts of self-worth haunt Perry and stymy his attempts to write his mother and brother about the war. In his initial confrontation with what author Stephen Crane termed "the great death," Perry feels himself ensnared in the machinery of war and contemplates going AWOL rather than return after recuperation from multiple shrapnel wounds. Validating his contribution to American patriotism is a complex mindset, the turmoil and despair that he carries inside. Myers builds meaning from Perry's clutch of Gates's hand on the flight from Osaka home to America, a tribute to human contact as an antidote to war.

See also **military, Richie Perry**

• *Further Reading*

Kazemek, Francis E. "The Literature of Vietnam and Afghanistan: Exploring War and Peace with Adolescents," *ALAN Review* 23, no. 3 (spring 1996): 6–9.
Moore, John Noell. "'Motherly Business' and the Moves to Manhood," *ALAN Review* 22, no. 1 (fall 1994): 51–55.
Myers, Walter Dean. *Fallen Angels.* New York: Scholastic, 1988.
_____. "Surviving Mean Streets," *Washington Post* (12 May 1991): 7.
Salvadore, Maria B. "Review: *Fallen Angels*," *School Library Journal* 34, no. 10 (June-July 1988): 118.

Fast Sam, Cool Clyde, and Stuff

Walter Dean Myers made his first foray into uplifting teen fiction with *Fast Sam, Cool Clyde, and Stuff* (1975), a spare, breezy urban odyssey based on episodes common to a Harlem neighborhood. Set over a year of character growth in Francis "Stuff" Williams, the first-person narrator, the plot stresses the positive aspects of a youth club. In the estimation of young adult novelist Robert Lipsyte, a critic for the *New York Times Book Review*, Stuff and his friends form the Good People, "an *ad hoc* gang devoted to consciousness raising" (Lipsyte, 1975, 28). The natural conversations range over a number of universal dwellers' concerns— survival, welfare, addiction, broken marriages, sex, death, and supportive camaraderie.

The energetic prologue follows up on changes in characters' vital statistics, including Gloria Chisholm, who is married and her parents reunited after a toxic period in their union. Stuff reports moving at age 12 to apartment 4S at 81 West 116th Street, where settling in among strangers requires enduring insults and ridicule of his limited ability at basketball. Vivid activities involve the neighborhood children in explaining bad grades on report cards, retrieving a stolen purse, and pleading for an emergency room physician to sew on part of an ear that Binky loses in a fight with Robin. The group also eases Clyde Jones through the death of his father and Kitty Jones through her widowed mother's first date. In each episode, unity prevails among friends, even after they fail to rescue Carnation Charley from drug addiction.

Myers's characters focus on each other's idiosyncrasies. The proposal of competing in a dance contest encourages subtle logic as Clyde and Sam determine which girls would make the best partners. Male fervor centers on block pride, which flags after multiple losses of Catholic relay races, a stoop ball contest, and the cleanest block award. A proposal that two boys dance as partners threatens macho images, which individuals establish by doing push-ups, tolerating torture, and bragging about having enough facial hair for a mustache. The episode concludes with the assembly of makeup and outfit to transform Clyde into Claudette, a cute girl dancer. Myers uses the farcical dance contest as a balance to more realistic coming-of-age trials involving issues of mortality and loss. In a review for *Language Arts*, Donald J. Bissett summarized the end result: "[Stuff's] honesty and openness with his friends and the merriment of the book's episodes combine to make intriguing reading" (Bissett, 1976, 521).

The author layers over name-calling and teasing some serious issues impacting children, particularly youthful experimentation with drugs and sex. The retreat of

Petey Johnson from graduation results from a wardrobe deficiency and the lack of funds to buy a new suit. More troubling to the gang is the break-up of Gloria's parents and her father's slapping her mother in full view of the neighborhood. To ease Gloria through the adjustment to separated parents, the gang tackles the neighborhood's common problems. Myers lightens up on the weighty discussion with the selection of a group name, which begins as Bloody Skulls and Golden Imperial Knights before settling on the 116th Street Good People. The high ideals of group action to save individuals endears the members to readers by illustrating willingness to confront human problems that have no easy solutions. In a review for *Bulletin of the Center for Children's Books*, critic Zena Sutherland applauded the effectiveness of varied "episodes and abundant vitality in the dialogue," a combination that allows Myers to maintain character motivation and plot logic at the teen level (Sutherland, 1976, 83).

Beyond childhood needs and behaviors, the novelist emphasizes responsible parenting. His narrative depicts Kitty Jones as a runaway after her mother's first date and dramatizes a confrontation with an angry father over Stuff's staying out until 2:15 A.M. More destructive to parent-child relations is the arrest of group members on false suspicion of drug use. Stuff and Sam weather the accusations with the help of on-the-scene parents who refuse to let the police interrogate their children alone. In the epilogue, Myers tapers off his survey of the mid-teens by portraying 17-year-old Stuff looking back over five years and concluding, "Maybe we all need Good People clubs" (Myers, 1975, 189). The statement captures the author's controlling motif of friendship as an anchor to youths as they advance to adulthood. Jim Naughton, an author-reviewer for the *Los Angeles Times*, credited Myers with "[managing] to evoke their sadness without robbing them of their dignity" (Naughton, 1989, 8). In 2004, schools throughout New York City used group reading of *Fast Sam, Cool Clyde, and Stuff* as a springboard for student discussion of the problems of childhood and the value of shared solutions.

- *Further Reading*

Bissett, Donald J. "Review: *Fast Sam, Cool Clyde, and Stuff*," *Language Arts* 53, no. 5 (May 1976): 520–521.

Lipsyte, Robert. "Review: *Fast Sam, Cool Clyde, and Stuff*," *New York Times Book Review* (4 May 1975): 28, 30.

Marks, Alexandra. "One City, One Curriculum; Consistency Is the Goal in New York City's Efforts to Improve Its Schools," *Christian Science Monitor* (20 January, 2004): 14.

Myers, Walter Dean. *Fast Sam, Cool Clyde, and Stuff*. New York: Viking, 1975.

Naughton, Jim. "Literary Crusader Writes Stories about Real Kids," *Los Angeles Times* (29 December 1989): 8.

Sutherland, Zena. "Review: *Fast Sam, Cool Clyde and Stuff*," *Bulletin of the Center for Children's Books* 29, no. 3 (January 1976): 82–83.

gambling

Myers describes gambling as a constant in human society. He speaks casually of the numbers racket, as though illegal betting were a normal part of urban life. In

It Ain't All for Nothin' (1978), Lonnie, the criminal father of 12-year-old Tippy, receives a visit from the numbers runner. The text notes that he "put in 065 and combinated it. He also played a 0 lead" (Myers, 1978, 120). A daily jackpot rewards the bettor who predicts a multi-digit number published in a common source, such as horse racing news. There are multiple ways of choosing a winner: by betting on a straight, which requires that the digits appear in the exact order of the winning number, or by boxing the bet, which pays less if the correct digits occur in any order, e.g., 605, 650, 056, 560, or 506.

In *The Young Landlords* (1979), Myers adds to the community around West 122nd Street in Harlem a numbers runner called "the Captain" Lloyd, who also invests in local buildings. The novelist wrings humor out of the fact that the New York State Lottery puts the numbers racket out of business, forcing kingpins to complain to the mayor about their plight. To reclaim stature in the community, runners board up abandoned buildings to protect children from injury and initiate an annual barbecue that serves chicken, ribs, hamburgers, and the fixings to all comers. Later, when Bubba applies for a job running numbers, Paul Williams realizes that the Captain deliberately makes the job look difficult and dangerous to prove to Bubba he is unfit for the task. In Paul's words, the Captain was "being a total businessman," a justification for winnowing out inept employees (Myers, 1979, 81).

More complicated than the Captain is Calvin F. "Cal" Jones, the volunteer basketball coach in *Hoops: A Novel* (1981) who gambled away his reputation while playing for the National Basketball Association. The example Cal sets for 17-year-old Lonnie Jackson, holder of an athletic scholarship, offers an unsteady crutch. Cal became a "shaver" when the lure of easy money proved too strong, but he admits a truism, "Nobody gives you something for nothing" (Myers, 1981, 59). His punishment of suspension and a $10,000 fine leads to debt and an absence from home when a fire kills his three-year-old son Jeffrey. Cal's marriage ends along with his celebrity as a sports star. Myers unfolds Cal's story late in the novel as a reminder to Lonnie that one faulty decision, one lapse of integrity can permanently alter a life.

In *The Outside Shot* (1984), the sequel to *Hoops*, gambling parallels motifs of team play and campus camaraderie at Montclare State College in Indiana. As Lonnie gets to know Alfredo "Fat Man" Corsi, the owner of a pizzeria and the arranger of pick-up games, the older man explains why gambling on sports appeals to local men. He creates a hypothetical gambler who perceives himself as an all-around loser. Only through betting does the gambler feel that he has a chance of reclaiming his self-esteem. Fat Man's downfall and Lonnie's exoneration establish for young readers the chancy nature of racketeering and justify Lonnie's personal satisfaction in distancing himself from the criminal side of college sports.

Myers perpetuates the social prestige of the numbers runner in varied settings. In *Fallen Angels* (1988), infantryman Harry "Peewee" Gates suggests that Walowick go to college and major in math, then invites his buddy back to Chicago to flourish in the numbers racket. When protagonist Perry reunites with Peewee in a veterans hospital, Peewee has already scoped out the institution's numbers racket. His speedy work implies that gambling is serious business to him. In another institutional setting in *The Glory Field* (1994) at the start of the second hour of the Reverend Bradley's

Sunday sermon at Bethel Tabernacle in Chicago, choir member Luvenia Lewis catches a glimpse of Norman Chesterfield, a seedy character dressed gangster style in white suit and yellow checked vest. The stereotype of the flashy-dressing gambler reflects the waste of ready cash on self-adornment. Myers suggests that flaunting criminal wealth among the poor denigrates the underclass who support the numbers racket.

The escapist nature of gambling confronts the reader eyeball-to-eyeball in "John Brambles, 55," a poem in Myers's verse anthology *Here in Harlem: Poems in Many Voices* (2004). Brambles, an appropriately named numbers runner, recognizes the hopes of bettors as "a static buzz," an eyeblink of solace for heartache (Myers, 2004, 73). From experience with the hopeful, he recognizes the lies that people tell themselves about luck to offer a glimmer of hope against poverty. The novelist uses Brambles's insight to illustrate the draw of low-end gambling to the poor, whom unwise spending makes even poorer.

• *Further Reading*

Myers, Walter Dean. *Here in Harlem: Poems in Many Voices*. New York: Holiday House, 2004.
_____. *Hoops*. New York: Delacorte, 1981.
_____. *It Ain't All for Nothin'*. New York: Viking, 1978.
_____. *The Young Landlords*. New York: Viking, 1979.

gangs

The importance to urban teens of group solidarity and belonging dominates Myers's young adult fiction, including the fantasy gang the "Royal Visigoths" in *Won't Know Till I Get There* (1982). The novelist remarked in a 1994 interview with the staff of the *Journal of Reading* that his own search for gang membership prefaced his enlistment in the military in August 1954 at age seventeen. He elaborated, "When I went into the Army, I had a very romantic concept, the same way teenagers feel in gangs today. I needed to explore my own feelings" (Chance, *et al.*, 1994, 247). He continues to examine the young male's need to identify with a source of strength, for example, the flight of 17-year-old Tyrone "Circle T" Curry from a fractious home situation to life among unsavory street toughs in *The Dream Bearer* (2003).

In Myers's first novel, *Fast Sam, Cool Clyde, and Stuff* (1975), a group of Harlem children gains support and acceptance through the dynamics of sharing and forbearance. Out of a spirit of "one for all and all for one," they form the 116th Street Good People. Myers indicates that the club offers protection and group solidarity against their antitheses, gangs like the Valiants. The Good People survive without violence or weapons, the hallmarks of urban teen violence in Myers's more dramatic later works. A subtext of territoriality abets the squabble between Binky and Robin, an outsider from 118th Street who gained a reputation for toughness by holding off seven of the Valiants at one time. In *Won't Know Till I Get There* (1982), the characters invent a tough-sounding gang name, the Royal Visigoths, which they advertise by spray-painting it on a train. The imaginary gang gets out of hand after four alleged members boast to police about their activities. Fantasizing about gang activity results in arrests and community projects for the foursome. Myers's ironic non-existent band satirizes the fantasy that encourages dreams of glory in would-be members.

Myers set his award-winning novel *Scorpions* (1988) in Harlem of the 1980s, a period of moral deterioration from poverty, gang violence, crack cocaine, and too many young males imprisoned for crime. Echoing the single-parent home and gang killings mentioned in *Fallen Angels* (1988), *Scorpions* amplifies the difficulties of a single-parent mother rearing Jamal Hicks and grieving for Randy Hicks, a 17-year-old son in prison for drug trafficking, attempted robbery, and murder of a deli owner. Randy's gang, the Scorpions, recruits "young dudes" for cynical reasons: The authorities "can't get you to testify" (Myers, 1988, 42–43). Jamal's replacement of his brother as gang leader and his receipt of a pistol from 16-year-old Mack precipitate crises that could destroy Jamal's future. Mack, the spokesman for gangland philosophy, insists on backing up tough talk with action: "You waste a couple of guys, and they know who you are" (*ibid.*, 207). Myers wrings irony from the fact that gun-play ends in death for a gang member named Angel. The cost of violence consumes Jamal after Tito commits murder and is deported to Puerto Rico along with his grandmother. Instead of leading a community support system, Jamal ends up isolated.

The twisted thinking of gang members earns Myers's probing. He presents the role of 14-year-old Osvaldo Cruz, a member of the Diablos (devils), in felony robbery and murder in *Monster: A Novel* (1999). On the stand at Steve Harmon's murder trial, Osvaldo hesitates to list the requirements for belonging to the Diablos. He mentions fighting another member "to show you got the heart" (Myers, 1999, 107). More sinister is proof of skill with a knife. Osvaldo reveals that new members have to leave a mark, a euphemism for cutting a person "where it shows" (*ibid.*, 108). Further interrogation elicits from Osvaldo that he sliced a stranger in the face, a heinous act that smacks of barbarous exhibitionism.

Gangs continue to figure in Myers's later fiction. In *Fallen Angels*, anti-hero Richard "Richie" Perry ponders how Black Pride began replacing gangs as a form of black identity and belonging. Nonetheless, groups like the Rovers from Brooklyn still stalk their prey late at night, shooting one victim on Manhattan Avenue. The story "Monkeyman" in *145th Street: Short Stories* (2000) describes the narrator's defiance of a Harlem gang. He clarifies exotic teen terms like "squad tract," a reference to a warning that the members intend to retaliate against an enemy like Monkeyman, who intervenes in a near knifing of Peaches (Myers, 2000, 75). The narrator summarizes the life span of a new gang: they overreach until the police arrest their leaders. The conclusion is ignominy: "Their reps and tattoos and colors don't keep them out of jail, they chill and their colors fade" (*ibid.*, 75). In a second short piece, "Kitty and Mack: A Love Story," a drive-by shooting causes a bystander to remark, "Those gang people don't care two cents for your life!" (*ibid.*, 92). The statement captures Myers's contempt for random, depersonalized gang violence.

Outlaw behavior dominates Myers's latest works. In *The Beast* (2003), a teen novel about heroin addiction, Gabriela "Gabi" Godoy is a bright young Dominican who loses her optimism after her mother Lucila suffers incurable cancer and her brother Rafe associates with a gang. The boy's choice of allegiance fills the void left by the single mother's precarious state of health. More fearful is the formation of the

Ordo Sagittae (Order of the Arrow), a cultic group that clusters informally around a sociopath, 16-year-old Leonard "Len" Gray, in *Shooter* (2004). Lacking direction or normal activities, the five members await the orders of Len, whose mental collapse compels him to fight back against Brad Williams, a pompous jock and bully. Like the anti-hero, the cult is a non-gang comprised of sycophants who aimlessly follow Len toward vindication for alienated students who have no way to achieve in a hostile school environment. Tenuous cult membership implodes after Len shoots Brad and kills himself, a collapse that embodies the vapid quality of gang loyalties.

See also **belonging, juvenile crime**

• *Further Reading*

Chance, Rosemary, Teri Lesesne, and Lois Buckman. "And the Winner Is ... : A Teleconference with Walter Dean Myers," *Journal of Reading* 38, no. 3 (November 1994): 246–249.

Myers, Walter Dean. *Monster: A Novel.* New York: HarperCollins, 1999.

_____. *145th Street: Short Stories.* New York: Delacorte, 2000.

_____. *Scorpions.* New York: Harper & Row, 1988.

The Glory Field

One of Myers's critically successful works, *The Glory Field* (1994) won kudos for its historic grandeur. The saga, which *Booklist* reviewer Hazel Rochman compares to Alex Haley's *Roots* (1976), covers some 250 years of family history succinctly charted on a two-page Lewis family tree and repeated at each stave. When the story opens in July 1753 off the shores of Sierra Leone, 11-year-old Muhammad Bilal, a native of Bonthe on Sherbro Island, is in no position to glory over his future patriarchy. His capture comes after he fends off and kills a wild animal with only a stick for a weapon. He admits a demoralizing historical fact, that black Africans speaking the Mande dialect, most likely traders from the Sewa River region, seized and bound him at hand and neck for the march to a slave pen. In a few pages, as Bilal accustoms himself to sea travel in the unlit underdeck, the narrative summarizes the terrors of what lies ahead and fears for the parents he leaves behind. Accompanying him is the personified Death, which swiftly winnows out the weak from survivors. Family legend accounts for Bilal's 109 years of life in descriptions of a proud, unruly spirit, which rejects the degradation of bondage. Myers promotes a family unity that treasures shreds of information about Bilal, a legendary role model who inspires his scions over the next eight generations.

Shifting over a century to March 1864, at the dawn of emancipation, Myers places the Lewis genealogy under the ownership of Manigault Lewis at Live Oaks Plantation on fictional Curry Island, South Carolina. The narrative stresses the class differences among elite planters enriched by harvests of cotton and sweet potatoes, the poor whites who work as patrollers, and the enterprising employees like overseer Joe Haynes, whose crippled leg keeps him out of the Confederate army. At the grave of Muhammad Bilal, new generations of slaves recertify their family connections to West Africa. At a tense time for the Lewises after Lem and his uncle Joshua's escape, field workers tend rows of sweet potatoes while singing call-and-response style a symbolic spiritual about tender lambs. The text refers directly to 16-year-old escapee Lem Lewis, the individualist who bears the traits of his great-grandfather Bilal. Myers implies a mystic transfer of courage and dignity to an untried teenager on the eve of his self-emancipation.

The ancestral story dramatizes the value of example in the lives of illiterate slaves. Their guidance in perilous times derives from the slave tales of foiled escapes and lashings that pervade oral history. Lizzy, a naive 13-year-old foster child of Joshua and Neela Foster Lewis, accepts responsibility for bearing water to Lem, whom slave catchers tie to a tree in the woods. Lizzy's choice of running away over staying at the plantation to be whipped and possibly killed expunges her innocence in minutes. On her run alongside Lem from baying hounds, the drama swells during the couple's confrontation with a black Union soldier. By connecting slave escape with the arrival of black regiments from the North, Myers expands on two strands of black history—the desperation and courage of slaves in the last days of bondage and the determination of Northern blacks to end the plantation system.

In the novel's third stave, Myers maintains his focus on teenagers as he moves into the Jim Crow era of 1900. The author justifies the choice of the Lewis family surname as a practical means of reuniting with any former field hands who might return to Curry Island in search of family. In honor of Moses Lewis's one-word exultation, "Glory!," the newly freed slaves of Live Oaks Plantation choose "Glory Field" for their eight-acre parcel, on which patriarch Muhammad Bilal had been enslaved (Myers, 1994, 74). Some 36 years after the three escapes from Manigault Lewis, Elijah, the 15-year-old son of Lizzy and Richard Lewis, plows the family's land. The narrative summarizes the terrors of the Reconstruction era as racist bankers, taxation, sharecropping, and night riders threaten the landed black family's ownership of property. Lifting spirits among the Lewis family are the traditions of cleaning family graves, prayers, and sharing church dinners of soul food, the greens, sweet potatoes, and rice dishes that nourished slaves 135 years earlier. The narrative establishes that biographical details from the past sustain the hopes of 20th-century blacks that they can rise above post-Civil War violence to a time of peace and prosperity.

Myers carries the courage of Muhammad Bilal into the fifth generation of Lewises by depicting Elijah as a brash sailor. To save a white child, Elijah and his cousin Abby row the *Pele Queen*, a 17-foot sailboat, into storm winds off Key Island. Because of white bias, the *Gazette* awards the glory to Sheriff Glover and makes no mention of Abby or Elijah's valor. Because white retaliation forces Elijah to flee to his Uncle Joshua and Aunt Neela in Chicago, the boy travels north on a crate, the only amenity in a blacks-only car of a train headed for Illinois. Picking up the narrative in May 1930, the author introduces Luvenia Lewis, the city-bred offspring of Elijah and Goldie Paige Lewis. The narrative, which saves to the falling action Luvenia's success in business, suggests that individuals have no inkling of the character traits that they pass to future generations.

The fourth stave of Myers's saga returns to the Lewis clan in Johnson City, South Carolina, in 1964, when 16-year-old Tommy Lewis boosts his team to victory in an All-City tournament. He wins the game for Curry Islanders against a school named for Charleston-born philosopher Martin Robinson Delany, the first black combat major in the Union Army. After a street demonstration by blacks, Jennie Epps identifies Tommy as a proud Lewis man. The action contrasts Tommy's choice to avoid confrontations with the courage of a peer, Skeeter Jackson, a white supporter whom klansmen brutalize. The text briefly bogs down in a recounting of white crimes against Medgar Evers and children at the Sixteenth Street Church in Birmingham, Alabama. Myers reinvigorates the action by picturing Tommy's intrusion on a press conference by chaining himself to the sheriff with Muhammad Bilal's shackles. The bold choice of public notoriety costs Tommy consideration for a scholarship, but his stance as a Lewis man earns him the regard of the black community. *Publishers Weekly* characterizes the theme as "the high cost—and the excruciatingly slow process—of justice" ("Review," 1994, 112).

The fifth stave of Myers's saga opens in Harlem in August 1994 on the budding musical career of 15-year-old Malcolm Lewis. The author contrasts the broken home of cousin Shep Lewis with Malcolm's stable parents, a vital support to their teenaged son. The narrative quotes the belief of Malcolm's father, Charles Lewis, that "A real man does what he knows is right," a credo that reflects on the previous example of Tommy abandoning hopes for a college education to promote civil rights (*ibid.*, 207). As a symbol of Shep's decline, the narrative pictures him selling bootleg audiocassettes outside the Apollo Theater, a famous landmark that slipped into ignominy much as Shep's addiction to crack lowers the standards of the once-proud Lewis clan. After Malcolm makes the arduous trip south with Shep for the annual sweet potato harvest, the redeeming quality of family solidarity washes over Malcolm. At a significant point in Malcolm's formative years, he hears about Tommy's death in Vietnam and about Robert Smalls's theft of a boat from the Confederates during the Civil War to aid the Union army. Planter Lewis takes pride in the shackles he buys from the sheriff's auction for $209. As a token of family regard for its patriarch, Muhammad Bilal, the Lewises maintain ownership of his leg irons, which pass to Malcolm. Myers's epilogue illustrates the importance of the honor to Malcolm, who improvises music that captures the endurance of a proud family line. In a review for *Horn Book*, critic Peter D. Sieruta commends Myers for supplying young adults with the rare intergenerational saga. Rochman summarizes the paradoxical themes in terms of proximity to family: "You can't make much progress if you don't leave home, but you can sure mess yourself up if you don't remember where home is" (Rochman, 1993, 319).

See also **Lewis genealogy**

• *Further Reading*

Myers, Walter Dean. *The Glory Field*. New York: Scholastic, 1994.
"Review: *The Glory Field*," *Publishers Weekly* 241, no. 36 (5 September 1994): 112.
Rochman, Hazel. "Review: *The Glory Field*," *Booklist* 91, no. 3 (1 October 1994): 319.
Sieruta, Peter D. "Review: *The Glory Field*," *Horn Book* 61, no. 2 (March-April 1995): 200.

Godoy genealogy

The nostalgia in *The Beast* (2003) expands with reflections by an elderly blind man, Gabriela "Gabi" Godoy's Dominican abuelo (grandfather). Myers implies that the source of Gabi Godoy's poet soul is the romanticism of an elderly man who sees images of home from the time before he lost his vision.:

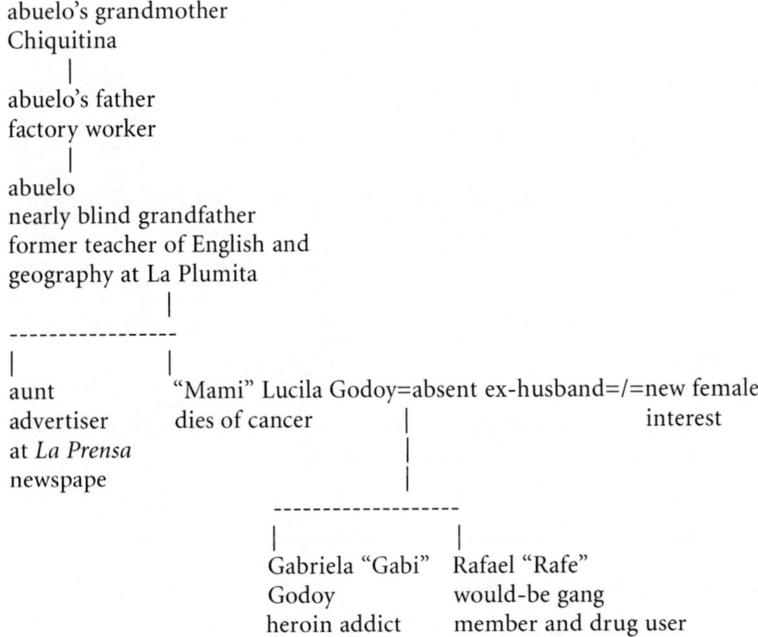

• *Further Reading*

Myers, Walter Dean. *The Beast.* New York: Scholastic, 2003.

The Golden Serpent

Myers earned positive critical review for an apologue, *The Golden Serpent* (1980), which he wrote in the style of a folk fable. Set in India in the early 20th century, the story takes the form of a conundrum about the hermit Pundabi, a guru who lives far up the slopes of the snow-capped Himalayan Mountains, far from the richly decorated architecture of the royal city. Because of his inaccessibility, he receives requests for advice that seekers write on linen strips, bake into loaves of bread, and convey to him for consideration through Ali, the guru's disciple-errand boy. The illustrations by Alice Provensen and Martin Provensen employ color to differentiate between social classes, with earth tones reserved for peasants and bright colors for the king and his motorcade and palace entourage.

As in the biblical stories of the Joseph and Daniel, the price of serving royalty pressures Pundabi to solve a mystery that has no name. The king's expectations of the beloved sage offer stark consequences— high pay for the right answer and prison for failure. By introducing the king to a handicapped boy, a trio of blind beggars, and a threadbare widow, Pundabi gives the king an opportunity to identify the source of discontent. At story's end, the king ignores the wide disparity between life in the palace and among citizens of the realm, leaving Pundabi to conclude that indifferent people are unaffected by the sufferings around them. Critic Ellen D. Warwick, in a review for *School Library Journal*, summarized the moral as "the blindness of power and the wisdom of simple living" (Warwick, 1981, 53).

• *Further Reading*

Briggs, Julia. "Review: *The Golden Serpent*," *Times Literary Supplement* (27 March 1981): 343.
Heins, Paul. "Review: *The Golden Serpent*," *Horn Book* 56 (December 1980): 686.
Warwick, Ellen D. "Review: *The Golden Serpent*," *School Library Journal* 27, no. 5 (January 1981): 53.

Gray, Leonard

The 16-year-old gunman in *Shooter* (2004), Leonard "Len" Gray is a white loner who bears strong similarities to the plotters of terrorism at Columbine High School, Littleton, Colorado, on April 20, 1999. The son of a right-wing militant and gun fancier, Len is a dedicated reader and marksman who pals around with Cameron Porter, a brilliant 17-year-old student at Madison High School in Harrison County. Len wears black, abuses prescription tranquilizers, and nurses caustic hostility, especially toward Jews and jock bullies. According to critic Nancy Chaplin in a review for *Kliatt*, he bears the emotional scars of the "bullied outsider with a taste for nihilistic, alternative music" (Chaplin, 2004, 51). Exacerbating his madness are the predations of his father against his mother and against Len, who refers to the elder Gray in his diary with the depersonalized all-caps pronouns HE and HIM. In the estimation of critic Lauren Adams, a reviewer for *Horn Book*, Len is "a disturbed mind about to go over the edge" (Adams, 2004, 335).

Through circular narrative, Myers discloses the touching relationship between Cameron and Len, which suggests an aimless follower's search for a leader. Cameron excuses Len's perverse behaviors without passing judgment on obvious delusions. To the county psychologist, Cameron describes how the two boys vandalized a church before Christmas. Len, who was hostile toward a creche with Caucasian bible characters, scrawled on the church walls in Magic Marker, **"GOD DOES NOT LIVE HERE!"** (Myers, 2004, 36). In Cameron's estimation, Len hated the church as one of the "symbols that we had to live by," an outside force that judged Len's misbehavior (*ibid.*, 44). As a result of psychiatric evaluation and treatment, Len rationalizes that "as long as we were nutcases and juveniles, [the authorities] couldn't touch us" (*ibid.*, 39). By romanticizing himself as an outlaw, Len recedes into the outsider's mask, a form of distancing that separates him from rules and morals.

Myers exemplifies Len as a dark-edged sociopath who envisions himself as St. Sebastian, a martyr pierced with arrows. At combat practice in Curry Woods near

Easter, Len empowers himself by using live turtles as targets, but conceals them in orange bags. Because the incident costs him friendship with Carla Evans, he humiliates her by posting anonymously on the school news web her therapy records about molestation by a step-brother. A more significant form of power for Len is suicide: "It was the ultimate power. Like being God" (*ibid.*, 56). Len rails at external limitations, calls parents fascists, and keeps an enemies list headed by Brad Williams, a symbol of the jock egotist. Searching for a suitable form of vengeance at being harassed and belittled, Len describes his gun as "a secret lover, quiet, powerful, waiting to work its magic" (*ibid.*, 225). His reliance on a Ruger illustrates his willingness to commit murder to silence Brad, the worst of the school's taunting athletes. Although the killing requires Len's suicide, he accepts it as the inevitable price of blotting out a tormentor.

See also **Cameron Porter, *Shooter***

• *Further Reading*

Adams, Lauren. "Review: *Shooter*," *Horn Book* 80, no. 3 (May-June 2004): 335.
Chaplin, Nancy. "Review: *Shooter*," *Kliatt* 38, no. 6 (November 2004): 50-51.
Myers, Walter Dean. *Shooter*. New York: Amistad, 2004.
_____. "Walter Dean Myers," *Read* 54, no. 13 (25 February 2005): 14–15.

Handbook for Boys

One of Walter Dean Myers's popular reprises of boyhood in Harlem, *Handbook for Boys: A Novel* (2002) is a triumph of his familiar blend of wry humor and realism. In an introductory letter to the reader, the author describes a familiar social quandary — teenagers who fail in school and give up. He warns, "At such times there is a desperate need for mentors ... but they are not often available" (Myers, 2002, n.p.). Myers opens the narrative with a rescuer, Duke Wilson, who offers six months of counsel to two court remands, 16-year-old Jimmy Lynch and 17-year-old Kevin. In the estimation of critic Joanne K. Cecere, a reviewer for *School Library Journal*, "[Jimmy]'s perspective is the vehicle that carries the story and by book's end readers know he will make it while Kevin has more to learn" (Cecere, 2002, 158). Aided by former courtroom guard Edward "Cap" Mills and Claudio "Mister M" Morales, regulars at the Harlem barbershop, Duke instills a sense of responsibility and accomplishment in the pair, to whom he offers college tuition if they complete high school. Reviewer Mary Hofmann, in a critique for *Book Report*, summarizes the suspenseful plot: "The boys resist, argue, rebel, and listen as Jimmy moves haltingly from resentment to admiration, with several close calls to recidivism" (Hofmann, 2002, 48).

Myers describes the unlike problems of the two delinquents with a tone that *Kirkus Reviews* calls "heartfelt urgency," an immediacy the author reprises in the pro-child ode "Wolf Song" (2005) ("Review," 2002, 575). Jimmy gets in a vicious fight with Martin at school. Kevin's decline begins with marijuana. Trapped by the vigilance of his mother, he goes to court on a charge of possession and receives three months' probation. To Frank Greene's complaint about being arrested for buying a stolen watch from an addict, Jimmy anticipates a lecture from Duke and learns about foolish dealings with criminals from an animal fable, "The Blind Monkey Strut" (Myers, 2002, 33). Duke follows up on his advice by introducing Jimmy to the philosophy of René Descartes.

Myers identifies Jimmy as one of a generation of hip blacks who knows about black history without respecting it. Jimmy denigrates his teacher, Miss Scott, and dismisses her lecture on civil rights marches in Alabama with, "I had heard most of the stuff before" (*ibid.*, 73). Duke reminds him that civil rights means more than segregated fountains and racist bombings— it also refers to joblessness and the jailing of a disproportionate number of blacks. Through Dr. Ernie Colfax, Myers interjects didactic commentary on frustration and curiosity as introductions to cocaine and heroin. The doctor concludes that addicts' lives end in pain, sometimes from AIDS. By the end of a progression of advisories on where and how black citizens have suffered, Jimmy acquires enough savvy to share with Ernesto, Duke's next court remand. In a review for *Kliatt*, Paula Rohrlick recommended the didactic work as "a great choice for counselors working with teens like Jimmy, and as a spark for debates" (Rohrlick, 2003, 20).

• *Further Reading*

Cecere, Joanne K. "Review: *Handbook for Boys: A Novel*," *School Library Journal* 48, no. 5 (May 2002): 157–158.
Hofmann, Mary. "Review: *Handbook for Boys: A Novel*," *Book Report* 21, no. 3 (November-December 2002): 48.
Myers, Walter Dean. *Handbook for Boys: A Novel*. New York: Amistad, 2002.
"Review: *Handbook for Boys*," *Kirkus Reviews* 70, no. 8 (15 April 2002): 575.
Rohrlick, Paula. "Review: *Handbook for Boys: A Novel*," *Kliatt* 37, no. 3 (May 2003): 20.

Harlem

Walter Dean Myers is one with the pulsing vitality of community life in Bedford-Stuyvesant, New York's Lower East Side, and Harlem, the hometown that he honors as America's black capital. In a community credited with the largest concentration of negroes in the nation, he played stickball and basketball with blacks from the South, Puerto Rico, and the West Indies. In *Handbook for Boys: A Novel* (2002), his fictional characters Duke Wilson and Jimmy Lynch stroll in a popular sliver of oasis, Jackie Robinson Park, which extends between Boardhurst and Edgecombe avenues from 145th to 154th street. Myers speaks admiringly in *Fallen Angels* (1988) through an old woman selling newspapers outside Sydenham Hospital on West 125th Street, "They ain't got this many black folks no place else in the world, 'cept maybe Africa and Haiti" (Myers, 1988, 75). More enthusiastic is the declaration of barber Duke Wilson: "Taking me out of Harlem would be like taking a fish out of water" (Myers, 2002, 7).

The author remembers home as a supportive neighborhood that he loved in childhood for its spirit of sharing and its love of music and humor. He explained to Allen O. Pierleoni in an interview for the *Sacramento Bee*, "It was my spiritual home, a community where standards were set" (Pierleoni, 2005). Myers got the idea of setting stories in Harlem from the novels of James Baldwin: "[He] wrote about my neighborhood; he gave *me* permission to write about my neighborhood" (Brown, 1999, 46). In Myers's collaboration with artist Jacob Lawrence on *The Great Migration: An American Story* (1993), the duo produced an historic retrospective on the gaudy, irrepressible community that energized black arts. Lawrence, whose family moved north from Virginia and the Carolinas, remarked on learning shape, pattern, and color from painting a vibrant urbanism —"peddlers, parades, fire escapes, apartment houses— all that was new to me" (Myers, 1993, n.p.). The immediacy of his primitive paintings inspired Myers to preserve memories of Harlemites.

In two biographies of Malcolm X, Myers examines the importance of Harlem to the development of leaders. The young adult biography *Malcolm X: By Any Means Necessary* (1993) introduces the sense of community that made the Harlem of 1957 a black paradise. In April, flower boxes and Jamaican garments enrich the red-brown brick walls with color. Conversation turns to baseball greats Cool Papa Bell and Buck Leonard. Into the benign atmosphere, Black Muslims march in impressive formation. In *Malcolm X: A Fire Burning Brightly* (2004), Myers cites the title figure's dedication to Harlem as a "seventh heaven," a place that deserves the moral purity of Islam (Myers, *Malcolm X: A Fire*, n.p.). After assassins killed Malcolm during a lecture, his funeral at Faith Temple Church on 147th and Amsterdam drew long lines of mourners.

Myers's love of home reached a height of celebration in an oversized picture-ode, *Harlem: A Poem* (1997), a visually engaging anthem to belonging and free expression among a melange of black people from the American South, the Caribbean, and Africa. In a profuse image of creative energy, illustrated text honors the black community for spawning Striver's Row, the Cotton Club, Apollo Theater, Smalls' jazz clubs, Minton's playhouse, and the Abyssinian Baptist Church, which the author attended in childhood. In the final stanzas, the poet extols the historical continuum that brought African culture from the Niger River to enrich American identity in Harlem. He extols black artistry for celebrating "memories of feelings, of place" (Myers, 1997, n.p.). In a review for *School Library Journal*, critic Melissa Hudak summarized the text as "an arresting and heartfelt tribute to a well-known, but little understood community" (Hudak, 1997, 121).

Against a reputation for poverty and crime created by Claude Brown's *Manchild in the Promised Land* (1965) and Alex Haley's *The Autobiography of Malcolm X* (1965), Myers found optimism and purpose in Harlemites similar to the upbeat themes of Langston Hughes's stories of Simple. Myers speaks through Richard "Richie" Perry, an infantryman in *Fallen Angels*, a visceral ache to escape the Vietnam War and return home. Richie's escapism is through immediate, palpable imagery: "I dreamt about the Apollo Theater. I dreamt that I was in the Apollo and the Shirelles were there" (Myers, 1988, 301). Among Myers's memories are visions ranging from boys shooting a basketball through a milk crate hoop and students researching black Civil War soldiers at the Schomburg library to views of Riverside Park from Grant's Tomb, a basketball tournament at the Felt Forum of Madison Square Garden, the A train station at 125th Street, and trolley rides to East Harlem to shop at La Marqueta, where he smelled fresh spices from blocks away. He declared to interviewer Roger Sutton, a critic for *School Library Journal*, "I loved those streets and not because of any sort of romantic notion, but because it was where I was raised. These were the people I knew, and my life was reasonably good as a young person" (Sutton, 1994, 26). Critics remark on Myers's ability to depict honesty and moral integrity in an atmosphere that others denigrate for squalor and lawlessness.

Myers is candid about problems in the black urban community, from wife beaters and snipers to the homeless, prostitutes, gangs, crackheads, winos, and the hitmen who shot Malcolm X at the Audubon Ballroom on Broadway between 165th and 166th streets. Tippy, the 12-year-old protagonist of *It Ain't All for Nothin'* (1978), remarks on a deadly shooting at Morningside Park, the same place where he buries Grandma Carrie Brown's canary Gregory. In *Hoops: A Novel* (1981), felonies involving loan sharking and the stealing and cashing of government checks target the oldest and poorest of Harlem residents. In the novel's falling action, 17-year-old basketball star Lonnie Jackson must accept Harlem sports for all its venality. In the summation of critic Zena Sutherland, a reviewer for *Bulletin of the Center for Children's Books*, "There are rough people in the business of basketball, and if he wants to get out of Harlem and become a pro, he'll have to cope with them" (Sutherland, 1981, 74). More menacing are the thugs armed with lengths of pipe who stalk an elderly homeless man in "The Treasure of Lemon Brown" (1983).

A parade of miserable scenes dramatizes juvenile crime in Myers's works. In *Monster: A Novel* (1999), 16-year-old Steve Harmon meets criminals Bobo Evans and James King in Marcus Garvey Park to chat idly about victimizing illegal aliens. After Steve's arrest, he resides in Manhattan Detention Center on a charge of abetting the felony robbery and murder of a drugstore owner at 145 Street in Harlem. A media report in his screenplay asserts, "In New York's Harlem, yet another holdup has ended in a grisly scene of murder" (Myers, 1999, 120). A neighborhood resident notes, "People getting killed and everything and it ain't right but I ain't shocked none" (*ibid.*, 121). The investigation branches out to Ryker's Island, the penal colony for 80 percent of New York City criminals, located east of Harlem in the East River. A pall of suspicion and criminality overcasts the novel and leaves the reader to decide whether Steve actively contributes to Harlem's lengthy criminal history.

Drugs and paranoia dog the Curry family in *The Dream Bearer* (2003). The urban folk tale depicts early morning movement on Frederick Douglass Boulevard as 12-year-old David and 17-year-old Tyrone, Reuben Curry's sons, help unload cans of floor polish from a pickup truck. Reuben's wife Evelyn, an employee at the Matthew Henson Community Project, tries to contain Reuben's erratic and frenzied behavior. She fails to stop him from hurling dishes out the window to the annoyance of neighbors, whom David worries may be discussing his father's mental illness in private. Balancing Reuben's threat is mention of more hospitable parts of the neighborhood — the YMCA on West 135th Street, George Bruce Branch of the public library on 125th Street, the Hudson River, and the Countee Cullen Library at 136th Street.

Myers depicts in characters his own excitement at reunion with his old neighborhood. In *The Beast* (2003), he portrays 16-year-old Anthony "Spoon" Witherspoon returning from Wallingford Academy in Connecticut to Harlem for Christmas break and regaining the rhythm of a macho strut down Nicholas Avenue. He spies a panhandler, touches fists with a brother, listens to the string music of a Spanish radio station, and pretends to interrupt "girls double Dutching" with their jump rope (Myers, *Beast*, 29). Of the sense impressions he treasures, the most stimulating are colors, "vibrant Gauguin hues almost bursting from the squared city canvas" (*ibid.*, 30). In a review of the novel for *School Library Journal*, critic Johanna Lewis echoed Myers's attempt at a balanced milieu in "the bright, clean, working-class hope and the slate-gray bankruptcy of drugs and crime" (Lewis, 2003, 157).

In *The Glory Field* (1994), Charles Lewis, a scion of the proud Lewis clan, describes Harlem's slide into squalor as the result of integration — after rich blacks moved out, they left behind those too poor to afford better neighborhoods. With surprisingly mature logic, Peaches observes in "Block Party — 145th Street Style," a short story anthologized in *145th Street: Short Stories* (2000): "Hurt happens here just like everywhere else" (Myers, 2000, 149). When cop cars pull up in the story "The Baddest Dog in Harlem," onlookers appreciate the break in monotony. The author explains, "Half the guys on the block don't have jobs and so they're always on the stoops or just standing around with nothing to do" (*ibid.*, 18). The story rises to perverse comedy as the police realize they have organized a shootout against a dog. Quickly sinking into tragedy, the story discloses that officers have killed a child who was watching cartoons on television. Myers remarks, "What a shame it was the way life could slip away so easily in Harlem" (*ibid.*, 25).

The survey of community decline parallels the Curry family crises in *The Dream Bearer* (2003), which, according to a review in *Kirkus Reviews*, features "an appreciation of the danger and the magic of Harlem" ("Review," 2003, 754). The narrative introduces 12-year-old David Curry as a bright student at Frederick Douglass Academy on Adam Clayton Powell Boulevard, a traveler of the A train, and a movie fan of Saturday shows at Magic Johnson's theater at 125th Street and Frederick Douglass Boulevard. A later episode sends the title figure, Moses Littlejohn, to Harlem Hospital on West 135th Street and Malcolm X Boulevard. A secondary motif involves the enthusiasm of David's mother Evelyn for turning an abandoned building into a shelter called the Matthew Henson Community Project, named for an explorer of the North Pole. Because the owner employs her husband Reuben to circumvent the plan, the author comments at length on the inner-city situation.

As David accompanies his father to work, the narrative examines 145th Street, which bears evidence of quality homes on one end and derelict structures between Frederick Douglass and Malcolm X boulevards. Of the cultural mix, David observes loud music and the work crews that take part in renovation, "mostly West Indian dudes with Rasta dreads and thick accents" (Myers, *Dream*, 42). Myers remarks on the difference a few blocks make as David searches for his brother, 17-year-old Tyrone, on 141st Street, a slum pocked with empty lots and suspicious characters hanging around a pool room. In a separate scenario, Myers speaks through Mr. Kerlin the source of blight: "Indifference is the enemy. Apathy is the enemy" (*ibid.*, 69).

In 2004, Myers published *Here in Harlem: Poems in Many Voices*, a salute through verse and photography to the diversity of Harlemites. The 53 first-person poems reflect the tone and metaphoric dash of Long Island poet Walt Whitman's urban verse and the style of Edgar Lee Masters's *Spoon River Anthology* (1915). Myers adopted the idea of imagining inhabitants of a fictional town and applied the idea to Harlem. Residents— a postman, basketball player, jazz guitarist, church attendees, and parents of young children — exude energy and pride in accomplishment. Myers's hustler, Sam DuPree, sports egotism that derives from place, "1–2-5 and Lenox A-ve-nue!," the heart of the Harlem Renaissance (Myers, *Here*, 64).

Significant to community culture and custom are rent parties, hair treatments, tryouts for a Cotton Club chorus line, call-and-response worship services, and the Harlem Hellfighters, veterans of World War II. In a deceptively simple stanza, "Hosea Liburd, 25," the author speaks through a laborer the demarcation of 125th Street, the subway stop that separates home from foreign territory. Out of terror at muscular blacks, white passengers look away from Hosea as though avoiding one of Harlem's violent beasts. A parallel homebody, live-in maid Caroline Fleming spends her time out of Harlem and wishing for Thursday, her day off. In the intervening days, she croons, "I long for my people," a passion shared by Myers (*ibid.*, 59).

See also **Here in Harlem: Poems in Many Voices, historical milieu, urbanism**

• *Further Reading*

Bader, Barbara. "Multiculturalism Takes Root," *Horn Book Magazine* 79, no. 2 (March/April 2003): 143–152.
Brown, Jennifer M. "Walter Dean Myers Unites Two Passions," *Publishers Weekly* 246, no. 2 (22 March 1999): 45–46.
Hudak, Melissa. "Review: *Harlem: A Poem*," *School Library Journal* 43, no. 2 (February 1997): 121.
Lewis, Johanna. "Review: The Beast," *School Library Journal* 49, no. 12 (December 2003): 157.
Myers, Walter Dean. *The Beast.* New York: Scholastic, 2003.
_____. *The Dream Bearer.* New York: Amistad, 2003
_____. *Fallen Angels.* New York: Scholastic, 1988.
_____. *The Great Migration: An American Story.* New York: HarperCollins, 1993.
_____. *Handbook for Boys: A Novel.* New York: Amistad, 2002.
_____. *Harlem: A Poem.* New York: Scholastic, 1997.
_____. *Here in Harlem: Poems in Many Voices.* New York: Holiday House, 2004.
_____. *Malcolm X: A Fire Burning Brightly.* New York: HarperCollins, 2004.
_____. *Malcolm X: By Any Means Necessary.* New York: Scholastic, 1993.
_____. *Monster: A Novel.* New York: HarperCollins, 1999.
_____. *145th Street: Short Stories.* New York: Delacorte, 2000.
Pierleoni, Allen O. "Wrongs and the Writer," *Sacramento Bee* (29 March 2005).
"Review: *The Dream Bearer*," *Kirkus Reviews* 71, no. 10 (15 May 2003): 754.
Sutherland, Zena. "Review: *Hoops: A Novel*," *Bulletin of the Center for Children's Books* 35, no. 4 (December 1981): 74.
Sutton, Roger. "Threads in Our Cultural Fabric," *School Library Journal* 40, no. 6 (June 1994): 24–28.

Harmon, Steve

In *Monster: A Novel* (1999), Myers analyzes Steve Harmon, the 16-year-old Harlemite and student at Stuyvesant High School at the time of his charge for aid-

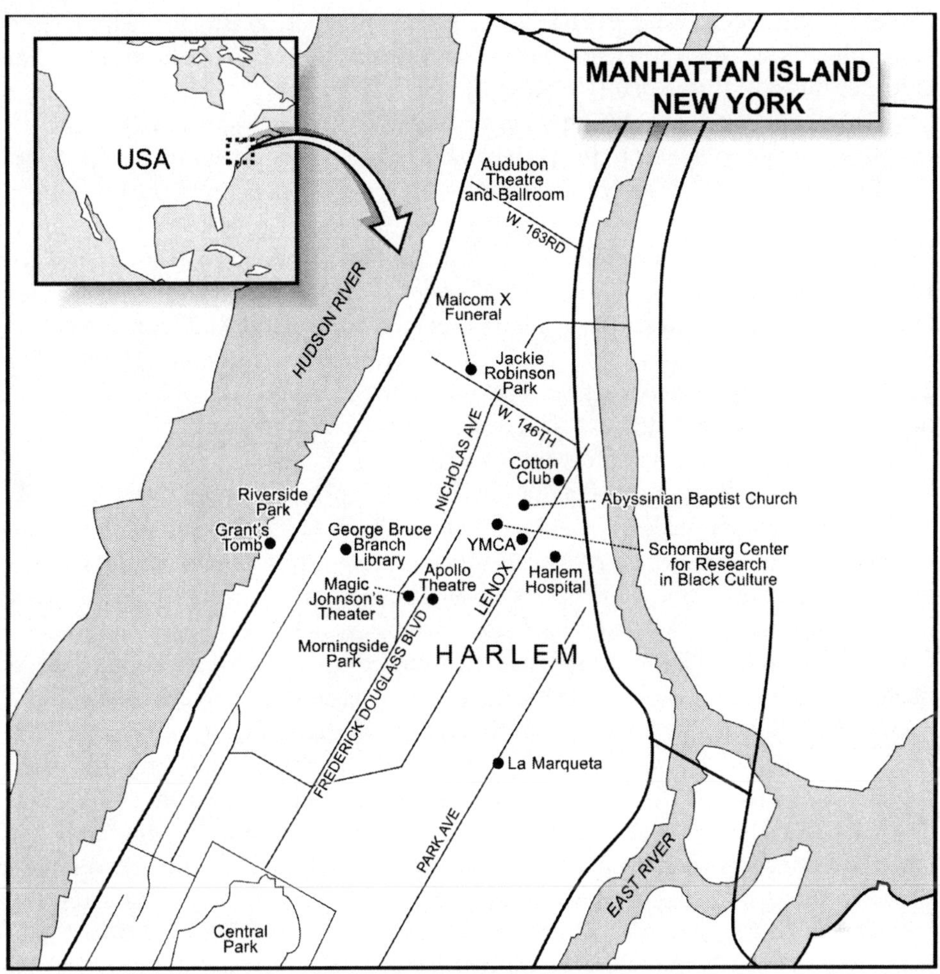

Walter Dean Myers honors Harlem as America's black capital.

ing Osvaldo Cruz, Richard "Bobo" Evans, and career criminal James King in felony robbery and murder of Alguinaldo Nesbitt on December 22. The assistant district attorney, Sandra Petrocelli, impresses on Steve the severity of his crime. In his notebook, he remarks, "I'll call it what the lady who is the prosecutor called me. Monster" (Myers, 1999, 5). The disquieting epithet serves Myers as a title that questions the demonizing of so young a child.

The distancing of Steve from actual stealing and shooting reprises the child endangerment in *It Ain't All for Nothin'* (1978), in which the criminal father forces 12-year-old Tippy to serve as lookout at a bank dropbox stickup. By pretending to write a screenplay on his incarceration and trial, Steve applies the observation methods taught in a school film workship by a mentor, George Sawicki. The metafictional approach depersonalizes a crime for which Steve may be guilty. When he writes in his journal, the lack of a fictional shield forces him to admit, "I can't write it enough times to make it look the way I feel. I *hate, hate, hate* this place!!" (*ibid.*, 46). Among cynical felons, Steve hears beatings in the night and voices crying for help. He gets some valuable advice: "Ain't no use putting the blanket over your head, man. You can't cut this out; this is reality" (*ibid.*, 8).

The turmoil of arrest and imprisonment places Steve in a shockingly cold environment, the type of threat to the young that Myers describes in his ode "Wolf Song" (2005). Steve's loss of identity forces him to stare at his reflection in the cell mirror. Myers implies pity for Steve's musings: "I see a face looking back at me but I don't recognize it. It doesn't look like me. I couldn't have changed that much in a few months" (*ibid.*, 1). He moves from cell to court in orange prison garb and shackles. He faces a possible death sentence, but the real terror is what critic Stephen Del Vecchio, a reviewer for *Teacher Magazine*, called "corrosive self-doubt" (Del Vecchio, 2000, 57). The experience costs Steve self-esteem and the respect of friends, neighbors, defense attorney Kathy O'Brien, Steve's younger brother Jerry, and their father, who ends his prison visit to Steve with sobs.

Myers dramatizes the effects of bullying and imprisonment of a young suspect among hardened criminals in Cell Block D at the Manhattan Detention Center. While mopping the corridors with a reeking disinfectant, Steve has time to ponder hanging out with street toughs and his efforts at a manly swagger. The narrative balances criminal elements in his life with a loving mother who leaves a bible with marked passages from the Psalms for Steve to read in his cell. Wracked with remorse, he subtly changes during his jailing and wonders about the example he sets for Jerry. Steve asserts, "I want to look like a good person. I want to feel like I'm a good person because I believe I am" (*ibid.*, 62). Myers words the statement with just enough ambiguity to create a psychological quandary in a character who is unsure of his own worth.

Critics agree that Myers deliberately puzzles the reader by casting doubt on Steve's complicity in the crime, for which the court exonerates him. He admits a common failing of teens— that his motive for hanging out with shady characters was self-esteem: "It was me, I thought as I tried not to throw up, that had wanted to be tough like them" (*ibid.*, 1300.) The difference between innocence and questionable friendship with criminals illustrates to the young that fraternization with lawbreakers forever incriminates Steve, even to himself. At a vulnerable pass in his life, an inconclusive court judgment forces Steve to re-establish his worth and dignity.

See also ***Monster: A Novel***

• *Further Reading*

Del Vecchio, Stephen. "Recommended for Kids," *Teacher Magazine* 11, no. 4 (January 2000): 57.

Myers, Walter Dean. *Monster: A Novel*. New York: HarperCollins, 1999.

Sullivan, Edward. "Review: *Monster: A Novel*," *School Library Journal* 45, no. 7 (July 1999): 98.

Here in Harlem: Poems in Many Voices

Although Walter Dean Myers certainly deserves his place among prose authors, his celebrity for young adult fiction and black biography and history overshadows his considerable aptitude for verse. Assuring his place among American poets is a picture-ode, *Harlem: A Poem* (1997), a brief preface at a virtuoso collection, *Here in Harlem: Poems in Many Voices* (2004). He remarked to Allen O. Pierleoni, an interviewer for the *Sacramento Bee*, on how clearly the poems took shape in his mind: "I remember the cab driver who seemed so tired one morning. It was because he had been a pallbearer the night before. 'I'm so tired of burying kids,' I remember him saying" (Pierleoni, 2005). An imitation of Edgar Lee Masters's format in *Spoon River Anthology* (1917), Myers's anthology of 54 poems glimpses Harlem in varied moods and modes. As an exuberant hymn to black belonging and cultural uniqueness, *Here in Harlem* inspired *Kirkus Review* to laud the anthology as a "Whitman-esque ode to time and the city" ("Review," 2004, 1092).

Myers dotted the text with candid black-and-white snapshots of the community and its people, including a cover photo of composer Duke Ellington and a head-and-shoulders portrait of singer Dorothy Dandridge. Like an over-eager child, the collection pushes ahead of the title page with the poem of English teacher George Ambrose, a fictional character whose name reprises that of Myers's birth father. The poet sets George's testimony on endpapers adorned with a 1929 map of ten blocks of upper Harlem, from West 136th Street to West 146th Street, stretching west beyond Seventh Avenue and East to the Harlem River. Myers toys with a variety of forerunners, tingeing the teacher's three stanzas with the stylized wording of the Song of Solomon and a sly dig at "Dixie," the musical credo of the racist South.

In the introduction, Myers states that the figures he depicts in verse are real Harlemites, citizens of his "sweet village" (Myers, 2004, viii). He juxtaposes heroes and celebrities among the ordinary folk "who sweat from day to day just to survive" (*ibid.*). A unifying device, the views of Clara Brown, breaks into six staves her personal disappointments and triumphs. She treasures the community as a metaphoric friend and absorbs its music as a gift to the soul. Her sassy self-regard arises in Part III, in which she shushes a meddler by "[telling] him to shut his fool self up on Easter Sunday" (*ibid.*, 37). In the next stave she scoffs at poverty with memories of a rented room "just about big enough to change your mind in" (*ibid.*, 53). Other female figures—a sultry passerby, a nurse at Harlem Hospital, the "private sun" of a grandmother in a rocking chair, and an exuberant Vassar College girl—extend Clara's presence with the array of feminine roles in Harlem (*ibid.*, 55).

The variances in human attainment envelope a stream of speakers in joy and despair. Hard-partying Helen Sweetland reflects on times when women wore taffeta and danced a pirouette of anticipation. Poet Ernest Scott patterns his verse after the "joyful noise" of authors James Baldwin and Richard Wright (*ibid.*, 58). Urban designer Jonathan Smalls exults in the landscape of "redbrick squares/Chipped with history" (*ibid.*, 48). With repetition and alliteration, college student Joshua de Grosse sinks so completely into neighborhood miseries that he can't escape to Homer's "wine-dark seas" (*ibid.*, 45). Terry Smith, a 24-year-old who is unemployed at Christmas time, hugs a fretful child and envisions the magi passing them by. Critic Nina Lindsay noted in a review for *School Library Journal* the collection's "multiplicity of times and peoples of Harlem," which she recommended as a source of individual recitation or choral reading (Lindsay, 2004, 166). *Kirkus Reviews* summed up

Myers's rhapsodic masterwork in few words: "Sure to be a classic" ("Review," 2004, 1092).

See also **Harlem**

• *Further Reading*

Lindsay, Nina. "Review: *Here in Harlem: Poems in Many Voices*," *School Library Journal* 50, no. 2 (Dec 2004): 166.

Myers, Walter Dean. *Here in Harlem: Poems in Many Voices.* New York: Holiday House, 2004.

Pierleoni, Allen O. "Wrongs and the Writer," *Sacramento Bee* (29 March 2005).

"Review: *Here in Harlem: Poems in Many Voices*," *Kirkus Reviews* 72, no. 22 (15 November 2004): 1092.

historical milieu

Myers receives critical attention for his skill at researching historical milieus, particularly the collapse of the rubber trade in a Quechuan village in *Ambush in the Amazon* (1986), the chronicling of the reign of Roderick, Spain's last Visigoth king in *Adventure in Granada* (1985), the uncertain future of eighth-century North Africa in *The Legend of Tarik* (1981), the displaced and out-of-work Vietnam vet Sweeby Jones in *Darnell Rock Reporting* (1994), and the Beale Street recording studios in Memphis, Tennessee, in *The Blues of Flats Brown* (2000). In 1994, critic Edna Reid stated in *African-American Voices in Young Adult Literature: Tradition, Transition, Transformation* that Myers is "recognized as one of modern young adult literature's premier authors of fiction about African-American experiences" (Smith, 1994, 383). Myers educates readers with little-known facts, such as the background of Nubians in Egypt in *Tales of a Dead King* (1983) and the role of the German child Nicholas in recapturing the Holy Lands from the Muslims in the teen mystery *The Nicholas Factor* (1983). At a stirring moment in the latter novel, Marlin Wilkes, founder and chairman of the Crusade Society, looks to leadership from "those who show us the way — the Gandhis, the Lincolns, the Bolivars, and the boy Nicholas," a ten-year-old German who led 20,000 marchers over the Alps on the Children's Crusade of 1212. (Myers, 1983, 45). In a later paragraph on prehistoric Peru, the narrative fosters suspense with the comment that "its secrets had been lost in the lush greenery of its jungles, and it was not until hundreds of years after whites had come that they discovered Machu Picchu" (*ibid.*, 54).

Influencing the author's fundamentals is Dr. Edward W. Robinson's belief in the value of history: "The masses of African-Americans suffer from partial *cultural* amnesia because of a certain deliberate program which wiped the slates of our memories clean of true African events prior to the cotton fields of America" (Robinson, 1987, 21). To capture a range of human achievement, Myers's allusions sweep a broad section of humanity reaching back to the biblical Exodus of Moses and the Hebrew children and to early African history of the Igbo, Kikuyu, and Songhai. In 1987, the author opened his fantasy-quest novel *Shadow of the Red Moon* with a summation of his regard for oral history. He describes the fictional Okalians as "[tracing] their history back to a time when stories were not written, but passed from generation to generation by word of mouth" (Myers, 1987, 1). In a salute to the contributions of storykeepers, he remarks: "It was the truth as they knew it to be, and the truth by which they would try to live" (*ibid.*). He attributes the Okalian ideal of greatness to their commitment to the past.

In an essay, "The Black Experience in Children's Books: One Step Forward, Two Steps Back," published in a 1979 issue of *Interracial Books for Children Bulletin*, Myers refuted claims by teachers and librarians "that the black experience need no longer be chronicled with truth and compassion" (Myers, 1979, 15). To spare future generations from floundering in ignorance, he forged a career writing fiction and nonfiction filled with honest glimpses of human scenes. His work portrays all races with equal respect, but he never stints on his pride in being African American, for example, the nostalgia of the blues harmonica player in "The Treasure of Lemon Brown" (1983) and the yearning for Harlem in an infantryman during the Vietnam War in *Fallen Angels* (1999). In *Now Is Your Time! The African-American Struggle for Freedom* (1991), Myers reminds readers that distancing themselves from their African roots is a serious neglect of their roots. He suggests, "If we listen closely to its rhythms, if we look at its art, we will find the echoes that link us with our heritage" (Myers, 1991, 272). Critic Randy Meyer, in a review for *Booklist*, praised the history for its "unifying theme of the constant struggle for freedom" (Meyer, 1991, 504). In commentary for the *Bulletin of the Center for Children's Books*, reviewer Betsy Hearne admires the writer's authorial voice for giving young readers "a personalized sense of the past" (Hearne, 1992, 134).

In *A Place Called Heartbreak: A Story of Vietnam* (1992), the young adult biography of Colonel Fred V. Cherry, Myers turns the story of America's first black prisoner of the Vietnam War into a commentary on national involvement. Over his seven-year, four-month incarceration at Hoa Lo and Cu Loc prisons, Cherry sustains himself and his American cellmates with news from home, including NASA's moon landing and the rise of heavyweight boxing champion Muhammad Ali. In Cherry's fifth year in Vietcong hands, he learns about the protest and shootings at Kent State and a demonstration at Jackson State College in Mississippi, where two black students died under fire from police machine guns. The tenor of the times for Americans produced ongoing clashes between those supporting and those opposing involvement in Southeast Asian combat. Significantly, Cherry thinks about a hero of the Civil War, Abraham Lincoln, on whose birthday the pilot returns to American-held territory.

One of Myers's successful collaborations, the picture book *The Great Migration: An American Story* (1993), co-authored by folk artist Jacob Lawrence, examines the peasant uprising of the World War I era that spurred field laborers from the agrarian South to urban industrialized centers in Chicago, Cleveland, Detroit, New York, and Pittsburgh. Against racist intimidation in segregated railway stations, wanderers grasped their tickets and meager belongings and moved north in hopes of broadening horizons and educational opportunities for the next generation of African Americans. In a fluid milieu, some realized their dreams while others confronted new forms of racism and suppression in crowded ghettoes. Out of this period of readjustment and acculturation to city ways came a unique black capital, Harlem, a vibrant impetus to American art, education, music, philosophy, religion, government, and sports. The political and economic context formed the backdrop of *Malcolm X: By Any Means Necessary* (1993) and earned the respect of critic Michele Landsberg, a reviewer for *Entertainment Weekly*, for explaining the spirit of the times that buoyed Malcolm to centrality in the downfall of segregation and the demand for civil rights.

A model of Myers's thorough research, *At Her Majesty's Request: An African Princess in Victorian England* (1999) tells the story of Sarah Forbes Bonetta, a Yoruban princess who grew up in England and Sierra Leone under the fostering of Queen Victoria. Myers supplied the text with a map of Africa noting the location of the slave-running Dahomian empire of King Gezo and added sketches and photos of Bonetta and her residences. Although there are great gaps in Bonetta's life story, Myers manages to outline a plausible biography, in part with details from Captain Frederick Edwyn Forbes's two-volume work *Dahomey and the Dahomans: Being the Journal of Two Missions to the King of Dahomey and Residence at His Capital in the Years 1849 and 1850* (1851). At the heart of Myers's description, Sarah faces limbo as a privileged black in London and as an anguished bartered bride who must marry a black man for whom she feels no love.

Myers, who in 1992 had displayed an interest in Buffalo Soldiers and black cowboys in *The Righteous Revenge of Artemis Bonner*, wrote for Scholastic Press a more realistic history, *My Name Is America: The Journal of Joshua Loper, a Black Cowboy on the Chisholm Trail, 1871* (1999). Covering from April 31 to September 1, 1871, the story of 16-year-old Joshua Loper opens in southern Texas at the beginning of a drive of 2,200 cattle due north to Abilene, Kansas. Geographic terms—Guadalupe River, devil's hole, Goliad, and the Goodnight Ranch—and trail dialect like jawboning, scrip money, and tailbone shock as well as information about gunfighter Wes Hardin, a game of monte, and the Pawnee lend authenticity to Myers's commentary. To stress Joshua's black upbringing, the author has him sing to the cattle a Negro spiritual, "O Mary, Don't You Weep." A poignant observation about black farm laborers reminds the reader that the end of slavery was not the end of misery: "They ain't got no money and no land and no learning.... What's free about that?" (Myers, 1999, 38). The author crafts a positive image of Buffalo Soldiers and other black wranglers who found jobs on the plains.

A second work in the "My Name Is America Series," *The Journal of Scott Pendleton Collins, a WWII Soldier, Normandy, France, 1944* (1999), covers the combat experience of the infantryman from May 25 to August 1944, the harrowing winding down of World War II. In the estimation of critic Randy Meyer, the author "captures nicely the shift from the fraternity and the boredom of life on the base to the terror and confusion of D-Day" (Meyer, 1999, 1830). As he did in previous histories, Myers salts the text with military terms—M-1, K rations, LCVP, noncom, strafe, half-track, mortar round, DUKWs, panzers, bangalore torpedo, 2300 hours, AWOL—and war slang like pillbox for artillery emplacement, Bouncing Betty land mines, and Kraut and Jerry for Germans. Aboard the troop transport *Thomas Jefferson*, the 17-year-old approaches Omaha Beach, which is destined to be the hottest landing zone of the European theater of operations. In the aftermath, he survives and joins a company that has to reform because of a high casualty rate. By selecting Collins's perspective on combat, Myers furthered his pet theme, the effect of dilemmas and adult decision making on a young man at the threshold of adulthood.

In 2001, Myers recouped sports history of the Birmingham Black Barons in *My Name Is America: The Journal of Biddy Owens: The Negro Leagues*, his third addition to Scholastic's "My Name Is America" series. In diary style, he opens on the involvement of the equipment manager, 17-year-old Biddy Owens, in road travel on May 1, 1948, and concludes the following October 3. Critic Shawn Brommer refers to the period's reputation for "institutional racism and blatant bigotry" for its Jim Crow treatment of blacks at hotels and diners (Brommer, 2001, 146). Among historical figures in the text are owner Tom Hayes, manager and second baseman Lorenzo "Piper" Davis, pitcher Bill Greason, catchers Herman Bell and Lloyd "Pepper" Bassett, right fielder Ed Steele, and infielder Wiley Griggs. Biddy mentions players for the Cleveland Buckeys, notably, center fielder Sam Jethroe, the first Negro League member to advance to a Boston National League team.

For his histories, Myers stresses minutia that flesh out the period and settings. Contributing to the daily realities in *The Journal of Biddy Owens: The Negro Leagues* are a Chicago pool hustler in a zoot suit and a round of tonk, a fast-paced card game like blackjack based on the value of the five cards dealt to each player. The ideal number is 15. Myers adds the racial realities of the day in Ku Klux Klan signs in Indianapolis, memories of pre–Civil War patty rollers (patrollers), and diners that serve German prisoners of World War II but not their black American guards. He also mentions Truman's integration of the American military and Jim Crow laws as evidence that racial politics affected the lives of youngsters like Biddy.

At age 67, Myers departed from his more familiar literary modes to write a young adult reference book. He compiled a series of explorers' biographies for *Antarctica: Journeys to the South Pole* (2004), which he developed from research at the Royal Geographical Society. To pique reader interest, the author incorporates historic photos and maps, first-person journal entries, and sidebars on seals, magnetic poles, and the causes of scurvy. Back matter includes data about Antarctica and a timeline of expeditions from 1773 to 1959.

Among Myers's young adult history books, his *U.S.S. Constellation: Pride of the American Navy* (2004) stands out for its pride in patriotism. The composition features words like "majestic," "valiant," and "exploits" to describe an emblem of naval service that was the nation's last all-sail vessel. Beginning with the stirring call to war implied by the Declaration of Independence, the biography of a ship describes its construction in Baltimore as part of a six-frigate fleet. Myers enlivens the action with commentary on attacks on the Barbary Coast of North Africa. The narrative reaches its peak of excitement in chapter 3, which describes intervention in the slave trade. Subsequent reportage on an integrated crew during the Civil War establishes for young readers that interracial cooperation increased the efficiency of the U.S. Navy before the emancipation of slaves. In his summation, Myers notes that photographs like the one taken in 1863 attested to the military service of black sailors. Another valuable bit of ephemera are the discharge papers of Thomas Bush, who mustered out of service on August 25, 1865.

In the same year, Myers published *Here in Harlem: Poems in Many Voices* (2004), a lifetime's love song to his motherland. Navigating familiar settings—the Apollo Theater, Cotton Club, Striver's Row, 125th Street and Lenox Avenue, and the Harlem Hospital—his lyric verses salute a stream of historic people and events. Manifesting Carl Jung's concept of the subconscious as a memory bank of past histories, Myers's city-bred folk exhibit the verbal and physical idiosyncrasies of Africa, the Khoisan's click-tongued language, Congo choreography, Masai gazes, and "leap genes and Songhai anthems" that black ancestors brought with them over the Middle Passage (Myers, 2004, 85). In the poet's hands, the past mellows out into flashes of blackness bred in the bone and destined to invigorate Harlemites for generations to come.

See also **Sarah Forbes Bonetta, Harlem, Martin Luther King, Jr., Malcolm X, Muhammad Ali, *Now Is Our Time!***

• *Further Reading*

Bosse, Malcolm. "Review: *The Legend of Tarik,*" *New York Times Book Review* (12 July 1981): 30.

Brommer, Shawn. "Review: *The Journal of Biddy Owens: The Negro Leagues,*" *School Library Journal* 47, no. 4 (April 2001): 146.

Hearne, Betsy. "Review: *Now Is Your Time! The African-American Struggle for Freedom,*" *Bulletin of the Center for Children's Books* 45 (January 1992): 134.

Landsberg, Michele. "Review: *Malcolm X: By Any Means Necessary,*" *Entertainment Weekly* no. 156 (5 February 1993): 63.

Meyer, Randy. "Review: *The Journal of Scott Pendleton Collins, a WWII Soldier, Normandy, France, 1944,*" *Booklist* 95 (1 June 1999): 1830.

____. "Review: *Now Is Your Time! The African-American Struggle for Freedom,*" *Booklist* 88 (1 November 1991): 504.

Myers, Walter Dean. *Antarctica: Journeys to the South Pole.* New York: Scholastic, 2004.

____. "The Black Experience in Children's Books: One Step Forward, Two Steps Back," *Interracial Books for Children Bulletin* 10, no. 6 (1979): 14–15.

____. *Here in Harlem: Poems in Many Voices.* New York: Holiday House, 2004.

____. *My Name Is America: The Journal of Joshua Loper, a Black Cowboy, The Chisholm Trail,* 1871. New York: Scholastic, 1999.

____. *The Nicholas Factor.* New York: Viking, 1983.

____. *Now Is Your Time! The African-American Struggle for Freedom.* New York: HarperCollins, 1991.

____. *Shadow of the Red Moon.* New York: Harper Collins, 1987.

____. *U.S.S. Constellation: Pride of the American Navy.* New York: Holiday House, 2004.

Phelan, Carolyn. "Review: *The Journal of Biddy Owens: The Negro Leagues,*" *Booklist* 97, no 12 (15 February 2001): 1149.

Price, Michael H. "A New Look at That Old Chisholm Trail," *Fort Worth Business Press* 17, no. 51 (17 December 2004): 28.

Renner, Coop. "Review: *The Journal of Joshua Loper, a Black Cowboy on the Chisholm Trail, 1871,*" *School Library Journal* 45, no. 7 (July 1999): 98.

Robinson, Edward W., et al. *The Journey of the Songhai People.* Philadelphia: Pan African federation, 1987.

Hoops

One of Myers's early ventures into teen sports fiction, *Hoops: A Novel* (1981) compares ethical issues from two perspectives, one adult and one youth. Home tension between 17-year-old Lonnie Jackson and his parents grows naturally from his evolving maturity and autonomy. In a familiar motif, he escapes to the gym to clutch a basketball, a tactile symbol of a competitive sport that gives his life meaning and promise. His confrontations with a volunteer coach, Calvin F. "Spider" Jones, result in angry explosions and an unintentional injury to Lonnie's hand from a .32 pistol. For its gritty, well-plotted action, E. L. Welschedel, a reviewer for *School Library Journal*, declared the novel an improvement on run-of-the-mill sports fiction.

As is true of many of Myers's works, sports and immaturity are lesser themes clustered around questions of coming of age. At one point, Lonnie interprets his adversarial relationship with Cal as "a manhood thing," a suggestion of challenge from the younger generation to their elders (Myers, 1981, 40). Cal conducts his subtle mentoring by alerting Lonnie to the dangers of life on the streets. As older teenagers turn into adults, he warns, "Things you were dreaming about start to curl up and die" (*ibid.*, 42). The fact that Cal speaks from experience ennobles him as a man willing to turn a failed career and wrecked marriage into lessons for the next cadre of sports stars.

To exploit suspense, Myers adopts the conventions of detective fiction by featuring Lonnie's notice of ready money in the hands of his friend Paul. Paul's sister Mary-Ann surmises that her brother needs cash "to keep up with those la-di-das from uptown" (*ibid.*, 67). The addition of an intrusion into Tyrone Giddins's office darkens the tone by depicting Lonnie and Mary-Ann committing a break-in to uncover criminal links between Paul and Tyrone. The couple's snooping reveals Tyrone's cashing of welfare checks, loan sharking, and bribery of a police officer, three examples of common urban felonies. Myers returns to teen concerns by examining Paul's avoidance of his father's job as an office flunky by elevating himself among pretentious people, an advancement based on the flashing of cash to superficial girlfriends. The story develops pathos for Paul, who is naively stealing checks for $15 each and passing them to Tyrone, who cashes them for the full amount. Myers emphasizes the deception to illustrate how unscrupulous adults lure youths into crime that endangers minors without implicating their adult manipulators.

The narrative returns to sports in the last quarter to situate Lonnie in competitive play at the city Tournament of Champions. The familiar milieu of practicing and playing other teams to earn scholarships seems petty compared to the financial stake of promoters like O'Donnel, a white racketeer who occupies a swank office on Madison Avenue. A break-in at the team office and the killing of Ox's parakeet Sparrow are hints at the treachery of outside forces betting on the tournament's outcome. Myers builds suspense as Cal insists that the team trust him. After convincing Tyrone that the game is a sure loss, Cal defies the conspirators who intend to profit from their bets. By paralleling Lonnie's victory with Cal's murder, Myers impresses on young readers that the ramifications of their behaviors range far beyond the scoreboard. The author furthers the themes and motifs of *Hoops* in a sequel, *The Outside Shot* (1984), which follows Lonnie's career in college sports.

See also **athletics, *The Outside Shot***

• *Further Reading*

Gill, Sam D. "Young Adult Literature for Young Adult Males," *ALAN Review* 26, no. 2 (winter 1999): 1.
Myers, Walter Dean. *Hoops.* New York: Delacorte, 1981.
Sutherland, Zena. "Review: *Hoops: A Novel,*" *Bulletin of the Center for Children's Books* 35, no. 4 (December 1981): 74.
Welschedel, E.1. Review: *Hoops: A Novel,*" *School Library Journal* 28 (December 1981): 86.
Zvirin, Stephanie. "Review: *Hoops: A Novel,*" *Booklist* 78, no. 2 (15 September 1981): 98.

humor

To assure readers a multi-dimensional account of human life, Myers creates spirited, upbeat characters who live much as he did in childhood. The street argot of friends and neighbors in *Fast Sam, Cool Clyde, and Stuff* (1975) and *Won't Know Till I Get There* (1982) activates and freshens dialogue. The first novel percolates with comedy as Clyde and Stuff list and rule out potential dates to pair with for a dance contest. Critic Donald J. Bissett, in a review for *Language Arts*, pegs the author's witty repartee as "clever, contemporary humor," especially for its incongruous blend of romance with religion (Bissett, 1976, 521). Blondell, a worthy dancer, is sidelined because of her mother's off-and-on religiosity. Stuff mutters, "I don't see how she keeps her dancing up what with being saved half the time" (Myers, 1975, 44). The cynicism about evangelistic faith emerges from a child who has already lost respect for religion based on the waxing and waning of fervor.

Myers's versatility takes wings in unlike settings and character situations. In the zany farce *Mojo and the Russians* (1977), the author wrings belly laughs from readers over a group of kids trying to escape a voodoo curse cast by Drusilla the mojo lady. In the opinion of critic Denise M. Wilms, a critic for *Booklist*, the story thrives on "snappy dialogue and the essential warmth between these friends" (Wilms, 1977, 379). A more serious form of humor is the death joke in *It Ain't All for Nothin'* (1978). Lonnie, a career criminal, tells his 12-year-old son Tippy about an execution. The punch line reminds a condemned man not to "sit down on the job" (Myers, 1978, 142). The inappropriate choice of humor for so young a listener magnifies a relationship between the ex-con and a boy who prefers living with his religious, right-living grandmother, Carrie Brown.

The author paces low-key humor throughout *Won't Know Till I Get There* (1982), a teenager's view of petty vandalism. In Steve Perry's first day in court, he encounters a street crook who rationalizes an "accidental" snatching of a woman's purse. In the thief's telling, "I must have hooked it when I ran by her, only by this time I'm around the corner and I don't know where it came from" (Myers, 1982, 24). Steve and the lawbreaker face a judge dubbed "Stick-'Em-In Jim" for his stern sentences to delinquents. When Steve examines his mother's face for obvious emotion, he spots her "Joan of Arc look ... like she doesn't care how hot the fire is, she can take it" (*ibid.*, 83). With similar quips, Myers lightens the ominous exposition of *Tales of a Dead King* (1983), which he sets at an archeological dig in Aswan, Egypt. Upon the arrival of protagonist John Robie to the site, he takes a room in a dowdy hotel. As a put-down, he mutters, "It looked like a place where they would give you a bowl of soup and a New Testament in the morning" (Myers, 1983, 7). The interspersing of realism with wisecracks allows Myers to stress prudence without sounding like a scold.

In a separate strand of Myers's writing, animal fable expresses a jovial humor mixed with hints of danger. For storybook fables *Mr. Monkey and the Gotcha Bird* (1984) and *How Mr. Monkey Saw the Whole World* (1996), the author allies with artists Leslie Morrill and Synthia Saint James to establish the fine line between everyday interaction in the natural world with examples of hectoring and victimization. Brightening the pages are pictures of the chirpy, offbeat humor of Mr. Monkey as well as the humiliation of Mr. Turtle standing naked and vulnerable without his shell. After unleashing Mr. Lion on the Gotcha Bird, Mr. Monkey retrieves his dignity and flaunts his exploitive self from a high-growing vine well out of the way of feline teeth. With an unsubtle dig at Mr. Lion, the hapless tool of the fable, Mr. Monkey chortles, "Next time you make supper and Monkey eat" (Myers, 1984, n.p.). Reflecting the cheery tone of Joel Chandler Harris's Uncle Remus tales, Myers's fable models the appeal and purpose of a genre that has instructed young readers from prehistory.

The balance of realism with jokes produces a relaxed pacing in Myers's young adult fiction. The early teen immersion in puns sustains a breezy atmosphere in the suspenseful novellas *The Hidden Shrine* (1985) and *Ambush in the Amazon* (1986), in which the Arrow brothers spar through situational comedy and witty put-downs. The favorites of 14-year-old Ken Arrow are tension cutters like a quip about piranhas being "fishy," the joke that concludes the Peruvian adventure (Myers, 1986, 83). The tension between a professional career and church teachings in *Crystal* (1987) creates questions in the mind of the title character, but Myers also uses fundamentalism as a source of humor. While 16-year-old model Crystal Brown styles the hair of Sister Gibbs, the 77-year-old woman joshes and gossips about "Sunday School Christians" (Myers, 1987, 29). Sister Gibbs punctuates her character assassinations with piety, "I'm telling you what the Lord loves and that's the truth!" (*ibid.*). At the completion of the beauty session, she chuckles over the incongruity of sex appeal in aged women: "How would it look? Me, a Christian woman, going around breaking these old men's hearts?" (*ibid.*, 30). Her light-heartedness shields Crystal during difficult moments, when Crystal longs for guidance on matters of chastity and self-esteem while choosing the right direction for her professional career. Myers's skillful banter illustrates that a light touch penetrates the age barrier to admit glimmers of sage advice.

Myers is adept at the exuberant peasant folklore that brought fame to Zora Neale Hurston. In *Darnell Rock Reporting* (1994), a barber named Preacher polishes off a serious newspaper interview on homelessness by telling a joke about a tenant farmer in Waycross, Georgia, and his mule. By convincing the angel of death that woeful complaints come from the mule, the farmer watches as the animal falls down. Relieved at evading the brush with sudden death, the farmer smiles at having to plow by himself. Critic Janice Del Negro, a reviewer for *Booklist*, lauded the storytelling scene as "a masterpiece of understatement" (Del Negro, 1994, 2044).

Myers maintains a reputation for the funny set-tos common to sibling rivalry. In a home incident in *Slam!* (1996), he depicts 17-year-old Greg "Slam" Harris's exasperation with his nine-year-old brother Derek, a cutup who "got more mouth than he got backup" (Myers, 1996, 4). In *The Young Landlords* (1979), the opening chapter employs a comedic example of misjudgment to describe a confrontation with a school bully. Taking advice about bullies being cowards under their bluster, 13-year-old Paul Williams faces off against James Hall. In a droll admission of miscalculation, Paul declares, "When he hit me the second and third times I was *sure* it was wrong" (Myers, 1979, 4). With Paul's remarks, the author eases some of the tension from a schoolyard motif all too familiar to undersized and vulnerable kids.

The author extracts universal comedy out of a parent-teen confrontation in *Hoops: A Novel* (1981). After 17-year-old Lonnie Jackson lands a job as factotum at the Grant Hotel, he sleeps in a vacant room. His mother echoes the standard sermon about his absence from her control, a familiar mother-son argument as young men ease into adulthood. He waits out the text of the usual chastisement as she heaps guilt on him for neglecting her "old gray head" (Myers, 1981, 85). He pours himself a rum and Coke until she reaches the end of her usual spiel. It concludes with his silent "Amen" and a hasty kiss before he departs once more to do as he pleases (*ibid.*). A subsequent exchange with Ox, a fellow ball player, about whether Superman really flies or just jumps over buildings serves as comic relief to Lonnie's concern about retaining Cal Jones as coach. The expanse of maturity that separates Ox from Lonnie illustrates how far Lonnie's character has developed in a matter of weeks.

Fictional situations among youth stress school, sports, and the temptations of sex, gangs, and street crime, the elements that empower *Scorpions* (1988). Through dialogue, the author eases anxiety in the Hicks home with running verbal zingers flung between 12-year-old Jamal and his eight-year-old sister. Their foolery is harmless sibling rivalry tinged with the venom of a tattletale little sister who envies her brother's freedom. Casual pranks get out of hand in *Fallen Angels* (1988), an historical novel about the Vietnam War in which rookie infantrymen embrace sportive jest as a release of tension. On the flight from Anchorage, Alaska, to Asia, a captain warns anti-hero Richard "Richie" Perry about venereal diseases "that'll rot your twinkie off" (Myers, 1988, 5). A black soldier's commentary on the level of action he has seen nets a positive response from jittery rookies. The soldier recalls that there was "more fighting in a juke joint outside of Fort Eustis" than he had seen in Vietnam (*ibid.*, 18).

In a combat story resonating with tragedy, Myers concentrates levity within the witty perceptions of one soldier. Perry's hoochmate, Harry "Peewee" Gates, contributes to the badinage with teasing of Jenkins, a new arrival. Gates invents an early rotation quota — a kill rate equal to the weight of the soldier. He claims to need eight more dead Viet Cong before he is eligible to go back to Chicago. In his theory of the best inductees, he thinks the army should hire criminals from the project to do the killing, "'cause that's all they like to do, anyway" (*ibid.*, 24). When a television crew interviews the men of Alpha Company of the 22nd Replacement Company, all give a somber reason for the war except Gates. To the question of why he came to Vietnam, he quips that he got off at the wrong stop: "I thought this was St. Louis!" (*ibid.*, 77). More than entertainment, his agile retorts evidence the centrality of a sense of humor to wartime survivalism.

To characterize the absurdities of war, Myers turns to whimsy. In the midst of constant violation of normal life, Alpha Company aids a civilian pacification team in showing Walt Disney movies at a nearby hamlet. The image of the team dressed in flak jackets while spreading American-style fun among local children illustrates the anomalies of a war zone. Monaco breaches the limits of humor at a tense time by terrorizing his hooch mates by pulling a pin from a grenade. After they learn that the weapon is a dummy, they direct their anger at the perpetrator of a childish stunt that mimics the life-and-death drama of patrols in hostile territory.

The author tones down realism in his children's books by layering terror with incongruity. In the tale of runaway dogs Flats and Caleb in *The Blues of Flats Brown* (2000), the narrative dramatizes the difficulties of the homeless who survive as street minstrels. When life improves for the duo after they record their songs to guitar and bones accompaniment, rumors spread that Flats has six fingers on each paw and a runaway wife in Mexico, a swipe at the frivolous gossip that accompanies musical celebrity. In the resolution, Myers returns their cruel owner to their lives. In a comically overstated confrontation, "Old A. J. Grubbs, bad breath and all, showed up at the recording studio sweating and acting ugly" (Myers, 2000, n.p.). The leveling of an ogre with jabs at his hygiene and conduct reduces the threat revealed in the opening pages, where Grubbs pits his animals in fiercely competitive matchups promoted for perverse entertainment of the dogs' owners.

Myers engineers contrast in characters through the sophisticated management of humor. He sprinkles *A Time to Love: Stories from the Old Testament* (2003) with glimmers of humanity that stress affection and merriment. In Delilah's first meeting with Samson, she teases him for blocking the sun with his muscular bulk. The remark causes him to emit a "laugh that filled the space around him," a quality that is both engaging and erotic to the 15-year-old Philistine (Myers, 2003, 2). A less fulfilling humor marks the life of Lot's wife, the mother of Saaria and Zillah. The latter daughter yearns for instrumental music and dancing in her life as much as she welcomes sunshine. Myers censures the jocularity outside Lot's home from depraved citizens of Sodom, who threaten Lot's peace with calls to join the city's lewd horseplay. That same year, Myers completed *The Dream Bearer* (2003), which contrasts the joviality of Sessi, a Kikuyu newcomer from Kenya, with street-wise American neighbors. To her, Loren Hart's little moron joke about throwing a clock out the window to see time fly means nothing. These gradations of humor reveal the susceptibility of characters to lightheartedness and to darker forms of pleasure.

Myers's artistry at matching character with humor is a basis of his appeal. Nuance and wit enhance the perceptions of first-person speakers in *Here in Harlem: Poems in Many Voices* (2004), his critically acclaimed verse anthology. Pairing a photo with the poem "Eleanor Hayden, 51," he wrests wry comedy out of the structured confrontation between a testy white woman and her tardy maid. In private, Eleanor chortles at the persnickety white mother of little Tiffany, whom Eleanor escorts to the Apollo Theater without the mother's knowledge. More satiric is "Delia Pierce, 32," a lengthy monologue spoken by a busybody who borders on cruelty for denigrating reputations, most of them female. By disclosing the capers that amuse Eleanor and the invective that dominates Delia's gossip, the poems unfold into psychological character assessments.

See also **irony, *The Mouse Rap***

• *Further Reading*

Bissett, Donald J. "Review: *Fast Sam, Cool Clyde, and Stuff*," *Language Arts* 53, no. 5 (May 1976): 520–521.
Del Negro, Janice. "Review: *Darnell Rock Reporting*," *Booklist* 90, no. 22 (August 1994): 2044.
Myers, Walter Dean. *Ambush in the Amazon*. New York: Viking Kestrel, 1986.
_____. *The Blues of Flats Brown*. New York: Holiday House, 2000.
_____. *Crystal*. New York: Viking Kestrel, 1987.
_____. *Darnell Rock Reporting*. New York: Delacorte, 1994.
_____. *Fallen Angels*. New York: Scholastic, 1988.
_____. *Fast Sam, Cool Clyde, and Stuff*. New York: Viking, 1975.
_____. *Here in Harlem: Poems in Many Voices*. New York: Holiday House, 2004.
_____. *Hoops*. New York: Delacorte, 1981.
_____. *It Ain't All for Nothin'*. New York: Viking, 1978.
_____. *Mr. Monkey and the Gotcha Bird*. New York: Delacorte, 1984.
_____. *Slam!* New York: Scholastic, 1996.
_____. *Tales of a Dead King*. New York: Morrow, 1983.
_____. *A Time to Love: Stories from the Old Testament*. New York: Scholastic, 2003.
_____. *Won't Know Till I Get There*. New York: Viking, 1982.
_____. *The Young Landlords*. New York: Viking, 1979.
Unsworth, Robert E. "Review: *Scorpions*," *School Library Journal* 35, no. 1 (September 1988): 201.
Wilms, Denise M. "Review: *Mojo and the Russians*," *Booklist* 74, no. 4 (15 October 1977): 379.

immaturity

The rate at which youths ready for adulthood influences much of Myers's writing, including the vulnerability of children in the ode "Wolf Song" (2005) and the passive criminal behavior of Steve Harmon, an alleged lookout at a robbery and shooting in *Monster: A Novel* (1999), and of Cameron Porter and Carla Evans, two teen accomplices to Len Gray's vandalism, terrorism, murder, and suicide in *Shooter* (2004). In an early glimpse of Myers's genius, he portrays the fear of death and homelessness in the nine-year-old orphan Stevie in "Gums," anthologized in *We Be Word Sorcerers: Twenty-five Stories by Black Americans* (1973). In the 1994 Margaret A. Edwards Award Acceptance Speech," which he delivered at the American Library Association annual convention in Miami, he listed the young victims of the past whom adults could not or would not spare—child laborers in the antebellum plantation system, young miners photographed by Lewis Hines, underaged migrant workers, and Japanese-Americans interned during World War II. Myers's sympathies for the indigent on Indian reservations and in New York slums scoped out to all children needing "to be brought into the light of recognition so that we can no longer avoid looking at their suffering" (Myers, 1995, 130).

A brief view of a chastened 14-year-old, Greg Ridley, follows an encounter with a grieving father in "The Treasure of Lemon Brown" (1983). The story, published in *Boys' Life*, reveals the treasure taped to Lemon's ankle—a battered harmonica and newspaper clippings about his music career that his son Jesse carried into combat in World War II. The father's advice to Greg helps the boy over a rough spot with his father, who scolds Greg for failing math. In *Sweet Illusions* (1986), a sequence of open-ended scenes pictures pregnant teens and the fathers of their unborn children as they ponder answers to difficult problems. In one episode, Ronald Turner blames the media for selling sex to youths too young to accept the consequences. He asserts, "It ain't just them, it's the whole damn system" (Myers, 1986, 83). In a more realistic view, Esther Greene, mother of Sandra Greene, puts the blame on immaturity. She concludes, "You can lay down for one minute of sex, a half minute, but a child is here forever" (*ibid.*, 64). The complaint exhibits one of Myers's pervasive themes, that young people respond to stimuli that overcharge their inexperienced moral foundations.

Facing the same temptations is 16-year-old model Crystal Brown in *Crystal* (1987), a story of difficult choices when intimacy with talent handlers seems a normal part of celebrity. She perceives the danger to the psyche after a colleague, 18-year-old Rowena, commits suicide rather than continue living the glamour and sleaze that accompany a fashion model's stardom. In the words of Zena Sutherland, a reviewer for *Bulletin of the Center for Children's Books*, Crystal "knows she's missing a social life that's normal in adolescence" (Sutherland, 1987, 175). The visceral "knowing" guides Crystal back to the formative classes and dating that will prepare her for adulthood.

Myers's canon features the shaping of conscience in varied studies of teen conduct. He sharpens his focus on right thinking in *Now Is Your Time! The African-American Struggle for Freedom* (1991) and *U.S.S. Constellation: Pride of the American Navy* (2004), two glimpses of demands on young blacks at precipitate moments in American history. In the fantasy-quest allegory *Shadow of the Red Moon* (1987), the author discloses his belief that the young will rescue their elders from catastrophe. The father of Jon, the 15-year-old hero, honors children as "the ones who must carry our dreams" (Myers, 1987, 7). An elder corroborates the consensus that the doomed nation's only hope is through intervention of the young, who "can save that precious ideal of what it means to be an Okalian" (*ibid.*, 9). The patriot's remark echoes other instances in Myers's writings in which he extols young characters for their willingness to raise human moral standards.

In frequent interviews, guest appearances, and speeches, the author remarks on the adult world's responsibility to protect the unwary from terrors they little suspect, the crux of *It Ain't All for Nothin'* (1978) and of *Monster: A Novel* (1999). His works charge grownups with an obligation to support the innocent as they develop from naivete to adulthood. The vulnerabilities of the idealist undergird the theme of the seriocomic novel *Darnell Rock Reporting* (1994). In the analysis of Janice Del Negro, a veteran reviewer, adult encouragement from a librarian, teachers, the media, and parents boosts Darnell from do-nothing student to local celebrity. She remarks, "We watch as Darnell takes his first tentative steps toward thinking and acting on his own" (Del Negro, "Review: *Darnell*," 2044). *Publishers Weekly* describes the work as "an optimistic — and realistic — portrayal of a boy learning to live by his convictions" ("Review: *Darnell*," 1994, 65).

Myers's interest in the wide-eyed observations of teens marks much of his nonfiction, notably, *A Time to Love: Stories from the Old Testament* (2003), a collection of six vignettes focusing on immature protagonists. The choice of 15-year-old Delilah, the young widow Ruth, Jacob's son Reuben, Lot's daughter Zillah, and Abraham's son Isaac to tell family stories illustrates the immediacy of dilemmas that are unfamiliar and frightening. To Zillah, her father's decision to toss her to a threatening mob presents from the female view a patriarch who devalues women. The most pathetic story in the collection, "Aser and Gamiel," dramatizes the efforts of a young Hebrew and his Egyptian friend to pay homage to God without violating family loyalties. Because Gamiel opts not to dishonor his father, the boy dies in the horrific passage of the angel of death over Egypt, which leaves unprotected firstborns dead and dying and terrifies their mothers into heart-rending wails. The tableau attests to the results of decisions bearing far more weight than youth are able to gauge.

Myers approaches inexperience through a variety of episodes and human interactions. In *Hoops: A Novel* (1981), he pictures a fault in the character growth of 17-year-old sports ace Lonnie Jackson during a crucial test, play in the citywide Tournament of Champions. Because of his father's abandonment of the family, Lonnie retreats from relationships with peers and adults. In the opinion of critic Stephanie Zvirin, a reviewer for *Booklist*, the boy is "skeptical of authority and afraid of emotional commitments" (Zvirin, 1981, 98). The hesitance to accept the sexual invitation of Mary-Ann and the coach-player camaraderie offered by Calvin F. "Spider" Jones reveals in Lonnie a missing element of manhood that locks him into past behaviors and outlooks. In a critique for *Voice of Youth Advocates*, reviewer Patricia Berry considers the appealing trust and loyalty between Cal and Lonnie "the best part of the book" (Berry, 1982, 36).

In *Scorpions* (1988), Myers pictures a surfeit of power in the hands of a child. Tragedy results from the attempts of two 12-year-olds to solve the problem of ridding Jamal Hicks of a pistol. The weapon, shoved into his hands by 16-year-old Mack as a token of advancement to gang leadership, poses an approach-avoidance quandary. Jamal, an undersized seventh-grader, discovers instant power from securing the pistol in his belt and allowing rumors to spread that he is armed and dangerous. Myers crafts the loss of innocence into a major injustice after Tito Cruz shoots two members of the Scorpions for pummeling Jamal. Although Jamal survives the police investigation, Tito is too young, too vulnerable to bear the emotional damage. In the final scene, Myers pictures the two boys parting forever after authorities send Tito and his grandmother back to Puerto Rico. Unlike the Greek myths of Phaeton and Icarus, the punishment for Jamal's breach of his safety zone falls on his friends, causing him to suffer remorse rather than a physical threat from a shooting or arrest.

The depiction of protagonist Greg "Slam" Harris, the 17-year-old basketball player in *Slam!* (1996), pictures an older male at a difficult pass, the last months of youth that precede manhood. In the words of critic Janice Del Negro, a reviewer for the *Bulletin of the Center for Children's Books*, Myers creates immediacy in the characterization of a "streetwise, life-naïve" boy (Del Negro, "Review: *Slam*," 216). Glib at wielding the latest slang, Slam hones an athletic frame to the court action of basketball. On the down side, his dealings with school assignments and coping with his grandmother's failing health require more adult responses than are forthcoming. The challenge of character growth creates an approach-avoidance dilemma—

how to extend the soaring joy of sinking baskets into the daily hassles of algebra class and visits to his grandmother's hospital room. The realism of lingo and life choices appeals to young readers, the audience whom Myers intends to shepherd toward maturity.

See also ***Bad Boy*****, betrayal, coming of age, education,** ***Fallen Angels***

• *Further Reading*

Berry, Patricia. "Review: *Hoops: A Novel*," *Voice of Youth Advocates* 5, no. 1 (April 1982): 36.

Del Negro, Janice. "Review: *Darnell Rock Reporting*," Booklist 90, no. 22 (August 1994): 2044.

_____. "Review: *Slam!*," *Bulletin of the Center for Children's Books* 50 (February 1997): 216.

Myers, Walter Dean. "1994 Margaret A. Edwards Award Acceptance Speech," *Youth Services in Libraries* 8, no. 2 (winter 1995): 129–133.

_____. *Shadow of the Red Moon*. New York: Harper Collins, 1987.

_____. *Sweet Illusions*. New York: Teachers and Writers Collaborative, 1986.

"Review: *Darnell Rock Reporting*," *Publishers Weekly* 241, no. 27 (4 July 1994): 65.

"Review: *A Time to Love: Stories from the Old Testament*," *Publishers Weekly* 250, no. 13 (31 March 2003): 64.

Smith, Karen Patricia, ed. *African-American Voices in Young Adult Literature: Tradition, Transition, Transformation*. Lanham, Md.: Scarecrow, 1994.

Sutherland, Zena. "Review: *Crystal*," *Bulletin of the Center for Children's Books* 40 (May 1987): 175.

Unsworth, Robert E. "Review: *Scorpions*," *School Library Journal* 35, no. 1 (September 1988): 201.

Zvirin, Stephanie. "Review: *Hoops: A Novel*," *Booklist* 78, no. 2 (15 September 1981): 98.

injustice

From the beginning of his career, Walter Dean Myers has taken as a personal responsibility the publication of works that supply minority children with images and characters indigenous to their unique world. In "The Black Experience in Children's Books: One Step Forward, Two Steps Back" (1979), an essay for *Interracial Books for Children Bulletin*, the author decried the dearth of children's works reflecting the everyday reality of the nonwhite world. With short stories, fables, biography, history, and lighthearted teen novels, he began incorporating outrage at miscarriages of justice, particularly the stereotyping of youths as villains, a motif in "The Vision of Felipe" (1978).

The theme of unfairness suits a variety of literary modes— the biographical play *And There Stood a Man* (1990), the storybook beast fables *Mr. Monkey and the Gotcha Bird* (1984) and *How Mr. Monkey Saw the Whole World* (1996), and the rise of boxer Cassius Clay above racism in *The Greatest: Muhammad Ali* (2001). Examples of Myers's narratives range from the bullying of strong over weak in the young adult novel *It Ain't All for Nothin'* (1978), the threat to the elderly homeless in the exemplum "The Treasure of Lemon Brown" (1983), and the victimization of the Quechua in the adventure novella *Ambush in the Amazon* (1986), one of the Arrow mystery series. Another of the four-book set, *Adventure in Granada* (1985), opens on police suspicions about Gypsies, whom society stereotypes as thieves. Myers explores more stirring examples of injustice from history in the chronicles *Now Is Your Time! The African-American Struggle for Freedom* (1991) and *U.S.S. Constellation: Pride of the American Navy* (2004). Both books detail the results of a diaspora that forced African slaves to acclimate to bondage in the Western Hemisphere.

Gradations of inequity empower themes in Myers's more thought-provoking works. An early publication, "How Long Is Forever?" (1968), published in *Negro Digest*, illustrates his dedication to the theme of racial equality. In a brutal assault, a white prison guard named Jenkins kicks the inmate Moses in the crotch. Moses restrains his impulse to retaliate because he knows "if there was anything at all against him" the parole board would refuse his request (Myers, 1969, 54). In *The Young Landlords* (1979), Myers creates counterpoint from the comic escapades of a teen action group that owns an apartment building. He overlays a more taxing moral judgment, the group's concern for Chris, a friend whom undercover police entrap and arrest for pillaging the electronics store where he works. Bubba, one of the neighborhood boys, repeats a faulty contention that people who look guilty must be guilty or else the police would not arrest them. The novel's outcome proves Bubba wrong without overstating a lesson in democratic ideals.

Meyers's skill at fable emerges in *The Golden Serpent* (1980), a picture book expressing the spiritual need to give to the less fortunate. In a veiled image of the American majority's blindness to suffering, an apathy that worsened during the consecutive terms of President Ronald Reagan, the narrative pictures a king of India who searches for the solution to a problem he is unable to identify. Guided by the wise hermit Pundabi, the king gazes unflinchingly at the serpentine coils of hunger and poverty that encircle his palace. After confronting three examples—a crippled boy, a starving widow, and three blind beggars—the king retreats to his lavish lifestyle with no inkling of the source of his discontent. Myers concludes the fable with a truism about wealth: those at the top of the social ladder gorge themselves on temporal pleasures but make no effort to satisfy a more insidious soul hunger.

Critics commend Myers for his accounts of parents who deliberately mislead or exploit their children. In *Somewhere in the Darkness* (1992), Jimmy Little falls into the hands of his ex-con father, Cephus "Crab" Little, who continues breaking laws in an effort to locate Rydell, the one witness who can exonerate Crab for murder. Crab's sketchy childhood lacked a consistent presence of a father figure. In Crab's words, "I used to see him about twice a month. He was a cook on the southern route" (Myers, 1992, 100). Although the quest to rectify Crab's involvement in crime ends with his capture and death in a prison infirmary, Jimmy observes the subtleties of right and wrong in his father's efforts to devote his final days of life to ushering his son into a respectable manhood. By emphasizing Crab's nobler impulses, the text rebuts the stereotype of the evil black criminal.

One of Myers's most compelling works is a single ode, "Migration," which concludes *The Great Migration: An American Story* (1993), a picture book he produced in collaboration with folk artist Jacob Lawrence. The text describes an epic gamble that life in the urban industrialized North offers more promise and less despair than scraping by in the racist agrarian South. The payoff for a World War I–era exodus offers blacks a mixture of solutions to police surveillance, illegal search and seizure, and threats of brutality and lynching. Although the cities of Chicago, Cleveland, Detroit, New York, Philadelphia, and Pittsburgh offer their own hybrids of slave-era coercion, African Americans winnow out opportunities for advancement in railroad and steel mill jobs and for better preparation for the next generation in Northern schools.

Overall, Myers's literary canon surveys shifts in opportunity that prophesy better times to come. In *Malcolm X: By Any Means Necessary* (1993), *Malcolm X: A Fire Burning Brightly* (2004), and *I've Seen the Promised Land: The Life of Dr. Martin Luther King, Jr.* (2004), the author investigates the issues of oppression and violence as they impact the careers of two bold black spokesmen for equality. In an interview with Paul Rockwell, a reviewer for the *Oakland Post*, Myers stressed the difference between reports of injustice in the white and black media: "The white press was hardly reporting Malcolm's travels to Africa, Malcolm's Hajj. But the black press was reporting that as a major growth of this man" (Rockwell, 1993, 4). By introducing subsequent generations to Malcolm and King, Myers extends the value of freedom fighting to the people who will reap the benefits.

See also **poverty, powerlessness, racism, segregation**

• *Further Reading*

Miller-Lachmann, Lyn. "Review: *The Great Migration: An American Story*," *School Library Journal* 39, no. 12 (December 1993): 127.

Myers, Walter Dean. *Adventure in Granada*. New York: Viking Kestrel 1985.

_____. "The Black Experience in Children's Books: One Step Forward, Two Steps Back," *Interracial Books for Children Bulletin* 10, no. 6 (1979): 14–15.

_____. *The Great Migration: An American Story*. New York: HarperCollins, 1993.

_____. "How Long Is Forever?," *Negro Digest* (June 1969): 52–57.

_____. *Somewhere in the Darkness*. New York: Scholastic, 1992.

Rockwell, Paul. "Malcolm X Biography a Must Read for Youth," *Oakland Post*, 29, no. 89 (28 February 1993): 4.

irony

To add force and enhance meaning in his writing, Myers orchestrates dramatic and situational irony, such as the wistful longing for a father in *It Ain't All for Nothin'* (1978), the search of criminals for a nonexistent trove in "The Treasure of Lemon Brown" (1983), the naivete of Father Santora about assignment to Khe Sanh in *Fallen Angels* (1988), and the fatal shooting of drugstore owner Alguinaldo Nesbitt with his own chrome-plated pistol in *Monster: A Novel* (1999). Early in Myers's career, he wrote a dilemma story, "How Long Is Forever?," for the June 1969 issue of *Negro Digest*. The action falls into distinct halves—an initial longing for freedom in Moses, a prison inmate incarcerated for complicity in robbery and murder, and the destruction of all hope for parole. The ache for home and a reunion with his aging mother prefaces a visceral reaction, his assault against Jenkins, a sadistic guard who taunts and pummels Moses. Myers applies irony to the falling action in the momentary thrill of vengeance that destroys Moses's chance for parole. He exults, "Hitting Jenkins was more than good; God, it was glorious" (Myers, 1969, 57). The rush of pent-up anguish maddens the protagonist, who, like the biblical Moses, aims his fist at a symbol of cultural enslavement.

Myers populates his writings with important characters who, on the surface, seem insignificant, like the bum, prostitute, and elderly woman whom Augie strangles in the short story "Dark Side of the Moon" (1971) and the homeless blues harmonica player in "The Treasure of Lemon Brown" (1983). In "Gums," anthologized in *We Be Word Sorcerers: Twenty-five Stories by Black Americans* (1973), the author builds on the lone lifestyle of the 69-year-old title figure and his nine-year-old grandson Stevie. To enhance the mounting terror of the frail old man and the hapless child, Myers gradually turns Death into a personified third character. The intrusion of mortality realigns the family structure, reducing Gums to a cowering babe sleeping in Stevie's arms. The picture of a nine-year-old boy pressed into the role of parent and protector adds pathos to the themes of powerlessness and poverty.

In Myers's sports story *Hoops: A Novel* (1981), irony enhances realism. The initial confrontation between 17-year-old basketball star Lonnie Jackson and a community wino seems inconsequential. As the narrative progresses, the drunk returns to Lonnie's life as coach and mentor Calvin F. "Spider" Jones, an athlete turned derelict after he loses his reputation within the National Basketball Association for point shaving and suffers the death of his son from an apartment fire. Situational irony mounts into dramatic irony after Cal saves Lonnie from risking his own reputation by negotiating with sports gamblers. In the falling action, Lonnie triumphs on the court, but sinks into grief after racketeers rough him up and stab Cal to death. The author implies that Lonnie deserves an opportunity to succeed, but that Cal's amorality stalks him to the grave.

Myers pursues complex ironies in the sequel novel, *The Outside Shot* (1984). After winning a scholarship based on his victory in the Tournament of Champions, Lonnie earns pocket money by providing twice-weekly therapy for an autistic child, nine-year-old Eddie Brignole, at University Hospital. The narrative describes the retreat of Lonnie from sports mania and his rise to manhood by involving himself wholeheartedly in Eddie's rehabilitation. In the resolution, Lonnie begins balancing a mature life by prioritizing sensible elements—college courses, his girlfriend Sherry Jewett, and the contentment of friendships and community volunteerism. Myers presents a female-centered glimpse of Lonnie's temptations in the story of a fashion model. Similarly overwhelmed by choices is 16-year-old model Crystal Brown in *Crystal* (1987). After learning of the suicide of Rowena, an 18-year-old colleague, Crystal abandons rides in limos and posing in expensive furs to become a normal teenager. Like Lonnie, Crystal is too steeped in right thinking from childhood to let flashy rewards derail her morality. In both novels, the author reminds young readers that the daily lessons of home, church, and school take on nobility in contrast to the tawdriness of instant celebrity.

Rich with situational irony is the picture book *The Great Migration: An American Story* (1993), which Myers wrote in collaboration with folk artist Jacob Lawrence. Through narrative art and a concluding ode, the text describes the failure of agrarianism to uplift black families in Alabama, the Carolinas, and Georgia from the squalor of slave times. During World War I, recruiters from railroad companies and steel mills in Chicago, Cleveland, Detroit, New York, and Pittsburgh scout likely workers for slots vacated by military inductees. As more black families board trains for urban areas, Southern land owners realize that the loss of cheap labor spells disaster for farms. Too late, hard-eyed law agents cannot reverse the exodus as streams of blacks bid farewell to a region noted for racism, lynching, and limited educational opportunity. The historical irony accounts for the vigor of black communities like Harlem, Myers's hometown.

Myers is more adept at the ironies that children encounter on their way to maturity. The reversal of roles from rescued to rescuer occurs in the intervention of 12-year-old David Curry in the life of a mystic mentor, Moses Littlejohn, the title figure and savior in the coming-of-age urban folk tale *The Dream Bearer* (2003). At the right moment, according to critic Jeff Zeleski's review in *Publishers Weekly*, "Moses subtly plants a seed of compassion in David for his father," thus triggering sympathy and forgiveness in a family that seems doomed to destruction ("Review," 2003, 52). As the elderly homeless man stumbles under the heavy burden of recovered memory, David returns the favor by insisting on aiding Moses, who requires immediate hospitalization. Myers creates symbolism in a parting scene in which the boy aids the old man with his suitcase as Moses departs Harlem for a warmer climate. The strong young hands on the old man's burden suggest that David gains from Moses an intuitive strength that will accompany the boy into manhood.

One of Myers's gems of irony envelops the story of Abraham and Isaac in the collection *A Time to Love: Stories from the Old Testament* (2003). The loving father-son relationship progresses as the two pick their way up a peak on Mount Moriah. As Isaac carries the rope and knife and aids his father on the upward slopes, the boy fears that Abraham, a pious servant of God, intends to sacrifice himself on a mountaintop altar. Out of fear and devotion, Isaac thinks, "O my precious father. O my precious father" (Myers, 2003, 78). The joy in paternal love lightens Isaac's limbs as he grasps one rock after another on the ascent. The shift to Isaac as the intended sacrifice makes no alteration in the tone as both son and father sorrow over an inevitable parting. On the return trip, Myers pictures the two rejoicing that God intervenes in time to spare the family the loss of Sarah's only son.

Myers's refinement of irony reaches an artistic height in *Here in Harlem: Poems in Many Voices* (2004), his finest verse anthology. In an impressionistic glimpse of subways riders in the poem "Hosea Liburd, 25," the author pictures 125th Street as the great divide between Harlem and the white section of Manhattan. After the subway departs, Hosea and his fellow passengers experience negative emotions based on racial differences. To Hosea, departure from Harlem strips him of manhood. To the horde of passengers, he represents the black beast, "huge in my beastness" (Myers, 2004, 14). The irony of everyday fears expresses a common source of urban stress that causes both the minority black and the majority whites to turn aside and seek invisibility.

See also **coming of age, gangs, music, *The Young Landlords***

• *Further Reading*

Myers, Walter Dean. *The Great Migration: An American Story*. New York: HarperCollins, 1993.

_____. "Gums" in *We Be Word Sorcerers: Twenty-five Stories by Black Americans.* New York: Bantam, 1973.
_____. *Here in Harlem: Poems in Many Voices.* New York: Holiday House, 2004.
_____. "How Long Is Forever?" in *Negro Digest* (June 1969): 52–57.
_____. *A Time to Love: Stories from the Old Testament.* New York: Scholastic, 2003.
Zaleski, Jeff. "Review: *The Dream Bearer*," *Publishers Weekly* 250, no. 23 (9 June 2003): 52.

It Ain't All for Nothin'

Dedicated to the author's brother and pal George Douglas "Mickey" Myers, Jr., the social novel *It Ain't All for Nothin'* (1978) examines the plight of the aged and of powerless children. Set at Manhattan Avenue and 125th Street, the story unfolds in the tentative voice of Tippy, a 12-year-old narrator who nursemaids his 69-year-old Grandmother Carrie Brown and joins her in daily prayer. The rending of the family's accord occurs naturally as Carrie becomes too frail to care for Tippy. After the child passes to Lonnie, his estranged father, the loss of regular hours and emotional support of a responsible parent threatens the boy. Worsening the situation is the realization that Lonnie and his cronies are jewelry thieves. To enhance the jeopardy of a morally corrupt homelife, the author populates Tippy's everyday world with shabby adults, including Jack, the numbers runner, and unnamed women who cohabitate with Lonnie.

In a narrative that critic Helen B. Andrejevic, reviewer for *Parents*, calls "even-toned, extremely well-written, and withal optimistic," Myers worsens the home scene for Tippy (Andrejevic, 1979, 20). Lonnie takes the boy on a grocery robbery and threatens him with a pistol, two forms of adult treachery reminiscent of Robert Cormier's thrillers. Emerging from Myers's text are two emotions— terror and excitement at being a part of the robbery, a subtextual warning that Tippy's new life bodes ill for his future. The menacing relationship turns to child abuse from brutal blows to the boy's head and stomach and a threat of murder if Tippy informs on Lonnie's whereabouts to the police. The boy's escape through sleep, movies, alcohol, and friendship with the hustler Motown fails to re-create the supportive atmosphere that Tippy enjoyed with Grandma Carrie.

Critic Ashley Jane Pennington states in a review for *Interracial Books for Children Bulletin* that Myers's crime novel is unremitting in "the stark realities of ghetto life. It pretties up nothing: not the language, not the circumstances, not the despair" (Pennington, 1979, 18). The intervention of Roland and Edna Sylvester interjects some structure in Tippy's upbringing, even on a short-term basis. Myers contrasts the erratic rhythms of laying low with Lonnie and his criminal friends during Tippy's bus ride with Roland, which introduces the boy to Central Park and downtown Manhattan. Tippy reaches a beneficial conclusion about morality: people feel less stress and more joy in life if they focus on "the right thing to do" (Myers, 1978, 115). Roland's praise for the boy's trophies for relay racing divide Tippy's thoughts— pride in achievement and regret that he has Lonnie for a parent.

The narrative takes a psychological twist after Tippy obeys his father and participates in the robbery of Mr. Walker, owner of a candy store. In the boy's mind,

Grandma Carrie's teachings and example refute Lonnie's immorality. Tippy feels pulled apart: "I was being me on the outside doing things like sneaking around ... and then I was being me inside looking at me on the outside doing what I was doing" (*ibid.*, 169). The separation into two selves, an idea that Myers develops further in *Monster: A Novel* (1999), worsens the powerlessness in Tippy, who is too young to abandon Lonnie and survive on his own. Pennington adds that the treachery of father against son causes the reader to "touch [Tippy's] pain — the hurt in his body and the hurt in his heart" (Pennington, 1979, 18).

Myers's style maintains the poignant intent to be true to a child's thinking. In the resolution, the author reveals a similar duality in the father, who wants to establish a normal home for his son, but who refuses to abandon the notion of easy money from robberies as the best method of getting a start. Lonnie's ambivalence predicts more crime and more spiritual unrest for Tippy. Of the story's brutal characterization, Andrejevic notes that Myers "deals unblinkingly with a milieu not often encountered in children's books" (Andrejevic, 1979, 20).

See also **crime, drugs and alcohol, Tippy's genealogy**

• *Further Reading*

Andrejevic, Helen B. "Review: *It Ain't All for Nothin*,'" *Parents* 54, no. 1 (January 1979): 20.

Myers, Walter Dean. *It Ain't All for Nothin'*. New York: Viking, 1978.

Pennington, Ashley Jane. "Review: *It Ain't All for Nothin'*," *Interracial Books for Children Bulletin* 10, no. 4 (1979): 18.

juvenile crime

Myers, an advocate for neglected and troubled children, muses on the rapid deterioration of innocence into crime. The subject of youthful involvement in crime permeates his earliest efforts: the adult story, "How Long Is Forever?," published in the June 1969 issue of *Negro Digest*, and "Dark Side of the Moon," a story in the fall 1971 issue of *Black Creation*. For Moses, the focus of the first story, a murderous assault springs from a threat to his life by Jenkins, a sadistic prison guard. The story's subtext illustrates how a badly flawed justice system exacerbates crime. The second story pictures Augie as too mentally skewed to stop the cycle of killings that begins with an attractive girl and escalates to a prostitute, a bum, and an old lady innocently walking her dog down Herkimer Street. The study of the human potential for murder anticipates the author's acclaimed exposés of teen crime in *Monster: A Novel* (1999) and *Shooter* (2004).

The author develops nuanced studies of gradual corruption in eleven-year-old Earl Goins's slide from disturbing the peace to vandalism and armed robbery in *Won't Know Till I Get There* (1982), Kevin's recidivism into marijuana possession in *Handbook for Boys: A Novel* (2003), and the debt to criminals that forces 17-year-old Tyrone Curry to borrow money from his mother in *The Dream Bearer* (2003). To Jim Naughton, an author-reviewer for the *Los Angeles Times*, Myers stated his concerns for a generation of at-risk children: "I see these kids at 11, I see them at 12 and then two years later I see them in trouble and I wonder about that" (Naughton, 1989, C1). Looking at delinquency as a father, citizen, and writer, Myers continues to explore social decline as a worthy subject for art.

Myers began describing the relationship between Harlem's children and the police in his first novel, *Fast Sam, Cool Clyde, and Stuff* (1975), a seriocomic teen tale. After Robin nips off part of Binky's ear in a fight, Clyde Jones and his friends escort the patient to a hospital emergency room to have the tissue reattached. The uproar created by kids demanding attention results in multiple arrests for disturbing the peace and rioting. The police overreact to the clutch of black children and use billy sticks and hands-on tactics of breaking up the fray. Another episode characterizes racial bias after the police become convinced that black boys stole a purse. Actually, the children ward off the purse snatchers and retrieve the owner's belongings. Myers maintains a light tone to balance a subtext of unfairness toward black children whom white authorities stereotype as drug users, thieves, and hooligans.

A lethal situation develops in the life of 12-year-old Tippy in *It Ain't All for Nothin'* (1978), a psychological novel depicting a child's perspective on adult lawlessness. Myers characterizes the powerlessness of a 12-year-old child reared by his Grandmother Carrie Brown and passed on to the welfare system when the elderly woman becomes too frail to manage a home or see to her own care and hygiene. The rapid decline of Tippy's situation introduces him to sleazy women, layabouts, and the alcohol and marijuana consumption of his father Lonnie. After Tippy realizes that Lonnie subsists on jewelry theft, the boy weeps uncontrollably at a situation beyond a child's ability to control or avoid. To his tears, Lonnie spouts a twisted rationalization for crime: "When it all come down it's about looking out for your manhood" (Myers, 1978, 55). By confusing thievery with independence and assertiveness, Lonnie implies that whatever he must do to survive is a justifiable facet of adulthood.

The down side of life with an alcoholic thief emerges as the shame of a dissolute parent rubs off on Tippy. The boy witnesses normal human relationships in Central Park and remarks wistfully on people "having a good time and liking the way they was" (*ibid.*, 114). Lonnie's offer to open a film rental agency carries a heavy price, the stealing of enough money to set him up in business. Myers indicates that Lonnie's immorality distances Tippy from his father. The boy wants an ego ideal who is "proud of himself and everything, the same way that I wanted to see me when I looked in the mirror" (*ibid.*, 124). The dissimilarity between Tippy's fantasy father and Lonnie forces the boy into escapism through alcohol, television, and sleep and into complicity with Lonnie's criminal ring.

In subsequent fiction, Myers illustrates how easily crime appears to solve teen problems. In *Hoops: A Novel* (1981), the rifling of a desk and the removal of checks and papers from the office of Tyrone Giddins helps 17-year-old Lonnie Jackson explain changes in his friend Paul, who has been stealing welfare checks to impress uptown girls with wads of cash. More troubling to Lonnie is the troubled past of Coach Calvin F. "Spider" Jones, a ruined sports figure who lost his place in the National Basketball Association for point shaving. Cal's death from a post-game knifing in the locker room proves to Lonnie that racketeers mean to win, whatever the cost in brutality and murder. The temptations shift from Cal to Lonnie in the sequel novel, *The Outside Shot* (1984), in which Alfredo "Fat Man" Corsi flashes easy money to college athletes who assure him a safe bet. As Lonnie teeters on the edge of complicity, investigators round up the major suspects, forcing Bill Larson out of college sports. By bringing Lonnie close to suspension and a possible arrest, Myers creates a lasting lesson in the brevity of reward from illicit point shaving.

The use of restitution as punishment in the seriocomic novel *Won't Know Till I Get There* (1982) suggests Myers's support of community projects that involve young hoodlums in positive experiences. For spray-painting "Royal Visigoths" on a train car, protagonist Steve Perry, his foster brother Earl Goins, Hi-Note, and Patty Bramwell spend a summer working at the Micheaux House for Senior Citizens, a run-down retirement home. The intergenerational novel balances the shame of Steve's vandalism against the delight of making friends with a challenging enclave of elders. The narrative pokes fun at the vainglory of street toughs by picturing Pietro Santini decked in a gang jacket and by Patty's suggestion that she and her pals spray paint the gang name on the limousine of a snooty city official. By the novel's end, good deeds absolve the foursome of their crime while revealing a streak of humanity.

From his study of prison inmates and his interaction with petty lawbreaking, Myers refuses to demonize criminals as lost causes. Instead, he views criminality as the result of misdirection and faulty logic. In the war novel *Fallen Angels* (1988), the anti-hero, infantryman Richard "Richie" Perry, considers writing letters to Howard, an old pal with whom he used to play basketball. After Howard enters the prison in Stormville, New York, for committing a robbery, he appreciates Perry's letters. Perry expects reciprocity from Howard, who might understand how much a soldier in Vietnam needs to hear from home folks. The symbiotic relationship humanizes Howard from criminal to true friend.

The involvement of Myers's characters in felonies influences the ambiguous *Monster: A Novel*. The innovative cautionary tale surveys 16-year-old Steven Harmon, the defendant at a juvenile trial, yet refrains from pinpointing the moment when abetting a robbery escalates into unpremeditated killing. Reader response to *Monster* caused Myers to address the ambiguities of guilt and justice, a topic he broached in *It Ain't All for Nothin'*. By leaving unsettled the issue of Steve Harmon's involvement with career criminals, the author places on the reader the responsibility for sifting details for proof of innocence or guilt. In an essay for *Horn Book*, Myers declared that American police and courts have migrated "from a moral system that was often too rigid to a system of graduated tolerances" (Myers, 2001, 701). He traces the slide in moral behavior to childhood, when authorities allow schoolyard bullying "because it is easier to let it go than to deal with it. We accept antisocial behavior as if there were no universal standards even within a single culture, until that antisocial behavior runs afoul of the legal system" (*ibid.*, 702). He regrets that the decline must run its course before society clamps down on infractions. He later commented that imprisonment of young felons weakens the democratic system: incarceration "has tremendous civil rights repercussions when [inmates] lose their right to vote.... It's something like one in four black men don't have the right to vote" (Corbett, 2000).

For his psychological study in *Shooter* (2004), Myers employs multiple narratives to reflect the ostracism and rage in a teenaged killer, 16-year-old sociopath

Leonard "Len" Gray. His twisted mind and actions parallel those of the shooters at Columbine High School in Littleton, Colorado, during a rampage on April 20, 1999. The author outlines formal interviews of the FBI agent Victoria Lash and of a county psychologist, Dr. Richard Ewings, with Carla Evans and Cameron Porter, Len's accomplices. The pair's culpability lies in the loose formation of a club, *Ordo Sagittae* (Order of the Arrow) by Len, a bully-turned-killer at suburban Madison High. More terrifying are the shooter's journal entries that let off angry outbursts revealing severe mental unrest and vindictiveness toward his parents and toward cliquish school jocks. The psychic pressure precipitates the murder of Brad Williams, a star football player, and leads to Len's suicide. The author hesitates to demonize any single mitigating factor as the cause of Len's rampage only weeks before his high school graduation.

See also ***Bad Boy: A Memoir*****, Leonard Gray,** ***Handbook for Boys*****, Steve Harmon,** ***Monster: A Novel*****, Cameron Porter,** ***Shooter*****, victimization, violence,** ***Won't Know Till I Get There***

• *Further Reading*

Corbett, Sue. "Walter Dean Myers Has Been Writing Poignant, Tough Stories for and about At-risk Kids," *Miami Herald* (26 January 2000).

Myers, Walter Dean. "Escalating Offenses," *Horn Book* 77, no. 6 (November-December 2001): 701–702.

____. *It Ain't All for Nothin'*. New York: Viking, 1978.

Naughton, Jim. "Stories from the Inner City; Walter Dean Myers, Writing about Reality for Black Children," *Washington Post* (9 December 1989): C1.

King, Martin Luther, Jr.

Myers commends Dr. Martin Luther King, Jr., as a peace-loving activist for social justice. Myers's writings salute the image of one man standing tall against racial inequities and shepherding human forces toward community and mutual respect. The author concludes his history book, *Now Is Your Time! The African-American Struggle for Freedom* (1991), with images of King and Malcolm X as stalwart leaders during the civil rights movement of the 1960s. The two spokesmen take on the historic aura of a new generation continuing the work of earlier black heroes, particularly orator Frederick Douglass and the soldiers of the 54th Massachusetts Regiment, America's first black fighting force. In 20th-century examples, Myers lauds the merger of physical stamina and courage with self-control, eloquence, and a world-framing vision that looks beyond the moment to a future when nonwhite citizens can grasp the rewards offered by the Constitution.

In the introduction to Myers's children's biography *Young Martin's Promise* (1992), editor Alex Haley describes King as "a young boy who felt the pain of unfair rules" (Myers, 1992, n.p.). Picture-book scenes of segregation begin in first grade in 1935, when Martin separates from his pals on Auburn Avenue to attend an all-black Atlanta school. Myers remarks on an incident at a shoe store, where a clerk orders the boy and his father to sit in the back of the room for fitting. To the elder King's refusal, the clerk charges him with being "high and mighty" (*ibid.*). The narrative characterizes the humiliating experience as the beginning of young Martin's war on segregation.

Myers also validates the hero worship of King by fictional characters. In *The Glory Field* (1994) in January 1964, residents of Johnson City, South Carolina, want to dramatize their demands for equal treatment by merchants by inviting King to appear in their defense. To promote the segregated status quo, Jed Sasser, a white employee of Clark's Five-and-Dime, accuses King of misreading local intent by trying to force more mixing of races in public places. Black support for King becomes a contentious element in the efforts to integrate Johnson City State College. Leonard Chase, a former athlete, advises Tommy Lewis to avoid the racial demonstrations. Chase declares that King knows too little about community events to advise blacks on securing justice and equality. The dramatic dialogue discloses some of the dissension among blacks about King's rise to freedom fighter and spokesman for the black race.

The author reveals his reverence for the famed preacher in a photo hanging in the Harlem barbershop in *Handbook for Boys: A Novel* (2002) and in a young adult biography, *I've Seen the Promised Land: The Life of Dr. Martin Luther King, Jr.* (2004). The latter expresses what syndicated columnist Lynne T. Burke extols as events that "changed the course of history" (Burke, 2004, 28). Critic Suzanne Rust, in an article for *Black Issues Book Review*, lauded Myers's version of the biography as "a stirring portrait of the man who guided American society towards the ideals of fairness and freedom" (Rust, 2004, 59). In similar analysis for *Library Media Connection*, reviewer Julie Scordato commended Myers's ability to coordinate illustrations that are "stark, expressive, moody, modernistic, almost graffiti-like" with a succinct text "distilled down to its essence" (Scordato, 2004, 72).

Without excess political or polemical discussion, the author depicts the rise of a nonviolent pulpit minister who uses his voice and example to inspire courage in the victims of segregation. On December 1, 1955, he supports Rosa Parks, a passenger arrested for refusing to sit at the back of a bus in Montgomery, Alabama. Myers states King's philosophy that "individuals had the responsibility of making democracy work" and acknowledges that King's example of accepting arrest and jailing promotes fairness (Myers, *I've*, n.p.). Study with Mohandas Gandhi, India's fount of nonviolent protest, sets King apart from militant blacks who prefer violence as the only means of achieving racial justice.

Myers stresses the value of King's public conduct "on the high plane of dignity and discipline" (*ibid.*). In 1963, as tempers flare on a daily basis and police direct billy clubs, fire hoses, and attack dogs against protesters, King maintains his belief in love and respect. An unnamed critic for *Kirkus Reviews* complimented the author for "highlighting King's nonviolent philosophy while viewing the Movement's angrier, more violent outbursts with a certain degree of — not sympathy, exactly, but understanding" ("Review," 2003, 1362). In August, at a high point in King's career as an orator, he delivers the "I Have a Dream Speech" during the March on Washington, a repudiation of the tactics of Adam Clayton Powell and Malcolm X, whom King meets on March 26, 1964. King's vision anticipates a time when his own children can be judged on character rather than race. On September 15, he mourns with the rest of the nation the murder of four little girls at a bombed-out Sunday school in Birmingham; in November the shooting death of President John F. Kennedy worsens national gloom. Myers summarizes the mounting consensus that "Violence seemed to rule the country" and adds the fearful question, "How long? How long?" (*ibid.*).

Myers documents the toll on King and his family from constant media attention and threats on their lives. In the words of critic Susan M. Moore, a writer for *School Library Journal*, the author intentionally "frames King's political efforts and his belief in nonviolent demonstration for change with information about the personal consequences to the man and his family" (Moore, 2004, 140). At the height of turmoil on college campuses in March 1968, King shakes off fatigue to support striking sanitation workers in Memphis, Tennessee. Myers freights his text with hints that King knows his time is limited. The leader's assassination a day after his "I've Been to the Mountaintop" speech proves that the King's suspicions are correct. Myers honors the fallen preacher "as a man, as a leader, and as a father" (*ibid.*). In *Here in Harlem: Poems in Many Voices* (2004), a young street preacher draws comparison to Dr. King, whom loving black community members identify familiarly as "Martin," an indication that the martyr holds a place in many hearts like a deceased member of the family (Myers, *Here*, 6, 7). In testimony to residual racism, *Shooter* (2004) pictures right-wing members of the Patriots gun club using photos of King as targets, a form of catharsis that eases pent-up hostilities toward the black leader. Ironically, the pictures in the gunsights of racists enhance King's reputation as a 20th-century prophet of the demise of bigotry.

See also ***Fallen Angels*****, injustice**

• *Further Reading*

Burke, Lynne T. 'Review: *I've Seen the Promised Land: The Life of Dr. Martin Luther King, Jr.*," *Reading Today* 21, no. 4 (February-March 2004): 28.

Moore, Susan M. "Review: *I've Seen the Promised Land: The Life of Dr. Martin Luther King, Jr.*," *School Library Journal* 50, no. 4 (April 2004): 140.

Myers, Walter Dean. *Here in Harlem: Poems in Many Voices.* New York: Holiday House, 2004.

____. *I've Seen the Promised Land: The Life of Dr. Martin Luther King, Jr.* New York: Amistad, 2004.

____. *Malcolm X: By Any Means Necessary*. New York: Scholastic, 1993.

____. *Young Martin's Promise.* Austin, Tex.: Raintree, 1992.

"Review: "*I've Seen the Promised Land: The Life of Dr. Martin Luther King, Jr.*," *Kirkus Reviews* 71, no. 11 (15 November 2003): 1362.

Rust, Suzanne. "Learning As We Climb: Stories about the Civil Rights Movement for Young Readers," *Black Issues Book Review* 6, no. 3 (May-June 2004): 58–60.

Scordato, Julie. "Review: "*I've Seen the Promised Land: The Life of Dr. Martin Luther King, Jr.*," *Library Media Connection* 23, no. 1 (August/September 2004): 72.

Lawrence, Jacob

One of Walter Dean Myers's urban heroes, narrative folk artist Jacob Lawrence, captured human strivings in a series of paintings that glimpse black history in the making. Lawrence was born at Atlantic City, New Jersey, during his parents' merger with a steady stream of transients on their way north from Virginia and the Carolinas. While living in a series of foster homes, he began integrating his artistic growth with the national story of African Americans. Of the grandeur of his people's history, he remarked, "It seemed almost inevitable that I would tell this story in my art" (Myers, 1993, cover).

Lawrence grew up in Philadelphia and New York City during the Great Depression and learned his profession in after-school studios that welcomed young artists. Further training at the Harlem Workshop and the American Artists School established his mastery of folk technique. Enlarging his understanding of black destiny were storytelling sessions at the 135th Street Branch of the New York Public Library and his readings at the library of the Schomburg Center for Research in Black Culture, a world-class collection of works on the global diaspora of black Africans that scholar Arturo Alfonso Schomburg opened in 1926. Lawrence's teaching career at the University of Washington and his visual contributions to black history earned him a National Medal of Arts.

On a grant in 1940 and 1941, the 22-year-old painter launched his career in an $8-per-month workshop by completing 60 canvases measuring 12 by 18 feet. He mused, "I can still remember all the panels spread out in my studio on tables made from boards and sawhorses" (*ibid.*, n.p.). With tempera on gesso, he painted the series in one effort, using the same mixture of colors on all the panels. The collection features a kinetic arrangement of stylized figures in muted tones who represent millions of upwardly mobile blacks. Known as "The Migration of the Negro," the sequential panels dramatize with scriptural gravity the courage and vulnerability of black individuals and families deserting their rural roots to establish more promising lives in the north. Edith Halpert's Downtown Gallery exhibited the understated series; *Fortune* magazine published 26 of the panels in November 1941. In March 1942, the series hung in separate collections in the Museum of Modern Art in New York City and the Phillips Collection in Washington, D.C. A half century later, a traveling exhibition, *Jacob Lawrence: The Migration Series*, graced museums in Atlanta, Birmingham, Denver, Milwaukee, New York, St. Louis, and Portland, Oregon.

Myers introduced young readers to the pathos and grandeur of the black diaspora in the picture book *The Great Migration: An American Story* (1993). The text opens in 1917, the year of Lawrence's birth, and covers the routes and traveling methods of ambitious blacks on their way from cropped-out Southern fields to the industrialized North to fill railroad and steel mill jobs left vacant by army inductees. Domestic scenes picture meager furnishings and a mother's paring knife slicing streak-o'-lean, a poor excuse for daily sustenance to the wide-eyed child who watches. More promising are picnic baskets that accompany families on the train and storefront churches that welcome newcomers. Of the compelling story that his parents told him in childhood, Lawrence adds, "Their struggles and triumphs ring true today" (*ibid.*). *Publishers Weekly* admired how the text "shows how momentous decisions made in individual households turned into an important part of U.S. history" ("Review: *The Great*," 1993, 61).

In 1996, Myers paired biography with Lawrence's panels to produce *Toussaint L'Ouverture: The Fight for Haiti's Freedom*, a vibrant young adult biography that depicts a self-educated freedom fighter and the eventual emancipation of Haitian blacks in the first black republic. In the introduction, the artist explains that he learned about black heroes in Harlem from street oratory. From stories of Frederick Douglass, Marcus Garvey, Toussaint L'Ouverture, Harriet Tubman, Nat Turner, and Denmark Vesey, the painter chose the Haitian as a first subject for "[defeating] those who would enslave him" (Myers, 1996, n.p.). In 41 panels featuring bold earth tones offset by stark white, Lawrence employed the patterning of quilts and the drama of murals to tell Toussaint's story. Critic Deborah Stevenson, in a review for the *Bulletin of the Center for Children's Books*, praised Lawrence's panels for "[conveying] the thoughtful somberness of the man and the time as well as the hazards and action of the battle" (Stevenson, 1997, 181).

See also **Toussaint L'Ouverture**

• *Further Reading*

Burns, Mary M. "Review: *The Great Migration: An American Story*," *Horn Book* 70, no. 1 (January 1994): 88–89.

Hodges, Alecia. "Jacob Lawrence's *The Great Migration*," *Arts & Activities* 129 no. 1 (February 2001): 36.

Levin, Ann. "Paintings Tell Vivid Story of a People on the Move," *Greensboro News Record* (14 March 1994): D6.

Myers, Walter Dean. *The Great Migration: An American Story*. New York: HarperCollins, 1993.

_____. *Toussaint L'Ouverture: The Fight for Haiti's Freedom*. New York: Simon & Schuster, 1996.

"Review: *The Great Migration: An American Story*," *Publishers Weekly* 240, no. 39 (27 September 1993): 61.

Rochman, Hazel. "Review: *Toussaint L'Ouverture: The Fight for Haiti's Freedom*," *Booklist* 93, no. 1 (1 September 1996): 123.

Stevenson, Deborah. "Review: *Toussaint L'Ouverture: The Fight for Haiti's Freedom*," *Bulletin of the Center for Children's Books* 50 (January 1997): 181.

The Legend of Tarik

Myers produced in *The Legend of Tarik* (1981) a searing glimpse of incipient manhood facing a lethal, character-molding challenge. He dedicated the work to Dr. Edward W. Robinson, Jr., a collector and disseminator of African history and culture and co-author of *The Journey of the Songhai People* (1992), a perusal of the West African diaspora. Unlike Robinson's fact-based example, Myers chose an allegory of youthful spirit set against a cynical serial killer called El Muerte (Death). By pacing the quest slowly through the preliminary stages and picking up the tempo as the inevitable clash nears, Myers correctly identifies a fact of naivete and inexperience — the waiting and training seem long and tedious, but the final advance on the worst of villains is brief, bloody, and inescapable. As is true in other of the author's depictions of teen heroes, Tarik seems puzzled by the outcome of a duel that he expects to cancel the hatred and satisfy the urgent mission that follows the murder of his family.

Set in Oulata, a medieval desert town of Mauritania in northwest Africa, the allegory opens around A.D. 775, over a century after the compilation of the Koran. Bearing epic elements of Christian, Islamic, African, and English lore, the narrative opens with the biblical "It came to pass" and develops into a monumental struggle against evil and the overthrow of death (Myers, 1981, 1). Of the author's suspense and imagination, critic E. R. Twichell, in a review for *Horn Book*, notes the deliberation of warrior training and the accelerated falling action. Of terrors that Tarik faces along the way to the final showdown, Twichell relishes the fact that Myers "has a talent for creating repulsive monsters" (Twichell, 1981, 434). Taking the opposing view, reviewer Alex Boyd, speaking for *Voice of Youth Advocates*, regrets the story's violence, which ranges from impalements to decapitation.

Paralleling the courage of Miguel de Cervantes's epic anti-hero in *Don Quixote* (1615) and of the Arthurian upstart in Alfred, Lord Tennyson's *Gareth and Lynette*, a test-of-manhood ballad from *Idylls of the King* (1885), Myers assembles the conventional machinery of quest lore — dreams and omens, a magic sword called Serq, a steed named Zinzinbadio, the loyal yeoman Capa, a shapeshifter who progresses from coaxing female to giant, a cyclopean serpent, and a source of future knowledge, the Crystal of Truth. The menacing presence of El Muerte (Death), the nickname of Artia Akwara, great grandson of the Alani-Vandal warrior Ganseric (also Gaiseric or Geiseric), acquires anecdotal traits like a magnet drawing iron filings, including a superhuman ability to exhume himself from burial. His literary foil is Nongo, the blind seer whose age and wisdom suggest Hod, the blind god of darkness in Norse mythology, the Greek seer Teiresias, and the harper Homer himself, whom tradition describes as blind.

The conflict sets El Muerte against the family of Kwesi Ntah, refugees from the Niger River north of Lake Debo to Oulata. After the slaughter of Mato and his wives, Kwesi and his surviving sons march in a coffle of slaves north to Encina, where El Muerte cuts down Kwesi and Umeme in the blood-sport ring. The remainder of the story describes the orphaned Tarik and his need for mentoring. Two sages, Docao and Nongo, prepare him for battle against El Muerte with fables, sword drill, and wise counsel on self-control. The contrast between Tarik's master of self and the revenge sickness that dehumanizes his companion Stria led critic Hazel Rochman to a conclusion: "The heroic quest is also an arduous search for self-knowledge and identity" (Rochman, 1981, 76).

• *Further Reading*

Bosse, Malcolm. "Review: *The Legend of Tarik*," *New York Times Book Review* (12 July 1981): 30.

Boyd, Alex. "Review: *The Legend of Tarik*," *Voice of Youth Advocates* 4, no. 4 (October 1981): 36.

Myers, Walter Dean. *The Legend of Tarik*. New York: Viking, 1981.

Rochman, Hazel. "Review: *The Legend of Tarik*," *School Library Journal* 27, no. 9 (May 1981): 76.
Twichell, Ethel R. "Review: *The Legend of Tarik*," *Horn Book* 57, 4 (August 1981): 434.

Lewis Genealogy

The pride of the Lewis family, the controlling theme of Myers's five-generation saga *The Glory Field* (1994), begins in the mid–18th century and swells to the late 20th century, when Planter Lewis passes on Muhammad Bilal's shackles to Malcolm Lewis, a Harlem musician. Along the way, family history acquires new sources of pride in the military service of Joshua and Lem in the Union army, Lizzy's work as an army cook, and freedom fighter Tommy, a casualty of the Vietnam War who was the first Lewis to attend college. The saga closes on the advancements of two liberated women—Jennie, a physician, and Luvenia, an entrepreneur who founds Mahogany Beauty Products.

Black Lewis clan

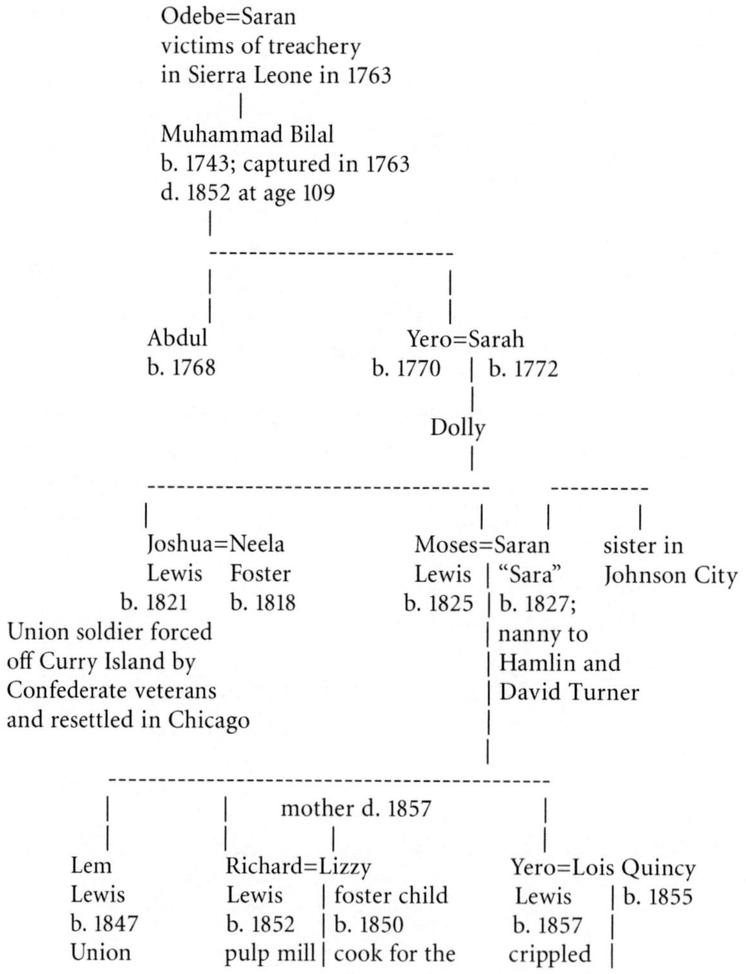

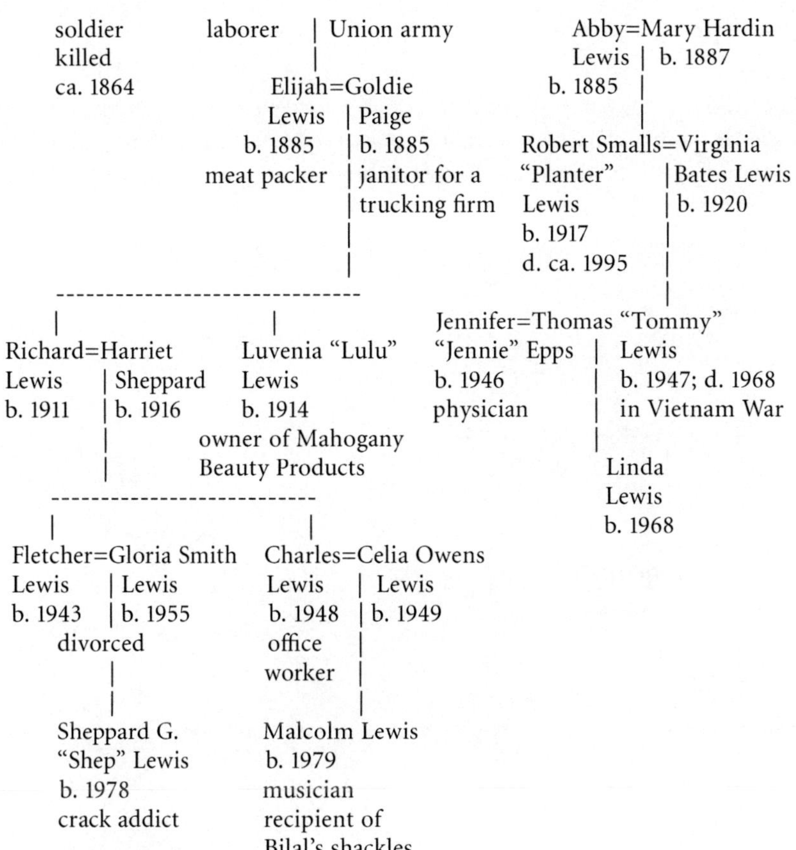

White Lewis clan

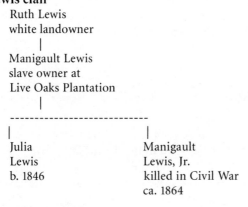

Ruth Lewis
white landowner
|
Manigault Lewis
slave owner at
Live Oaks Plantation
|

Julia Lewis b. 1846	Manigault Lewis, Jr. killed in Civil War ca. 1864

• *Further Reading*

Myers, Walter Dean. *The Glory Field.* New York: Scholastic, 1994.

Little genealogy

Myers informs the reader of *Somewhere in the Darkness* (1992) of the murky unknowns in the life of 14-year-old Jimmy Little, a motherless boy living in Harlem who is unaware of having a half-brother. By revealing facts of the family tree, the novel establishes the tenuous links that force the boy to rely heavily on Mama Jean, his foster mother:

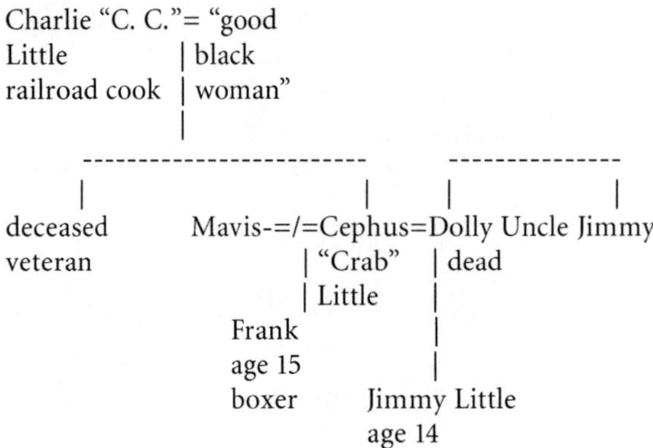

- *Further Reading*

Myers, Walter Dean. *Somewhere in the Darkness.* New York: Scholastic, 1992.

Littlejohn, Moses

The sudden appearance of "Mr. Moses" Littlejohn, a *deus ex machina* in the life of 12-year-old David Curry in *The Dream Bearer* (2003), contrasts the preceding scenes that precipitate self-doubt and depression. Unlike the boy's weeping mother, Evelyn Curry, and the aggressive, troubled father Reuben, Moses bears positive wisdom about a young man's obligation to ambition. On a hot mid–July day, he appears strange in a brown overcoat. He is dark and white-haired in rumpled pants and pushing a shopping cart, standard equipment for homeless people. David, who has the street instincts of the city-bred, chooses to leave Moses to himself lest he turn out to be "a mass murderer or something" (Myers, 2003, 24). The on-the-spot-judgment suits the style of Myers, who was reared in Harlem among a mix of people who could easily harm children.

David begins to see images of the title figure from *The Rime of the Ancient Mariner* (1789) in Moses, who is roughly bearded and elderly with a faraway gaze and tragic note in his voice. After the man's claim to be 303 years old, David and his friend Loren Hart keep their distance. Moses eases their suspicions of insanity by joking, "What would crazy be for a black man?" (*ibid.*, 27). He describes the imploding action of anger, which piles so deep in the psyche that it confuses sources of hostility. He also warns Loren to be more cautious about hasty judgments based on peripheral evidence, such as the old man's shaggy appearance. Moses warns the unwary, "You got to be careful what you believe these days," a kernel of wisdom that suits Harlem in the early 21st century (*ibid.*, 28–29).

Myers empowers Moses with the magical qualities of the shiny man in August Wilson's urban black plays *Joe Turner's Come and Gone* (1988) and *Gem of the Ocean* (2003). A charismatic guide through the black diaspora, the mystic figure bestows good fortune from serendipity, the positive side of fate. Echoing the supernatural powers of the Yoruban deity Ogun, a god of iron, Moses also reflects the trickster guile and heavenly shield of the mythic hero-divine High John the Conqueror, who protected captive Africans during the Middle Passage and throughout enslavement and the diaspora. In Moses's childhood, the gift of dream-bearing came at age 12, the dividing line between childhood and manhood, a common separation of intuitive powers in Gothic convention. Moses's receipt of visionary powers began as an emotional burden that he accepted from Aaron, the 400-year-old giver, who "was tired and needed to pass his dreams on to somebody new" (*ibid.*, 29). Aaron's protracted journey suggests both the storytelling curse of the Ancient Mariner and the unending search of the Wandering Jew, the mythic pariah and symbol of otherness who longs for death to end an unremitting earthly trek.

Moses's value to David derives from the promotion of ambition and hope. When the two meet at a shady spot in the park, Moses speaks of "dreams that fill up the soul, dreams that can be unfolded like wings and lift you off the ground" (*ibid.*, 58). The introduction of a crooning sound creates an eerie backdrop to his reliving of the chaining of his father, a coastal tableau that appears to come from the slave trade along West Africa's Bight of Benin. Myers implies that the three centuries of Moses's life are actually the burden of black history, which Moses reduces to the inchoate howl of his father as captors hurry him out to sea to a slaving vessel early in the 18th century. Another dream of picking cotton in the heat sets Moses at a South Carolina plantation in the early 1750s, a scenario that suggests a Jungian racial consciousness that is indigenous to American blacks. Of the ephemeral source of such dreams, Moses surmises that "footprints" of the past "might be the only things we got that's real" (*ibid.*, 85).

Myers contrasts the two strands in David's life by picturing a meeting between Reuben and Moses at the basketball court and a second encounter in the park. Reuben dismisses the elderly homeless man as possibly criminal or diseased—"dead people waiting for a place to lay down" (*ibid.*, 92). The old man's mutterings grow more fervid after Moses shares his vision of ineluctable doom for Cammie, an innocent black in the hands of a white lynch mob. David's friend Sessi, a Kikuyu immigrant from Kenya, offers an African view of the elderly as oracles. Her description enhances Myers's portrayal of Moses as an intuitive truth teller.

See also **dreams, wisdom**

• *Further Reading*

Anderson, George K. *The Legend of the Wandering Jew.* Providence, R.I.: Brown University Press, 1965.

Appiah, Kwame Anthony. *In My Father's House: Africa in the Philosophy of Culture.* New York: Oxford University Press, 1992.

Drewel, Margaret Thompson. *Yoruba Ritual.* Indianapolis: Indiana University Press, 1992.

Myers, Walter Dean. *The Dream Bearer.* New York: Amistad, 2003.
Snodgrass, Mary Ellen. *August Wilson.* Jefferson, N.C.: McFarland, 2004.
Tibbets, Sally. "Review: *The Dream Bearer,*" *Kliatt* 38, no. 2 (March 2004): 48.
Tidjani-Serpos, Noureini, "The Postcolonial Condition: The Archeology of African Knowledge," *Research in African Literatures,* Vol. 27, No. 1, Spring 1996, pp. 3–18.

Loper genealogy

Myers describes a black family in Texas in *My Name Is America: The Journal of Joshua Loper, a Black Cowboy, The Chisholm Trail, 1871* (1999) that spans the pre–Civil War era into the heydey of Western trail drives:

Kissee Loper=Nehemiah Loper
ex-slave of | free-born man who was wounded
Muhlen | while fighting for the Union Army
d. 1900 | in 1860; postmaster; d. 1898
|
Joshua Loper=Carrie Lynch
b. ca. 1855 | teacher
cow hand and | m. September 1886
railroad worker| d. September 1933
d. 1920 |
|
Samuel Loper
b. July 1887
owner of barbershops
in Austin, Texas

• *Further Reading*

Myers, Walter Dean. *My Name Is America: The Journal of Joshua Loper, a Black Cowboy on the Chisholm Trail, 1871.* New York: Scholastic, 1999.

Malcolm X

Walter Dean Myers pursued a literary interest in the evolution of Malcolm Little into Malcolm X. In 1993, the author issued a bestselling young adult biography, *Malcolm X: By Any Means Necessary*, a precise work featuring photos, a chronology, index, and suggested readings. Introduced as "one person riding the crest of social discontent," the famed orator grew up in tense times for blacks who promoted racial equality (Myers, 1993, n.p.). Influencing Malcolm's immersion in issues of self-determination is his father's promotion of Marcus Garvey, founder of the Universal Negro Improvement Association. The suspicious death of Earl Little in 1931 under a trolley car prefaces Malcolm's turbulent life and assassination at age 39. In an interview with Paul Rockwell, a reviewer for the *Oakland Press*, the author revealed that white-owned media emphasized the violent aspects of the leader's career. Myers stressed that "Malcolm was meeting with African leaders, with [Kwame] Nkrumah, with African leaders from North Africa and Central Africa," a contribution to the world's black population through diplomacy and consensus building that resulted in the Organization of Afro-American Unity (Rockwell, 1993, 4).

Myers honored the distinguished career of Malcolm X in a second young adult biography, *Malcolm X: Fire Burning Brightly* (2000). The illustrated text outlines the troubled childhood and dabblings in crime in young manhood that precede a change of heart. One incident involving a junior high English teacher who belittles Malcolm for wanting to study law precipitates his defiance of judgments based on skin color. According to Carol Jones Collins in an article published in *African-American Voices in Young Adult Literature: Tradition, Transition, Transformation* (1994), the youth's slide into "criminal activity, a prison term, and the sudden and complete conversion to the Black Muslim faith" is a "familiar story" (Smith, 1994, 14). Because the jailhouse conversion coincides with the civil rights movement, Malcolm turns his energies and talents into a force for social revolution.

Myers uses Malcolm as a model of achievement. Largely self-educated during his term at Charlestown State Prison for robbery, from age 21 to 27, the freedom fighter studies the works of assertive male innovators—Aristotle, Plato, Mohandas Gandhi, Adolf Hitler, Vladimir Lenin, Karl Marx, Erwin Rommel, and Patrick Henry. Malcolm comes under the sway of the Nation of Islam, led by Elijah Muhammad. In his autobiography, Malcolm remarks, "I was totally unprepared for the Messenger Elijah Muhammad's physical impact upon my emotions" (Myers, 1993, 80). Through readings and letters, Malcolm embraces Allah and Islam. He readies himself for parole in August 1952, when he begins his work as an organizer, recruiter, and inspirational speaker. Myers observes that the ex-con's themes "speak to today's time.... The reasons might be different, but the disillusionment is the same" ("Review," 1992, B1).

At the beginning of Malcolm's drive for justice and racial equality, he founds a newspaper, *Muhammad Speaks*, as the "voice of the Nation of Islam" (Myers, 1993, 160). He gains public attention in April 1957 by leading a protest of the police mistreatment of a black prisoner, Johnson Hinton, a Muslim brother whose injuries in custody required the positioning of a steel plate in his skull (*ibid.*, xi). Malcolm urges audiences to avoid the immorality, ignorance, and low standards of hygiene that make blacks feel inferior to whites. Restless and belligerent, he defies the nonviolence of Dr. Martin Luther King, Jr.'s followers with a call to arms: "Up, you mighty race, you can accomplish what you will!" (Myers, 2004, n.p.). In spring 1964, he makes the obligatory pilgrimage to Mecca and discovers a model for racial peace, "a spirit of unity and brotherhood that my experiences had led me to believe never could exist between the white and the non-white" (Myers, 1993, 153).

Energized by his epiphany in the Middle East, Malcolm takes the name El Hajj Malik el Shabazz, meaning "the pilgrim Malcolm the Negro." By agitating for global action against racism, he aims toward "establishing a non-religious and non-sectarian constructive program for human rights" (*ibid.*, 159). As his stature grows among people of African descent, he becomes "the most dangerous man in America," a lightning rod for violence that the F.B.I. monitors round the clock (*ibid.*, 157). Death threats to Malcolm and his family are common as media attention demonizes his intent. Although three black gunmen assassinate him at age 39, his martyrdom assures the survival of his principles. Myers accounts for Malcolm's loss as the result of too bright a flame that cannot hold its intensity: "His light was too soon extinguished" (*ibid.*). At the funeral in Harlem at Faith Temple Church on 147th and

Amsterdam, actors Ruby Dee and Ossie Davis eulogize the orator before the procession to Ferndale Cemetery in Hartsdale, New York. A wave of encomia and analyses of Malcolm's works spawns the legacy that remains.

Mention of Malcolm X in Myers's fiction tends to associate the name with outsized striving, hatred, and turbulence. A brief mention in the picture-ode *Harlem: A Poem* (1997) pairs the martyr with Marcus Garvey as sources of black blues. In *The Glory Field* (1994), Jed Sasser, a white employee of Clark's Five-and-Dime, makes an *ad hominem* argument that ridicules any person "that calls himself 'X'" (Myers, 1994, 145). Revealing more of his ignorance, Jed claims that Dr. Martin Luther King, Jr., is not actually a preacher and accuses Malcolm X and Elijah Muhammad with being Satan worshippers. Myers turns Jed into the butt of situational irony with Jed's claim of an accurate, but unnamed source: "Some people just know that kind of thing" (*ibid.*, 248).

Myers perused the influence of Malcolm X in subsequent works. Tyrone Curry, a handsome, but wayward 17-year-old in *The Dream Bearer* (2003), resembles Malcolm X. In a later scene, Reuben Curry, Tyrone's crazed alcoholic father, muses on his birth a year after the assassination of Malcolm X. Reuben maintains, "They had to kill Malcolm because they couldn't control him" (Myers, 2003, 75). The comment is indicative of Reuben's paranoia about the nameless "they" and of public suppositions that some controlling force murdered the forceful leader because he threatened a governmental power structure. Myers refers to a given in legends—the need of people to surmise that conspiracies and phantom enemies complicate the lives of the great.

In *The Beast* (2003), a chance conversation on a train from New York City to New Haven, Connecticut, offers 17-year-old protagonist Anthony "Spoon" Witherspoon a white man's views on racism. The speaker attests that white people knew little about segregation or black hatred of whites until Malcolm X amplified simmering black rage. The next year, Myers referred familiarly to the famed religious leader and freedom fighter in *Here in Harlem: Poems in Many Voices* (2004) as "Malcolm," an indication of the orator's prominence as a personal hero and role model to Harlemites (Myers, 6, 7). In *I've Seen the Promised Land: The Life of Dr. Martin Luther King, Jr.* (2004), the author contrasts the methods of King and Malcolm X, which pit nonviolent protest in the South with the more explosive demonstrations of anger and hatred in Northern cities.

See also **Harlem**

• *Further Reading*

Garner, Judith M. "Review: *Malcolm X: By Any Means Necessary*," *Book Report* 11, no. 5 (March/April 1993): 48.

Myers, Walter Dean. *The Dream Bearer*. New York: Amistad, 2003,

_____. *The Glory Field*. New York: Scholastic, 1994.

_____. *I've Seen the Promised Land: The Life of Dr. Martin Luther King, Jr*. New York: Amistad, 2004.

_____. *Malcolm X: A Fire Burning Brightly*. New York: HarperCollins, 2004.

_____. *Malcolm X: By Any Means Necessary*. New York: Scholastic, 1993.

"Review: *Malcolm X: By Any Means Necessary*," (Indianapolis) *Recorder* (28 November 1992): B1.

Roback, Diane. "Picture Book Reprints," *Publishers Weekly* 251, no. 2 (12 January 2004): 56.

Rockwell, Paul. "Malcolm X Biography a Must Read for Youth," *Oakland Post*, 29, no. 89 (28 February 1993): 4.

Smith, Karen Patricia, ed. *African-American Voices in Young Adult Literature: Tradition, Transition, Transformation*. Lanham, Md.: Scarecrow, 1994.

Willett, Gail Pettiford. "Review: *Malcolm X: By Any Means Necessary*," *Horn Book* 69, no. 5 (September 1993): 626.

metafiction

Myers's ability to break free of narrative convention speaks well of his strong upbringing in a variety of storytelling and improvisational modes, including the optical storytelling and verse coda of *The Great Migration: An American Story* (1993), which he wrote in collaboration with folk artist Jacob Lawrence. Early in Myers's career, he dabbled in metafiction with a slangy take on the good fairy. Mabel Mae Jones, the hip black makeover artist in *The Dragon Takes a Wife* (1972), violates the quick fix of medieval wonder tales by trying out a variety of solutions to invigorate Harry, a diffident fire-breathing dragon. After three strategies—hotter flame, larger body, and invisibility—Mabel Mae steps outside the paradigm of fairy tales to turn Harry into a border on the page. The fourth failure offers Mabel Mae an opportunity to address the real issue, that Harry sees himself as a loser.

For *Monster: A Novel* (1999), Myers chose an experimental, nonsequential approach to narrative that mirrors the tensions of a televised police psychodrama. The introspective reportage reflects a similar conceit, Steve Perry's personal journal, the basis for the seriocomic novel *Won't Know Till I Get There* (1982). Patty Campbell, writing for *Horn Book*, classed *Monster* as a landmark on a par with J. D. Salinger's *The Catcher in the Rye* (1951), S. H. Hinton's *The Outsiders* (1967), and Robert Cormier's *The Chocolate War* (1974). To get at the truth about juvenile crime, Myers allows the main character to examine himself and his alienation from society through a system of interleaving—confessional writing in his journal interspersed with the plotting and cinematic techniques of a film of his own life. In the critique of John A. Staunton, a reviewer for *Journal of Adolescent & Adult Literacy*, the author "intersperses a variety of surface effects—marginalia, drawings, photographs, mug shots, and video stills—to offer an analysis of the complex identities that emerge in the context of such surfaces" (Staunton, 2002, 791). The metafictional method creates an objectivity in the boy that reprieves him from addressing his guilt in a robbery-murder of Alguinaldo Nesbitt, a drugstore owner.

Of the backdrop of prison cells and felons, Myers "discovered the language of the prison subculture, in which sexual terminology was used to discuss power concepts by men denied both power and heterosexual sex" (Myers, 2001, 61). A familiarity with prison argot enabled the author to get inside characters and comprehend their thought patterns. Through the film club's camera, Steve examines Harlem objectively and seeks through cinematography to comprehend the hostile environment that brings him close to a life sentence or execution by lethal injection. Contributing to the impersonal view of crime is Steve's familiarity with film terms—fade in, group shot, close-up, long shot, voice-over, pan, cut to, split-screen montage, and sidebar. Staunton commented, "These highly structured cinematic blockings are witness to Steve's own internal division about being scared or being tough, about being a good student and a good person or being a 'look-out' at a 'getover'" (Staunton, 2002, 792).

The author confided to Hazel Rochman, an interviewer for *Booklist*, his fascination with a criminal's ability to separate self from crime, an extreme form of rationalizing that allows the perpetrator to hold on to self-esteem. At the novel's disquieting conclusion, Steve is still searching for the real persona amid the fictional character in his film and the judgments of adults at the trial. He predicts a long search comprised of "a thousand times to look for one true image" (Myers, 1999, 281). Hanging in the balance is Myers's pivotal question — Is Steve guilty of doing nothing at the scene of the crime or did he "sign that everything was cool"? (*ibid.*, 179). The suspenseful text offers a number of discussion topics for young readers concerning the guilt of abetting crimes and the hard-handedness of the justice system toward teen suspects.

Furthering the vehicle of conflicting testimony is *Shooter* (2004), a psychological novel that mimics the motivations and crimes committed at a student terrorist spree at Columbine High School, Littleton, Colorado, on April 20, 1999. Myers's metafictional approach questions the input of psychologists, school personnel, and law enforcement officers to a threat analysis report. The contrasting results commend the gentle county psychologist Richard Ewings for reassuring Cameron Porter during non-judgmental testimony. By patching in media reports and the meandering diary of shooter Leonard "Len" Gray, the narrative juxtaposes the complex motives of a community tragedy that bears implications for other schools and institutions. The novel offers teachers, students, and parents a springboard for mature debate on outlawry committed by disaffected students and of the bullying and belittling that forces Len and Cameron to the outskirts of school participation.

See also **Leonard Gray, *The Great Migration*, Steve Harmon, *Monster*, Cameron Porter, *Shooter*, *Won't Know Till I Get There***

• *Further Reading*

Campbell, Patty. "The Sand in the Oyster Radical Monster," *Horn Book* 75, no. 6 (November 1999): 769.

Gepson, Lolly. "Review: *Shooter*," *Booklist* 101, no. 6 (15 November 2004): 608.

Myers, Walter Dean. "And Then I Read....," *Voices-from-the-Middle* 8, no. 4 (May 2001): 58–62.

____. *Monster: A Novel.* New York: HarperCollins, 1999.

Rochman, Hazel. "Interview: Walter Dean Myers," *Booklist* 96, no. 12 (15 February 2000): 1101.

Staunton, John A. "Review: *Monster: A Novel*," *Journal of Adolescent & Adult Literacy* 45, no. 8 (May 2002): 791–793.

military

Myers speaks knowledgably about military life and the impact of wars on black history. Soldiery forms the subtext of *The Great Migration: An American Story* (1993), which is set during World War I; of "The Treasure of Lemon Brown" (2001), which dramatizes the grief of the title character for his son Jesse, a casualty of World War II; and of *Darnell Rock Reporting* (1994), a seriocomic novel about the plight of unemployed Vietnam vets. Two of Myers's histories, *Now Is Your Time! The African-American Struggle for Freedom* (1991) and *U.S.S. Constellation: Pride of the American Navy* (2004), reflect the role of blacks in the army and navy and the importance of integrated teamwork to American military successes. In the latter, Myers cites the importance of stamina or "personal toughness," which is essential in a setting where "the sea was unforgiving" (Myers, 2004, 44). From veterans, young powder monkeys quickly acquire a respect for military responsibility, especially for its importance to the preservation of an entire unit or ship. The motif of elders mentoring to youngsters supports Myers's life-long promotion of intergenerational tutoring.

Myers' winsome poem, "To a Child of War," anthologized in *On the Wings of Peace* (1995), analyzes the costs of combat beyond the battlefield. Illustrated with James E. Ransome's three views of a "Methuselah-eyed" child in pensive pose, the poem attempts to console the young noncombatant for losses that no human gift can assuage (Myers, 1995, 40–41). The poet links the world's charity with the treasures of the wise men, who offered the Christ Child myrrh, a "sweet incense" known in ancient times as a burial gift. Myers acknowledges that the claws of war harden the young, who have no way of restoring innocence shattered by battle. In the closing lines, he leaves doubt that any child scarred by military incursion can "wait/With sweet forgiveness" (*ibid.*, 41).

For the background and action of "The Vision of Felipe" (1978), a short story published in *Black Scholar*, the author turned his observations during a 1976 vacation to Peru into a reflection on the waves of destruction that emanate from guerrilla violence. By setting the story in Lima during the brutal 12-year dictatorship of Juan Velasco Alvarado, Myers illustrates how unwary peasants risk wounding during bursts of random violence. As a result of late-night gunfire, the title character, a homeless ten-year-old orphan, dies in the street from a stray bullet that lodges in his chest. The author, who prefers minimalist impressionism to carnage, pictures a lone tennis shoe and blood stains as the remains of a child who sought a new life in the city. Because the struggle for food and shelter outrank political concerns, the child seems oblivious to the purpose of military patrols or the intent of a curfew. Thus Felipe sets the pattern for other of Myers's wandering, displaced child victims.

A youngster's questions about killing turns into a lesson on war in *Won't Know Till I Get There* (1982). At Micheaux House for Senior Citizens, a 13-year-old delinquent, Earl Goins, serves a summer sentence within a Harlem community by aiding residents. To his question about killing, Jack Lasher displays pictures of his unit at Camp Polk before their deployment to Mindanao in the Philippines. On the subject of how he killed the enemy, Jack replies that wartime shooting targets noises rather than people. To movement in a log, Jack shoots into the woods, killing a young Japanese soldier. On eye-to-eye contact with the enemy, Jack admits, "There was a life and it was gone, and I was the one that did it" (Myers, 1982, 88). Easing the memory of killing another human being is a friendly encounter between Jack and a Japanese POW from Bataan who becomes a U.S. citizen. The former prisoner has one advantage — his memories do not include looking at the face of someone he shot.

In a review for the *Washington Post*, Myers commends the soldier's experience as a reason for pride and a source of male bonding among those with "warrior status" (Myers, 1991, 7). In the settling-in period for the 22nd Replacement Company in *Fallen Angels* (1988), recruits share basic training stories and develop an unsubtle barracks pecking order. One black barracks mate warns other black recruits about unity of race: "I can't trust no whitey to watch my back when the deal go down" (Myers, 1988, 16). To a self-important white ranger who threatens rookie infantryman Harry "Peewee" Gates, the retaliation is swift and deadly. Before the ranger can test his mettle against the Viet Cong, he lessens Peewee with "boy," an insufferable racist slur against self and manhood (*ibid.*, 12). Peewee batters him in the crotch and flicks a knife from his pillow before the ranger can regain control. The speed of the fracas suggests a home-grown survivalism that supports homeboys like Peewee in adaptation to the coming months of combat. For Perry, no preparation is enough. He carps, "There was never anything there until it was on top of your ass" (*ibid.*, 295). After recovery from a wound in mid–January 1968, he argues with himself: "No. I said no to myself. I wouldn't go back. I would go AWOL" (*ibid.*, 216). The argument between the trained soldier and the inner survivor reflects a duality in infantrymen that Myers implies is normal.

A comment on identification of combat dead arose in a 1994 interview for the staff of the *Journal of Reading*. To an issue in the text that unretrieved dog tags might conceal the circumstances of death, Myers acknowledged that wartime is too messy for simple cataloguing. He charged the military with subterfuge: "I've seen cases in which people were killed and the paperwork didn't go through for several weeks, and the Army would change the date of death" (Chance, *et al.*, 247). He added that people like the fictional Perry and Walowick may have eyewitness knowledge of a casualty that army headquarters smudges as missing in action.

Myers equates an elite regiment of black soldiers during the Civil War with a rescue mission to slaves. In *The Glory Field* (1994), the sudden encounter with a black Union soldier in March 1864 snatches Lizzy from the terrors of a pack of hounds chasing her through open fields to the safety of the U.S. Army. By campfires, men croon a sweet spiritual while they attend to "the work of soldiering," which involves cleaning leather boots and saddles (Myers, 1994, 65). An elderly conscript takes pride in the 440,760 blacks who swell the Northern army. A woman recalls how service turned boys into men "strutting so tall and proud" (*ibid.*, 129). In the saga's third stave, Grandma Saran remembers that her former master, Manigault Lewis, buries his own son, Manigault, Jr., with honors after the boy's service to the Confederate army. The demise of the son's contemporary, Lem Lewis, while fighting for a black Union regiment, angers the planter, who orders blacks to toss Lem's body into the river. The Lewis family, newly freed from slavery, chooses to start a new burial ground at Glory

Field with the interment of Lem in an unmarked grave. The addition sanctifies the ground with the remains of a family martyr.

A later work, the young adult biography *Toussaint L'Ouverture: The Fight for Haiti's Freedom* (1996) explores a different kind of military. Reflecting on the rise of François Toussaint to a Caribbean liberator of slaves, Myers pictures the innate leadership of a tactician who instinctively protects his ragtag followers by leading them to higher ground. Because better trained, better equipped French soldiers led by General Charles Leclerc outnumber the Haitian irregulars, Toussaint chooses to draw out the conflict. By staying in the high country just out of reach, he wears down the French, who suffer tropical diseases and severe casualty rates. The strategy gains the Haitian general enough time to negotiate for his people's freedom. Although Leclerc deceives Toussaint and holds him in prison until the islander's death, the black general's legend grows greater than the man and fuels a revolt that resonates throughout the West Indies and the Western Hemisphere.

See also **Fallen Angels, historical milieu, Richie Perry**

• *Further Reading*

Chance, Rosemary, Teri Lesesne, and Lois Buckman. "And the Winner Is ... : A Teleconference with Walter Dean Myers," *Journal of Reading* 38, no. 3 (November 1994): 246–249.

Masciere, Christina. "Browser: Cultural Adventures," *New Orleans Magazine* 31, no. 1 (October 1996): 74.

Myers, Walter Dean. *Fallen Angels*. New York: Scholastic, 1988.

_____. *The Glory Field*. New York: Scholastic, 1994.

_____. "Surviving Mean Streets," *Washington Post* (12 May 1991): 7.

_____. "To a Child of War," *On the Wings of Peace*. New York: Clarion, 1995.

_____. *U.S.S. Constellation: Pride of the American Navy*. New York: Holiday House, 2004.

_____. *Won't Know Till I Get There*. New York: Viking, 1982.

Monster: A Novel

In Myers's 1994 Margaret A. Edwards Award Acceptance Speech, which the author delivered at the American Library Association annual convention in Miami, he anticipated the writing of *Monster: A Novel* (1999), a contemplative journal of 16-year-old Steven Harmon during his trial for complicity in robbery and murder. Myers comments on society's preference for distancing itself from troubled youths and for giving "silent assent ... to their destruction" (Myers, 1995, 132). He accounts for his choice of young felons as characters as a way to give alienated youth sources of morals and right thinking about real-life temptations. With compassion for those shut away in adult prisons, he singles out the undervalued, the throwaway children who need greater articulation of emotion and higher ideals to support them through coming of age.

Myers challenges the American justice system by describing his narrator/protagonist's youth and inexperience and by suggesting in Steve and his cronies a growing amorality that critic Linda D. Behen, a reviewer for *Book Report* labels "the dark side of human nature" (Behen, 1999, 61). At night, Steve sobs in Cell Block D of the

Manhattan Detention Center while he hears young inmates being beaten and gang raped. His normal biological functions—eating, sleeping, using the toilet—occur under the scrutiny of guards. He has already learned a fearful truism of the insider: "If anybody knows that you are crying, they'll start talking about it and soon it'll be your turn to get beat up when the lights go out" (Myers, 1999, 1). Prison rules exacerbate the dehumanizing process by forcing inmates to wear orange uniforms and by forbidding Steve the touching of his father's hand during visitation. On the van ride to the courtroom, Steve lurches in shackles. Long before he is exonerated, prison treatment brutalizes his spirit.

Adults move in and out of the case and view Steve and his ordeal impersonally, as though he were a monster already convicted of abetting the theft of five cartons of cigarettes and the shooting of drugstore owner Alguinaldo Nesbitt through the torso with his own chrome-plated pistol. Two criminals, Richard "Bobo" Evans and James King, display aberrant personality traits and behaviors in court, where they glower at Steve. Steve's attorney, Kathy O'Brien, advises, "You'd better put some distance between yourself and whatever being a tough guy represents" (*ibid.*, 216). In *Bad Boy: A Memoir* (2001), Myers develops a reason for the enmity that forces young toughs into negative modes of behavior: "Each of us is born with a history already in place.... While we live our own individual lives, what has gone before us, our history, always has some effect on us" (Myers, 2001, 1).

Myers uses suspense and metaphor as two literary means of heightening emotions. The crime, which leaves victim Alguinaldo Nesbitt to drown in his own blood, takes place three days before Christmas. Like Tippy in *It Ain't All for Nothin'* (1978), Steve apparently serves as lookout, a pose that distances him from the actual crime. The symbolic court date of July 6 places the boy in the hands of a bored judge, defense attorney Kathy O'Brien, and a Assistant District Attorney Sandra Petrocelli two days after Independence Day. Myers uses a mix of ethnic names—José Delgado, Salvatore Zinzi, Asa Briggs, Wendell Bolden, Officer Williams, Detective Gluck—to Americanize the episode. Glazing the scene with cynicism is a guard's report to Steve that observers are contributing to a pool on the outcome of the jury trial.

At the heart of Myers's approach to teen crime is his concern for the immaturity and malleability of perpetrators, two motives that he develops further in *Shooter* (2004). In an interview with Hazel Rochman for *Booklist*, he stressed that "It's incredible that these kids could go from being in high school now and not much later be faced with a life sentence" (Rochman, 2000, 1101). The handcuffing of Steve to a U-bolt on the court bench suggests that he has no choice in participation in a trial for a crime he claims not to have committed. Contributing to the seamy background of the investigation is a tip to police detectives from Zinzi, a criminal at Riker's Island. The jail, opened in 1932 due east of Harlem in the East River, is the world's largest penal colony, which houses 80 percent of New York City's criminals and suspects. Zinzi offers inside information in exchange for a shorter sentence. The deal-making between lawbreakers and police creates an eerie background of shadowy witnesses who further sully Steve's reputation while he sits at the table with his defense attorney and says nothing.

See also **Steve Harmon, Christopher Myers**

• *Further Reading*

Behen, Linda D. "Review: *Monster: A Novel*," *Book Report* 18, no. 2 (September/October 1999): 61.
Myers, Walter Dean. *Bad Boy: A Memoir*. New York: HarperCollins, 2001.
_____. *Monster: A Novel*. New York: HarperCollins, 1999.
_____. "1994 Margaret A. Edwards Award Acceptance Speech," *Youth Services in Libraries* 8, no. 2 (winter 1995): 129–133.
Rochman, Hazel. "Interview: Walter Dean Myers," *Booklist* 96, no. 12 (15 February 2000): 1101.
Staunton, John A. "Review: *Monster: A Novel*," *Journal of Adolescent & Adult Literacy* 45, no. 8 (May 2002): 791–793.

The Mouse Rap

Exploiting a hidden treasure motif complicated by memories of New York gangsters from the 1930s, Myers packs *The Mouse Rap* (1990) with the exuberance and exhibitionism of the early teens. He begins each of the first 13 chapters with rap and concludes the last chapter the same way, with breezy, slangy verse. The bouncy patter between groups of children keeps pace with a plot-counterplot about Tiger Moran's stashed belongings and an invitation to 14-year-old Frederick "The Mouse" Douglas to dance in a talent contest with a neighborhood trio called the Selects. Contributing incongruity is the boy's diminutive size. Myers upends expectations about Bobby Burdette's challenge to Mouse by sending Beverly in a flying Kung Fu stance, knocking Bobby to the ground in a daze. Bobby's surprise downfall introduces a string of unexpected ends to minor crises, a literary strategy that appeals to young readers.

The author prefers a light touch in scenes of pick-up basketball in the park, walks with Beverly and Sheri, and watching television and eating tacos prepared by Ceil Bonilla's mother. Heavier concerns flit across Mouse's mind every time he ponders the likelihood that his estranged father, Paul Douglas, will stop working in the Middle East and reunite with his former wife, a telephone company employee who is cool to being wooed a second time. In chapter 9, the unease fills Mouse like a heavy liquid to the point of overflowing after he has accustomed himself to "all the my-father-don't-live-here moves" (Myers, 1990, 124). Affable, yet vulnerable, he continues dodging his father's invitations to avoid "little price tags … that read 'risk' and 'not sure' and 'confusion'" (*ibid.*, 159). With the aplomb of a child who knows how to release tension, Mouse withdraws to the safety of television and capers with his friends.

Critic Diane Roback admires the Keystone Cops style of comedy that ends *The Mouse Rap*. The narrative keeps agile rap flowing and characters in cartoon-like motion to the end. At the re-enactment of a bank heist that Booster's grandmother, gang moll Katie Donahue, took part in, Mouse tries to disarm Booster and succeeds in sending a pistol skidding across the bank floor. A guard tackles an innocent man and a skinny woman drops a jar of dimes before police begin streaming in at both entrances. In the retreat, the uproar jogs Booster's memory about Tiger Moran's money. Because two elderly accomplices, Sudden Sam and Gramps "Slick" Jones, get into a fist fight, Beverly excuses their actions as a competition for her favors. A rapid resolution of the mysterious lost cash sustains the humor, with Mouse once more in control of loose elements in his young life. Reviewer Gerry Larson, in a critique for *School Library Journal*, notes that Myers's "banter reveals both independence and vulnerability" in Mouse, whose emotions are as unstable as his adventures are colorful (Larson, 1991, S37).

• *Further Reading*

Larson, Gerry. "Review: *The Mouse Rap*," *School Library Journal* 37, no. 2 (February 1991): S37.
Myers, Walter Dean. *The Mouse Rap*. New York: HarperCollins, 1990.
Roback, Diane. "Review: *The Mouse Rap*," *Publishers Weekly* 237, no. 13 (30 March 1990): 64.

Muhammad Ali

Myers's emphasis on the importance of heroes to youths tends to favor athletic stars like Jackie Robinson, Jack Johnson, Larry Doby, and Joe Louis over political figures, celebrities, religious leaders, writers, actors, and musicians. In 2001, the author honored an enduring American figure in a biography, *The Greatest: Muhammad Ali*. The Olympic gold-medalist progresses from professional heavyweight boxing champ to civil rights freedom fighter and survivor of Parkinson's disease, the possible result of "the cruelest of sports" (Myers, 2001, xi). Along the way to stardom, he inspires men like baseball player Reggie Jackson and aspiring athletes to take pride in racial heritage. A review in the *Los Angeles Daily News* summarizes Ali's impact as one "who dared to be boastful and arrogant in an age when African-Americans were told to be quiet and respectful" ("World," 2001).

Myers recounts Ali's rise from childhood, a starting place that allows young readers to identify with struggles along the way. Named Cassius Marcellus Clay, Jr., at his birth in Louisville, Kentucky, on January 17, 1942, he chooses boxing as a sport after someone steals his Schwinn bicycle when he is twelve. A decade later, he achieves international notoriety by facing Sonny Liston, a world heavyweight champion bearing an intimidating criminal record for assault and armed robbery in service to the Mafia. Among Clay's admirers is Malcolm X, who visits the boxer's training camp in Miami on January 15, 1964. As described in *Malcolm X: By Any Means Necessary* (1993), Malcolm prays silently in Ali's dressing room before the fight with Liston and cheers on the underdog.

In Myers's biography, Clay's rise to sports celebrity coincides with a number of shifts in black philosophy — the rise of the Nation of Islam, the establishment of a "Black Is Beautiful" movement, and the August 1963 March on Washington, at which Dr. Martin Luther King, Jr., delivers his "I Have a Dream" speech. During the Vietnam War, black soldiers like Colonel Fred V. Cherry, a seven-year prisoner of war in Hoa Lo prison outside Hanoi, craves news of Ali, a sports hero in Myers's *A Place Called Heartbreak: A Story of Vietnam* (1992). At a height of competitive fame, Clay alters his name to Muhammad Ali, but his notoriety plunges to a low in June 1967 when he refuses to enter the army as an act of Muslim piety and obedience to the Koran. After his career wanes, he returns to prominence on July 22, 1996, at age 52 to ignite the Olympic torch at the summer games in Atlanta, Georgia.

Myers's affectionate, but realistic commentary won him compliments from readers, teachers, librarians, and reviewers. Critic Ann W. Moore, a reviewer for *School Library Journal*, praised Myers for producing a memorable biography about "an American icon" (Moore, 2001, 57). An unsigned critique in *Booklist* honored the choice of Ali as "a courageous iconoclast whose story continues to inspire new generations" ("Review," 2002, 766). Critic Khafre K. Abif, reviewing for *Black Issues Book Review*, approved Myers's adulation of a sports figure who "made a huge impact on the American consciousness" (Abif, 2001, 80).

• *Further Reading*

Abif, Khafre K. "Review: The Greatest: Muhammad Ali," *Black Issues Book Review* 3, no. 3 (May 2001): 80.

Moore, Ann W. "Review: The Greatest: Muhammad Ali," *School Library Journal* 51, no. 1 (January 2005): 57.

Myers, Walter Dean. *The Greatest: Muhammad Ali*. New York: Scholastic, 2001.

_____. *Malcolm X: By Any Means Necessary*. New York: Scholastic, 1993.

"Review: The Greatest: Muhammad Ali," Booklist 98 (1 January 2002): 766.

"A World to Learn From," *Los Angeles Daily News* (6 February 2001).

music

Music is dear to Walter Dean Myers and essential to his appreciation of black history. In a comment for *Instructor* magazine, he recalled growing up in Harlem and "[listening] to music that ranged from the blues to jazz to the spirituals we sang in the corner church" (Lewis, 1996, 73). In the short story "Jeremiah's Song," collected in *The Giver and Related Readings* (1987), the author muses on the dividing line between music as amusement and music as worship. The elderly title character strums guitar and croons "The Delta Blues" until the appearance of the pious Sister Todd. In her presence, he shifts to a more seemly "Precious Lord" or "Just a Closer Walk with Thee" (Myers, 1987, 187). It is fitting that, at Grandpa Jeremiah's funeral, mourners conclude the service with the jubilant slave shout "Soon-a Will Be Done" and weep at the grave site at the playing of "Precious Lord." The use of music as a tribute fittingly enwraps the old man's remains in godly praise.

The author's tiny home office sports a picture of Billie Holiday, one of the blues greats from the 1930s to the 1950s. From the beginning of his career, the author included the rhythms and lyrics of songs that hold the same meaning in the lives of fictional characters that they bear in Myers's life. The shift in technology in *Mojo and the Russians* (1977) sets children apart from Drusilla, the elderly mojo lady run down by Michael "Mean" Dean's bicycle. She mutters, "If they ain't ripping and running down the street they got them radio and tape things stuck up to their ears and popping their fingers like nobody in the world every heard no music before except them" (Myers, 1977, 18). Her grumble establishes the full of immersion of a generation in meaningful sound.

Later fictional scenes involve the performance of musical lines and rhythms at crucial moments in the action. In *It Ain't All for Nothin'* (1978), Grandma Carrie Brown instructs her 12-year-old grandson Tippy on the importance of Christian faith in his life. After he confesses that his derelict father Lonnie is a thief, Carrie reminds the boy of the availability of heavenly guidance. She suggests a familiar hymn as a prayer: "Precious Lord, take my hand, lead me on, let me stand" (Myers, 1978, 59). In *The Nicholas Factor* (1983), Gerald McQuillen, a college student enlisted by John Martens of the National Security Agency to spy on the Crusader Society, ponders the job of infiltrating a campus group with neo-Nazi ties. As his thoughts fluctuate through the night, he listens on an FM station to a Bob Marley album of early reggae. The visceral stimulus gives Gerald focus and emotional release. He remarks, "I found myself not listening to [the lyrics], shutting them out so that the driving force of the music filled me" (Myers, *Nicholas* 15). As Martens ratchets up the risk of spying, Gerald again turns to music by pulling off the highway and turning up the radio enough to drown out concerns that Gerald is not equal to the challenge. The use of familiar musicians as a psychological bolster establishes the value of musicians as role models to the young and untried.

Myers stresses instances of music as a spiritual salve during stirring moments. In *Now Is Your Time! The African-American Struggle for Freedom* (1991), a history reflecting Myers's heritage and genealogy, he mentions the importance of group sings among black laborers, who join in "Bound for the Promised Land" and "Crossing over Jordan," both musical reminders of a time of rest and recuperation from slave labor. Concerning the Bower, the plantation that owned his great grandmother, the author quotes a member of General J. E. B. Stuart's staff on the contributions of slaves to hospitality on his visit in September 1862: "The Negroes would ask for the lively measures of a jig or a breakdown, and then danced within the circle ... like dervishes or lunatics" to spectator applause (Myers, 1991, 147). More plaintive is the spiritual "Oh, Freedom!," which Myers cites along with photos of young drummers and fifers for the 54th Massachusetts Regiment, formed by Colonel Robert Gould Shaw to aid the Union army. As the men march in parade, the band plays "John Brown's Body" in tribute to John Brown, an abolitionist who led an unsuccessful raid on the federal arsenal at Harpers Ferry, Virginia, on October 16, 1859. These musical renditions serve as protests of racism and reassurances of grace to the godly.

Much as he himself enjoys song and the history of music in the lives of his forebears, Myers relaxes and serenades his fictional characters with music. Early in his career, he depicted flute sounds as a release for disappointment in *The Dragon Takes a Wife* (1972), a picture-fable that presaged Myers's later works on the natural flow of the blues as an antidote to human frustration. At a sad moment in the seriocomic novel *Fast Sam, Cool Clyde, and Stuff* (1975), Myers describes the healing aspect of "Mood Indigo," which Stuff plays on his saxophone to lift the spirits of Kitty Jones. His union with the instrument results in an epiphany for Stuff: "It was the first time, really, that my friends meant more to me than my mother" (Myers, 1975, 105). A happier occasion acknowledges Sam's athletic scholarship to the University of Arizona. The partying begins with chips and cookies and includes Angel's father and his Puerto

Rican friends, who provide guitar music. The celebratory element of music elevates it from amusement to spiritual uplift.

The author also chooses music to highlight and enhance drama. To promote community affairs and raise money, the Action Group in *The Young Landlords* (1979) organizes recorded music to please a variety of tastes and to encourage dancing at a street fair. The project promotes repair to 356 West 122nd Street, a tenement in need of upgrading. A short story, "The Treasure of Lemon Brown" (1983), published in *Boys' Life*, characterizes the blues as a form of identity to the homeless title character, a harmonica player and singer who has traveled Louisiana, Georgia, and Mississippi before arriving at a boarded-up tenement basement in Harlem. He boasts, "If I sang at a funeral, the dead would commence to rocking with the beat" (Myers, "Treasure," 35). His battered harmonica bears a double meaning in its return from a combat zone in the personal effects of his son Jesse, who died during World War II. Myers creates irony out of a treasure that comforts an old man who has no one to live for.

Of subtler significance to plot is the role of music in shaping character. Myers uses a church choir performance to open *Crystal* (1987), a young adult novel that portrays 16-year-old model Crystal Brown making life choices about the amorality of talent handlers who enrich themselves off her youth and sexual allure. In *Fallen Angels* (1988), memories of singer Diana Ross and of the Shirelles' performance at the Apollo Theater in Harlem relieve Infantryman Richard "Richie" Perry of homesickness and stirs him to courage during the Vietnam War. In a somber turn of phrase in the picture-ode *Harlem: A Poem* (1997), Myers adds to the rhythm of community life the bluesy rhapsody from Smalls's jazz club juxtaposed against the "cracked reed/soprano sax laughter" of music honoring the deceased while funeral cars bear the coffin to the cemetery (Myers, 1997, n.p.). In each instance, familiar songs bear elements of identity and belonging to people who feel threatened and saddened.

Myers honors the place of spirituals in slave lore in *The Glory Field* (1994), in which call-and-response serves as solacing communication among fearful field hands. As they tend sweet potatoes and sing, their words express fear for two runaways, Lem and Joshua Lewis. The narrative illustrates changing times in the third stave, in which guitarist Abby Lewis declares his allegiance to the "new breed" of musicians who play ragtime, a late–19th-century phenomenon and forerunner of jazz (Myers, 1994, 96). The Lewis family perpetuates its penchant for melody during the Great Depression, when 16-year-old Luvenia Lewis, Abby's second cousin, joins the choir at Bethel Tabernacle in Chicago in a processional to the humming of "Over My Head." In the fourth stave, Luvenia's second cousin, 16-year-old Tommy Lewis, observes a black demonstration in fictional Johnson City, South Carolina, where marchers sing "O Freedom!," a paean to liberation. Another singing of the anthem recurs after the march in response to arrangements for another worthless meeting between community leaders. In the final stave, Myers introduces multiculturalism in Malcolm Lewis's band, which includes an Indian satirist, Caucasian pianist, and native American bass guitarist.

Music remains a staple in Myers's more recent works. In *My Name Is America: The Journal of Joshua Loper, a Black Cowboy on the Chisholm Trail, 1871* (1999), the title figure sings to the cattle the soothing phrases of 19th-century classics—"Just Before the Battle, Mother," "Lorena," and "Jeannie with the Light Brown Hair"—and segues into improvisations that relieve boredom and fatigue. For a picture book, *The Blues of Flats Brown* (2000), the author envisions a hip dog, Flats Brown, a crooner-guitarist from the Mississippi bayou accompanied by his pal Caleb on the bones on "The Freaky Flea Blues," "The Bent Tail Blues," "The Junkyard Heap," "The Bad Barking Blues," and "The Mangy Muzzle Stomp." In the words of critic Shelle Rosenfeld, a reviewer for *Booklist*, the duo's songs "draw out and comfort the hidden hurt in even the coldest hearts" (Rosenfeld, 2000, 1242). At a climactic confrontation with A. J. Grubbs, his former owner, Flats stakes his freedom on a heart-rending soul tune, "The Gritty Grubbs Blues," an example of Christian forgiveness. Like the prayers for early Christians for their persecutors, the sympathy implied for the junkyard owner redeems him from barbarity and sets Flats free from persistent stalking.

In a subsequent picture book, *Blues Journey* (2003), the author illustrates the range of events and emotions that inspired blues improvisers to compose paradoxically uplifting and deflating tunes and lyrics. Sources of human misery extend from slavery to chain gangs, injustice and lynching, share-cropping and net-fishing, and civil rights freedom marches. Enhancing black history are allusions to the creaking deck of a slave ship, to fleeing north on a rail car to avoid arrest in Memphis, and to the Parchman farm, a notorious 2,000-acre penal plantation in Sunflower County, Mississippi, that worked black convicts like field hands. As described by Ilene Cooper, a reviewer for *Booklist*, a "deceptively simple rhyme scheme tracks the deeper feelings of lives that have been bruised" (Cooper, 2003, 1082).

More plaintive than picture books is Myers's inclusion of music in realistic teen fiction. He dramatizes the displacement and alienation that Chanelle suffers from divorced parents in the novel *The Beast* (2003). While studying among mostly white students at Wallingford Academy in Connecticut, she finds peace in Sunday evening candlelight services, where she can sing hymns. Her friend, 16-year-old Anthony "Spoon" Witherspoon, perceives that music is Chanelle's support in hard times. The theme reverberates in *A Time to Love: Stories from the Old Testament* (2003), a collection of biblical episodes that express a full range of human behaviors. In the account of Zillah and Lot, the daughter identifies her mother's yearning for sunshine and her wish that "every minute would be filled with music" (Myers, *A Time*, 88). In the marketplace, the unnamed wife of Lot enjoys instrumental music in contrast to the ominous mutterings of Lot and his brother Abraham. A lover of beauty and merrymaking, the wife takes time to admire a sensuous dancer decked in gold bangles and instrumental music, performances that the wife admires as facets of the "good life" (*ibid.*, 92). In another story about Abraham, after his terrifying struggle with son Isaac up a pinnacle in Moriah to offer a burnt sacrifice to God, the patriarch clings to a stern piety. After God intervenes in a ritual that might have required the killing of Isaac, the two rejoice on their way down after a ram miraculously takes Isaac's place on the altar. On the walk home under a half-moon, Abraham seems less critical of the "good life." Isaac reports, "We sing a song of praise to the night sky," a line that anticipates the lyrical reverence of David's psalms (*ibid.*, 84).

The author extends the concept of worship through sacred music as a given in black culture. In *Here in Harlem: Poems in Many Voices* (2004), a preacher values the singing and shouts of an ecstatic congregation. Even the sweep of a black hand on piano keys at a rent party the poet compares to "[scratching] God's broad back" (Myers, *Here*, 51). Church organist Effie Black carries the melding of sacred with profane to a street scene, where songs unite strollers and sitters in harmonies she calls "the sweet voice of a living God" (*ibid.*, 60). Less pious, but no less integral to peace of mind is the burst of music from young sailors enjoying peace in *U.S.S. Constellation: Pride of the American Navy* (2004). Myers cites Wilburn Hall, a ship's officer, who recalls a moment of relaxation, when "Songs were heard forward, messenger boys were skylarking in the gangways" (Myers, 2004, 25). By equating melody with worship and peace, Myers elevates the beauties of black musicmaking to pinnacles of humanity.

• *Further Reading*

Cooper, Ilene. "Review: *Blues Journey*," *Booklist* 99, no. 12 (15 February 2003): 1082.
Lewis, Valerie. "Meet the Author," *Instructor* 105 (May/June 1996): 72–73.
Myers, Walter Dean. *Blues Journey*. New York: Holiday House, 2003.
_____. *The Blues of Flats Brown*. New York: Holiday House, 2000.
_____. *Fast Sam, Cool Clyde, and Stuff*. New York: Viking, 1975.
_____. *The Glory Field*. New York: Scholastic, 1994.
_____. *Harlem: A Poem*. New York: Scholastic, 1997.
_____. *Here in Harlem: Poems in Many Voices*. New York: Holiday House, 2004.
_____. *It Ain't All for Nothin'*. New York: Viking, 1978.
_____. "Jeremiah's Song," *The Giver and Related Readings*. Boston: McDougal Littell, 1987.
_____. *Mojo and the Russians*. New York: Viking, 1977.
_____. *The Nicholas Factor*. New York: Viking, 1983.
_____. *Now Is Your Time! The African-American Struggle for Freedom*. New York: HarperCollins, 1991.
_____. *A Time to Love: Stories from the Old Testament*. New York: Scholastic, 2003.
_____. "The Treasure of Lemon Brown," *Boys' Life* 73 (March 1983): 34–40.
_____. *U.S.S. Constellation: Pride of the American Navy*. New York: Holiday House, 2004.
Rosenfeld, Shelle. "Review: *The Blues of Flats Brown*," *Booklist* 96, no. 13 (1 March 2000): 1242.

Myers, Christopher

The youngest of Walter Dean Myers's three children, Christopher "Chris" Myers was steeped in black history, music, and storytelling in childhood. He showed artistic promise by age four, when he entered elementary school. Introduced to art in 1987 at age 13, he graduated from high school three years without achieving the maturity of his peers. After graduating from Brown University, he returned to a neighborhood seriously altered by the decline in some of his classmates into drugs and crime. He first collaborated with his father on *Shadow of the Red Moon* (1995), a fantasy-quest novel illustrated with ten pen-and-ink drawings. Although the work is immature, it displays a vigor and intensity from deft use of texturizing and chiaroscuro, the play of light against dark. Still motivated by coursework, Chris

Myers took part in the Whitney Museum of American Art one-year Independent Studio Program, which he completed in 1996. Influenced by the styles of Romare Bearden and Jacob Lawrence, Myers developed modernist expressions in colored markers, woodcut, clipped newspaper, and photo-collage.

Chris Myers's artistic vision emerged in the vibrant, kinetic images in the picture-ode *Harlem: A Poem* (1997), a visual panorama that critic Michael Cart lauded as "metaphorical moments" in community life (Cart, 1997, 1021). In concert with his father's anthem to freedom, Chris used collage, gouache, and ink to supply a riveting image — a white turbaned West African newcomer spreading his burned-umber arms to feel the liberation of a new land. Dressed in an orange tunic splotched with lighter and darker tones, the figure releases centuries of anguish in African people longing for a welcoming community of fellow blacks. Echoing the paean are three black birds, wings extended, who caress the free air above.

According to critic Teri Lesesne, Christopher Myers's striking collage illustrations enhance and illumine the rhythmic chorus created by the elder Myers in this tribute to a community "whose legacy is immeasurable" (Lesesne, 1998, 51). Christopher Myers contributed surreal black-and-white photos, cropped and edited, to his father's chilling juvenile crime study in *Monster: A Novel* (1999). In this same period, Chris published his own picture books, beginning with *Black Cat* (1999), an urban rap story that he illustrated with photographs. The read-along book earned a Coretta Scott King honor listing. He next wrote *Wings* (2000), winner of a Charlotte Zolotow honor citation. The book restyles the Greek myth of Icarus to Ikarus Jackson, an outsider whose individuality sets him apart from his peers. For *Fly!* (2001), Christopher Myers bases character growth on a boy's relationship with an elderly man, a motif common to the fiction of Walter Dean Myers. In 2003, Chris's father dedicated to his son *The Beast*, a novel that commiserates with youth growing up in a period of moral malaise and rising drug addiction and violence.

The publication of *A Time to Love: Stories from the Old Testament* (2003) revealed Chris Myers's growing competence with illustration and his instinct for enhancing his father's narratives. The artist's modes include modernistic pencil drawings, collage, and photos, for which he used family members and young Palestinian women as models. Of particular worth are the Egyptian profiles that echo a lengthy tradition of projectionless side views and the familiar Nile symbols, white garments, gold wheat, oxen, birds, and blue-green lotus, a pervasive emblem of exotic beauty. Of his research into graphic methods of depicting the divine, Chris Myers described study of classic religious works in the Brooklyn Museum and the Metropolitan Museum of Art and his focus on painters Rembrandt von Rijn, Marc Chagall, and Henry Ossawa Tanner, a black painter from Pittsburgh best known for his vignettes of African American peasant life. Myers solves the problem of painting God's image by picturing his works in normal human relations. The artist asserts, "This is where God lives" (Myers, 2003, 127).

In the dedication, Chris thanks his mother for escorting him to "holy places like church and museums" (*ibid.*, v). He credits her with introducing him to art, love, and God and with serving as a hand model. The importance of hands to the narrative reaches a dramatic peak in the seizure of Joseph by his own brothers. Chris

Myers's mixed media drawings picture spare, large-handed males lifting Joseph, whose body tones range from rust and deep orange to luminous shades of yellow. A subsequent picture of Joseph immured in a pit contrasts his bound hands with the fists of nine brothers reaching down with curved blades in their grasp. As the author moves the story toward resolution, the artist returns to strong hands for another luminous image of a forgiving Joseph, who sweeps ten guilty brothers into his arms. Jana Riess, a reviewer for *Publishers Weekly,* exudes enthusiasm for the experimental work: "This fresh aesthetic approach underscores the collection's implicit message: there are numberless ways to behold sacred stories" ("Review," 2003, 64).

• *Further Reading*

Beram, Nell S. "Review: *Fly!,*" *Horn Book* 78, no. 2 (March-April 2002): 203.

Campbell, Patty. "The Sand in the Oyster Radical Monster," *Horn Book* 75, no. 6 (November 1999): 769.

Cart, Michael. "Review: *Harlem: A Poem,*" *Booklist* 98, no. 12 (15 February 1997): 1021.

Decandido, Graceanne A. "Review: *A Time to Love: Stories from the Old Testament,*" *Booklist* 99, no. 18 (15 May 2003): 1656.

Lesesne, Teri. "Books for Children," *Emergency Librarian* 25, no. 5 (May/June 1998): 49–51.

Myers, Walter Dean. *Harlem: A Poem.* New York: Scholastic, 1997.

_____. *A Time to Love: Stories from the Old Testament.* New York: Scholastic, 2003.

Riess, Jana. "Review: *A Time to Love: Stories from the Old Testament,*" *Publishers Weekly* 250, no. 13 (31 March 2003): 64.

Shinn, Dorothy. "Museum Showcases Illustrator," *Beacon Journal* (2 March 2003).

Myers, Walter Dean

Walter Dean Myers claims that he has "the best job in the world" because writing lets him do what he loves (Jones, 2001, 48). As of 2005, he had published 80 books, a greater total of pages than any other African American author. He summarized his own uniqueness as spokesman for young readers: "Very few men think about writing stories for young people.... And very few black men are writing at all" (Naughton, "Literary," 8). He maintains a varied output of science fiction and fantasy, biography and history, mystery-adventure stories, fairy tales, war fiction, drama and verse, and novels about African American teens living in New York's inner city communities. According to R. D. Lane, Myers turns the tide against youth fiction that creates racial bias and mythologizes the black soldier in war movies and the misfit lawbreaker of James Dean cult films. Instead, insists Lane, "Myers celebrates children by weaving narratives of the black juvenile experience in ways that reverse the effects of mediated messages of the black experience in public culture" (Lane, 1998, 127). As a result, the author succeeds with fans by conceptualizing the young black male's life choices.

Myers successfully blends memories of his Harlem youth with historical changes in the 'hood. Drawing on boxes of heirloom sepia-toned photographs and reference works and on field trips to Harlem settings, he focuses on middle-class families beset by serious issues—gangs, drugs, suicide, teen pregnancy, foster care and adoption, single parenting, and parental neglect. In one example, *The Young Landlords* (1979), he laces an upbeat story about community rehabilitation with Paul Williams's comments on his father's relentless nagging. The scene, which recurs in the exemplum "The Treasure of Lemon Brown" (1983), illustrates frustrations that reduce communication between male parent and son. Myers explained in *Scholastic Scope* his regard for narrative: "In fiction, kids can see things happen to someone else. They can cope with scary issues more easily" (Feder-Feitel, 2004, 14). He has earned critical regard for redefining the image of the black teen by evenhandedly depicting humorous mixups, non-sexual boy-girl friendships, intergenerational relations, and complex family dynamics without resorting to depressing images of burned-out ghettoes, virulent emotions, and dead-end lives.

Myers follows a routine that suits the rhythms of work. A resident of Jersey City, New Jersey, he lives and works in a modest house with his wife Constance and with Christopher, the youngest of his three children. In his off hours, the author plays the flute, works crossword puzzles, tends the family cat, travels, and writes plays and short fiction for fun. He is a pre-dawn riser who collects ideas while lying in bed after a restful night. Five days a week, he dons a 20-pound vest to enhance the exercise he gets from a five-mile walk from 5:00–7:00 A.M. After a shower, he goes to his small upstairs office and composes seven pages, down from his goal of ten pages when he first started writing professionally. His writing fleshes out a six-part story outline consisting of characterization and conflict, exposition, character recognizing internal weakness, character growth, falling action, and wrap-up. He draws believable human actions from "a resume. Actually it is an application form," a template that frames the figures in his fiction (Naughton, "Walter," C1).

Critics admire Myers's ability to make people come to life on the printed page. He explains that complication is necessary for depth: "Life is far too complex for a simple shootout to solve our problems" (Myers, 2001, 62). For verisimilitude, he follows a character collage that Constance constructs from photos and hangs over his computer work station. After a quick first draft, he studies the pictures and begins rewriting, filling in details from his own experience with fathers and sons, basketball, the army, and Harlem history. For organization, he keeps a detailed kitchen flow chart of each stage of his tasks, including selecting names from sports rosters and high school yearbooks. He graces even the starkest narratives with grandeur. One of his grimmest novels, *Fallen Angels* (1988), allows anti-hero Richard "Richie" Perry to look up from a nest of sandbags at jets streaking overhead, which take on the shapes of "dark birds in a sweeping arc across a silver sky" (Myers, 1988, 101).

Of his motivation, Myers holds fast to the aims of a mentor. He observed to Allen O. Pierleoni, an interviewer for the *Sacramento Bee*, "I'm trying to give a voice to the imperfect model in order to reach imperfect kids" (Pierleoni, 2005). Myers relies heavily on introspection for characterization of folk tales, poetry, ghost stories, history, and biography. Whether describing the Vietnam War, a cattle drive on the Chisholm Trail, or neighborhood squabbles, he focuses on the young adult perspective. He has told interviewers that writing helps him to look back on his own boyhood difficulties and to interpret why he was a behavioral problem.

Myers believes that writing and analyzing literature help young people understand the causes of their troubles. He emphasizes that each person is responsible for his decisions and actions, the crux of *Monster: A Novel* (1999), a milestone in innovative teen fiction. To get at the causes of felonies, he sorts out the steps preceding criminal acts and incarceration. From interviews with prison inmates, he concluded that "there always seemed to be interim stages. Decisions to bend, not break, the law" (Campbell, 1999, 769). These increments of amorality "give permission for the next experience. Eventually a line would be crossed in which the probability of being caught was the only governing restriction" (*ibid.*). For his mastery of humanistic themes and realistic situations, he earned the regard of the Harlem Writers Guild and of critic Barbara Bader, who attested that his teen novels "spoke in a black voice to readers of all complexions and increasingly turned his protagonists into universal figures" (Bader, 2003, 145).

See also **chronology, writing**

• *Further Reading*

Bader, Barbara. "Multiculturalism Takes Root," *Horn Book Magazine* 79, no. 2 (March/April 2003): 143–152.

Campbell, Patty. "The Sand in the Oyster Radical Monster," *Horn Book* 75, no. 6 (November 1999): 769.

Corbett, Sue. "Walter Dean Myers Has Been Writing Poignant, Tough Stories for and about At-risk Kids," *Miami Herald* (26 January 2000).

Feder-Feitel, Lisa. "Writing About What's Real," *Scholastic Scope* 52, no. 12 (9 February 2004): 14.

Jones, Lynda. *Five Famous Writers.* New York: Scholastic, 2001.

Lane, R. D. "'Keepin' It Real': Walter Dean Myers and the Promise of African-American Children's Literature," *African American Review* 32, no. 1 (22 March 1998): 125–138.

Myers, Walter Dean. "And Then I Read....," *Voices-from-the-Middle* 8, no. 4 (May 2001): 58–62.

_____. *Fallen Angels.* New York: Scholastic, 1988.

Naughton, Jim. "Literary Crusader Writes Stories about Real Kids," *Los Angeles Times* (29 December 1989): 8.

_____. "Walter Dean Myers, Writing about Reality for Black Children," *Washington Post Book World* (9 December 1989): C1.

Pierleoni, Allen O. "Wrongs and the Writer," *Sacramento Bee* (29 March 2005).

Price, Anne, and Juliette Yaakov. *Middle and Junior High School Library Catalog.* New York: H. W. Wilson, 1995.

Now Is Your Time!

Myers combined an interest in American history and his own family background for the compilation of *Now Is Your Time! The African-American Struggle for Freedom* (1991). Dedicated to nine notable historians and researchers, the text stresses the centrality of the past to an appreciation of the present. The introduction states that "What we understand of our history is what we understand of ourselves" (Myers, 1991, ix). The title comes from a Civil War poster recruiting colored males for a regiment of the Union army from Burlington County, New Jersey. The ad encourages recruits to take an active role in ending slavery: "Every blow you strike at the call of your Government against this accursed Slaveholders' Rebellion, you Break the Shackles from the Limbs of your Kindred and their Wives and Children" (*ibid.*, 158). The sentiment chimes true to Myers's assertion that people must take an active interest in ridding themselves of ignorance and half-truths.

In a lyric overview, the author embraces his people's struggles as the source of his own sinew and heart. His identification with African American struggles commits him to "the darkest moments of my people" and to the perseverance that kept them alive and thriving (*ibid.*, x). He avoids an exclusionary approach by comparing the lot of agricultural slaves with that of white prisoners and the indentured poor from England and Ireland who labored for little more than room and board. All sources of cheap labor helped to enrich a land-owning class that laid the foundation for American wealth. The main difference between slavery and indenturing was the prospect of investing with additional interest by breeding slave offspring for labor or for sale, a concept that dehumanized black laborers to the level of livestock.

Myers exhibits pity for the newly captured Africans who lost status, family, language, and culture through the exploitative white Americans. A chapter on Abd al-Rahman Ibrahima, a Fulan prince born in Guinea in 1762, describes the lot of the newly captured. Educated in Koran at Timbuktu, a cosmopolitan African city near the Niger River in modern-day Mali, he fell into the hands of Mandingo warriors. After they sold him to slavers, he survived the Middle Passage. As a laborer for Thomas Foster, Ibrahima bore the derisive name Prince and worked under the whip in tobacco fields outside Natchez, Mississippi. Through the intercession of Dr. John Cox, printer Andrew Marschalk, and President James Monroe, abolitionists returned Ibrahima and his wife to Africa, where the prince died months later at age 67. Myers commends the former slave's doomed struggle to reunite with family and the noble image of a freedom fighter whose progeny remained slaves in the plantation South.

Myers embroiders his history with a variety of notable figures, including insurrectionists Cinqué and Nat Turner, scientist and inventor Lewis Howard Latimer and Benjamin Banneker, painter George W. Latimer, justice Thurgood Marshall, freedom fighters John Brown and Dred Scott, patriot Crispus Attucks, leaders Malcolm X and Dr. Martin Luther King, Jr., crusading journalist Ida B. Wells, innkeeper Samuel Fraunces, and sculptor Meta Vaux Warrick. A subsequent chapter on Revolutionary War veteran James Forten displays Myers's pride in ties to American history. The son of a Philadelphia sailmaker, Forten sailed on the *Royal Louis*, a warship owned by Stephen Decatur. After capture by the British, Forten survived imprisonment in the English hulks off Long Island, New York. Myers took a personal interest in the biography of Dolly Dennis, the author's great grandmother living at the Bower, Adam Stephen Dandridge's plantation at Leetown, Virginia. The narrative muses on her observations of the opulence of Virginia Aristocrats, who extended hospitality to General J. E. B. Stuart and his staff in September 1862 while Dandridge's staff occupied squalid slave quarters.

Critical reception of Myers's unique blend of historical events, biographical vignettes, and reportage established the author's skill at chronological narrative. One appreciative reviewer for *Teaching PreK–8* acknowledged the break with white dominated chronicles by supplying "a history of the United States from the African-American point of view" ("New," 1992, 125). Critic Lois Anderson, a reviewer for

Horn Book, cited the author's "intuitive, investigative" style, which includes captioned photos and documents, bibliography, and index (Anderson, 1992, 217). A review in *Publishers Weekly* described the novelist's skills at "[portraying] the quests of individual Africans against the background of broader historical movements" ("Review," 1991, 82).

See also **Appendix A**

• *Further Reading*

Anderson, Lois F. "Review: *Now Is Your Time! The African-American Struggle for Freedom*," *Horn Book* 68, no. 2 (March-April 1992): 217-218.

Andrews, Loretta Kreider. "Review: *Now Is Your Time! The African-American Struggle for Freedom*," *School Library Journal* 38, no. 4 (March 1992): 263–264.

Myers, Walter Dean. *Now Is Your Time! The African-American Struggle for Freedom.* New York: HarperCollins, 1991.

"New and Noteworthy," *Teaching PreK–8* 22, no. 8 (May 1992): 125.

"Review: *Now Is Your Time! The African-American Struggle for Freedom*," *Publishers Weekly* 238, no. 48 (1 November 1991): 82.

old age

Myers demonstrates compassion and respect for the aged in his earliest writings, setting a pattern that continues into his more recent works. In "Dark Side of the Moon," a short story published in the fall 1971 issue of *Black Creation*, the narrative follows Augie, a crazed high school student, from the rape and asphyxiation of Sheila, a fellow student, to more outrageous serial crimes. His paranoid gaze darts across the street to a fantasy figure—an "old wizened lady with warts on her chin" whom he envisions screaming "Murderer! Murderer!" (Myers, 1971, 28). On a flight from the neighborhood, Augie strangles a subway bum and murders Denise, a prostitute who trades sex for ten dollars. As madness extinguishes logic from Augie's thoughts, he imagines that Mrs. Fletcher, an elderly woman walking her dog on Herkimer Street, intuitively suspects him of crime. The story concludes on Augie's intent to kill her, his fourth victim, an old woman too obscure to deserve a media report on her death.

The author counters the perplexities of youth with the wisdom of old relatives and neighbors. In "Gums," a short story anthologized in *We Be Word Sorcerers: Twenty-five Stories by Black Americans* (1973), Myers sets up a familiar motif in his fiction—a failing 69-year-old grandparent who expresses to Stevie, his nine-year-old grandson, an old man's understanding of death's unpredictability. The terror of a personified Death results from Gums's advancing feebleness. He explains to Stevie, "I ain't been too well lately, I can't face up to death like I used to when I was young" (Myers, 1973, 183). More pointed is the commentary of Grandma Carrie Brown in *It Ain't All for Nothin'* (1978). After a fall that ends her ability to work, she confronts social workers with the hard truths of geriatric deterioration: "I'm just what you gonna be one day—I'm old. And if you don't like it, it don't make no difference" (Myers, 1978, 29). Her bitterness derives from frustration that 12-year-old Tippy can no longer depend on her for support and mothering. It is not surprising that the boy lapses into confusion. In the words of critic Ashley Jane Pennington in a review for *Interracial Books for Children Bulletin*, "He wonders how his grandmother's benevolent God can allow such dreadful things to happen" (Pennington, 1979, 18).

The outrage of youth at the loneliness and institutional warehousing of elderly residents of Micheaux House for Senior Citizens adds poignance to the social novel *Won't Know Till I Get There* (1982). Steve Perry's first response to his punishment for vandalizing a train is an admission: "I never really notice old people anyway. I mean, I look at them, but I don't see them" (Myers, 1982, 29). With the aid of Patty Bramwell, Steve's co-conspirator, the staff introduces Picture Day, a way of sharing identities. From Mabel Jackson, Steve learns the consequence of getting old and frail: "You lose your strength, you get scared easy" (*ibid.*, 45). According to critic Diane Gersoni Edelman in a review for the *New York Times Book Review*, Myers uses the seriocomic novel to denounce "the stereotypical view of [old people] as sexless, sedentary and non-productive; the loss of government benefits when they marry; discrimination against them in business" (Edelman, 1982, 27).

Less depressing are Myers's portraits of elderly people who maintain their interest in human affairs, such as the mentoring of 14-year-old Greg Ridley by the aged homeless title figure in "The Treasure of Lemon Brown" (1983). Brown's warm memories of a son who died during World War II reassure Greg that a father's love endures adversity. The author wrings humor out of 77-year-old Sister Gibbs in *Crystal* (1987), in which she gossips about the sex lives of sinners. At mention of her own sex appeal to Brother Pugh, Gibbs snickers, "If that old man knew what to say, he wouldn't know what to do!" (Myers, 1987, 29). The vigor of old people interests 14-year-olds in Gramps "Slick" Jones, Sheri Jones's grandfather, a former worker on a moving van in *The Mouse Rap* (1990). He shares memories of Tiger Moran, a local gangster in the 1930s during the heyday of gang kingpins Al Capone and Dutch Schultz. Gramps introduces Sheri and her friends to Sudden Sam, a resident of the Bartlett Nursing Home, who passes the Harlem Treasure Crew on to gang moll Katie Donahue's grandson in Queens. The comic search for Moran's money ends with the recovery of $50,000 in $100 bills, but more valuable to Gramps and Sam is their notoriety to news reporters. Myers's subtext ennobles the young characters for restoring two elderly men's enthusiasm for life.

Similarly upbeat is the relationship between Flats Brown and Caleb, an aged hound who shares Flats's trials as the dogs of junkyard owner A. J. Grubbs in *The Blues of Flats Brown* (2000). Like the charitable descriptions of Slick Jones, Myers's depiction of Caleb balances the good with the not-so-good: "Caleb was old and had a touch of arthritis in his hip, but he had a good heart" (Myers, 2000, n.p.). Inevitably, life on the run proves too demanding for Caleb. Myers creates a poignant parting of the duo with Caleb waving as the Midnight Special speeds Flats toward New York City. In honor of his aged pal, Flats sings "The Dog Gone Long Gone Blues." Myers indicates that the loss of the elderly from long-term relationships is a jolting experience.

As Flats learns from his friendship with Caleb, loving the aged demands compassion for their waning stamina and health, a responsibility that recurs in Myers's people-friendly writings. In *The Beast* (2003), Gabriela "Gabi" Godoy regrets her family's financial decline after the arrival of her abuelo (grandfather), a blind Dominican who entertains himself with Spanish-language radio broadcasts. In "Einstein the Second" (2003), a story published in *Boys' Life*, Myers selects as a model of humanity Biddy Owens, a "seriously old" Harlemite who once played for Birmingham's Black Barons in the Negro Baseball League (Myers, "Einstein," 30). His kindness to children and animals earns the love of Kwame, who figures out a ruse to get the old ball player to enter a hospital to repair a bad leg. In these fictional situations, the author depicts the rewards for tending the elderly as a serendipity, an unforeseen blessing.

A stronger influence on youth is Moses Littlejohn, the mystic rescuer in *The Dream Bearer* (2003), who bears the gravity and reserve of Samuel Taylor Coleridge's Ancient Mariner. Myers places the old wanderer at an informal encounter in the life of 12-year-old David Curry, whose daily life rollercoasters from normal events to crises generated by the paranoia of his father Reuben. Moses is both bearer of wisdom and creator of opportunity. David learns from him how adults shoulder the grievous history of past events dating to enslavement of Africans and continuing through the lynchings of the Jim Crow era. After Moses collapses from the weight of his recovered memories, David's compassion overflows the bounds of caution, forcing him to seek Reuben's assistance in getting medical care for Moses. Myers's parallel plots illustrate how the young man's benevolence toward a fragile elder generates forbearance in David when Reuben spirals out of control after losing his job. From aiding Moses in recovery, David finds the grace to forgive and shelter Reuben, whose memories and emotionals burdens jeopardize his manhood and the well-being of the Curry family. One of the author's strongest humanistic statements, *The Dream Bearer* illustrates that mercy and tolerance flow in an unending current through human affairs.

One of Myers's winsome retellings from the female point of view is the story of Ruth and Naomi in *A Time to Love: Stories from the Old Testament* (Scholastic, 2003). The return of Naomi to her hometown in Judah reunites her with her people, but forces her widowed daughters-in-law Orpah and Ruth into an uncomfortable status of Moabites among strangers. Naomi regrets being elderly and husbandless, but she recognizes promise in the younger women. With the generosity of a biblical matriarch, she sends Orpah and Ruth to join caravans returning to Moab. To Ruth, Naomi urges a realistic view of women's lives: "There is no sin in choosing to be young, in wanting the joys of life" (Myers, *A Time*, 63). The widow's largeheartedness prompted a beloved biblical story, the bond between two unrelated women whose lineage produces David, the first king of Jerusalem, and his kinsman Jesus.

Myers's little human dramas accentuate the unique empowerment of children through contact with their elders. In *Angel to Angel: A Mother's Gift of Love* (1998), the poem "Don't Mess with Grandmama and Me" creates a series of confrontations with frogs, rats and mice, and creepy things in the basement and the bushes. In each stanza, the child takes courage from the grandmother, who will face the unknown and "will turn it inside out," a child's statement of valor (Myers, 1998, n.p.). The text earned the regard of Lorraine E. Hale, daughter of Clara McBride Hale, a foster mother to foundlings who earned the title "the Mother Teresa of New York." The author makes his most incisive comparison of the young and the old in *Here in Harlem: Poems in Many Voices* (2004), a verse collection illustrated with candid black-and-white snapshots. In the poem "Mali Evans, 12," the speaker admires the gray hair and grand stroll of Mrs. Purvis, whose queenly posture and genteel manners belie a spirit "tree-tough and deep-rooted" (Myers, 1997, 2). The image of resilient plant life echoes in the many genealogies the author sketches in his writings to outline the flow of strength and wisdom from one generation to another.

See also **Lewis genealogy, wisdom, women**

• *Further Reading*

Edelman, Diane Gersoni. "Review: *Won't Know Till I Get There*," *New York Times Book Review* (13 June 1982): 26–27.

Larson, Gerry. "Review: *The Mouse Rap*," *School Library Journal* 37, no. 2 (February 1991): S37.

Myers, Walter Dean. *Angel to Angel: A Mother's Gift of Love*. New York: HarperCollins, 1998.

_____. *The Blues of Flats Brown*. New York: Holiday House, 2000.

_____. *Crystal*. New York: Viking Kestrel, 1987.

_____. "The Dark Side of the Moon," *Black Creation* (fall 1971): 26–29.

_____. "Einstein the Second," *Boys' Life* 93, no. 11 (November 2003): 30–36.

_____. "Gums" in *We Be Word Sorcerers: Twenty-five Stories by Black Americans*. New York: Bantam, 1973.

_____. *Here in Harlem: Poems in Many Voices*. New York: Holiday House, 2004.

_____. *It Ain't All for Nothin'*. New York: Viking, 1978.

_____. *A Time to Love: Stories from the Old Testament*. New York: Scholastic, 2003.

_____. *Won't Know Till I Get There*. New York: Viking, 1982.

Pennington, Ashley Jane. "Review: *It Ain't All for Nothin*,'" *Interracial Books for Children Bulletin* 10, no. 4 (1979): 18.

opportunity

Myers comments frequently on opportunities that await bright, enterprising young people, such as a stage career in *The Dancers* (1972), shining shoes as a source of income for homeless orphans in "The Vision of Felipe" (1978), a spread for *La Femme* magazine and a possible movie contract for 16-year-old model Crystal Brown in *Crystal* (1987), Steve Harmon's three-year study of cinematography in *Monster: A Novel* (1999), a reprieve from juvenile hall in *Handbook for Boys: A Novel* (2003), and the chance for black youths to serve the nation as sailors fighting slavery in *U.S.S. Constellation: Pride of the American Navy* (2004). The conflicts between gambling and sportsmanship haunt 17-year-old protagonist Lonnie Jackson, a potential scholarship winner in *Hoops: A Novel* (1981) and its sequel, *The Outside Shot* (1984). The narratives accentuate the losses of Coach Calvin F. "Spider" Jones, a point shaver ousted from the National Basketball Association, and of Bill Larson, a star guard on the Montclare State College basketball team who disobeys rules about signing professional contracts while holding amateur status. Lonnie learns from Cal's experience the far-reaching tentacles of felonious gambling; from Larson's dishonesty,

Lonnie realizes that the risks are too great to trade team loyalty for ready money from a local hustler, Alfredo "Fat Man" Corsi. In all these models, young people begin to recognize the complexity of opportunities that come with strings attached.

In the didactic teen novel *Won't Know Till I Get There* (1982), Myers engineers a variety of opportunities for protagonist Steve Perry, the son of a devoted couple. After the family accepts 13-year-old Earl Goins, a hardened delinquent, into their apartment, Steve and Earl enter a court-ordered community action program that requires them to aid a retirement home, the Micheaux House for Senior Citizens. Synergy generates opportunity in multiple directions: the teens discard stereotypes of old people as juiceless relics; the retirees negate preconceptions about delinquency by joining the teens in money-making efforts to rescue the institution from abandonment. Most important to the Perry family is their acceptance of Earl as their adopted son, a conclusion applauded in *Voice of Youth Advocates* by critic Susan Williamson.

In 1993, Myers teamed with folk artist Jacob Lawrence to produce a picture book of black history, *The Great Migration: An American Story* (1993). The combination of Lawrence's kinetic paintings and Myers's contemplative ode "Migration" produces a stirring account of African American zeal. During World War I, peasants from the agrarian South abandon fields withered by drought and weevil damage to relocate their families in the urban industrialized North. The gamble carries the older generation to jobs on railroads and in steel mills in Chicago, Cleveland, Detroit, New York, Philadelphia, and Pittsburgh. Led on by newspaper accounts and the promises of industrial recruiters, families accept the discomforts of ghetto life as they groom their children for better times. The new surroundings generate hope that better schools and less fear of lynching and financial oppression will offer expand horizons for vigorous young blacks.

In a seriocomic novel, *Darnell Rock Reporting* (1994), Myers sets up a fruitful confab between older men and teenagers. During the title figure's interview with 51-year-old Sweeby Jones, a down-and-out Vietnam vet, other men in the barbershop comment on means of avoiding joblessness and homelessness. The narrative contrasts Sweeby with Sidney Rock, Darnell's father, who exited the Vietnam War with the intent to take a civil service exam and land a federal job with the Post Office. Unlike Sidney, Sweeby lacked the educational background to pass the test. Drifting from good jobs downhill to inertia, he lives on the street until Darnell's newspaper interview revives hope. The author's depiction of a teen reporter's interest in a street wanderer highlights the role of serendipity in Sweeby's life, which takes an upward turn after he finds a small job at a hospital.

Myers illustrates other examples of the unpredictable nature of opportunity. For the title character in *The Blues of Flats Brown* (2000), fame and a recording contract derive from songs about the events of his life on the road. After migrating to New York City from Mississippi, he entertains night-clubbers with the lonesome soul sounds of a nomad from the South. Singing from the heart, Flats wins a fan base to whom he communicates a universal truth about the pain of physical distance from cultural roots. In *My Name Is America: The Journal of Biddy Owens* (2001), Myers produces another example of unforeseen good from loss. He describes the title character's admission about the erratic returns from professional baseball, "I love this game, but it don't love me" (Myers, 2001, 88). More promising is his meeting with Morehouse and Spelman students. Biddy, who is already writing sports news for the Birmingham Black Barons, decides that he wants to be smart and respected like college students. More compelling is a teen's opportunity to own and shoot illegal firearms in *Shooter* (2004). For disaffected students who picture themselves as outlaws, the possession of guns bolsters wavering self-esteem and catapults a sociopath, 16-year-old Leonard "Len" Gray," into a media circus surrounding the crazed gunman in an early-morning school terrorism plot. The perversion of opportunity into a means of avenging Len and his friends, Cameron Porter and Carla Evans, against the cliquish jock set furthers Len's conspiracy to make schools "Stop the Violence," a generalized complaint hurled at institutions that discount the feelings and worth of outsiders (Myers, 2004, 239). The author wrings irony from Len's assault on society's respected institution of public learning, which turns to madness the children it fails.

See also **education, military, self-destruction**

• *Further Reading*

Betancourt, Jeanne. "Review: *Crystal*," *New York Times Book Review* (13 September 1987): 48.
Myers, Walter Dean. *The Blues of Flats Brown*. New York: Holiday House, 2000.
_____. *The Great Migration: An American Story*. New York: HarperCollins, 1993.
_____. *My Name Is America: The Journal of Biddy Owens*. New York: Scholastic, 2001.
_____. *Shooter*. New York: Amistad, 2004.
Smith, Karen Patricia, ed. *African-American Voices in Young Adult Literature: Tradition, Transition, Transformation*. Lanham, Md.: Scarecrow, 1994.
Williamson, Susan. "Review: *Won't Know Till I Get There*," *Voice of Youth Advocates* 5, no. 5 (December 1982): 34.

The Outside Shot

Reprising the successful sports and coming-of-age motifs of *Hoops: A Novel* (1981), Myers produced *The Outside Shot* (1984), a sequel that follows high school senior basketball star Lonnie Jackson to fictional Montclare State College in Indiana. The author develops more sophisticated scenes that appeal to an older reader with a broader horizon than neighborhood pick-up games in the park. Varying Lonnie's daily practice and classes in freshman math, psychology, and U.S. history are two three-hour therapy sessions per week at University Hospital with nine-year-old Eddie Brignole and friendship with roommates Colin, Juice, and Sly and with middle-class track athlete Sherry Jewett. Quickly, Lonnie faces more opposition than he knew in early adolescence in Harlem — Sherry's independence, rivalries with teammates, sportswriter John Bowers's negative sports commentary in the *Eagle*, and Lonnie's potential failure in math. Most problematic is Coach Leeds' anger that Lonnie pursues an intuitive, self-directed game rather than learn the team's patterned plays. As in *Hoops*, Lonnie's concerns about court performance initially overshadow the pressing issues of campus life, thus casting doubt that he sincerely seeks a college education and manhood.

To exhibit depth in his main character, Myers introduces a series of unforeseen events into the plot. After helping Eddie overcome autism, Lonnie views at the Brignole home evidence that Carl, the boy's father, undermines the child's self-esteem. At the Young farm, Lonnie spends a weekend with his roommate Colin and gets a taste of the demands of milking and tilling and the pleasures of rural solitude and open spaces. Dates with Sherry produce roller-coaster emotions in Lonnie, who is unsure how to maneuver her toward a lasting romance. A shock to the predictability of campus life occurs on December 2, when police question Lonnie and Colin after Ray York kills himself. Lonnie, who knew Ray only from pick-up basketball games, visits the York home to comfort Alethea, Ray's widow. On return to campus, Lonnie confesses to an epiphany, that he had pictured himself in the same predicament as Ray, a former ball player who never makes the transition to adult life. Myers retains images of Ray as a prod to Lonnie's deepening introspection.

The progression toward a resolution once more hinges on issues of integrity and team loyalty. Alfredo "Fat Man" Corsi rewards Lonnie three $50 bills for ramping up the score in the game against Gary Tech. The money is so unacceptable to the player that he mails it to Alethea York as a gift, an admirable gesture from a college student who works at a low-paying hospital job for spending money. Myers works out a convenient trade between Lonnie and June Brignole — home therapy for Eddie in exchange for math tutoring from June to get Lonnie past a difficult introductory course. Investigation of gambling on point spreads terrifies Lonnie, who accepts encouragement from Earl "Sweetman" Johnson, a former pro player and member of a brotherhood of athletes. A suspension sidelines Lonnie, who withdraws into self-pity and alcohol, the downhill slope that ended Calvin F. "Spider" Jones's career in *Hoops*. The hurried conclusion exonerates Lonnie and assures the reader that he looks beyond adolescent sports competitions to more mature concerns. Myers stresses the development of integrity in black-and-white terms—"what to go for and what to walk away from" (*ibid.*, 185). Writing for *School Library Journal*, critic Carolyn Caywood summarized Lonnie's advancement toward honesty for its own sake as "a very American rite of passage" (Caywood, 1984, 136).

See also **athletics, *Hoops***

• *Further Reading*

Caywood, Carolyn. "Review: *The Outside Shot*," *School Library Journal* 31 (November 1984): 135–136.

Myers, Walter Dean. *The Outside Shot*. New York: Delacorte, 1984.

Owens genealogy

Myers establishes a close and loving family for the title character in *My Name Is America: The Journal of Biddy Owens: The Negro Leagues* (2001):

Grandpap Booker T. Smith
African Methodist Episcopal
minister
|

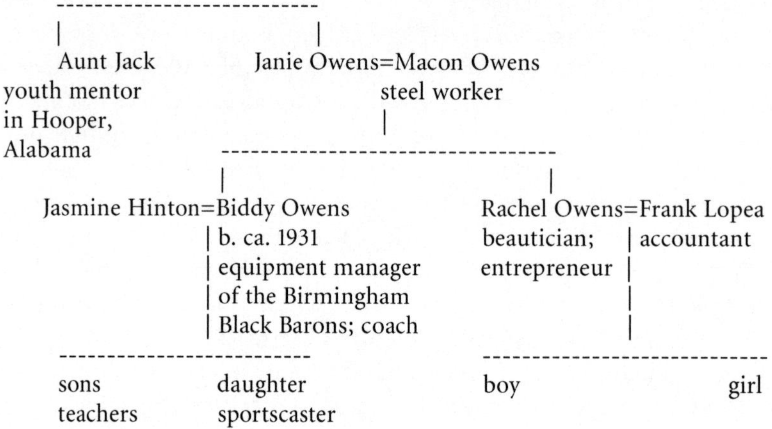

• *Further Reading*

Myers, Walter Dean. *My Name Is America: The Journal of Biddy Owens.* New York: Scholastic, 2001.

parenthood

As a result of his mother's death and his placement with foster parents, Myers began perusing the responsibilities of parents in his youth, a motif of his biblical ode "Wolf Song" (2005). In his 1994 Margaret A. Edwards Award Acceptance Speech at the American Library Association annual convention in Miami, he admitted to alienation in a straightforward question: "Was it normal for me to feel apart from my parents?" (Myers, "1994," 131). Four years later in the introduction to *Angel to Angel: A Mother's Gift of Love* (1998), he singles out mothering as a crucial influence on babies. He asks readers, "Will anyone ever know how close we are to our mothers? How much the bonding between mother and child affects our lives?" (Myers, 1998, n.p.). The photos supply positive models of the importance of a loving parent to an active, healthy childhood.

The separation of child from parent takes varied forms in his writings—the orphaning of 10-year-old Felipe in "The Vision of Felipe" (1978), a disappointed father's rejection of a girl baby in *The Nicholas Factor* (1983), the estrangement of 14-year-old Jimmy Little, the child of an incarcerated felon in *Somewhere in the Darkness* (1992), and the divorce of Inez, the poorly paid waitress and single mother of Jimmy Lynch in *Handbook for Boys: A Novel* (2002). In the Arrow series of detective novellas, a distant work schedule for Dr. Carla Arrow, an anthropologist in *Ambush in the Amazon* (1986), requires faith in her sons, 17-year-old Chris and 14-year-old Ken, to care for themselves. In *Duel in the Desert* (1986), another of the series, the boys explore a field site in the company of Mussa Tawfik. Before the threesome spends the night at the edge of the Sahara Desert, Mussa receives a lecture from his father, Professor Tawfik. Ken describes the comments as "the Arabic version of Mom's 'Be careful' speech" (Myers, 1986, 11). Myers implies that cautionary words from parents are universal, whether in English or Arabic.

More serious is the four-generation alienation in *Sweet Illusions* (1986), a collection of fictional views of childbearing and single parenthood. One short, open-ended narrative pictures Hector Rojas living apart from his mother in Ponce and his emotional estrangement from his daughter Maria, a 16-year-old who is pregnant with her first child. In a later chapter, Karen Harris adopts the child of Gloria Stokes. Karen's altruism toward teen mothers is moving. She states, "My heart goes out to the mother, but I think we'll be good parents. We have a great deal of love to share" (Myers, *Sweet*, 115). Whatever the obstacle to an active parent-child fellowship in these vignettes, the loss of acceptance, affection, and guidance threatens emotional stability to all parties. Myers stresses to the reader that the burden of early parenthood leaves serious decisions and subtle moral considerations to the judgment of youths who lack the logic and character development to cope.

From early memories of home and his observation of friends' parents, the author creates realistic familial situations in his teen novels. His home scenes include the alcoholism and thievery of Lonnie, 12-year-old Tippy's birth father in *It Ain't All for Nothin'* (1978), the sarcastic father chiding 15-year-old Paul Williams for leaving a Kentucky Fried Chicken bag crumpled on the floor in *The Young Landlords* (1979), and a grandmother scolding her recalcitrant grandson from her hospital bed in *Slam!* (1996). Balancing negative situations are such positive evidence of parenting as a loving mother's farewell to her son as he leaves for war in *Fallen Angels* (1988) and Mama braiding Rachel Owens's hair in *My Name Is America: The Journal of Biddy Owens* (2001). An exemplum, Myers's short story "The Treasure of Lemon Brown" (1983), published in *Boys' Life*, depicts 14-year-old Greg Ridley's father in the role of disciplinarian. For poor performance in math, the father scorns the notion of playing basketball at the community center. With the finality that comes from disappointment and anger, he shouts, "Now you just get into your room and hit those books" (Myers, 1983, 34). Contrasting the gruff command are the gentle words of the title figure, a blues singer whose son Jesse fought in World War II. Concerning the importance of a role model to Jesse, Lemon Brown remarked, "If you know your pappy did something, you know you can do something too" (*ibid.*, 37). The remark emphasizes Myers's intent to provide readers with positive examples of black home life and with patterns of family formation that youth can emulate.

In addition to normal interaction, the author acknowledges the sufferings of the underclass in vignettes of sick and enfeebled, poor and unemployed, widowed, overwhelmed, alcoholic, and befuddled parents who juggle responsibility and decision making against the demands of survival. The noble gesture of the Perry family in adopting a delinquent, 13-year-old Earl Goins in *Won't Know Till I Get There* (1982), rebut the stereotype of black families as weak and fractious. The input of Carol and Daniel Brown in the scheduling of work for 16-year-old model Crystal Brown in *Crystal* (1987) exemplifies the importance of daily questioning of whereabouts and of relationships with adults who might exploit her. Characters like Mabel Perry, the single parent in *Fallen Angels*, display the quiet day-to-day commitment to children whose fathers desert them. Her older son, Richard "Richie" Perry, who is fatherless from age 15, embraces manhood in his late teens by joining the army and sending home allotment checks from Vietnam, the support that his absent father neglects. The missing element in the life of younger brother Kenny is emotional support and counsel from an older male, which Richie attempts to supply with letters home from a war zone. The surrogate fathering ennobles Richie as a survivor of a broken home who intends to shield Kenny from loss and aimlessness.

Myers focuses on escapism as a deterrent to steady parenting. Worsening the problems of poverty and unpredictable employment in *Scorpions* (1988) is the undependable Jevon Hicks, an absentee father who takes to drink after he loses his job. He baits his 12-year-old son Jamal with demands to start "acting like a man," advice that Jevon could well apply to his own behavior. (Myers, 1988, 94). Instead of building self-esteem in his son, Jevon manages to confuse the boy about choosing behaviors that demonstrate masculinity. In contrast to Jevon's macho posturing, Mrs. Hicks enfolds her son and daughter in her arms and rocks them as a sign of family unity. Myers summarizes her value to the children in the words of Mack: "When she gone, it's a hurting thing" (*ibid.*, 208). The pain the author refers to is an incessant mother hunger that gnaws at the motherless child into adulthood.

The situation in *Somewhere in the Darkness* (1992) involves a parent who wants to rid himself of blame for a crime he planned but did not commit. In the story, prison escapee Cephus "Crab" Little attempts to make up for absent parenting by posturing as the authoritarian father, the decision maker. His misdirected effort results from the failure of his own father, Charlie C. C. Little, a railroad cook who was out of town too often to establish a firm sense of fatherhood in Crab. Unfortunately for Crab's son, Jimmy Little, Crab relies heavily on thievery and lying to salvage his son's filial respect. To save the novel from a perpetual downward spiral, Myers indicates that Jimmy surmises that C. C.'s absence from home and Crab's lies are a poor basis for father-son alliances. Jimmy's intent to improve on the actions of the past two generations offers the reader hope that a troubled boy can opt for a total restructuring of the fathering model when he establishes a family.

Myers applauds notable attempts at surrogate guidance. In *Won't Know Till I Get There*, he characterizes the Perrys as idealists who intend to accept a troubled foster child into the family to make up for their failure to conceive more children. Their everyday interaction with Earl Goins dampens the Perrys' enthusiasm for reclaiming a hardened delinquent. Myers dramatizes the necessity for adult mediation in choosing where Earl will spend his last two years of legal minority. The fact that his mother reclaims him bodes well for his self-esteem, as does the Perrys' intent to serve as his legal guardians. In *It Ain't All for Nothin'* competent parenting saves Tippy from bearing ethical decisions alone. Tippy is fortunate in having Roland Sylvester, a sympathetic bus driver, and his wife Edna to advise on issues involving Tippy's return to the custody of his dissolute father.

Surrogate parenting undergirds two of Myers's sports novels, *Hoops: A Novel* (1981) and *The Outside Shot* (1984), in which 17-year-old Lonnie Jackson looks to basketball as a means of exiting ghetto life. Under the influence of Calvin "Spider" Jones, a coach who sullied his reputation while playing professionally, Lonnie matures and develops character. In the second novel, Lonnie moves on to college in Indiana at Montclare State College and discovers that disreputable officials and point-shaving tempt him to accept cash in exchange for disloyalty to the team. Providing experience and advice are Sweet Man Jones and a professional coterie known as the

Brotherhood. Lonnie shares the mentoring by befriending a troubled nine-year-old, Eddie Brignole, who flourishes under special attention. The concentric circles of adult wisdom that radiate outward epitomize the author's belief that intervention at the right moment can save youth from repeating family flaws in the next generation.

Myers maintains the value of an older, wiser adviser in *The Nicholas Factor* (1983), a foreign intrigue novel that places John Martens, a federal representative of the National Security Agency, at the service of Gerald McQuillen, a freshman at a college in Santa Barbara, California. Still puzzling over his relationship to his father, a race car driver recently killed in a crash, the young adventurer accepts an assignment to Peru with the elitist Crusade Society, whom Martens suspects of evil intent. In fatherly fashion, the NSA agent clarifies the ethics of clandestine investigation to aid Gerald when the heady mystery threatens his values. According to reviewer Lucy V. Hawley, a critic for *School Library Journal*, "One develops a deep regard for Gerald," who returns to his widowed mother a stronger, more self-confident person (Hawley, 1983, 138).

Myers sustains his interest in complicated parenting issues. The issue of adoption in *Me, Mop, and the Moondance Kid* (1988) reveals the need of older orphans for structure. Protagonist Tommy "T. J." Jackson explains, "The [Dominican] Academy is all right, but it's not like having your own home and your own parents and everything" (Myers, 1988, 15). In *Scorpions*, one of Myers's critically acclaimed young adult novels, Mrs. Hicks battles for Jamal, a 12-year-old whose brother Randy languishes in prison for committing robbery and murder. A pair of literary foils, Tito Cruz and his grandmother, seem yoked to the same destiny after Tito fires a gun and is deported back to Puerto Rico. The text stops short of explaining the two boys' fates. Instead, the author stresses that serious consequences await faulty choices, an issue that undergirds *Monster: A Novel* (1999), a novel that reveals the helplessness of good parents in shielding their older son from criminality. Myers indicates that parents like those of Steve Harmon, a 16-year-old accused of complicity in a felony robbery and murder, counter a serious temptation — the draw of the mean streets of Harlem, where young punks define manhood for the impressionable.

The image of supportive parenting permeates Myers's verse-photo anthology, *Glorious Angels: A Celebration of Children* (1995). He opens the collection with a posed studio portrait of a mother and three children and a poem that celebrates the offspring "that glance into my very soul" (Myers, *Glorious*, n.p.). Subsequent snapshots of women and children from a variety of racial groups picture fathers who recognize a new opportunity in a fresh generation. By extending the role of parent to an array of settings, the author emphasizes the responsibility of adults toward the young who are "Wonderful/and forever Glorious" (*ibid.*). The ebullient language that describes parents' attitudes toward children exhibits the enthusiasm that Myers feels for his own family.

A more pathetic glimpse of parenting in *The Dream Bearer* (2003) pictures the trials of 12-year-old David and 17-year-old Tyrone Curry in a home scene fractured by the outbursts of Reuben, a drunken, mentally unstable father who feels emasculated by circumstance. Myers applies to Reuben the feral responses of an animal in the low growl that accompanies arguments with his wife in the wee hours of the morning. The sophistication of David in detecting alcohol on his father's breath and in diagnosing symptoms of missed dosages of medication suggests that the child has had to leapfrog into early manhood to protect himself and his mother from serious harm. Evelyn Curry's explanation of her husband's unpredictable blowups is frail: "People grow away from each other" (Myers, *Dream*, 24). At a low point, she admits her need in prayer, "Lord Jesus, give us strength" (*ibid.*, 73). Myers's pity for Evelyn derives from close association with parents who reach the end of their ability to cope with worsening situations.

Even amid the decline of family unity, Myers portrays Reuben as a battler against "little bits of anger buzzing like flies around his head," but he is capable and committed in his lucid moments (*ibid.*, 101). To the question of Tyrone's involvement in drugs, the father extends worthy advice: "It's never wrong for us to look out for each other" (*ibid.*, 45). When David has an opportunity to analyze his father's inner demons at close range, he pictures abstract mental torments in Reuben, who dreams of "monsters that scared him" (*ibid.*, 81). With a child's perspective, David identifies with a terror that haunts his own nightmares. Critic Paula Rohrlick, in a review for *Kliatt*, describes the narrative as a "haunting, sad, and yet hopeful tale" for David's ability to pity his self-destructive father (Rohrlick, 2004, 20).

The relationship of parent to child dominates episodes of Myers's bible vignettes in *A Time to Love: Stories from the Old Testament* (2003), which contains two pivotal patriarchal episodes—Abraham's intent to sacrifice Isaac and the troubling account of Lot's betrayal of his daughters Saaria and Zillah. In the story of brothers Joseph and Reuben, the author pictures the joy in Jacob, the father, who plans to celebrate a reunion with Joseph, whom the other sons—Reuben, Asher, Simeon, Judah, Dan, Gad, and Levi—sold into slavery in Egypt. The symbol of paternal love is the famed coat of many colors, which Myers describes as linen trimmed in gold and "luminescent against the distant sky" (Myers, *A Time*, 30). The narrative stresses the coat as an emblem of preferential treatment, the source of strife among the brothers, and as a torment to Jacob, who wails piteously for a favorite son who appears to have died violently. In a view of the foster parent, the collection pictures Ruth the Moabite as the beloved and loving daughter-in-law of Naomi. The mark of mothering arises in the pair's meeting, when Naomi pulls Ruth close and calls her "my daughter" (*ibid.*, 57). Myers stresses the importance of acceptance to a lasting relationship, especially among people from different Mideastern tribes. He places in Ruth's comments the simplest expression of commitment: "You are my mother now" (*ibid.*, 58). The bond ennobles both Ruth and the role of the volunteer mother.

In a troubling psychological novel, Myers develops the importance of adult supervision to three accomplices in *Shooter* (2004), a teen novel loosely based on student terrorism at Columbine High School, Littleton, Colorado, on April 20, 1999. The leader, Leonard "Len" Gray, acquires stature and self-importance from access to his father's guns, ammunition, and shooting privileges at the Patriots club, a right-wing organization. Accompanying the expertise at weaponry is an inflated notion of his abusive father's training as an army Ranger. Len's friend, Cameron Porter, enjoys shooting at the club, but he fails to meet the stringent standards of athleticism of his father, Norman Porter, who demands the boy's participation on the basketball team. Carla Evans, the third of the triad, receives lackadaisical parental control from her separated mother and father and consequently enters foster care. The merger of the three disaffected youths into the cultish *Ordo Sagittae* (Order of the Arrow) channels their unease among mocking classmates into a conspiracy to retaliate. The author's failure to present the parents' defense of their children suggests lethal sins of omission.

See also **Fast Sam, Cool Clyde, and Stuff, Sarah Bonetta Forbes, Perry genealogy, women**

- *Further Reading*

Apol, Laura. "Reappearing Fathers, Reappearing Pasts: History, Gender, and Identity in Hamilton's 'Plain City' and Myers' 'Somewhere in the Darkness,'" *ALAN Review* 29, no. 2 (winter 2002): 21–25.

Cooper, Ilene. "Review: *Glorious Angels: A Celebration of Children*," *Booklist* 92, no. 1 (1 September 1995): 79–80.

Hawley, Lucy V. "Review: *The Nicholas Factor*," *School Library Journal* 30, no. 1 (September 1983): 138.

Lane, R. D. "'Keepin' It Real': Walter Dean Myers and the Promise of African-American Children's Literature," *African American Review* 32, no. 1 (22 March 1998): 125–138.

Larsen, Gerry. "Review: *Somewhere in the Darkness*," *School Library Journal* 38, no. 4 (April 1992): 146.

Lothrop, Patricia D. "Review: *A Time to Love: Stories from the Old Testament*," *School Library Journal* 49, no. 5 (May 2003): 158.

Myers, Walter Dean. *Angel to Angel: A Mother's Gift of Love*. New York: HarperCollins, 1998.

_____. *The Dream Bearer*. New York: Amistad, 2003.

_____. *Duel in the Desert*. New York: Viking Kestrel, 1986.

_____. *Glorious Angels: A Celebration of Children*. New York: Bantam, 1995.

_____. *Me, Mop, and the Moondance Kid*. New York: Delacorte, 1988.

_____. "1994 Margaret A. Edwards Award Acceptance Speech," *Journal of Youth Services in Libraries*, 8, no. 2 (winter 1995): 129–133.

_____. *Scorpions*. New York: Harper & Row, 1988.

_____. *Sweet Illusions*. New York: Teachers and Writers Collaborative, 1986.

_____. *A Time to Love: Stories from the Old Testament*. New York: Scholastic, 2003.

_____. "The Treasure of Lemon Brown," *Boys' Life* 73 (March 1983): 34–40.

Rohrlick, Paula. "Review: *The Dream Bearer*," *Kliatt* 38, no. 6 (November 2004): 19–20.

Perry genealogy

In *Won't Know Till I Get There* (1982), the lengthy trials of Earl Goins after his mother gives him up catapults him into crime and a juvenile home that introduces him to the institutional lifestyle. After foster homes and tentative adoption arrangements fail, he makes a lasting impact on the Perry family, who adopt him to rear with their birth son Steve.

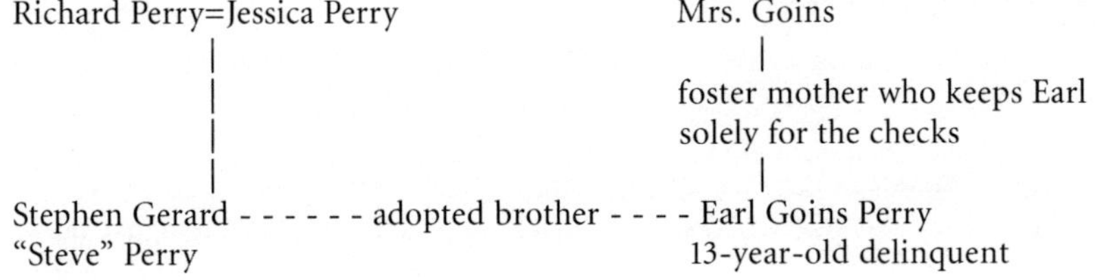

• *Further Reading*

Myers, Walter Dean. *Won't Know Till I Get There.* New York: Viking, 1982.
Rochman, Hazel. "Review: *Won't Know Till I Get There,*" *School Library Journal* 28, no. 9 (May 1982): 72–73.

Porter, Cameron

The focus of *Shooter* (2004), 17-year-old Cameron Porter, a middle-class black student at Madison High School in Harrison County, cooperates with officials investigating a shooting six months after the event. Handsome, well-groomed, and tested in the 140 IQ range, he is bright, but misdirected. He expresses discomfort in the presence of his father, Norman Porter, a goal-driven quality control manager in industry who threatens his son for the shooting incident. Cameron's asocial behavior furthers a single friendship with Leonard "Len" Gray, whom he likes because Len "really understood how I felt just about all the time and didn't try to punk me out or dump on me" (Myers, 2004, 82). The nebulous statement of friendship reveals Cameron's inability to make social judgments based on human behavior.

Myers pities Cameron for his incomplete formation of logic and for his naivete about following leaders intent on nefarious purpose. Cameron joins Len in desecrating a church with Magic Marker slogans by scribbling on a wall **"JESUS WOULDN'T EVEN RENT THIS SPACE"** (*ibid.*, 36). Cameron's justification for following Len's example is a desire not to disappoint a friend, but Cameron is unable to explain the terms of friendship with a crazed boy who victimizes animals and people as forms of catharsis for unrelenting rage and alienation. The disconnects between good sense and inborn suspicion turn Cameron into the tool of a psychopath.

Myers begins the novel with Cameron's interrogation to illustrate the dangers of passivity, a character behavior that the author placed at the crux of *Monster: A Novel* (1999). As the only black bystander, Cameron has the intelligence to think for himself, but he chooses to drift through perils without examining the repercussions, including the right-wing Patriots club's use of a photo of Dr. Martin Luther King, Jr., as a target. Questioning by psychologists reveals Cameron's suicidal urges, his lack of values, and his confession that he "just screwed up everybody" (*ibid.*, 42). Whereas he merely daydreams about shooting the bullying jocks who taunt him, Len arms himself with a Ruger and plots "to break a hole in the wall of silence so big it couldn't be fixed" (*ibid.*, 85). At that point, Cameron comes to himself long enough to protect Carla and to hide in a classroom while Len acts out his plot. The last-minute save rescues Cameron from criminality, but suggests a need for extensive psychological treatment for a string of lapses in judgment.

See also **Leonard Gray, *Shooter***

• *Further Reading*

Myers, Walter Dean. *Shooter.* New York: Amistad, 2004.
Rochman, Hazel. "Review: *Shooter,*" *Booklist* 100, no. 12 (15 February 2004): 1070.
Ward, Elise Virginia. "Review: *Shooter,*" *Black Issues Book Review* 6, no. 4 (August 2004): 60.

poverty

Myers hovers on a fine line between pride in underprivileged people and pity for their sufferings. In an interview with Elizabeth Mehren, a journalist for the *Los Angeles Times*, he accounts for his motivation: "It's liberalism, wanting to reach out and help the poor black child, like the missionaries" (Mehren, 1997, E1). In 1976, he published in *Black Scholar* an encomium to a noted black photographer, "Gordon Parks: John Henry with a Camera." Significant to Parks's value as a role model when he worked for the Farm Security Administration during the Great Depression was his ability to turn black-and-white candid shots of poor people into dignified images of suffering. Myers noted that Parks contributed to all of American history: "The poverty and struggle he had seen there had touched both black and white alike" (Myers, 1976, 28). The compliment also fit the author.

In comparison to Parks, Myers is similarly greathearted in his studies of human need. An early example, "Gums," published in *We Be Word Sorcerers: Twenty-five Stories by Black Americans* (1973), describes the plight of the title character, a grandfather who rears his orphaned grandson, nine-year-old Stevie. Their protection from destitution is thin: "[Gums] got his check from the railroad and social security so they made out pretty good and didn't have to go on welfare" (Myers, 1973, 181). In private, Stevie bears an adult level of worry that Gums is showing signs of senile dementia. Without a grandfather to provide for him, Stevie despairs of surviving alone. The author's pity for rudderless children like Stevie shapes much of his canon. Myers reprises Stevie's situation in a teen character novel, *It Ain't All for Nothin'* (1978), in which 12-year-old Tippy regrets that his Grandma Carrie Brown must call Social Services when the family runs out of food. To Tippy, "It was a shameful thing" to depend on government handouts (Myers, 1978, 25). With as much pride as she can muster, Carrie states to social workers her lifetime credo: "I ain't asking for nothing 'cause I don't want to work" (*ibid.*, 28). After social workers remand Tippy to the custody of Lonnie, his birth father, the boy flees undependable nutrition and frequent beatings and spends part of one night in an abandoned building. The terrors of living alone in the dark send him back to Lonnie's apartment to work out a more bearable solution. The author's choice of family drama indicates respect for children who must function far beyond their skills and powers to cope.

Two years later, the author published the short story "The Vision of Felipe" (1978) in *Black Scholar*. He based the title character, a homeless ten-year-old orphan on the streets of Lima, on personal observation when the Myers family traveled to Peru in 1976. The boy's snatch of a mango from a market fruit display illustrates how perpetual hunger clouds the consequences of hasty thievery. In discussions of poverty, Felipe reasons that, even in the United States, "They had to have some poor people to do the work" (Myers, 1978, 6). The child's observation captures the disparity between the wealthy who travel and spend and the poor who support their social parasitism on South American poor, who serve as colorful backdrops for photos. Myers followed with *The Golden Serpent* (1980), a humanistic fable set in India. The story dramatizes a ruler's inability to commiserate with the have-nots of his realm. By illustrating what reviewer Ellen D. Warwick called "the triumph of caring over indifference," the picture book expresses to young readers the importance of sensitivity to society's neediest people (Warwick, 1981, 53).

In another survey of world suffering, Myers reported on his experiences with the hungry and homeless. The author turned his observations in Peru to pointed commentary in *The Nicholas Factor* (1983), a spy thriller. The narrative takes Gerald McQuillen from college in Santa Barbara, California, to Iquitos, a Quechuan village, where "the poverty of the people came through my clothes with the cold rain and dampened everything within me" (Myers, 1983, 77). Like Parks, Myers speaks from eyewitness experiences with urchins begging in the streets and with mothers who produce babies who suffer malnutrition from lack of protein. Andwele Kofe, Gerald's companion from Cameroon, summarizes, "So they have babies to replace the lives they love, and so it goes on" (*ibid.*, 91). That same year, Myers turned his attention to suffering closer to home. The exemplum "The Treasure of Lemon Brown" (1983), set in Harlem, depicts the tattered memorabilia that link the title wanderer with his son, Jesse Brown, who died in combat during World War II. Strapped to Lemon's ankle are the harmonica and press clippings that accompanied Jesse to war and returned with his body to become Lemon's family treasures. The view of children as the treasures of destitute parents accounts for the author's respect for the poor in attempting to maintain normal home environments for their young.

In 1993, Myers teamed with folk artist Jacob Lawrence on a picture book, *The Great Migration: An American Story* (1993), a wrenching retrospect on starvation diets and big-eyed children whose parents do well to survive in the racist agrarian South. The narrative lauds the spunk of ambitious blacks who pull up stakes from the land that enslaved their ancestors. Through the diaspora, exemplified by the lengthy train travel to urban industrial centers in Chicago, Cleveland, Detroit, New York, Philadelphia, and Pittsburgh, nomads leave behind despair as they settle themselves in America's emerging black communities. Because of the demand for factory labor during World War I, they upgrade their standard of living and invigorate the next generation for opportunity in the North. The author considers it crucial to black history for readers to validate the courage of former generations in flight from no-win situations.

The problems of homelessness and hunger in urban settings beset the title character in *Darnell Rock Reporting* (1994). Myers contrasts the polar opposites of public opinion in twins, Tamika and Darnell. Tamika denounces a poor man for shoplifting a potato from a market. Her father, Sidney Rock, observes that street wanderers might "get caught on purpose to have someplace to stay" (Myers, 1994, 5). When Darnell identifies a friend of the thief as 51-year-old Sweeby Jones, one of Sidney's buddies during the Vietnam War, the situation becomes personal. From Sweeby, Darnell learns the truth about homelessness: "Unless you out here, you don't know. You just don't know" (*ibid.*, 91). Myers's skillful dialogue bears the ring of authenticity, suggesting that he interviewed real victims to explore their perspective.

Myers returned more pointedly to the concept of the social parasite in *How Mr. Monkey Saw the Whole World* (1996), an African beast fable that depicts the upper echelon of society as a buzzard, a suggestion of Joseph Mobutu, the long-time profiteer and dictator of Zaire. The fictional predator profits off the misery of less fortunate animals by flying upside down to terrorize them into giving up precious food, an overturning of the logic of commodity distribution. Enhancing the cruelty of empty promises to the hare, antelope, and crab of precious stores is a famine that depletes the food supply that the buzzard pillages. The text concludes with the joy of sharing and with the self-congratulatory laugh of the monkey, the fable's hero. The title implies that the monkey's world view exonerates him for using the same forms of terror against the predator that the predator used on his victims.

With similar compassion, Myers's teen novels depict the effects of want on children whose parents struggle to cope with unemployment and financial loss. In *The Outside Shot* (1984), Lonnie Jackson learns from his college roommate, Colin Young, about the dismal prospects of farming ten acres of played-out soil in rural Cisne, Illinois. Making a joke about white poverty, Colin mimics God's answer to his prayers, "Them's be the breaks, brother!" (Myers, 1984, 11). In another image of scrimping to stay alive, Myers describes the home situation of 12-year-old Jamal Hicks in *Scorpions* (1988), which forces him to buy food on credit from Evans's store. Jamal complains that Evans was "loudmouthing me," an embarrassment in a close-knit community (Myers, *Scorpions*, 19). The humiliation of asking for eggs and bread is so onerous that Jamal prefers to go hungry. More painful is the taunting of Dwayne, a classmate who ridicules Jamal's sneakers as "Brand X" from the Salvation Army (*ibid.*, 21). The text identifies assaults on self-esteem as more damaging even than hunger.

More pathetic than Jamal's wardrobe predicament is the abandonment of Mabel Perry in *Fallen Angels* (1988), a war novel that depicts her fatherless son Richie reneging on his dream of going to college and becoming a pharmacist. When a high school counselor suggests City College, Richie silently pictures himself washing his few outfits and drying them on the oven door "to have something to wear to high school" (Myers, *Fallen*, 14). Lacking funds for college, he joins the army and fights in the Vietnam War to assure Mabel and his little brother Kenny a steady round of allotment checks for their support in his absence. On the upside of Richie's military experience, he can agree with friend Harry "Peewee" Gates, who applauds the fairness of government issue: "This is the first place I ever been in my life where I got what everybody else got" (*ibid.*, 15). Johnson, a native of Savannah, Georgia, looks at service from the perspective of unemployment: "If the man give me a job back home I wouldn't be doing this job over here" (*ibid.*, 34). The comment suggests Myers's rage that young men put themselves on the firing line as an antidote to poverty.

Other constraints on human lives produce poignance in Myers's fiction. In *Somewhere in the Darkness* (1992), Myers describes Cephus "Crab" Little renting a room for himself and his 14-year-old son Jimmy. The boy climbs the stairs of the seedy rooming house and unlocks the door to 3B on a dirty efficiency containing two beds and small kitchen appliances. The squalor of the setting makes him think of his foster mother, Mama Jean, who attacks such filth with a pail of soapy water. The living conditions of runaway dogs Flats and Caleb in the picture book *The Blues of Flats Brown* (2000) envisions a realistic hand-to-mouth misery: "They lived where they could and made enough money to eat by Flats playing [guitar] on the street" (Myers, 2000, n.p.). In both texts, poverty demands reader attention.

The issue of a decline in the black standard of living occurs in *The Beast* (2003). While 17-year-old Anthony "Spoon" Witherspoon begins a freshman year on scholarship at Wallingford Academy in Connecticut, Gabriela "Gabi" Godoy, the Dominican girlfriend he leaves behind in Harlem, experiences a downward spiral, beginning with loss of phone service and the arrival of a blind grandfather from the West Indies to live with her family. In a warm letter, she quips, "*Habla* poverty?," but the reality of her homelife devastates her (Myers, 2003, 15). Events worsening the scenario begin with her mother Lucila's hospitalization with cancer and Gabi's retreat into heroin after her mother dies. The onslaught of difficulties rings true to comments Myers has made about his own youth. He remarked in an essay for the *Washington Post* on the destructiveness of want: "At home the poverty that so disappointed me was crushing my mother and bruising the already fragile relationship between her and my hard-working father" (Myers, 1991, 1). The realism of the author's narratives humanizes the sufferers and generates in readers awareness and empathy for society's underclass.

See also **realism**

• *Further Reading*

Mehren, Elizabeth. "Fountain of Stories for Youth: Walter Dean Myers," *Los Angeles Times* (15 October 1997): E1.

Myers, Walter Dean. *The Beast.* New York: Scholastic, 2003.

_____. *The Blues of Flats Brown.* New York: Holiday House, 2000.

_____. *Darnell Rock Reporting.* New York: Delacorte, 1994.

_____. *Fallen Angels.* New York: Scholastic, 1988.

_____. "Gordon Parks: John Henry with a Camera," *Black Scholar* 7, no. 5 (1976): 27–30.

_____. *The Great Migration: An American Story.* New York: HarperCollins, 1993.

_____. "Gums" in *We Be Word Sorcerers: Twenty-five Stories by Black Americans.* New York: Bantam, 1973.

_____. *It Ain't All for Nothin'.* New York: Viking, 1978.

_____. *The Nicholas Factor.* New York: Viking, 1983.

_____. *The Outside Shot.* New York: Delacorte, 1984.

_____. "School Days; Least Likely to Succeed," *Washington Post* (4 August 1991): 1.

_____. *Scorpions.* New York: Harper & Row, 1988.

_____. "The Vision of Felipe," *Black Scholar* (November-December 1978): 2–9.

Warwick, Ellen D. "Review: *The Golden Serpent,*" *School Library Journal* 27, no. 5 (January 1981): 53.

powerlessness

Myers's urban settings portray the gap between criminals and tough young punks and the young children, teens, women, handicapped, aged, wanderers, and prisoners who struggle for survival. Disenfranchisement empowers the exemplum "The Treasure of Lemon Brown" (1983), the poem "Wolf Song" (2005), and two psychological novels, *Monster: A Novel* (1999) and *Shooter* (2004), fictional accounts of youths who turn to crime to advance their personal agendas. In an early story, "Dark Side of the Moon," published in the fall 1971 edition of *Black Creation*, the author examines the dichotomy of random violence and frail victims. As the mind of Augie, a high school student, rationalizes rape, strangling, then random murders, the author intensifies sympathy for Sheila, a fellow student, then advances to compassion for a nameless subway bum, a prostitute named Denise, and Mrs. Fletcher, a pedestrian who gives no offense to her stalker. Contributing to the pathos of these powerless victims is society's lack of outrage for crimes targeting the unwary.

A similar disgust fuels Myers's earliest fiction. The short story "The Vision of Felipe" (1978) pictures the victimization of street urchins in Lima, Peru. During the brutal 12-year dictatorship of Juan Velasco Alvarado, street urchins like Felipe risk death in the bursts of gunfire that accompany guerrilla revolt against the military junta. Felipe's death from a bullet to the chest epitomizes the senselessness of displays of force and the waste of young wanderers who have no adults to feed, shelter, and guide them. Closer to home, the author sets *It Ain't All for Nothin'* (1978) in Harlem, but reprises Felipe's powerlessness in 12-year-old Tippy, the son of a career criminal. After Tippy's grandmother becomes too arthritic and frail to care for him, the boy passes to social workers who place him in the custody of Lonnie, his neglectful father. On the cusp of manhood, Tippy displays courage and wisdom in turning his father and his gang over to police and choosing for foster parents Edna and Roland Sylvester, mentors who offer stability in a safe environment.

The author good-naturedly introduces the ongoing issue of bullying in *The Young Landlords* (1979), which pictures 15-year-old Paul Williams pummeled by James Hall, a high school student with a reputation for intimidating weaker classmates. In *Scorpions* (1988), the reassurance of gang membership appeals to 12-year-old Jamal Hicks, who is too small to be much of a threat to 14-year-old Dwayne, a belligerent punk. In courting Jamal for leadership of the Scorpions, Mack promises to be his Ace man or protector. Mack shapes his value to Jamal into a jingle: "If I got your back, they got to give you some slack, 'cause I'm the Mack" (Myers, 1988, 43). The rhymed doggerel introduces a paradox — a promise of shielding Jamal from an unnamed danger that he would not incur if he avoided gang dealings altogether. Myers echoes the exchange between Mack and Jamal with a pointed symbol, a dog leading a blind man across a street.

Like an element of folk fable, Jamal's pistol exacerbates rather than solves his problems. The tension between Dwayne Parsons and Jamal mounts with Dwayne's insults to Jamal's ragged clothes and Jamal's self-saving retorts. To even the age and size difference, Jamal arms himself with the pistol Mack provides. The shift in power is rapid and deadly. Jamal locks himself into the school storeroom with Dwayne, terrorizes him with the pistol, and kicks him repeatedly. After Tito's grandmother seizes the weapon, Jamal recovers it, finding it heavier than before. Like King Midas and the golden touch, Jamal longs to rid himself of the curse, but he keeps the pistol as a source of power against escalating dangers.

In one of his most successful works, Myers collaborated with folk artist Jacob Lawrence on the picture book *The Great Migration: An American Story* (1993). Through narrative art, caption, and concluding ode, the text tells the story of black sharecroppers who cut their ties to the agrarian South, the farmlands of the Carolinas, Alabama, and Georgia that once enslaved America's black Africans. Through an act of self-empowerment, families make new lives for themselves in the industrialized urban North by risking a shift in lifestyle. Myers followed black history to the next stage in *Malcolm X: By Any Means Necessary* (1993), *Malcolm X: A Fire Burning Brightly* (2004), and *I've Seen the Promised Land: The Life of Dr. Martin Luther King, Jr.* (2004), which portray the rise of two bold, but disparate freedom fighters who infuse followers with hope that the days of powerlessness are at an end.

Just as Myers's beast fables *Mr. Monkey and the Gotcha Bird* (1984), *The Story of the Three Kingdoms* (1995), and *How Mr. Monkey Saw the Whole World* (1996) picture the struggle of weak against the strong opportunists of the natural world, his history books picture the reality of slaver and captive. In his overview of the slave era, he describes scenes of shackling, starving, and whipping hapless Africans held under the lash of the Southern plantation system. These pictorial reminders dramatize the centuries-long migration of "Mr. Moses" Littlejohn, the title figure in *The Dream Bearer* (2003) who resembles the wandering Jew. Moses's young friend, 12-year-old David Curry, listens to details of a dream about the lynching of Cammie by a white mob. David surmises that powerlessness once proved a heavy burden to outnumbered blacks "watching something terrible like that and not being able to do anything about it" (Myers, 2003, 120). David's surmise opens his eyes to the humiliations of the past that stirred rage in America's underclass.

Myers frequently returns to recovered memories of humiliations and intimidation of past eras. In *U.S.S. Constellation: Pride of the American Navy* (2004), ship's officer Wilburn Hall provides an eyewitness account of the terrors of the Middle Passage. After the *Constellation* waylays the *Cora* on its departure from the Bight of Benin, slaves mob the deck shouting in fear. To Hall, the tableau reminds him of "the horrors of hell" (Myers, 2004, 28). Worsening the officer's understanding of the flesh trade is the revolting conditions that killed off captives before they could be sold—"the sickening stench of hundreds of naked beings crowded into a space so small, in so warm a climate, without ventilation" (*ibid.*). Myers carries the historic event forward to the repatriation of the *Cora*'s cargo in Liberia, a welcoming microcosm for former slaves. Although the reclamation of slaves in Africa affected only a few, the author's commendation to survivors exhibits his pride in his people's defiance of bondage.

See also **juvenile crime, old age, opportunity, violence**

• *Further Reading*

Myers, Walter Dean. "The Dark Side of the Moon," *Black Creation* (fall 1971): 26–29.
_____. *The Dream Bearer.* New York: Amistad, 2003.
_____. *The Great Migration: An American Story.* New York: HarperCollins, 1993.
_____. *Scorpions.* New York: Harper & Row, 1988.
_____. *U.S.S. Constellation: Pride of the American Navy.* New York: Holiday House, 2004.
Staunton, John A. "Review: *Monster: A Novel*," *Journal of Adolescent & Adult Literacy* 45, no. 8 (May 2002): 791–793.

racism

When Walter Dean Myers began writing, he set out to project normality in stories about black children and communities. His personal credo compelled him toward a public stand against racist books and literature that either stereotyped or omitted nonwhite people. In the essay "The Black Experience in Children's Books: One Step Forward, Two Steps Back," issued in *Interracial Books for Children Bulletin* in 1979, he revealed his own experience with race-inspired censorship: "Our survival as black artists will depend at times on tolerance of racism and at all times on keeping a low profile" (Myers, 1979, 15). For the sake of his own children, he chose to write books rich in humanity that values race as well as mind and spirit.

Myers's intent was to legitimize the lives of blacks and to assert to the white world that black people have worth and dignity. His realistic dramas supplant the caricatures and false portraits of the young adult fiction that fuels racial bias. In *The Outside Shot* (1984), he places a freshman basketball player, Lonnie Jackson, twice weekly at a University Hospital job helping a handicapped white child, nine-year-old Eddie Brignole. To stir the boy out of his malaise, Lonnie plays an active game of ball around Eddie's chair and menaces him with a humorous quip. Lonnie declares that he differs from other people at Montclare State College: "I'm black and mean, jim" (Myers, 1984, 24). The playful badinage helps to initiate trust and friendship in their relationship. Lonnie's performance on the basketball court is another story. Both Hauser, a racist player, and Coach Leeds express their regret that Lonnie left Harlem to accept a scholarship in Indiana. By balancing his activities, Lonnie shoves racism into a small corner of his life.

In most of Myers's fiction, racism is a subtext that frequently bubbles to the surface in unexpected places. Denigration seems normal, almost commonplace in *Fallen Angels* (1988), a Vietnam War text in which white infantryman vilify gooks, slants or slant-eyes, and niggers. To Brunner's comments about gooks, Johnson retorts, "How come when you say 'gooks' it sounds like 'nigger' to me?" (Myers, *Fallen* , 54). Brunner brushes off the accusation with a smirk, "You hear what you want to hear" (*ibid.*) At the height of the Tet offensive in December 1967, black soldier Richard "Richie" Perry muses on the irony of war against Asians while riots in Harlem and other American cities pit blacks against whites. At a pivotal time in his youth, his expanded perspective humanizes white-on-Asian violence and enlarges the dimension of Richie's combat experience.

Because Myers grew up in a multicultural setting, he extends his perspective on bigotry to Latinos and women. Racism toward Hispanics occurs in *Scorpions* (1988), where a wino charges 12-year-old Jamal Hicks with befriending Tito Cruz, a Puerto Rican classmate. The wino degrades the entire race for "[drinking] that tequila and [getting] crazy" (Myers, *Scorpions*, 184). Another insidious slur emerges in *The Glory Field* (1994), in which 16-year-old Luvenia Lewis longs for a college education. After asking Mrs. Deets for a pledge of steady work, Luvenia weeps at the stereotype of the black female in Chicago during the Great Depression. Mrs. Deets speaks the white opinion: "You have a trade.... You are a maid" (Myers, 1994, 166). The clash that demonstrates racial hatred in the fourth stave of *The Glory Field* begins in fictional Johnson City at Cadet Park. After Sheriff Moser tones down march plans by the Ku Klux Klan, disgruntled members enter a coffee shop complaining about black persistence: "The more you ease up on them, the more they push up into your face!" (*ibid.*, 264). In counterpoint, Myers concludes the stave with black marchers entering the same area while singing "O Freedom!," a slave anthem that continues to reflect inhuman situations. A dual issue of anti-black and anti–Indian feeling undergirds *My Name Is America: The Journal of Joshua Loper, a Black Cowboy on the Chisholm Trail, 1871* (1999). On the trail, Joshua learns the reason for buffalo hunting. According to the Captain, the government promotes the skinning of buffalo and the sale of hides as a way of "controlling the Indians," a euphemism for starving out Plains tribes (Myers, 1999, 104). Myers indicates that white Americans owe more than one group an apology for perpetrating white supremacy on minorities.

Characters in the author's writings bear a constant burden of alienation and rage. In *My Name Is America: The Journal of Biddy Owens* (2001), members of the Birmingham Black Barons discuss the difference between black stadiums and those "built for white folks ball," including the New York Polo Grounds and Chicago's Comiskey Park (Myers, 2001, 8). The title character admires two heroic black athletes, Jackie Robinson, player for the Brooklyn Dodgers, and Larry Doby, a member of the Cleveland Browns. A confrontation with a white store owner threatens to escalate until pitcher Jimmy Newberry ends the face-off. Biddy words the team's anger at having to return home hungry because they can't eat in white-owned facilities: "Just about any white person could mess with you if you were black" (*ibid*., 11). His naivete emerges on a first visit to Cleveland, where he assumes that the absence of Southern "whites only" signs indicate a more inclusive environment. Racism violates constitutional rights in subsequent scenes, when a white woman examines an impromptu lineup in a movie house in search of a purse snatcher and when a white conductor refuses to let the team board a train. The progression of incidents gradually enlightens Biddy into a national outrage, the continuing mistreatment and exclusion of nonwhite people.

Myers takes pride in the upsurge of black activism. He epitomized in *The Greatest: Muhammad Ali* (2001) the turning point of civil rights struggles in 1963. By picturing the March on Washington, the "I Have a Dream" speech of Dr. Martin Luther King, Jr., and the conversion of Cassius Clay to the Nation of Islam, the sports biography celebrates a cataclysm that struck American racism at its roots. A more personal picture of acceptance of outsiders arises in *A Time to Love: Stories from the Old Testament* (2003), in which Naomi returns to Bethlehem and fears for her Moabite daughters-in-law, who get a taste of clannishness and suspicion from border guards. Myers portrays Naomi as farsighted in her fear of what lies ahead. Of national enmities, she regrets, "It's a terrible thing, but it's the way of the world" (Myers, *A Time*, 57). The thinly veiled comment reflects on exclusion and vilification of racial groups into prehistory.

One of Myers's most troubled fictions, *The Dream Bearer* (2003), ventures into a damning truth, the color bias that exists within the mixed-race family. Loren Hart, the child of a black father and white mother, denounces exclusion after his mother refuses to give character references for the Mutus, a Kikuyu family from Kenya. Loren reveals that the Curry family offers their signatures, but his mother refuses because she dislikes black immigrants. Loren retorts, "She just didn't like Africans" (Myers, *Dream*, 61). Rather than discuss their differences, the mother grounds Loren until he cleans the bathroom. The potential for disunity in the family recedes into the background, but the rancor remains in the narrative's forefront.

Even more insidious is the color bias that pits one black American against another. At a significant point in *Here in Harlem: Poems in Many Voices* (2004), Myers's verse paean to his childhood home, he reveals a troubling form of discrimination. Clara Brown, who speaks six intercalary staves that loop through the 54 poems, recalls girlhood hopes that she and sister Vicky might join the chorus line at the Cotton Club. Clara certifies that they dance with style. On her way past the pianist, she hears the hard-edged truth that the club managers "only hire light-skinned girls" (Myers, 2004, 11). A more hurtful form of racism, the preference for light over dark sets Clara's eyes to tearing and her lip at a quiver. Voicing the author's theme, she concludes that "being black wasn't no simple thing" (*ibid.*).

See also **injustice, Martin Luther King, Malcolm X, powerlessness, reclamation, segregation, victimization, violence**

• *Further Reading*

Myers, Walter Dean. "The Black Experience in Children's Books: One Step Forward, Two Steps Back," *Interracial Books for Children Bulletin* 10, no. 6 (1979): 4–15.

_____. *The Dream Bearer*. New York: Amistad, 2003.

_____. *Fallen Angels*. New York: Scholastic, 1988.

_____. *The Glory Field*. New York: Scholastic, 1994.

_____. *Here in Harlem: Poems in Many Voices*. New York: Holiday House, 2004.

_____. *My Name Is America: The Journal of Biddy Owens*. New York: Scholastic, 2001.

_____. *My Name Is America: The Journal of Joshua Loper, a Black Cowboy on the Chisholm Trail, 1871*. New York: Scholastic, 1999.

_____. *The Outside Shot*. New York: Delacorte, 1984.

_____. *Scorpions*. New York: Harper & Row, 1988.

_____. *A Time to Love: Stories from the Old Testament*. New York: Scholastic, 2003.

Sutton, Roger. "Threads in Our Cultural Fabric," *School Library Journal* 40, no. 6 (June 1994): 24–28.

reading

Like young adult author Gary Paulsen, novelist Walter Dean Myers gained an understanding of self and of ambition from becoming a reader in boyhood. He observed, "In my imagination I could also be a participant in adventures that were beyond the limits of 'self'" (Myers, May 2001, 60). In early childhood, he valued the liberty of a neighborhood lending library, in which he could browse and select works without adult supervision. He told Adam Graham, an interviewer for the *Detroit News*, "I was not a social person, so I ended up spending a lot of time with myself. But books were always a friend" (Graham, 2002). He later commented that reading took him deep inside to a place he loves to explore. He reprised the delight in the printed word in young characters like Kenny Perry in *Fallen Angels* (1988), who delays obligatory bedtime by reading comic books by flashlight under his blanket. The image suggests the author's familiarity with ploys to extend his own time for reading for pleasure. He admitted in his 1994 Margaret A. Edwards Award Acceptance Speech to the American Library Association annual convention in Miami to asking himself, "Was I somehow peculiar?" (Myers, 1995, 131).

Teachers directed Myers toward works more character-shaping than comic books, his usual source of diversion. In 1971, he alluded to Betty, Jughead, and Veronica, the white teenagers in Archie comic books, who tease the mind of Augie, a disturbed rapist in Myers's short story "Dark Side of the Moon." Because Myers failed to learn in a traditional classroom setting, Bonnie Liebow, his English teacher at Stuyvesant High School, lured him from teen pulp works by outlining a reading list that challenged and educated him. Gradually, he taught himself by studying the themes and styles of great 19th-century European and American writers, including Honoré de Balzac, Thomas Mann, and Emile Zola. One title Myers has frequently cited is Samuel Taylor Coleridge's quest poem *The Rime of the Ancient Mariner* (1798), a fable based on sin and redemption. As Myers internalized "poems with their rhythms as pacing aids and end rhymes as targets," the rewards of reading emerged in his writing (Myers, May 2001, 60). From his efforts, he gained a mystical experience that "holds an enduring fascination" (*ibid.*, 61).

Myers began a career of nurturing the emotional and mental health of young readers by writing the kinds of literature that enlarges on real teen situations. The impetus among teen readers grew from need. In Myers's words, "For many young people the only place in the world they find themselves included is in the pages of novels" (Myers, 1995, 131). As he advanced from writing adult fiction to young adult novels, he found it difficult to particularize the age that would most appreciate his work. He explained in an interview with the staff of the *Journal of Reading*, "It's increasingly difficult to target an age group because of the discrepancy in reading levels at the various schools" (Chance, *et al.*, 1994, 247).

Myers locates in fictional characters a hunger for good reading. Sherry Jewett, the romantic interest in *The Outside Shot* (1984), helps protagonist Lonnie Jackson recover from a drinking binge by reading aloud to him while he rests in bed. In *Fallen Angels* (1988), the author pictures protagonist Richard "Richie" Perry and other soldiers reading *Stars and Stripes*, the *New York Times*, *Playboy*, *Reader's Digest*, *Ebony* magazine, and copies of *Valley of the Dolls*. Richie recalls the film *Shane* (1945), a screen version of Jack Schaefer's young adult classic novel filmed in 1949. In "Telling Our Children the Stories of Their Lives," an essay published in *American Visions*, Myers justified the importance of worthy literature to youth: "Children need books, in and out of school, that depict people who look like them because they are being told on a daily basis that these books are indicators of importance" (Myers, 1991, 30).

Myers contributed to the knowledge of reading in January 1991 when he delivered "Travelers and Translators," the main address at the Ohio State University Children's Literature Conference in Columbus. His text stressed that reading comprehension is less important than opportunities to explore self, others, and experience. He commended reading as a personal, social, and political endeavor that introduces diverse people and ideas. He identified three types of readers— travelers, searchers, and translators. Travelers absorb texts with a strong sense of their place in history. Searchers, the second group, are less sure-footed, less adventuresome in following narrative to a vision of other times and places. Unlike travelers, searchers tend to get by without actually educating themselves. The third group, translators, relate narrative to a limited reality. Typically annoyed and confused by books, they reject reading that deals with unknown times and events. For the author, the challenge of appealing to all three groups has undergirded most of his career.

Myers's close association with his own children and with school groups extenuates his interest in the responses of youth to literature. In *Darnell Rock Reporting* (1994), he describes at-risk junior high students discussing with their teacher, Mrs. Finley, "a story about an old man who went fishing," a reference to Ernest Hemingway's Caribbean fable *The Old Man and the Sea* (1952) (Myers, 1994, 22). Chris McKoy, a student in a "ladder" or below-level class, falters on the issue of writing about an unremarkable peasant fisherman. Lee Chiang, showing support for a writer's subjects, declares, "[Hemingway] can write about what he wants to" (*ibid.*). A comment on reading from the perspective of delinquent teens occurs in *Handbook for Boys: A Novel* (2002). Using reverse psychology, the male mentors in Duke's barbershop instruct Jimmy Lynch that reading is essential to business and the professions. Duke confides in private that "being alive in America is like having a box of tools that I can use to build any kind of life I want" (Myers, 2002, 86). One of the tools is reading, the activity that saved the author in childhood and directed his active mind toward a career.

In 2003, Myers posed clues to characters in *The Beast* by analyzing their reading tastes. As 17-year-old protagonist Anthony "Spoon" Witherspoon nears Harlem for Christmas break from Wallingford Academy in Connecticut, he carries in his overnight bag a treasure. He remembers days at Mt. Morris Park with his Dominican girlfriend Gabriela "Gabi" Godoy, when he reads from Nobel Prize–winning author Derek Walcott and Gabi recites short pieces by a Cuban-American, Carolina Hospital, who lives in Miami. The infusion of verbal emotion in an unfamiliar language still uplifts Spoon. He recalls, "I'd become suddenly heroic, had been able to fly, to soar over the family gray of the city" (Myers, *Beast*, 113). The exchange of verse readings spawns a love of literature in Spoon, an indication of his sensitivity to beauty in language and to oral interpretation.

The expression of self through love of literature continues throughout the relationship between Spoon and Gabi. He presents her a used copy of Langston Hughes's translation of the verse of Gabriela Mistral, an influential Chilean feminist, poet, and educator for whom Gabi was named. During affectionate conversation at a post–Christmas walk in the park, Gabi quotes Mistral's line from "Suavidades" (Serenity), anthologized in her first collection, *Desolación* (1922). The citation describes how a love song dispels the world's evils. The extreme idealism enables Spoon to particularize Gabi's state of mind and to comprehend why she retreats from home problems into heroin and the contemplation of idyllic innocence that has nothing in common with reality. The depiction of literature as escapism reflects Myers's own experience of fleeing a speech defect into the silent world of books.

See also **realism**

• *Further Reading*

Chance, Rosemary, Teri Lesesne, and Lois Buckman. "And the Winner Is ... : A Teleconference with Walter Dean Myers," *Journal of Reading* 38, no. 3 (November 1994): 246–249.

Enciso, Patricia E. "Taking Our Seats: The Consequences of Positioning in Reading Assessments," *Theory Into Practice* 40, no. 3 (1 June 2001): 166–174.

Gill, Sam D. "Young Adult Literature for Young Adult Males," *ALAN Review* 26, no. 2 (winter 1999): 1.

Graham, Adam. "Author's Just a Kid at Heart," *Detroit News* (6 May 2002).

Myers, Walter Dean. "And Then I Read....," *Voices-from-the-Middle* 8, no. 4 (May 2001): 58–62.

_____. *The Beast.* New York: Scholastic, 2003.

_____. *Darnell Rock Reporting.* New York: Delacorte, 1994.

_____. *Handbook for Boys: A Novel.* New York: Amistad, 2002.

_____. "1994 Margaret A. Edwards Award Acceptance Speech," *Youth Services in Libraries* 8, no. 2 (winter 1995): 129–133.

_____. "Telling Our Children the Stories of Their Lives," *American Visions* 6, no. 6 (December 1991): 30–32.

_____. *A Time to Love: Stories from the Old Testament.* New York: Scholastic, 2003.

Tolson, Nancy. "Making Books Available: The Role of Early Libraries, Librarians, and Booksellers in the Promotion of African American Literature," *African American Review* 32, no. 1 (1998): 9–16.

Wilder, Ann, and Alan B. Teasley. "Making the Transition to Lifelong Reading: Books Older Teens Choose," *ALAN Review* 27, no. 1 (1999): 42–46.

realism

The popularity of real life situations and characters with young readers has supported a burgeoning market in young adult fiction and nonfiction. Literary experts Kathryn Latrobe and Trisha Hutcherson note that the genre "became a phenomenon in almost a single year, 1967" (Latrobe & Hutcherson, 2002, 73). As the market for realism grew, Walter Dean Myers was evolving into a top-rank fiction writer alongside Alice Childress, Virginia Hamilton, Ntozake Shange, and Mildred Taylor. He became a natural at writing the kind of stories, histories, and novels that met the demand, such as *It Ain't All for Nothin'* (1968), a gritty social novel that places 12-year-old Tippy as lookout for his father Lonnie's gang as they rob a liquor store owner at an urban bank night-drop. In the falling action, the boy comforts Bubba, a gang member slowly dying of a gunshot wound to the side. In terror for the future, Tippy chooses to turn Lonnie over to the police. In a review for *Interracial Books for Children Bulletin*, critic Ashley Jane Pennington regrets that Myers's realism "[underscores] the fact that Tippy and the people who populate this world cannot escape" random violence and repetitive crime (Pennington, 1979, 18).

Through realism, Myers explores universal human fears. In "Gums," anthologized in *We Be Word Sorcerers: Twenty-five Stories by Black Americans* (1973), the author pits the real terrors of homelessness and loss against the personification of Death, a stalker of the title figure. While 69-year-old Gums rapidly retreats into paranoia from senile dementia, his nine-year-old grandson Stevie shoulders the responsibilities of caring for a house-bound old man. As Gums works up charms against the advance of mortality, Stevie cowers in the corner and contemplates a future without a grandfather or without a source of income from an adult provider. Mental phantasms return Stevie to the deaths of his parents in a car wreck. Such overwhelming obstacles to childhood confidence resonate in much of Myers's fiction, which maintains a Dickensian sympathy for children whom society fails.

The appeal of Myers's writings to youth solves the problem of teachers, parents, and librarians of finding relevant materials that develop regular reading habits in the young. The appeal of realistic contemporary fiction derives from the similarities between the problems of characters and of readers, the foundation of Myers's seriocomic novel *Fast Sam, Cool Clyde, and Stuff* (1975). By identifying with fictional teens like Sam, Clyde, and Stuff, readers perceive the universality of such school and community problems as unstable homes, sexual experimentation, fighting, drug use, and run-ins with authorities. The result of Myers's hopeful fiction, according to Maria Salvadore, coordinator of children's services for the District of Columbia public library, is the "sense of control through self-exploration" that inspires teen readers, especially at-risk students whom institutions must steer away from malaise toward success (Naughton, 1989, 8).

Another aspect of realism is its exposure of youth to a variety of solutions to such adult problems as separation and divorce, alcoholism, unemployment, and the illness and deaths of loved ones, the motif in Myers's short story "The Vision of Felipe" (1978), the exemplum "The Treasure of Lemon Brown" (1983), short takes on teen pregnancy in *Sweet Illusions* (1986), commentary on superstition in "Angela's Eyes" (2000), and the reclamation of juvenile delinquents in *Handbook for Boys: A Novel* (2003). By imagining fictional characters controlling fear, anger, and grief, readers develop hope from bibliotherapy for their own quandaries with homelessness, domestic abuse, abandonment, teen parenthood, and adoption. By comparing immature responses to those of adults, particularly authority figure like police officers and teachers, teen fiction nurtures cross-generational understanding and rapport. As a result, according to *ALAN Review* editor Rita Karr and Leslie Verzi Julian, immersion in young adult books "unlocks that door of resistance to reading and resistance to learning, and ultimately opens a pathway to success in school" (Karr & Julian, 1999, 1).

Walter Dean Myers heads a long list of authors who flourish at believable dialogue and compelling themes and who vivify narrative with sense impressions, such as the burning pain from a bullet in the chest of the title character in "The Vision of Felipe" and the near-drowning of Ken Arrow during pursuit of a fake monster in *Ambush in the Amazon* (1986). The author perplexes 16-year-old model Crystal Brown with the suicide of a colleague in *Crystal* (1987). She realizes the reality of a career in fashion modeling that pits sexual sleaze against the hype, limo rides, glamorous wardrobe, and a fan base. Because of strong personal morals, Crystal retreats from a movie contract that requires a sexual commitment to a talent handler. Crystal's choice of self-worth over fame sets an example for young readers who may find themselves in similarly tempting situations that exploit the youth, health, and beauty of teens.

In the tradition that dates to Homer's *Iliad* (850 B. C.), Myers saturates a Vietnam War novel, *Fallen Angels* (1988), with real combat. He relies on fierce diction — sapper, cosmolene, cordite, shrapnel, muzzle flashes. On arrival in 1967, protagonist Richard "Richie" Perry quails at the rumble of artillery. He thinks to himself, "My stomach felt queasy.... This was Nam" (Myers, 1988, 9). Terms that imply protection and sanctuary include gung ho, pickup zone, tet trust, F-100s streaking overhead, and the Paris peace table, the image of sensible negotiators trying to align the raw edges of peace. Weaponry ranges from the standard M-16 to punji sticks, trip flares, rocket-propelled grenades, gunships, Molotov cocktails, and the suicide missions of booby-trapped children, who explode like land mines. For immature readers, Myers's authentic combat story rebuts any unfounded dreams of glory in uniform.

The conventions of Myers's war fiction require technical terms—interdiction patrol, skirmish line, and Graves Registration—which dot the narrative with the technicalities of surveillance, injury, and death. The reader feels the weight of a flak jacket, the boredom of days in the hooch awaiting mail call, tense silences in foxholes, flights into fantasy, and the terror of investigating a spider hole. As the pace of destruction picks up, Richard experiences the full range of horrors—the eyeball-to-eyeball look at a Viet Cong, the sight of dismembered bodies, the smell of gunfire, and the sounds of bubbles from the shrapnel wound to the chest that kills Jenkins. Perry's experience of being airlifted to medical aid increases the tempo of death within life as medics zip some of his buddies's remains into body bags. Contributing post-war realism is Myers's story of 51-year-old Sweeby Jones, a homeless, out-of-work Vietnam vet in *Darnell Rock Reporting* (1994). Like Richie, Sweeby gets a taste of war that threatens to consume the rest of his civilian life.

Like Maya Angelou, Judy Blume, and the anonymous author of *Go Ask Alice* (1971), Myers has earned his share of criticism for exposing youth to harsh, vulgar language as well as to sexuality, racism, and the seamy underside of urban life. He develops internal strengths in teen characters from their ability to make rational decisions about dilemmas deriving from peer pressure and media temptations. To slip past the need for profanity common to street language, in *The Mouse Rap* (1990), he has the protagonist, 14-year-old Frederick "The Mouse" Douglas, refer to an older man who "[starts] with the *S* word, then [switches] to the *F* word" (Myers, 1990, 145). In defiance of racism in *Hoops: A Novel* (1981), drugs and guns in *Scorpions* (1988), soldiers' profanity in *Fallen Angels* (1988), and astrology in "Who Needs an Aries Ape" (1992), censors have removed Myers's works from public and school libraries and from required and supplemental reading lists. The publicity has broadened Myers's audience by attesting to his willingness to address such serious issues as the suicide of mill worker Ray York, a late-in-life basketball hopeful in *The Outside Shot* (1984), the trial of a juvenile, 16-year-old Steven Harmon, for murder in *Monster* (1999), and the shooting rampage that results in murder and suicide in *Shooter* (2004). Against the minority of parents, teachers, and librarians who repudiate realism, millions read Myers's works for the truths that he reveals for the sake of a better world.

Myers's focus on human failings compounds the surface of realism with the internal demons of victims, for example, the self-doubt of Steve Harmon about his role in murder in *Monster: A Novel* (1999) and the terrors of Isaac and Zillah in scriptural vignettes in *A Time to Love: Stories from the Old Testament* (2003). One of the author's heart-rending cautionary tales is the fear of 12-year-old David Curry for his mentally ill father Reuben in the urban folktale *The Dream Bearer* (2003). The Curry family's crises generate a rollercoaster existence from police raiding the house after midnight to Reuben's assault on 17-year-old Tyrone, who refuses to divulge his daily whereabouts to his parents. In an historical setting, the author subjects innocent whites to the plight of naked, foul-smelling slaves during the Middle Passage in *U.S.S. Constellation: Pride of the American Navy* (2004). In the latter text, a memoir of sailor John Hoxse recalls a gunshot wound to his arm: "I was then taken up, laid on a table, my wounds washed clean, and my arm amputated and thrown overboard" (Myers, 2004, 16). The matter-of-fact commentary illustrates Myers's ability to envigorate his histories with horrific truths that deserve telling.

See also **gangs, juvenile crime, military, old age, parenthood, self-destruction, sex, urbanism, victimization, violence**

• *Further Reading*

Bissett, Donald J. "Review: *Fast Sam, Cool Clyde, and Stuff*," *Language Arts* 53, no. 5 (May 1976): 520–521.
Carter, Betty. "Review: *U.S.S. Constellation: Pride of the American Navy*," *Horn Book* 80, no. 4 (July-August 2004): 80.
Donelson, Kenneth L., and Aileen Pace Nilsen. *Literature for Today's Young Adults*. Boston: Allyn & Bacon, 2004.
Karr, Rita, and Leslie Verzi Julian. "Middle School Readers: Common Views, Different Worlds," *ALAN Review* 26, no. 2 (winter 1999): 1.
Kaywell, Joan F. *Adolescent Literature As a Complement to the Classics*. New York: Christopher-Gordon, 1992.
Latrobe, Kathryn, and Trisha Hutcherson. "An Introduction to Ten Outstanding Young-Adult Authors in the United States," *World Literature Today* (summer 2002): 70–79.
Myers, Walter Dean. *Fallen Angels*. New York: Scholastic, 1988.
_____. "Gums" in *We Be Word Sorcerers: Twenty-five Stories by Black Americans*. New York: Bantam, 1973.
_____. *The Mouse Rap*. New York: HarperCollins, 1990.
_____. *U.S.S. Constellation: Pride of the American Navy*. New York: Holiday House, 2004.
Naughton, Jim. "Literary Crusader Writes Stories about Real Kids," *Los Angeles Times* (29 December 1989): 8.
Pennington, Ashley Jane. "Review: *It Ain't All for Nothin*,'" *Interracial Books for Children Bulletin* 10, no. 4 (1979): 18.
Smith, Karen Patricia, ed. *African-American Voices in Young Adult Literature: Tradition, Transition, Transformation*. Lanham, Md.: Scarecrow, 1994.

reclamation

Reclamation of wayward souls invigorates Myers's fiction, giving it life and hope, as with a junkie's soft side in "The Fare to Crown Point" (1971), the prison epiphany that redirects the life of the title figure in *Malcolm X: By Any Means Necessary* (1993), the tactics of General François Toussaint L'Ouverture during the flight of ex-slaves from the French army to the mountains in *Toussaint L'Ouverture: The Fight for Haiti's Freedom* (1996), and the retrieval of 705 slaves from the *Cora* for repatriation to Africa in *U.S.S. Constellation: Pride of the American Navy* (2004). In "How Long Is Forever?," a somber tale of lost opportunity published in the June 1969 issue of *Negro Digest*, the author creates an explosive tension in Moses, an inmate incarcerated for robbery and murder. Coursing through his thoughts are dreams of freedom within months, depending on the whim of the parole board. A counter current forces him to tolerate the dehumanization of gibes and buffeting from Jenkins, a sadistic white prison guard. Myers depicts the loss of control in Moses as a "brewing storm" (Myers, 1969, 57). In the falling action, murderous blows at Jenkins destroy Moses's chance for release and topple him into an ecstatic lunacy. Myers aims his story at a justice system impaired by racism that mirrors the power of the overseer during the slave era.

In *It Ain't All for Nothin'* (1978), the author presents community synergy as the hope of 12-year-old Tippy, a neglected child forced into robberies by his father Lonnie, an ex-con and career criminal. Recovery from beatings, poor nutrition, and terror comes slowly to the boy, who tries to put on a brave face for the sake of 69-year-old Carrie Brown, his ailing grandmother. Because of Tippy's immaturity, he escapes into the available retreats for a pre-teen—sleep, television, movies, and running away. Binges on alcohol do nothing to retrieve him from a perilous home situation. Myers pictures Carrie's basic home training in godliness and right thinking as the impetus to a hard decision for a boy, to turn Lonnie and his gang in to the police and to accept the fostering of Edna and Roland Sylvester, loving friends who observe the turmoil in Tippy. The community forces of social services, police, friends, and neighbors enable the boy to nest in a stable environment while he maintains a frail lifeline of letters to his father in prison.

The importance of community to human redemption empowers the author's writings about urban areas, notably in his ode "Wolf Song" (2005). In *Crystal* (1987), 16-year-old model Crystal Brown caroms back and forth between glamorous Manhattan settings and her home in a Brooklyn ghetto. The allure of limo rides, beautiful clothes and makeup, and notoriety for magazine spreads competes with the advice of Sister Gibbs, who reminds Crystal that a conscience is a built-in extension of community values. From another perspective, in the seriocomic novel *Darnell Rock Reporting* (1994), Myers presents the unpredictable outcome of interest in 51-year-old Sweeby Jones, a homeless, out-of-work Vietnam vet. Although Darnell witnesses the collapse of his ideal plan to turn basketball courts into gardens for street wanderers to tend, media and city council interest energizes others to suggest methods of helping the poor. From reading of his plight in the newspaper, Sweeby decides to continue seeking work. After landing a small job at the hospital, he develops hope that he can once more support himself. The author commends Darnell for his part in redirecting Sweeby toward reinvolvement in the community.

Myers delineates the redemptive power of first love in "Kitty and Mack: A Love Story" in *145th Street: Short Stories* (2000). Eddie "Mack" McCormick, whom the narrator describes as "stuck on himself," falls hard for Kitty, a beauty who is smart, personable, and headed for a career in law. She wows Mack in English class by reading aloud a sonnet in Shakespearean format that she wrote in imitation of Elizabeth Barrett Browning's "Sonnet 43" from *Sonnets from the Portuguese* (1850). In the narrator's opinion, Kitty rids Mack of "attitude," a slang term suggesting a cocky, conceited pose (Myers, 2000, 90). After a drive-by shooting results in the amputation of Mack's foot, Kitty determines to save him from despondence by sitting in her grandfather's barbershop behind a sign in the window declaring her love. By being as stubborn as Mack, Kitty maintains her love and faith in his future.

The author's most direct attack on self-destructive behaviors takes shape in *Handbook for Boys: A Novel* (2002). By following the day-by-day education of Jimmy Lynch and Kevin under the mentorship of barber Duke Wilson, Myers works in warnings about sex, drugs, irresponsibility, limited ambitions, and teen crime. In an urban setting, Duke selects examples of worthy or poor life choices from people passing on the street, operating businesses in Harlem, or coming to his barbershop for haircuts. The pairing of Jimmy with Kevin emphasizes that wise counsel takes root in Jimmy's thinking, but Kevin retains his love of marijuana, which ends his chance for parole and saddles him with months of incarceration he could have avoided. Myers emphasizes the moral value of an elder-to-youth relationship as well as the discipline of a concerned mother as two elements in Jimmy's reclamation from fighting and a negative attitude toward school.

In *The Beast* (2003), Myers challenges 17-year-old Anthony "Spoon" Witherspoon to banish his temptation to quit Wallingford Academy in Connecticut. Rather than pursue his dream of a professional education, the protagonist longs to remain home from Christmas break to rescue his Dominican girlfriend, Gabriela "Gabi" Godoy, from heroin. The romantic image of himself as her hero falls short of the reality of reclaiming a heroin user. Gabi strengthens him for the leavetaking with a promise to apply "this Dominican woman's brain and ... this Catholic heart" to rid herself of addiction (Myers, 2003, 145). Exhausted from grief at Gabi's mother's burial and from fear that Gabi may retreat into drugs, Spoon accepts an adult burden of doubt that his girlfriend can turn religious strength into the daily courage she will need during rehabilitation.

See also **gambling, opportunity, religion, self-destruction**

• *Further Reading*

Myers, Walter Dean. *The Beast.* New York: Scholastic, 2003.

_____. "How Long Is Forever?," *Negro Digest* (June 1969): 52–57.

_____. *145th Street: Short Stories.* New York: Delacorte, 2000.

Silvey, Anita. "Review: *Malcolm X: By Any Means Necessary*," *Horn Book* 69, no. 5 (September/October 1993): 626–627.

Smith, Karen Patricia, ed. *African-American Voices in Young Adult Literature: Tradition, Transition, Transformation.* Lanham, Md.: Scarecrow, 1994.

religion

Myers recognizes the human propensity for religious hunger and spiritual upheaval. In his Margaret A. Edwards Award Acceptance Speech at the American Library Association annual conference in Miami in 1994, he admitted a childhood curiosity "if it was really okay to worry about the existence of God" (Myers, 1995, 131). His canon balances violence, disappointment, and hurt with strands of personal and scriptural values, such as the fake shrine of an old form of Buddhism in

The Hidden Shrine (1985) and the vibrant hallelujahs expressed in collage and verse in a picture-ode, *Harlem: A Poem* (1997). In the latter, gesturing worshippers embrace the spirit with joy, "reflecting the face of God" (Myers, *Harlem*, n.p.). The statement opposes the white tradition of a Caucasian god pictured in art, statuary, and holiday cards. Boldly reclaiming deity for his own people, Myers's black minister raises a powerful hand in the tradition of Harlem's "jive and Jehovah artists" (*ibid.*). Christopher Myers's illustration positions the minister's face toward a doorway bright-gold with promise.

Spirituality takes a variety of forms in Myers's fiction. He treats various religions with respect, including black Muslims and Hari Krishnas in *It Ain't All for Nothin'* (1978). The protagonist, 12-year-old Tippy, tries to emulate the faith of his 69-year-old Grandma Carrie Brown, but the family's decline weakens his resolve. When he tries to pray, his brain rebels: "I was mad at God and I tried to push being mad out of my head" (Myers, 1978, 60). For the first time threatened by a dissolute life style, Tippy regrets having to depend on his father Lonnie, a thief and alcohol and drug abuser. The boy's attempt at confession to a priest goes awry, further confusing Tippy about God's relationship with humanity. Unsure why the almighty is "doing me wrong," the boy says, "This is *me*, God, this is Tippy. I ain't done nothing wrong!" (*ibid.*, 85). At a crisis in his relationship with Lonnie, Tippy is true to Carrie's example. He prays that God will shield him from his father's thievery.

The author frequently ties religion to other elderly female characters, as with Sister Gibbs of the Victory Tabernacle in *Crystal* (1987) and Sister Boone, a neighbor in *The Outside Shot* (1984) who urges college freshman Lonnie Jackson to "keep your mind on Jesus" (Myers, 1984, 1). In the seriocomic novel *Won't Know Till I Get There*, Mabel Jackson rebukes a difficult young man who is wearing a crucifix. In her opinion, "Only side of the church that fool know is the outside" (Myers, 1982, 159). Mrs. Hicks, the sorrowing single parent in *Scorpions* (1988), accepts the condolence of the Reverend Biggs. At a troubling time in the family's lives, he leads them in prayer for Randy Hicks, a prisoner whom another inmate stabbed. Biggs's prayer, filled with cliches and biblical grammar, comforts the mother, but does little to reassure 12-year-old Jamal Hicks, who ponders how to rid himself of a pistol without upsetting her. He confuses the issues of being the man of the house with arming himself against trouble. Spiritual intervention does nothing to clarify the question of whether a gun strengthens or weakens him. Neither does his mother's insistence that the family attend Bethel Tabernacle regularly.

Myers's half-hearted reliance on formal ritual emerges in numerous scenes in which characters take no comfort from prayer. In a telling moment in *Fallen Angels* (1988), anti-hero Richard "Richie" Perry, a raw recruit on his first deployment to Vietnam, prays the Lord's Prayer and accepts from hoochmate "Brew" Brewster an indexed bible. Perry suffers guilt for ignoring God until the deployment to Vietnam and wonders "if Buddha was answering prayers on the other side" (Myers, 1988, 279). Perry rejects the ritualized prayer of the chaplain, Father Santora, a noncombatant who has never ventured into a battle zone. Myers implies a dramatic irony in the chaplain's transfer to Khe Sanh, the site of some of the war's bloodiest fighting.

More comforting to Perry and the other men of Alpha Company of the 22nd

Replacement Company is the prayer of their 23-year-old platoon leader, Lieutenant Carroll, a man devoid of vaunting ambition and vainglory. In three simple lines, he pays homage to the dead and asks that soldiers fear death but that they stop fear from enveloping them. After Carroll's death from a hit to the armpit, Monaco, the company point man, repeats the plaintive prayer as a token of respect for a fallen leader and as a source of strength for battle-weary men. On Perry's return flight home, he experiences a helter-skelter commemoration to the men who died in action. He concludes that nonstandard prayer suits the occasion: "I just wanted God to care for them, to keep them whole" (*ibid.*, 309). The reverie contrasts the conditions of casualties whom he saw zipped into body bags.

Myers's novels expose spiritual courage from unlikely and unexpected sources. For Richie Perry, memories of his mother, Mabel Perry, commend her as the mom who tucked her children into bed and led them in prayer. In a later novel, *Somewhere in the Darkness* (1992), it is Miss Mackenzie, a friend of the Little family, who speaks comforting words. She reassures Jimmy Little that prayer is a refuge for the suffering and sorrowing. After Jimmy's father dies in a prison hospital, the solace continues at the funeral, where a woman sings "Precious Lord," a familiar gospel hymn that perceives God as a personal guide and comforter.

Myers acknowledges that the pervasive black faith in God accompanied African Americans on their rise from dray labor to more promising jobs in urban industrialized areas. In *The Great Migration: An American Story* (1993), an epic journey that parallels the Hebrew exodus, Myers wrote the concluding ode "Migration" to accompany the folk art panels painted by Jacob Lawrence. The poetic coda pictures the small patrimony that families pack for the long train ride North. They leave behind the family dead interred at "a church built/With sweat and faith and knotted pine" (Myers, 1993, n.p.). Along with rope-bound suitcases and insufficient bag lunches are "Bibles older than freedom," an image that attests to the power of faith that blacks exerted before emancipation (*ibid.*).

The author extends the range of the diaspora in the short story "Sunrise over Manaus," collected in *From One Experience to Another* (1997). Elena Alacar Cabrera, a Brazilian exotic dancer, recounts how religious faith followed her from South American to Manhattan. On her departure, her father gave her a carved cross with the observation, "If I took care of Jesus then he would take care of me" (Myers, "Sunrise," 81). As a gesture of concern, she gives the cross to James Simms, a new friend whom she meets at a mental health clinic. In an ironic touch, Myers shows James warding off a confrontation with his mother by placing the cross in front of her. The statue symbolizes an emotional tie between James and Elena, who returns to Manaus to escape thoughts of suicide. The narrative indicates how a religious talisman develops meaning in the lives of James and Elena at serious lows in their expectations.

Biblical knowledge infuses Myers's writings with wisdom and lyricism as well as history. The mother of 16-year-old protagonist Steve Harmon in *Monster: A Novel* (1999) visits him at the Manhattan Detention Center and leaves a bible with a passage marked for his perusal. The gift is ambiguous in that it implies her reliance on God and her doubts of Steve's innocence. In Myers's sports biography *My Name Is*

America: The Journal of Biddy Owens: The Negro Leagues (2001), Aunt Jack quizzes her nephew on Daniel in the lion's den and fumes when niece Rachel chooses to play jazz rather than church music. In *My Name Is America: The Journal of Joshua Loper, a Black Cowboy, The Chisholm Trail, 1871* (1999), the title character's mother, a "good religious woman," asks Joshua to pray with her before he departs on a cattle drive (Myers, 1999, 4). Joshua obeys his mother and takes temporary refuge in a Negro prayer meeting at the edge of Indian Territory, where nine members pray for the wranglers' salvation and safety.

In *Scorpions* (1988), Myers retreats from investing older women with a supernatural touch of godliness. The narrative depicts the failure of an unnamed grandmother to save Tito, her Puerto Rican grandson, from gang violence. By hero-worshipping Jamal Hicks, Tito commits murder among gang members. His punishment is severe — loss of his status as legal alien. On his return to his father in the Caribbean, his grandmother also suffers shame and disillusion from deportation. The double loss to Jamal's community attests to the extensive damage wreaked by teen brigands.

Myers parallels superstition and plantation religion in the saga *The Glory Field* (1994), a narration on the fictional Lewis clan. In 1864, the only sanctuary is the former slave dormitory that Moses Lewis occupies. In 1900, Curry Islanders frame a real church from recycled boards of dismantled slave cabins. By 1930, the Lewises attend Bethel Tabernacle in Chicago, a church established in a former synagogue on Indiana Avenue. After the singing of a lively spiritual, "Standing in the Need of Prayer," the Reverend Bradley delivers a call-and-response sermon on lost sheep and forgiveness. In the fourth stave, set in fictional Johnson City, South Carolina, in 1964, Miss Mary Hardin Lewis chides her grandson, 16-year-old Tommy Lewis, with making a wry comment involving Noah's ark. She reminds him that the Bible makes no mention that "thou shalt have a fast mouth" (Myers, 1994, 250).

Myers's writings account for variation in concepts of God and godliness. At a dramatic moment in *The Beast* (2003), the author dramatizes the divide between Catholics and fundamentalists. As 17-year-old Anthony "Spoon" Witherspoon steers Gabriela "Gabi" Godoy, his Dominican girlfriend, through a Catholic funeral mass for Gabi's mother Lucila, he observes how Gabi clings to the unchanging words. In a separate section, Spoon's parents sit and view the proceedings from a Baptist point of view. Spoon, who knows little about Catholicism, attempts to wrest comfort from the ritual, but he departs in silence with no appreciable uplift in mood.

After years of immersion in scripture, Myers paraphrased six stories of conflict and temptation in *A Time to Love: Stories from the Old Testament* (2003). The stern, uncompromising religion of the first 39 books of the bible tinges the stories of Lot's wife, Abraham and his son Isaac, and Reuben and his brother Joseph with human dilemmas. For obedience, Abraham is spared the ritual killing of Isaac; for her disobedience, Lot's wife turns to a pillar of salt, a punishment that Myers hesitates to condemn, but implies is too harsh a penalty for loving life. In a more compelling psychological study, Myers portrays Reuben as a devoted brother who is too afraid of the rest of the vindictive family to halt the sale of Joseph into slavery in Egypt. The final vignette, a fanciful picture of Gamiel, a victim of the last plague of Egypt, brandishes images of a huge round sun, the muttering of prayers, and a "gathering gloom," the author's atmospheric vision of a death angel primed to carry off Egypt's unprotected firstborns (Myers, 2003, 119). As Gamiel's friend Aser awaits with faith and belief for God's release of the Hebrews from bondage to Pharaoh, a wail and rattling shutters sweep through the darkness. Aser's separation from Gamiel is permanent as the Egyptian boy sinks into a moribund state.

Myers peruses black religion from a cultural stance in his verse anthology *Here in Harlem: Poems in Many Voices* (2004). Enlivened with mention of the Reverend Adam Clayton Powell and black-and-white photos of religious leader Al Sharpton and a pulpit address by Winnie Mandela, the collection includes fanatics like Ann Carter and doubters like Richmond Leake. The latter, a 53-year-old newsstand dealer, accuses God of ignoring needy blacks while "listening to folks in India" (Myers, 2004, 42). Contrasting Carter and Richmond is a boy evangelist, 14-year-old Jimmy Wall. He belts out his sermon "with the clarity of I am," a reference to the self-identification of Jehovah in Exodus, where Moses encounters the almighty in a burning bush (*ibid.*, 29). In another first-person poem, deacon Macon R. Allen admires the shouting of praises in a lively church worship punctuated with the jingle of tambourines and the mopping of sweaty brows. He peoples his ideal service with a "jump-up preacher" and ebullient glossolalia, the spontaneous ecstatic utterance common to Pentecostalism (*ibid.*, 5). For focus, Allen stresses the rejuvenation of Lazarus from the dead and the concept of end-time, the theme of the spiritual "Sinner, Please Don't Let This Harvest Pass." Tied to the agrarian roots of black slaves, the song grips the imagination with a pictorial image of the human need for oneness with God.

See also **humor, music**

• *Further Reading*

Decandido, Graceanne A. "Review: *A Time to Love: Stories from the Old Testament*," *Booklist* 99, no. 18 (15 May 2003): 1656.

Myers, Walter Dean. *Fallen Angels.* New York: Scholastic, 1988.

_____. *The Glory Field.* New York: Scholastic, 1994.

_____. *The Great Migration: An American Story.* New York: HarperCollins, 1993.

_____. *Harlem: A Poem.* New York: Scholastic, 1997.

_____. *Here in Harlem: Poems in Many Voices.* New York: Holiday House, 2004.

_____. *It Ain't All for Nothin'.* New York: Viking, 1978.

_____. *My Name Is America: The Journal of Joshua Loper, a Black Cowboy, The Chisholm Trail, 1871.* New York: Scholastic, 1999.

_____. "1994 Margaret A. Edwards Award Acceptance Speech," *Journal of Youth Services in Libraries*, 8, no. 2 (winter 1995): 129–133.

_____. *145th Street: Short Stories.* New York: Delacorte, 2000.

_____. *The Outside Shot.* New York: Delacorte, 1984.

_____. "Sunrise over Manaus" in *From One Experience to Another.* New York: Forge, 1997.

_____. *A Time to Love: Stories from the Old Testament.* New York: Scholastic, 2003.

_____. *Won't Know Till I Get There.* New York: Viking, 1982.

rootlessness

Myers's love for community and cultural belonging dominates his work, providing contrast for his images of pathetic wanderers and seekers, such as the drug addict in "The Fare to Crown Point" (1971), the grieving blues musician in "The Treasure of Lemon Brown" (1983), an exemplum on nostalgia and pride published in *Boys' Life*, and Leonard "Len" Gray, Cameron Porter, and Carla Evans, alienated high school students in *Shooter* (2004). In "The Vision of Felipe" (1978), which the author issued in *Black Scholar*, the narrative pictures the absence of family and stability in the life of the ten-year-old title figure, a homeless orphan. Lacking direction and advice after his grandmother's death, he opts for a city life and travels from Iquitos, Peru, by barge 600 miles to the southwest to Lima. The text illustrates the worth of humble intangibles in the humanity that the boy gained from his grandmother. His reverence for life inspires a sympathy for others. Although a soldier robs him of pocket change, Felipe views the crime as the act of an unhappy man. After Felipe acquires cash from working and begging from tourists, he maintains an altruistic outlook that impels him to donate coins to a destitute mother and her sickly infant.

In the same year, Myers wrote a young adult social novel, *It Ain't All for Nothin'* (1978). The story pictures 12-year-old Tippy, a mirror image of Felipe, as the child of Lonnie, a career criminal. After days of wandering the streets to escape Lonnie's drinking, foul moods, and trysts with women, Tippy must flee his father, whose aberrant behavior turns to punches and kicks to the boy's stomach. At an impasse in his home life, the boy takes the subway to 43rd Street in downtown Manhattan and attempts to comfort himself with solitude in an abandoned building. Tippy concludes that the romance of running away from home is largely imaginary.

Myers describes Tippy's rootlessness as mimicry of the lifestyle of Motown, a street urchin who lives alone in Brooklyn. Living on the run generates necessities, which Tippy satisfies by buying a candy bar for food and a flashlight for protection from rats and unidentifiable sounds. A series of solutions to homelessness and parental neglect rattle around in his head, from fleeing "to California or maybe Ohio or someplace like that" to seeking shelter with a local woman (Myers, 1978, 178). Without protection, Tippy admits, "I was even scareder than I thought I was going to be" (*ibid.*, 179). Myers allows a glimmer of humor in the situation as Tippy slips down the stairs and leaps from the front door. His sudden appearance unsettles derelicts on the street, who hurl a bottle as Tippy flees down the street.

The rootless life has an unanticipated value in Myers's picture book *The Blues of Flats Brown* (2000). After the title character eludes his owner, A. J. Grubbs, and sets out from the junkyard to make a new life on the run, the creation of blues lyrics from experience turns Flats into a nightclub and recording star. At a low point in his fortunes, Flats escapes down an alley, through a tent revival, and onto the Midnight Special headed to New York City. To earn his living, he sings from the heart the struggles of life on the street, which become the elements of big-city blues. Revered in legend, he reunites with his pal Caleb and continues to perform soul music at the Atlantic shores in Savannah, Georgia. Through the final setting, the author implies that Flats draws material and listeners from places where wanderlust flourishes.

See also **belonging, betrayal, community, diaspora, displacement**

• *Further Reading*

Myers, Walter Dean. *The Blues of Flats Brown*. New York: Holiday House, 2000.
__________. *It Ain't All for Nothin.'* New York: Viking, 1978.
__________. "The Vision of Felipe," *Black Scholar* (November-December 1978): 2–9.
Smith, Karen Patricia, ed. *African-American Voices in Young Adult Literature: Tradition, Transition, Transformation*. Lanham, Md.: Scarecrow, 1994.

Scorpions

Myers tackles vital social issues of public safety in *Scorpions* (1988), one of his prize-winning novels. The story contrasts the situations of two brothers, Jamal and Randy Hicks. While Randy serves a 15 to 20 year sentence at Greenhaven prison in Stormville, New York, for robbing a delicatessen and murdering the owner, 12-year-old Jamal tries to be man of the house for the sake of his mother and for his eight-year-old sister Sassy. As in Paul Laurence Dunbar's novel *The Sport of the Gods* (1902), the Harlem setting precipitates frustrations that overwhelm the central character. Because of the heartache to Jamal's mother, who fails to borrow $1,000 to finance an appeal of Randy's case, the younger boy hopes that Randy never returns home to cause even worse troubles. The immediate conflict arises from the menace of the Scorpions, Randy's old gang, who are the underage leg men for drug dealers. Jamal explores a boarded-up crack house and earns a bloodied mouth for leaning on a silver Mercedes, a symbol of the wealth acquired by traffickers. In contrast to the Hicks family's poverty, the proceeds of drug sales seem like easy money earned with little effort. The depiction of a pre-teen trying to navigate the underground milieu explains how ghetto children grow experienced with criminality beyond their perception of the consequences.

Myers earned awards for *Scorpions* because of the simplicity and earnest tone of his text. Lending immediacy are the implications of a youth's response to deadly temptations. In a neighborhood where childhood ends abruptly and sometimes fatally, Jamal's mother remains alert to peril. Because she works late for Mr. Stanton, Jamal often has no adult supervision to shield him from folly and potential self-destruction. When she arrives home, her keen senses catch the gestures and nuances of Jamal's cool responses. With rhetorical effect, she warns him, "As God is my secret judge I don't *need* to be played with" (Myers, 1988, 51). A cozy afternoon at the Cruz house poses a second parent, Abuela, offering cookies and milk to Tito and Jamal, who are doing homework on Tito's bed. When she leaves the room, the classmates discuss adult problems— how to earn money to finance an appeal of Randy's case and whether to accept a gun from the Scorpions. The shift in topics illustrates the duality of children who know what to say in front of adults and what to keep to themselves.

The novel stresses one of Myers's pervasive motifs, the fantasy life of deprived children who escape financial need and insecurity in daydreams. Jamal reads comic books with Tito, watches *ThunderCats* on television, and takes an hour-long walk to the marina at 79th Street to imagine owning a yacht, a symbol of affluence and freedom. After a one-sided fight against Dwayne Parsons in the school storeroom, Jamal is so overcome with the power of owning a pistol that he flees to the marina to fantasize about running away until he can grow to manhood and return metamorphosed in suit and tie. He envisions being important enough to invite movie stars on his yacht. He pictures himself in a dual role as wealthy enough to give a small boat to a poor child like himself. Tito's fit of coughing from asthma pushes Jamal farther into never-never-land, a warm imaginary place in Puerto Rico where he and Tito can race their impressive craft. Subsequent flights of fancy involve buying a car, a dream that lies beyond the reach of most Harlemites, including Jamal's unemployed absent father Levon.

The falling action interweaves emotions and encounters that move the novel toward tragedy. While facing Angel and Indian, his tormentors, near the swings in Marcus Garvey Park, Jamal looks upward and realizes that he seldom studies the stars. Myers implies that there are so many perils and distractions at ground level from peer pressure that Jamal has no idle moments for enjoying the pleasures of childhood. After Tito shoots Angel and Indian, Mack's lie about being the shooter eases the tension on Jamal. The settlement of an ongoing challenge with two shots from the pistol replicates the rapid-fire violence on television, where programs rarely depict the messy aftermath.

Myers is clever at surprising both his characters and his readers. The price of conspiracy and armed violence comes from an unforeseen development, Tito's inability to bear guilt for killing Angel. For catharsis, Tito spills his confession to the police. Myers concludes the story with the deportation of two loving neighbors, Tito and his grandmother, who set out on the journey home to Puerto Rico. Left behind, Jamal alone bears the life-altering legacy he inherited from Randy, a reputation for toughness that precedes Jamal into the teen years. In acknowledgement of the boy's residence in Harlem, a critic for *American Visions* concludes that "the real protagonist in this novel is 'the street,'" the venomous scorpion that poisons childhood innocence ("Books," 1993/1994, 35).

• *Further Reading*

"Books," *American Visions* 8, no. 6 (December 1993/January 1994): 35–36.
Cox, Ruth. "Young Men Making Choices," *Teacher Librarian* 27, no. 2 (December 1999): 47–49.
Myers, Walter Dean. *Scorpions*. New York: Harper & Row, 1988.
West, Mark I. "Harlem Connections: Teaching Walter Dean Myers's *Scorpions* in Conjunction with Paul Laurence Dunbar's *The Sport of the Gods*," *ALAN Review*, 26, no. 2 (winter 1999): 1.

segregation

A devout libertarian, Myers began writing about segregation in his early magazine articles, which stressed the injustice of social barriers based on race. In "Gordon Parks: John Henry with a Camera" (1976), an encomium for *Black Scholar*, Myers quotes his subject on the futility of creating art for a single race of people: "If I try to limit what I do, segregate myself in terms of race, it seems that I'm achieving what I don't want anyone else to achieve" (Myers, 1976, 28). Parks concluded that self-segregation would decrease his opportunities to touch all people's hearts. Similarly, Myers focuses on black lives, but flourishes at universal themes.

The motif of the separation of whites from nonwhites permeates Myers's urban fiction, often in brief references like the posting of a Virginia law of 1849 against unlawful assembly of whites with blacks in *Handbook for Boys: A Novel* (2002). Of particular impact are the comments of a white train passenger in *The Beast* (2003) who summarized Malcolm X as the voice of black rage at segregation. The author makes a simple statement of the rules of racial separation in *The Greatest: Muhammad Ali* (2001). Ali had grown up in the segregated South and was accustomed to policies banning blacks from parks and restaurants. Myers stresses that Ali "had felt the humiliation of seeing water fountains from which he could not drink because of the color of his skin" (Myers, 2001, 33). In *The Outside Shot* (1984), the sequel to *Hoops: A Novel* (1981), Myers contrasts Ali's simplicity with the experience of Lonnie Jackson, a freshman on a sports scholarship. He endures the isolation of extreme minority at Montclare State College in Indiana. After a nonleague basketball game against Grambling, a traditionally black college in west-century Louisiana, Bill "Go-Go" Larson comments that integration keeps the school from securing good players, black or white. In his opinion, "That's what integration does for you" (Myers, 1984, 95).

Myers enlightens other characters by wresting them from the urban North to the racist South. In *Somewhere in the Darkness* (1992), 14-year-old Jimmy Little visits the South for the first time. He is aware of Dr. Martin Luther King, Jr.'s push for black voting rights, but Jimmy knows little about Jim Crow and the segregated South. His father, Cephus "Crab" Little, a native of Arkansas, describes the soda shop in the old days when blacks could buy a soda at the counter, but they had to drink it outside. To Jimmy's questions about segregation, Crab summarizes, "It's when they divided the world into white people and niggers" (Myers, *Somewhere*, 121). He refers to the unsubtle events that reveal the white belief that blacks are inferior. In the early 1990s, suspicions about black strangers require police questions and the following of cars. In Crab's opinion, "Down here they'd rather see a snake than a stranger" (*ibid.*, 124). The image suits an agrarian milieu where both snakes and blacks are anathema to whites.

Myers collaborated with folk artist Jacob Lawrence on the picture book *The Great Migration: An American Story* (1993), a visual history of black departure from the rural South roots dating back to enslavement. Concluding the 60-panel story of the displacement of black Southerners from agricultural environs to the urban life of industrialized Northern cities is Myers's ode "Migration." He emphasizes the racism of Alabama, the Carolinas, and Georgia, where migrants of the World War I period wait for trains in stations divided into white and colored sections. With body language, "hard-eyed men with guns in their belts/Stare daggers into the waiting room" (Myers, 1993, n.p.). Despite the misery of Southern segregation, departing blacks reflect tearfully on the cemeteries they leave behind at black churches, evidence of community roots that can't be ferried north in suitcases.

Myers stresses the unfairness of the racial divide in his children's books. In the biography *Young Martin's Promise* (1992), the author pictures young Martin Luther

King, Jr., growing up in an integrated Atlanta neighborhood. When King begins school in 1935, the bus that takes him to first grade carries only black children to an all-black school. The scene dramatizes a flaw in the educational system that breaks up black and white companions and neighbors who have played together throughout their early childhood. The narrative charges the system with abetting the social stigma against black children as playmates and friends.

Supporting segregation during tense times in fictional Johnson City, South Carolina, are Miss Harriet Robbins and Jed Sasser, white employees of Clark's Five-and-Dime in *The Glory Field* (1994). Jed rejects the philosophies of Dr. Martin Luther King, Jr., for promoting racial mixing. Harriet, who is Jed's manager, corroborates his argument with a vague truism —"that white people are a certain way, and coloreds are a certain way" (Myers, 1994, 246). After ameliorating her remarks with Tommy Lewis, a black 16-year-old, she admits that she would work for him but not socialize with him. Tommy recalls that she treats black employees fairly, yet she enforces the company rule that blacks may order food from the counter, but must eat elsewhere. In a subsequent appraisal of local racism, Tommy notes that local rules bar black women from drinking from whites-only water fountains, yet allows those same women to bathe and breastfeed white children. The social scenario is a familiar motif of literature set in the South, where black nannies like Mammy in Margaret Mitchell's *Gone with the Wind* (1936) and Berenice Sadie Brown of Carson McCullers's *The Member of the Wedding* (1946) are revered like members of the family.

Myers refuses to simplify integration as a cure-all for multicultural societies. His intuitive verse neighborhood in *Here in Harlem: Poems in Many Voices* (2004) describes the lasting effects of racial separation. In "Etta Peabody, 60," the speaker recalls watching Errol Flynn and Hopalong Cassidy movies at the Alhambra Theater between 125th and 126th streets in Harlem. She describes the black balcony as "Nigger Heaven," a witty term for racial denigration that turns insult into reward (Myers, 2004, 33). More detrimental to human relationships is laborer Hosea Liburd's ride on the A train among whites whose "fear-wide eyes" survey young, muscular blacks (*ibid.*, 14). Unknown to white passengers is Hosea's rapidly diminishing manhood as the subway carries him farther from familiar territory.

See also **historical milieu, racism, slavery**

• *Further Reading*

Myers, Walter Dean. *The Glory Field*. New York: Scholastic, 1994.
_____. "Gordon Parks: John Henry with a Camera," *Black Scholar* 7, no. 5 (1976): 27–30.
_____. *The Great Migration: An American Story*. New York: HarperCollins, 1993.
_____. *The Greatest: Muhammad Ali*. New York: Scholastic, 2001.
_____. *Handbook for Boys: A Novel*. New York: Amistad, 2002.
_____. *Here in Harlem: Poems in Many Voices*. New York: Holiday House, 2004.
_____. *The Outside Shot*. New York: Delacorte, 1984.
_____. *Somewhere in the Darkness*. New York: Scholastic, 1992.
_____. *Young Martin's Promise*. Austin, Tex.: Raintree, 1992.
Rust, Suzanne. "Learning As We Climb: Stories about the Civil Rights Movement for Young Readers," *Black Issues Book Review* 6, no. 3 (May-June 2004): 58–60.

self-destruction

The theme of self-destructive urges enlarges the drama of some of Myers's best scenarios, including the retreat from community in Vietnam War vet Sweeby Jones in *Darnell Rock Reporting* (1994), the author's own life history, *Bad Boy: A Memoir* (2001), and *The Beast* (2003), the story of a girl who retreats from hard times into heroin. In the dilemma story "How Long Is Forever?," written for the June 1969 issue of *Negro Digest*, the author sets up a lose-lose situation between Jenkins, a jeering white prison guard, and Moses, a rehabilitated prisoner anticipating parole. Longing for freedom and a reunion with his aged mother, Moses withstands daily sexual threat and sadism: one belittles his manhood; the other threatens his life. Myers indicates that self-defense erupts into murderous vengeance, a visceral retaliation that Moses is powerless to halt.

In the author's social novel *It Ain't All for Nothin'* (1978), he contrasts the tender feelings and responsive conscience of 12-year-old Tippy to Lonnie, his birth father. Once the boy enters the father's custody, their father-son relationship falls victim to Lonnie's rationalization of crime. At first, he taunts Tippy with a reminder that he must develop macho behaviors if he wants to be a man. Later in the novel, as Lonnie's crimes worsen in terms of risk and personal injury, he justifies immoral choices as the only way to make a start on a new life. As father and son say goodbye after the trial that sends Lonnie back to prison, the father claims noble intentions. His reaction is infantile: "Damn! I don't even know what the hell happened" (Myers, 1978, 224). The disclaimer offers a lame excuse for a bungled robbery in which shooting kills one robber and threatens the life of Tippy, whom Lonnie forces to act as lookout. With a child's grasp of reality, Tippy recognizes that, whatever his hopes for a father-son relationship, "It really ain't going to be that way" (*ibid.*, 226).

Myers amplifies his concern for extreme anger in *The Legend of Tarik* (1981), a quest novel based on medieval crusader lore. The story incorporates ancient wisdom and parables that enhance the motifs of knighthood and a vengeance quest. As in Myers's Harlem novels, the hero, the black African knight Tarik ibn Ziyad, requires the mentoring of two elders, Nongo the teacher and the priest Docao. Once Tarik learns to let his brain rule his emotions, he ably subdues El Muerte (death), an allegorical stalker. Accompanying Tarik is Stria, an attractive female adventurer obsessed with hatred of the villain for slaughtering the innocent, but lacking the necessary training in self-control. In the falling action, Tarik is pleased with the outcome of his quest and with the accompanying self-knowledge. Stria, his literary foil, witnesses El Muerte's demise, but she feels only emptiness after the satisfactory conclusion to the quest. Myers implies that her emotional collapse results from the destructiveness of unremitting hatred.

Self-destructive habits dominate the conflicts of Myers's sports novels. In *Hoops: A Novel* (1981), Calvin F. "Spider" Jones turns in an erratic performance as the coach of a community team by getting drunk, conspiring with racketeers, and dwelling on the failures of his past. After missing practices and games, Cal redeems himself in the team's estimation by playing the final game of the Tournament of Champions to win. Cal's death from a post-game locker room stabbing illustrates the difference between foolish risks and heroism. By refusing to throw the game at the bidding of villain Tyrone Giddins, Cal reclaims his self-respect while giving community boys an opportunity to impress college scouts. In the sequel, *The Outside Shot* (1984), alcohol returns to prominence in the basketball playing of Bobby Wortham, a valuable center who ruins his game with booze. Neil states a sports principle: "You can't be bringing down the team by boozing it up" (Myers, 1984, 66). In despair at being suspended during an investigation of a point shaving scandal, Lonnie emulates Cal by retreating to La Hispania to sink into pitchers of beer. Myers elevates the importance of love to Lonnie by depicting his girlfriend, Sherry Jewett, rescuing him from self-pity and sobering him up to face authorities at the administration office. From his brush with criminality, Lonnie learns a lesson about right choices.

In 2004, Myers studied the self-destructive behavior of sociopathic teens in *Shooter*, a psychological novel paralleling the terrorism at Columbine High School in Littleton, Colorado, on April 20, 1999. The county psychologist, Dr. Richard Ewings, elicits from 17-year-old Cameron Porter the fact that he and 16-year-old Leonard "Len" Gray wanted to be arrested for vandalizing a church before Christmas. Contributing to the alienation of Cameron and Len is the bullying of the pair by jocks for Len's alleged insult to a girl. For Cameron, the best view of school is "outside looking at the place, not inside dealing with it" (Myers, 2004, 50). The gravitation of Cameron to Len's twisted thinking results in a murder-suicide during Len's shooting spree at school. Although Cameron survives Len's spray of bullets and the intervention of a SWAT team, the impact on Cameron's psyche suggests that he has damaged himself beyond repair. To a lesser degree, Carla Evans, Len's girlfriend, cuts herself off from reclamation by drifting away from adult control by her mother, father, and foster parents. Like Cameron, she allows deep-seated antipathy to excuse Len's perverse behaviors. By bringing blood-red paint to school to aid in a vandalism plot, she edges close to Len's vengeful conspiracy until Cameron secures her in a closet from the range of fire. Myers leaves unsettled the direction that Carla and Cameron will take in the aftermath of teen terrorism.

See also **drugs and alcohol, gangs, reclamation, sex, *Slam!***

• *Further Reading*

Myers, Walter Dean. *It Ain't All for Nothin.'* New York: Viking, 1978.
_____. *The Outside Shot.* New York: Delacorte, 1984.
_____. *Shooter.* New York: Amistad, 2004.
Smith, Karen Patricia, ed. *African-American Voices in Young Adult Literature: Tradition, Transition, Transformation.* Lanham, Md.: Scarecrow, 1994.

sex

Critics have questioned the discussion of sex and the sparse evidence of coitus in Myers's teen novels, for example, Sam's idle boasting that he "did it to a girl" in the seriocomic novel *Fast Sam, Cool Clyde, and Stuff* (1975) and the intimate badinage between Gerald McQuillen and Jennifer Wells in *The Nicholas Factor* (1983) (Myers, 1975, 123). The former novel characterizes one of the hard truths of coming of age — that girls are more emotionally and intellectually mature than their male peers. To Clyde Jones's timid efforts to introduce carnality into a conversation, Gloria replies, "I thought the conversation was going to be about sex, not 'you know'" (*ibid.*, 128). Gloria's awareness of the consequences of promiscuous intercourse emerges in her statement that "Half the people who have sex don't get pregnant. The boys" (*ibid.*, 129). Her hesitance to condemn premarital sex concludes with a valuable concept — that physical intimacy is "too important to be just doing without thinking about" (*ibid.*, 130). She backs up her arguments for serious consideration of actions by refuting Clyde's contention that sexual desire comes naturally to males.

With similar stress on the idle chatter of maturing males, the short story "The Vision of Felipe" (1978) depicts the naive boy-talk of two street urchins, twelve-year-old Daniel and ten-year-old Felipe. They discuss "push-push" as an escape from more urgent worries, immediate sources of food and shelter for the homeless in Lima, Peru (Myers, 1978, 5). Myers dramatizes the personalized concern of older teens about when and how to lose their virginity. Worrying infantryman Richard "Richie" Perry in *Fallen Angels* (1988) is his lack of sexual experience. The thought of dying without experiencing intercourse rankles on his mind during deadly patrols during the Vietnam War. While lying in ambush on a jungle trail at midnight, he presumes, "Maybe it wasn't important" (Myers, 1988, 124). The narrative indicates that the not knowing disturbs more than his lack of intimacy with females. Like Daniel and Felipe, Richie receives little comfort from mental pictures of carnal acts.

Although the author's youths are wise to physical maturity and desire, his narratives are surprisingly devoid of sex acts. In *It Ain't All for Nothin'* (1978), immorality surrounds 12-year-old Tippy after social workers pass him from his grandmother Carrie Brown's care into the custody of Lonnie, his birth father. Life with an ex-con exposes the boy to irresponsible drinking, marijuana smoking, and casual sex. Women — Denise, Peggy, an anonymous nurse, Lois, Jackie — pass through Lonnie's squalid apartment without meaning or consequence. Denise, Bubba's retarded moll, divulges to Tippy her pregnancy and hope for a legitimate relationship with the child's father. With Tippy as stand-in, she performs a make-believe wedding ceremony, a ritual that has no meaning to either participant. Far too involved for a pre-teen, the boy develops no urge to participate in dead-end carnal acts that diminish the meaning of love.

For *Hoops: A Novel* (1981), according to critic Stephanie Zvirin, a reviewer for *Booklist*, "sex and violence emerge naturally as part of the setting" (Zvirin, 1981, 98). In the character exposition, 17-year-old sports ace Lonnie Jackson obviously loves Mary-Ann and experiences yearning for intimacy, but his mental involvement with basketball limits the time he concentrates on sex. At a low point in the action, he rests at his room at the Grant Hotel and tries to converse with his girl. Her uninhibited mood draws Lonnie into kissing and stroking her back and thigh, but his disinclination for intercourse interrupts the moment with an argument. Her insistence on sex attests to the female libido, a subject that gained attention after the women's movement of the 1960s. Lacking from the relationship is commitment from Lonnie, whose hesitance to admit love for a woman suggests that he needs more time to grow into manhood.

The scene changes in *The Outside Shot* (1984), the sequel to *Hoops*. At Montclare State College in Indiana, Lonnie tries to advance his romance with Sherry Jewett, a track athlete from Milwaukee. His use of what passes for smooth moves in Harlem fall flat at the local theater. Turned down and left standing after the movie, he vacillates between hurt feelings and anger. Subsequent ups and downs in their relationship bemuse Lonnie, who lacks the experience with middle-class people to behave well in Sherry's estimation. By abstaining from precipitate sexual involvement, he wins her love and admiration. Myers implies that Lonnie is more likely to enter a satisfying relationship if he lets his friendship take precedence over sex.

Myers captures the importance of morals and ideals to urban teens. The role models and female advice in *Crystal* (1987) directs a star-struck model out of a maze of influences. Above the pro-career cheerleading of her mother and the professional direction of her agent, 16-year-old Crystal Brown values more the example of Rowena, an 18-year-old colleague who commits suicide rather than work in the amoral conditions of posing for sexy fashion magazine spreads. Crystal realizes that Rowena's death is the price of devaluing personal principles. In *The Beast* (2003), 17-year-old Anthony "Spoon" Witherspoon cautiously reunites with his Dominican girlfriend Gabriela "Gabi" Godoy. Tentatively, he restores some of the warmth that the two shared before his departure to Wallingford Academy in Connecticut. In the subtext, old friends ponder the moral downfall of Clara, a contemporary whose pregnancy generates gossip. Because peers once admired her high standards, they express shock that she gave in to casual sex. In the words of Scott, "Things drift with the tide and she drifted with it" (Myers, 2003, 81). The dismissal of Clara as a victim of self-destructive behavior depicts the double standard that judges pregnant women but not the males who caused them to conceive.

Myers reprises the approach-avoidance quandary of pretty females in *Here in Harlem: Poems in Many Voices* (2004). The sexual implications of water imagery infuse the narrative of 17-year-old Marcia Williams, one of the speakers of the verse anthology. To heighten her maidenhood, she pictures herself floating, yet capable of outpacing the neap tide. At the sea's frothy edge, she contemplates the dangers of flirtation, yet she decks her hair in seaweed. The uncertainty of courtship stirs her emotions. With some hesitation, she responds to the siren song, a metaphoric depiction of the surging hormones that press her far from shore toward womanhood. Another model of emotional turmoil infuses the poem "Lydia Cruz, 15," whose name implies the crux of the hormone-rich teen years. Retreating to her mother for moral courage, Lydia reaches upward toward education at the same time that her eyes stray back to a broad-shouldered, two-legged peril, a hustler who knows how to turn a good girl into a "hussy child" (Myers, 2004, 82). The glance captures the author's concern for temptations that exceed the wisdom of youth.

See also **immaturity**

• *Further Reading*

Myers, Walter Dean. *The Beast.* New York: Scholastic, 2003.
_____. *Fallen Angels.* New York: Scholastic, 1988.

_____. *Fast Sam, Cool Clyde, and Stuff*. New York: Viking, 1975.
_____. *Here in Harlem: Poems in Many Voices*. New York: Holiday House, 2004.
_____. *Hoops*. New York: Delacorte, 1981.
_____. *It Ain't All for Nothin'*. New York: Viking, 1978.
_____. "The Vision of Felipe," *Black Scholar* (November-December 1978): 2–9.
Zvirin, Stephanie. "Review: *Hoops: A Novel*," *Booklist* 78, no. 2 (15 September 1981): 98.

Shooter

An innovative and insightful spin-off of the student terrorism incident at Columbine High School south of Denver, Colorado, on April 20, 1999, *Shooter* (2004) probes the cause of conspiracy, stalking, murder, and suicide. Myers turns the arbitrary eye of the justice system primarily on Cameron Porter, an inoffensive 17-year-old at Madison High School in Harrison County. In metafictional collage style, the plot unfolds piecemeal in a threat analysis report from adult authorities and journalists who wrestle with the sources of student rage. Cameron's antipathy toward the hostile school environment reveals paranoia: "And if you get a label — that you're easy — then they're going to find you" (Myers, 2004, 2). Out of loyalty to his twisted friend, Leonard "Len" Gray, Cameron protects him from bullying by jocks and goes along with a plan to commit suicide. The implications of a follower enabling a crazed leader bode ill for both boys and for their emotionally disturbed friend, Carla Evans.

Myers manipulates point of view to illustrate the many sides of the shooting. The inquiry methods of psychologists, FBI agent, and sheriff illustrate the bias of adults in getting to the truth. In a review for *Booklist*, critic Lolly Gepson notes the effectiveness of nonjudgmental questioning at eliciting details from Cameron and Carla, both alienated students and members of the *Ordo Sagittae* (Order of the Arrow), a confederacy of misfits. Missing from the inquiry are comments from parents, whose lax attitude toward discipline allowed hostilities to grow unchallenged. The most telling remark is the brief disclaimer of Superintendent Jonathan Margolies, who ignores the potential for tragedy by exonerating the school and staff for past events.

Nancy Chaplin, in a critique for *Kliatt*, remarked that "the similarities to Columbine are huge" (Chaplin, 2004, 51). The buildup of hate and anger in *Shooter* seems to flourish best in the dark outside the purview of parents, teachers, and authorities. Another reviewer, Francisca Goldsmith, writing for *School Library Journal*, characterizes the motivation as "ranging from 'typical' bullying to parental psychological abuse to wasting the intelligence of some students because they lacked the social skills to take part of their own accord in the standard menu of institutional reputation-building activities" (Goldsmith, 2004, 155). Snowballing toward a terrifying conclusion is Len's diary, a manic, self-aggrandizing record of his mental decline through "choppy sentences and nonsensible connections," both revealing the eddy of suppressed rage as it surges toward retribution (Gepson, 2004, 608). Lauren Adams, a reviewer for *Horn Book*, summarizes Myers's revelation that "the blame for such horrific violence transcends the individual" (Adams, 2004, 335).

See also **Leonard Gray, Cameron Porter**

• *Further Reading*

Adams, Lauren. "Review: *Shooter*," *Horn Book* 80, no. 3 (May-June 2004): 335.
Chaplin, Nancy. "Review: *Shooter*," *Kliatt* 38, no. 6 (November 2004): 50-51.
Gepson, Lolly. "Review: *Shooter*," *Booklist* 101, no. 6 (15 November 2004): 608.
Goldsmith, Francisca. "Review: *Shooter*," *School Library Journal* 50, no. 5 (May 2004): 154–155.
Myers, Walter Dean. *Shooter*. New York: Amistad, 2004.

Slam!

One of Walter Dean Myers's likeable teenagers, protagonist Greg "Slam" Harris, the 17-year-old basketball player in *Slam!* (1996), fights maturity battles in his head and daily activities. His life lacks balance and control. Cool and easy on the court as a guard, he is confused and disgruntled when the school principal, Mr. Tate, calls Mrs. Harris in for a conference on Slam's poor classroom performance at the mostly white Latimer Arts Magnet School in the Bronx. In contrast to a serious, up-front mother, Slam faces an unpredictable father, Jimmy Harris, a thin, nervous man who drinks to overcome low self-esteem from joblessness. In Slam's opinion, Mr. Harris survives by "scoping and hoping," a hit-or-miss lifestyle that fuels the cycle of lost jobs, family blow-ups, and frequent separations from his wife (Myers, 1996, 5).

The story follows Slam's maturation through mishaps and wins. He is cool enough to sew up his little brother Derek's split pants, but lacking in tact while talking with Grandma Ellie, who is dying from a spreading cancer. Too bull-headed to follow Coach Nipper's advice about patterned play, Slam walks off the court in frustration with less able teammates. He is, in the opinion of critic Shirley Zimmer, "a hot dog, a kid who won't think of the team first and his personal stats second" (Zimmer, 1996, 42). "Goldy" Goldstein, the assistant coach, advises that Slam abandon childish self-pity, but Slam continues to rationalize his faults and to cultivate dreams of glory in the NBA. In U.S. history class, Slam lets his mind drift away from the Constitution to thoughts of Karen. To direct him toward more productive aims, Myers introduces volunteerism from Richie Randall, a member of the Guardians. The proposal of outside help annoys Slam because he lacks the introspection to perceive flaws in his plans.

Myers enlarges on Slam's self-absorption in the school project with Marjorie Flatley. To Slam, the best documentary they could create is "the story of Slam the Great" (*ibid.*, 77). As he reflects on the future, he sees himself as a loner playing professional ball: "No wife. No kids" (*ibid.*, 100). After performing for younger children at the hoop in the park, Slam works his way around to the truth. He admits to Mtisha Clark, "I ain't doing nothing right in my life these days" (*ibid.*, 120). Although she tries to help him understand algebra, he appears to fear math.

The theme of lifetime satisfaction digs at the protagonist, forcing him to look beyond the temporal victories of the teen years. Myers speaks through Goldy, who advises that Slam put himself wholeheartedly into what he loves doing. The advice applies to Jimmy, the unemployed father who is so distraught at breaking his arm that he lies on the sidewalk weeping. Goldy's wisdom is an epiphany to Slam during a game at Hunter College. After the coach calls him a "prima donna," Slam stalks off to the locker room in turmoil, unsure whether he is angry at the coach or at himself (*ibid.*, 203). Myers again speaks through Goldy a remonstrance of Slam's sulking by accusing him of naivete. Gradually, Slam sees the importance of playing well for the team rather than for self. His shift in perspective reveals the stirrings of maturity.

A significant change in Slam incorporates loyalties and self-respect, but not until he debates an internal war that threatens his stability. As the critic Maeve Visser Knoth explains, "Walter Dean Myers never presents easy solutions in his novels" (Knoth, 63). As old friend Ice moves into scary territory inhabited by dealers and users, Slam edges toward less lethal boys like Ducky for friendship. In a blow-up in English class, Slam realizes that raising his fist against Mr. Parrish is foolish. Goldy labels Slam's behavior self-destructive, but obviously not so risky as Ice's venture into major crime. Goldy's final word on athletics informs Slam of the realities of playing life by the rules. Goldy warns, "You *will* play, and you *will* win or lose" (*ibid.*, 218). To Slam's credit, he apologizes to Mr. Parrish before momentary hostility worsens their relationship. Slam also opens his mind to derelicts, whom he videotapes on a vacant lot on Malcolm X Boulevard. From relatively young street bums, Slam draws conclusions about playing life to win. The overview of lives in Harlem center Slam in a ghetto matrix that can either make or break him. Myers implies that Slam possesses the foresight to choose a positive path.

• *Further Reading*

Knoth, Maeve Visser. "Review: *Slam!*," *Horn Book* 73, no. 1 (January-February 1997): 63–64.

Myers, Walter Dean. *Slam!* New York: Scholastic, 1996.

Zimmer, Shirley. "Review: *Slam!*," *Book Report* 15, no. 3 (November/ December 1996): 42.

slavery

Myers scatters throughout his books African American oral traditions of bondage that reduced Bambara, Fula, Hausa, Mandingo, and Yoruba captives to automata. In the seriocomic novel *Won't Know Till I Get There* (1982), Mabel Jackson summarizes unending toil through her grandfather's words: "You did your can to can't till you couldn't do no more" (Myers, 1982, 156). *Now Is Your Time! The African-American Struggle for Freedom* (1991), Myers's ebullient history book, presents the story of Ibrahima, a prince and Koranic scholar. The reduction of such workers to the status of investments created a symbiotic relationship, with workers supplying the labor and the offspring that owners could sell or mortgage. In Myers's words, "In that evolved value there existed a relationship and an interdependency that did not exist between any other people in the country" (Myers, 1991, 34). To get the most value from these investments, owners seasoned their captives through threats, beatings, and patrolling to prevent uprisings and escapes. In Ibrahima's case, bondage did not stop him from regaining his freedom. At age 67, he returned to

West Africa, but died in Liberia without locating his family. To Myers, even a partial victory is worthy of inclusion in black history.

A brief reference to a handmade quilt, a common artistic mode for slave women, occurs at a dramatic moment in *Somewhere in the Darkness* (1992). While Cephus "Crab" Little seeks counsel from a conjuror, High John, in Marion, Arkansas, the elderly man digresses by spreading a quilt, which dates before the Civil War. Bemused, he wonders how black people living in the antebellum South could "make something so pretty" (Myers, 1992, 133). The image permeates feminist literature like Toni Morrison's *Beloved* (1987) with honor to history's needleworkers who turn scraps into a useful household item. In slaves times, bondswomen found beauty in the patterns that took shape in bright colors.

Myers carefully reminds readers that the end of slavery in 1865 did not conclude the anguish of bondage that had plagued Americans since the arrival of the first slave to Virginia in 1619. Long after the Civil War, families attempted to reunite members sold from plantation to plantation. In *Malcolm X: By Any Means Necessary* (1993), Myers notes that blacks "advertised for the loved ones from whom they had been separated" (Myers, 1993, 84). Inhibiting the search were black illiteracy, insufficient transportation and funds for travel, and the lack of support by white law enforcement officers, who arrested wanderers for vagrancy. Nonetheless, the urge to reunite kept blacks on the move, singly and in families.

In an eerie reprise of post-Civil War oppression, Myers collaborated with folk artist Jacob Lawrence for the picture book *The Great Migration: An American Story* (1993), the pictorial recreation of the black diaspora. The text stresses that the privations black sharecroppers abandon in the agrarian South of 1917 bear a stark resemblance to servitude. Still shackled to white landowners and corrupt law officers, blacks face the terrors of lynching, capricious arrest and jailing, and the exhaustion and slow starvation of families. Their children, denied of adequate nutrition, shrivel spiritually and mentally from poor educational opportunities, a result of the laws that forbade literacy training in slaves.

In *The Glory Field* (1994), a tale of the Lewis clan that parallels the scope of Alex Haley's *Roots* (1965) and *Queen: The Story of an American Family* (1993), Myers applies the horrors of kidnap and the Middle Passage. In the 1700s, the family's founder, Muhammad Bilal, endures capture and transport to America, where he is enslaved at Glory Field, a South Carolina plantation. Balancing terror with courage, the narrative describes the bludgeoning of Kaiman, who refuses to go willingly into the hold. Muhammad is barely able to suppress a scream when his turn comes for loading into the slave vessel. The narrative commends the patriarch's pride as well as evolving African American customs, including Sunday worship, call-and-response spirituals, protective amulets, and meals of cold greens, hoecake, and pan bread. The basics of soul food recur in 1900 at a church dinner and at a breakfast of fried hominy, bacon, and sassafras tea after Abby and Elijah Lewis return safely from a storm aboard the *Pele Queen*. Contributing to family solidarity is the fact that the Lewis clan manages to stay together without any trades or sell-offs of their members.

Bondage takes a stronger role in subsequent works. In 1996, Myers produced *Toussaint L'Ouverture: The Fight for Haiti's Freedom*, a text featuring the island's visual history painted by Jacob Lawrence. Because of the Haitian liberator's importance to Hispaniola, the narrative opens on beatings and coercion that nearly eradicate the Carib and Taino Indians. Replacing them as free labor are African imports, who provide the income that maintains colonial overlords in style. In *My Name Is America: The Journal of Joshua Loper, a Black Cowboy, The Chisholm Trail, 1871* (1999), Isaiah, the trail cook, describes the anger of his owner and reveals a lash-scarred back to the title character, who knows about slavery mainly from his mother's memories. The subject of hard times and the sale of slave children permeates "A Story in Three Parts" in *145th Street: Short Stories* (2000), in which Miss Pat tells Big Time about Doll's life on an Alabama Plantation. When a speculator buys black children from the master to sell in Montgomery, female field hands ignore the overseer's whip as they crowd around the house to plead for their little ones. Miss Pat notes that slaves "have the same feelings as everybody else" (Myers, 2000, 121). Like the infanticide in Toni Morrison's *Beloved*, the action concludes with Doll's murder of her boys to spare them more misery.

The subject of the Middle Passage generates baleful blues lyrics in the author's *Blues Journey* (2003), in which the singer hears "the top deck groaning" and the silent death of a "brother" (Myers, 2003, n.p.). Key to the loss of African heritage was the banning or removal of personal reminders of a distant homeland—long hair, literacy, Islamic names, symbolic jewelry and scarification, family connections, and ritual healing and worship. In *The Dream Bearer* (2003), Myers presents the same era through the mystic dreams of the title figure, "Mr. Moses" Littlejohn, a clairvoyant whose reliving of the past three centuries of black struggles enables him to see his own father captured and forced into the tender that bears him howling and gesturing to the slaving vessel in the West African bay. The name "Moses" suggests the leader of the Hebrew people from bondage; his last name implies a human version of the mythic High John the Conqueror, a protector of unwilling travelers in the diaspora who spread hope for divine intervention on the part of belabored African Americans.

In the naval history accompanying *U.S.S. Constellation: Pride of the American Navy* (2004), Myers honors the last sail-equipped frigate as a warship against the slave trade and a military asset during the Civil War. He describes through the eyes of a 21-year-old officer, Wilburn Hall, the commandeering of the *Cora*, a Havana-based slaver, on September 26, 1860. In a mad dash near the Bight of Benin, "There seemed no way to stop the chase without sinking her, and humanity forbade a shot in her hull" (Myers, *U.S.S.*, 27). The exultation of capturing a prize sinks to disgust at the odor and state of the slave deck, which left Hall "faint and sick at heart" (*ibid.*, 28). His eyewitness account reached print in 1894 in *Century* magazine. In *I've Seen the Promised Land: The Life of Dr. Martin Luther King, Jr.* (2004), the author reprises the vision of the famed preacher and boycott leader at the August 1963 March on Washington. Before the statue of Abraham Lincoln, King predicted a time when "the sons of slaves and the sons of slave owners could sit down together at the table of brotherhood" (Myers, *I've Seen*, n.p.).

See also **diaspora, *The Glory Field*, Martin Luther King, *Now Is Our Time!*, victimization**

• *Further Reading*

Corbett, Sue. "Tales of Slavery Introduce a Month of Black History," *Miami Herald* (30 January 1998): 3F.
Myers, Walter Dean. *Blues Journey*. New York: Holiday House, 2003.
____. *I've Seen the Promised Land: The Life of Dr. Martin Luther King, Jr.* New York: Amistad, 2004.
____. *Malcolm X: By Any Means Necessary*. New York: Scholastic, 1993.
____. *Now Is Your Time! The African-American Struggle for Freedom*. New York: HarperCollins, 1991.
____. *145th Street: Short Stories*. New York: Delacorte, 2000.
____. *Somewhere in the Darkness*. New York: Scholastic, 1992.
____. *U.S.S. Constellation: Pride of the American Navy*. New York: Holiday House, 2004.
____. *Won't Know Till I Get There*. New York: Viking, 1982.
Phelan, Carolyn. "Review: *The Dream Bearer*," *Booklist* 99, no. 21 (July 2003): 1891.

Somewhere in the Darkness

Myers glimpses serious familial dysfunction in *Somewhere in the Darkness* (1992), a quest novel about father and son. Fourteen-year-old Jimmy Little, a dreamy, motherless tenth grader, drifts into a pattern of missing school and wandering the neighborhood. By retreating into fantasies of knights and dragons and the rescue of maidens, he eludes hard evidence that he wastes an intelligent mind. Myers indicates that Jimmy's malaise is more serious than immaturity and simple misbehavior. In childhood, the boy suffered asthma attacks; in his teens, the initiate copes with loss and uncertainty through mental escapes like hanging out on the streets, watching television, and lying about illness. His inner fatigue suggests a serious depression "as if something tired was growing in him" (Myers, 1992, 17). By imagining himself as an actor in an *I Love Lucy* rerun, he eludes a family fractured by his mother's death and his father's imprisonment.

Without warning, the sudden reappearance of Cephus "Crab" Little in Jimmy's life sets the plot in motion. Critic R. D. Lane attributes the unexpected return of the father to "patriarchal notions of masculinity ... [and] Crab's aspiration for retribution," a disclosure of an injustice that Crab expects to exonerate him for a lengthy absence in Jimmy's life (Lane, 1998, 131). After a nine-year sentence to New York's Green Haven prison for robbery and murder of an armored car driver, Crab escapes from the infirmary in "the slam" and removes Jimmy from a stable home and the love of Mama Jean, his foster parent (*ibid.*, 65). Before making the abrupt removal of his son, Crab postures as the man of the house by repairing a clogged drain. The single good deed makes little impact on Jimmy, who looks to his foster mother as the sole adult in his life. Myers characterizes her strength in her gift of $50 and her promise of a welcome to Jimmy any time he wants to return to New York. Like other of the author's stalwart females, Mama Jean displays love through actions rather than words. With simple faith, she assures Jimmy that God will protect the family. The creation of a loving mother figure follows Jimmy throughout his journey west to Chicago and south to Arkansas. When his courage wanes, he reminds himself that Mama Jean is just a phone call away.

Significant to the novel is the emergence of sympathy in Jimmy for a man he has never known. As the boy attempts to make sense of events that occurred long before, he suspects his father of wrongdoing, an ambiguous series of actions that imply the robbery of a gas station near Cleveland, Ohio. More obvious are Crab's use of a stolen credit card and the alias Robert Daniels to rent a car and Crab's lies to Mama Jean and Mavis Stokes about a job in Chicago and to the police in Marion, Arkansas, about traveling to the town of Forrest. Episodes of back pain and doses of aspirin inform Jimmy of Crab's desperation as his life ebbs away from kidney disease. The boy's concern for his frail father's weeping in his sleep extends to sympathy for years in prison "locked in a cell, in the darkness" (*ibid.*, p. 139). The pressures of serious questions force Jimmy out of a life of daydreams to consider his future with a wanted man, a dubious legacy for a boy far from home.

Myers exemplifies the psychological truism that children tend to duplicate their parents' mistakes or to retreat to the extreme opposite behavior, a factor that may make an alcoholic's child either drink heavily or refuse all contact with addictive substances. At the end of Jimmy's trek west and south with Crab, Myers establishes hope for a cessation of father-son alienation. Unlike Charlie "C. C." Little, the railroad cook who had a limited kinship with Crab because of long trips to Louisiana, Jimmy intends to be an in-house father. In contrast to Crab, who was unable to express paternal feelings in letters from prison, Jimmy intends to have a strong relationship with his own son. Jimmy bases his future parenthood on truth and an eye-to-eye honesty that makes a connection, "something that would be there even when they weren't together" (*ibid.*, 167).

See also **Little genealogy**

• *Further Reading*

Fader, Ellen. "Booklist: For Older Readers," *Horn Book* 68, no. 3 (May 1992): 344–345.

Lane, R. D. "'Keepin' It Real': Walter Dean Myers and the Promise of African-American Children's Literature," *African American Review* 32, no. 1 (22 March 1998): 125–138.

Myers, Walter Dean. *Somewhere in the Darkness.* New York: Scholastic, 1992.

soul food

A significant part of Myers's depiction of black and white culture involves the cooking, serving, and eating of typical foods, which contrast the undistinguished Cokes sipped along with packaged doughnuts and burgers that teen characters continually ingest. The seriocomic narrative of *Won't Know Till I Get There* (1982) portrays Steve Perry and his foster brother Earl Goins eating a breakfast of eggs and scrapple, a fried pork mush. In *The Outside Shot* (1984), when Colin Young brings protagonist Lonnie Jackson home for the weekend at Cisne, Illinois, Mrs. Young displays motherly love by serving country fare — roast pork in gravy with buttermilk cornbread. In the short story "Jeremiah's Song," collected in *The Giver and Related Readings* (1987), a gift of rhubarb pie with cheese on top comforts the title character, who recovers from a stroke. Scenes of mothering in *Scorpions* (1988) stress the black woman's role in preparing streak-o'-lean, snap beans, and peppery devil fish, which Mrs. Hicks simmers in chicken stock. In *The Great Migration: An American Story* (1993), families who board trains in 1917 from the agrarian South to railroad and steel mill centers in Chicago, Cleveland, Detroit, New York, Philadelphia, and Pittsburgh carry picnic baskets of the meals that once sustained slaves in the antebellum South. Because of the racism still rampant in Alabama, the Carolinas, and Georgia, families do their best to feed their young, but adults despair of rural life, the source of soul food.

Meals of down-home dishes enhance the joys of folk culture. Pleasing the title figure in *The Righteous Revenge of Artemis Bonner* (1992) on his arrival in Tombstone, Arizona, is his aunt's meal of mustard greens, hog jowls, and buttermilk biscuits. At an Arkansas diner in *Somewhere in the Darkness* (1992), Jimmy Little accepts a waitress's offer of biscuits with white ham gravy. Awaiting Greg "Slam" Harris and his mother in *Slam!* (1996) is his father's meal of black beans and oxtails; Slam later videotapes a West Indian cook making cow feet stew and dirty rice. For herders in *My Name Is America: The Journal of Joshua Loper, a Black Cowboy, The Chisholm Trail, 1871* (1999), Isaiah Cotton, the camp cook, serves Southwestern specialties—beans with fatback and corn pone with hot lard drippings. In *My Name Is America: The Journal of Biddy Owens: The Negro Leagues* (2001), Aunt Jack displays her love for Biddy with hearty breakfasts of eggs, bacon and sausages, and grits topped with red-eye gravy, a Southern specialty made by pouring hot coffee into a pan of pork drippings. Because the two substances remain separate, the coffee forms a brick-red eye in the grease. In later scenes, Aunt Jack makes potato salad and collard greens with ham hocks. As a token of welcome when Biddy returns home for Father's Day, his mother and aunt roast a turkey and serve it with macaroni, spinach, deviled eggs, and candied yams. The meals continue to please Biddy at home and on the road, especially peach cobbler and fried chicken with lemon-pepper sauce. In Myers's reflective verse anthology *Here in Harlem: Poems in Many Voices* (2004), even the fragrance of collards and curried chicken "warm-edge" the thinking of 14-year-old Gerry Jones.

See also **The Glory Field**

• *Further Reading*

Jones, Evan. *American Food.* Woodstock, N.Y.: Overlook Press, 1990.
Myers, Walter Dean. *Here in Harlem: Poems in Many Voices.* New York: Holiday House, 2004.
Snodgrass, Mary Ellen. *Encyclopedia of Kitchen History.* London: Fitzroy Dearborn, 2003.

stereotypes

Myers deals directly with the problem of racial, educational, cultural, and gender stereotypes, such as unfounded police suspicions of the Gypsy postcard seller, Pedro Barcia, in *Adventure in Granada* (1985) and the implied worthlessness of the delinquent boy Darnell and the homeless Vietnam vet Sweeby Jones in *Darnell Rock*

Reporting (1994). In the seriocomic novel *Won't Know Till I Get There* (1982), Steve Perry ponders the limited expectations for elders and certain occupations. He admits, "I know this is wrong, but that's the way it is" (Myers, 1982, 161). For his candid portrayal of the human tendency toward hasty labeling, the author has won respect from readers, parents, teachers, librarians, and critics for insisting on a fair depiction of urban youth. In 1979, in a challenging essay—"The Black Experience in Children's Books: One Step Forward, Two Steps Back" in *Interracial Books for Children Bulletin*—he criticizes children's literature "made meaningless by stereotype" (Myers, 1979, 15). In place of shallow, racist perceptions, he demands literature that "upholds and gives special place" to the readers' humanity" (*ibid.*). To the effort, he adds his own books, which look at varied cultural situations with an eye toward realistic characterization, setting, and dialogue.

The author often takes children's side against faulty perceptions of youthful indiscretions. In his first novel, *Fast Sam, Cool Clyde, and Stuff* (1975), Myers portrays an edgy hospital staff and police who jump to conclusions about a clutch of noisy black children seeking attention for Binky, whose ear Robin bit off during a fight. More damning is the school faculty that assumes that Cool Clyde is not college material, a common misconception of black teens. A discussion of sex reveals sensible dialogue between Cool Clyde, Fast Sam, and Stuff and a trio of girls, BeBe, Gloria, and Maria. To negate assumptions that black teens lack wisdom about their bodies, Myers recognizes appropriate upbringing and common sense in the group's conclusion that experimenters must accept the consequences.

The author's sensitivity to teens reaches out to 15-year-old Paul Williams, protagonist of *The Young Landlords* (1979). Surrounding an active plot about youth taking charge of a run-down tenement are vignettes of Paul's relationship with a snide, know-it-all father. The author acknowledges Paul's scruffy behaviors at home, but stresses that the boy is more likely to volunteer help around the house for his mother, the parent who encourages Paul. Instead of lobbing potshots at typical teen behaviors, Myers pictures a boy who is sensitive to a prickly home environment and eager to lighten the load for his mother. Subtextually, Myers defeats other givens about Harlemites with a variety of entertaining characters. Patricia Lee Gauch, in a critique for the *New York Times Book Review*, selects as her favorites "the Captain, a cool, pig-eyed numbers man; ...'slap slap' Kelly, whose slick talk is pure music, and best of all, Askia Ben Kenobi, the wild black mystic" (Gauch, 1980, 20).

Evenhanded characterization of Harlem youth painting picket signs portrays Paul Williams's valid complaint against a slum lord. Because Bubba misspells "tenant," the group retains its integrity by withdrawing the sign from public display. Paul explains, "We didn't want to look ignorant, just mad" (Myers, 1979, 26). Even with the best of intentions, the group gets a hard going-over by Mrs. Petey Darden, who looks at the teens as though they might "change into something weird at any moment" (*ibid.*, 31). Less humorous are the cynicism and lackadaisical attitude of police who answer Mrs. Lulu Jones's call about hoodlums wrecking the building. When Bubba observes his friends taken into custody and handcuffed, he draws the lack-logic conclusion that the teens must have broken laws "or they wouldn't have you in the police car" (*ibid.*, 37). His willingness to believe the worst echoes similar leaps to judgment in adults.

Myers soars above stereotypes in his masterwork, *Fallen Angels* (1988), a study of the Vietnam War through the eyes of untried youth. The swirling emotions and observations that impact the anti-hero, infantryman Richard "Richie" Perry, form lasting values as combat shapes his manhood. His jocular buddy Lobel, who retreats into fantasies of movie roles, summarizes Hollywood's abuse of black soldiers in war films. Lobel disdains the part of the "good black guy who everybody thinks is a coward" because, inevitably, the predictable role ends in death when the man redeems himself by saving others (Myers, 1988, 76). Lobel criticizes another overdone scenario—the black soldier who loves a white woman. Lobel smirks that the film kills off the man "so they can show it in Georgia" (*ibid.*).

In a saga, *The Glory Field* (1994), the author fleshes out black-white relationships with an array of familiar stereotypes. In 1864, Julia Lewis utters the typical complaints that black slaves are lazy, a phony excuse by which she summons her friend Lizzy to the main house. More demeaning is Luvenia Lewis's understanding of urban white expectations in 1930. After Florenz Deets makes up a pregnancy as an excuse to drive her father's car, Luvenia pictures the white stereotype of the black who claims pregnancy or arrest as excuses for leaving a job. Luvenia hopes to separate herself from excuses that "grew like vapors" in people's minds (Myers, 1994, 183).

One of the most damning of Myers's urban teen fictions, *Monster: A Novel* (1999) dramatizes the young black male facing a court trial for a mature crime. In place of the pervasive assumptions about black teens from broken homes and poverty, the author portrays Steve Harmon as the son of a concerned, college-educated father and religious mother. Grounded in family love, the boy inexplicably feels himself drawn to the criminal element, depicted in the steely-eyed glowers and joint-smoking of James King, the career criminal who partners with Richard "Bobo" Evans and Osvaldo Cruz. To tease readers into a debate about the typical juvenile delinquent, the author presents adult viewers and Steve himself in a quandary over the boy's culpability. To the far end of the spectrum, a lawyer sees him as a monster; his teacher rebuts that description by describing Steve as honest and intelligent. The ambiguous ending leaves in doubt the capability and intent of the American judicial system to winnow out the truth about young black offenders.

Myers contributes to a pervasive media stereotype, the disaffected sociopath, in *Shooter* (2004), a psychological novel. Based on his study of teen terrorism at Columbine High School, Littleton, Colorado, on April 20, 1999, the metafiction layers psychological evaluations and FBI and sheriff interrogations with commentary by the school superintendent, journalists, and the shooter, 16-year-old Leonard "Len" Gray. His whirling mental faculties, beset by depression and the abuse of prescription tranquilizers, impels him toward murder as a suitable vengeance against his tormentor, Brad Williams, a bullying, self-important jock. The patterned hostilities between acclaimed sports figures and black-clad outlaws recurs in news stories and fiction that exploits the cliques and cults of 21st-century high schools. Myers retrieves from the narrative a black follower, 17-year-old Cameron Porter, who rationalizes his drift into conspiracy and perverse behaviors as his debt to Len, Cameron's only friend. The resulting shooting that claims Len and Brad cuts Cameron loose from his idol and establishes an individuality that is tentatively salvageable. By leaving

Cameron to account for the plot, Myers indicates that Cameron may yet reclaim himself from spiritual rootlessness and expunge his record for complicity in a reckless shooting spree.

See also **anti-hero, black identity**

• *Further Reading*

Campbell, Patty. "The Sand in the Oyster Radical Monster," *Horn Book* 75, no. 6 (November 1999): 769.

Gauch, Patricia L. "Review: *The Young Landlords*," *New York Times Book Review* (6 January 1980): 20.

Myers, Walter Dean. "The Black Experience in Children's Books: One Step Forward, Two Steps Back," *Interracial Books for Children Bulletin* 10, no. 6 (1979): 14–15.

_____. *Fallen Angels*. New York: Scholastic, 1988.

_____. *The Glory Field*. New York: Scholastic, 1994.

_____. *Won't Know Till I Get There*. New York: Viking, 1982.

_____. *The Young Landlords*. New York: Viking, 1979.

Rochman, Hazel. "Review: *Won't Know Till I Get There*," *School Library Journal* 28, no. 9 (May 1982): 72–73.

Staunton, John A. "Review: *Monster: A Novel*," *Journal of Adolescent & Adult Literacy* 45, no. 8 (May 2002): 791–793.

storytelling

Early in his life, Myers appraised oral stories as a lasting gift he could pass on to his children and grandchildren. After he mastered narrative technique in his youth from his parents and grandfather, retired wagoneer William "Pap" Dean, the author began incorporating oral tradition in his storybooks and novels as naturally as he applied essay style or rhymed couplets. He complained to Allen O. Pierleoni in an interview for the *Sacramento Bee* on the absence of storytelling among families: "We're not celebrating ordinary people or our roots enough. We need to teach young people to listen to the stories the older people have to tell. That is how wisdom is passed on" (Pierleoni, 2005).

Myers's skill at updating conventional plot and characterization found an outlet in *The Dragon Takes a Wife* (1972), a vigorous, upbeat narrative for children that preceded a stream of fable, biography, and history. Attesting to the value of wisdom literature is "The Treasure of Lemon Brown" (1983), an exemplum that helps 14-year-old Greg Ridley to value his father's teachings. In a short story, "Jeremiah's Song," which Myers issued in *The Giver and Related Readings* (1987), the elderly title character praises treasured narratives as "the songs of my people" (Myers, "Jeremiah," 185). To the nine-year-old narrator, Grandpa Jeremiah declares that stories are an ongoing human montage: "You think on what those folks been through … and you add it up with what you been through" (*ibid.*, 192). By bridging history, stories encourage hearers to study the courage of those who "got bent and … got twisted" (*ibid.*).

Storytelling remained a staple in Myers's subsequent works. In 1980, he presented the paradox of hunger and pain in a prosperous society in a picture book, *The Golden Serpent*, an Eastern fable set among the have-nots of medieval India that applied as well to the sprawling slums of New York City. The next year, Myers combined a number of literary strains to produce *The Legend of Tarik* (1981), a moody quest story about mentoring and vengeance, dueling and honor. Critic Hazel Rochman, in a review for *School Library Journal*, listed the elements that undergird the heroic myth—"a reborn hero, rites of passage, monsters, perilous journeys, an ultimate duel between good and evil; and there are Islamic, Classical, Christian, and traditional African elements" (Rochman, 1981, 76). Two beast fables, *Mr. Monkey and the Gotcha Bird* (1984) and *How Mr. Monkey Saw the Whole World* (1996), employ rhythmic dialect narrative and the suspenseful shifts in power common to Caribbean oral tradition. Like Aesop in ancient Greece and Uncle Remus in Georgian stories of Br'er Fox and Br'er Rabbit, the narrator moves directly to the moral lesson to freight each story with practical information about survival in a dangerous milieu.

Myers pays tribute to the storyteller in the prologue to *Shadow of the Red Moon* (1987), a fantasy-quest allegory that departs from the author's usual style into sci-fi. His words credit the preserver of oral legends with supporting a threatened people until they achieve "their triumph, their rise to greatness" (Myers, *Shadow*, 1). The author engages the reader with the elements of classical epic structure, which tell of the calamitous weather and plague that threaten Okalian survival. At a critical moment when an atavistic race attempts to overthrow the Okalians, Jon clings to the Orenllag, an earthly version of oral tradition, as his guide. He asserts, "What was written there was true," an acknowledgement of historical handholds to floundering survivors (*ibid.*, 129).

A more scholarly approach in Myers's history *Now Is Your Time! The African-American Struggle for Freedom* (1991. The text summarizes the importance of the griot as the gatherer of African history, the repository of oral tradition stretching back before the recording of data in print. The author allies himself with the truth gatherer and dedicates his talents to enlightening the world about "the legions who have passed this way without yet having their stories told" (Myers, 1991, x). The opportunity to commend the story keeper emerged in Myers's 1994 Margaret A. Edwards Award Acceptance Speech at the American Library Association annual conference in Miami. He told the audience that he delighted in the good fortune "to be able to do what I want to with my life, to write, to tell my stories" (Myers, 1995, 133).

Among the works that pleased Myers was the picture book *The Great Migration: An American Story* (1993), a collaboration with folk artist Jacob Lawrence that combines narrative art with captions and a poetic coda, the ode "The Migration." In spare images of gnarled hands and tattered luggage, Myers summarizes the lot of powerless Southern dray labor. At a chancy pass in the African American diaspora, adults hope for a more vigorous generation of African Americans nurtured on higher wages and better schools in the urban North. In response to the appeal of movement and ambition, critic Hazel Rochman, reviewing for *Booklist*, admired the work for its command of storytelling.

Examples of oral tradition recur in Myers's fables and historical fiction. At the 1994 Lewis family reunion in the black American saga *The Glory Field* (1994), the final stave depicts Malcolm Lewis sharing a sofa-bed with Stephen Vernon Lewis, a small boy who relates the story of Mufaro's daughters, an African folk version of Cinderella. In *The Story of the Three Kingdoms* (1995), the author pictures a people who use fireside gatherings as a time for the wise to instruct the young and uninformed. In *My Name Is America: The Journal of Joshua Loper, a Black Cowboy, The Chisholm Trail, 1871* (1999), a former slave's memories enlighten the title character about "how people had been beat or tracked down by hounds when they tried to run off" (Myers, 1999, 30). Balancing hard times is an Old West ghost story about a black wrangler named Little Tom who froze to death in the saddle along the Powder River in Montana.

Myers shares with characters his love of stories told well. In "A Story in Three Parts" in *145th Street: Short Stories* (2000), Big Time Henson acknowledges his great-grandmother Pat's recall of Harlem in the 1920s and her treasury of family narratives from slave times. For *A Time to Love: Stories from the Old Testament* (2003), the author shifts vignettes by teenaged narrators into first person to tell of Delilah's conflicted love for Samson, Isaac's reverence for his father Abraham, jealousy between Joseph and his brother Reuben, and Zillah's explanation of the bizarre death of her mother, Lot's wife. In the Gothic mode, *The Dream Bearer* (2003) meshes the too-real struggles within the Curry family with the recovered slave memories of "Mr. Moses" Littlejohn, a mystic character who encourages 12-year-old David Curry to give in to the power of dreams as guides and mainstays. The advice suggests a similar moment in the author's life when storytellers convinced him that ancient wisdom is an appropriate foundation for a writing career.

See also **fable, metafiction, supernatural**

• *Further Reading*

Devine, Katherine. "Review: *The Dream Bearer*," *School Library Journal* 49, no. 9 (September 2003): 73.

Mehren, Elizabeth. "Fountain of Stories for Youth: Walter Dean Myers," *Los Angeles Times* (15 October 1997): E1.

Myers, Walter Dean. "Jeremiah's Song," *The Giver and Related Readings*. Boston: McDougal Littell, 1987.

_____. *Mr. Monkey and the Gotcha Bird*. New York: Delacorte, 1984.

_____. *My Name Is America: The Journal of Joshua Loper, a Black Cowboy: The Chisholm Trail, 1871*. New York: Scholastic, 1999.

_____. "1994 Margaret A. Edwards Award Acceptance Speech," *Journal of Youth Services in Libraries*, 8, no. 2 (winter 1995): 129–133.

_____. *Now Is Your Time! The African-American Struggle for Freedom*. New York: HarperCollins, 1991.

_____. *145th Street: Short Stories*. New York: Delacorte, 2000.

_____. *Shadow of the Red Moon*. New York: Harper Collins, 1987.

Pierleoni, Allen O. "Wrongs and the Writer," *Sacramento Bee* (29 March 2005).

"Review: *The Dream Bearer*," *Black Issues Book Review* 5, no. 5 (September-October 2003): 70.

Rochman, Hazel. "Review: *The Great Migration: An American Story*," *Booklist* 90 , no. 28 (15 November 1993): 621.

_____. "Review: *The Legend of Tarik*," *School Library Journal* 27, no. 9 (May 1981): 76.

Silvey, Anita, ed. *Children's Books and Their Creators*. Boston: Houghton Mifflin, 1995.

supernatural

Walter Dean Myers showcases the human desire for answers and salvation from mystic forces, a motif that permeates the quest parable *The Legend of Tarik* (1981) and the impact of mortality in the Gothic short story "Angela's Eyes" (2000). In the former, a blend of literary modes buoys the age-old confrontation between good and evil. Like Miguel de Cervantes's Don Quixote arming for an expedition or like a Western walkdown in Dodge City, the face-off requires careful preparation and a series of predictables, including prophecy, dreams, mysticism, and foreknowledge. In the review of Malcolm Bosse, a critic for the *New York Times Book Review*, Myers equips his paladin with "a magic sword, a powerful horse, and the Crystal of Truth" (Bosse, 1981, 30). The allegory reaches its height not in supernatural conventions, but in the elemental courage and self-control of the title character, a young Mauritanian knight who willingly harnesses all forces at hand to avenge his family's slaying.

Myers frequently pairs the supernatural with such nonstandard forms of religion as voodoo and dream interpretation. For *Black Scholar*, he wrote "The Vision of Felipe" (1978), a narrative about poverty and hopelessness in a ten-year-old Peruvian orphan. After his barge journey 600 miles southwest to Lima, he scrapes by on discarded and fallen fruit and handouts from tourists. Following his vision in late October of his body arranged in a coffin under the eyes of family mourners, the boy centers his ambitions on a white shirt, a dignified burial garment. The vision becomes reality on All Saint's Day, an emotional holiday among Hispanic Catholics, when survivors honor the graves of the family's dead and process with images of skeletons. Myers depicts Felipe's pathetic demise from after-curfew gunfire as the touching loss of a sensitive boy who maintains his love of other people in the face of hunger and imminent death.

For Drusilla, the charm-worker in *Mojo and the Russians* (1977), Myers derived details from local mojo shops. He had a kooky aunt who dabbled in a domestic variety of voodoo, which involved searching for ghosts by dusting the floor with flour. He also recalled a Brazilian practitioner who hexed a disloyal mate by boiling his photo and some of his hair in a pot of fragrant herbs and spices. After Michael "Mean" Dean's bicycle skids into Drusilla, she threatens him with a hex: "I gonna make his tongue split like a lizard's and his eyes to cross. ... Make his monkey ears fall off!" (Myers, 1977, 4). Her exaggerated mutterings elicit more laughs than terror.

By compounding mojo with childish guile, Myers turns the novel into a rollicking comedy. The children attempt their own mojo on Long Willie, whom they suspect of spying for the Russian embassy. Their method is more psychological than supernatural — they play a tape recording for Long Willie while he sleeps. Through hypnopedia, the subliminal message implies that his actions could lead to "whitemale," the Harlem version of blackmail. Because the novel depicts harmless mischief, the tone and atmosphere are humorous and non-threatening.

The manipulation of the unknown in *Ambush in the Amazon* (1986) turns the adventure novella into a mystery. Myers builds on an initial encounter with a *monstruo* (Myers, 1986, 10). As the heroes, Ken and Chris Arrow and their Quechuan interpreter Tarija, investigate a huge hairy beast with vicious paws and a revolting smell, they put themselves into danger among locals in the Peruvian village of Los Cauchos. Tarija explains the chilling basis of local superstition: "If the monster does not want gifts it means that he wants a bride" (*ibid.*, 21). After a thrill-packed series of encounters, the trio discloses that there is nothing supernatural about two villains dressed in monster suits. The author advances from suspense to titters as local authorities apprehend the duo. As a result, "[The villains] looked a lot less fierce with their hands tied behind their backs" (*ibid.*, 80).

In a realistic novel, *Somewhere in the Darkness* (1992), Myers describes the desperation of Cephus "Crab" Little, an escapee from Green Haven prison. As he faces death from kidney failure, he longs to free himself of a false murder charge while he can still influence his 14-year-old son Jimmy. On their flight to Marion, Arkansas, they search for Rydell Depuis, the only witness who can correct an injustice. Because Crab fled the prison infirmary in fear of dying in jail, he consults a conjuror named High John, an elderly man with a lined face. Myers uses the supernatural element to enhance a pathetic truth — that Crab clings to life solely to complete a fatherly quest that will right a wrong and restore his dignity in Jimmy's eyes.

Myers builds tension in the scene as Crab and Jimmy enter the conjuror's house. High John's effectiveness as a counselor shines through his acceptance of Crab and his boy. The conjuror asserts, "A man finds peace in his sons" (Myers, 1992, 132). He replies to Crab's questions as though the answers appear from some mystic source. In High John's words, "There's a veil and a cloud" (*ibid.*). High John's physical examination of Crab is standard medical procedure — he touches the painful side, examines the yellowed whites of the eyes, and touches the inflamed lymph nodes in the underarm. High John's prescription of sassafras tea precedes a gently negative prognosis— Crab is living on borrowed strength. To Jimmy's questions, Crab explains notions of the supernatural as a gift passed on by folk tradition from the past.

For *The Dream Bearer* (2003), Myers returns to Gothic mode. He pairs a 12-year-old Harlemite, David Curry, with "Mr. Moses" Littlejohn, a 300-year-old man who calls to mind Aunt Ester, the superannuated seer-griot in August Wilson's play *Gem of the Ocean* (2003). The audiocassette of *The Dream Bearer*, which Peter Francis James performed for Recorded Books in 2004, contrasts David's concerns for a mentally ill father and a drug-addicted brother with lighter moments of friendships with Sessi, an immigrant from Kenya. Limiting the influence of the supernatural is the collapse of Mr. Moses, whose human body exhibits the mortal limitations that all people experience. In a farewell gesture, David carries the old man's suitcase, a suggestion of the boy's willingness to shoulder the burden of the story keeper.

See also **storytelling, superstition**

• *Further Reading*

Bosse, Malcolm. "Review: *The Legend of Tarik,*" *New York Times Book Review* (12 July 1981): 30.
Myers, Walter Dean. *Ambush in the Amazon*. New York: Viking Kestrel, 1986.
_____. *Mojo and the Russians.* New York: Viking, 1977
_____. *Somewhere in the Darkness.* New York: Scholastic, 1992.

superstition

Myers's novels lend little credence to superstition, but he includes examples of folk beliefs to heighten verisimilitude and enhance humor. The terror plaguing the title figure in "Gums" in *We Be Word Sorcerers: Twenty-five Stories by Black Americans* (1973) causes the sickly grandfather to rely on folk charms against death. As he recedes daily into senile dementia, he attempts more bizarre methods of outfoxing the personified Death, including yelling passwords at the locked door, lighting candles, and sitting up in the dark to ward off the approach of death by night. A pagan shield blended with Christianity is a mark on the floor that delineates a safe zone: "He had said the Lord's Prayer over the chalk and Death couldn't mess with the Lord's Prayer" (Myers, 1973, 185). Gums's frail weapons against mortality increase the pathos of the human fear that progresses as life dwindles.

Myers turns superstitions into idiosyncrasies in other works. In *The Young Landlords* (1979), the teen Action Group that purchases 356 West 122nd Street interviews tenants, including Askia Ben Kenobi, who reads their aura with outstretched hands. The weirdness of his hooded robe, red light, spooky music, and incense takes on a comic air that frightens nobody. The kids flee Askia only after he karate chops through a banister. Harry "Peewee" Gates, an infantryman in *Fallen Angels* (1988), milks laughs out of his mother's belief in a "mojo lady" who cures swollen feet (Myers, 1988, 58). To Perry's retort that his Baptist mother avoids mojo workers, Gates identifies his mother as a "sore-feet Baptist" who is willing to try folk cures. During a pacification mission, Gates makes a joke about a Vietnamese woman who massages salve into his hair, an act that resembles the white assumption that rubbing a negro's head brings good luck. These efforts at drollery divert the soldiers' thoughts from combat.

More dramatic examples occur at a crucial point in the slave saga *The Glory Field* (1994). Some 121 years after the enslavement Muhammad Bilal, the Lewis patriarch from Bonthe, Sierra Leone, the family maintains folk beliefs imported from West Africa. As Lizzy prepares to flee Live Oaks Plantation in 1864, a family members places an amulet around her neck to ward off illness and misadventure. In 1900, Elijah hears Grandma Saran Lewis referring to people who hear the wind calling them. These models of pagan beliefs derive from an African people who lived close to nature from prehistory and who brought their assurances from the motherland over the fearful Middle Passage. Myers suggests that survivors claim the efficacy of supernatural intervention in a time that witnessed multiple deaths of black people.

In *145th Street: Short Stories* (2000), Myers reflects 21st-century views of folk superstitions. Terrors of death produce laughs in an urban fool tale, "Big Joe's Funeral." While plotting his own funeral, Big Joe gets a dressing down from his girlfriend Sadie, who warns, "You don't mess with dying. ... You go laying up in some coffin and death liable to reach out and snatch you right away from here!" (Myers, 2000, 4). In a second story, "Angela's Eyes," events imply to neighbors that Angela Luz Colón foresees death in her dreams. Terror spreads among the superstitious that Angela's glance foretells doom. As a result, Angela's name surfaces in quiet conversations "like a muted drum" (*ibid.*, 47). During a gathering at a bodega, Angela's mother compares the charges against her daughter to jungle beliefs. The owner, Mr. Rodriguez, concludes a valuable truism about jobless, hopeless people: "All they have for entertainment is what they can make up" (*ibid.*). As neighbors continue pressing Angela about the nature of her dreams, she accepts as good advice Mr. Rodriguez's suggestion that she let go of her grief. Angela misinterprets his remark by assuming he speaks of her dreams. The Gothic narrative leaves unaddressed the question of her channeling of mystic powers.

Myers returns to superstition in the opening chapter of *The Beast* (2003), in which Gabriela "Gabi" Godoy, a Dominican beauty, hesitates to bid farewell to her boyfriend, 17-year-old Anthony "Spoon" Witherspoon. She recalls a visit to the island and the projection of a fortune teller, who promised that Gabi would be well remembered. Like the Pythia's pronouncements in ancient Delphi, the statement is ambiguous— it doesn't indicate by whom, where, and when the remembering would take place. Gabi's mother couches her interpretation in terms of love and promises that any man who leaves Gabi will return. The discussion of fortune telling is an appropriate introit to a story of rescue from drug addiction. Paralleling Gabi's search for reassurance from prognostication is her mother's dependence on lighting candles at church and readings of tea leaves as she weathers chemotherapy for stomach cancer. The Gothic elements illustrate how vulnerable people grasp at any source of power, whether real or imagined.

In this same period, the author and his son, artist Chris Myers, teamed up to produce *Blues Journey* (2003), a storybook perusal of the varied meanings of indigenous black music. The frequent mention of mystic events such as a "blood moon," moral crossroads, blackbirds in flight, slave-chasing dogs, and evil storms suggests how thoroughly superstition permeates life (Myers, 2003, n.p.). In one verse, the "root woman" predicts approaching death, which the seeker brushes off with a comparison to unlikely occurrences— a mule reading scripture and Christmas arriving in June (*ibid.*). In a less humorous vision of good combating evil, another stanza pictures the climb of the preacher to the mountaintop, but the devil continuing to thrive.

In *A Time to Love: Stories from the Old Testament* (2003), Myers recreates the mystic wonders of the bible in wondrous personal experiences. In the story of Joseph and Reuben, a luminosity marks Joseph as a figure tapped in youth by God to reunite his squabbling brothers. In the account of Abraham and Isaac, the sudden appearance of a ram caught in a thicket is an unforeseen acknowledgement of God's acceptance of Abraham's act of faith. An eerier event, the urgency of two holy men during the rescue of Lot's family from Sodom, takes on the atmosphere of the ghosts in Charles Dickens's *The Christmas Carol*. In Myers's handling, the grim-voiced guides refuse to engage in trivial conversation or to accede to excuses as they carry out the will of the almighty. For disobedience to God, Lot's wife recedes from the sight of her husband and daughters, who trudge on to Zoar. Myers pictures her demise as "a frozen nightmare on that barren plain," a suitable punishment to anyone who doubts Jehovah's powers (Myers, 2003, 101).

See also **supernatural**

• *Further Reading*

Myers, Walter Dean. *The Beast.* New York: Scholastic, 2003.
_____. *Fallen Angels.* New York: Scholastic, 1988.
_____. "Gums" in *We Be Word Sorcerers: Twenty-five Stories by Black Americans.* New York: Bantam, 1973.
_____. *145th Street: Short Stories.* New York: Delacorte, 2000.
_____. *A Time to Love: Stories from the Old Testament.* New York: Scholastic, 2003.
Smith, Karen Patricia. *African-American Voices in Young Adult Literature: Tradition, Transition, Transformation.* Lanham, Md.: Scarecrow, 1994.

suspense

Through inventive plots and intriguing pacing, Myers creates suspense, such as the question of a stable home for 12-year-old Tippy in *It Ain't All for Nothin'* (1978), the stalking of a serial killer in the allegory *The Legend of Tarik* (1981), the search for a viable motherland in the sci-fi allegory *Shadow of the Red Moon* (1987), and the choice of a tempting, but amoral career outside familiar territory in *Crystal* (1987). The poignant conclusion to *Hoops: A Novel* (1981), draws strength and impact from a mounting tension in 17-year-old Lonnie Jackson, a sports ace battling the criminal elements of the basketball underworld. In the falling action, his honorable choice results in a terrible price, the death of Calvin F. "Spider" Jones, the paternal coach who leads the team to victory in the Tournament of Champions.

Myers tends to involved plots in serious quests. In the seriocomic novel *Won't Know Till I Get There* (1982), both Earl Goins and the residents at the Micheaux House for Senior Citizens live in precarious situations. The retirees make new lives for themselves, but the issue of Earl Goins's adoption remains unsettled until the final pages, when his mother gives him up to loving parents. A departure from Myers's teen stories set in Harlem is the suspenseful novel *The Nicholas Factor* (1983), a spy thriller featuring blackmail and multiple poisonings in the Amazonian jungles of Peru. The mysterious meeting that opens the novel raises questions about why John Martens, an investigator for the National Security Agency, enlists Gerald McQuillen as an undercover agent to observe and photograph neo–Nazis infiltrating the campus Crusade Society. A reviewer for *Publishers Weekly* notes the importance of the crusader motif, an historical reference to "religious zealots who felt a holy obligation to impose their will" ("Review," 1983, 70). Against the fluff of founder and society chair Marlin Wilkes's bromide—"We aren't dropouts, we're dropins"—Alfredo Santana, Gerald's Costa Rican contact, injects a chilling Hitleresque dictum that "the need to anchor oneself to humanity's ungifted and unwashed residue becomes less compelling" (*ibid.*, 19, 21). The brainwashing continues during the society's expedition to Lima, where Andwele Kofe, a Crusader from Cameroon, poses a thought-provoking question: "Are we not conquered by our inability to run our own lives?" (*ibid.*, 72).

At the outset, the mechanics of *The Nicholas Factor* seem like routine plot development with tinges of suspicious activity. Myers develops the involvement of Kohler, a surly German medic who packs along aluminum cases of test tubes. By managing a power struggle between Kohler and Marlin Wilkes, the founder and chairman of the society, the author swells the tensions of young do-gooders on a mission to a Quechuan settlement. The first break in the action, the poisoning of Andwele, precedes disclosure of grave illness at a distant site from a pyrethrin that Kohler distributes to the Quechua, allegedly for water purification. By punching up the pace with an escape by boat, plane, and car, the author sweeps readers along to a stirring conclusion with a humanitarian touch, the rescue of at least some of the Quechua from the machinations of a genocidal maniac.

Also in 1983, Myers published *Tales of a Dead King*, an exotic thriller set in Aswan, Egypt. The pairing of Karen Lacey and John Robie at a deserted Egyptian village sets in motion the resolution of a search for John's great uncle, Egyptologist Erich Leonhardt. Contributing to suspense are a coded message, desert stalkers, and attempts to terrify Karen with a snake in her bed and to scare off both teen searchers by the thud of a knife in the wall. To enhance the couple's guesswork, the author misleads them by casting doubts on the motives Captain Gamael, a police official who rescues them. By proving Karen and John equal to the search, Myers envigorates one of his favorite motifs, the gumption of young people in dangerous situations.

Meyers's adventure novellas bank on suspense for narrative pacing and unity. The first chapter of *The Hidden Shrine* (1985), one of the Arrow brothers series, opens on a boat confrontation in Hong Kong that forces overboard 14-year-old Ken and 17-year-old Chris Arrow and their 16-year-old guide Won Li. With the search for temple robbers already in progress at Cheung Chau island, the narrative ramps up the suspense. The second of the series, *Adventure in Granada* (1985), places the Arrow brothers in Spain in the company of a Gypsy postcard seller, Pedro Barcia, a victim of police stereotyping during the investigation of the disappearance of the Cruzada Cross. Similarly tense and focused on the pilfering of valuable artifacts, *Duel in the Desert* (1986), set at the rim of the Sahara in Goulamime, Morocco, begins with Chris awakening to blood on his body. A fast-moving story of child kidnap and the theft of a valuable chalice, the plot concludes with Chris rescuing his brother from a knife blade held to his throat. In all of the Arrow brothers novellas, the element of foreign language adds mystery and complicates communication with suggestions of hostility and menace.

The author opens *Ambush in the Amazon* (1986), another of the four-book Arrow series, on a conversation in which Ken awakens his brother Chris in the night after hearing a noise at Los Cauchos, a village in the Amazon jungle. Within the first page, Chris fears that a malodorous "something" has ripped into the tent netting and attacked him with the hairy paws of a *monstruo* (Myers, 1986, 10). Building tension after the initial scene are an underwater attack by a crocodile, a 14-year-old translator who glows in the dark, and escape from a burning boat in piranha-infested waters. The narrative builds on the fears of a mysterious animal with a sighting of a humanoid walking upright: "The quick, black eyes darted back and forth, the mouth was a red gash filled with fierce rows of jagged teeth" (*ibid.*, 48). The discovery of villains in monster suits concludes the story with a logical answer and heroism for Tarija, the female translator.

Some works, like *Somewhere in the Darkness* (1992), *Monster: A Novel* (1999), and *The Dream Bearer* (2003), remain partially unresolved, leaving readers to mull over serious issues like a father's death in prison, the guilt of felony murder, father-son hostilities, and untreated paranoia. These conclusions stress the reality of human difficulties, which cling to lives with a cruel persistence. More certain is the outcome of *Toussaint L'Ouverture: The Fight for Haiti's Freedom* (1996), a picture book biography that carries the life of François Toussaint from enslavement in childhood to his rise as General Toussaint L'Ouverture, leader of Haiti's liberators. Within months of his death in a French dungeon cell at Castle Joux, his people embrace liberation and form the first black republic. Myers chooses Toussaint as an example of mortal deeds that generate an immortality that continues to direct the actions of followers after the hero's death.

Less intense than Toussaint's struggles is the suspenseful flight of the title character and his pal Caleb in a seriocomic children's work, *The Blues of Flats Brown* (2000). The picture book explains that the blues-playing duo must escape from their owner, A. J. Grubbs, before he commits them to another dog fight for the amusement of brutal humans. Myers turns from straight narrative to legend on the final page, where the guitar-playing crooner with Caleb on the bones entertains listeners along the Atlantic shore of Savannah, Georgia. The peaceful ambience of a park bench concert satisfies suspense with a reassurance that Flats and Caleb are safe.

See also ***The Legend of Tarik, Monster: A Novel, Shooter***

• *Further Reading*

Morgans, Patricia A. "Review: *The Nicholas Factor*," *Best Sellers* 43, no. 4 (July 1983): 155.
Myers, Walter Dean. *Adventure in Granada*. New York: Viking Kestrel 1985.
_____. *Ambush in the Amazon*. New York: Viking Kestrel, 1986.
_____. *The Blues of Flats Brown*. New York: Holiday House, 2000.
_____. *The Nicholas Factor*. New York: Viking, 1983.
_____. *Toussaint L'Ouverture: The Fight for Haiti's Freedom*. New York: Simon & Schuster, 1996.
Ramsay, Marie. "Review: *Shadow of the Red Moon*," *Book Report* 15, no. 1 (May/June 1996): 38.
"Review: *The Nicholas Factor*," *Publishers Weekly* 223, no. 11 (13 March 1983): 70.
Spencer, Pam. "Winners in Their Own Right," *School Library Journal* 38, no. 3 (March 1992): 163–167.
Sutherland, Zena. "Review: *Hoops: A Novel*," *Bulletin of the Center for Children's Books* 35, no. 4 (December 1981): 74.

Tarik's genealogy

The family history in Myers's quest story *The Legend of Tarik* (1981) examines events that heighten the West African diaspora. Setting the plot in motion is the serial killer El Muerte (Death), the great grandson of the Alani-Vandal warrior Ganseric (also Gaiseric or Geiseric), who murders the family of Kwesi Ntah, Mauritanian refugees from the Niger River north of Lake Debo to Oulata, and cuts down Kwesi and Umeme in the blood-sport ring at Encina. The family tree illustrates Tarik's losses and the burden of vengeance:

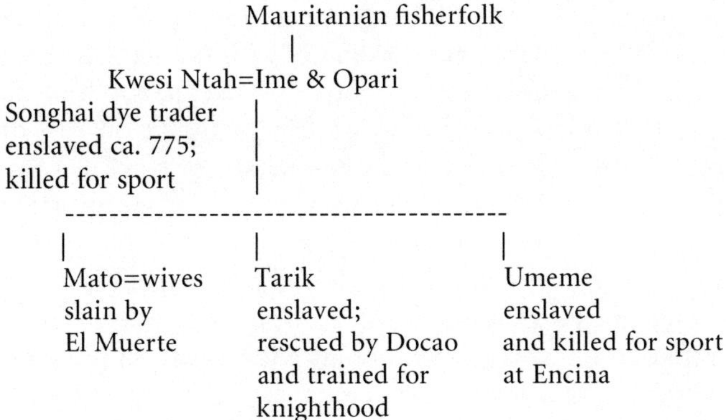

• *Further Reading*

Myers, Walter Dean. *The Legend of Tarik*. New York: Viking, 1981.

Tippy's genealogy

In *It Ain't All for Nothin'* (1978), a dicey home life in Harlem emerges in a diagram the shows the passage of 12-year-old Tippy from Carrie Brown, his 69-year-old maternal grandmother, to Lonnie, a thief serving a second prison term, to the Sylvesters, Edna and Roland, foster parents worthy of a child lovingly reared in his grandmother's Christian care.

```
Grandma
Carrie Brown    distant
hospitalized    father
     |               |
Esther Brown=Lonnie  =/=Lois
died in        | ex-con  =/=Peggy
childbirth     | and
               | womanizer
               |
               | Roland=Edna (foster parents)
                       | Sylvester
                       | bus driver
                       |    |
                       Tippy
```

• *Further Reading*

Myers, Walter Dean. *It Ain't All for Nothin'*. New York: Viking, 1978.

Toussaint L'Ouverture

Along with a series of American heroes—Colonel Fred V. Cherry, Dr. Martin Luther, King, Jr., Muhammad Ali, and Malcolm X—Myers chose foreign examples of courageous blacks. His young adult biography *Toussaint L'Ouverture: The Fight for Haiti's Freedom* (1996) depicts the Haitian liberator as a model freedom fighter and creator of the first black republic. The story coordinates with the stark stylized paintings of Jacob Lawrence, a visual historian who dramatized the Haitian leader's libertarian spirit with a series of 41 earth-toned drawings capturing the horrors of Caribbean colonialism. Like Myers, Lawrence learned the details of black heroics from street orators in Harlem. The first whom the painter chose to honor was the Haitian who "fought and contributed much to our continuous struggle for liberty" (Myers, 1996, n.p.). His panels, which debuted in 1940, found permanent residence in the Amistad Research Center in New Orleans.

According to the narrative, the terrors of whippings and cruelty impress on François Toussaint the racial divide that made white colonists the rulers of blacks. Ironically, he earns the name L'Ouverture (the opener) from forcing a breach in the French battle line. His abilities as a strategist and leader spread hope to slaves in the United States and encourage fighters in Santo Domingo to make their own stand against slavery. Through suspense and immediacy, Myers stresses that international powers can ill afford a model of black liberty in the West Indies. At the command of Napoleon Bonaparte, French forces battle the ex-slaves to a standstill. Imprisoned at age 59 at Castle Joux, the general dies days before his 60th birthday, but his example sustains the libertarian spirit throughout the Caribbean and into the United States.

- *Further Reading*

Masciere, Christina. "Browser: Cultural Adventures," *New Orleans Magazine* 31, no. 1 (October 1996): 74.

Myers, Walter Dean. *Toussaint L'Ouverture: The Fight for Haiti's Freedom*. New York: Simon & Schuster, 1996.

Rochman, Hazel. "Review: *Toussaint L'Ouverture: The Fight for Haiti's Freedom*," *Booklist* 93, no. 1 (1 September 1996): 123.

urbanism

A revered contributor to urban reality fiction, Walter Dean Myers continues to build a reputation for depicting the lures and perils that endanger the inner-city resident, ranging from the rapid rise of fashion model Crystal Brown in *Crystal* (1987) and the despair of out-of-work Vietnam War vet Sweeby Jones in *Darnell Rock Reporting* (1994) to thugs threatening a homeless man in "The Treasure of Lemon Brown" (1983) and teens involved in felony robbery and murder in *Monster: A Novel* (1988). The author succeeded with a short story "The Vision of Felipe" (1978), published in *Black Scholar*. By describing the destitution of the title character, a ten-year-old orphan, on the streets of Lima, Peru, Myers creates empathy for the hungry and homeless who arrive in urban areas without street survival skills. Through friendship with 12-year-old Daniel, a city-bred urchin, Felipe learns how to scavenge food and which tourists are most likely to offer coins. From Daniel comes a city-dweller's plan for prosperity — save enough money for a shoe shine box and go into business. In *It Ain't All for Nothin'* (1978), the escapes offered on Harlem streets help 12-year-old Tippy cope with ex-con Lonnie, an abusive, drunken father. Eventually, immersion in television and movies, alcohol, the park, and an abandoned building at 43rd Street in downtown Manhattan fail the boy in distancing him from the inevitable mayhem of life with a career criminal. Myers applauds Tippy's choice to cooperate with police to end the downward spiral of his life and save him from death as an unwilling accomplice of criminals.

The next year, Myers turned to Harlem for the city complexities found in a crowded black community in the teen novels *Mojo and the Russians* and *The Young Landlords*. Patricia Lee Gauch, in a critique of the latter novel for the *New York Times Book Review*, lists urban ills as "the hot-goods industry, police lethargy, newspapers' predilection for story over facts" (Gauch, 1980, 20). Although only peripherally linked, these weaknesses contribute to the crime and citizen apathy that undergird Myers's city-based fiction. The author followed with longer fiction—*Hoops: A Novel* (1981), *Motown and Didi: A Love Story* (1984), *Crystal* (1987), and *Scorpions* (1988)—which rounds out city-bred personalities and matches wrongheadedness and pride with compassion and good sense. For *The Mouse Rap* (1990), the author creates humor from the unusual background of Booster, a scion of a gangster family. After a subway ride to Willets Point, 14-year-old Mouse encounters a mugger who threatens him with a knife. Booster, who is two years younger than Mouse, is so enured to random violence that he pulls out a pistol and cocks the hammer. Mouse ends the edgy encounter by departing while giving further thought to Booster as "Al Capone, Jr." (Myers, 1990, 139).

In a retrospect on black history, Myers teamed with folk artist Jacob Lawrence to produce the picture book *The Great Migration: An American Story* (1993), a tribute to the African American diaspora. The tension of black families posed under armed guard in segregated railway depots anticipates a lessening of injustice and a retreat from powerlessness as newcomers seek their fortune in the urban centers of Chicago, Cleveland, Detroit, New York, Philadelphia, and Pittsburgh. Captions admit that the North had its own ways of brutalizing and demeaning blacks, but the subtext indicates that, overall, the risk of traveling north from the agrarian South was worth the effort and pain of uprooting. In Harlem, the pinnacle of black communitarianism, black families not only achieve spiritual uplift and economic betterment, but also create their own artistic expression of the American dream. Historian and critic Henry Louis Gates, Jr., saluted the Great Migration as the reinvention of black Americanism.

Picturing a low point in American history, Myers employs urbanism in his Vietnam War novel *Fallen Angels* (1988), which describes the black infantrymen that serve the confrontation as cannon fodder. He describes the adaptation of two city boys, infantrymen Richard "Richie" Perry from Harlem and Harry "Peewee" Gates from Chicago, to army patrols in a combat zone. Both youths suffer from poverty and a lack of educational opportunity, both enter the war under clouded motivation—Perry because of an institutional error that fails to limit his involvement because of a knee injury and Gates because of a casual visit to a recruiter with a friend who intends to enlist. In both instances, urban teens find themselves processed and shipped out to a jungle war that exceeds their imagination.

Urbanism follows the soldiers to Indochina and membership in Alpha Company of the 22nd Replacement Company at Tan Son Nhut airbase in Hue City. Memories of Kenny Perry's difficulties with a bully worry infantryman Richie, who feels cut off from the urban scene in Vietnam, too far from Harlem to aid his small brother. A later reference to the family residence in Harlem portrays it as a neighborhood where kids had to be tough enough "to get to the store with money for a loaf of bread" (Myers, 1988, 118). In a verbal swipe at Chicago, Pee Wee's hometown, Sergeant Simpson states that Walowick is safer in a war zone than he would be living in a dangerous city. When Richie links up with Pee Wee at a military hospital at Chu Lai, Pee Wee retains his urban smarts by masterminding the numbers racket, a favorite entertainment of city dwellers. For all Pee Wee's lightheartedness, Richie divulges, "We weren't all right. We would have to learn to be alive again" (*ibid.*, 304).

In *Somewhere in the Darkness* (1992), Myers sets up a different contrast between city and the outback. After Cephus "Crab" Little collects his son, 14-year-old Jimmy Little, from a New York apartment, the two drive to Cleveland, Chicago, then south to Tennessee and Arkansas. Near Crab's hometown of Marion, he discusses with his son the differences between city life and towns in the South. There is no need to lock groceries in the trunk of the car because random theft is rare. The building of homes sometimes begins with a vacated concrete foundation or pilings and the hammering together of old wood into a livable structure. Even though life seems breezy and laid back, Crab adds that "You keep hearing the call of the city," a reference to dreams of good jobs and easy money (Myers, 1992, 124).

In a book review for the *Washington Post*, Myers acknowledges the dangers of "the mean streets of urban America" (Myers, 1991, 7). In *Slam!* (1996), one of his best received sports novels, he describes Greg "Slam" Harris using his ears during bouts of insomnia. Outside, he hears boom boxes, buses and garbage trucks, and smashing wine bottles. Of the shriek of sirens, he describes holding his breath as the police cars and emergency vehicles hurry by. He releases his tension after he knows "it ain't any of your people who's getting arrested or being taken to the hospital" (Myers, 1996, 2–3). With the insouciance of a born-in-the-city kid, Slam's little brother Derek decides not to shop for cold-cuts because of a drive-by shooting on 141st Street. The two boys exhibit a wealth of urban experience, despite their youth.

Myers backs away from pat answers to the complexities of territorial gangs and bullying by offering young characters community models to follow and wisdom from older, more experienced heads like Roland Sylvester, Felipe's grandmother, Lemon Brown, and Coach Cal. The offer of big money to Crystal for modeling and posing for pornographic pictures and to Lonnie Jackson for point-shaving depicts cash as a means of escaping the ghetto and of living in more comfortable homes in better neighborhoods. At stake is self-respect, which Crystal and Lonnie ultimately value above the payoff. From Lemon Brown, Greg Ridley learns that even the city's elderly homeless can live in a boarded up basement while retaining treasures from family loss and memories that never fade.

More devastating is the psychic isolation and self-questioning of 16-year-old Steve Harmon, the protagonist/narrator of the innovative cautionary tale *Monster: A Novel* (1999). The author earned a list of kudos from critics who recommended the quandary of the young juvenile delinquent as a source of reader debate. The narrative, a metafictional blend of personal journal and objective scriptwriting, presents the aimless drift into trouble that begins with a yearning for attention and acceptance. Still on the cusp of manhood, Steve hovers on the outer rim of respect from thugs who commit a felony robbery and murder. He struggles to account for his presence at the crime scene and retreats from accusing himself of participating as the lookout. To retain self-esteem, he pictures himself as a cinematographer capturing the amorality and criminality of his peers on the city streets of Harlem. Myers leaves up to the reader whether the camera exonerates Steve as an observer rather than condemn him as a culprit.

The author earned a long list of critical kudos for his overview of the causes of delinquency in *Handbook for Boys: A Novel* (2002). The dramatic situation pictures Kevin and Jimmy Lynch as court remands of Duke Wilson, a wise barber who teaches the boys about life at the same time that he directs their daily tasks of sweeping. Central to their reclamation are life lessons drawn from passersby on the street and customers in the shop. In the opinion of critic Lynda Jones, a writer for *Black Issues Book Review*, the novel "weaves together a sad but true tale that depicts the challenges that many inner-city kids face each day" (Jones, 2002, 78). The stress on urban temptations— sex, drugs, and easy money from crime — makes the novel a valuable classroom tool for discussion of right thinking.

See also **diaspora, displacement, Harlem, Steve Harmon, *Monster: A Novel***

• *Further Reading*

Fader, Ellen. "Review: *Darnell Rock Reporting*," *Horn Book* 71, no. 2 (March 1995): 194, 200.
Gauch, Patricia L. "Review: *The Young Landlords*," *New York Times Book Review* (6 January 1980): 20.
Jones, Lynda. "Review: *Handbook for Boys: A Novel*," *Black Issues Book Review*, 4, no. 3 (May/June 2002): 78.
Myers, Walter Dean. *Fallen Angels*. New York: Scholastic, 1988.
_____. "Mean Streets *Do or Die*, by Leon Bing," *Los Angeles Times* (11 August 1991): 1.
_____. *The Mouse Rap*. New York: HarperCollins, 1990.
_____. *Slam!* New York: Scholastic, 1996.
_____. *Somewhere in the Darkness*. New York: Scholastic, 1992.
_____. "Surviving Mean Streets," *Washington Post* (12 May 1991): 7.

vengeance

Myers charges his plots with currents of retaliation and exonerates characters for striking back, such as the title character's war on death in the short story "Gums" (1973) and the tense male-to-male verbal sparring between rivals Hi-Note and Earl Goins in *Won't Know Till I Get There* (1983). The author learned to expect retribution in childhood from his grandfather, William "Pap" Dean, who told Old Testament stories of divine wrath, like the destruction of Sodom and Gomorrah, the death of Samson in his battle with the Philistines, and the transformation of Lot's wife into a pillar of salt. In an early dilemma story, "How Long Is Forever?," published in the

June 1969 issue of *Negro Digest*, the author dramatizes the daily sadism that Jenkins, a white prison guard, directs against Moses, an inmate anticipating parole. The tension between Moses's longing for liberty and his desire to defend himself against an evil bully increases suspense to the final confrontation. In the last paragraph, the author portrays the embrace of violence as a bursting dam. For Moses, "there was no use in stopping" because he has nothing left to lose (Myers, 1969, 57). By condemning himself to a longer sentence, he frees his fists to crush his oppressor. Myers depicts the price of vengeance in the hysterical laughter that erupts from the mental breakdown of a desperate man.

As Myers acquired sophistication as well as narrative subtlety, he began blending literary modes to express complex ideas. One of his challenging hero stories, *The Legend of Tarik* (1981), examines the fierce quest lore dating to the Crusades to determine the nature and depth of satisfaction in payback. The title character, an untested Mauritanian orphan, requires extensive counsel and training before he is ready to avenge the slaughter of his family by El Muerte (death), a symbolic scourge who strikes fear into all who stand in his path. For the sake of contrast, Myers pairs Tarik with Stria, a wound-tight paladin more obsessed with vengeance than is her male counterpart. Of Tarik's overthrow of a sadist, critic Hazel Rochman, in a review for *School Library Journal*, notes the lack of "joy in his victories" (Rochman, 1981, 76). The vicious battles produce a kill, but they leave the young knight "[questioning] whether a righteous end must require such bloody means" (*ibid.*). Myers's subtext implies that Tarik, like the biblical shepherd David, gains more from introspection and control of his emotions than he does from felling a North African Goliath.

The author produced a clever spoof of Western retribution plots in *The Righteous Revenge of Artemis Bonner* (1992), a quest novel that resembles in tone, dialogue, and structure Charles Portis's classic young adult Western *True Grit* (1968). The centrality of payback looms in Myers's title and opening sentence: "I, Artemis Bonner, in order to explain why I am going to kill a low-lifed and sniveling scoundrel called Catfish Grimes, am writing down the whole story, and the truth as well" (Myers, 1992, 1). The droll tone emulates first-person adventure tales that related to Easterners an exaggerated view of Western danger and mayhem. The choice of Tombstone, Arizona, as a setting for the murder of Uncle Ugly Ned links 17-year-old Artemis's narrative to one of the most colorful border towns, where armed walkdowns and barroom shootouts established the town's reputation for lawlessness and where Boot Hill was a fitting resting place for the wayward. Contributing to verisimilitude are frequent capital letters for emphasis, as in "wishing us God's Holy Grace," "both Proper and Fit," and "a no-good card cheat, rat, and Evil-doer" (*ibid*, 2, 11, 3). A boost to satire of Old West lore is Artemis's choice of period clichés, for example, "Her who brought me into this world," "slipped away like a thief in the night," and "had forced the hand of cruel fate" (*ibid.*, 6, 19, 3).

To balance the elements of murder and requital, Myers tweaks the reader from time to time with sentimentality and frontier humor. Endearing the hero Artemis to the reader are his great-heartedness in sending $100 to his mother and another dollar to the New York Colored Orphans Home. The hero's bold generalization about women being poor shots concludes with Lucy Featherdip hitting the handle of his pistol with her first shot and mangling his ear with her second. In typical Western style, Uncle Ugly's tombstone sports an upbeat jingle: "Here Lies Ugly Ned Bonner/ Once Alive—/Now a Goner" (*ibid.*, 10). The light-hearted repartee bears nuggets worth pondering, such as the fierce look in the eyes of Indians who resent the theft of their land. Contributing to Myers's coming-of-age motif is Artemis's discovery that he is capable of cunning.

Myers yanks humor back in its place with Artemis's interview with Moby, a hired killer who offers to murder two people for five dollars. In the falling action, Artemis dispenses justice to Catfish, whom the undertaker drags away. Aunt Mary caps the deed with a sincere wish that Catfish's "miserable butt sizzle in the Fires of Hell forever," a far-reaching vengeance that follows the victim to the afterlife (*ibid.*, 134). Myers tricks the reader just as Catfish tricked Artemis into shooting him with phony bullets. The novel ends with Artemis and Frolic plotting another trek out west in hopes of bringing Catfish to justice. Like a cartoon cliffhanger, the story defuses the simmering requital theme by overwhelming the hero's murderous intent with bumbling actions.

More realistic is the wartime hatred that mounts during *Fallen Angels* (1988), Myers's masterwork of the Vietnam War. The emergence of terms like "gook," "slants," and "slant eyes" poses a paradox—hatred for the enemy encourages racism from a mixed American force comprised of a span of races. Dramatizing the need for retaliation is a scene in chapter 12 in which sappers threaten the bunker occupied by Alpha Company of the 22nd Replacement Company. Captain Stewart counters the Viet Cong suicide squad by vowing to keep the enemy awake all night from incoming fire. In a later battle, his last chance for promotion, he sends men on patrol at the Song Nha Ngu River with orders to intercept more VC. Anti-hero Richard "Richie" Perry and his buddies interpret Stewart's meaning in personal terms—the captain's intent to earn promotion to major by intensifying a firefight that could result in unnecessary loses to his unit. Contributing to the author's defamation of Stewart is the captain's urging that Perry raise the VC body count by 50 percent.

By mapping out *Shooter!* a fictional echo of teen terrorism at Columbine High School, Littleton, Colorado, on April 20, 1999, Myers dramatizes the need of outlaw students to exact punishment on bullies. At the crux of the *Ordo Saggitae* (Order of the Arrow), a cultish club, is the persistent cruelties and threats of Brad Williams, a strutting jock. He miscalculates the venom of his target, 16-year-old Leonard "Len" Gray, an outsider who stokes vengeance to a killing point. By forcing Len and his friends, Cameron Porter and Carla Evans, to the fringe of student achievement, Brad unintentionally engages Len's admiration for guns as the cure. Myers builds suspense as Len introduces Cameron and Carla to the right-wing Patriots gun club and as he builds his personal arsenal. Because of parental and faculty disinterest in student tiffs, Len's mounting rage goes unaddressed. The superintendent is quick to distance himself and the school system from Brad's murder and Len's suicide, the outcome of psychological dysfunction that adult intervention might have averted.

See also **The Legend of *Tarik*,** **Tarik genealogy**

• *Further Reading*

Bosse, Malcolm. "Review: *The Legend of Tarik*," *New York Times Book Review* (12 July 1981): 30.
Myers, Walter Dean. "How Long Is Forever?," *Negro Digest* (June 1969): 52-57.
____. *The Righteous Revenge of Artemis Bonner*. New York: HarperCollins, 1992.
____. "The Vision of Felipe," *Black Scholar* (November-December 1978): 2–9.
Rochman, Hazel. "Review: *The Legend of Tarik*," *School Library Journal* 27, no. 9 (May 1981): 76.

victimization

A championing of justice in Myers's fiction requires frequent images of victimization, from the slave era in *U.S.S. Constellation: Pride of the American Navy* (2004) and Jim Crow in *Now Is Your Time! The African-American Struggle for Freedom* (1991) to the potential theft of Quechuan property in *Ambush in the Amazon* (1986) and Lonnie's child neglect and contribution to the delinquency of 12-year-old Tippy, the anti-hero of *It Ain't All for Nothin'* (1978). The author introduces the tensions of weak vs. strong in an early dilemma story, "How Long Is Forever?," written for the June 1969 issue of *Negro Digest*. The victim, inmate Moses, symbolizes the enslavement of the Hebrew people and the unforeseen emergence of the epic champion to lead former slaves out of Egypt toward a promised land. Realism reduces the fictional Moses to a one-on-one daily battery by Jenkins, a sadistic white guard. Myers enhances the theme of injustice by dramatizing Moses's loss of self-control and his descent into madness, retaliation, and hysterical laughter as the victim destroys his hopes for parole.

In *Mojo and the Russians* (1977), Myers develops the character of Kwami, who conceals his vulnerability under tough talk. He weathers his father's insistance that he not mount a poster of the white bionic woman on his wall. When the father accuses Kwami of causing his mother's chest pains from cleaning Kwami's dirty room, the boy needs the consolation of friends. The next year, Myers published "The Vision of Felipe" (1978) in *Black Scholar*. The story of a ten-year-old homeless orphan scavenging the streets of Lima, it describes Felipe's naivete of urban ways and his need of 12-year-old Daniel as friend and mentor. Even with a street-wise cohort, Felipe loses the two dollars he gets from begging to a cruel soldier. The victimization of two children by a soulless adult creates empathy for the poor, especially those too young to fend for themselves.

Fictional depictions of victimization cover the gamut of human responses to disappointment and menace. Less threatening than Felipe's situation is the placement of Earl Goins in *Won't Know Till I Get There* (1982) with a foster mother who agrees to take him only for the monthly checks reimbursing her for parenting. However, beyond the insult to Earl, the emotional damage toughens him and makes it hard for the Perrys to establish him in a loving home environment. Similarly easy-going in style is the reverse psychology of the predator in *Mr. Monkey and the Gotcha Bird* (1984), which plays on Mr. Fish's ego with the enticement, "Who see in water? Everybody see in tree. Maybe you no double smart" (Myers, 1984, n.p.). Myers also interjects stories with angry words that go no farther than threats. In *Sweet Illusions* (1986), a series of open-ended stories about teen pregnancy, a father, Edward Shaw, takes his daughter Ellen's side without hearing from the teen father. Edward snarls, "If I could get at the guy I would kill him. I'm not a violent men, but if I could get at this guy I would kill him" (Myers, 1986, 95).

Myers sets scenes of victimization within a greater context of heroism and survival, particularly in the story of a homeless blues musician in "The Treasure of Lemon Brown" (1983) and in the awkward sleuthing of Ken and Chris Arrow in *The Hidden Shrine* (1985) and *Ambush in the Amazon* (1986). A more desperate situation threatens Didi in *Motown and Didi: A Love Story* (1984). After she begs police to arrest Touchy to stop his dealing of heroin, officers tip off the dealer. When Touchy's hit men try to assault her on a tenement roof, Motown arrives in time to rescue her. Myers implies that the last-minute save intervenes before life-threatening harm befalls Didi. Within the amoral plexus of the beauty industry in *Crystal* (1987), 16-year-old model Crystal Brown must protect herself from a gradual slide into sexual favors. To exploiters who photograph her and book contracts for fashion shoots and movies, she chooses to abandon a promising career rather than end up like Rowena, an 18-year-old colleague who chooses to kill herself rather than live with constant devaluation. In *Fallen Angels* (1988), infantryman Lobel escapes a verbally abusive father who calls his son a faggot. Lobel views his experience in the Vietnam War from two perspectives— his father must respect him for fighting America's enemy and fear him for learning how to fight. Myers overturns the image with irony by impressing on Lobel that basic training has turned him into a skillful killer "to prove that he wasn't queer" (Myers, 1988, 118).

Victimization occurs in random urban scenes in *The Mouse Rap* (1990), beginning with the sudden appearance of a mugger armed with a knife at a subway platform in Queens. In a later scene, 14-year-old Frederick "The Mouse" Douglas plays an ordinary game of basketball at the park with friends Styx and Toast when the trio teams up with three older men. The pick-up game turns to harsh language, then violence breaks out with a punch to Mouse's stomach. The aggressor, who looks "as big as King Kong's daddy," knocks Mouse down (Myers, 1991, 147). The author eases back on the tension by turning what looks like a broken leg into a prosthesis that the attacker swings like a weapon. The humor of the unexpected precedes a rout, with Mouse fleeing the park. Myers waits until the next scene to add that Mouse broke the artificial foot.

See also **betrayal, juvenile crime, vengeance, violence**

• *Further Reading*

Myers, Walter Dean. *Fallen Angels.* New York: Scholastic, 1988
____. *The Mouse Rap.* New York: HarperCollins, 1990.
____. *Sweet Illusions.* New York: Teachers and Writers Collaborative, 1986.
Smith, Karen Patricia, ed. *African-American Voices in Young Adult Literature: Tradition, Transition, Transformation.* Lanham, Md.: Scarecrow, 1994.

Vietnam War

Like many Americans, Walter Dean Myers had a personal stake in the Vietnam War after his younger brother, Thomas Wayne "Sonny" Myers, emulated the author by joining the military. In 1968, before age 21, Sonny died in combat shortly after deployment. For two decades, the author incubated his thoughts and emotions about the waste of young lives in war. He approached the subject tentatively in "Bubba," a short story of racism and loss published in the November 1972 issue of *Essence*. The motif of a youth trapped in an old man's war recurs in *The Nicholas Factor* (1983), a spy thriller set on a college campus in Santa Barbara, California. On the issue of combat slaughter, Marlin Wilkes, the founder and chairman of the Crusade Society, acknowledges, "We had kids dying in Korea and Vietnam who had never heard of those places until a few weeks before they died there" (Myers, 1983, 18–19). The poignance and injustice of wasted lives continued to goad Myers in later writings.

Myers's masterwork, *Fallen Angels* (1988), places a contemplative Sonny character, Richard "Richie" Perry, in the war at a crucial point of his teen years. His motives are noble — a way to earn money for his alcoholic mother and his little brother Kenny and to acquire training that he is too poor to obtain from college. In compelling narrative, the author describes an institutional blunder that sends Perry to combat despite a knee injury from playing basketball. The value of camaraderie and self-preservation advance his understanding of manhood.

In 1992, Myers wrote *A Place Called Heartbreak: A Story of Vietnam* about the wartime captivity of Colonel Fred V. Cherry, an Air Force officer who became America's first black prisoner of war. The enemy downed his F-105 jet bomber outside Hanoi on October 22, 1965, on Cherry's return to North Vietnam from Takhli Air Force Base in Thailand. After ejecting from his plane, he remained in enemy hands seven years and four months until February 12, 1973, a period that saw the rise of heavyweight boxing champ Muhammad Ali as a black hero. In the book's introduction, editor Alex Haley remarks on the public response to combat: "I couldn't help but notice how some journalists reported the war as if *it* was a sporting event" (Myers, 1992, n.p.).

The narrative describes the terrors of protracted incarceration among brutal staff. In enemy hands, a prisoner's sense of healthy competition quickly gives place to fear of torture or death from barbaric medical treatments and multiple surgeries on a broken ankle, shoulder, and rib. At Hoa Lo Prison, the infamous Hanoi Hilton, Cherry endures protracted torment in a room called Heartbreak. The misery continues at Cu Loc Prison, dubbed "the Zoo." To enticements to turn against white Americans, Cherry retorts, "I am black ... *And* I am American" (*ibid.*, 43). At the end of his ordeal, he admits, "War is a miserable thing" (*ibid.*, 64).

In a seriocomic teen novel *Darnell Rock Reporting* (1994), Myers broaches the problem of aimlessness and defeat mong Vietnam veterans. The title character, who takes an interest in homelessness, meets Sweeby Jones, a 51-year-old street wanderer who fought in the war with Sidney Jones, Darnell's father. Sidney relates a humorous incident at Cu Chi when Sweeby sang opera into a tunnel and forced a Viet Cong soldier to surrender. With a winner's disdain for a loser, Sidney sneers, "Anybody can learn how to be a failure" (Myers, 1994, 54). Rather than dismiss Sweeby as hopeless, Darnell proposes a garden on the old basketball court where the homeless can grow vegetables. Myers expresses Darnell's idealism in simple terms, "[The homeless] feel better when they can help themselves" (*ibid.*, 76).

Myers returned to issues of the Vietnam War with a brief comment in *The Beast* (2003) and with an anti-war picture book, *Patrol: An American Soldier in Vietnam* (2003), a succinct tone poem on the mind webs that entangle youths on both sides of the conflict. In *The Beast*, a chance comment on a train from New York City to New Haven, Connecticut, simplifies the struggle in Vietnam as a need for peasant education. The unnamed man states, "The Vietnamese were struggling to survive. That's your basic cause for all war" (Myers, 2003, 154). In the picture book, the author's depictions of a black soldier contrast his movements in elegant, lush jungle with his search for a hidden enemy. The text enhances terror with the soldier's sweaty body, unshed tears, letters home, and shadows that cause him to shoot at nothing. Giving the narrative universality and a sense of family tradition is the idea of sheltering under "a tree older than my grandfather" (Myers, 12). Contrasting mental images of family are exploding grenades and overhead bombing, which rumbles and spreads mechanized extinction below. Myers expands on family with close-ups of the enemy—elderly men and women and babies. The brief work closes on emotional exhaustion, a mind fatigue that bodes ill for the young American's spiritual health.

• *Further Reading*

Chance, Rosemary, Teri Lesesne, and Lois Buckman. "And the Winner Is ... : A Teleconference with Walter Dean Myers," *Journal of Reading* 38, no. 3 (November 1994): 246–249.

Gearan, Jay. "School Assignment Becomes Quest for Family History," Worcester, Mass., *Telegram & Gazette* (28 May 2000): 1.

Gray, Jerry. "'He Knows I Have Come to Kill Him': A Young Soldier Meets the Enemy in Vietnam, and Discovers an Unsettling Truth," *New York Times Book Review*107, no. 40 (19 May 2002): 35.

Myers, Walter Dean. *The Beast*. New York: Scholastic, 2003.

_____. *Darnell Rock Reporting*. New York: Delacorte, 1994.

_____. *The Nicholas Factor*. New York: Viking, 1983.

_____. *Patrol: An American Soldier in Vietnam*. New York: HarperCollins, 2003.

_____. *A Place Called Heartbreak: A Story of Vietnam*. Austin, Tex.: Raintree, 1992.

"Novel Depicts Black Soldier in Vietnam," [Portland, Ore.] *Skanner* 13, no. 38 (22 June 1988): 7.

violence

Walter Dean Myers earns respect for literary depictions of violence, especially in the lives of teenagers, such as Greg Ridley in "The Treasure of Lemon Brown" (1983), Steve Harmon in *Monster: A Novel* (1999), Leonard "Len" Gray, Carla Evans, and Cameron Porter in *Shooter* (2004), and the tender youth he describes in the poem "Wolf Song" (2005). In his early writings, the author carefully separates violence from innocence. The year that he earned recognition as a children's author for

Where Does the Day Go? (1969), he wrote for *Negro Digest* an adult vengeance tale, "How Long Is Forever?" (1969). Enmeshed in a prison scenario, Moses, the protagonist, yearns for parole while holding at bay the sadist Jenkins, a guard who lacerates and emasculates with crude remarks. After the guard indicates his intent to rape Moses, the troubled inmate loses control and pummels Jenkins beyond death. Similarly disturbing, Myers's story "Dark Side of the Moon," published in the fall 1971 issue of *Black Creation*, follows Augie, a troubled teen, from masturbating over fantasies of Sheila to raping and strangling her on an apartment roof. Unlike Moses, who commits violence after daily goading, Augie loses himself in a spiral of violence that targets a prostitute, a subway bum, and an old lady walking her dog. Myers's immersion in the psychology of violence follows his study with John Oliver Killens, organizer of the Harlem Writers Guild, who helped Myers develop his writing into a creative art.

In much of his canon, Myers has juxtaposed art and violence, particularly in the illustrated beast fables *Mr. Monkey and the Gotcha Bird* (1984) and *How Mr. Monkey Saw the Whole World* (1996), two storybook lessons in the need for guile in small, weak creatures. In an essay for *Black Scholar*, "Gordon Parks: John Henry with a Camera" (1976), Myers mused on the privations and struggles of blacks who lived under the rule of Jim Crow. His thoughts turned to people who endured desperate situations and who still took time to write songs and paint pictures. Myers summarized Parks's observation on the resilience of creativity: "You last longer with art than with a gun or a knife" (Myers, 1976, 30).

Myers creates fictional milieus in which urban violence is an everyday companion, such as the mugging of two Peruvian street beggars, aged ten and twelve, in "The Vision of Felipe" (1978). Daniel reacts to the soldier with murderous anger: "I'd shoot him a million times. Rat-tat-tat-at-at-tat. And right through his heart" (Myers, 1978, 4). In the social novel *It All Ain't for Nothin'* (1978), violence becomes a way of life for 12-year-old Tippy, who passes from the care of a nurturing grandmother, Carrie Brown, to Lonnie, the boy's birth father. Dodging kicks to the stomach and blows to the head, the boy lives in the shadows of his father's unpredictable outrages. When violence escalates to forced participation in thefts, Tippy witnesses the slow death of Bubba, a gang member shot in a foiled street robbery of a liquor store owner at a bank night-drop. In an act of self-preservation, the boy turns his father and his gang over to police and retreats to the care of Edna and Roland Sylvester, a normal couple who offer stable foster care.

Throughout his career Myers has warned readers that terrible ends can await misguided and short-sighted characters who toy with violence. A model of the author's motif is Coach Calvin F. "Spider" Jones, the failed basketball star in *Hoops: A Novel* (1981) who loses his reputation after a National Basketball Association point-shaving scandal. To his credit, Jones challenges racketeers during the Tournament of Champions, when he refuses to throw a game by leading his team to a televised win. Cal's bloody death in the locker room from a retaliatory stabbing impresses on player Lonnie Jackson that professional criminals compound gambling felonies by murdering Cal in front of an arena filled with witnesses. In *Motown and Didi: A Love Story* (1984), Didi risks retaliation from drug dealers by informing on them to police and surviving a rooftop assault after Motown intervenes. Didi's brother gorges on heroin from Touchy, his supplier, and dies of an overdose. That same year, Myers used Ray as a foil for Lonnie Jackson, the scholarship basketball player in *The Outside Shot* (1984). Ray's failure to succeed in athletics ends in a suicidal shooting, a pathetic choice of self-destruction as an antidote to disappointment.

Wartime carnage forms the dramatic basis of *Fallen Angels* (1988), in which antihero Richard "Richie" Perry faces deployment to a hot war zone in Vietnam. Myers introduces destruction gradually, beginning with chopper flights above the fighting before plunging the rookies from Alpha Company of the 22nd Replacement Company into personal encounters with firefights. Contributing to terror are air drops of napalm, a gel form of gasoline, and of white phosphorus, a corrosive powder that eats away flesh of the men of First Platoon, whom Perry's squad accidentally targets. The tagging of men too far gone to save and the zipping of 15 corpses into body bags familiarizes the greenies with the fragility of human life.

Myers stresses the indelible memories of killing in flashbacks that haunt Richie. After a patrol retrieves the corpse of a Viet Cong, Richie muses, "I didn't want to see some of the things I was seeing" (Myers, 1988, 81). To cope with terror and shock, he debates whether combat experiences are real or fantasy. The image of the slain man returns that afternoon, causing Richie to perceive the enemy as a human being, a member of a family. During a pacification mission to a hamlet, Richie realizes that the youngest Vietnamese children have known only chaos and murder all their lives. Interaction with Asians as people rather than as enemies limits the urge for vengeance in Richie. Myers attests to the overriding humanity in Richie, a belief system that will serve him well in adaptation to civilian life.

Empowering the untried soldiers to kill is evidence that the Viet Cong torture American POWs by tying them to trees and extracting their entrails. Another boost to the gung-ho spirit is a rumor that General William Westmoreland, commander of ground troops, wants Americans to inflict higher VC body counts, a suggestion of political manipulation of the news media to prove that the U.S. is succeeding. After a month of fighting, Perry undergoes treatment for multiple shrapnel wounds, but the recovery time sidelines him only briefly. By January, he returns to war with a greater appreciation of his mission than he originally brought to Vietnam. Myers reprised the terrors and random violence of war in *A Place Called Heartbreak: A Story of Vietnam* (1992), a young adult biography honoring the courage of Colonel Fred V. Cherry, the first black prisoner of war of the Vietnam War.

In 1999, Myers returned to soldiery in *My Name Is America: The Journal of Scott Pendleton Collins, a WWII Soldier, Normandy, France, 1944*, a novelized biography that begins with the carnage of D-Day. The slaughter is so severe that 17-year-old Scott chooses not to think about the bodies that clog the shore and litter the landscape. Hightower, an avid infantryman, brags that Hitler "thought he could walk over the United States the way he walked over Poland and the Netherlands" (Myers, 1999, 38). Scott's friend Bobby Joe jokes about the situation outside Couvains, France: "If I ran right into myself I'd shoot me two or three times before I said hello" (*ibid.*, 40). Scott, who is neither a boaster nor a joker, summarizes the violent ends of combat from a personal perspective: "It's all meant to kill you. That's why everybody is over here: they want to kill me" (*ibid.*, 43). He reserves pity for himself and wonders how he has managed to survive. Contributing to the surreal experience of hovering death are signs of normalcy — the sight of a woman calmly hanging out the wash, a newspaper article about George Burns and Gracie Allen, and a platoon marching to a Glenn Miller tune from a radio.

The upsurge of violence invests many of Myers's urban settings. In a cautionary flashback, the author reveals moral corruption in the conscience of Steve Harmon, the protagonist of *Monster: A Novel* (1999). Critic Debbie Carton, a reviewer for *Booklist*, calls Steve "an intriguingly sympathetic but flawed" 16-year-old (Carton, 1999, 1587). The boy remembers tossing a rock in the park at age twelve, striking a female passerby. Instead of apologizing for an unintentional rock throw that glanced off a lamppost, he blamed Tony, his companion. The imbroglio with the woman's date caused Tony to fantasize vengeance with an uzi, a response that John A. Staunton, a critic for the *Journal of Adolescent & Adult Literacy*, calls the "culture of male toughness," the breeding ground of gangs and random violence (Staunton, 2002, 792). Myers uses the episode to reveal the beginnings of Steve's callousness in his preteens. A second flashback pictures Steve with James King on 141st Street in Harlem discussing a "getover" with Peaches and Johnny, who consider robbing an illegal alien. Both episodes dramatize the pattern of strong against weak, the basis of macho posturing.

The following year, Myers reprised urban barbarism in a children's picture book, *The Blues of Flats Brown* (2000). In the opening scenes, junkyard owner A. J. Grubbs forces his elderly, arthritic dog Caleb to fight a bulldog as a form of human entertainment. The story depicts Caleb and his friend Flats as runaways from a situation that can get them killed. To Flats's question about A. J.'s meanness, Caleb surmises that the owner deteriorates morally from living around junk. Caleb proposes that A. J. is "Just a throwed away man" (Myers, 2000, n.p.). When A. J. returns to his dogs' lives, the two "hot pawed it out the front door" after Caleb bites his cruel owner on the leg (*ibid.*). The action attests to desperation as a cause of violence, the same motivation that keeps soldiers alive in combat.

Myers choreographs neighborhood violence as though it were a structured dance with each participant playing an assigned role. In the story "Big Joe's Funeral" in *145th Street: Short Stories* (2000), the arrival of cops to stop Cassie's husband from beating her seems almost routine for the community. The violence ends with his arrest, his little girls crying in the street, and Cassie perpetuating the cycle of spousal abuse by borrowing bail money to retrieve him from jail. More chilling than husband-wife fights is gang violence. The patterned action, like knights battling in the lists, accords members a reputation for toughness in protecting their reputation and territory. In the story "Monkeyman," Fee comes directly to the point in a discussion of the danger the Tigros pose to the title character: a gun is "the only thing they respect" (Myers, 2000, 77). Like the rumble scenes in Irving Shulman's *West Side Story* (1961), the students in the story go through the motions of anticipating and talking up a face-off that the Tigros predict in graffiti resembling wanted posters. At a formal duel, Clean relies on the false impression that he once belonged to the Crips in Los Angeles. Because Clean's challenge to Monkeyman comes to nothing, a gang assassin stabs

Monkeyman in the back. The vicious blow satisfies the cycle of slaughter by putting the victim in the hospital for three weeks while certifying to the neighborhood that the Tigros are a sincere threat to their detractors.

Myers zeroes in on weapons as a source of confidence to city-dwellers. In *The Beast* (2003), he describes a disgruntled customer at a diner complaining about underdone sausages. To his threat to leave without paying, the clerk at the register flashes a shotgun, a visual retort that forces the customer to pay and leave in a huff. The protagonist, 17-year-old Anthony "Spoon" Witherspoon, realizes from the clerk's casual gesture and from the cynicism of police and nurses in an emergency room across from the diner that Harlem has changed in the five months Spoon has been in school at Wallingford Academy in Connecticut. Worsening his holiday on home turf is a burst of gunfire and a flash of badges from investigating police as they handcuff Leon and haul him away. Spoon's friend Scott jokes, "You're out of the 'hood two days and you forget the routine" (Myers, *Beast*, 76).

After visiting Columbine High School following the student shooting-suicide, Myers concluded that "the problem with so many young people is that violence gets to be a resource. When nothing else works for you, violence always does, and you're always drawn to it" (Rochman, 2000, 1101). He exhibits fantasy gunplay in *The Dream Bearer* (2003), in which 17-year-old Tyrone Curry predicts that his paranoid father Reuben will die from a bullet fired by "somebody ... that don't care if he's crazy" (Myers, *Dream*, 17). Tyrone inadvertently predicts retribution in his own life after he moves from home to the streets and tries to survive among despicable companions. In *Here in Harlem: Poems in Many Voices* (2004), the author creates voices to describe the deadly attraction of guns and knives as easy solutions to daily problems. An artist, Reuben Mills, pictures a black portrait tinged orange from "reflections on a switch-blade knife" (Myers, 2004, 27). Speaking through undertaker J. Milton Brooks, Myers regrets the tragedy of teenagers readied for coffins and burial. Without success, Brooks tries to shut his eyes to "old men shuffling children to the grave" (*ibid.*, 18).

See also **Leonard Gray, Steve Harmon, juvenile crime, military, *Monster: A Novel*, Cameron Porter, *Shooter*, vengeance, victimization**

• *Further Reading*

Carton, Debbie. "Review: *Monster*," *Booklist* 95, no. 17 (1 May, 1999): 1587.
Myers, Walter Dean. *The Beast*. New York: Scholastic, 2003.
_____. *The Blues of Flats Brown*. New York: Holiday House, 2000.
_____. *The Dream Bearer*. New York: Amistad, 2003.
_____. *Fallen Angels*. New York: Scholastic, 1988.
_____. "Gordon Parks: John Henry with a Camera," *Black Scholar* 7, no. 5 (1976): 27–30.
_____. *Here in Harlem: Poems in Many Voices*. New York: Holiday House, 2004.
_____. *My Name Is America: The Journal of Scott Pendleton Collins, a WWII Soldier, Normandy, France, 1944*. New York: Scholastic, 1999.
_____. *145th Street: Short Stories*. New York: Delacorte, 2000.
_____. "The Vision of Felipe," *Black Scholar* (November-December 1978): 2–9.
Rochman, Hazel. "Interview," *Booklist* 96, no. 12 (15 February 2000): 1101.
Staunton, John A. "Review: *Monster: A Novel*," *Journal of Adolescent & Adult Literacy* 45, no. 8 (May 2002): 791–793.

wisdom

Myers comments verbally and in print on his admiration for role models and for useful advice, for example, a grandfather's value to youth in "Jeremiah's Song" (1987) and a chance meeting with a homeless musician in "The Treasure of Lemon Brown" (1983), in which 14-year-old Greg Ridley learns to treasure the example of his stern father. In the encomium "Gordon Parks: John Henry with a Camera" (1976), which Myers wrote for *Black Scholar*, the text honors a real source of wisdom. The author concentrates on aspects of excellence in Parks's multifaceted career. In a personal interview with his subject, Myers savored thought-provoking statements, such as Parks's insistance that "If you use the best of you, you can survive the worst of you" (Myers, 1976, 30). Myers paused on a nugget of wisdom that a would-be artist should treasure: "History doesn't judge you on your excuses, but on your accomplishments" (*ibid.*, 28). The essay applies the advice to the generation of black children who see Parks's photos and films and who read his poems with pride that they are the work of a black man.

Myers expresses a similar desire to impact readers with life-affirming art. His works project hope for ghetto youth in mentoring by older men and women, such as the informative father in *Where Does the Day Go?* (1968), Myers's first children's book, and in Lavelle, a balding old man who tends Harlem street kids in *The Beast* (2003). In 1978, Myers chronicled the sequence of events following a grandmother's death in "The Vision of Felipe," an urban story published in *Black Scholar*. Because the main character is orphaned at age ten, his neighbor offers sound advice: "It was always good to leave death behind" (Myers, 1978, 2). The remark corroborates Felipe's belief that he will prosper by leaving Iquitos and journeying the 600 miles southwest to Lima. The boy bears the wisdom of his grandmother, who taught him to eat well and to "see with my heart because my eyes did not love truth" (Myers, 1978, 3).

Myers tailors wisdom for young children. One of his picture books, *The Golden Serpent* (1980), muses on the disparities between a life of giving with a life of luxury. By contrasting Pundabi, a generous savant, with a self-absorbed king, the narrative illustrates how wealth isolates society's top echelon from pockets of suffering and want. The story's mystery derives from the king's discontent and his inability to recognize selfishness as the phantom malaise that haunts his spirit. Pundabi returns to his mountain top pondering his assumption that affluence blinds some people to the soul's need to aid the less fortunate. Rather than force a happily-ever-after conclusion, the narrative leaves to the young reader a universal conundrum, the survival of misery within a contented society, an anomaly that Myers witnessed during his childhood in Harlem.

The author is skilled at manipulating the conventions of various genres to suit the expression of good advice to the young. In 1981, he composed a medieval quest tale, *The Legend of Tarik*, which pairs the young survivor in the title with a wise duo—the aged warrior-priest Ovolli Docao and the blind teacher Nongo, a native of Meroe, Sudan. Through nested fables, Nongo readies Tarik to avenge the deaths of his family. In the seriocomic novel *Won't Know Till I Get There* (1982), Steve Perry depends on his affable mother, Jessica Perry, for guidance in the matter of adopting a foster son, 13-year-old Earl Goins. With a smile, she expresses an uplifting aside: "That we're not machines. None of us. We can't just plug in the facts and come out with nice, neat answers" (Myers, 1982, 114). Her wise acceptance of human uniqueness enables the family to love Earl and to welcome him into the family.

The pairing of mentor with naif functions well in Myers's ventures into other human dramas. In the young adult spy thriller *The Nicholas Factor* (1983), protagonist Gerald McQuillen works for John Martens, an investigator for the National Security Agency who provides money and advice on appearing innocent while making useful photos. As Gerald sets off for Peru, Martens comments on fear: "Panic is your brain telling your body that it's in a whole lot of trouble" (Myers, 1983, 60). The author also contributed to children's wisdom lore two worthy beast fables, *Mr. Monkey and the Gotcha Bird* (1984) and *How Mr. Monkey Saw the Whole World* (1996). In both jungle stories, the innate wisdom of the weak generates guile to protect scrawny Mr. Monkey against predators who threaten his survival. Like the Br'er Rabbit cautionary and trickster tales of Joel Chandler Harris, Myers's animal stories characterizes savvy as the only solution to a battle pitting weak against strong.

Myers is cautious about overstating the qualities of the wise. In *Hoops: A Novel* (1981), he establishes a coach-player relationship between Coach Calvin "Spider" Jones and 17-year-old Lonnie Jackson, a rising sports star in need of guidance. Myers profits from Cal's shame and self-destructive drinking to illustrate that grown men suffer the consequences of their youthful indiscretions. Because Cal gradually discloses his talents and failures to Lonnie, the man keeps the youth interested. Because Lonnie has much to learn about channeling his physical acumen toward success, Cal relays compact adages rather than lengthy sermons. To Lonnie's flirtation with a café clerk, Cal replies, "People see in you what they need. … You got to be what *you* need" (Myers, 1981, 102). By rationing out wisdom in small doses, he teases Lonnie's mind with pithy thoughts that require mental incubation before they benefit his behavior and self-image. In *The Outside Shot* (1984), the sequel to *Hoops*, Lonnie admits that, at a low point in his youth, Earl "Sweet Man" Jones had counseled him to give up self-pity and take control of his game and his life. Lonnie admits that wise counsel was painful, but therapeutic, a conclusion that Myers cultivates in later teen fiction.

Wisdom flows around anti-hero Richard "Richie" Perry, one of Myers's most fully realized characters. In *Fallen Angels* (1988), a sudden deployment of the rookie infantryman from camp in Massachusetts to Tan Son Nhut, Vietnam, plunges him into the madness of a war zone. Myers describes by-the-book officers as humane, but fallible sources of guidance and indicates that obedience without question saves Perry and other greenies from peril. At significant moments in his maturation from Harlem teenager to soldier, he seeks enlightenment. From Lieutenant Carroll, he receives a prayerful acknowledgement of fear as a normal reaction to carnage. From Father Santora, a war virgin who remains behind the firing line to administer religious counsel, Perry rejects a dry ritual prayer. During emotional unrest on patrol outside Chu Lai, Perry reverts unexpectedly to the words of a classroom teacher, Mrs. Liebow, who encouraged him to grasp life and live it to the full. In her opinion, the willingness to reach for excellence "separated heroes from humans" (Myers,

1988, 36). For his own reasons, Myers opts to honor the teaching profession over organized religion as a pragmatic source of strength and direction.

The narrative implications of age and experience in women connects them with an acquired intuition about human emotion, a motif that echoes the author's respect for the counsel of Florence Dean, his beloved foster mother. In *Crystal* (1987), the author pairs the 16-year-old title character with 77-year-old Sister Gibbs, a pillar of Brooklyn's Victory Tabernacle. Gibbs advises Crystal on relying on scripture: "You can't read the Bible and not know how to live your life" (Myers, 1987, 30). Similarly, Jimmy Little receives spiritual help from Miss Mackenzie, an old friend of his father, Cephus "Crab" Little, in *Somewhere in the Darkness* (1992). When hope appears to ebb for Crab, the elderly woman summons divine aid and declares, "What God can't do ain't worth doing" (Myers, 1992, 163). Myers discloses insight into a life of hard times in Grandma Dolly, the matriarch of Live Oaks Plantation in *The Glory Field* (1994). On the night that planter Manigault Lewis orders Lem Lewis to be tied to a tree in the woods as punishment for running away, Dolly looks out for the tender feelings of Lizzy, a foster child of the Lewis family who tries to tiptoe out at night to visit Lem. Dolly warns Lizzy that women's lives are filled with good-byes. The advice summarizes the hard truth of women's bondage, which forces them to breed children for the auction block, the subject of Toni Morrison's *Beloved* (1987). In a subsequent scene of *The Glory Field*, Saran, Lizzy's foster mother, eases some of the fear of running away by urging Lizzy to trust in God and intuition and to remember that "death comes when it wants to" (Myers, 1994, 50).

The role of mentors permeates Myers's later fiction with wisdom from a variety of sources and stances. In a salute to storytelling in *The Story of the Three Kingdoms* (1995), the author declares that in "stories could be found wisdom and in wisdom, strength" (Myers, 1995, n.p.). In realistic mode, Greg "Slam" Harris, protagonist of *Slam!* (1996), takes advice from the assistant coach and from his Grandma Ellie. The former encourages mature thinking about team membership; Grandma reminds Slam that going to school is a privilege that black people have not always enjoyed. Another urban adviser, George Sawicki, teacher of 16-year-old protagonist Steve Harmon in *Monster: A Novel* (1999), influences the boy for three years during film workshops at Stuyvesant High School. At Steve's trial for felony robbery and murder, Sawicki unhesitatingly characterizes his student as honest. George's faith in Steve illustrates the trust that mentors place in youth, even foolish young men like Steve.

Myers advocates an informal style of elder-to-youth tutelage. In *Handbook for Boys: A Novel* (2002), three teenage males— Jimmy Lynch, Kevin, and Ernesto—come under the advice and encouragement of 68-year-old Duke Wilson, Edward "Cap" Mills, and Claudio "Mister M" Morales at Duke's Barber Shop in Harlem. As court remands, the boys choose to undergo a version of "scared straight" rather than serve time at a juvenile hall. They have an opportunity to perform useful work sweeping, dusting, and hanging pictures while learning from their elders how to survive and flourish in the real world. Duke speaks from experience of racial inequity in his own youth, when "you had to take what opportunities you could find" (Myers, 2002, 9). The statement illustrates his pragmatism, which is devoid of bitterness and self pity.

At novel's end, Duke's example produces the next generation of mentorship in Jimmy, who encourages Ernesto to listen and learn.

In *The Dream Bearer* (2003), a story of rage and compassion, Myers supplies 12-year-old David Curry with one of the author's mystic seers, the 300-year-old mentor, "Mr. Moses" Littlejohn. The old man's name implies gravity and godliness as well as humility. Moses offers flashes of insight into human behavior through conversation with David and his friend Loren. To Loren's implication that Moses is a wino, the old man retorts, "You looking, boy, but you ain't seeing," a suggestion for the unobservant and hasty judges (Myers, 2003, 28). Moses explains the value of dreams in uplifting the spirit and directing the self toward fulfillment. His explanation of thwarted hopes helps David understand his father's frustrations. In the falling action, David illustrates the reciprocal nature of wisdom in his aid to Moses, who feebly carries his luggage on the next leg of his journey.

See also **"Mr. Moses" Littlejohn, women**

• *Further Reading*

Myers, Walter Dean. *Crystal.* New York: Viking Kestrel, 1987.
_____. *The Dream Bearer.* New York: Amistad, 2003.
_____. *Fallen Angels.* New York: Scholastic, 1988.
_____. *The Glory Field.* New York: Scholastic, 1994.
_____. "Gordon Parks: John Henry with a Camera," *Black Scholar* 7, no. 5 (1976): 27–30.
_____. *Handbook for Boys: A Novel.* New York: Amistad, 2002.
_____. *Hoops.* New York: Delacorte, 1981.
_____. *The Nicholas Factor.* New York: Viking, 1983.
_____. *Somewhere in the Darkness.* New York: Scholastic, 1992.
_____. *The Story of the Three Kingdoms.* New York: HarperCollins, 1995.
_____. "The Vision of Felipe," *Black Scholar* (November-December 1978): 2–9.
_____. *Won't Know Till I Get There.* New York: Viking, 1982.
Roback, Diane. "Review: *Handbook for Boys: A Novel,*" *Publishers Weekly* 249, no. 16 (22 April 2002)" 70–71.
Smith, Karen Patricia, ed. *African-American Voices in Young Adult Literature: Tradition, Transition, Transformation.* Lanham, Md.: Scarecrow Press, 1994.

women

Myers tends to present female characters in a fair light, from the beloved Peruvian grandmother in "The Vision of Felipe" (1978), the hip-strutting, corn-rowed sisters in *Harlem: A Poem* (1997), and the unnamed mother who brings a bible to her son Steve's jail cell in *Monster: A Novel* (1999) to the photos in *Angel to Angel: A Mother's Gift of Love* (1998), a loving picture book of maternity. In realistic mode, he pictures the anguished Evelyn Curry, wife of a mentally ill husband in *The Dream Bearer* (2003) and the grieving mother in *Here in Harlem: Poems in Many Voices* (2004) who responds to the death of her son by "[turning] her heart so it read closed on/Both sides" (Myers, 2004, 16). The variances in maternal style and commitment ingather a broad range of women for maximum validation of the many faces of womanhood.

In the introduction to his volume of black history, *Now Is Your Time! The*

African-American Struggle for Freedom (1991), the author describes the diminution of slave women in the pet-like names Binkey, Minty, Blind Jenny, and Big Lucy and Little Lucy. Of Eve, the property of Louis Manigault at Gowerie plantation near Savannah, an account book devalues her in terms of dollars: "Old, Quite old, cost nothing" (Myers, 1991, 80). The author lauds "womenfolk" for their quilting, narratives, art, music, and possessiveness of children, whom slave owners could mistreat or sell at their whim (*ibid.*, x). In reference to Maria Perkins, a slave in Charlottesville, Virginia, Myers pities the sale of her son Albert, which she reports to her husband Richard in a letter. The author's outrage is apparent in his commentary: "It is a situation that no kind treatment can assuage, a wound of the soul that will never heal" (*ibid.*, 75).

Myers, who was fostered in boyhood by Florence Dean, honors women who rear needy children, for example, Jessica Perry in *Won't Know Till I Get There* (1982), who adds juvenile delinquent, 13-year-old Earl Goins, to her family. The role of a grandmother parenting a young grandson dominates the social novel *It Ain't All for Nothin'* (1978). Tippy, the 12-year-old narrator, opens chapter one with an encomium to 69-year-old Grandma Carrie Brown, a large, but feeble woman who works when she is able. Her credo establishes her importance to the boy's self-image: "[When] you didn't have a man to hold on to, you had to reach inside yourself and find something strong" (Myers, 1978, 1). In addition to the work ethic, Carrie teaches her grandson to lean on Jesus through daily prayer, the source of her strength.

Myers's generosity to females grows out of a fundamental humanism he developed in childhood. In *The Nicholas Factor* (1983), the narrative allows 16-year-old Jennifer Wells, a member of the Crusade Society, to erupt in feminist anger that she came to Peru to plan a charity mission "and they ask me do I know shorthand" (Myers, 1983, 66). For two works from the Arrow series, *The Hidden Shrine* (1985) and *Ambush in the Amazon* (1986), the author supplies 17-year-old Chris and 14-year-old Ken Arrow with a working mom, anthropologist Carla Arrow. In *Duel in the Desert* (1986), she has a female colleague, Dr. Susan Goldsmith, who studies family life on the edge of the Sahara Desert; in *Adventure in Granada* (1985), Carla's in-country contact is another learned female, Profesora Velázquez. Significant to Carla's motherhood in *Ambush in the Amazon* is the introduction of the boys to the Amazon jungle, which they accomplish on their own while she departs for an assignment in Bolivia. The basis of the mother-sons relationship is trust. A parallel to Carla's role in the adventure novella is 14-year-old Tarija, the Quechuan translator who unravels the mystery of a hairy, vicious *monstruo* that threatens their lives (Myers, 1986, 10). The importance of the two females to Chris and Ken's adventure illustrates the value of education to women, even in a patriarchal society like the isolated village of Los Cauchos.

More positive is Myers's response to girls who survive teen pregnancy and single motherhood in *Sweet Illusions* (1986). In the final chapter, he salutes Gloria Stokes Turner, who directs an outreach to pregnant teens. Because she makes the hard decision to surrender her child for adoption and to return to school, Gloria exemplifies the fight in Myers's female characters who don't let a costly mistake ruin their chances for self-fulfillment. The theme recurs in the young adult novel *Crystal* (1987), in which the glamour of limo rides and expensive outfits lures 16-year-old model Crystal Brown from the right thinking advocated by 77-year-old Sister Gibbs. The elderly woman's Christian principles shield Crystal at a difficult pass in her professional career when casual sex is the expected payback from a young would-be actor to a talent packager. Myers pictures Crystal fleeing the hospital, where a colleague kills herself rather than pursue a soul-damaging career. The womanly wisdom that Crystal absorbs in girlhood holds steady as she rejects a movie contract rather than accept exploitation.

A year later, when Myers wrote *Me, Mop, and the Moondance Kid* (1988), he gave the role of family organizer to the mother of Tommy "T. J." Jackson. For Family Discussion Day, she requires that everybody listen for five minutes to another family member's contribution. For her own remarks, she introduces the foods that comprise a nourishing diet, but she adds to the other people at the dinner table, "You can talk about anything you want.... Even if it doesn't exactly fit our topic" (Myers, *Me, Mop*, 27). When her husband chastises T. J. for giving in to pain during a baseball game, the mother reminds him, "Winning or losing a game of Little League baseball isn't all that important," a salient observation to a sports-crazed father who should know better (*ibid.*, 41).

The author depicts women as sources of comfort and succor. He accords an honorable military death to medic Judy Duncan, a minor character in his Vietnam War novel *Fallen Angels* (1988). On infantryman Richard "Richie" Perry's first pacification mission to a Vietnamese village, he looks at the creased, withered faces of women whose "dark, life-weary eyes ... had seen everything" (Myers, *Fallen*, 111). Unnamed comforters— a North Vietnamese nurse and two teenage domestics— offer fresh fruit to prisoner of war Colonel Fred V. Cherry in *A Place Called Heartbreak: A Story of Vietnam* (1992). Their acts of mercy ease his pain from torture and multiple surgeries on a broken ankle, shoulder, and ribs. In *Now Is Your Time! The African-American Struggle for Freedom*, Myers extols not only his great grandmother Dolly Dennis but also black heroes journalist Ida B. Wells, a campaigner against lynching, and Meta Vaux Warrick, a noted sculptor of black themes. In *The Beast* (2003), 17-year-old protagonist Anthony "Spoon" Witherspoon values a chance acquaintance with Monica, a skinny crack user who pushes aside a muscular attendant at a drug parlor to help Spoon rescue Gabriela "Gabi" Godoy, his Dominican girlfriend. In these instances, the author respects female strengths for their resilience against human trauma.

The author is especially appreciative of female grace and vigor in Gloria Wiggens, the powerhouse of *The Young Landlords* (1979). She organizes the Action Group to spruce up 356 West 122nd Street, a forlorn building that blights a Harlem neighborhood. To implications that the boys in the group are the only ones who can fix a broken toilet, she retorts "Don't come off telling me about what's women's work and what's men's work" (Myers, 1979, 47). In subsequent scenes, Gloria takes charge of interviewing Jonathan Pender for the job of accountant and attempts to tighten a stripped screw on a bathroom door. When the theme switches to romance, she exhibits more maturity than Paul Williams, who woos her with two words, "You're okay" (*ibid.*, 135). Gloria rephrases his vague compliment with a precise statement of character: "I care for people" (*ibid.*). Myers correctly gauges the maturational differences between male and female teenagers by picturing Gloria as the alpha member of the pair.

The depiction of early female blossoming strengthens *Hoops: A Novel* (1981). The author creates a bright female, Mary-Ann, as a foil for her easily duped older brother Paul. The protagonist, 17-year-old Lonnie Jackson, admires her savvy and admits that "she seemed a lot older in the head" than her brother (Myers, 1981, 95). The normal lag in male maturity dampens his enthusiasm after she suggests marriage. Still boyish about serious matters, Lonnie flees from her as though escaping suffocation. His alliance with Aggie, Cal Jones's ex-wife, links Lonnie to a more experienced female. As she lashes out at Cal for preferring sports over family, she educates Lonnie on serious male misconceptions that women accept the stereotype of the dependent female waiting at home until her man returns. She phrases the philosophy of the independent woman in a song, "Hurry Home, Sweet Daddy," which warns that the man who exploits his woman may lose her (*ibid.*, 137). According to Aggie, self-protection from exploitation and heartbreak is "something black women learn" (*ibid.*).

In *The Outside Shot* (1984), the sequel to *Hoops*, Myers pairs Lonnie Jackson with a new type of female, Sherry Jewett, a competitive track athlete from Milwaukee. From experience with both white and black dates, she refrains from committing herself to intimacy with Lonnie. She extracts wisdom from her mother's advice not to commit to a man because "your one and his one make an easy two" (Myers, 1984, 142). By pursuing a deeper relationship with her, Lonnie develops an adult perspective that he failed to develop in *Hoops*. His ability to admit fear suppresses his former "bad-Harlem-cat act," a mask worn by cocky males (*ibid.*, 178).

Myers perpetuates the image of strength in urban females in later teen novels. In *Motown and Didi: A Love Story* (1984), Didi faces adult decisions involving her father's abandonment of the family, her mother's physical and emotional decline, and her brother Tony's drug use. With firm resolve, she demands that police stop Touchy from selling heroin to her brother. Echoing Didi's blend of tough talk and vulnerability is Jennifer, the romantic interest in *The Nicholas Factor* (1983). Tougher and less honorable is the part of Lucy Featherdip in the evil plots of Catfish Grimes, the villain in *The Righteous Revenge of Artemis Bonner* (1992). Myers allows Artemis to belittle and stereotype women as the weaker sex until Lucy wallops him, bites his ear, and helps Catfish lure the boy into an unfair gun battle. At the end of Myers's Western spoof, Lucy remains in control of the plot by writing Artemis a letter deflating his heroism and once more involving him in the stalking of his Uncle Ugly's killer.

In his presentation of widows and elderly women, Myers tends toward stereotypes of wisdom with age. He explains through Tito Cruz in *Scorpions* (1988) that Puerto Ricans revere the *abuela* (grandmother) as the family matriarch. Mrs. Hicks supports Tito's grandmother as one of a legion of caregivers—the lone females who rear fatherless boys. Distracting Mrs. Hicks from her duty to two fatherless children are her concerns for Randy, her son who is incarcerated for robbery and murder and hospitalized after an inmate stabs him. In *Somewhere in the Darkness* (1992), Jimmy Little returns from a harum-scarum cross-country trek with his father, prison escapee

Cephus "Crab" Little, to the security of Mama Jean, Jimmy's great-hearted legal guardian. A fount of dignity and self-respect, she anchors the boy to rightness as he searches for manhood. Critics find in her acquiescence to Crab's demands for the boy the stereotype of the submissive black female who believes that the father has a greater claim on Jimmy than she. Without challenge to Crab's abrupt reappearance in Jimmy's life, she allows the boy to leave a protected environment with little more than the promise to return if he needs a home.

For *The Glory Field* (1994), Myers evens out a nine-generation family tree with male and female role models. Directly from the West African line of slave Muhammad Bilal comes his granddaughter Dolly, a matriarch who steadies her enslaved family during hard times. The Lewis courage receives vigor and stout-heartedness from Saran, wife of Moses Lewis, who supports Lizzy, another outsider, on her flight north to freedom from Live Oaks Plantation in fictional Curry Island, South Carolina. The Lewis males' penchant for marrying strong women continues through Elijah, Abby, Robert, and Tommy. Simultaneously, the Lewis name gains an entrepreneur in Luvenia Lewis, a Chicago matriarch who establishes Mahogany Beauty Products. Luvenia's success parallels that of a real black entrepreneur, Madame C. J. Walker, the first black female millionaire in American history.

Young girls in Myers's fiction tend to exhibit the good sense of their elders. In *Slam!* (1996), Mtisha helps to steady and sooth Greg "Slam" Harris, who lacks her self-control. After Slam's run-in with Ice, an old friend who has turned to dealing dope, the two exchange blows. Mtisha calls Slam to report that Ice wants to quit the business, but she doubts his sincerity. She comments to Slam, "All you guys are just heartbreaks waiting to happen," a stop-action remark that critic Bill Ott calls the novel's "sobering coda" (Myers, 1996, 264; Ott, 1996, 579). Mtisha's ability to view the future as an adult aids her in winnowing out males who are poor choices for husbands. With a woman's instinct, she supports Slam, the immature youth who shows promise and character.

Myers showcases a variety of female strengths in the collection *145th Street: Short Stories* (2000). In "Monkeyman," the author describes Peaches as a faithful friend; in "Kitty and Mack: A Love Story," Mack's girlfriend possesses the understanding and maturity to wait out his distress over an amputated foot. In the humorous story "Big Joe's Funeral" (2000), Mother Fletcher, who is well over 90 years old, observes Big Joe's fakery and misunderstands LaToya, Peaches, and Squeezie's hand-lettered sign assuring the public that Joe is still alive. Mother Fletcher shouts "Glory, hallelujah!" and asserts, "The flesh fades but the spirit lives on to its eternal reward!" (Myers, 2000, 7). She returns in "A Christmas Story" as the knitter of sweaters for kind police officers. When Officer Bill O'Brien appears at her door on Christmas, she makes a significant point about a white man policing a black neighborhood: "It's good for you to see we have holidays here, too" (*ibid.*, 114). She states her personal creed that she must be ready to provide human goodness, a gesture toward the author's belief in community altruism.

One of Myers's most perceptive images of women occurs in *A Time to Love: Stories from the Old Testament* (2003). He defends Lots's wife for loving beauty and models female bonding in the story of Naomi and her daughters-in-law Orpah and

Ruth. On a long walk home from Moab, the trio bears private burdens. Ruth regrets the death of her husband Mahlon before they produced children. Naomi, bereft of husband, sons, and grandchildren, returns to Bethlehem in grief and want. The importance of males to female well-being takes shape in Naomi's plaint, "I went out full, and the Lord hath brought me home again empty" (Myers, 2003, 60). Her statement characterizes the plight of women in a patriarchal society.

See also **Sarah Forbes Bonetta, parenthood, religion, wisdom**

• *Further Reading*

Hayn, Judith, and Deborah Wherrill. "Female Protagonists in Multicultural Young Adult Literature: Sources and Strategies," *ALAN Review* 24, no. 1 (fall 1996): 1.

Myers, Walter Dean. *Ambush in the Amazon.* New York: Viking Kestrel, 1986.

_____. *Fallen Angels.* New York: Scholastic, 1988.

_____. *Hoops.* New York: Delacorte, 1981.

_____. *Here in Harlem: Poems in Many Voices.* New York: Holiday House, 2004.

_____. *It Ain't All for Nothin'.* New York: Viking, 1978.

_____. *Me, Mop, and the Moondance Kid.* New York: Delacorte, 1988.

_____. *The Nicholas Factor.* New York: Viking, 1983.

_____. *Now Is Your Time! The African-American Struggle for Freedom.* New York: HarperCollins, 1991.

_____. *145th Street: Short Stories.* New York: Delacorte, 2000.

_____. *The Outside Shot.* New York: Delacorte, 1984.

_____. *The Righteous Revenge of Artemis Bonner.* New York: HarperCollins, 1992.

_____. *Slam!* New York: Scholastic, 1996.

_____. *A Time to Love: Stories from the Old Testament.* New York: Scholastic, 2003.

_____. *The Young Landlords.* New York: Viking, 1979.

Ott, Bill. "Review: *Slam!*," *Booklist* 93, no. 6 (15 November 1996): 579.

"Review: *The Dream Bearer*," *Black Issues Book Review* 5, no. 5 (September-October 2003): 70.

West, Mark I. "Harlem Connections: Teaching Walter Dean Myers's *Scorpions* in Conjunction with Paul Laurence Dunbar's *The Sport of the Gods*," *ALAN Review*, 26, no. 2 (winter 1999): 1.

Won't Know Till I Get There

A seriocomic examination of foster parenting and intergenerational relations between teens and retirees, *Won't Know Till I Get There* (1982) extended Walter Dean Myers's streak of award-winning realistic fiction. In one of his early forays into metafiction, he speaks through the tentative, boyish observations of Stephen Gerard "Steve" Perry, who keeps a journal at the prompting of his English teacher. A believer in the student-teacher relationship, the author reflects his guidance by fifth-grade reading instructor Mrs. Conway at Public School 43, ex–Marine Irwin Lasher at Public School 125, ninth-grade teacher Mrs. Finley, and Bonnie Liebow, a beloved inspiration at Stuyvesant High School. From them, he learned to trust the instincts that his pen gleaned from fleeting thoughts.

Myers parlays his choice of an articulate narrator into what Mary M. Burns, a reviewer for *Horn Book*, calls "a contemporary Huckleberry Finn, as Stephen comments wisely and wryly upon society" (Burns, 1982, 415). The remarks reach from the community inward to the turmoil in his own family and his place in it. The writing of candid observations reflects on society's tendency toward stereotyping, a theme that caught the eye of critic Hazel Rochman, a reviewer for *School Library Journal.* In her opinion, the labels "old, Black, female, enemy, delinquent, deserting mother — turn out to be widely differing, surprising and interesting individuals" (Rochman, 1982, 73). The opening of the mind to human possibilities develops into the novel's main strength.

The narrative examines a shift in family structure, which the author lightly compares to the trials of the title character in Charles Dickens's *Oliver Twist* (1839). After the Perrys, Jessica and Richard, accept 13-year-old Earl Goins as a foster son, Steve states his purpose in recording events: "What the journal is about — how come there's four of us now" (Myers, 1982, 2). With a touch of boyish humor, he addresses each entry to TWIMC (Two Whom It May Concern), personalized to Twimsy. Additional examples of wit and nimble commentary include Steve's survey of a social worker's questions, a family visit to the Guggenheim Museum, and his accidentally-on-purpose steaming of a registered letter that reveals confidential data about Earl's criminal record. The humor lightens a situation that threatens the Perry family's stability after they receive into their home a delinquent whom Steve typifies as "King Kong with sneakers" (*ibid.*, 9).

Myers moves quickly to conflict with the arrest of Steve, Earl, and two friends, Hi-Note and Patty Bramwell, for spray-painting on a train the name of an imaginary gang, the Royal Visigoths. In Earl's overview, "I'm in trouble because of what the gang you ain't got didn't do" (*ibid.*, 20). In juvenile court, the judge's choice of community service at Michaux House for Senior Citizens rearranges the teens' priorities by introducing them to people who have already survived faulty choices and their consequences. After young and old break down age barriers, their synergy focuses on saving the center by working in a grocery store deli and by cleaning streets in front of businesses. At a high point in the narrative, Eileen Lardner invests $1,000 in a cleaning serving operated by London Brown, the center's maintenance man. The narrative summarizes one view of success from a newspaper account: "A group of local residents have proved that integration works as they band together to clean up their neighborhood" (*ibid.*, 138).

Myers creates a scene in the falling action that exemplifies the sensitivity of young people. After the Perry family offers adoption to Earl, the boy can barely speak for happiness. Steve describes how his father exploits the good feeling of offering a home to a delinquent: "Sometimes you can take something that seems so simple ... and it ends up not being simple at all" (*ibid.*, 143). The evolving good feeling, over a bumpy trial period of foster parenting, results in a worthy four-member home guaranteed by a judge until Earl reaches manhood. The truism of June Davenport summarizes Earl's gain and his mother's loss: "Human beings choose the way they want to live" (Myers, 1982, 176).

See also **humor**

• *Further Reading*

Burns, Mary M. "Review: *Won't Know Till I Get There,*" *Horn Book* 58 (August 1982): 415.

Edelman, Diane Gersoni. "Review: *Won't Know Till I Get There*," *New York Times Book Review* (13 June 1982): 26–27.
Myers, Walter Dean. *Won't Know Till I Get There*. New York: Viking, 1982.
Rochman, Hazel. "Review: *Won't Know Till I Get There*," *School Library Journal* 28, no. 9 (May 1982): 72–73.

writing

Myers became a writer out of self-defense. Because of a speech defect, he had to suppress his words until he found a suitable outlet. Of the frustration, he explained, "I had an inner life I couldn't share" (Myers, 2005, 14). Solitude encouraged the author to develop his language skills. He confided to Adam Graham, an interviewer from the *Detroit News*, the pleasure of composing: "You can do it in the dark and no one knows. It's not like going out there and playing basketball where everyone's watching you; it's private" (Graham, 2002). He risked being the oddball among his peers by composing poems and stories, an activity he assigns to an alter ego, the failing student and title character in *Darnell Rock Reporting* (1994). According to critic Rosemary Chance, a reviewer for *Emergency Librarian*, in the process of becoming an interviewer for a local newspaper, Darnell, "a boy who hasn't had many successes, learns that he can write and that he can stand up for what he believes" (Chance, 1995, 57). Another reviewer, Brenda B. Little, in a critique for *Book Report*, sums up Darnell's reclamation from do-nothing student to a beneficiary of the "power of the written word" (Little, 1995, 48).

Myers admitted his own apprenticeship in writing: "I spent years doing it on the QT" (Due, 1992, 1C). His motive was a form of empowerment. In an article for May/June 1996 issue of *Instructor* magazine, he explained: "Stories gave me a whole new world, a world which I could control to an extent" (Lewis, 1996, 73). The manipulation of fictional people on the page aided him in understanding the world and in solving problems in his own life. For verisimilitude, he imagined himself in tight situations that he saw "like movies that play in my head," a visual trick that he accords Steve Harmon in *Monster: A Novel* (1999), a powerful metafictional crime novel (*ibid.*).

Contributing to Myers's imaginative scenarios is his ability to abandon adult constraints and become a kid again, a skill that produces gripping realism for a boy confronting death and homelessness in "Gums," anthologized in *We Be Word Sorcerers: Twenty-five Stories by Black Americans* (1973), and furthers jovial, character-rich interaction in *Fast Sam, Cool Clyde, and Stuff* (1975). Another departure from standard writing style is the plotting of poignant vignettes for his history overview, *Now Is Your Time! The African-American Struggle for Freedom* (1991). Preparing the reader for his innovative method is an exuberant introduction in which Myers identifies himself personally and historically with "the joy and the light and the music and the genius and the muscle and the glory of these I write about" (Myers, 1991, x).

In his 1994 Margaret A. Edwards Award Acceptance Speech to the American Library Association annual convention in Miami, the author recalled wondering whether literary interests made him peculiar. He asks himself, "Were there other boys my age who secretly wrote poems and hid them?" (Myers, 1995, 131). More perplexing was his interest in his own Harlem neighborhood above "some European concept" (*ibid.*). Subconsciously, he was following Ernest Hemingway's belief that the best writing evolves from the home territory that the writer knows best. The technique turned Myers into an authority on urban teen fiction.

For *Scholastic Scope*, a popular magazine in high school classes, Myers suggested methods of learning to write. He proposed journal-keeping for life issues that stymy or embarrass young writers. In his first young adult novels, he models journaling as a means of sorting out feelings. In *Won't Know Till I Get There* (1982), Stephen "Steve" Perry keeps a diary that reveals from a son's perspective the tangle of emotions involved in his parents' attempt to adopt a delinquent boy, 13-year-old Earl Goins. On the opening page, Steve accounts for his choice of personal writing by citing his English teacher: "Writing helps [people] bring things together, to see where they fit in life" (Myers, 1982, 1). Myers further elevates journal keeping in *At Her Majesty's Request: An African Princess in Victorian England* (1999), in which he cites passages from Queen Victoria's diary, and in *My Name Is America: The Journal of Joshua Loper, a Black Cowboy, The Chisholm Trail, 1871* (1999), in which the racist trail boss named Captain belittles Joshua's diary as "your scribble book" (Myers, 1999, 16). The text of *My Name Is American: The Journal of Biddy Owens: The Negro Leagues* (2001) derives from a notebook in which the title character summarizes team events for the Birmingham Black Barons. By validating these writings as historic documents, Myers justifies personal composition as a worthy endeavor, whether informal or professional.

A poignant form of composition infuses *Fallen Angels* (1988), Myers's masterwork about young infantrymen fighting the Vietnam War. For verisimilitude, he studied military dispatches from actual firefights and traveled for a month across America on Amtrak to interview people about their impressions of the Vietnam War. In a 1994 interview with Rosemary Chance, Teri Lesesne, and Lois Buckman for the *Journal of Reading*, he recalled, "I sat down with people on street corners, in parks, and in bars, speaking with them about their personal experiences. I got the voices from these people" (Chance, *et al.*, 1994, 247). The person-to-person approach accounts for the humanism in the novel, which negates stereotypes of the brave warrior killing his enemy.

Because the anti-hero, Richard "Richie" Perry, abandons his dream of a college education and the chance to "write like James Baldwin," he chooses military service as an alternative (Myers, 1988, 15). At a terrifying loss of Jenkins to a land mine, Lieutenant Carroll, the 23-year-old platoon leader for Alpha Company of the 22nd Replacement Company, prays that his men accept fear as normal, but that they not let terror debilitate them. The prayer returns to the narrative after Carroll's death from a hit in the armpit. Rather than thoughts of military courage, Perry recalls that Carroll exhibited gentleness to the men, an unusual quality that calms and settles them. At the insistence of Sergeant Simpson, Perry undertakes the necessary condolence letter to Carroll's wife Lois in Hays, Kansas. With simple, yet moving assurance, Perry informs her of her husband's valor and honor. Perry's ability to word the letter illustrates his sensitivity to human traits that elevate fighters above the ongoing destruction. The knack for letters fails him when he words a message to his little brother Kenny. Perry admits, "Writing that I had done a good job killing just didn't work" (*ibid.*, 190).

Also for *Scholastic Scope*, Myers wrote a short story, "The Beast" (2004), an excerpt from the novel *The Beast* (2003). It depicts two old friends, Gabriela "Gabi" Godoy and 17-year-old Anthony "Spoon" Witherspoon, reuniting after Spoon's return for Christmas break from five months at Wallingford, a private school in Connecticut. His observations about Gabi's heroin dependence produces a profitable dialogue about the emotional difficulties that empower "the beast." The author attributes the couple's differences to teen angst, which Gabi combats through poetry: "Teens have so many questions: 'Am I okay? What's my life really about?'" (Myers, 2003, 13). She composes a poem, "Nubian Clouds," that alludes to her mother, a *campesina* (peasant) undergoing chemotherapy for stomach cancer. Gabi's reasoning for composition is personal: "I think it helps, even if you don't come up with answers, at least to begin to organize your thoughts and begin to express your feelings. Any writing, seriously approached, is useful in this respect" (*ibid.*).

In 2004, Myers returned to the metafictional style of *Monster: A Novel* (1999) by incorporating a sociopath's diary with psychological and law enforcement evaluations and media reports in *Shooter* (2004), a teen crime novel. To explain a high school shooting incident similar to that at Columbine High School, Littleton, Colorado, on April 20, 1999, the author describes the swirl of antipathies in the mind of 16-year-old Leonard "Len" Gray, a senior only weeks from graduation. Capping his hostility is a toxic relationship with his father, a former army Ranger and member of the Patriots, a conservative gun club. Len permeates his writing with puns and word play, such as summarize/winterize, the Inconvenience store, Drab Brad (Myers, 2004, 217, 218). To his mother's suggestion that he "lighten up," he sneers, "What should I cut off to make myself lighter? Maybe a leg or an arm?" (*ibid.*, 215). His delusions of maiming and slaying reach murderous proportions in his journal, which ends on the day that he shoots tormentor Brad Williams and kills himself with one shot to the mouth. A tense examination of a diseased mind, the novel concludes with Len's observations in a diary, a catharsis for his persecution complex and for the vengeance he exacts against bullying at school. The verisimilitude of Len's wording earns critical acclaim for prodding young readers to examine the thinking of a sociopath. As Myers explained in a 2001 panel discussion on *Authors on the Web*, "All that's needed is your best and truest voice" (Myers, "YA Grows Up," 2001).

See also **fable, irony, storytelling**

• *Further Reading*

Chance, Rosemary. "Voices from Diverse Cultures," *Emergency Librarian* 22, no. 4 (March/April 1995): 57–58.

_____, Teri Lesesne, and Lois Buckman. "And the Winner Is ... : A Teleconference with Walter Dean Myers," *Journal of Reading* 38, no. 3 (November 1994): 246–249.

Due, Tananarive. "Kids' Books for the Real World," *Miami Herald* (17 February 1992): 1C.

Feder-feitel, Lisa. "Writing About What's Real," *Scholastic Scope* 52, no. 12 (9 February 2004): 14.

Graham, Adam. "Author's Just a Kid at Heart," *Detroit News* (6 May 2002).

Lewis, Valerie. "Meet the Author," *Instructor* 105 (May/June 1996): 72–73.

Little, Brenda B. "Review: *Darnell Rock Reporting*," *Book Report* 13, no.4 (January/February 1995): 48–49.

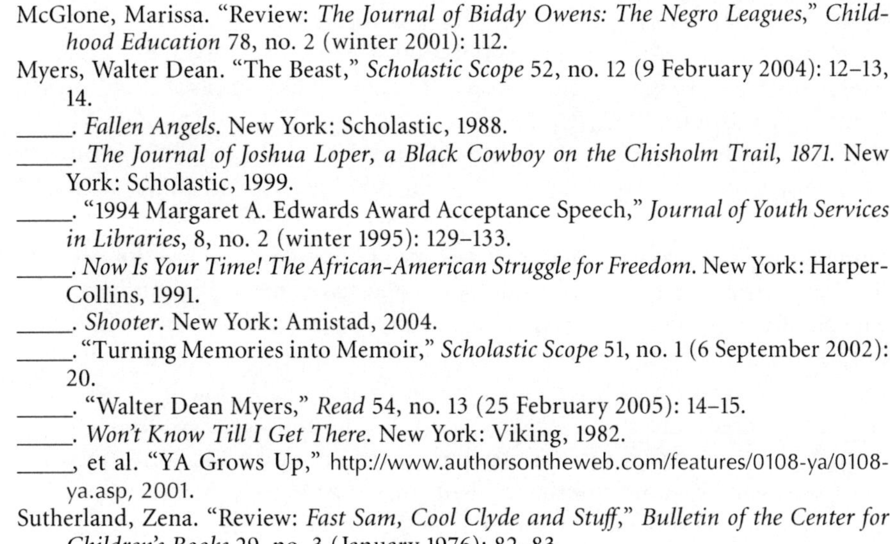

McGlone, Marissa. "Review: *The Journal of Biddy Owens: The Negro Leagues*," *Childhood Education* 78, no. 2 (winter 2001): 112.

Myers, Walter Dean. "The Beast," *Scholastic Scope* 52, no. 12 (9 February 2004): 12–13, 14.

_____. *Fallen Angels*. New York: Scholastic, 1988.

_____. *The Journal of Joshua Loper, a Black Cowboy on the Chisholm Trail, 1871*. New York: Scholastic, 1999.

_____. "1994 Margaret A. Edwards Award Acceptance Speech," *Journal of Youth Services in Libraries*, 8, no. 2 (winter 1995): 129–133.

_____. *Now Is Your Time! The African-American Struggle for Freedom*. New York: HarperCollins, 1991.

_____. *Shooter*. New York: Amistad, 2004.

_____. "Turning Memories into Memoir," *Scholastic Scope* 51, no. 1 (6 September 2002): 20.

_____. "Walter Dean Myers," *Read* 54, no. 13 (25 February 2005): 14–15.

_____. *Won't Know Till I Get There*. New York: Viking, 1982.

_____, et al. "YA Grows Up," http://www.authorsontheweb.com/features/0108-ya/0108-ya.asp, 2001.

Sutherland, Zena. "Review: *Fast Sam, Cool Clyde and Stuff*," *Bulletin of the Center for Children's Books* 29, no. 3 (January 1976): 82–83.

The Young Landlords

Myers opens *The Young Landlords* (1979), a "blend of social commentary and whodunit," with humorous irony by offering advice from a numbers runner, the Captain, to youngsters who accept no responsibility for their future (Naughton, 1989, 8). The Captain promotes "Good-Doing conversations," the impetus to Gloria Wiggens's Action Group, which consists of 15-year-old Paul Williams, the protagonist, plus Bubba, Dean Michaels, Jeannie, and Omar (Myers, 1979, 7). The six members postpone action on a plan for world peace and choose to upgrade 356 West 122nd Street, a crumbling building once known as the Stratford Arms. In Dean's words, 356 is "oppressing my people" for its ragged appearance (*ibid.*, 10). Gloria organizes the painting of picket signs, one of which charges that "Roaches and Rats and Filth Really Hurt," a muted commentary on the origins of slums (*ibid.*, 26). Without preaching, the author enlarges on the fictional situation to denounce absentee landlords like Joseph Harley, who allows a blighted property to mar the urban scene. The alliance of childhood idealism with community spirit lets Myers to promote productivity among youth who need worthy projects to channel their energies.

Myers attempts a two-stranded plot amply stocked with humor. After the burden of urban property maintenance passes from Harley to Paul, the oldest of the five members who complain about slum conditions, the group learns that their friend Chris has been arrested for theft. The narrative pits the brainstorming of solutions to upgrading property against the juvenile detective work on Chris's behalf. The slim tether between parallel plots is the offer of $1,000 to anyone who can clear Chris of complicity in a felony. By offsetting serious cash flow problems with Bubba's boneheaded remarks, Myers maintains a positive tone. Contributing hope and vision to the profitless ownership of rental property, accountant Jonathan Pender reminds the Action Group that "abandoning a building is largely inhumane if there are tenants living in it" (*ibid.*, 69). The low-key pep talk inspires Gloria to stick to the original goal of uplifting a beleaguered neighborhood. The narrative juxtaposes absurd obstacles to her aims, ranging from a street orator proclaiming revolution to the police bomb squad arriving after Petey Darden's still explodes in the basement.

The clutch of human variables that figure into tenement management stymies the Action Group. Myers builds a cast of misfits: Askia Ben Kenobia, a crazed karate expert; Ella Fox, a gullible ex-wife of a grifter; Mr. Hyatt, the drunk taken away by ambulance; Miss Brown, who fantasizes about boxing legend Jack Johnson; and the Robinson sisters, Tina and Johnnie Mae, who have trouble operating a gas range. The possibilities of evicting renters in arrears angers Gloria, but Paul phrases their options in a professional manner—it's easier to hope for the best than to run a profitable business. Myers speaks through Gloria his belief that altruistic people are the wrong choices for successful managers, but he allows her to supply the idea for a block party, which morphs into a rent party and food fight. More successful is a street fair that draws most of the residents into reviving the area to make it more livable. At novel's end, Paul states the lesson that problems are easier to solve for people who have no responsibility for them. Jack Forman, a reviewer for *School Library Journal*, describes the novel as "slick and easy-going comedy/adventure" and trivializes the resolution by comparing it to a Nancy Drew mystery (Forman, 1979, 160). His critique overlooks the value of synergy to serious issues and shortchanges the centrality of persistence to the Action Group's success.

• *Further Reading*

Flanagan, K. M. "Review: *The Young Landlords*," *Horn Book* 55, no. 5 (October 1979): 535.

Forman, Jack. "Review: *The Young Landlords*," *School Library Journal* 26, no. 2 (October 1979): 160.

Myers, Walter Dean. *The Young Landlords*. New York: Viking, 1979.

Naughton, Jim. "Literary Crusader Writes Stories about Real Kids," *Los Angeles Times* (29 December 1989): 8.

Appendix A: Time Line of Historical and Fictional Events in Myers's Works

Each entry contains an abbreviated title for identification of the source of each event. Key: AHMR = *At Her Majesty's Request*, 1999; ALRF = *Amistad: A Long Road to Freedom*, 1998; B = *The Beast*, 2003; BDH = "The Baddest Dog in Harlem," 2000; ES = "Einstein the Second," 2003; FA = *Fallen Angels*, 1988; GF = *The Glory Field*, 1994; GMA = *The Greatest: Muhammad Ali*, 2001; HH = *Here in Harlem*, 2004; ISPL = *I've Seen the Promised Land*, 2004; JBO = *The Journal of Biddy Owens*, 2001; JJL = *The Journal of Joshua Loper*, 1999; JSPC = *The Journal of Scott Pendleton Collins*, 1999; M = *Monster: A Novel*, 1999; MXBAMN = *Malcolm X: By Any Means Necessary*, 1993; MXFBB = *Malcolm X: A Fire Burning Brightly*, 2004; NIYT = *Now Is Your Time!*, 1991; P = *Patrol: An American Soldier in Vietnam*, 2002; PCH = *A Place Called Heartbreak*, 1992; RRAB = *The Righteous Revenge of Artemis Bonner*, 1992; SD = *Somewhere in the Darkness*, 1992; Sh = *Shooter*, 2004; SW = *Social Welfare: A First Book*, 1976; TDK = *Tales of a Dead King*, 1983; TL = *Toussaint L'Ouverture*, 1996; USSC = *U.S.S. Constellation*, 2004; VF = "The Vision of Felipe," 1978; WKTIGT = *Won't Know Till I Get There*, 1988; YL = *The Young Landlords*, 1979; YMP = *Young Martin's Promise*, 1992

1619 A Dutch ships brings African slaves to Virginia to work cotton, rice, and tobacco fields (MXBAMN). • The streamlining of the slave trade introduces a terrifying ordeal called the Middle Passage (GF).

1743 May 20: François Dominique Toussaint is born in Haiti (TL).

1753 July: Muhammad Bilal, a fictional African from Sierra Leone and patriarch of the Lewis family, is kidnapped during the rise of world slavery (GF).

1781 Revolutionary War veteran James Forten, a 15-year-old powderboy on the *Royal Louis*, is imprisoned in the English hulks off Long Island, New York (NIYT, USSC).

1788 Prince Ibrahima of Guinea is enslaved in West Africa and sold to a tobacco farmer near Natchez, Mississippi (NIYT).

1791 August 22: During a slave uprising in Haiti, Toussaint L'Ouverture leads his master and mistress to safety (TL).

1794 George Washington names the U.S.S. *Constellation* (USSC).

1797 September 7: The U.S.S. *Constellation* first puts to sea from Baltimore (USSC).

1800 General Toussaint L'Ouverture controls most of Haiti (TL).

1802 June 7: General Charles Leclerc imprisons Toussaint L'Ouverture in Castle Joux (TL).

1803 April 7: Toussaint L'Ouverture dies in his dungeon cell (TL).

1804 January 1: Haitians obtain independence from the French (TL).

1808 January 1: The United States halts the importation of slaves (USSC).

1828 Pedro Blanco, a Spanish merchant who establishes a slave warehouse at Lomboko, Sierra Leone, enters the world flesh trade (ALRF).

1829 Ibrahima dies in Liberia without contacting his family (NIYT).

1831 August 22: Insurrectionist Nat Turner kills 56 people during a slave uprising in Virginia (NIYT).

1839 July 2: Slave rebellion breaks out aboard the slaver *Amistad* (ALRF, NIYT). • August 7: Foone, a slave from the *Amistad*, drowns himself in a pond at the canal basin in Farmington, Connecticut (ALRF). • September: Curiosity seekers pay an entrance fee to gawk at slaves from the *Amistad* during their incarceration in New Haven, Connecticut (ALRF).

1841 March 9: An appeal to the U.S. Supreme Court ends in acquittal for the 35 surviving slaves from the *Amistad* (ALRF, NIYT).

1842 January: Slaves from the *Amistad* arrive safely aboard the *Gentleman* at Freetown, Liberia (ALRF). • October 4: George W. Latimer and his wife Rebecca escape from slavery in Norfolk, Virginia, by hiding in the prow of a ship (NIYT).

1848 Sarah Forbes Bonetta is orphaned during the Okeadon War waged against the Yoruba of Sierra Leone (AHMR).

1849 Captain Frederick Edwyn Forbes rescues Sarah Forbes Bonetta from King Gezo (AHMR).

1850 A Missouri court declares Dred Scott a free man (NIYT). July: Sarah Forbes Bonetta arrives at Gravesend, England, to become the godchild of Queen Victoria (AHMR).

1854 August 26: Parts of the U.S.S. *Constellation* go into the second ship sailing under that name (USCC).

1855 The U.S.S. *Constellation* becomes the last sail-equipped frigate in the U.S. Navy (USSC).

1857 March 6: Chief Justice Roger Brooke Taney declares Dred Scott ineligible for the rights of a white man (NIYT).

1859 April 20: The U.S.S. *Constellation* is deployed against the slave trade (USSC). • October 16: John Brown leads a raid on the federal arsenal at Harpers Ferry, Virginia (NIYT).

1860 September 26: The U.S.S. *Constellation* captures the *Cora* and rescues 705 slaves for return to Liberia (USSC).

1861 April 12: The firing on Fort Sumter, South Carolina, begins the Civil War (NIYT, USSC).

1862 February 26: The U.S. Navy deploys the U.S.S. *Constellation* during the Civil War (USSC). • August 14: Sarah Forbes Bonetta marries African missionary James Pinson Labulo Davies at St. Nicholas Church, Brighton, England (AHMR). • September: General J. E. B. Stuart receives the hospitality of Stephen Dandridge at the Bower near Leetown, Virginia (NIYT). • October 21: Charlotte Forten, granddaughter of James Forten, teaches at a freedman's school near Fort Wagner, South Carolina (NIYT).

1863 Sarah Forbes Bonetta gives birth to Victoria Davies, whom the mother names after the English queen (AHMR). • February 16: Colonel Robert Gould Shaw recruits black soldiers for the 54th Massachusetts Regiment of the Union army (NIYT). • A Civil War poster recruits colored males for the Union army from Burlington County, New Jersey (NIYT). • July 16: Colonel Robert Gould Shaw dies in action as the 54th Massachusetts

Regiment tries to take Fort Wagner, South Carolina (NIYT). • Early September: The 54th Massachusetts Regiment seizes Fort Wagner, South Carolina (NIYT).

1865 Philosopher Martin Robinson Delany becomes the first black combat major in the Union army (GF). • April: Some 180,000 black soldiers fight for the Union cause (NIYT). • April 9: General Robert E. Lee surrenders to General Ulysses S. Grant at Appomattox Courthouse, Virginia (NIYT). • Late: Thousands of black cowboys staff Texas cattle ranches and drive herds north over the cattle trails to rail heads in Kansas (RRAB). • December: The 13th Amendment abolishes slavery (MXBAMN, NIYT).

1866 Congress establishes the Buffalo Soldiers, the first peace-time black military units (RRAB).

1867 Nathan Bedford Forrest launches the Ku Klux Klan (NIYT). • O. W. Wheeler herds 2,400 steers from San Antonio, Texas, over the Chisholm Trail to Abilene, Kansas (JJL). • January 2: The Free Baptist Church at Martinsburg, West Virginia, opens the first freedman's school (NIYT).

1868 July 29: The 14th Amendment extends citizenship to blacks (MXBAMN, NIYT).

1870 Hiram Rhoades Revels of Mississippi becomes the first black U.S. senator (FA). • February 3: The 15th Amendment grants blacks the right to vote (NIYT).

1871 April 31: At age 16, Joshua Loper, author of *The Journal of Joshua Loper*, sets out on a cattle drive from southern Texas to Abilene, Kansas (JJL). • September 1: Joshua Loper completes his first cattle drive and returns home from Abilene, Kansas (JJL).

1880 March: The U.S.S. *Constellation* ferries potatoes and flour to Ireland to ease the potato famine (USSC). • August: Sarah Forbes Bonetta dies of tuberculosis in Funchal, Madeira (AHMR).

1881 Booker T. Washington opens Tuskegee Institute in Alabama (HH). • Lewis Howard Latimer co-patents a lamp filament (NIYT).

1892 Homer Adolph Plessy's suit against a New Orleans railway results in the Supreme Court's "separate but equal" ruling (NIYT). • May: Crusading journalist Ida B. Wells leads a campaign against lynching (NIYT).

1897 Jack Johnson becomes a professional boxer (GMA, YL).

1900 May 20: Sergeant William H. Carney receives the Congressional Medal of Honor for bravery at the siege of Fort Wagner, South Carolina, on July 16, 1863 (NIYT).

1908 December 26: Jack Johnson becomes the first black heavyweight boxing champion (GMA, YL).

1909 April 6: Arctic explorer Matthew Alexander Henson reaches the North Pole (B).

1912 The National Association for the Advancement of Colored People (NAACP) is formed (NIYT).

1916 The period known as the Great Migration coincides with the loss of labor to military service in World War I (GM).

1922 Meta Vaux Warrick displays her sculpture *Awakening Ethiopia* at the Making of America Exposition in New York (NIYT). • November 25: Howard Carter discovers the tomb of King Tut (TDK).

1926 The Paul Laurence Dunbar Apartments, the first large garden complex in Manhattan, opens at Seventh Avenue and West 149th Street, Harlem (B).

1930 Wallace Fard founds the Nation of Islam (GMA, MXBAMN, MXFBB).

1931 September 28: Elder Earl Little, the father of Malcolm X, dies in a suspicious trolley accident (MXFBB).

1933 Black athletes form the Negro Baseball League (JBO).

1935 Martin Luther King, Jr., enters first grade at a segregated school in Atlanta (YMP).

1936 Thurgood Marshall is lead counsel for the NAACP (NIYT). • June 19: German heavyweight boxer Max Schmeling defeats Joe Louis at Yankee Stadium in New York City (GMA).

1937 June 22: Joe Louis wins the heavyweight boxing championship from James Braddock at Comiskey Park in Chicago (GMA, MXBAMN).

1938 The Reverend Adam Clayton Powell, Jr., pastor of Harlem's Abyssinian Church, fights for black employment rights (HH). • June 22: Joe Louis defeats German heavyweight boxer Max Schmeling in one round at Yankee Stadium in New York City (GMA).

1939 Black children labor on Southern farms (SW).

1940 Folk artist Jacob Lawrence begins painting 60 panels of narrative art describing the Great Migration of 1916–1919 (GM).

1942 April: Two of Jack Lasher's brothers die during the Bataan death march in the Philippines (WKTIGT).

1944 June 6: On D-Day, Scott Pendleton Collins arrives at Omaha Beach in Normandy, France (JSPC).

1945 Jackie Robinson plays for the Brooklyn Dodgers (JBO). • March 10: Jack Lasher takes part in the battle of Mindanao in the Philippines (WKTIGT).

1946 February 27: Malcolm Little enters Charlestown State Prison to serve a ten-year prison term for breaking and entering and armed robbery (MXBAMN). • June 10: Heavyweight boxing champ Jack Johnson dies in a car crash in Raleigh, North Carolina (YL).

1947 Malcolm Little begins his conversion to Islam (MXBAMN). • July 5: Larry Doby plays for the Cleveland Browns (JBO).

1948 May 1: Batboy William Ulysses "Biddy" Owens departs on a road trip with the Birmingham Black Barons, a team in the Negro Baseball League (JBO). • Summer: Biddy Owens plays for Birmingham Black Barons (ES, JBO). • October 3: Biddy Owens ends his trip with the Negro Baseball League (JBO). • Late fall: The Negro Baseball League competes for the last time (JBO).

1949 Congress votes to restore the U.S.S. *Constellation* (USSC).

1952 Pilot Fred V. Cherry flies F-89G fighter bombers in Korea (PCH). • August 7: Malcolm Little gains parole from Charlestown State Prison and joins the Nation of Islam at its Detroit headquarters (MXBAMN, MXFBB). • August 31: Malcolm Little changes his name to Malcolm X (MXBAMN). • As Malcolm X, he and Elijah Muhammad lead the Nation of Islam, which offers blacks an alternative to Christianity (GF).

1954 American soldiers advise the South Vietnamese (PCH). • May: Americans become more involved in Vietnam after the fall of Dien Bien Phu (FA, GMA, P). • May 17: The Supreme court overturns segregation in a case known as *Brown v. the Board of Education* (GMA, MXBAMN, MXFBB, NIYT).

1955 December 1: Dr. Martin Luther King, Jr., supports a bus boycott in Montgomery, Alabama, after Rosa Parks is arrested for refusing to sit in the back of a bus (ISPL, MXBAMN). • The first American soldiers die in Vietnam (PCH).

1956 June: The U.S. District Court strikes down separate but equal on public transportation (ISPL).

1957 Langston Hughes translates the poetry of Gabriela Mistral (B). • April: Malcolm X demands medical care for Johnson Hinton, a detainee whom police injure (MXBAMN). • September 4: Dorothy Counts integrates Harding High School in Charlotte, North Carolina (NIYT).

1959 February: Dr. Martin Luther King, Jr., studies for a month with Mohandas Gandhi (ISPL). • June: The Shirelles perform at the Apollo Theater (FA). • July 13–17: Louis Lomax and Mike Wallace film a documentary on the rise of the Nation of Islam called "The Hate That Hate Produced" (GMA, MXBAMN).

1960 Dr. Martin Luther King, Jr., pushes for black voting rights (SD). • 1960s: The Black Is Beautiful movement popularizes positive attitudes toward African Americans in the spirit of Marcus Garvey (GMA). • Summer: Cassius Clay wins a gold medal for boxing at the Summer Olympics in Rome (GMA). • October 19: Students lead lunch counter sit-ins in Atlanta that result in the jailing of Dr. Martin Luther King, Jr. (NIYT).

1961 Freedom Riders leave Washington, D.C., to tour the South (GMA). • March: FBI agents infiltrate audiences at the speeches of Malcolm X (MXBAMN).

1962 Cassius Clay meets Malcolm X in Detroit (GMA). • September 25: Sonny Liston defeats heavyweight champion Floyd Patterson in the first round at Comiskey Park in Chicago (GMA). • November 15: Cassius Clay defeats his former trainer, Archie Moore, in the fourth round in Los Angeles (GMA).

1963 June 12: Ku Klux Klansmen martyr freedom fighter Medgar Evers in the driveway of his home in Jackson, Mississippi (GF, GMA). • June 18: Cassius Clay defeats English boxer Henry Cooper in London (GMA). • July 31: Malcolm X denounces nonviolent methods in the fight for civil rights (GMA, ISPL). • August 28: Black demonstrators join the March on Washington to promote civil rights (GMA, ISPL, MXBAMN, NIYT). • Late in the day, Martin Luther King, Jr., delivers the "I Have a Dream" speech from the steps of the Lincoln Memorial (GMA, ISPL, MXBAMN). • September 15: Four children — Addie Mae Collins, Denise McNair, Carol Robertson, and Cynthia Wesley — die in a bombing of Sunday school classes at the Sixteenth Street Church in Birmingham, Alabama (GF, GMA, ISPL, MXBAMN). • November 21: An assassin shoots President John F. Kennedy, a supporter of racial justice (ISPL, MXBAMN).

1964 January 15: Malcolm X visits Cassius Clay at his Miami training camp (GMA). • March 8: Malcolm X leaves the Nation of Islam (MXBAMN, MXFBB). • March 26: Malcolm X meets Dr. Martin Luther King, Jr. (MXBAMN). • May 21: Malcolm X completes a pilgrimage to Mecca (MXBAMN, MXFBB). • July 2: At the White House, President Lyndon B. Johnson signs the Civil Rights Act (GMA). • August 7: Congress passes the Tonkin Gulf Resolution supporting President Lyndon Johnson's troop build-up in Vietnam (FA). • December 10: Dr. Martin Luther King, Jr., receives the Nobel Peace Prize (ISPL).

1965 February 11: Formal bombing begins against North Vietnam (FA). • February 14: Assailants fire-bomb the Queens home of Malcolm X (MXBAMN). • February 21: Assassins shoot Malcolm X as he delivers a speech at the Audubon Ballroom in Harlem (GMA, ISPL, MXBAMN, MXFBB, NIYT). • February 25: Muhammad Ali defeats Sonny Liston for the world heavyweight boxing championship in Miami, Florida (GMA, MXBAMN). • May 25: Muhammad Ali defeats Sonny Liston in the first minute of the first round in Lewiston, Maine (GMA). • October 22: Colonel Fred V. Cherry becomes America's first black prisoner of the Vietnam War (PCH). • November 22: Muhammad Ali defeats Floyd Patterson in Las Vegas, Nevada (GMA).

1966 February 17: Muhammad Ali claims the status of conscientious objector and refuses induction into the army (GMA). • February: Richard "Richie" Perry joins the army to secure allotment checks for his mother and brother Kenny (FA).

1967 April 4: During an address at Riverside Church in Harlem, Dr. Martin Luther King, Jr., protests the Vietnam War and recommends draft evasion (FA). • April 15: Anti-war demonstrations in large American cities energize the move to stop the bombing in Vietnam (FA). • August 30: Congress supports Lyndon Johnson's appointment of Thurgood Marshall to the Supreme Court (NIYT). • September 15: Richie Perry travels from Harlem to Tan Son Nhut air base (FA). • Thanksgiving: Richie Perry sends his brother Kenny a silk jacket from Vietnam (FA).

1968 Mid-January: Richie Perry leaves the hospital to return to duty in Tam Ky (FA). • January 23: A North Korean patrol boat captures the *Pueblo*, an American spy ship (FA). • January 31: North Vietnamese soldiers launch the Tet offensive, the height of the Vietnam War (FA). • February 24: South Vietnamese regulars capture Hue (FA). • March: Protests against racial injustice involve college campuses (ISPL). • March 8: Richie Perry's medical profile arrives shortly before he is wounded a second time (FA). • March 28: Dr. Martin Luther King, Jr., leads a march through Memphis in support of striking sanitation workers (ISPL). • April 3: Dr. Martin Luther King, Jr., delivers a speech in Memphis describing his vision from the mountaintop (ISPL). • April 4: An assassin kills Dr. Martin Luther King, Jr., in Memphis, Tennessee (NIYT). • April 22: Following the death of Dr. Martin Luther King, Jr., rioting breaks out in Harlem (FA). • May 7: Thomas Wayne "Sonny" Myers dies in Vietnam (FA). • October 3: A military junta under dictator Juan Valesco Alvarado takes control of Peru (VF).

1969 June 20: Neil Armstrong becomes the first human to walk on the moon (PCH).

1970 May 4: National Guardsmen kill four Kent State student demonstrators and wound nine others (PCH). • May 14: Police open fire with machine guns at Jackson State in Mississippi, killing two black students, James Earl Green and Lafayette Gibbs, and wounding twelve others (PCH).

1972 December 18: Colonel Fred V. Cherry occupies a cell at Hoa Lo Prison in Hanoi, Vietnam, when 126 American bombers attack (PCH).

1973 January 27: A cease-fire ends the Vietnam War (FA). • February 12: On the birthday of Abraham Lincoln, Colonel Fred V. Cherry obtains release from a Hanoi prison (PCH).

1982 Mid-July: A year after Rich "Goose" Gossage and pitcher Rudy May play for the Yankees during a World Series win, Patty Bramwell's cousin tries out against the two sports heroes (WKTIGT).

1983 Congress names the most recent national holiday, Martin Luther King Day (YMP).

1986 January 20: Americans celebrate the first Martin Luther King Day (ISPL).

1989 February: Roberto Duran adds the middleweight championship to three world titles—lightweight (1972–79), welterweight (1980), and junior middleweight (1983) (BDH). • August: Alguinaldo Nesbitt is licensed to carry a gun to protect his Harlem drugstore (M).

1996 July 22: Muhammad Ali ignites the Olympic flame at the summer games in Atlanta, Georgia (GMA). • November 17: The U.S.S. *Constellation* begins restoration (USSC).

1999 April 20: The student terrorism at Columbine High School in Littleton, Colorado, gives Myers the idea for *Shooter* (2004) (Sh).

Appendix B: Writing and Research Topics

1. With a flow chart, contrast the thematic contributions of James Baldwin, Toni Cade Bambara, Alice Childress, Langston Hughes, Zora Neale Hurston, Ann Petry, Sonia Sanchez, and John Edgar Wideman to black literature for teen readers with the works of Walter Dean Myers. Include achievement, adaptation, athletics, belonging, betrayal, coming of age, crime, death, displacement, dreams, drugs and alcohol, education, gangs, humor, immaturity, injustice, insanity, music, old age, opportunity, parenthood, poverty, powerlessness, racism, religion, rootlessness, segregation, self-destruction, sex, slavery, superstition, urbanism, vengeance, victimization, violence, wisdom, and women.

2. Discuss reasons for Walter Dean Myers's focus on male youth, including Chris and Ken Arrow, David Curry, Peewee Gates, Earl Goins, Len Gray, Steve Harmon, Prince Ibrahima, Lonnie Jackson, Joshua Loper, Jimmy Lynch, Gerald McQuillen, the Nagasaki Knights, Biddy Owens, Richie Perry, Steve Perry, Cameron Porter, Greg Ridley, Darnell Rock, Paul Williams, Anthony Witherspoon, and Clyde, Sam, and Stuff. Does the author's stress on one gender indicate that boys are more susceptible to temptation? to crime? to failure? to sexual adventurism? to self-destruction?

3. Characterize elements of black dialect and slang in "Gums," *Monster: A Novel*, *The Young Landlords*, *Won't Know Till I Get There*, "The Treasure of Lemon Brown," *The Mouse Rap*, *Mr. Monkey and the Gotcha Bird*, "The Going On," or *Fallen Angels*. Note the difference between dialect in daily conversation and in the folk expressions that serve elders and authority figures as wise adages.

4. Explain why Walter Dean Myers's teen stories express black issues and conflicts, such as homelessness in Harlem in "The Treasure of Lemon Brown," vying for athletic scholarships in *Hoops*, poverty in *The Beast* and *Bad Boy: A Memoir*, drug addiction in *The Outside Shot*, slums in *The Young Landlords*, and the complicity in the post–Columbine High School conspiracy to murder and terrorize a high school in *Shooter*. Outline controversies that Myers's male-dominated works may have omitted or understated, particularly lack of opportunity for female athletes and scholars, women's right to vote and seek office, equal opportunities for women in the military and in politics, planned parenthood and birth control, workplace stress on women, sexual harassment, denigration of women as thinkers and leaders, and abortion rights.

5. Summarize comic elements in Myers's works. Include animal situations in *How*

Mr. Monkey Saw the Whole World, illogic in *Smiffy Blue, Ace Crime Detective*, situational humor and sarcasm about religion in *Fast Sam, Cool Clyde, and Stuff*, mismatched fighters in *The Young Landlords*, parent-child confrontations in *Hoops*, intergenerational comedy in *Won't Know Till I Get There*, combat wit in *Fallen Angels*, sports mix-ups in *Me, Mop, and the Moondance Kid*, the refusal to steal horses in *The Righteous Revenge of Artemis Bonner*, death jokes in *My Name Is America: The Journal of Scott Pendleton Collins, a WWII Soldier, Normandy, France, 1944*, silly puns in the Arrow brothers' detective series, incongruity in "Big Joe's Funeral," and sexual badinage between Samson and Delilah in *A Time to Love: Stories from the Old Testament.*

6. Compose a letter to local educators and librarians proposing how use of the books of Walter Dean Myers during a celebration of Black History Month can benefit reluctant and ESL readers. Cite examples of high drama, history, parent-child miscommunication, community involvement, role models, risk-taking, and intergenerational mediation as sources of a debate, mural, musical, puppet shows, shadow art, or improvisational pantomime.

7. Cite lines that disclose Walter Dean Myers's opinions on the value of reading, keeping a journal, obedience to authority figures, community improvement projects, part-time jobs, foster parenting and adoption, school plays, music, religious involvement, and competitive sports as worthy involvements for disadvantaged students. Outline your own opinion.

8. Identify and explain references to Christmas in *The Beast* or *Shooter* and in J. D. Salinger's *The Catcher in the Rye*. Why do 17-year-old Anthony "Spoon" Witherspoon, Leonard "Len" Gray, Cameron Porter, Carla Evans, and Holden Caulfield share a disillusion with the holidays and with their role at cliquish schools? Why do holidays magnify problems? How does each character channel negative feelings?

9. Account for the image of Death in *The Legend of Tarik, Brainstorm,* and the short story "Gums." Contrast the stalking phantasm with the realistic view of dying in *Fallen Angels, Somewhere in the Darkness, A Time for Love, Crystal, Shooter,* "The Treasure of Lemon Brown," and *It Ain't All for Nothin.'*

10. Contrast the parenting in several of Myers's works. Include the following models:

- single parenting in *Fast Sam, Cool Clyde, and Stuff*
- the mother as peacemaker in *Me, Mop, and the Moondance Kid*
- parents as preservers of tradition in *Shadow of the Red Moon*
- Lot's disloyalty to daughters Saaria and Zillah in *A Time for Love*
- Evelyn Curry's compassion for sons Tyrone and David in *The Dream Bearer*
- a family's venture into foster parenting in *Won't Know Till I Get There*
- the substitution of grandparents for parents in *It Ain't All for Nothin'* and "Gums"
- concern for the future generation in "Wolf Song"
- the trusting Carla Arrow, mother of Ken and Chris in *Ambush in the Amazon, Duel in the Desert,* and *The Hidden Shrine*
- the grieving father in "The Treasure of Lemon Brown"
- supportive parents in *Monster: A Novel* and *Fallen Angels*
- a parent's treachery against a child in *It Ain't All for Nothin'*
- a mother's abandonment of her son in *Won't Know Till I Get There*
- Queen Victoria as a surrogate parent and arranger of a wedding in *At Her Majesty's Request: An African Princess in Victorian England*
- the author's mother as storyteller and instructor in *Bad Boy: A Memoir*
- bad motherly advice to a budding model in *Crystal*
- the absence of discipline and understanding in *Shooter.*

11. Select blues lyrics from Myers's works that derive from slavery, sharecropping, the Jim Crow era, the urban migration,

and blighted slums. Analyze emotions, ambitions, losses, and frustrations that weigh heavily on black people, for example, petty ghetto crime, imprisonment and service on chain gangs, declining agricultural income, bewilderment at the social and economic challenges of trying to find work in the city, the white-dominated justice and penal systems, endangerment of male self-esteem, and the dissolution of the black family. Contrast stanzas exhibiting an identifiable time frame with the universality of songs about love gone wrong.

12. Outline the history of American baseball, beginning with informal rules and pick-up games and continuing through the rise of the Negro League, Satchel Paige, Josh Gibson, Jackie Robinson, Hank Aaron, Larry Doby, and Wes Covington. Explain why Joshua Logan is thrilled to be a part of the league's last year. Conclude why Patty Bramwell's cousin Eddie in *Won't Know Till I Get There* is fortunate to get a try-out against Rich "Goose" Gossage and pitcher Rudy May of the Yankees.

13. Compare the strengths of the nuclear family in two of Myers's works, for example:

- the choice of destiny in *Cages*
- Carla Arrow's trust in her two sons' wisdom in *Ambush in the Amazon, Duel in the Desert,* or *The Hidden Shrine*
- the loss of family unity after a son's death in World War II in "The Treasure of Lemon Brown"
- support for pregnant teens in *Sweet Illusions*
- parental visits to the Manhattan Detention Center in *Monster: A Novel*
- the salvation of a mentally disturbed father in *The Dream Bearer*
- the importance of adoption to Tommy "T. J." Jackson in *Me, Mop, and the Moondance Kid*
- Steve Perry's role in the adoption proceedings begun by his parents, Jessica and Richard Perry, in *Won't Know Till I Get There.*

14. Compare the source of anger and mistrust in Kaye Gibbons's *Ellen Foster*, Toni Cade Bambara's story "Blues Ain't No Mockin' Bird," James Baldwin's "Sonny's Blues," Angelina Weld Grimké's "The Closing Door," Terry McMillan's *Mama*, Dick Gregory's *Nigger*, Sue Kidd's *The Secret Life of Bees*, Toni Morrison's *The Bluest Eye*, Margaret Walker's *Jubilee*, August Wilson's *Fences*, or Richard Wright's story "Almos' a Man" to a similar discontent in *The Dream Bearer, Won't Know Till I Get There, The Righteous Revenge of Artemis Bonner, Shooter*, "The Treasure of Lemon Brown," or *It Ain't All for Nothin'*, or *Autobiography of My Dead Brother.*

15. Compare the ambitions and yearnings in unwanted or neglected children in *Me, Mop, and the Moondance Kid* or *Somewhere in the Darkness* to those of Earl Goins in *Won't Know Till I Get There*, teens in *Cages*, a young model in *Crystal*, Greg Ridley in "The Treasure of Lemon Brown," or conspirators Leonard "Len" Gray, Carla Evans, and Cameron Porter in *Shooter*. Determine which text best presents the precarious state of self-esteem.

16. Compare losses in Robert Newton Peck's *A Day No Pigs Would Die*, Marjorie Kinnan Rawlings's *The Yearling*, William Gibson's *The Miracle Worker*, John van Druten's *I Remember Mama*, or John Steinbeck's *The Red Pony* with losses in either *It Ain't All for Nothin,'* "The Fare to Crown Point," "Migration," "Sunrise over Manaus," *Crystal, Monster: A Novel, Shooter, Brainstorm,* "The Treasure of Lemon Brown," "Stranger," *My Name Is America: The Journal of Scott Pendleton Collins, Sweet Illusions, Cages*, "Season's End," or *Fallen Angels*. Note what types of solace ease emotional pain and trauma.

17. Compile a brochure or audio tape to accompany a walking tour of Harlem, noting locales that Walter Dean Myers mentions in his works, particularly Bedford-Stuyvesant, Striver's Row, Cotton Club, Apollo Theater, Smalls' and Minton's jazz clubs, Abyssinian Baptist Church, Schomburg library, Riverside Park, the A train station at

125th Street, La Marqueta, Morningside Park, Frederick Douglass Boulevard, YMCA on West 135th Street, George Bruce Branch of the public library on 125th Street, Hudson River, Countee Cullen Library, Adam Clayton Powell Boulevard, Magic Johnson's theater, Harlem Hospital, and Matthew Henson Community Project.

18. Summarize the sources of advice and counsel in *Crystal*. Note details of community and family response and the friendship of 18-year-old model Rowena in helping 16-year-old Crystal Brown map out a career in the beauty industry and movies. Contrast Sister Gibbs as an elderly mentor with the value of "Mr. Moses" Littlejohn in *The Dream Bearer*, the trainer in *The Legend of Tarik*, Duke Wilson in *Handbook for Boys: A Novel*, counselors in *Sweet Illusions*, or the title figure in "The Treasure of Lemon Brown."

19. Contrast the parental perversion of sports in *Shooter* with similar incidents and attitudes in Pat Conroy's *The Great Santini*.

20. Select contrasting scenes and describe their pictorial qualities, for example:

- Cameron Porter and Leonard "Len" Gray discharging a Ruger at a dumpster in *Shooter*
- retreating from armed thugs in "The Treasure of Lemon Brown"
- the dangers to youth in "Wolf Song"
- seeking a monster in *Ambush in the Amazon*
- locking out death in "Gums"
- detective work in *The Nicholas Factor*
- holding a block party in *The Young Landlords*
- the search for prophecy in "Angela's Eyes"
- a hospital reunion in *Fallen Angels*
- feelings of belonging in *Here in Harlem*
- the job of the powder monkey in *U.S.S. Constellation*
- parental disappointment in *Here in Harlem*
- the rescue of a drug addict in *The Glory Field*
- a prison visit in *Monster: A Novel*
- pursuit of a villain in *The Hidden Shrine*
- locating gangsters in *The Mouse Rap*
- the flight of a family from destruction in *A Time to Love.*

21. Discuss the cultural continuum as the burden of Aaron and "Mr. Moses" Littlejohn in *The Dream Bearer* and of the title figure in Lois Lowry's *The Giver.*

22. Compare self-destructive behaviors in *The Righteous Revenge of Artemis Bonner*, "The Fare to Crown Point," *The Beast, Three Swords for Granada, Scorpions, The Glory Field*, "The Vision of Felipe," "How Long Is Forever," and "Sunrise over Manaus." Determine which characters are most at risk of serious injury or death.

23. Write an extended definition of *legend* using High John the Conqueror, Malcolm X, Dr. Martin Luther King, Jr., Muhammad Ali, Billie Holiday, Duke Ellington, and Toussaint L'Ouverture as models. Note how the U.S.S. *Constellation*, the Great Migration, the Negro Baseball League, Muhammad Bilal, Sarah Forbes Bonetta, and Flats Brown can also qualify as legends.

24. Compare the skill of Grandma Carrie Brown in *It Ain't All for Nothin,'* Sister Gibbs in *Crystal*, Queen Victoria in *At Her Majesty's Request*, and the mothers in *Angel to Angel* and *Me, Mop, and the Moondance Kid* as comforters and spiritual healers to that of the mother in William Armstrong's *Sounder*, the title character in Ernest Gaines's *The Autobiography of Miss Jane Pittman*, the title character in Gary Paulsen's *Nightjohn*, or August Boatwright in Sue Kidd's *The Secret Life of Bees.* Describe rhythmic, physical, and vocal methods of releasing hurt and insecurity.

25. Typify family dynamics in Walter Dean Myers's *Shadow of the Red Moon, The Nicholas Factor*, or *Scorpions* and in Zora Neale Hurston's *Their Eyes Were Watching God*, August Wilson's *Fences*, Margaret Walker's *Jubilee*, Toni Morrison's *The Bluest Eye*, Isabel Allende's *The House of the Spirits*,

Laura Esquivel's *Like Water for Chocolate*, Amy Tan's *The Kitchen God's Wife*, Alice Walker's *The Color Purple*, or Lorraine Hansberry's *A Raisin in the Sun*. Emphasize the male's need to satisfy ambitions and personal needs.

26. Improvise a conference of Saran, Crab, Lonnie Jackson, Crystal Brown, Gabi Godoy, Earl Goins, Pundabi, and Artemis Bonner on the subject of human happiness in regards to money. As a model, explain through dialogue why Saran takes in a foster daughter, how Pundabi investigates poverty, why Crab ends up in prison, why Lonnie Jackson considers the rewards of gambling, why Gabi retreats from poverty into drugs, how Artemis risks his life, and why Crystal abandons a movie career.

27. Contrast the use of vision quests in *Black Elk Speaks*, the biography of Black Elk, clairvoyance in Marion Zimmer Bradley's *The Mists of Avalon* or Mary Stewart's *The Crystal Cave*, or prophecies of greatness in T. H. White's *The Sword in the Stone* with "Mr. Moses" Littlejohn's reflections on three centuries of carrying the burden of black history in *The Dream Bearer*.

28. List and describe a variety of narrative forms and styles in Walter Dean Myers's writings, including one-act play, saga, call-and-response, dialogue, anecdote, history lecture, satire, genealogy, scripture, eulogy, testimony, animal fable, quip, witticism, adage, song, ode, elegy, boast, lament, sermon, fool tale, cautionary tale, rap, short story, picture book, folk fable, detective story, sci-fi, legend, wisdom lore, biography, and debate.

29. Compare "Mr. Moses" Littlejohn, Martin Luther King, Jr., Lemon Brown, Pundabi, Malcolm X, Duke Wilson, Colonel Fred V. Cherry, Roland Sylvester, and Gordon Parks as advisers and bearers of wisdom with the advisory roles of Sojourner Truth, Marcus Aurelius, Isaiah, the Cumaean Sibyl, Mother Teresa, Confucius, Marian Wright Edelman, Cesar Chavez, Solomon, Dr. Elie Wiesel, Barbara Jordan, Jeremiah, Eleanor Roosevelt, Dr. Ruth Westheimer, the Dalai Lama, Pope John XXIII, and Black Elk.

30. With a partner, select unlike characters to pantomime, for instance, Mabel Mae Jones/Motown, Luvenia Lewis/Colonel Fred V. Cherry, Elijah Muhammad/Carla Arrow, Grandpa Jeremiah/Greg Ridley, Gerald McQuillen/Mr. Monkey, *monstruo*/Ibrahima, Frederick Douglass/Caleb, Grandma Carrie Brown/King Gezo, Sarah Forbes Bonetta/Muhammad Ali, Tarik/Mouse Douglas, or Cinqué/Gabi Godoy.

31. Recap the predicaments and points of view of these women in Myers's writings: Stria, Mabel Mae Jones, Carrie Brown, Queen Victoria, Evelyn Curry, Delilah, Dolly Dennis, Gloria Wiggens, Mildred Smith, Gabi Godoy, Luvenia Lewis, Tito's grandmother, and Florence Dean.

32. Characterize the importance of secondary character placement in Myers's works. For example, note the significance and number of appearances of Docao, Askai Ben Kenobia, Big Joe, Mtisha, Brad Williams, Old Man Jenkins, "Cap" Mills, Kathy O'Brien, Lieutenant Carroll, Robert Gould Shaw, Tito, Sweeby Jones, Stria, Tamika Rock, Father Santora, George Sawicki, peasants in *The Golden Serpent*, and George Dean, Jr.

33. Summarize the pragmatic values of Myers's heroes. Characterize the good sense of Lonnie Jackson, Samson, Scott Pendleton Collins, Gloria Wiggens, Chris Arrow, David Curry, Abraham, Richie Perry, Slam Harris, Crystal Brown, Tippy, Mouse Douglas, Paul Robeson, Pundabi, or Muhammad Ali.

34. Contrast characters in terms of the analyses of their fathers, a recurrent motif in *Somewhere in the Darkness, Malcolm X: By Any Means Necessary, It Ain't All for Nothin,' Sweet Illusions, Won't Know Till I Get There, The Dream Bearer*, and *Shooter*.

35. Locate examples of journeys and quests as symbols of ambition, vengeance, and persistence. Choose from *I've Seen the*

Promised Land, The Legend of Tarik, At Her Majesty's Request, Turning Points, A Place Called Heartbreak, U.S.S. Constellation, The Golden Serpent, The Great Migration, Somewhere in the Darkness, Fallen Angels, Shooter, Slam!, My Name Is America: The Journal of Scott Pendleton Collins, My Name Is America: The Journal of Joshua Loper, "Migration," *Mop, Moondance and the Nagasaki Nights,* and *My Name Is America: The Journal of Biddy Owens.*

36. Collect wisdom lore and adages from Walter Dean Myers's works, such as John Martens's comment on fear: "Panic is your brain telling your body that it's in a whole lot of trouble" and Gordon Parks's assertion, "If you use the best of you, you can survive the worst of you." Match them with similar statements in compendia of world quotations from native Americans, Africa, Australia, India, Japan, and China.

37. Locate models of versification in Walter Dean Myers's poetry. Include these: euphony, caesura, alliteration, controlling metaphor, internal rhyme, couplet, allusion, spondee, simile, rhyme scheme, cacophony, lyricism, personification, repetition, and abstract theme.

38. Compare violence in "Briefcase," *Fallen Angels,* "The Vision of Felipe," *My Name Is America: The Journal of Scott Pendleton Collins,* "Wolf Song," *The Legend of Tarik, Shooter, Mr. Monkey and the Gotcha Bird,* or *Monster: A Novel* to punishments in Ernest Gaines's *The Autobiography of Miss Jane Pittman,* threats in Lorraine Hansberry's *A Raisin in the Sun,* assault in Toni Morrison *The Bluest Eye,* sudden death in Zora Neale Hurston's *Their Eyes Were Watching God,* racism in August Wilson's *The Piano Lesson,* and physical suffering in William Armstrong's *Sounder.*

39. List and discuss the effectiveness of Gothic elements from *The Glory Field,* "Angela's Eyes," *Ambush in the Amazon, The Legend of Tarik, Shadow of the Red Moon,* "Gums," "Things That Go Gleep in the Night," *Monster: A Novel, The Dream Bearer,* "How Long Is Forever," and *The Mouse Rap,* including suspense, melodrama, superstition, violence, prophecy, *chiaroscuro,* and the supernatural. Explain how Gothic conventions function in realistic works, like *Fallen Angels, One More River to Cross,* "Sunrise over Manaus," *Motown and Didi,* and *Shooter.*

40. Compare the vision of a nurturing, supportive community in Myers's Harlem settings to the Louisiana Quarters of Ernest Gaines's *A Lesson Before Dying,* the North Carolina poor in Kaye Gibbons's *Charms for the Easy Life,* the Florida outback in Marjorie Kinnan Rawlings's *The Yearling,* frontier Arkansas in William Portis's *True Grit,* or the South Carolina ghetto of Dubose Heyward and George Gershwin's *Porgy and Bess,* the first American opera. Include music, soul food, superstition, faith, shared labor, ritual, fear, betrayal, love, and trust.

Bibliography

Primary Sources

Adventure in Granada. New York: Viking Kestrel, 1985.
Ambush in the Amazon. New York: Viking Kestrel, 1986.
Amistad: A Long Road to Freedom. New York: Dutton, 1998.
"And Then I Read...," *Voices-from-the-Middle* 8, no. 4 (May 2001): 58–62.
And There Stood a Man (unpublished play), performed at Rutgers University, 1990.
Angel to Angel: A Mother's Gift of Love. New York: HarperCollins, 1998.
Antarctica: Journeys to the South Pole. New York: Scholastic, 2004.
At Her Majesty's Request: An African Princess in Victorian England. New York: Scholastic, 1999.
Bad Boy: A Memoir. New York: HarperCollins, 2001.
The Beast. New York: Scholastic, 2003.
"The Beast," *Scholastic Scope* 52, no. 12 (9 February 2004): 12–13, 14.
"The Beast Is in the Labyrinth," *Places I Never Meant To Be: Original Stories by Censored Writers*. New York: Simon & Schuster, 1999.
"The Black Experience in Children's Books: One Step Forward, Two Steps Back," *Interracial Books for Children Bulletin* 10, no. 6 (1979): 14–15.
The Black Pearl and the Ghost; or, One Mystery After Another. New York: Viking, 1980.
"Block Party—145th Street Style," *Big City Cool: Short Stories About Urban Youth*. New York: Persea, 2002.
Blues Journey. New York: Holiday House, 2003.
The Blues of Flats Brown. New York: Holiday House, 2000; reissue, 2001.
Brainstorm. New York: Franklin Watts, 1977; London: Watts, 1977; New York: Dell, 1979.
"Briefcase," *Twelve Shots: Outstanding Short Stories About Guns*. New York: Delacorte, 1997.
Brown Angels: An Album of Pictures and Verse. New York: HarperCollins, 1993.
"Bubba," *Essence* (November 1972): 56, 74, 76.
"Cages," *Center State: One-Act Plays for Teenage Readers and Actors*. New York: HarperCollins, 1990.
"A Cowboy's Diary," *Storyworks* 6, no. 5 (February/March 1999): 26–31.
Crystal. New York: Viking Kestrel, 1987, reissued by Harper Trophy, 2002.
The Dancers. New York: Parents Magazine, 1972.
"The Dark Side of the Moon," *Black Creation* (fall 1971): 26–29.
Darnell Rock Reporting. New York: Delacorte, 1994.
The Dragon Takes a Wife. Indianapolis: Bobbs-Merrill, 1972; New York: Scholastic, 1995.
The Dream Bearer. New York: Amistad, 2003; reissued by Harper Trophy, 2004.
Duel in the Desert. New York: Viking Kestrel, 1986.
"Einstein the Second," *Boys' Life* 93, no. 11 (November 2003): 30–36.
"Escalating Offenses," *Horn Book* 77, no. 6 (November-December 2001): 701–702.
Fallen Angels. New York: Scholastic, 1988.
"The Fare to Crown Point" in *What We Must SEE: Young Black Storytellers*. New York: Dodd, Mead, 1971.
Fast Sam, Cool Clyde, and Stuff. New York: Viking, 1975.
Fly, Jimmy, Fly! New York: Putnam, 1974.

"Gifts," *Horn Book* 62, no. 4 (July-August 1986): 436–437.
The Gifts We Bring. New York: HarperCollins, 2002.
Glorious Angels: A Celebration of Children. New York: Bantam, 1995.
The Glory Field. New York: Scholastic, 1994.
"The Going On," *Black World* (March 1971): 61–67.
The Golden Serpent. New York: Viking, 1980; London: McRae, 1981.
"Gordon Parks: John Henry with a Camera," *Black Scholar* 7, no. 5 (1976): 27–30.
The Great Migration: An American Story. New York: HarperCollins, 1993.
The Greatest: Muhammad Ali. New York: Scholastic, 2001.
"Growing Pains," *Scholastic Scope* 51, no. 1 (6 September 2002): 18–19.
"Gums" in *We Be Word Sorcerers: Twenty-five Stories by Black Americans.* New York: Bantam, 1973.
Handbook for Boys: A Novel. New York: Amistad, 2002.
Harlem: A Poem. New York: Scholastic, 1997.
Harlem Blues. New York: Rageot, 1996.
Here in Harlem: Poems in Many Voices. New York: Holiday House, 2004.
The Hidden Shrine. New York: Viking Kestrel, 1985.
Hoops. New York: Delacorte, 1981.
"How I Came to Love English Literature," *English Journal* 74, no. 7 (November 1985): 93–94.
"How Long Is Forever?," *Negro Digest* (June 1969): 52–57.
"How Mr. Monkey Saw the Whole World," *Cricket* 20, no. 6 (February 1993): 5–10.
How Mr. Monkey Saw the Whole World. New York: Doubleday, 1996.
"I Actually Thought We Would Revolutionize the Industry," *New York Times Book Review* (9 November 1986): 50.
It Ain't All for Nothin.' New York: Viking, 1978; reissued by Amistad, 2003.
I've Seen the Promised Land: The Life of Dr. Martin Luther King, Jr. New York: Amistad, 2004.
"Jeremiah's Song" in *The Giver and Related Readings.* Boston: McDougal Littell, 1987.
"Juby," *Black Creation* (April 1971): 26–27.
The Legend of Tarik. New York: Viking, 1981; Scholastic, 1982.
"Let Us Celebrate the Children," *Horn Book* 65 (1989): 46–48.
Malcolm X: A Fire Burning Brightly. New York: HarperCollins, 2000; reprint, 2004.
Malcolm X: By Any Means Necessary. New York: Scholastic, 1993.
Me, Mop, and the Moondance Kid. New York: Delacorte, 1988.
Mr. Monkey and the Gotcha Bird. New York: Delacorte, 1984.
Mojo and the Russians. New York: Viking, 1977; Avon, 1979.
Monster: A Novel. New York: HarperCollins, 1999.
Mop, Moondance, and the Nagasaki Knights. New York: Delacorte, 1992.
Motown and Didi: A Love Story. New York: Viking Kestrel, 1984.
The Mouse Rap. New York: HarperCollins, 1990.
My Name Is America: The Journal of Biddy Owens: The Negro Leagues. New York: Scholastic, 2001.
My Name Is America: The Journal of Joshua Loper, a Black Cowboy on the Chisholm Trail, 1871. New York: Scholastic, 1999.
My Name Is America: The Journal of Scott Pendleton Collins, a WWII Soldier, Normandy, France, 1944. New York: Scholastic, 1999.
"My Own Harlem," *Read* 54, no. 13 (25 February 2005): 6–13.
The Nicholas Factor. New York: Viking, 1983.
"1994 Margaret A. Edwards Award Acceptance Speech," *Youth Services in Libraries* 8, no. 2 (winter 1995): 129–133.
Now Is Your Time! The African-American Struggle for Freedom. New York: HarperCollins, 1991.
145th Street: Short Stories. New York: Delacorte, 2000.
One More River to Cross: An African American Photograph Album. New York: Harcourt Brace, 1995.
The Outside Shot. New York: Delacorte, 1984; Dell, 1987.
Patrol: An American Soldier in Vietnam. New York: HarperCollins, 2002.
A Place Called Heartbreak: A Story of Vietnam. Austin, Tex.: Raintree, 1992.
"Pulling No Punches," *School Library Journal* 47, no. 6 (June 2001): 44.
Remember Us Well: An Album of Pictures and Verse. New York: HarperCollins, 1993.
"Reverend Abbott and Those Bloodshot Eyes" in *When I Was Your Age: Original Stories About Growing Up.* New York: Candlewick, 1996.
The Righteous Revenge of Artemis Bonner. New York: HarperCollins, 1992.
"School Days; Least Likely to Succeed," *Washington Post* (4 August 1991): 1.

Scorpions. New York: Harper & Row, 1988.
"Season's End" in *The Color of Absence: Twelve Stories About Loss*. New York: Simon & Schuster, 2001.
Shadow of the Red Moon. New York: Harper Collins, 1987; Scholastic, 1995.
Shooter. New York: Amistad, 2004.
Slam! New York: Scholastic, 1996.
Smiffy Blue, Ace Crime Detective: The Case of the Missing Ruby and Other Stories. New York: Scholastic, 1996, reissued, 1999.
Social Welfare: A First Book. New York: Franklin Watts, 1976.
Somewhere in the Darkness. New York: Scholastic, 1992.
The Story of the Three Kingdoms. New York: HarperCollins, 1995.
"Stranger" in *No Easy Answers: Short Stories About Teenagers Making Tough Choices*. New York: Delacorte, 1997.
"Sunrise Over Manaus" in *From One Experience to Another*. New York: Forge, 1997.
"Surviving Mean Streets," *Washington Post* (12 May 1991): 7.
Sweet Illusions. New York: Teachers and Writers Collaborative, 1986.
Tales of a Dead King. New York: Morrow, 1983.
"Telling Our Children the Stories of Their Lives," *American Visions* 6, no. 6 (December 1991): 30–32.
"Things That Go Gleep in the Night" in *Don't Give Up the Ghost: The Delacorte Book of Original Ghost Stories*. New York: Delacorte, 1993.
Three Swords for Granada. New York: Holiday House, 2002.
A Time to Love: Stories from the Old Testament. New York: Scholastic, 2003.
"To a Child of War" in *On the Wings of Peace*. New York: Clarion, 1995.
Toussaint L'Ouverture: The Fight for Haiti's Freedom. New York: Simon & Schuster, 1996.
"The Treasure of Lemon Brown," *Boys' Life* 73 (March 1983): 34–40; reprinted in *The Pigman and Related Readings*. New York: Glencoe, 2001.
"Turning Memories into Memoir," *Scholastic Scope* 51, no. 1 (6 September 2002): 20.
Turning Points: When Everything Changes. New York: Troll Communications, 1996.
U.S.S. Constellation: Pride of the American Navy. New York: Holiday House, 2004.
"The Vision of Felipe," *Black Scholar* (November-December 1978): 2–9.
Where Does the Day Go? New York: Parents Magazine, 1969.
"Wolf Song," *Horn Book* 81, no. 3 (May-June 2005): 304.
Won't Know Till I Get There. New York: Viking, 1982; Penguin, 1988.
The World of Work: A Guide to Choosing a Career. Indianapolis: Bobbs-Merrill, 1975.
"Writing for the Uninspired Reader," *English Journal* 94, no. 3 (January 2005): 36–38.
"Writing, Rewriting, Rejection and Recognition: Some Lessons from a Writer's Workshop" in *Authors Insights: Turning Teenagers into Readers and Writers*. New York: Boynton/Cook, 1992.
The Young Landlords. New York: Viking, 1979.
Young Martin's Promise. Austin, Tex.: Raintree, 1992.

Secondary Sources

Abif, Khafre K. "Review: *The Greatest: Muhammad Ali*," *Black Issues Book Review* 3, no. 3 (May 2001): 80.
Adams, Lauren. "Disorderly Fiction," *Horn Book* 78, no. 5 (September/October 2002): 521–528.
_____. "Review: *Shooter*," *Horn Book* 80, no. 3 (May-June 2004): 335.
Agosto, D. E., et al. "The All-White World of Middle-School Genre Fiction: Surveying the Field for Multicultural Protagonists," *Children's Literature in Education* 34, no. 4 (2003): 257–275.
Allen, Jamie. "Banned Books Week Spotlights Battle Over Censorship," http://www.cnn.com/books/news/9909/27/banned.books/, September 27, 1999.
Ammon, Bette D. *Handbook for the Newbery Medal and Honor Books, 1980–1989*. Hagerstown, Md.: Alleyside Press, 1991.
Ammon, Richard. "Review: *Blues Journey*," *General Music Today* 17, no. 3 (spring 2004): 33–34.
Anderson, George K. *The Legend of the Wandering Jew*. Providence, R.I.: Brown University Press, 1965.
Anderson, Lois F. "Review: *Brown Angels: An Album of Pictures and Verse*," *Horn Book* 70, no. 1 (January 1994): 82.
_____. "Review: *Now Is Your Time! The African-American Struggle for Freedom*," *Horn Book* 68, no. 2 (March-April 1992): 217–218.
Andrejevic, Helen B. "Review: *It Ain't All for Nothin*,'" *Parents* 54, no. 1 (January 1979): 20.
Andrews, Loretta Kreider. "Review: *Now Is Your Time! The African-American Struggle for Freedom*," *School Library Journal* 38, no. 4 (March 1992): 263–264.
Andrews, William L. *The African-American*

Novel in the Age of Reaction: Three Classics. New York: Signet, 1992.

Apol, Laura. "Reappearing Fathers, Reappearing Pasts: History, Gender, and Identity in Hamilton's "Plain City" and Myers' "Somewhere in the Darkness," *ALAN Review* 29, no. 2 (winter 2002): 21–25.

Appiah, Kwame Anthony. *In My Father's House: Africa in the Philosophy of Culture*. New York: Oxford University Press, 1992.

"Author: Teen Problems Start at Home" (Santa Rosa, California), *Press Democrat* (22 June 2004).

"Authors Derrick Bell, Walter Dean Myers," *Amsterdam News* 84, no. 2 (9 January 1998): 21.

Bader, Barbara. "Multiculturalism in the Mainstream," *Horn Book Magazine* 79, no. 3 (May 2003): 18–19.

_____. "Multiculturalism Takes Root," *Horn Book Magazine* 79, no. 2 (March/April 2003): 143–152.

Baker, Augusta. "The Changing Image of the Black in Children's Literature," *Horn Book* 51 (February 1975): 79–88.

Banfield, Beryle. "Commitment to Change: The Council on Interracial Books for Children and the World of Children's Books," *African American Review* 32 (spring 1998): 17–22.

Barker, Carol Y. "Review: The Dream Bearer," *School Library Journal* 50, no. 1 (January 2004): 67.

Bauza, Margarite. "Mom's Dispute May Revise Reading Policies," *Detroit News* (21 December 2004).

Baxter, Kathleen. "Review: *The Greatest*," *School Library Journal* 47, no. 12 (December 2001): 39.

Beavin, Kristi. "Review: *Bad Boy*," *Booklist* 98 (July 2001): 473.

_____. "Review: *Monster*," *Booklist* 98 (January 2001): 123.

Beecham, Katherine. "Review: *Blues Journey*," *Five Owls* 17, no. 3 (spring 2004): 81–82.

Beetz, Kirk H., ed. *Beacham's Guide to Literature for Young Adults*. Vol. 6. Washington, D.C.: Beacham Publishing, 1989.

_____. *Beacham's Guide to Literature for Young Adults*. Vol. 8. Washington, D.C.: Beacham Publishing, 1999.

_____. *Beacham's Guide to Literature for Young Adults*. Vol. 11. Farmington Hills, Mich.: Gale Group, 2001.

Behen, Linda D. "Review: *Monster: A Novel*," *Book Report* 18, no. 2 (September/October 1999): 61.

Beram, Nell S. "Review: *Fly!*," *Horn Book* 78, no. 2 (March-April 2002): 203.

Berry, Patricia. "Review: *Hoops: A Novel*," *Voice of Youth Advocates* 5, no. 1 (April 1982): 36.

Betancourt, Jeanne. "Review: *Crystal*," *New York Times Book Review* (13 September 1987): 48.

Bishop, Rudine Sims. *Presenting Walter Dean Myers*. Boston, Mass.: Twayne, 1990.

_____. *Shadow and Substance: Afro-American Experience in Contemporary Children's Fiction*. Urbana, Ill.: National Council of Teachers of English, 1982.

_____. "Walter Dean Myers," *Language-Arts* 67, no. 8 (December 1990): 862–866.

Bissett, Donald J. "Review: *Fast Sam, Cool Clyde, and Stuff*," *Language Arts* 53, no. 5 (May 1976): 520–521.

Black Literature Criticism. Vol. 3. Detroit: Gale Research, 1992.

Block, Francesca Lia, Amy Ehrlich, and Susan Cooper, eds. *When I Was Your Age: Original Stories About Growing Up*. Cambridge: Candlewick Press, 1996.

"Books," *American Visions* 8, no. 6 (December 1993/January 1994): 35–36.

"Books for Adolescents," *Journal of Reading* 38, no. 3 (November 1994): 246–249.

Bosse, Malcolm. "Review: *The Legend of Tarik*," *New York Times Book Review* (12 July 1981): 30.

Bousquin, Marilyn. "Review: *At Her Majesty's Request: An African Princess in Victorian England*," *Horn Book* 75, no. 1 (January 1999): 82.

Boyd, Alex. "Review: *The Legend of Tarik*," *Voice of Youth Advocates* 4, no. 4 (October 1981): 36.

Bradburn, Frances B. "Walter Dean Myers," *Wilson Library Bulletin* (January, 1993): 88.

Bray, Rosemary L. "Review: *Harlem*," *New York Times Book Review* (20 July 1997): 22.

Briggs, Julia. "Review: *The Golden Serpent*," *Times Literary Supplement* (27 March 1981): 343.

Brommer, Shawn. "Review: *The Journal of Biddy Owens: The Negro Leagues*," *School Library Journal* 47, no. 4 (April 2001): 146.

Brown, Jennifer M. "Walter Dean Myers Unites Two Passions," *Publishers Weekly* 246, no. 2 (22 March 1999): 45–46.

"Bully Business," *Scholastic Choices* 20, no. 3 (November-December 2004): 5.

Burke, Lynne T. 'Review: *I've Seen the Promised Land: The Life of Dr. Martin Luther King, Jr.*," *Reading Today* 21, no. 4 (February-March 2004): 28.

Burnett, Jeanie. "Review: *Blues Journey*," *Childhood Education* 80, no. 3 (spring 2004): 163.

Burns, Mary M. "Review: *The Great Migration: An American Story*," *Horn Book* 70, no. 1 (January 1994): 88–89.

_____. "Review: *Won't Know Till I Get There*," *Horn Book* 58 (August 1982): 415.

Bush, Elizabeth. "Review: *How Mr. Monkey Saw the Whole World*," *Bulletin of the Center for Children's Books* 49 (June 1996): 348.

_____. "Review: *U.S.S. Constellation: Pride of the American Navy*," *Bulletin of the Center for Children's Books* 58, no. 1 (September 2004): 32–33.

Bush, Margaret A. "Review: *Scorpions*," *Horn Book* 64 (July/August 1988): 504.

Campbell, Patty. "The Sand in the Oyster Radical Monster," *Horn Book* 75, no. 6 (November 1999): 769.

Cart, Michael. "Review: *Harlem: A Poem*," *Booklist* 98, no. 12 (15 February 1997): 1021.

Carter, Betty. "Review: *U.S.S. Constellation: Pride of the American Navy*," *Horn Book* 80, no. 4 (July-August 2004): 80.

Carton, Debbie. "Review: *Monster*," *Booklist* 95, no. 17 (1 May, 1999): 1587.

Caviston, John F. "Review: *Fast Sam, Cool Clyde, and Stuff*," *School Library Journal* 21, no. 7 (March 1975): 108–109.

Caywood, Carolyn. "Review: *The Outside Shot*," *School Library Journal* 31 (November 1984): 135–136.

Cecere, Joanne K. "Review: *Handbook for Boys: A Novel*," *School Library Journal* 48, no. 5 (May 2002): 157–158.

"Center Offers Mentoring Program for Aspiring Writers," *Reading Today* 13, no. 5 (April/May 1996): 12.

Chance, Rosemary. "Voices from Diverse Cultures," *Emergency Librarian* 22, no. 4 (March/April 1995): 57–58.

_____, Teri Lesesne, and Lois Buckman. "And the Winner Is...: A Teleconference with Walter Dean Myers," *Journal of Reading* 38, no. 3 (November 1994): 246–249.

Chaplin, Nancy. "Review: *Shooter*," *Kliatt* 38, no. 6 (November 2004): 50–51.

Chollet, Laurence. "A Teller of Tales Recreating the Past for the Children of Today," *New Jersey Record* (22 January 1995): E1.

Christenbury, L., ed. *Books for You: An Annotated Booklist for Senior High Students*. Urbana, Ill.: National Council of Teachers of English, 1995.

Coates, Karen. "Review: *The Beast*," *Bulletin of the Center for Children's Books* 57, no. 5 (January 2004): 199.

Codell, Cindy Darling. "Review: *At Her Majesty's Request*," *School Library Journal* 45, no. 1 (January 1999): 149.

Collins, Carol Jones. "Review: *The Glory Field*," *School Library Journal* 40, no. 11 (November 1994): 121–122.

Connors, Cathy. "Walter Dean Myers Captures Childhood in Its Beautiful Innocence of an Era," *New York Amsterdam News* (16 April 1994): 17.

Contemporary Black Biography. Vol. 8. Detroit: Gale Research, 1994.

Cooper, Ilene. "Review: *Angel to Angel: A Mother's Gift of Love*," *Booklist* 94, no. 12 (15 February 1998): 1006.

_____. "Review: *Blues Journey*," *Booklist* 99, no. 12 (15 February 2003): 1082.

_____. "Review: *Glorious Angels: A Celebration of Children*," *Booklist* 92, no. 1 (1 September 1995): 79–80.

_____. "Review: *The Righteous Revenge of Artemis Bonner*," *Booklist* 92, no. 1 (1 September 1995): 321.

Corbett, Sue. "'Monster' Writer Walter Dean Myers' Newest Work Is Destined to Be a Classic," *Tulsa World* (13 February 2000).

_____. "A Storyteller for Urban Teens," *Miami Herald* (21 January 2000): 1E.

_____. "Tales of Slavery Introduce a Month of Black History," *Miami Herald* (30 January 1998): 3F.

_____. "Walter Dean Myers Has Been Writing Poignant, Tough Stories for and about At-risk Kids," *Miami Herald* (26 January 2000): 8D.

Cox, James A., and Diane C. Donovan. "Reviewer's Choice: *The Beast*," *Children's Bookwatch* 14, no. 2 (February 2004): 1.

Cox, Ruth. "Extreme Measures," *Teacher Librarian* 31, no. 4 (April 2004): 68.

_____. "Preteen and Young Teen Protagonists," *Teacher Librarian* 31, no. 2 (Dec 2003): 16.

_____. "Young Men Making Choices," *Teacher Librarian* 27, no. 2 (December 1999): 47–49.

Creech, Sharon. *Love That Dog*. New York: Joanna Cotler Books, 2001.

Crouch, Marcus. "Review: *Scorpions*," *Junior Bookshelf* (March 1990): 190–191.

Crowe, Chris, and Nathan Phillips. "Monsters' Ink: How Walter Dean Myers Made Frankenstein Fun," *English Journal* 92, no. 5 (May 2003): 87–90.

Curley, Suzanne. "Review: *The Glory Field*," *Los Angeles Times Book Review* (1 January 1995): 10.

Davis, Kenneth C. "Review: *The Glory Field*,"

New York Times Book Review (22 January 1989): 29.

Davis, T., and T. Harris, eds. *Dictionary of Literary Biography: Afro-American Fiction Writers After 1955*. Detroit, Mich.: Gale, 1984.

Decandido, Graceanne A. "Review: *A Time to Love: Stories from the Old Testament*," *Booklist* 99, no. 18 (15 May 2003): 1656.

_____, and Alan P. Mahony. "Westchester Librarians Study Multiculturalism," *School Library Journal* 37, no. 11 (November 1991): 14–15.

Del Negro, Janice. "Review: *Darnell Rock Reporting*," *Booklist* 90, no. 22 (August 1994): 2044.

_____. "Review: *Slam!*," *Bulletin of the Center for Children's Books* 50 (February 1997): 216.

Del Vecchio, Stephen. "Recommended for Kids," *Teacher Magazine* 11, no. 4 (January 2000): 57.

Devine, Katherine. "Review: *The Dream Bearer*," *School Library Journal* 49, no. 9 (September 2003): 73.

Dimmit, Jean Pollard. "The First Printz Award Designations: Winners All," *ALAN Review* 28, no. 2 (winter 2001): 54–59.

Dirda, Michael. "Review: *Now Is Your Time! The African-American Struggle for Freedom*," *Washington Post Book World* (8 March 1992): 11.

Donelson, Ken. "'Filth' and 'Pure Filth' in Our Schools—Censorship of Classroom Books in the Last Ten Years," *English Journal* (February 1997: 21–25.

_____, and Aileen Pace Nilsen. *Literature for Today's Young Adults*. Boston: Allyn & Bacon, 2004.

Doyle, Miranda. "Review: *Bad Boy: A Memoir*," *School Library Journal* 47, no. 5 (May 2001): 169.

Drew, Bernard A. *The One Hundred Most Popular Young Adult Authors*. Englewood, Colo.: Libraries Unlimited, 1996.

Drewel, Margaret Thompson. *Yoruba Ritual*. Indianapolis: Indiana University Press, 1992.

Due, Tananarive. "Kids' Books for the Real World," *Miami Herald* (17 February 1992): 1C.

Eble, Mary. "Review: *Where Does the Day Go?*," *School Library Journal* (15 April 1970): 111.

Edelman, Diane Gersoni. "Review: *Won't Know Till I Get There*," *New York Times Book Review* (13 June 1982): 26–27.

Edwards, Anthony. "Review: *One More River to Cross: An African American Photograph Album*," *MultiCultural Review* 5 (September 1996): 73.

Enciso, Patricia E. "Taking Our Seats: The Consequences of Positioning in Reading Assessments," *Theory Into Practice* 40, no. 3 (1 June 2001): 166–174.

Engberg, Gillian. "Review: *The Greatest: The Life and Career of Muhammad Ali*," *Booklist* 98, no. 1 (1 September 2001): 101.

Estes, Cheri. "Review: *The Dragon Takes a Wife*," *School Library Journal* 41, no. 3 (March 1995): 185.

Fader, Ellen. "Booklist: For Older Readers," *Horn Book* 68, no. 3 (May 1992): 344–345.

_____. "Review: *Darnell Rock Reporting*," *Horn Book* 71, no. 2 (March 1995): 194, 200.

_____. "Review: *How Mr. Monkey Saw the Whole World*," *Horn Book* 72, no. 4 (March 1995): 452.

Fakih, Kimerly Olson. "Interview: Walter Dean Myers," *Publishers Weekly* 247, no. 21 (10 April 2000): 101.

_____. *Literature of Delight: A Critical Guide to Humorous Books for Children*. Englewood, Colo.: Libraries Unlimited, 1993.

_____. "Review: *Me, Mop, and the Moondance Kid*," *Publishers Weekly* 234, no. 20 (11 November 1988): 58.

Fazioli, Carol. "Review: *Bad Boy*," *School Library Journal* 49, no. 11 (November 2003): 84.

Feder-Feitel, Lisa. "Writing About What's Real," *Scholastic Scope* 52, no. 12 (9 February 2004): 14.

Feiwel, Jean, and Kimberly Colen. *Walter Dean Myers*. New York, N.Y.: Scholastic, 1993.

Flanagan, K. M. "Review: *The Young Landlords*," *Horn Book* 55, no. 5 (October 1979): 535.

Flynn, Kellie. "Review: *Now Is Your Time! The African-American Struggle for Freedom*," *Voice of Youth Advocates* 15 (February 1992): 398.

Follos, Alison. "Review: *Bad Boy: A Memoir*," *School Library Journal* 50, no. 11 (November 2004): 66.

_____. "Review: *Blues Journey*," *School Library Journal* 50, no. 11 (November 2004): 65.

Foner, Laura. "Review: *Blues Journey*," *Horn Book* 80, no. 1 (January-February 2004): 16.

Forbes, Frederick E. *Dahomey and the Dahomans: Being the Journal of Two Missions to the King of Dahomey and Residence at His Capital in the Years 1849 and 1850*. London: Longman, Brown, Green, and Longmans, 1851.

Foreman, Carol. "Review: *Walter Dean Myers*," *School Library Journal* 50, no. 9 (September 2004): 223.

Forman, Jack. "Review: *The Greatest: The Life and Career of Muhammad Ali*," *Horn Book* 77, no. 1 (January 2001): 115.

_____. "Review: *The Greatest: Muhammad Ali*," *Horn Book* 77, no. 1 (January 2001): 115.

_____. "Review: *The Young Landlords*," *School Library Journal* 26, no. 2 (October 1979): 160.

Frazier, Kermit. "Review: *Bad Boy*," *New York Times Book Review* (21 October 2001): 3.

Frederick, Helen Vogel. "Review: *Now Is Your Time!: The African-American Struggle for Freedom* and *Somewhere in the Darkness*," *Christian Science Monitor* (1 May 1992): 10.

Gallo, Donald R. "A Man of Many Ideas: Walter Dean Myers," *Writing* 26, no. 5 (February/March 2004): 10–11.

_____, ed. *Speaking for Ourselves: Autobiographical Sketches by Notable Authors of Books for Young Adults.* Urbana, Ill.: National Council of Teachers of English, 1990.

Garner, Judith M. "Review: *Malcolm X: By Any Means Necessary*," *Book Report* 11, no. 5 (March/April 1993): 48.

Garrett, A., and H. McCue, eds. *Authors & Artists.* Detroit, Mich.: Gale, 1990.

Gauch, Patricia L. "Review: *The Young Landlords*," *New York Times Book Review* (6 January 1980): 20.

Gearan, Jay. "School Assignment Becomes Quest for Family History," Worcester, Mass., *Telegram & Gazette* (28 May 2000): 1.

Gebhart, Ann O. "The Emerging Self: Young-Adult and Classic Novels of the Black Experience," *English Journal* 82 (September 1993): 50–54.

Gentle, Maria. "The Printz Award for Young Adult Literature," *Book Report* 20, no. 1 (May/June 2001): 27.

Gepson, Lolly. "Review: *Shooter*," *Booklist* 101, no. 6 (15 November 2004): 608.

Gill, Sam D. "Young Adult Literature for Young Adult Males," *ALAN Review* 26, no. 2 (winter 1999): 1.

Goldsmith, Francisca. "Review: *Shooter*," *School Library Journal* 50, no. 5 (May 2004): 154–155.

_____. "Review: *U.S.S. Constellation: Pride of the American Navy*," *School Library Journal* 50, no. 9 (September 2004): 79.

Graham, Adam. "Author's Just a Kid at Heart," *Detroit News* (6 May 2002).

Gray, Jerry. "'He Knows I Have Come to Kill Him': A Young Soldier Meets the Enemy in Vietnam, and Discovers an Unsettling Truth," *New York Times Book Review* 107, no. 40 (19 May 2002): 35.

Greever, Ellen A., and Patricia Austin, "Making Connections in the Life and Works of Walter Dean Myers," *Teaching and Learning Literature with Children and Young Adults* 8, no. 1 (September-October 1998): 42–54.

Griffin, Maureen. "Review: *Patrol: An American Soldier in Vietnam*," *Kliatt* 39, no. 1 (January 2005): 28.

Griffin, Nancy. "Review: *The Dragon Takes a Wife*," *New York Times Book Review* (19 April 1972): 8.

Gropman, Jackie. "Review: *One More River to Cross: An African-American Photograph Album*," *Booklist* 42, no. 8 (August 1996): 186.

Hanson, Elaine. "Review: *Slam!*," *Booklist* 97, no. 21 (July 2001): 2030.

Hatfield, Jean. "Review: *Monster*," *Booklist* 97, no. 5 (1 November 2000): 557.

Hawley, Lucy V. "Review: *The Nicholas Factor*," *School Library Journal* 30, no. 1 (September 1983): 138.

Hayn, Judith, and Deborah Wherrill. "Female Protagonists in Multicultural Young Adult Literature: Sources and Strategies," *ALAN Review* 24, no. 1 (fall 1996): 1.

Hearn, Michael Patrick. "Review: *Brown Angels, an Album of Pictures and Verse*," *Washington Post Book World* (3 July 1994): 14.

Hearne, Betsy. "Review: *The Great Migration: An American Story*," *Bulletin of the Center for Children's Books* 47 (November 1993): 89.

_____. "Review: *Now Is Your Time! The African-American Struggle for Freedom*," *Bulletin of the Center for Children's Books* 45 (January 1992): 134.

Hedblad, Alan, ed. *Something About the Author.* Vol. 41. Detroit, Mich.: Gale Research, 1985.

Heins, Ethel L. "Review: *Fallen Angels*," *Horn Book* 64, no. 4 (July-August, 1988): 503.

_____. "Review: *Mojo and the Russians*," *Horn Book* 54, no. 2 (April 1978): 166–167.

Heins, Paul. "Review: *Fast Sam, Cool Clyde, and Stuff*," *Horn Book* (August 1975): 388.

_____. "Review: *The Golden Serpent*," *Horn Book* 56 (December 1980): 686.

Higgins, Marilyn. "Review: *Slam!*," *School Library Journal* 47, no. 3 (March 2001): 89.

Hiron, Barbara, and Blake Rodman. "Noteworthy," *Teacher Magazine* 9, no. 1 (August/September 1997): 65.

"His Goal Is to Make Young Blacks See Themselves in Books," *Philadelphia Daily News* (4 February 2000).

Hodges, Alecia. "Jacob Lawrence's *The Great Migration*," *Arts & Activities* 129 no. 1 (February 2001): 36.

Hofmann, Mary. "Review: *Handbook for Boys: A Novel*," *Book Report* 21, no. 3 (November-December 2002): 48.

Holtze, Sally Holmes. *The Fifth Book of Junior Authors*. New York: H. W. Wilson, 1983.

"Home to Harlem," *QBR* 11, no. 5 (September/October 2004): 26–27.

Hooper, Brad. "Review: *One More River to Cross*," *Booklist* 95, no. 12 (15 February 1999): 1012.

Horner, Shirley. "Author Seeks to Inspire Black Youth," *New York Times* (21 August 1988): 10.

Hudak, Melissa. "Review: *Harlem: A Poem*," *School Library Journal* 43, no. 2 (February 1997): 121.

_____. "Review: *Toussaint L'Ouverture: The Fight for Haiti's Freedom*," *School Library Journal* 42, no. 11 (November 1996): 116.

Hurlburt, Tom S. "Review: *Darnell Rock Reporting*," *School Library Journal* (September 1994): 220.

_____. "Review: *Slam!*," *School Library Journal* 42, 11 (November 1996): 123.

Hurst, Alison. "Review: *Fallen Angels*," *School Librarian* 40, no. 9 (August 1990): 118–119.

Hurst, Carol Otis. *Long Ago and Far Away...: An Encyclopedia for Successfully Using Literature with Intermediate Readers*. Allen, Tex.: DLM, 1991.

James, Karen. "Review: *The Blues of Flats Brown*," *School Library Journal* 46, no. 3 (March 2000): 210.

Johnson, Diane. *Telling Tales: The Pedagogy and Promise of African-American Literature for Youth*. Westport, Conn.: Greenwood, 1990.

Johnson, Nancy J., and Cyndi Giorgis. "Imagination," *Reading Teacher* 56, no. 5 (February 2003): 504–511.

Jones, Howard. *Mutiny on the Amistad*. Oxford: Oxford University Press, 1987.

Jones, Lynda. *Five Famous Writers*. New York: Scholastic, 2001.

_____. "Review: *Handbook for Boys: A Novel*," *Black Issues Book Review*, 4, no. 3 (May/June 2002): 78.

_____. "Review: *Patrol: An American Soldier in Vietnam*," *Black Issues Book Review* 4, no. 5 (September-October 2002): 61.

Jones, Trevelyn E., et al. "Review: *Malcolm X: A Fire Burning Brightly*," *School Library Journal* 46, no. 12 (December 2000): 54.

Jordan, Denise M. *Walter Dean Myers: Writer for Real Teens*. Berkeley Heights, N.J.: Enslow, 1999.

Junior Discovering Authors on CD. Detroit: Gale Research, 1994.

Kalamu ya Salaam. "Enriching the Paper Trail: An Interview with Tom Dent," *African American Review* 27, no. 2 (summer 1993): 327–344.

Karr, Rita, and Leslie Verzi Julian. "Middle School Readers: Common Views, Different Worlds," *ALAN Review* 26, no. 2 (winter 1999): 1.

Kaywell, Joan F. *Adolescent Literature As a Complement to the Classics*. New York: Christopher-Gordon, 1992.

Kazemek, Francis E. "The Literature of Vietnam and Afghanistan: Exploring War and Peace with Adolescents," *ALAN-Review* 23, no. 3 (spring 1996): 6–9.

Kelly, David. "I Can Pop I Can Break I Can Slide and Jerk," *New York Times Book Review* 139, no. 4824 (20 May 1990): 44.

Kiefer, Barbara. *Getting to Know You: Profiles of Children's Authors Featured in "Language Arts" 1985–1990*. Urbana, Ill.: National Council of Teachers of English, 1991.

Knight, Elaine E. "Review: *Three Swords for Granada*," *School Library Journal* 48 no. 9 (September 2002): 230.

Knoth, Maeve Visser. "Review: *Slam!*," *Horn Book* 73, no. 1 (January-February 1997): 63–64.

Kraco, Karen. "Reading for Culture and Understanding," *Minneapolis-St. Paul Magazine* 29, no. 9 (September 2001): 177.

Kutenplon, Deborah, and Ellen Olmstead. *Young Adult Fiction by African American Writers, 1968–1993: A Critical and Annotated Guide*. New York: Garland, 1996.

Kutzer, M. D. ed. *Writers of Multicultural Fiction for Young Adults*. Westwood, Conn.: Greenwood Press, 1996.

Laing, E. K. "Review: *Malcolm X: By Any Means Necessary*," *Christian Science Monitor* (5 February 1993): 11.

Laminack, Lester L., et al. "Striving to Keep Up with New Children's Books," *Language Arts* 82, no. 5 (May 2005): 398–403.

Landsberg, Michele. "Review: *The Great Migration*," *Entertainment Weekly* no. 194 (29 October 1993): 76.

_____. "Review: *Malcolm X: By Any Means Necessary*," *Entertainment Weekly* no. 156 (5 February 1993): 63.

Lane, R. D. "'Keepin' It Real': Walter Dean Myers and the Promise of African-American Children's Literature," *African American Review* 32, no. 1 (22 March 1998): 125–138.

Larson, Gerry. "Review: *Amistad: A Long Road to Freedom*," *School Library Journal* 44, no. 5 (May 1998): 158.

_____. "Review: *Crystal*," *School Library Journal* 33, 10 (June/July 1987): 111.

_____. "Review: *The Journal of Joshua Loper, a Black Cowboy on the Chisholm Trail, 1871*," *School Library Journal* 45, no. 4 (April 1999): 140.

_____. "Review: *The Mouse Rap*," *School Library Journal* 37, no. 2 (February 1991): 37.

_____. "Review: *Somewhere in the Darkness*," *School Library Journal* 38, no. 4 (April 1992): 146.

Latrobe, Kathryn, and Trisha Hutcherson. "An Introduction to Ten Outstanding Young-Adult Authors in the United States," *World Literature Today* 76 (summer 2002): 70–79.

Lempke, Susan Dove. "Review: *How Mr. Monkey Saw the Whole World*," *Booklist* 92, no. 15 (1 April 1996): 1373.

Lesesne, Teri. "Books for Children," *Emergency Librarian* 25, no. 5 (May/June 1998): 49–51.

_____. "Review: *Angel to Angel: A Mother's Gift of Love*," *Teacher Librarian* 26, no. 3 (January-February 1999): 42–43.

Lester, Jasmine. "Review: *The Beast*," *Journal of Adolescent & Adult Literacy* 48, no. 4 (December 2004): 347.

Levin, Ann. "Paintings Tell Vivid Story of a People on the Move," *Greensboro News Record* (14 March 1994): D6.

Lewis, Johanna. "Review: *The Beast*," *School Library Journal* 49, no. 12 (December 2003): 157.

Lewis, Valerie. "Meet the Author," *Instructor* 105, no. 8 (May/June 1996): 72–73.

"Lewis Family Threads Drawn Together Over Time," Portland, Ore., *Skanner* 21, no. 7 (22 November 1995): 13.

Lindgren, Merri V., ed. *The Multicolored Mirror: Cultural Substance in Literature for Children and Young Adults*. Madison, Wisc.: Cooperative Children's Book Center, 1991.

Lindsay, Nina. "Review: *Here in Harlem: Poems in Many Voices*," *School Library Journal* 50, no. 2 (Dec 2004): 166.

Lindsey, David A. "Review: *A Place Called Heartbreak: A Story of Vietnam*," *School Library Journal* 39, no. 6 (June 1993): 120.

Lipson, Eden Ross. *New York Times Parent's Guide to the Best Books for Children*. New York: Turtleback, 2000.

Lipsyte, Robert. "Novels with the Power to Change Young Lives," *New York Times* (28 April 2003): E1.

_____. "Review: *Fast Sam, Cool Clyde, and Stuff*," *New York Times Book Review* (4 May 1975): 28, 30.

Little, Brenda B. "Review: *Darnell Rock Reporting*," *Book Report* 13, no.4 (January/February 1995): 48–49.

_____. "Review: *The Glory Field*," *Book Report* 13, no. 3 (November/December 1994): 47.

Long, Joanna Rudge. "Review: *Patrol: An American Soldier in Vietnam*," *Horn Book* 78, no. 4 (July-August 2002): 449–450.

Lothrop, Patricia D. "Review: *A Time to Love: Stories from the Old Testament*," *School Library Journal* 49, no. 5 (May 2003): 158.

Lukehart, Wendy. "Review: *Blues Journey*," *School Library Journal* 49, no. 4 (April 2003): 188.

MacDonald, Sandy. "Children's Books," *New York Times Book Review* (19 September 2004): 16.

MacPherson, Karen. "Living to Tell," *Washington Post Book World* (13 May 2003): 3.

Major Authors and Illustrators for Children and Young Adults, 2nd ed. Farmington Hills, Mich.: Gale Group, 2002.

Manning, Patricia. "Review: *Antarctica: Journeys to the South Pole*," *School Library Journal* 50, no. 2 (Dec 2004): 166.

Marcus, Leonard S. "Review: *Malcolm X: A Fire Burning Brightly*," *Parenting* 14, no. 1 (February 2000): 70.

Marks, Alexandra. "One City, One Curriculum; Consistency Is the Goal in New York City's Efforts to Improve Its Schools," *Christian Science Monitor* (20 January, 2004): 14.

Marowski, D. G., ed. *Contemporary Literary Criticism*. Vol. 35. Detroit, Mich.: Gale, 1991.

Martin, Hillias J. "Review: *The Dream Bearer*," *School Library Journal* 49, no. 6 (June 2003): 146.

Masciere, Christina. "Browser: Cultural Adventures," *New Orleans Magazine* 31, no. 1 (October 1996): 74.

Matthews, Steven. "Review: *It Ain't All for Nothin'*," *School Library Journal* 26 (October 1978): 158.

McClelland, Kate. "Review: *On the Wings of Peace*," *School Library Journal* 41, no. 10 (October 1995): 150.

McCoy, W. Keith. "Review: *Fallen Angels*," *Voice of Youth Advocates* 11 (August 1988): 133.

McCullough, Michael. "Review: *The Greatest: The Life and Career of Muhammad Ali*," *School Library Journal* 47, no. 1 (January 2001): 152.

McElmeel, Sharron L., and Carol Simpson. "Profile: Walter Dean Myers," *Book Report* 20, no. 2 (September/October 2001): 42–44.

McGlone, Marissa. "Review: *The Journal of Biddy Owens: The Negro Leagues*," *Childhood Education* 78, no. 2 (winter 2001): 112.

"Meet Walter Dean Myers, Making Intellect Cool," *NEA Today* (December 1991): 9.

Mehren, Elizabeth. "Fountain of Stories for Youth: Walter Dean Myers," *Los Angeles Times* (15 October 1997): E1.

Meyer, Randy. "Review: *The Journal of Scott Pendleton Collins, a WWII Soldier, Normandy, France, 1944*," *Booklist* 95 (1 June 1999): 1830.

_____. "Review: *Now Is Your Time! The African-American Struggle for Freedom*," *Booklist* 88 (1 November 1991): 504.

Micklos, J., Jr., "Author Walter Dean Myers Stresses Realism in His Writing," *Reading Today* 8, no.4 (February-March 1991): 38.

Millard, Holly. "Review: *The World of Work*," *Library Journal* 100, no. 8, 15 April 1975): 755.

Miller-Lachmann, Lyn. "Review: *The Great Migration: An American Story*," *School Library Journal* 39, no. 12 (December 1993): 127.

Monks, Merri M, and Donna Reidy Pistolis. *Hit List: Frequently Challenged Books for Young Adults*. Chicago: Young Adult Library Services, 1996.

Moore, Ann W. "Review: *The Greatest: Muhammad Ali*," *School Library Journal* 51, no. 1 (January 2005): 57.

Moore, Claudia. "Review: *Monster: A Novel*," *School Library Journal* 46, no. 12 (December 2000): 81.

Moore, John Noell. "'Motherly Business' and the Moves to Manhood," *ALAN Review* 22, no. 1 (fall 1994): 51–55.

Moore, Susan M. "Review: *I've Seen the Promised Land: The Life of Dr. Martin Luther King, Jr.*," *School Library Journal* 50, no. 4 (April 2004): 140.

Morgans, Patricia A. "Review: *The Nicholas Factor*," *Best Sellers* 43, no. 4 (July 1983): 155.

Mueller, Mary. "Review: *U.S.S. Constellation: Pride of the American Navy*," *School Library Journal* 50, no. 8 (August 2004): 140.

Muse, Daphne. "Detectives, Dubious Dudes, Spies and Suspense in African American Fiction for Children and Young Adults," *Black Scholar* 28, no. 1 (1998): 33–39.

Myers, Walter Dean. "The Intimidating Foe of Bullying," *Newark Star-Ledger* (23 April 2004): 21.

_____. "Jersey City Class Hears Call for 'Lifetime Learning,'" *Newark Star-Ledger* (23 May 1994).

_____. "Mean Streets; *Do or Die*, by Leon Bing," *Los Angeles Times* (11 August 1991): 1.

_____. "Private Interview" (email), February 25, 2005.

_____. "Private Interview" (email), March 16, 2005.

_____. "Private Interview" (email), May 22, 2005.

_____. "Walter Dean Myers," *Read* 54, no. 13 (25 February 2005): 14–15.

_____, et al. "YA Grows Up," http://www.authorsontheweb.com/features/0108-ya/0108-ya.asp, 2001.

"Myers, Teen Panel Headline Denver YA Conference," *School Library Journal* 40, no. 6 (June 1994): 17.

Naughton, Jim. "Literary Crusader Writes Stories About Real Kids," *Los Angeles Times* (29 December 1989): 8.

_____. "Review: *Slam!*," *Washington Post Book World* (12 January 1997).

_____. "Walter Dean Myers, Writing About Reality for Black Children," *Washington Post Book World* (9 December 1989): C1.

Needham, Nancy R. "Making Intellect Cool," *NEA Today* 10, no. 5 (December 1991): 9.

Nelmes, Margot. "Older Readers," *Reading Time* 55, no. 5 (February 2002): 488.

"New and Noteworthy," *Teaching PreK–8* 22, no. 8 (May 1992): 125

Nilsen, Alleen Pace. "Love and the Teenage Reader," *English Journal* (March 1976): 90–92.

_____. "Review: *Fast Sam, Cool Clyde, and Stuff*," *English Journal* 65, no. 2 (March 1976): 90–92.

"Novel Depicts Black Soldier in Vietnam," Portland, Ore., *Skanner* 13, no. 38 (22 June 1988): 7.

Osagie, Iyunolu Folayan. *The Amistad Revolt: Memory, Slavery, and the Politics of Identity in the United States and Sierra Leone*. Athens: University of Georgia Press, 2000.

Ott, Bill. "Review: *The Greatest: The Life and Career of Muhammad Ali*," *Booklist* 97, no. 1 (1 January 2001): 952.

_____. "Review: *Slam!*," *Booklist* 93, no. 6 (15 November 1996): 579.

Owens, William A. *Black Mutiny: The Revolt on the Schooner Amistad*. New York: Plume, 1997.

Palmer, Jean. "Review: *Monster: A Novel*," *Kliatt* 35, no. 4 (July 2001).

Patrick-Wexler, Diane. *Walter Dean Myers*. New York: Steck-Vaughn, 1996.

Pennington, Ashley Jane. "Review: *It Ain't All for Nothin*,'" *Interracial Books for Children Bulletin* 10, no. 4 (1979): 18.

Perkins, Linda. "Review: *The Glory Field*," *Wilson Library Bulletin* 69, no. 3 (November 1994): 120–121.

Perren, Susan. "Children's Books: *Shooter*," *Globe & Mail* (31 July 2004), D11.

Peters, John. "Review: *The Journal of Joshua Loper, a Black Cowboy on the Chisholm Trail, 1871*," *Booklist* 95, no. 12 (15 February 1999): 1070.

Phelan, Carolyn. "Review: *At Her Majesty's Request: An African Princess in Victorian England*," *Booklist* 95, no. 15 (1 April 1999): 1405.

_____. "Review: *The Dream Bearer*," *Booklist* 99, no. 21 (July 2003): 1891.

_____. "Review: *Here in Harlem: Poems in Many Voices*," *Booklist* 101, no. 5 (1 November 2004): 480.

_____. "Review: *The Journal of Biddy Owens: The Negro Leagues, Birmingham, Alabama, 1948*," *Booklist* 97, no. 12 (15 February 2001): 1149.

_____. "Review: *The Story of the Three Kingdoms*," *Booklist* 91, no. 19–20 (1 June 1995): 1788.

_____. "Review: *U.S.S. Constellation: Pride of the American Navy*," *Booklist* 100, no. 21 (July 2004): 1841.

Phillips, Nathan. "'Monsters' Ink: How Walter Dean Myers Made Frankenstein Fun," *English Journal* 92, no. 5 (May 2003): 87–90.

Pierleoni, Allen O. "Wrongs and the Writer," *Sacramento Bee* (29 March 2005).

Pietrofesa, John J. "Review: *The World of Work*," *Personnel & Guidance Journal* 55, no. 3 (November 1976): 150–151.

Polette, Nancy J. *Gifted Books, Gifted Readers: Literature Activities to Excite Young Minds.* Englewood, Colo.: Libraries Unlimited, 2000.

Price, Anne, and Juliette Yaakov. *Middle and Junior High School Library Catalog.* New York: H. W. Wilson, 1995.

Price, Michael H. "A New Look at That Old Chisholm Trail," *Fort Worth Business Press* 17, no. 51 (17 December 2004): 28.

Raines, Shirley C. *450 More Story Stretchers for the Primary Grades: Activities to Expand Children's Favorite Books.* Mt. Rainier, Md.: Gryphon House, 1994.

Ramsay, John G. "When Jesse Reads *Slam!*," *Education Week* 18, no. 7 (14 October 1998): 44.

Ramsay, Marie. "Review: *Shadow of the Red Moon*," *Book Report* 15, no. 1 (May/June 1996): 38.

Rausch, Tim. "Review: *Shadow of the Red Moon*," *School Library Journal* 41, no. 12 (December 1995): 106.

Raymond, A. "Walter Dean Myers: A 'Bad Kid' Who Makes Good," *Teaching Pre-K–8* 20, no. 2 (October 1989): 53–55.

Renner, Coop. "Review: *The Journal of Scott Pendleton Collins, a WWII Soldier, Normandy, France, 1944*," *School Library Journal* 45, no. 7 (July 1999): 98.

"Review: *Antarctica: Journeys to the South Pole*," *Kirkus Reviews* 72, no. 21 (1 November 2004): 1046.

"Review: *At Her Majesty's Request: An African Princess in Victorian England*," *Kirkus* 67 (1 June 1999): 887.

"Review: *At Her Majesty's Request: An African Princess in Victorian England*," *Publishers Weekly* 246, no. 6 (8 February 1999): 215.

"Review: *Bad Boy: A Memoir*," *Bulletin of the Center for Children's Books* 55 (September 2001): 29.

"Review: *Bad Boy: A Memoir*," *Horn Book Guide* 12 (fall 2001): 416.

"Review: *Bad Boy: A Memoir*," *Ruminator Review* (fall 2001): 43.

"Review: *Blues Journey*," *School Library Journal* 50, no. 4 (April 2004): 46.

"Review: *The Blues of Flats Brown*," *Publishers Weekly* 247, no. 4 (24 January 2000): 311.

"Review: *Darnell Rock Reporting*," *Publishers Weekly* 241, no. 27 (4 July 1994): 65.

"Review: *The Dragon Takes a Wife*," *Kirkus Reviews* (1 March 1972): 256.

"Review: *The Dream Bearer*," *Black Issues Book Review* 5, no. 5 (September-October 2003): 70.

"Review: *The Dream Bearer*," *Kirkus Reviews* 71, no. 10 (15 May 2003): 754.

"Review: *The Glory Field*," *Booklist* 91, no. 15 (1 April 1995): 1403.

"Review: *The Glory Field*," *Bulletin of the Center for Children's Books* 48 (November 1994): 97.

"Review: *The Glory Field*," *Children's Book Review Service* 23 (November 1994): 34.

"Review: *The Glory Field*," *English Journal* 84, no. 5 (September 1995): 117.

"Review: *The Glory Field*," *Horn Book Guide* 6 (spring 1995): 90.

"Review: *The Glory Field*," *Instructor* 105 (October 1995): 80.

"Review: *The Glory Field*," *Instructor* 105 (November 1995): 51.

"Review: *The Glory Field*," *Journal of Reading* 38 (November 1994): 249.

"Review: *The Glory Field*," *Kliatt* 30, no. 5 (September 1996): 4.

"Review: *The Glory Field*," *Library Media Connection* 13 (November 1994): 47.

"Review: *The Glory Field*," *Los Angeles Times* (1 January 1995): 10.

"Review: *The Glory Field*," *New York Times Book Review* 99 (13 November 1994): 42.

"Review: *The Glory Field*," *Publishers Weekly* 241, no. 36 (5 September 1994): 112.

"Review: *The Glory Field*," *Reading Teacher* 49 (September 1995): 56.

"Review: *The Glory Field*," *School Library Journal* 40, no. 11 (November 1994): 121–122.

"Review: *The Glory Field*," *Social Education* 59 (April 1995): 219.

"Review: *The Glory Field*," *Village Voice Literary Supplement* (October 1994): 22.

"Review: *The Glory Field*," *Voice of Youth Advocates* 17 (October 1994): 214.

"Review: *The Great Migration: An American Story*," *Publishers Weekly* 240, no. 39 (27 September 1993): 61.

"Review: *The Greatest: Muhammad Ali*," *Booklist* 98 (1 January 2002): 766.

"Review: *The Greatest: Muhammad Ali*," *Horn Book Guide* 12 (fall 2001): 398.

"Review: *Handbook for Boys*," *Kirkus Reviews* 70, no. 8 (15 April 2002): 575.

"Review: *Handbook for Boys: A Novel*," *Publishers Weekly*, 249 no. 16 (22 April 2002): 70–71.

"Review: *Handbook for Boys: A Novel*," *Publishers Weekly* 249, no. 31 (5 August 2002): 28.

"Review: *Here in Harlem: Poems in Many Voices*," *Kirkus Reviews* 72, no. 22 (15 November 2004): 1092.

"Review: *Here in Harlem: Poems in Many Voices*," *Publishers Weekly* 251, no. 46 (15 November 2004): 61.

"Review: *How Mr. Monkey Saw the Whole World*," *Publishers Weekly* 243, no. 8 (19 February 1996): 215.

"Review: "*It Ain't All for Nothin*,"" *Kirkus Reviews* (15 October 1978): 1143.

"Review: "*I've Seen the Promised Land: The Life of Dr. Martin Luther King, Jr.*," *Kirkus Reviews* 71, no. 11 (15 November 2003): 1362.

"Review: "*I've Seen the Promised Land: The Life of Dr. Martin Luther King, Jr.*," *Publishers Weekly* 251, no. 2 (12 January 2004): 53–54.

"Review: *Malcolm X: A Fire Burning Brightly*," *Booklist* 96, no. 12 (15 February 2000): 1103.

"Review: *Malcolm X: A Fire Burning Brightly*," *Bulletin of the Center for Children's Books* 53 (April 2000): 288.

"Review: *Malcolm X: A Fire Burning Brightly*," *Children's Book Review Service* 28 (May 2000): 115.

"Review: *Malcolm X: A Fire Burning Brightly*," *Horn Book* 76, no. 3 (May 2000): 336.

"Review: *Malcolm X: A Fire Burning Brightly*," *Horn Book Guide* 11 (fall 2000): 399.

"Review: *Malcolm X: A Fire Burning Brightly*," *New Advocate* 14 (fall 2001): 343.

"Review: *Malcolm X: A Fire Burning Brightly*," *Reading Teacher* 54 (November 2000): 339.

"Review: *Malcolm X: A Fire Burning Brightly*," *Riverbank Review* 3 (fall 2000): 43.

"Review: *Malcolm X: A Fire Burning Brightly*," *Social Education* 65, no. 14 (May 2001): 23.

"Review: *Malcolm X: By Any Means Necessary*," Indianapolis *Recorder* (28 November 1992): B1.

"Review: *Malcolm X: By Any Means Necessary*," *Publishers Weekly* 239, no. 51 (23 November 1992): 64.

"Review: *Monster: A Novel*," *Horn Book* 75, no. 3 (May 1999): 337.

"Review: *Monster: A Novel*," *Horn Book* 76, no. 1 (January 2000): 42.

"Review: *Monster: A Novel*," *Publishers Weekly* 247, no. 30 (24 July 2000): 32.

"Review: *The Nicholas Factor*," *Publishers Weekly* 223, no. 11 (13 March 1983): 70.

"Review: *Now Is Your Time! The African-American Struggle for Freedom*," *Kirkus Reviews* (1 December 1991): 1537.

"Review: *Now Is Your Time! The African-American Struggle for Freedom*," *Publishers Weekly* 238, no. 48 (1 November 1991): 82.

"Review: *Shooter*," *Kirkus Reviews* 72, no. 8 (15 April 2004): 398.

"Review: *Shooter*," *Publishers Weekly* 251, no. 12 (22 March 2004): 87.

"Review: *The Story of the Three Kingdoms*," *Publishers Weekly* 242, no. 19 (8 May 1995): 296.

"Review: *A Time to Love: Stories from the Old Testament*," *Publishers Weekly* 250, no. 13 (31 March 2003): 64.

"Review: *U.S.S. Constellation: Pride of the American Navy*," *Children's Bookwatch* 14, no. 7 (July 2004): 8.

"Review: *U.S.S. Constellation: Pride of the American Navy*," *Kirkus Reviews* 72, no. 11 (1 June 2004): 539.

"Review: *U.S.S. Constellation: Pride of the American Navy*," *Publishers Weekly* 251, no. 26 (28 June 2004): 52.

"Review: *U.S.S. Constellation: Pride of the American Navy*," *Voice of Youth Advocates* 27, no. 3 (August 2004): 240.

"Review: *Won't Know Till I Get There*," *Black Issues Book Review* 1 (November, 1999): 75.

"Review: *Won't Know Till I Get There*," *Bulletin of the Center for Children's Books* 35 (June 1982): 193.

Rich, Anna. "Review: *Monster*," *Booklist* 97, no. 6 (15 November 2000): 657.

Richards, Chris. "African American Authors Offer a Peek at the Write Stuff," *Washington Post* (8 July 2004): C5.

Riess, Jana. "Review: *A Time to Love: Stories from the Old Testament*," *Publishers Weekly* 250, no. 13 (31 March 2003): 64.

Roback, Diane. "Picture Book Reprints," *Publishers Weekly* 251, no. 2 (12 January 2004): 56.

_____. "Review: *The Blues of Flats Brown*," *Publishers Weekly* 247, no. 4 (24 January 2000): 311.

_____. "Review: *Handbook for Boys: A Novel*," *Publishers Weekly* 249, no. 16 (22 April 2002)" 70–71.

_____. "Review: *I've Seen the Promised Land: The Life of Dr. Martin Luther King, Jr.*," *Library Media Connection* 23, no. 1 (August/September 2004): 72.

_____. "Review: *The Mouse Rap*," *Publishers Weekly* 237, no. 13 (30 March 1990): 64.

_____, and Jennifer M. Brown. "Forecasts: Children's Books," *Publishers Weekly* 246, no. 6 (8 February 1999): 215–216.

Robinson, Edward W., *et al*. *The Journey of the Songhai People*. Philadelphia: Pan African federation, 1987.

Rochman, Hazel. "Interview: Walter Dean Myers," *Booklist* 96, no. 12 (15 February 2000): 1101.

_____. "Review: *Amistad*," *Booklist* 94, no. 12 (15 February 1998): 1003.

_____. "Review: *Antarctica: Journeys to the South Pole*," *Booklist* 101, no. 6 (15 November 2004): 573.

_____. "Review: *Bad Boy: A Memoir*," *Booklist* 97, no. 17 (1 May 2001): 1673.

_____. "Review: *The Glory Field*," *Booklist* 91, no. 3 (1 October 1994): 319.

_____. "Review: *The Great Migration: An American Story*," *Booklist* 90, no. 28 (15 November 1993): 621.

_____. "Review: *I've Seen the Promised Land: The Life of Dr. Martin Luther King, Jr.*," *Booklist* 100, no. 8 (15 December 2003): 752.

_____. "Review: *The Legend of Tarik*," *School Library Journal* 27, no. 9 (May 1981): 76.

_____. "Review: *Malcolm X: A Fire Burning Brightly*," *Booklist* 96, no. 12 (15 February 2000): 1103.

_____. "Review: *145th Street: Short Stories*," *Booklist* 96, no. 8 (15 December 1995): 778.

_____. "Review: *Scorpions*," *Booklist* 97, no. 16 (15 April 2001): 1549.

_____. "Review: *Shadow of the Red Moon*," *Booklist* 92, no. 6 (15 November 1995): 548.

_____. "Review: *Shooter*," *Booklist* 100, no. 12 (15 February 2004): 1070.

_____. "Review: *Toussaint L'Ouverture: The Fight for Haiti's Freedom*," *Booklist* 93, no. 1 (1 September 1996): 123.

_____. "Review: *Won't Know Till I Get There*," *School Library Journal* 28, no. 9 (May 1982): 72–73.

Rockwell, Paul. "Malcolm X Biography a Must Read for Youth," *Oakland Post*, 29, no. 89 (28 February 1993): 4.

Rohrlick, Paula. "Review: *The Dream Bearer*," *Kliatt* 38, no. 6 (November 2004): 19–20.

_____. "Review: *Handbook for Boys: A Novel*," *Kliatt* 37, no. 3 (May 2003): 20.

_____. "Review: *Shooter*," *Kliatt* 38, no. 3 (May 2004): 11.

Rosenfield, Shelle. "Review: *The Blues of Flats Brown*," *Booklist* 96, no. 13 (1 March 2000): 1242.

Rotella, Mark. "Review: *The Beast*," *Publishers Weekly* 250, no. 48 (1 December 2003): 57–58.

Rush, Theresa G., ed. *Black American Writers: Past and Present*. Metuchen: N.J.: Scarecrow, 1975.

Russell, Mary Harris. "Review: *I've Seen the Promised Land: The Life of Dr. Martin Luther King, Jr.*," *Chicago Tribune Books* (18 January 2004): 5.

Rust, Suzanne. "Learning As We Climb: Stories about the Civil Rights Movement for Young Readers," *Black Issues Book Review* 6, no. 3 (May-June 2004): 58–60.

_____. "Love and Tenderness: Sweet Poetry for the Child in All of Us," *Black Issues Book Review* 7, no. 2 (March/April 2005): 66–67.

_____. "Review: *Shooter*," *Black Issues Book Review* 6, no. 3 (May/June 2004): 60.

Saccardi, Marianne. "Review: *How Mr. Monkey Saw the Whole World*," *School Library Journal* 42, no. 5 (May 1996): 96.

Salvadore, Maria B. "Review: *Fallen Angels*," *School Library Journal* 34, no. 10 (June-July 1988): 118.

Sarkissian, Adele, ed. *Something About the Author*. Vol. 2. Detroit, Mich.: Gale, 1986.

Sasges, Judy. "Review: *Scorpions*," *Voice of Youth Advocates* 11 (August 1988): 133.

Scheps, Susan. "Review: *The Story of the Three Kingdoms*," *School Library Journal* 41, no. 7(July 1995): 67.

Schmidt, Nancy J. "Children's Literature About Africa," *Lion and the Unicorn* 21, no. 2 (April 1997): 284–287.

Schoener, Allon, and Henry Louis Gates, eds. *Harlem on My Mind: Cultural Capital of Black America 1900–1968*. New York: New Press, 1995.

Scordato, Julie. "Review: "*I've Seen the Promised Land: The Life of Dr. Martin Luther King, Jr.*," *Library Media Connection* 23, no. 1 (August/September 2004): 72.

Senick, G., ed. *Children's Literature Review.* vols. 4, 16. Detroit, Mich.: Gale Research, 1982, 1989.

Shapiro, Stephanie, "Getting the Drift: Author Walter Dean Myers Understands How Youngsters Without a Moral Rudder in Their Lives Can Wander toward Trouble," *Chicago Sun*, January 29, 2000.

Sharon, Keith. "Ordinary Guy Calls Forth Creative Spirits," *Jersey Journal* (11 April 1991): 17.

Shinn, Dorothy. "Museum Showcases Illustrator," *Beacon Journal* (2 March 2003).

Short, Lynda N. "Review: *Monster*," *School Library Journal* 46, no. 9 (September 2000): 84.

Sieruta, Peter D. "Review: *The Glory Field*," *Horn Book* 61, no. 2 (March-April 1995): 200.

Silvey, Anita. "Review: *Malcolm X: By Any Means Necessary*," *Horn Book* 69, no. 5 (September/October 1993): 626–627.

_____, ed. *Children's Books and Their Creators.* Boston: Houghton Mifflin, 1995.

Smith, Amanda, "Walter Dean Myers," *Publishers Weekly* 239, no. 32 (20 July 1992): 217–218.

Smith, Henrietta M., ed. *The Coretta Scott King Awards Book, 1970–1999.* Chicago, Ill.: American Library Association, 1999.

Smith, Karen Patricia, ed. *African-American Voices in Young Adult Literature: Tradition, Transition, Transformation.* Lanham, Md.: Scarecrow, 1994.

Smith, Vicky. "Are There Seats at the Round Table?: An Examination of Black Characters in Heroic Fantasy," *New Advocate* 13, no. 4 (fall 2000): 333–345.

Snodgrass, Mary Ellen. *August Wilson.* Jefferson, N.C.: McFarland, 2004.

Something About the Author Autobiography Series. Vol. 2. Detroit: Gale Research, 1986.

Spencer, Pam. "Winners in Their Own Right," *School Library Journal* 38, no. 3 (March 1992): 163–167.

Spielberg, Steven, Maya Angelou, and Debbie Allen. *Amistad: "Give Us Free."* New York: Newmarket, 1998.

Stallworth, B. Joyce. "The Young Adult Literature Course: Facilitating the Integration of Young Adult Literature into the High School English Classroom," *ALAN Review* 26, no. 1 (fall 1998): 1).

Staunton, John A. "Review: *Monster: A Novel*," *Journal of Adolescent & Adult Literacy* 45, no. 8 (May 2002): 791–793.

Steinberg, Sybil S. "Review: *Slam!*," *Publishers Weekly* 243, no. 48 (25 November 1996): 76.

Stevenson, Deborah. "Review: *Antarctica: Journeys to the South Pole*," *Bulletin of the Center for Children's Books* 58, no. 4 (December 2004): 177–178.

_____. "Review: *Here in Harlem: Poems in Many Voices*," *Bulletin of the Center for Children's Books* 58, no. 4 (December 2004): 178.

_____. "Review: *Shooter*," *Bulletin of the Center for Children's Books* 57, no. 10 (June 2004): 429.

_____. "Review: *Toussaint L'Ouverture: The Fight for Haiti's Freedom*," *Bulletin of the Center for Children's Books* 50 (January 1997): 181.

Subryan, Carmen. "Walter Dean Myers," *Dictionary of Literary Biography: Afro-American Fiction Writers After 1955.* Detroit: Gale Research, 1984.

Suhor, Charles. "From the Front Line: Censorship Calls Down," *SLATE Newsletter* (September 2003): 1.

Sullivan, Edward. "Review: *Monster: A Novel*," *School Library Journal* 45, no. 7 (July 1999): 98.

_____. "Review: *145th Street: Short Stories*," *School Library Journal* 46, no. 4 (April 2000): 140.

Sutherland, Zena. "Review: *Crystal*," *Bulletin of the Center for Children's Books* 40 (May 1987): 175.

_____. "Review: *Fast Sam, Cool Clyde and Stuff*," *Bulletin of the Center for Children's Books* 29, no. 3 (January 1976): 82–83.

_____. "Review: *Hoops: A Novel*," *Bulletin of the Center for Children's Books* 35, no. 4 (December 1981): 74.

_____, Dianne L. Monson, and May Hill Arbuthnot, eds. *Children and Books.* Glenview, Ill: Scott, Foresman, 1972.

Sutton, Roger. "Review: *Blues Journey*," *Horn Book* 79, no. 3 (May-June 2003): 363–364.

_____. "Review: *Here in Harlem*," *Horn Book*, 81, no. 1 (January/ February 2005): 104.

_____. "Review: *Monster: A Novel*," Horn Book 75, no. 3 (May/June 1999): 337.

_____. "Review: *Scorpions*," *Bulletin of the Center for Children's Books* (July-August 1988): 235.

_____. "Threads in Our Cultural Fabric," *School Library Journal* 40, no. 6 (June 1994): 24–28.

Sychterz, Terre. "Review: *The Beast*," *Childhood Education* 80, no. 4 (summer 2004): 214.

Taxel, Joel. "Children's Literature at the Turn of the Century: Toward a Political Economy of the Publishing Industry," *Research in the Teaching of English* 37 (November 2002): 145–197.

Telgen, D., ed. *Something About the Author*. vol. 71. Detroit, Mich.: Gale, 1993.

Thornhill, Samantha. "Star Poets and Poet Stars," *Black Issues Book Review* 7, no. 2 (1 March 2005): 26–28.

Tibbets, Sally. "Review: *The Dream Bearer*," *Kliatt* 38, no. 2 (March 2004): 48.

Tidjani-Serpos, Noureini, "The Postcolonial Condition: The Archeology of African Knowledge," *Research in African Literatures* 27, no. 1, (spring 1996): 3–18.

Todd, Tracy. "Review: *The Dream Bearer*," *Booklist* 100, no. 9–10 (1 January 2004): 892–893.

Tolson, Nancy. "Making Books Available: The Role of Early Libraries, Librarians, and Booksellers in the Promotion of African American Literature," *African American Review* 32, no. 1 (1998): 9–16.

Trice, Linda. "A Writer's Life," *Footsteps* 7, no. 2 (March/April 2005): 24–26.

Trosky, S., ed. *Contemporary Authors: New Revision Series*. Vol. 42. Detroit, Mich.: Gale, 1995.

Tuccillo, Diane. "Review: *Shooter*," *Voice of Youth Advocates* 27, no. 2 (June 2004): 133.

Twichell, Ethel R. "Review: *The Legend of Tarik*," *Horn Book* 57, 4 (August 1981): 434.

Unsworth, Robert E. "Review: *Scorpions*," *School Library Journal* 35, no. 1 (September 1988): 201.

Vanca, Lynn K. "Review: *Darnell Rock Reporting*," *School Library Journal* 42, no. 1 (January 1996): 65.

Vasilakis, Nancy. Review: *Mop, Moondance, and the Moondance Kid*," *Horn Book* 65, no. 1 (January-February 1989): 73–74.

_____. "Review: *Mop, Moondance, and the Nagasaki Knights*," *Horn Book* 68, no. 6 (November-December 1992): 739.

Veeder, Mary. "Review: *Fallen Angels*," *Chicago Tribune Books* (13 November 1988): 6.

"Walter Dean Myers," *St. James Guide to Young Adult Writers*, 2nd ed. Detroit: St. James Press, 1999.

Ward, Elise Virginia. "Review: *Shooter*," *Black Issues Book Review* 6, no. 4 (August 2004): 60.

Ward, Martha E., et al. *Authors of Books for Young People*. Metuchen, N.J.: Scarecrow Press, 1979.

Warwick, Ellen D. "Review: *The Golden Serpent*," *School Library Journal* 27, no. 5 (January 1981): 53.

Watkins, Mel. "Review: *Fallen Angels*," *New York Times Book Review* (22 January 1989): 29.

Weech, Eunice. "Review: *Malcolm X: A Fire Burning Brightly*," *School Library Journal* 46, no. 2 (February 2000): 114.

Weischedel, Elaine Fort. "Review: *Hoops: A Novel*," *School Library Journal* 28 (December 1981): 86.

_____. "Review: *Me, Mop, and the Moondance Kid*," *School Library Journal* 35, no. 4 (December 1988): 110.

West, I. "Harlem Connections: Teaching Walter Dean Myers's *Scorpions* in Conjunction with Paul Laurence Dunbar's *The Sport of the Gods*," *ALAN Review*, 26, no. 2 (winter 1999): 1.

Whalin, Kathleen. "Review: *Glorious Angels: A Celebration of Children*," *School Library Journal* 41, no. 9 (September 1995): 196.

Whitfield, Jamie. "In the Ring with Walter Dean Myers," *BookPage* http://www.bookpage.com/, February 2001.

Wildberger, M. E. *Approaches to Literature Through Authors*. Phoenix, Ariz.: Oryx, 1993.

Wilder, Ann, and Alan B. Teasley. "Making the Transition to Lifelong Reading: Books Older Teens Choose," *ALAN Review* 27, no. 1 (1999): 42–46.

Willett, Gail Pettiford. "Review: *Malcolm X: By Any Means Necessary*," *Horn Book* 69, no. 5 (September 1993): 626.

Williams, Helen E. "Review: *Mr. Monkey and the Gotcha Bird*," *School Library Journal* 31, no. 5 (January 1985): 66.

Williams, Karen. "Review: *Brown Angels: An Album of Pictures and Verse*," *Christian Science Monitor* (17 December 1993): 12.

_____. "Review: *The Glory Field*," *Christian Science Monitor* (4 November 1994): 10.

_____. "Review: *Harlem: A Poem*," *Christian Science Monitor* (29 May 1997): 1.

Williamson, Susan. "Review: *Won't Know Till I Get There*," *Voice of Youth Advocates* 5, no. 5 (December 1982): 34.

Wilms, Denise M. "Review: *Mojo and the Russians*," *Booklist* 74, no. 4 (15 October 1977): 379.

Wilson, Brian E. "Review: *The Blues of Flats Brown*," *School Library Journal* 48, no. 11 (November 2002): 8.

"A World to Learn From," *Los Angeles Daily News* (6 February 2001).

"Writer Tells Kids: Future Is in Books, Not on the Streets," *Bergen* (N.J.) *Record* (9 March 2005).

Yeager, Elizabeth Anne, *et al.* "Now Is Your Time!: A Middle School History Unit," *Social Education* 61, no. 4 (April-May 1997): 207–209.

Yearwood, Stephenie. "Popular Postmodernism: 'Walk Two Moons,' 'Holes,' and 'Monster,'" *ALAN Review* 29, no. 3 (spring-summer 2002): 50–53.

"Youth Author Has Reasons to Write," *Syracuse Post-Standard* (21 April 2005).

Yunghans, Penelope. *Prize Winners: Ten Writers for Young Readers*. Greensboro, N.C.: Morgan Reynolds, 1995.

Zaleski, Jeff. "Review: *The Dream Bearer*," *Publishers Weekly* 250, no. 23 (9 June 2003): 52.

Zeigler, Hannah B. "Review: *The Righteous Revenge of Artemis Bonner*," *Horn Book* 69, no. 2 (1 March 1993): 209.

Zimmer, Shirley. "Review: *Slam!*," *Book Report* 15, no. 3 (November/December 1996): 42.

Zimmerman, Jean W. "Review: *Young Martin's Promise*," *School Library Journal* 39, no. 5 (May 1993): 100.

Zvirin, Stephanie. "Parents in Prison," *Booklist* 99, no. 5 (1 November 2002): 505.

_____. "The Printz Award Revisited," *Booklist* 97 (1 January 2001): 932.

_____. "Review: *At Her Majesty's Request: An African Princess in Victorian England*," *Booklist* 96, no. 13 (1 March 2000): 1249.

_____. "Review: *Hoops: A Novel*," *Booklist* 78, no. 2 (15 September 1981): 98.

_____. "Review: *Monster*," *Booklist* 97, no. 17 (1 May 2001): 1611.

_____. "Review: *The Righteous Revenge of Artemis Bonner*," *Booklist* 89, no. 3 (1 October 1992): 321.

Index